Christian Wilhelm Michael Grein

A handy Anglo-Saxon dictionary

Christian Wilhelm Michael Grein
A handy Anglo-Saxon dictionary
ISBN/EAN: 9783337101411
Printed in Europe, USA, Canada, Australia, Japan
Cover: Foto ©Paul-Georg Meister /pixelio.de

More available books at **www.hansebooks.com**

ANGLO-SAXON DICTIONARY:

BASED ON

GROSCHOPP'S GREIN.

EDITED, REVISED, AND CORRECTED,

WITH

GRAMMATICAL APPENDIX, LIST OF IRREGULAR VERBS,

AND

BRIEF ETYMOLOGICAL FEATURES.

BY

JAMES A. HARRISON,
PROFESSOR OF ENGLISH AND MODERN LANGUAGES IN WASHINGTON AND LEE UNIVERSITY, VIRGINIA;

AND

W. M. BASKERVILL, PH.D., LIPS.,
PROFESSOR OF ENGLISH LANGUAGE AND LITERATURE IN VANDERBILT UNIVERSITY, NASHVILLE, TENN.

Copyright, 1885.

A. S. BARNES & CO.,
NEW YORK AND CHICAGO.

INTRODUCTION.

In preparing this edition of GROSCHOPP'S REVISED GREIN'S POETICAL LEXICON OF THE ANGLO-SAXON LANGUAGE, the editors have worked from advanced sheets, with the express sanction of the German scholar's executors.

In the course of their work they found it necessary to introduce several new and important features, which, it is hoped, will increase the value of the book as a practical Lexicon, and commend themselves to the students of Anglo-Saxon. These are—

1. A Grammatical Appendix, intended to convey in brief but explicit form a working OUTLINE OF ANGLO-SAXON GRAMMAR, such as students often find it convenient to consult in the process of their language studies.

2. Cognate words from the Icelandic, Gothic, Old High German, and Modern German, intended to show some of the etymological connections of the Anglo-Saxon poetic vocabulary.

3. A List of the Irregular Verbs occurring in Anglo-Saxon Poetry.

4. The use of **antique type** in the definitions of words, by which the modern English derivative may be directly traced to the Anglo-Saxon original.

Compound words have been separated by hyphens, so as to show their constituent elements.

While the editors are far from claiming that their American presentation of Groschopp-Grein's work is an *Etymological Dictionary*, they invite kindly attention to this feature as one helpful to students of Old English.

At present it is impossible to make a complete Dictionary of the so-called Anglo-Saxon period. Only the poetical monuments have been carefully edited. The prose of that period is still partly locked up in Mss. Even the prose works of Aelfred and Aelfric are not to be found in complete, trustworthy editions. Already the Bosworth-Toller Dictionary needs a careful revision, although it is only half finished. Hence the present work will contain only such words as are used in Anglo-Saxon Poetry. It will, however, contain all words in Anglo-Saxon Poetry, and thus afford students of Old English a cheap and handy volume by means of which any poem of that time can be read and studied.

In all poetry the diction and the constructions are peculiar; but in Anglo-Saxon as in Icelandic poetry there are special peculiarities. After a student has learned to construe Aelfred and Aelfric with ease, he finds almost as much difficulty in reading Caedmon and Cynewulf as in learning a new language. And moreover, as in the beginning of every literature, so here, poetry is far more important than prose. Beowulf will give as much information about the manners and the customs, the life and the religion of the Old English as can be found in all their prose writings; while Genesis, Exodus, Daniel, Elene, and Andreas will show their highest culture under Christian influences and education.

INTRODUCTION.

Even in Germany, where careful study has long been given to this period of the English language, such a work as the present could not be found till the German edition from which this is adapted recently appeared. It had long been felt that *Grein's Lexicon of Anglo-Saxon Poetry* (*Sprachschatz der Angelsächsischen Dichter*) was too unhandy and too costly; and, on this account, the publishers of that work engaged Dr. Groschopp to adapt it for more general use. He therefore retained all the words found in Grein's larger work, leaving out only Proper Names and the copious references. Several important changes were at the same time introduced. In Grein's larger work the definitions are given sometimes in Latin, sometimes in English, and occasionally in German. In Dr. Groschopp's edition they are given throughout in German. With every substantive is given the manner of its declension, that is, whether strong or weak: verbs are treated in like manner. To ablauting verbs is added the number of the class to which each belongs; and here *Koch's division has been followed. Then again no difference is made between long and short vowels. Breaking and Diphthongs stand together: æ comes after ad; ea and eo after e; and ia, ie, io, after i. Compound verbs are placed under the simple forms; and Zupitza's method of accentuation is adopted with reference to êa and êo. The Rune wên is reproduced by w instead of by v.

But it is not intended that this work should be merely a translation from Dr. Groschopp's German edition. In the preparation of the *Handy Dictionary* Grein's original work, Bosworth-Toller (as far as completed), Bosworth and other lexical helps have been utilized. Glossaries of certain poems have been especially helpful. Mistakes have been corrected, misprints removed, and additional definitions given whenever it was necessary.

In a short while we hope to add to the texts already published in *The Library of Anglo-Saxon Poetry*, other texts, believing that, if the proper material is furnished, the study of the oldest English will flourish as it should in all our Colleges and Universities.

JAMES A. HARRISON,
Washington and Lee University, Lexington, Va.

W. M. BASKERVILL,
Vanderbilt University, Nashville, Tenn.

B. is responsible for the Dictionary from A. to L., and for the *Outline of Anglo-Saxon Grammar*. H. is responsible for the Dictionary from L. to Z., and for the *List of Irregular Verbs*.

---

*Koch's system will be found in the *Outline of Anglo-Saxon Grammar*, p. 255.

ABBREVIATIONS.

m. masculine.
f. feminine.
n. neuter.
w. weak.
st. strong.
w. v. weak verb.
st. abl. v. strong ablauting verb.
st. red. v. strong reduplicating verb.
adj. adjective.

pron. pronoun.
subs. substantive.
num. numeral.
adv. adverb.
part. participle.
interj. interjection.
compar. comparative.
superl. superlative.
instr. instrumental.
w. with.
ind. indicative.

subj. subjunctive.
imper. imperative.
Goth., Gothic.
O. H. Ger., Old High German. [man.
Ger., German.
Scan., Scandinavian.
Icel., Icelandic.
B.-T., Bosworth-Toller's Anglo-Saxon Dictionary.
H.-S., Harrison & Sharp's Edition of Beowulf.

ABBREVIATIONS USED IN THE DICTIONARY.

The following abbreviations refer to poems in Grein's *Bibliothek* (Library of Anglo-Saxon Poetry):—

Ælf. Tod. Poem on the Death of Alfred, son of Ethelred, given in the Chronicle under the year 1036.
Ædelst. Poem on the victory of Athelstan, taken from the Chronicle.
Alm. Almosen, from the Codex Exoniensis, p. 467.
An. The legend of St. Andrew.
Ap. The fates of the Apostles, from the Codex Vercellensis.
Az. Azarias, from the Codex Exoniensis, p. 185.
B. Beowulf.
Bo. Botschaft des Gemahls, from the Codex Exoniensis, p. 472.
By. The Death of Byrhtnoth.
Cræ. Manna Cræftas, from the Codex Exoniensis, p. 292.
Cri. Cynewulfs Crist, from the Codex Exoniensis, p. 1.
Dan. Daniel, in Thorpe's Cædmon, p. 216.
Deôr. Deors Klage, from Codex Exoniensis, p. 377.
Dôm. Dômes dæg, from Codex Exoniensis, p. 445.
Edg. Eádgár: poems from the Chronicle, under the years 973, 975.
Edm. Eádmund, from the Chronicle, under the year 942.
Edw. Eádweard, from the Chronicle, under the year 1065.
El. Elene, from the Codex Vercellensis.
Exod. Exodus, in Thorpe's Cædmon, p. 177.
Fä. Fæder lárcwidas, in Codex Exoniensis, p. 300.
Fin. The Fight at Finnsburg.
Gen. Genesis, in Thorpe's Cædmon, p. 1.
Gn. G. Versus gnomici (Cotton MS).
Gn. Ex. Versus gnomici, from Codex Exoniensis, p. 333.
Gû. Legend of St. Guthlac, from Codex Exoniensis, p. 104.
Hö. Höllenfahrt Christi, from Codex Exoniensis, p. 459.
Hy. Hymnen und Gebete.
Jud. The Poem of Judith.
Jul. The Legend of St. Juliana, in Codex Exoniensis, p. 242.
Kl. Klage der Frau, in Codex Exoniensis, p. 442.
Kr. Das heilige Kreuz, from the Codex Vercellensis.
Leâs. Bî manna leáse, from the Codex Vercellensis.
Men. Menologium.
Met. The Meters of Alfred.
Môd. Manna mod, in the Codex Exoniensis, p. 313.
Pa. Panther, in the Codex Exoniensis, p. 355.
Ph. Phönix, in the Codex Exoniensis, p. 197.
Phar. Pharao, in the Codex Exoniensis, p. 468.
Ps. Psalms, from Thorpe's Edition.
Ps. C. The 50th psalm, from one of the Cotton MSS.
Rä. Riddles from the Codex Exoniensis.
Reb. Rebhuhn, from the Codex Exoniensis, p. 365.
Reim. Reimlied, from the Codex Exoniensis, p. 352.
Ruin. Ruine, from the Codex Exoniensis, p. 476.
Rûn. Rûnenlied, in Archæologia, vol. 28.
Sal. Salomo und Saturn.
Sat. Crist und Satan, in Thorpe's Cædmon, p. 265.
Seef. Seefahrer, in the Codex Exoniensis, p. 306.
Seel. Reden der Seelen, in the Codex Exoniensis, p. 367.
Sch. Wunder der Schöpfung, in the Codex Exoniensis, p. 346.
Wid. Vîdsîđ, in Codex Exoniensis, p. 318.
Wy. Manna wyrde, in Codex Exoniensis, p. 327.
Wal. Walfisch, in Codex Exoniensis, p. 360.
Wand. Wanderer, in Codex Exoniensis, p. 286.

ANGLO-SAXON DICTIONARY.

A

â, *adv.* **aye, 1.** always.—**2.** ever, forever.

â (=ǽ), *st. f.* law.

â-, (Ger. *er-*, O. H. Ger. *ir-*, same as *ur-*, Goth. *uz-*).

abal, *st. n.* strength. (O. H. Ger. *aval.*)

â-bylgnes, *st. f.* offense, wrong.

â-byligd, *st. f.* anger, indignation.

ac, ach, ah, *conj.* **1.** but, sed.—**2.** but also, but yet; sed tamen, sed etiam. (Goth. *ak.*)

ac, *interrog. particle,* not? why, wherefore, nonne, numquid.

âc, *st. m.* **oak**; and name of the Rune a: a ship made of oak, Rûn. 25, 4. (Ger. *eiche.*)

âc-, ach. See **âg-, ac.**

âclian, *w. v.*
  ge-âclian, to frighten, excite.

âcol, *adj.* frightened, terrified, excited by fear.

âcol-môd, *adj.* of a fearful mind, timid.

âcsian, âcsigan, *w. v.* to **ask**, inquire, demand.

âc-trêo, *st. n.* **oak-tree.**

âd, *st. m.* funeral-pile, fire. (Goth. *aiths;* Ger. *eid.*)

adela, *w. m.* dirt, filth; cp. **addle-pool.** (N. Ger. *adel.*)

adesa, *w. m.* **adze.**

âd-faru, *st. f.* way, path to the funeral-pile.

âd-fȳr, *st. n.* pile-fire, fire of the funeral-pile.

âdl, *st. f.* disease, sickness.

âdle, *w. f.* disease, sickness.

âd-lêg, *st. m.* flame of the funeral-pile.

âd-loma, *w. m.* one crippled by the fire; fire-lame.

âdl-wêrig, *adj.* weary with sickness.

âdl-þracu, *st. f.* force or virulence of disease.

âd-wylm. See **êdwylm.**

ǽ, *st. f.* life. Az. 165.

ǽ, *indecl.* **1.** law, right.—**2.** marriage. **3.** religious usage, rite, ceremony. (Ger. *ehe.*)

ǽ, *interj.* See **êa.**

ǽ-bebod, *st. n.* injunction of the law; command.

ǽ-boda, *w. m.* messenger, preacher of the law.

ǽ-bylg, *st. n.* anger, wrath, indignation.

ǽ-bylgd, *st. n. f.* offense, fault, wrong.

ǽ-bylignes, *st. f.* state or condition of being angry; anger, wrath.

æcer, *st. m.* **acre**, field, sown land. (Ger. *acker.*)

æc-lǽca. See **âglǽca.**

ǽ-cræft, *st. m.* lawcraft, knowledge of the law, religion.

ǽ-cræftig, *adj.* law-crafty, skilled in the law.

ǽdr, ǽdre, êdre, *st. & w. f.* artery, blood-vein, vein;—vein of fresh water, fountain, river, stream. (Ger. *ader.*)

ædre, edre, *adv.* **1.** at once, forthwith.— **2.** fully, entirely. Gû. 1172, 1351.
ǽ-fæst, -fest, *adj.* firm in observing the law; pious, upright, religious.
ǽfen, ǽfyn, êfen, *st. n.* the even, evening, eventide. (Ger. *abend*.)
ǽfen-glôm, *st. m.* **even-gloom,** twilight, gloaming.
ǽfen-grom, *adj.* fierce at eve, night-enemy. (B.-T.)
ǽfen-grôm, *st. m.* evening guard; one that watches at night.(Grein.)
ǽfen-lâc, *st. n.* evening sacrifice, evening prayer.
ǽfen-lêoht, *st. n.* evening light.
ǽfen-lêoð, *st. n.* evening song. (Ger. *abend-lied*.)
ǽfen-ræst, *st. f.* evening rest. [hard.
ǽfen-sceop, *st. m.* evening singer,
ǽfen-scima, *w. m.* evening shimmer, evening splendor.
ǽfen-spræc, *st. f.* evening speech, a speech made in the evening.
ǽfen-steorra, -stiorra, *w. m.* evening star, Hesperus.
ǽfen-tid, *st. f.* eventide, evening.
ǽ-fest. See **ǽfæst.**
ǽfest, ǽfst, ǽfstu, *st. f. n.?* without favor, envy, hate, zeal, jealousy, enmity. (Ger. *ab-gunst*.)
æf-grynde, *st. n.* abyss. (Ger. *abgrund*.)
ǽfian, *w. v.* to be in a colorless or miserable condition (Leo) Cri. 1357.
æf-lâst, *st. m.* a departure from the way? Exod. 473.
æf-nan, *w. v.* to do, perform, accomplish, perfect.
    ge-æfnan, 1. to accomplish, perfect, do, make.— **2.** prepare, get ready. B. 3106.— **3.** effect, excite, bring upon one's self. Gû. 1211.— **4.** bear, suffer, endure.
ǽfre, *adv.* **1.** ever.— **2.** always.
ǽ-fremmend, *part.* fulfilling the law; religious.

ǽfst, ǽfstu. See **ǽfest.**
æft. See **eft.**
æftan, *adv.* behind, from behind.
æftan-weard, *adj.* behind, in the rear, following.
æftan-tid, *st. f.* eventide, evening.
æfter, I. *prep.* **1.** *w. dat.* (*a*.) local: after, long, along, through, over, = geond. (*b*.) temporal: after, through, throughout, during. (*c*.) causal: (showing purpose and consequence), in consequence of, after, according to, on account of, for the purpose of, after, about (with verbs of saying, speaking, asking, &c.)— **2.** *w. acc.* after, according to.
æfter, II. *adv.* after, then, afterward, thereupon, later.
æftera, æftra, *w. compar. adj.* the hinder, other, second.
æfter-lêan, *st. n.* after-loan, reward, recompense, restitution.
æfter-weard, *adj.* **afterward,** behind, in the rear, following. [age.
æfter-yld, *st. f.* advanced age, old
æftra. See **æftera.**
æf-þanca, -þonca, *w. m.* enmity, insult, offense, hate, envy, displeasure, jealousy.
æf-þunca, *w. m.* the same as the above.
ǽ-fyllend, *part.* fulfilling the law, faithful.
æg, *st. n.; pl.* **ægru,** egg. (Ger. *ei*.)
æg-lǽc, -lǽca. See **âg-.**
æg-flota, *w. m.* a floater on the water, a ship.
æg-hwanan, -hwonon, *adv.* everywhere, from all sides.
æg-hwâ, *pron.* every one, everything. The *gen. n.* is often used adverbially = at all, in general, altogether, quite, entirely.
æg-hwǽr, *adv.* **1.** everywhere.— **2.** in every way, in every respect.— **3.** in every direction. Rä. 41, 69.— **4.** anywhere. Ps. 102, 15.

æg-hwæder, æg-der, *pron.* 1. each (of two), either, both; æghwæder-ge, as well — as also, both — and. — 2. each (of several). B. 1636.

æg-hwider, *adv.* in all directions, on every side, in every way.

æg-hwilc, -hwelc, -hwylc, *pron.* every, whosoever, whatsoever, all, every one.

æ-glêaw, *adj.* skilled in the law; wise.

ægne. See âgen.

ægnian, *w. v.* to frighten, disquiet, vex, torment.

ægder. See æghwæder.

æg-weard, *st. f.* sea-ward; guardianship over the sea.

æ-gype, *adj.* mocking? scoffing? Ps. 106,10. — trifling, worthless. (B.-T.)

æht, *st. f.* deliberation, council.

æht, *st. f.* pursuit. B. 2957. — others; persecution, hostility. (Ger. *acht*.)

æht, *st. f.* 1. possessions, property, riches, goods. — 2. possession, power. (Goth. *aihts*.)

æhtan, *w. v.*
    ge-æhtan, to value, prize, speak of with praise.

æht-gesteald, *st. n.* possession.

æht-gestrêon, *st. n.* possessions, riches.

æht-geweald, *st. f.* power of possession, firm possession, the right to do with a thing as one pleases; right, possession, power.

æht-spêdig, *adj.* wealthy, rich.

æht-wela, *w. m.* wealth, riches.

æht-welig, *adj.* wealthy, rich.

æ-hwær = âhwær, *adv.* everywhere.

æ-lærend, *part. & subs.* a teacher of law or faith.

ælan, *w. v.* 1. to set on fire, kindle, consume. — 2. burn, blaze (up).
    in-ælan, to set on fire, kindle.
    on-ælan, to set on fire, kindle.

æl-beorht (æll-), *adj.* all bright, shining on all sides.

ælc, *pron.* each, every, any, all.

æl-ceald, *adj.* all cold, everywhere, altogether cold.

æl-cræftig, *adj.* all-crafty, all-mighty, all-powerful.

æld, ældu, *st. f.* age, a century, generation, old age.

ælde, *st. m. pl.* men, human beings.

ældran, *compar. w. m. pl.* parents.

ældu. See æld.

æled, *st. m.* fire, firebrand, conflagration. (O. N. *eldr*.)

æled-fŷr, *st. n.* flame of fire, fire.

æled-lêoma, *w. m.* firebrand, torch, gleaming fire.

ælf, ylf, *st. m. & f.* elf, fairy, goblin, nymph. (Ger. *elf, elbe*.)

æl-fæle, *adj.* all fell, thoroughly bad, very baleful.

æl-fær, -fer, *st. f.* the whole army. (Grein, *ælfaru*.)

ælf-scin, *adj.* shining like an elf or a fairy, elfin-bright.

ælf-sciene, -scŷne, *adj.* beautiful as an elf, of elfin beauty.

æl-fylce, *st. n.* 1. strange land, foreign land. — 2. foreign band, hostile army, enemy.

æl-grêne, *adj.* all green, on all sides green.

æling, *st. f.* burning.

æl-mehtig. See ælmeahtig.

ælmes-georn, *adj.* giving alms willingly, benevolent, liberal.

ælmesse, ælmysse, *w. f.* alms, alms-giving, benefit.

æl-meaht, -miht, *adj.* almighty.

æl-meahtig, -mehtig, -mihtig, *adj.* almighty.

ælmysse. See ælmesse.

æl-þêodig, *adj.* strange, foreign.

æl-wiht, *st. n. f.* 1. a being of another kind, monster. — 2. all created things, creature.

æ-men, *adj.* depopulated, uninhabited.

æmetan, æmetian, æmtian, *w. v.* to be at leisure, be vacant, be moderate, refrain from.

ǽne, *adv.* **1.** once.— **2.** alone. *acc. instr. sg. m.* See **ân.**

ǽnga (= **ânga**), *w. adj.* sole, only? Sal. 382.

ænge, *adj.* narrow, anxious, troubled.

ænge, *adv.* narrowly, anxiously, sadly.

ængel. See **engel.**

ǽnig, *pron.* any, one, any one.

ǽninga, *adv.* continually, uninterruptedly, of necessity, by all means.

ǽn-lîc, *adj.* only, incomparable, excellent, beautiful, elegant.

ǽnne, *acc. sg. m.* See **ân.**

æpl, æppel, eapl, (Sat. 411), *st. m.* **1.** apple, fruit generally.— **2.** something round, a round object, ball. (Ger. *apfel.*)

æpled, æppled, *adj.* appled, shaped like an apple, made into balls or bosses. [orchard.

æppel-bearu, *st. m.* a fruit-garden,

æppel-fealu, *adj.* apple-fallow, yellow like an apple, reddish-yellow.

ǽr, I. *conj. w. ind. & subj.* ere, before,— used also correlatively with **ǽr,** *adv.*— II. *prep. w. dat.* before. III. *adv.* **1.** ere, before, sooner, earlier,— nô þŷ ǽr. See þŷ.— **2.** early, betimes, premature. (Ger. *eher.*)

ǽr, *st. n.* brass.

ǽr = **âr,** *st. f.* honor. See **ǽrfæst, ǽrlêast.**

ǽr-âdl, *st. f.* early disease. Gû. Ex. 31.

ǽr-boren, *part.* the earlier born, firstborn.

ǽr-cwide, *st. m.* old saying, prophecy.

ǽr-dæg, *st. m.* early day, early morn. In the *pl.* former days, olden time.

ǽr-dêad, *st. m.* early death.

ærdon, By. 191: Wülcker = **rǽdon.** See **rǽdan;** Grein = **ærndon,** from **ærnan,** to run.

ǽren, *adj.* brazen, made of brass. (Ger. *ehern.*)

ǽrend-bôc, *st. f.* message, letter.

ǽrende, *st. n.* errand, message, tidings, business, care.

ǽrend-gâst, *st. m.* a message-bringing spirit, angel.

ǽrend-gewrit, *st. n.* written message, letter, epistle.

ǽrendian, *w. v.* to take or carry a message, news, tidings.

ǽrend-raca, *w. m.* messenger, ambassador, apostle, angel.

ǽrend-secg, *st. m.* messenger, ambassador, apostle, angel.

ǽrend-sprǽc, *st. f.* message, verbal message.

ǽrest. See **ǽrist.**

ǽrest, ǽrost, *superl.* **1.** *adj.* the first, erst.— **2.** *adv. &* uninflected *adj.* at first, before all, first of all; also *w. gen. pl.* (Ger. *der erste,* &c.)

ǽr-fæder, *st. m.* deceased father, late father.

ǽr-fæst, *adj.* honorable, gracious, merciful. (Ger. *ehrfest.*)

ǽr-gescôd, *part.* furnished with brazen scabbard, with brazen covering, sheathed in brass (Groschopp);— brass-shod, shod with brass, ære calceatus. Grein, B.-T.

ǽr-gestrêon, *st. n.* old treasure, possessions dating from old times, riches accumulated in olden time.

ǽr-geweorc, *st. n.* an ancient work, work of the olden time.

ǽr-gewinn, *st. n.* former pains, labor, an ancient struggle.

ǽr-gewyrht, *st. n.* former work, deed of old, a work done formerly.

ǽr-glæd, *adj.* brass-bright, gleaming in brazen arms.

ǽr-gôd, *adj.* good above others, of prime goodness (Grein, B.-T.); good in honors, well furnished with dignity and advantages (Leo);

good since old times, long invested with dignity or advantages. (Harrison & Sharp.)

ǽ-riht, *st. n.* law-right, faith, belief.

ǽring, *st. f.* early dawn, daybreak, early morning.

ǽ-rest, -rist, *st. f.* **1.** resurrection, awakening, rising up.— **2.** origin, relation to the beginning? B.2157. (Goth. *urrists.*)

ǽr-léast, -lést, *st. f.* dishonor, disgraceful deed, impiety.

ǽr-mergen, *st. m.* early morning, daybreak.

ǽr-morgen, *st. m.* early morning, daybreak.

ærn. See ern.

ǽror, ǽrror, ǽrur, *compar.* **1.** *adv.* earlier, before, formerly.— **2.** *prep. w. dat.* before, sooner than.

ǽrra, *compar. adj.* earlier, former.

ǽr-sceaft, *st. f.* what was wrought in former times, old work, ancient building.

ǽr-wela, *w. m.* ancient wealth, riches from the olden time.

ǽr-woruld, *st. f.* the former world, old world. (Cf. Ger. *Ur-welt.*)

ǽs, *st. n.* carcass, carrion, food, meat. (Ger. *aas.*)

æsc, *st. m.* ash. **1.** ash-tree; and name for the Rune æ.— **2.** ash-spear; lance, spear made of ash.— **3.** a vessel made of ash.— **4.** a small ship, skiff. (O. H. Ger. *asc.*)

æsc-berend, *part. & subs.* ash-spear bearer, lance-bearer.

æsce, *w. f.* ashes.

æsc-here, *st. m.* a spear-bearing army.

æsc-holt, *st. n.* ash wood, ashen shaft, lance.

æsc-plega, *w. m.* play of spears, battle.

æsc-róf, *adj.* renowned in the battle of spears, able in battle, illustrious.

æsc-stéde, *st. f.* firmness, constancy in battle. (Grein.)

æsc-stede, *st. m.* place of trial (Leo); ash-spear place, place of battle (B.-T.) Môd. 17. [war.

æsc-tir, *st. m.* spear-glory, glory in

æsc-þracu, *st. f.* stress of spears; battle.

æsc-wiga, *w. m.* a spear-warrior, warrior.

ǽ-springe, -sprynge, *st. m.* **1.** water-spring, fountain.— **2.** what is yet to spring forth, yet to happen, fate, destiny. Sch. 77.

ǽ-swic, *st. m.* offense, scandal, shame, infamy, disgrace.

æt, I. *prep.* **1.** *w. dat.*(*a.*) local: where? at, near, by, in, on, upon, with, in respect to, as to;—with verbs of taking, from, away from. Whither? to, toward, at, on.—(*b.*) temporal: at, at the time of, near, in, on, to.—(*c.*) causal: at, to.— **2.** *w. acc.* to, unto, up to, as far as, into.— II. *adv.* at, to, near.

ǽt, *st. m.* **1.** food, meat.— **2.** feeding, eating. (O. H. Ger. *âz.*)

æt-fele, adhesion, Ps. 72, 23, mihi autem adhærere deo.(Grein, B.-T.); devoting, dedicating; adhering? (Groschopp.)

æt-foran, *prep. w. dat.* before, in the presence of.

æt-gædere, -gædre, *adv.* united, together, at the same time.

ǽt-gifa, -geofa, *w. m.* food-giver, nourisher.

æt-grǽpe, *adj.* laying hold of, grabbing at, seizing; *w.* weorþan = to seize.

æt-hwâ, *pron.* each. Pa. 15.

æt-hwega, *adv.* to a certain degree, tolerably, somewhat, a little.

æt-hwon, *adv.* almost, nearly.

ǽtor-cyn, *st. n.* poisonous kind.

ǽtren, ǽttren, ǽttern, ǽttryn, *adj.* poisonous, poisoned. (Ger. *eiterig.*)

ǽtren-môd, adj. venom-minded, sly, cunning, deceitful.
æt-rihte, -ryhte, adj. right at, near, present.
æt-rihte, adv. almost, nearly.
æt-samne, -somne (et-), adv. united, at once, together.
æt-stǽl, st. m. aid, assistance (Grein); station, camp-station (B.-T.)
æt-steall, st. m. standing face to face with hostile intent, hostile opposition (Grein); camp-station (B.-T.)
ǽttren, ǽttryn. See ǽtren.
æt-wela, w. m. wealth of food, supply of food; food.
æt-wist, st. f. presence, existence, substance, sustenance.
ǽdan, êdan, w. v. to lay waste, devastate.
   â-ǽdan, to make desolate, lay waste.
ǽdel = œdel. See êdel.
ædel-cund, adj. of noble origin, noble.
ædel-cyning, st. m. the noble king, Christ.
ædel-dugud, st. f. noble comitatus, attendance, fellowship.
ædele, edele, adj. noble, noble-minded, excellent, illustrious, vigorous, famous. (Ger. edel.)
ædelian, w. v. (Ger. edeln.)
   ge-ædelian, to ennoble, make illustrious, improve.
   un-ædelian, to degrade, debase.
ædeling, st. m. a man of noble birth, noble, prince, God, Christ, man;— pl. men, people.
ædel-ic (= ædel-lic), adj. noble, excellent.
ædel-nes, st. f. nobility, excellence.
ædel-stenc, st. m. noble odor, sweet smell.
ædel-tungol, st. n. noble star.

ædelu, ædelo, st. f. & st. n. pl. noble qualities, especially of the mind; talents, genius, nature, noble origin, nobility, descent, origin, noble descendants, family, race. (Ger. adel.)
ǽdm, êdm, st. m. breath, breathing, vapor. (Ger. athem.)
ǽwan, w. v. to despise, scorn, contemn.
ǽ-welm, st. m. spring, fountain, source, beginning.
ǽwisc, st. f. offense, shame, disgrace, dishonor. (Goth. aiwisks.)
ǽwisc-môd, adj. ashamed, cast down in mind, disgraced, oppressed.
ǽ-wita, w. m. one acquainted with the law, a law-expert, counselor.
æx, st. f. an ax, hatchet. (Ger. axt.)
afara, -era, -ora. See eafora.
afor, adj. grim, dire, rough, impetuous, strong.
âgan, r. pret.-pres., pret. ind. sg. 1. 3. âh.— 2. âhst; pl. âgon, âgan, âgun; subj. sg. âge; pl. âgen, âgon (Ps. 108, 27); pret. âhte, to have, possess, own (older form owe). (Goth. aigan.)
âge, w. f. possessions, property. Sat. 147.
âgen, adj. own, peculiar, proper.
âgend, part. & subs. owner, possessor, lord, master.
âgend-frêa, w. m. owner, possessor, lord;— w. f. mistress. Gen. 2237.
âg-lâc, -lǽc, st. m. trouble, misery, pressure, misfortune, sharp fighting, bitter hostility.
âglâc-hâd, st. m. misery-hood, state or condition causing sadness or affliction.
âg-lǽca, -lǽcea, -lêca (âh-, ǽg-, âc-) w. m. bringer of trouble, evil spirit, demon, monster, devil;— great hero, mighty warrior.

âg- (âc-) lǽc-cræft, *st. m.* evil, destructive art.
âglǽc-wif, *st. n.* female monster, destruction-bringing woman.
âgnian, *w. v.* to appropriate, possess, prove or claim as one's own. (Ger. *eignen.*)
   ge-âgnian, same as the above.
agof = agob, transposition of the word boga. Rä. 24, 1.
ah, âh-, âh. See ac-, âg-, âgan.
â-hafenes, *st. f.* a lifting up, elevation.
âhsian, *w. v.* 1. to ask, to demand.— 2. to obtain, experience, endure.
   ge-âhsian, to find out by asking, get by hearsay.
âhst. See âgan.
âht (= âwiht), *st. n.* aught, anything, something.
âhte. See âgan.
â-hwǽr, *adv.* anywhere, everywhere; —used specially in negative sentences.
â-hwǽrgen, *adv.* same as the above.
â-hwǽder, *pron.* some one, something, any one.
al. See eal.
alan, *st.* abl, *v.* IV. to nourish, produce. (Goth. *alan.*)
   of-alan, to take away, diminish. Reim. 24.
ald, aldor. See eald, ealdor.
alet, *st. m.* fire.
algian, alh, all. See ealgian, ealh, eal.
â-lihting, *st. f.* illumination, enlightening.
almægen, -wealda, -wight. See eal-.
â-lýsend, *part. & subs.* redeemer, deliverer. (Cf. Ger. *erlöser.*)
â-lýsing, *st. f.* redemption. (Ger. *erlösung.*)
â-lýsnes, *st. f.* redemption.
âm, *st. m.* weaver's beam, yarn-beam. Rä. 36, 8 (Grein); the reed or slay of a weaver's loom. (B.-T.)

ambeht, -biht, -bieht, -byht (an-, om-, on-), *st. n.* office, service, command, commission.
ambeht (with same parallel forms), *st. m.* servant, serving-man.
ambeht-hêra, *w. m.* servant, obedient servant, bond-slave.
ambeht-mæcg, *st. m.* serving-man, servant.
ambeht-scealc, *st. m.* same as above.
ambeht-secg, *st. m.* same as above.
ambeht-þegn, *st. m.* same as above.
an. See unnan.
an. I. *prep. w. dat. & acc.* in, on, among, with respect to, into, to (frequently separated from the word governed). See on.— II. *adv.* away, forth? Met. 20, 30.
ân, *num. st. & w.* 1. one, a certain one of many, an only one.— 2. a, an, —almost in the sense of our so-called indefinite article.— 3. alone, only, sole.— 4. alone, sole, unique, distinguished, excellent.— 5. alone, lonely, solitary.— 6. *gen. pl.* ânra, in connection with pronouns,— single, each, every, all.— 7. on ân, in one, in accordance with, once for all, continually, ever.— 8. uninflected in ân-forlǽtan, to leave alone, leave, give up, forsake, relinquish.
ân-âd, *st. n.* waste, desert, solitude. (Ger. *einöde.*)
an-bid, *st. n.* expectation, hope, awaiting.
anbiht, -bieht, -byht. See ambeht.
ân-boren, *part.* only born, only begotten.
an-brôce, *w. f.* wood, timber, building material. El. 1029.
ân-bûend, *part. & subs.* lone dweller, hermit, anchorite.
ân-cenned, *part.* only begotten.
ancor, oncor, *st. m.* anchor. (Ger. *anker.* From Gr. ἄγκυρα.)
ancor-bend, *st. m.* anchor-band, anchor-rope.

ancor-râp, *st. m.* anchor-rope, cable.
and, ond, *conj.* and.
and, *prep.* I. *w. dat.* (in numbers), with. II. *w. acc.* over, against, with, into, on, before. (O. H. Ger. *ant-*, *int-*. Ger. *ent-*.)
anda, onda, *w. m.* grudge, anger, hate, envy, jealousy, discontent, excitement, vexation, horror, an endeavor to hurt. (O. H. Ger. *anado, anto*.)
ân-dæge, *adj.* for one day.
and-bid, *st. n.* hope, expectation.
and-cwis, *st. f.* answer.
andettan, -etan, ondetan, *w. v.* to confess, acknowledge.
    mægen-andettan, earnestly, strongly to confess.
andet-nes, *st. f.* acknowledgment, confession.
and-feng, *st. m.* a taking up, a receiving, defense. Sat. 245.
and-fenga, -fengea, -fencgea (ond-), *w. m.* one that undertakes a thing, taker-up, defender, receiver, harborer. [fit.
and-fenge, *adj.* acceptable, approved,
and-fenge, -fencge, *st. m.* undertaker, defender, protector.
and-gete, *adj.* open, plain, manifest, clear, easily recognized.
and-git, -giet, -gyt (ond-), *st. n.* insight, perception, intellect, understanding, knowledge.
and-gite, -giete (ond-), *w. f.* same as the above.
andgiet-tâcen, *st. n.* a sensible token, a sign by which something is recognized, sign, token.
and-lang, -long (ond-), *adj.* along, continuous, whole, entire, throughout, extended, all-along. (Ger. *entlang*.)
and-lata? Cri. 1436.
and-lêan (ond-), *st. n.* retribution, retaliation, like for like.
and-leofa, *w. m.* recreation, refection, food? Sat. 522.

and-leofen, -lifen, *st. f.* food, nourishment.
and-raca, *w. m.* servant, representative? deputy? Exod. 15. (**and-saca** *ms.*)
andrysnlic. See **ondrysnlic.**
and-rysno (ond-), *st. f.* what is to be considered, the becoming, due attention, etiquette. (Grein, Heyne, &c.)
an-drysno (on-), *st. f.* fear, awe, reverence. (B.-T.)
and-saca (ond-), *w. m.* adversary, enemy, denier, apostate.
and-sæc (ond-), *st. f. n.?* contention, denial, refusal, resistance, strife.
and-slyht (ond-). See **hand-slyht.**
and-swaru (ond-), *st. f.* answer, accosting, reply, address.
and-weard, *adj.* present, lying over against, standing over against, opposite to, against. (O. H. Ger. *antwart*.)
andweard-lic, *adj.* present, actually present.
andweard-lice, *adv.* in the presence of, present, actually.
and-weorc, *st. n.* matter, material, stuff, ground, cause.
and-wig, *st. m.* resistance, battle.
and-wit, *adj.* expert, skillful, acquainted with, experienced.
and-wist, *st. f.* place, station; (the support of the earth, Kemble). An. 1542.
and-wlita, *w. m.* look, face, countenance, appearance. (Ger. *antlitz*.)
and-wrâd, *adj.* hostile, enraged.
and-wyrde, *st. n.* answer. (Ger. *antwort*.)
â-nêhst, -nýhst, *adv.* next, at last, in the last place.
an-feng, *st. m.* apprehension, laying hold of, reception, receiving.
ân-fête, *adj.* one-footed, with one foot.
ân-feald, *adj.* one-fold, simple, single, plain, modest.

ân-floga, w. m. the alone, lonely flier.
an-forht, adj. fearful, timid.
anga, onga, w. m. point, sting.
ânga, w. adj. only, sole.
ange, onge, adj. narrow, straitened, sore, anxious, troubled. (Ger. *enge*.)
ân-genga, -gengea, w. m. the alone, solitary goer, solitary.
ân-getrum, st. n. an illustrious company? Exod. 334.
an-gin, st. n. beginning, commencement, undertaking, endeavor, attempt, cause, action.
ang-môd, adj. anxious in mind, sad, sorrowful.
ang-nes, st. f. anxiety, uneasiness, fear, anguish.
an-gryslic, adj. grisly, frightful, horrible, horrid, terrible. Ps. 104, 33. Bed. 5, 2.
ân-haga, -hoga, w. m. lone dweller, recluse, solitary.
an-hoga, w. m. care, sorrow, solicitude, anxiety. Gû. 970.
ân-horn, st. m. unicorn.
ân-horna, w. m. unicorn.
ân-hȳdig, adj. constant, firm, determined, brave.
âninga, adv. unceasingly, straightway, by all means, entirely, altogether, at all events.
ân-lêpe, adj. single, singular, alone, solitary, private, a single one.
an-leofa, w. m. food, nourishment.
an-lic, adj. like, similar, of like age, equal.
ân-lic = ǽnlic, adj. only, unique, incomparable, excellent.
an-lice, adv. similarly, of like manner.
an-licnes, st. f. likeness, similarity, image, comparison, parable.
ân-mêde, st. n. unanimity, concord, harmony.
an-medla, w. m. pride, arrogance, insolence.

an-môd, adj. steadfast, daring, courageous, brave, grim, fierce.
ân-môd, adj. of one mind, with one accord, harmonious.
ân-môdlice, adv. unanimously, with one accord.
ân-nes, st. f. oneness, unity.
ân-pæd, st. m. lonely, narrow path, lonely way.
ân-rǽd, adj. of one counsel, firm, determined, resolute.
ân-seld, st. m. lonely seat, lonely dwelling.
ân-stapa, w. m. lonely wanderer, solitary.
an-sund, adj. whole, unhurt, sound. (Cf. Ger. *gesund*.)
an-sȳn, -sien, -sion, st. f. face, appearance, look, countenance, aspect, sight, view, presence. (Ger. *ansehen*.)
an-sȳn, st. f. want, lack. Ps. 142, 6.
ân-tid, st. f. first hour? one and the same time? (Grein); one time, *i. e.* the same time (Heyne). B. 219.
ânunga, adv. without ceasing, throughout, entirely, altogether, wholly.
an-weald, -wald, st. m. power, might, rule, dominion, empire. (Cf. Ger. *ge-walt*.)
an-wealda, -walda, w. m. one who has rule or power, ruler, Lord.
ân-wig-gearu, adj. ready for single combat.
an-wlôh, adj. adorned, ornamented.
ânȳhst. See ânêhst.
apostol, st. m. apostle.
apostol-hâd, st. m. apostlehood, apostolic office.
Aprelis, m. April.
âr, st. f. oar. Gû. Ex. 188.
âr, st. m. messenger, ambassador, herald, apostle, angel, servant, man. (Goth. *airus*.)
âr, st. f. 1. honor, worth, dignity, renown, glory, respect, reverence.—

2. grace, favor, compassion, benefit, help. (Ger. *chrc.*)
âra = geâra, *adv. gen. pl.* once, formerly.
âr-cræftig, *adj.* strong in honor, honorable, (Grein); respectful, polite. (B.-T.)
âre, *w. f.* = **âr,** *st. f.* honor, &c.
âr-fæst, *adj.* **1.** honorable, honest, just, upright, pious, virtuous, respectful.— **2.** favorable, good, kind, compassionate.—**3.** ready for help? B. 1168.
âr-fæstnes, -festnes, *st. f.* uprightness, honesty, mildness, pity, mercy, compassion.
âr-geblond, *st. m.* waves of the sea raised by oars, oar-disturbed sea, mingling of the oars.
âr-gifa, *w. m.* honor-giver, giver of benefits, benefactor.
âr-hwæt, *adj.* eager for honor, desirous of renown.
ârian, *w. v.* **1.** to honor, reverence, adore.— **2.** to be gracious, favorable to, have mercy.— **3.** to spare, pity. (Ger. *chren.*)
  ge-ârian, 1. to honor.— **2.** to have mercy, be gracious, help.
âr-lêas, *adj.* **1.** honorless, impious.— **2.** notorious, infamous, disgraceful, wicked.— **3.** without compassion, cruel. Jul. 4. (Ger. *chrlos.*)
âr-lêaslice, *adv.* impiously, cruelly, wickedly.
âr-lêast, *st. f.* impiety, cruelty, dishonor, iniquity.
âr-lic, *adj.* honorable, honest, becoming, agreeable, pleasant, lovely, merciful. (Ger. *chrlich.*)
âr-lice, *adv.* honestly, honorably, becomingly, graciously, mercifully, pleasantly.
arod, *adj.* ready, prepared.
âr-scamu, *st. f.* holy awe, respect, reverence.

âr-stæf, *st. m.* benefit, kindness, assistance, help, favor, grace.
âr-wela, *w. m.* wealth of oars, the sea.
âr-wyrde, *adj.* worthy of honor, venerable. (Ger. *ehrwürdig.*)
âr-ŷd, *st. f.* waves stirred up by the oar, oar-wave.
asce, *w. f.* ashes. (O. H. Ger. *asca;* Goth. *azgo;* Ger. *asche.*)
âscian, *w. v.* to ask, demand, seek out, find out by inquiry.
  ge-âscian, to find out by asking, hear of, learn.
âscung, *st. f.* asking, inquiry, question, interrogation.
aspide, *st. m.* asp, adder, serpent.
assa, *w. m.* ass, a male ass.
atelic (= **atol-lic**), *adj.* dire, dreadful, terrible.
atol, atul, *adj.* ugly, deformed, foul, dire, horrible, loathsome, terrible, hostile.
atol, *st. n.* cruelty, horror, terribleness, evil, wretchedness.
âtor, âttor, *st. n.* poison, venom. (Ger. *eiter.*)
âtor-tân, *st. m.* poisonous twig, poisoned rod.
âttor. See **âtor.**
âttor-soeada, *w. m.* poisonous enemy, poisonous dragon.
âttor-spere, *st. n.* poisonous spear, poisoned spear.
âd, *st. m.* **oath.** (Ger. *eid.*)
âd-loga, *w. m.* oath-breaker, perjurer.
âdolian, *w. v.* to make noble, ennoble.
adol-ware, *st. m. pl.* citizens.
âdor (= **âwder**), *pron.* other, one of two.
âd-swaru, *st. f.* oath-swearing, oath.
âd-sweord, *st. f.* same as the above.
âdum, *st. m.* son-in-law. (Ger. *eidam.*)
â-uht (= **âwiht**), *st. n.* aught, anything.
âwa, âwo, *adv.* **1.** always.— **2.** ever, any, some. Sal. 322.

â-wærged, *adj.* accursed, wicked, malicious.
â-weg, *adv.* away, forth.
â-wêr (= âhwǽr), *adv.* anywhere, somewhere.
â-werged, -wyrged, *adj.* accursed, malicious, malevolent.
â-wiht, -wuht, -wyht, *st. n.* aught, anything, anything at all; — *acc.*, often used adverbially. [turbed.
â-wyged, *adj.* moved, disquieted, dis-
âwđer (= â-hwǽđer), *pron.* either, other, one of two, one or the other.
axe, *w. f.* ashes.

B

bâ. See begen.
bâd, *st. f.* pledge, pawn.
bæc, bec, *st. n.* back; ofer bæc bûgan, to turn back, flee; under bæc, on bec, backwards.
bæcling, found only in the adverbial phrase on bæcling, backwards.
bǽdan, *w. v.* to demand, compel, constrain, incite, encourage.
 â-bǽdan, to have a demand for, compel, restrain, exact.
 ge-bǽdan, 1. *w. gen.* of thing, to bring about, force, compel. Gn. Ex. 105.— 2. *w. acc.* of person, and *w. tô*, or *gen.* of thing, to induce one to do a thing, to force, compel. 3. to drive, send forth, let fly. B. 3117.— 4. to press hard, compel, restrain, overcome, repress.
bǽde-wêg, *st. n.* cup, drinking-vessel.
bæl, *st. n.* fire of the funeral-pile, fire, flames, funeral pile. (O.N. *bál.*)
bæl-blǽse, *w. f.* fire-blaze, a blaze.
bæl-blŷse, *st. f.* same as the above.
bælc, *st. m.* balk, covering, cloud. (Ger. *ge-bälk.*)
bælc, *st. m.?* belch, stomach, pride, arrogance, presumption.
bælcan, *w. v.* to cry out, to make an arrogant noise.
bældan, *w. v.* to animate, arouse, encourage.
bæl-egesa, *w. m.* terror, dread of the flames.

bæl-fŷr, *st. n.* fire of the funeral-pile, bale-fire.
bæligan, *w. v.*
 â-bæligan, to insult, provoke, make angry.
bæl-stede, *st. f.* place of the funeral fire, the burning of the corpse.
bæl-þracu, *st. f.* force or violence of the flame.
bæl-wudu, *st. m.* wood for the funeral-fire.
bæl-wylm, *st. m.* funeral-fire flames, billow-like flames.
bændan, *w. v.*
 ge-bændan, to bind, fetter, tie.
bær, *adj.* bare, naked. (Ger. *baar.*)
bǽr, *st. f.* bier. (Ger. *bahre.*)
bǽran, *w. v.*
 ge-bǽran, to demean one's self, to behave, bear one's self. (O. H. Ger. *gebárón, -ón;* Ger. *geberden.*)
bærnan, *w. v.* to burn, burn up, consume. (Ger. *brennen.*)
 for-bærnan, to burn up, consume. (Ger. *ver-brennen.*)
 ge-bærnan, to burn.
 on-bærnan, to set on fire, kindle.
bǽtan, *w. v.* to restrain with a bit, bit, curb, tame.
 ge-bǽtan, same as the above.
 ymbe-bǽtan, to throw a restraint around, put a check upon.
bætera. See bettra.

bæd, *st. n.* bath. (Ger. *bad.*)
bæd-weg, *st. m.* bath-way, the sea.
bald, baldor, balu. See beald, bealdor, bealu.
bân, *st. n.* bone, bones of the human body. (Ger. *bein.*)
bana, bona, *w. m.* killer, murderer.
bân-côfa, *w. m.* bone-chamber, the body.
ban-côda, *w. m.* a baneful disease, deadly sickness? Etmüller, bân-côda, ossium morbus, *disease of the bones*. Gû. 998.
bân-fæt, *st. n.* bone-vat, vessel for the bones, the body.
bân-fâg, -fâh, *adj.* variegated with bones, adorned with bone-work, or perhaps with deer-antlers. (Grein, H. & S.) ban-fâh, death or mur-der-stained. (B.-T.) B. 780.
ban-, bon-gâr, *st. m.* murderous spear.
bân-gebrec, *st. m.* bone-breaking? An. 1444.
bân-helm, *st. m.* a helm or shield for the protection of the bones of the body, *i. e.*, a helmet for the body. Fin. 30.
bân-hring, *st. m.* bone-structure, joint, bone-joint.
bân-hûs, *st. n.* bone-house, body.
bân-lêas, *adj.* boneless, without bones.
bân-loca, *w. m.* bone inclosure, body.
bannan, bonnan, *st. red. v.* to order, command, call, call together, sum-mon. (Ger. *bannen.*)
   â-bannan, to order, call, summon, call off.
   ge-bannan, to bid, order, name, call, summon.
bân-sele, *st. m.* bone-hall, body.
bâsnian, *w. v.* to expect, await, wait.
basilisca, *w. m.* basilisk.
basu, *adj.* purple, crimson.
bât, *st. m.* boat, skiff, ship, vessel. (Ger. *boot.*)

bât-weard, *st. m.* boat-warder, watcher over the ship.
baðian, *w. v.* 1. to bathe, wash, cherish, foment. — 2. to bathe one's self, bathe.
bi-baðian, to bathe.
be, *prep*, *w. dat. & instr.* 1. local: by, near by, near, at, on, with. — 2. likewise local, but of motion from the subject in the direction of the object, on, upon, by. — 3. causal: by, with, for, through, by reason of, on account of, in accordance with. — 4. from, concerning, about, (after verbs of saying, &c.). — 4. temporal: while, during, be þe (him) lifigendum, *during thy (their) life.* — 8. in various phrases: be âwihte, *in any respect;* be fullan, *in excess;* be sumum dæle, *in some part, partly;* þâ tid be getale, *the movable Easter festival;* be ânfealdum, *single.* — 7. frequently separated from its case. Rä. 28, 17; Ps. 72.
be-æftan, *adv.* 1. after, hind. — 2. without.
be-bod, *st. n.* command, order. (Ger. *ge-bot.*)
bec. See bæc.
bêc, *pl. of* bôc.
bêcn, *st. n.* beacon, sign.
bêcnan, *w. v.* to beckon, point out, signify, denote.
bêcnung, *st. f.* indicating, signifying: hence — mark, sign.
bed, bedd, *st. n.* bed, resting-place. (Ger. *bett.*)
bed-, bedd-rest, *st. f.* bed-rest. bed.
be-foran, I. *prep.* 1. *w. dat. (a.)* local: before, in the presence of, in front. (*b.*) temporal: before, prior to, sooner than. — 2. *w. acc.* before. — II. *adv.* 1. local: before, in front, at hand, openly. — 2. temporal: before, formerly, earlier, sooner.
bêg. See bêag.

bêgan, *w. v.* to bow, bend, depress.
 â-bêgan, to bend in, crook, curve.
 for-bêgan, to give a wrong bend to, oppress, humble, degrade.
 ge-bêgan, to bow, bend, depress.
bêgan, *w. v., w. inf.* to prosecute zealously? Ps. 143, 14.
be-gang, -gong, *st. m.* (literally the extent of going), district, way, course, circuit.
begen, bâ, bû, *num.* both, *nom. m.* begen; with things, bâ, bû; *f.* bâ; *n.* bû; *gen. m. f. n.* bega, begea, begra; *dat.* bâm, bǣm; *acc. m.* bû; *f.* bâ; *n.* bû; — frequently associated with twegen.
be-hindan, I. *adv.* behind, in the rear. — II. *prep., w. dat.* (post positive), behind, after.
bêhd, *st. f.* token, witness, sign, proof.
belced-sweora, *adj.* inflated, having an inflated neck. Rä. 79, 1.
belcettan, *w. v.* to belch, eructate, utter, give forth.
belgan, *st. abl. v.* I. (*w. acc. reflex.*), to swell with anger, become angry, enraged; *w. acc.* to cause one's self to swell with anger, &c. (Ger. *balgen.*)
 â-belgan, to make angry, irritate, insult, hurt, distress.
 ge-belgan, to make angry, irritate, provoke, exasperate.
bell, the forehead? Dietrich.
bellan, *st. abl. v.* I. to bellow, bark, grunt. (Ger. *bellen.*)
bême, *w. f.* trumpet.
bên, *st. f.* boon, request, prayer, petition. (O. N. *bón.*)
ben, benn, *st. f.* wound. (Icel. *ben;* Goth. *banja.*)
bêna, *w. m.* petitioner, asker, demander.
benc, *st. f.* bench. (Ger. *bank.*)
benc-sittende, *part.* sitting on a bench, bench-sitter.
benc-swêg, *st. m.* bench-rejoicing; a joyous, convivial noise, coming from those sitting on the benches in the mead-hall.
benc-þel, *st. n.* bench-board, *i. e.*, the wainscotted space where the benches stand.
bend, *st. m. f.* band, bond. [fetter.
bendan, *w. v.* 1. to bend.— 2. to bind, ge-bendan, to bend.
be-neoðan, *prep.* beneath, under.
ben-geat, *st. n.* wound-gate, the opening of a wound.
bennian, bennegean, *w. v.* to wound.
 ge-bennian, to wound.
bên-tîd, *st. f.* prayer-time.
bera, *w. m.* bear. (Ger. *bär.*)
beran, *st. abl. v.* II. to bear, carry, bring forward, carry off, bear out, offer, extend, wear, support, suffer. At times the object is wanting, — weapons, shield, &c. (O. H. Ger. *beran;* Goth. *bairan.*)
 â-beran, 1. to bear, suffer, endure.— 2. to take away, remove.
 ǣt-beran, 1. to bring to, carry to, produce.— 2. to take away, carry off. B. 2127.
 for-beran, 1. to hold, suppress. 2. to make allowance for, humor.
 ge-beran, 1. to bear, bring forth. 2. to lead. Gû. 468.
 ôd-beran, 1. to carry, carry to, draw to, bring hither.— 2. to carry off or away.
 on-beran, to take away, carry off, abduct, weaken.
 tô-beran, to tear asunder, scatter, destroy, remove, distract, dissipate.
 ymb-beran, to bear around, surround.
berht, *adj.* bright, shining.
berhtan, *w. v.*
 ge-berhtan, to light up, enlighten, brighten.
berhtm-hwæt, *adj.* swift as an eyewink, in a moment.

berian, *w. v.* to make bare, bare, vacate.
berian, *w. v.*
   ge-berian, to happen, occur.
berige, *w. f.* berry. (O. H. Ger. *beri;* Goth. *basi;* Ger. *beere.*)
berne-lâc, *st. n.* burnt offering.
berstan, *st. abl. v.* I. **1.** to burst, break, break to pieces.—**2.** to make a noise, crack, crash, resound. (Ger. *bersten.*)
   for-berstan, to break, break in two, burst asunder, fail, vanish.
   tô-berstan, to break to pieces.
berstan, *w. v.* to make a noise, crush, resound? to break to pieces? Rä. 5, 8.
bet, *adv.* better; þê(þŷ)bet, the better.
bêtan, *w. v.* to better, restore, cure, improve, repair. (Ger. *bessern.*)
   ge-bêtan, 1. to better, improve. —**2.** to make away with, remove, relieve.—**3.** avenge, vindicate.
   un-bêtan, not to make better; *part.* **unbêted,** unatoned for, unexpiated.
betast, betost, *superl. adj.* **best,** the best.
betend, *part. & subs.* atoning, renewing; renewer, restorer.
bêt-lic, *adj.* grand, superior, excellent, magnificent.
betst, *superl.* **1.** *adj.* **best,** the best. **2.** *adv.* best, in the best manner.
be-tweoh, *prep.* between, among.
be-tweohs, -tweox, *prep. w. dat.* between, among.
be-twêonan, *prep. w. dat.* between, among.
be-twêonum, *prep. w. gen. dat. & acc.* between, among.
be-twinum, *prep.* between, among.
be-twuh, -twux, *prep.* between, among.
be-ûtan, *prep. w. dat.* **but,** without, outside of.

bêacen, *st. n.* **beacon,** token, mark, sign, standard, banner, wonder, miracle,—used especially with reference to the cross and to the sun.
bêacnian, *w. v.* to beckon, show, point out, indicate, represent pictorially.
   ge-bêacnian, to show, indicate, announce, make known.
beadu, beado, *st. f.* fight, battle, contention, strife. (O. H. Ger. *badu-, pato-.*)
beadu-caf, *adj.* ready, prepared for battle.
beadu-cræft, *st. m.* the art of war, skill in war, war-strength.
beadu-cræftig, *adj.* war-crafty, skillful in war, warlike.
beadu-cwealm, *st. m.* murder, violent death.
beadu-folm, *st. f.* battle-hand,—hence, a bloody hand.
beadu-grima, -grimma, *w. m.* war-mask, helmet.
beadu-hrægl, *st. n.* war-shirt, coat-of-mail, corselet.
beadu-lâc, *st. n.* war-play, battle, combat.
beadu-lêoma, *w. m.* battle-light, sword.
beadu-mægen, *st. n.* battle-troop, host (Grein); battle-strength, military power. (B.-T.)
beadu-mêce, *st. m.* battle-sword.
beadu-ræs, *st. m.* battle-rush, storm of battle, attack.
beadu-rinc, *st. m.* warrior, soldier.
beadu-rôf, *adj.* bold in war, strong in battle.
beadu-rûn, *st. f.* battle-secret, mystery of battle, quarrel; **beadurûn onbindan,** to loose the battle-mystery, begin battle.
beadu-scearp, *adj.* battle-sharp, sharp for the battle.
beadu-scrûd, *st. n.* battle-shroud, corselet, shirt of mail.

beadu-serce, *w. f.* battle-sark, corselet, shirt of mail.
beadu-searo, *st. n.* war-equipment weapons.
beadu-þreat, *st. m.* war-band, army.
beadu-wang, *st. m.* battlefield.
beadu-wǣpen, *st. n.* war-weapon, weapons.
beadu-weorc, *st. n.* battle-work, warlike operation, battle.
bêag, bêah, bêg, *st. m.* ring, bracelet, collar, chain, crown, diadem. (O.H. Ger. *pouc;* O. N. *baugr.*)
bêag-gifa, -gyfa, *w. m.* ring or ornament giver, king, prince, lord.
bêag-gifu, *st. f.* ring-giving, giving of rings or ornaments.
bêag-hord, *st. m.* ring-hoard, treasure consisting of ornaments, rings.
bêag-hroden, *part.* adorned with rings, or with diadems.
bêag-sel, *st. n.* ring-hall, house or hall in which rings and other ornaments are distributed.
bêag-sele, *st. m.* the same.
bêag-þegu, *st. f.* the receiving of the ring.
bêag-wriđa, *w. m.* ring-wreath, bracelet, armlet.
bêah. See **bêag.**
beald, bald, *adj.* **bold,** strong, powerful, skillful, brave, courageous, of good courage, free, liberal. (Goth. **balþs.**)
bealde, balde, *adv.* freely, trustingly, confidently, courageously, boldly, immediately, without hesitation.
bealdian, *w. v.* to show one's self bold, be brave.
beald-lîce (bald-), *adv.* = bealde, boldly.
bealdor, baldor, *st. m.* lord, master, prince, hero.
bealu, bealo, balu, *st. f.* **bale,** evil, mischief, hurt, injury, woe, affliction, wickedness, depravity. (O.H. Ger. *balo.*)

bealu, balu, *adj.* baleful, destructive, dangerous, bad, abandoned, treacherous, malicious.
bealu-ben, *st. f.* destruction-bringing wound, deadly wound.
bealo-blonden, *part.* blended or mixed with destruction, pernicious.
bealo-clom, *st. m. f.* hard, oppressive bond, dire chain.
bealo-cræft, *st. m.* magic art; wicked, pernicious art.
bealo-cwealm, *st. m.* violent death, death by the sword or disease. B. 2265.
bealu-dǣd, *st. f.* evil deed, sin.
bealo-ful, *adj.* **baleful,** full of evil, dire, cruel, wicked, pernicious.
bealo-fûs, *adj.* prone to sin, inclined to sin.
bealo-hycgende, *part.* thinking of death, meditating destruction.
bealo-hŷdig, *adj.* thinking of death, meditating destruction.
bealu-inwit, *st. n.* deceit, cunning, treachery.
bealu-lêas, *adj.* baleless, free from sin, innocent.
bealu-nîđ (bala-), *st. m.* zeal for destruction, unworthy or pernicious striving, deadly enmity, destruction.
bealo-râp, *st. m.* a sinful bond, hard, oppressive fetter.
bealo-searu, *st. n.* wicked machination or snare.
bealu-sîđ, *st. m.* **1.** mischief, hurt, calamity, adversity. See f. 28.— **2.** fatal journey, death. Exod. 5.
bealo-sorg, *st. f.* sorrow on account of expected misfortune; hard, oppressive sorrow.
bealo-spell, *st. n.* a message of dire misfortune, evil tale.
bealo-þanc, -þonc, *st. m.* malicious, evil thought.

bêam, *st. m.* **beam, 1.** tree.—**2.** cross, gallows.—**3.** pillar, column, pillar of cloud, pillar of fire.—**4.** wood, piece of wood, ship. Rä. 11, 7.—**5.** beam, post, rafter. Rä. 71, 11. (Ger. *baum.*)

bêam-sceadu, *st. f.* shadow of the tree; tree-shade.

bêam-telg, *st. m.* tree-dye, ink.

beard, *st. m.* beard. (Ger. *bart.*)

bearg, bearh, *st. m.* a barrow-pig, pig, a castrated boar. (Ger. *borgschweine.*)

bearhtm, *st. m.* **1.** splendor, brightness, clearness.—**2.** noise, tumult, clamor, cry, sound, tone.

bearm, *st. m.* barm, lap, bosom; figuratively, possession, property. (Goth. *barms;* O. H. Ger. *barm;* cf. Ger. *erbarmen.*)

bearm, *st. m.?* emotion, excitement. Ps. 118, 139.

bearn, *st. n.* (what is borne), bairn, child, boy, son, offspring, descendant, progeny. (Scot. *bairn;* Goth. *barn.*)

bearn-gebyrdu. *st. f.* childbirth, bearing; birth of a son.

bearn-gestrêon, *st. n.* child-procreation, riches in children.

bearu, bearo, *st. m.* a wood, grove, tree, forest, thicket. (O. N. *börr.*)

bearo-næs, *st. m.* woody shore.

bêatan, *st. red. v.* **1.** to beat, thrust, strike, shake, tremble.—**2.** to hurt, injure. Dan. 265.

   â-bêatan, to beat, strike, break or beat to pieces, to make to fall.

   ge-bêatan, to beat, strike, hit.

   of-bêatan, to beat to death, kill.

bêo. See **bêon.**

bêo, bi, *w. f.* bee. (Ger. *biene.*)

bêo-, bio-, bia-brêad, *st. n.* bee-bread, honeycomb.

bêod, *st. m.* table. (Goth. *biuds.*)

beodan = **bidon,** *pret.* of **bidan.**

bêodan, biodan, *st. abl. v.* VI. **1.** to bid, command, order.—**2.** to offer, proffer, give, grant.—**3.** to bring, prepare. Seef, 54.—**4.** to threaten.—**5.** to bid, announce, proclaim, inform, deliver a message, perform a commission.—**6.** to betoken, signify. (Ger. *bieten;* Goth. *biudan.*)

   â-beodan, 1. to order, command, commission, direct.—**2.** to present, announce, make known, offer, tender, wish.—**3.** to order, command.

   be-bêodan, bi-bêodan, 1. to order, command, bid.—**2.** to intrust to, recommend.—**3.** to offer.—**4.** to announce, proclaim, make known.

   for-bêodan, to forbid.

   ge-bêodan, 1. to command, order, direct.—**2.** to deliver up, give over to, surrender. Dan. 414.—**3.** to offer, show.—**4.** to offer.—**5.** to threaten. Dan. 223.

   on-bêodan, to announce, proclaim, make known.

bêod-gæst, *st. m.* table guest, familiar friend.

bêod-genêat, *st. m.* table-companion.

bêod-gereordu, *st. n. pl.* table-meal, feast. [moved.

beofian, *w. v.* to tremble, quake, be

   â-beofian, same as the above.

bêo-hâta, *w. m.* (the queen-bee), leader, prince.

bêon, bion, *irreg. v. pres. ind. sg.* **1.** bêom, bêon, bêo.—**2.** bist, byst.—**3.** bið, byd, beoð (Hy. 7, 96); *pl.* bêoð, bioð, biað; *subj. sg.* bêo, bio; *pl.* bêon; *imper. sig.* bêo; *pl.* bêoð, to be,—generally with a future signification *will be.*

bêor, *st. n.* beer. (Ger. *bier.*)

beoran = **beran,** to bear, carry. Sal. 206.

beorc, *st. f.* birch, birch-tree; and name for the Rune B. (Ger. *birke.*)

beorcan, *st. abl. v.* I. to bark.

beorg, beorh, biorg, *st. m.* **barrow,** mountain, hill, mound. (Ger. *berg.*)
beorgan, *st. abl. v.* I. to save, protect, shelter, guard, defend, shield, spare, preserve;— *w. reflex. dat.* to beware of, avoid. (Ger. *bergen;* Goth. *bairgan.*)
be-beorgan, *w. reflex. dat.* to be on one's guard, take care.
ge-beorgan, to save, protect, defend; to protect one from something, ward off, spare, preserve.
ymb-beorgan, to surround protectingly.
beorgan, *w. v.* to taste, drink.
beorg-hlid, *st. n.* mountain-height, elevation, hill.
beorg-sedel, *st. m. n.?* mountain dwelling. Gû. 73.
beorg-stede, *st. m.* mountain place, place on a mountain, mound, mountain.
beorh. See **beorg.**
bêor-hyrde, *st. m.* beer-keeper, butler.
beorht, *st. n.* brightness, shining object, light, glance, twinkling.
beorht, *adj.* 1. **bright,** brilliant, glistening, clear, lucid, plain, beautiful.— 2. celebrated, excellent, noble, splendid, sublime, holy, divine. (Goth. *bairhts.*)
beorhtan, *w.v.* to light, shine, lighten.
beorhte, *adv.* brightly, lucidly, clearly, distinctly.
beorhtian, *w. v.* 1. to glisten, shine. 2. to sound clearly.
beorht-lic, *adj.* brilliant, bright, shining, splendid.
beorht-lice,*adv.*brilliantly,**brightly,** clearly, excellently.
beorhtm, *st. m.* noise, tumult.
beorht-nes, -nys, *st. f.* **brightness,** clearness, brilliancy, splendor.
beorht-rodor, *st. m.* bright firmament, ether.

beorhtu, *st. f.* brightness, clearness.
beorma, *w. m.* **barm,** yeast, leaven. Ger. *barme, bärme.*)
beorn, biorn, *st. m.* noble, distinguished man, hero, warrior; a man. (Scan. *björn.*)
beornân, *st. abl. v.* I. to **burn,** glow, blaze up, burn up. (Ger. *brennen.*)
â-beornan, to kindle, inflame, take fire.
for-beornan, to burn up, to be burnt up, burn. (Ger. *verbrennen.*)
ge-beornan, same as the above.
beorn-cyning, *st. m.* king of warriors, king of heroes.
beorne, byrne, *w. f.* **burnie,** shirt of mail. (Ger. *brünne.*)
beorn-þrĕat, *st. m.* band of men or warriors.
beorn-wiga, *w. m.* steel-clad warrior, or noble warrior, hero.
bêor-scealc, *st. m.* keeper of the beer, cup-bearer.
bêor-sele, *st. m.* beer-hall, a hall in which beer is drunk.
bêor-setl, *st. m.* beer-settle, beerbench.
bêor-þegu, *st. f.* beer-drinking, beer-banquet.
beordor, *st. n.* childbirth, fetus? See **hysebeordor.**
bêot, *st. n.* proud, boastful speech, by which one is pledged or bound; threat, promise, pledge.— 2. peril? danger? Dan. 265.
bêotian, *w. v.* 1. to threaten.— 2. to promise, pledge.
ge-bêotian, to promise, to bind one's self, make one's self responsible for.
bêot-word, *st. n.*= **bêot.**
bêod. See **bêon.**
bi (most frequently met with in shortened form **be),** *prep. w. dat.* 1. local: **by,** near, at, on, upon, about, of, in, with.— 2. causal: by,

through, by reason of, after, according to.— **3.** of, about, concerning (w. verbs of saying, &c.)— **4.** in comparison with. Ph. 338.— **5.** temporal: by, during, **bi me lifgendum**, during my lifetime.

bi, big, in improper word-composition **by.**

bi. See **bêo.**

bi-bod, *st. n.* command, order, decree.

bi-brêad, *st. n.* bee-bread, honeycomb.

biogan. See **byogan.**

bid, *st. n.* lingering, delay, abiding.

bidan, *st. abl. v.* V. **1.** to bide, delay, linger, wait, abide, remain, live, dwell.— **2.** to await, expect, wait for.— **3.** to reach, arrive at, know, experience, find. (Goth. *beidan;* O. H. Ger. *bîtan.*)

 â-bidan, to tarry, delay, remain behind, await, expect, experience.

 ge-bidan, 1. to remain, delay, abide, tarry.— **2.** to expect, wait for, await.— **3.** to reach, arrive at, know, experience, find.

 ofer-bidan, to outlast, surmount, outlive.

 on-bidan, to wait, await, expect.

biddan, *st. abl. v.* III. to bid, desire, beg, ask, pray, order, require. (Ger. *bitten.*)

 â-biddan, to implore, obtain by entreaty.

 ge-biddan, to beg, ask, pray, pray to,— often with *reflex. dat.*

bid-fæst, *adj.* firm, forced to stand out.

bidian, *w. v.*

 an-bidian, to await.

biding, *st. f.* biding, waiting, delaying;— abode.

bid-steal, *st. m.* halt, stand.

bifian, *w. v.* to tremble, shake, be moved. (Ger. *beben.*)

 â-bifian, same as the above.

bi-foran, I. *prep. w. dat.* (temporal and local), **before.**— II. *adv.* **1.** local: before, in the presence of.— **2.** before, formerly.

big. See **bi.**

bigan. See **bŷgan.**

bi-gang, -gong, *st. m.* extent, way, course, circuit.

bi-genga, -gengea, *w. m.* cultivator, inhabitant, dweller.

bi-hâta, *w. m.* the queen-bee, leader.

bil, bill, *st. n.* bill, battle-axe, sword; — a *bill* was a broad two-edged sword. (Ger. *beil.*)

bile-wit. See **bilwit.**

bil-gesliht, *st. n.* sword-fight, battle of swords.

bil-hete, bill-, *st. m.* sword-hate, hate made known by the sword.

bil-swæd, *st. n.* sword-track, wound.

bil-wit, bile-wit, byly-wit, *adj.* mild, gentle, merciful, calm, composed.

bin, binn, *st. f.* bin, manger, crib. (Ger. *benne.*)

bindan, *st. abl. v.* I. to bind, tie. (Ger. *binden.*)

 ge-bindan, to bind, tie, fetter.

 in-bindan, to unbind, untie, loose.

 on-bindan, same as the above.

bindan, *w. r.* to feign, dissimulate. Luc. C. 24, 28.

bindere, *st. m.* binder.

binn. See **bin.**

binnan, *prep.* within, inside of, in, into. (Ger. *binnen.*)

bired. See **beran.**

birhtu, *st. f.* brightness, clearness.

bi-rihte, -ryhte, *prep.* right by, near by, beside.

bi-sæce, *st. m.?* a visit. Gû. 188.

bisceop, biscop, *st. m.* bishop.

bisceop-hâd, *st. m.* office of a bishop, episcopate.

bisen. See **bysen.**

bises, *st. m.* an intercalary day, leap-year.

bisgan, bisgu, bisig. See **bysgan, bysgu, bysig.**

bismer, bismor, bysmer, *st. n.* mockery, disgrace, opprobrium, reproach, pollution, infamy, blasphemy.

bismerian, bysmrian, *w. v.* to mock, deride, reproach, blaspheme.

    ge-bysmrian, to deride, provoke, enrage.

bismer-léas, *adj.* reproachless, free from shame, infamy, blameless, spotless.

bismer-, bismor-, bysmer-lice, *adv.* scandalously, shamefully, reproachfully, infamously, irreverently.

bi-spel, *st. n.* parable, fable, allegory, example. (Ger. *beispiel.*)

bist. See **béon.**

bitan, *st. abl. v.* V. to bite, cut, cut into, wound. (Ger. *beiszen.*)

    â-bitan, to bite, gnaw, corrode, eat.

    on-bitan, to bite, taste, feed upon.

bite, *st. m.* bite, cut.

biter, bitor, bitter, *adj.* bitter, sharp, cutting, biting, harsh, painful;— exasperated, angry, embittered. (Ger. *bitter.*)

bitian, *w. v.*

    grist-bitian, to bite the teeth together, gnash the teeth.

bitre, bitere, bittre, *adv.* bitterly, sharply, severely, furiously.

bi-tweon, *prep.* between.

bi-twéonum, *prep.* between.

biered, biersted, biesgian. See **beran, berstan, bysgian.**

biad, bio, bion, biod. See **béon.**

blac, blæc, *adj.* black, dark.

blâc, *adj.* 1. brilliant, shining, gleaming.— 2. pale (of the white death-color), bleak.

blâc-ern, *st. n.* lighthouse, lamp, candlestick, light, candle.

blâc-hléor, *adj.* pale-faced, fair.

blâcian, *w. v.* to become white, pale.

blæc. See **blac.**

blǽc. See **blâc.**

blǽcan, *w. v.* to bleach, whiten, fade.

blǽc-ern. See **blâcern.**

blæd, *st. n.* blade, leaf. Gen. 994. (Ger. *blatt.*)

blǽd, *st. m.* 1. blowing, blast.— 2. inspiration? Ph. 548.— 3. breath, spirit. Hexam. 11.— 4. life.— 5. riches, fullness, success, happiness, renown, glory, worth, dignity, honor. (O. H. Ger. *blât.*)

blǽd, *st. f.* blade, leaf, twig, flower, blossom, fruit, foliage, grass.

blǽd-âgend, *part. & subs.* having an abundance of renown, glory;— possessing abundance, prosperous.

blǽd-dagas, *st. m. pl.* happy, prosperous day, happy life.

blǽd-fæst, *adj.* fast or fixed in renown, celebrated, prosperous, happy.

blǽd-gifa, *w. m.* glory-giver, giver of prosperity or happiness.

blǽd-wela, *w. m.* wealth of glory or riches, happiness bringing wealth.

blæst, *st. m.* blast, flame, torch, blaze.

blǽst, *st. m.* blowing, wind.

blǽtan, *st. red. v.* to bleat. (O. H. Ger. *blâzan.*)

blanca, blonca, *w. m.* white or gray horse.

bland, *st. n.* blending, mixture, confusion.

blandan, *st. red. v.* to blend, mix. (O. H. Ger. *blandan.*)

    ge-blandan, to blend, mix, exchange, disturb, disquiet.

    on-blandan, to mingle, blend, disturb.

blanden-, blonden-feax, *adj.* with mixed hair, having gray hair, old.

blât, *st. m. n.?* an inarticulate sound of sorrow. An. 1281.—B.-T. make *blát* an adjective = livid.

blât, *adj.* livid, pale.

blâtan, *st. red. v.* to be livid, pale, as with envy.

blâte, *adv.* lividly, pallidly.

blâwan, *st. red. v.* to blow. (Ger. *blähen*.)
    â-blâwan, same as the above.
    to-blâwan, to blow to pieces, scatter.

blêd = blǽd, *st. m.*

blêd = blǽd, *st. f.*

blêdan, *w. v.* to bleed, let blood. (Ger. *bluten*.)

blêd-hwæt, *adj.* rich in flowers or fruits (Grein);—a shoot growing quickly (B.-T.). Rä. 2, 9.

bledsian, *w. v.* to bless, consecrate.
    ge-bledsian, to bless, benefit, favor, make to prosper.

blencan, *w. v.* to deceive, cheat.

blendan, *w.v.* to blind. (Ger. *blenden*.)
    â-blendan, same as the above.

bletsian, *w. v.* to bless, consecrate, ordain.
    ge-bletsian, to bless, consecrate, benefit, make to prosper.
    un-gebletsian, *part.* ungebletsod, unblessed.

bletsung, *st. f.* blessing, benediction.

blêat, *adj.* naked, bare, miserable, wretched. (Ger. *bloss*.)

blêate, *adv.* wretchedly, miserably.

blêað, *adj.* cowardly, unwarlike, timid. (Ger. *blöde*.)

blêo-bord, *st. n.* colored board, chessboard.

blêo-brygd, *st. m.? n.?* variation of color, variegated color.

blêo-fâg, *adj.* variable in color, variegated, many-colored.

blêoh, blioh, blêo, *st. n.* color, appearance, complexion, delight, joy.

blêowe? Rä. 84, 6, blow, blew.

blican, *st. abl. v.* V. 1. to lighten, shine, glitter, sparkle, dazzle.—2. to appear, become visible. Sal. 144. (Ger. *bleichen*.)

blids. See **bliðs**.

blin, *st. f.* cessation, interruption, end.

blind, *adj.* blind. (Ger. *blind*.)

blind-nes, *st. f.* blindness.

blinnan, *st. abl. v.* I. to cease, leave off, forego, to lose, be deprived of. (Chaucer, *blynne*.)

blis, bliss, blyss, *st. f.* 1. bliss, joy, joyousness, happiness, pleasure. 2. complaisance, courteousness, kindness, grace, favor.

blissian, *w. v.* 1. to rejoice, gladden, make glad.—2. to rejoice, be glad, exult.
    ge-blissian, to rejoice, gladden, make glad.—2. to bless? Cri. 380. 3. to make joyous, delightful.

bliwum, *dat. pl.* See **blêoh**.

blið, *adj.* agreeable, sweet, pleasant.

blîðe, *adj.* 1. blithe, joyous, glad, merry.—2. gentle, friendly, pleasant, kind, mild, agreeable.—3. quiet, peaceful. An. 385.; Ps. 106, 28. (Goth. *bleiþs*.)

blîðe, *adv.* 1. joyously, merrily, gladly. 2. graciously, kindly, mildly.

blîðe-môd, *adj.* 1. of joyous mind, glad, cheerful.—2. calm, tranquil, mild, gentle.

blîð-heort, *adj.* 1. blithe of heart, joyous.—2. well-wishing, friendly, merciful.

bliðs, blids, *st. f.* joy, gladness.

bliðsian, *w. v.* to rejoice, be glad, merry.

blôd, *st. n.* blood. (Ger. *blut*.)

blôd-egesa, *w. m.* bloody terror, horror.

blôd-fâg, *adj.* colored with blood, bloody.

blôd-gyte, -gete, -geote, *st. m.* gush of blood, blood-flowing.

blôd-hrêow, *adj.* bloody, bloody-minded, cruel.
blôdian, *w. v.*
ge-blôdegian, to make bloody, stain with blood.
blôdig, *adj.* bloody. (Ger. *blutig.*)
blôdig-tôđ, *adj.* with bloody tooth, cruel.
blôd-rêow, *adj.* bloodthirsty, cruel.
blôstm, *st. m.? f.?* blossom, flower.
blôstma, *w. m.* blossom, flower.
blôtan, *st. red. v.* to sacrifice, kill for a sacrifice. (Goth. *blotan.*)
on-blôtan, to sacrifice, kill for a sacrifice.
blôt-mônađ, *st. m.* month of sacrifice, November.
blôwan, *st. red. v.* to blow, bloom, blossom.
ge-blôwan, to blow, bloom, blossom, sprout, — also used figuratively.
blŷgan, *w. v.* to scare, frighten.
un-geblŷgan, *part.* ungeblŷged, intrepid, fearless, bold.
blys. See blis.
bôc, *st. f.* beech-tree, book, writing. (Ger. *buche.*)
bôc, *irreg. f.* (*dat. sg.*, *nom. acc., pl.* bêc), book; — in *pl.* generally the Scriptures. (Ger. *buch.*)
bôc-cræftig, *adj.* book-crafty, learned, especially with reference to the Scriptures.
bôcere, *st. m.* writer, scribe, learned man, author, teacher.
bôc-stæf, *st. m.* letter, character.
bôc-wudu, *st. m.* beech-wood.
bod, *st. n.* command, order, commandment, message. (Ger. *ge-bot.*)
boda, *w. m.* messenger, herald, ambassador, apostle, angel; — seer, prophet. (Ger. *bote.*)
bodian, *w. v.* to bode, announce, make known, tell, preach, prophesy.
ge-bodian, to tell, announce, make known.

bod-scipe, *st. m.* 1. commandment. — 2. message, announcement. (Cf. Ger. *botschaft.*)
bôg, bôh, *st. m.* bough, branch (of a tree).
bôg, *st. m.* arm, shoulder; — cf. elbow. (Ger. *bug.*)
boga, *w. m.* bow. (Ger. *boge.*)
bôh. See bôg.
bohte. See bycgan.
bolca, *w. m.* gangway of a ship. (Icel. *bálki.*)
bold, *st. n.* building, dwelling, house, dwelling-place, edifice.
bold-âgend, *part. & subs.* house-owner, property-holder.
bold-getimbru, *st. n. pl.* building, edifice; — lit., the timbers of a house.
bold-wela, *w. m.* rich, splendid dwelling, paradise, heaven.
bolgen-môd, *adj.* angry at heart, enraged.
bolla, *w. m.* bowl, cup, pot, drinking-vessel. (Ger. *bolc.*)
bolster, *st. m.* bolster, pillow. (Ger. *polster.*)
bôn (= bôgan), to boast.
bona, bongâr, bonnan. See bana, bangâr, bannan.
bora, *w. m.* bearer.
borcian, *w. v.* to bark.
bord, *st. n.*, lit. board; hence, 1. board, table. — 2. plank, side of a ship, ship. — 3. shield. (Ger. *bord.*)
borde, *w. f.* a lady's chamber? Gn. Ex. 64 (Grein); — board, table. (B.-T.)
bord-gelâc, *st. n.* shield-storming, missile, dart.
bord-hæbbende, *part. & subs.* shield-having, shield-bearer.
bord-haga, *w. m.* shield-hedge, cover of shields.
bord-hrêođa, -hrêđa, *w. m.* shield-covering, shield, buckler.

bord-rand, *st. m.* edge of a shield, shield.
bord-stæð, *st. n.* seashore.
bord-weall, *st. m.* **1.** shield-wall, wall of shields, buckler, shield.—**2.** quay. Rä. 34, 6.
bord-wudu, *st. m.* shield-wood, shield.
borg-sorg, *st. f.* sorrow on account of lending, or of security. (*ms. burg sorg.* Reim 63.)
bôsm, *st. m.* bosom, breast, lap, inner parts. (Ger. *busen.*)
bôt, *st. f.* **1.** boot, help, cure, remedy.—**2.** alleviation, redress.—**3.** boot, amends, reparation.—**4.** satisfaction, restoring, compensation.—**5.** penance, repentance, offering.—**6. tô bôte, to boot,** besides, moreover. (Ger. *busze.*)
botl, *st. n.* house, dwelling.
botl-gestrêon, *st. n.* riches in houses, goods, riches.
botl-wela, *w. m.* wealth of houses, village.
botm, *st. m.* bottom. (Ger. *boden*, O. H. Ger. *bodam.*)
brâd, *adj.* broad, stretched out, roomy, wide, spacious, copious. (Ger. *breit.*)
brâd, *st. n.* breadth.
brâde, *adv.* far and wide, broadly, widely.
bræd, *st. f.* heat, glow, smell; or the fleshy part of animal bodies. Ph. 240.
brǣdan, *w. v.* **1.** to broaden, make broad, stretch out, expand.—**2.** to be extended or developed, rise, grow. (Ger. *breiten.*) [tend.
 ge-brǣdan, to stretch out, ex-
 geond-brǣdan, to spread over, cover entirely.
 ofer-brǣdan, to be spread over, cover.
 tô-brǣdan, to spread out, multiply, open.

brǣdra, *compar.* of **brâd.**
brǣdu, *st. f.* breadth, width.
brægdan (=**bregdan**), to sing according to time, sing.
brægd-boga, *w. m.* deceitful bow.
brægd-wis, *adj.* crafty, sly, cunning.
brægn-loca, *w. m.* brain-house, head. (*ms. hrægnloca.*)
bræsne, *adj.* mighty, powerful.
bræwum, *dat. pl.* See **brêaw.**
brand, brond, *st. m.* **1.** brand, firebrand, burning piece of wood.—**2.** burning, flame, fire.—**3.** a glowing object, torch.—**4.** sword. B. 1451.—**5.** warrior. B. 1020. (Ger. *brand.*)
brand-hât, *adj.* burning hot, ardent, passionate.
brand-hord, *st. n.* burning treasure, *i. e.*, care, anxiety.
brand-stæfn, *adj.* having a prow supplied with a pole or beam (Grein);—the shining prowed. (B.-T.). An. 501.
brant, bront, *adj.* going high, raging, foaming, high, steep.
brecan, *st. abl. v.* II. **1.** to break, break to pieces, break through, violate.—**2.** to vex, press, not to let rest.—**3.** to break in upon, take by storm.—**4.** to break out, spring out.—**5.** to make a way for one's self by force, to sail. (Ger. *brechen.*)
 â-brecan, to break open, force, break to pieces, violate, conquer, take by storm.
 be-brecan, to rob or spoil by breaking off, plucking.
 for-brecan, to break to pieces, destroy, violate.
 ge-brecan, to break, break to pieces, destroy, oppress.
 tô-brecan, to break in pieces, break through.
 þurh-brecan, to break through. (Ger. *durchbrechen.*)

brecan, *w. v.* to roar, break.
brêc-hrægl, *st. n.* clothes for the thigh, breeches.
brecđ, *st. f.* breach, breaking, sorrow.
brêdan, *st. abl. v.* I. **1.** to swing round, swing, move, draw out, draw, drag.— **2.** to braid, knit, knot, plait, weave.
   â-brêdan, to swing, draw, take away, draw back.
   for-brêdan, to change, transform.
   ge-brêdan, 1. to swing, draw, unsheath.— **2.** to breathe (drawing in and giving forth breath).— **3.** to knit, plait.
   ofer-brêdan, to draw over, cover.
   on-brêdan, to tear open, throw open violently.
   ôđ-brêdan, to withdraw, deprive.
   tô-brêdan, 1. to divide.— **2.** to spread out, stretch out.— **3.** to awake from sleep.— **4.** to turn to, turn about.
bredian, *w. v.*
   ge-bredian, to restore flesh, make fleshy.
bredwian, *w. v.*
   â-bredwian, to strike down, kill.
brêgan, *w. v.* to frighten, terrify.
   â-brêgan, same as above.
bregdan, *st. abl. v.* I. **1.** to swing, vibrate, draw, unsheath, brandish. — **2.** to knit, knot, plait, weave. — **3.** to change color, be particolored.— **4.** to modulate.— **5.** to turn or be transformed into. (O. H. Ger. *brettan*.)
   â-bregdan, to swing, draw, take away, draw back.
   for-bregdan, to draw over, cover.
   ge-bregdan, to swing.
   ofer-bregdan, to draw over, cover.
   on-bregdan, to start up.
   tô-bregdan, 1. to divide, tear in pieces, rend, lacerate.— **2.** slǽpe tôbregdan, to awake, wake up.
brego, bregu, brega, breogo, *st. m.* prince, lord, master. (Icel. *bragr*.)
brego-rîce, *st. n.* principality, kingdom.
brego-rôf, *adj.* powerful like a ruler, of heroic strength.
brego-stôl, *st. m.* throne, rule, power.
brego-weard, *st. m.* ruler, prince, lord, master.
brêgum, *dat. pl.* See **brêaw**.
brehtm, *st. m.* sound, noise, tumult; —sudden, quick movement.
brêman, *w. v.* to celebrate, make famous.
brember, *st. m.* bramble. (Cf. Ger. *brom-beere*.)
brême, *adj.* widely known, celebrated, renowned, noble, illustrious.
brême, *adv.* famously, gloriously.
brêmen, *adj.* celebrated, illustrious, noble, glorious.
brênan, *w. v.* to make or dye brown, Rûn. 15 (Grein); — **breneđ,** burns, = berneđ, 3*d sig. pres.* of bernan. (B.-T.)
brengan, *w. v., pret.* **brôhte,** to bring, bear, lead, advance, present, offer.
   ge-brengan, same as above.
brenting, *st. m.* ship, craft.
brêr, *st. m.* briar, thorny plant. (Chaucer, *brere*.)
brerd, *st. m.* brim, edge, margin, shore, bank.
bresne, *adj.* brazen, mighty, powerful, strong.
bretta (=**brytta**), *w. m.* ruler, lord.
brêđer. See **brôđor**.
brêađ, *st. n.* bread. (Ger. *brot*.)
breađian, *w. v.*
   ge-breađian, to make fleshy, restore.
brêagas, *nom. acc. pl.* See **brêaw**.

breahtm, *st. m.* noise, cry, tumult, rejoicing. (O. H. Ger. *braht*.)
breahtum-hwæt, *adj.* quick as the wink of an eye, swift.
brēatan, *st. red. v.* to break through, demolish, cut in pieces, tear, destroy, kill.
  â-brēatan, same as above.
brēaw, *st. m.* eyelid.
breodian, *w. v.* to cry out.
breodwian, *w. v.* to strike, beat down.
breogo, breomo, breotone. See **brego, brim, bryten**.
brēost, *st. n.* breast, heart, mind, thought, disposition. (Ger. *brust*.)
brēost-cearu, *st. f.* breast-care, heart-sorrow.
brēost-côfa, *w. m.* the breast as the seat of the feelings;—affections, breast, heart, mind.
brēost-gehygd, *st. f. n.* thought of the heart or mind, inner thought, secret thought.
brēost-geþanc, *st. m.* heart-thought, thought of the mind.
brēost-gewǣdu, *st. n. pl.* breast-weeds, coat of mail.
brēost-hord, *st. n. m.* breast-hoard, thought, heart, soul.
brēost-loca, *w. m.* breast-inclosure, mind, heart.
brēost-net, *st. n.* breast-net, shirt of chain-mail, coat of mail.
brēost-sefa, *w. m.* breast-thought, mind.
brēost-toga, *w. m.* breast-leader, chief.
brēost-weordung, *st. f.* ornament worn on the breast, ornament.
brēost-wylm, *st. m.* heaving of the breast, emotion, sorrow.
brēotan, *st. abl. v.* VI. to break, break to pieces, destroy, kill. (O. H. Ger. *bretôn*.)
  â-brēotan, same as above.
breoton. See **bryten**.
brēodan, *st. abl. v.* VI.
  â-brēodan, to perish, be destroyed;—deteriorate.
brice, brice, briced. See **bryce, brýce, brecan**.
bricg. See **brycg**.
brid, *st. m.* bird, the young (of any of the feathered tribe).
bridel, *st. m.* bridle, rein. (O. H. Ger. *brittil*.)
bridels, *st. m.* bridle, rein.
bridels-hring, *st. m.* bridle-ring.
brigd, *st. n.* change, variety of colors. Pa. 26.
brihtan, *w. v.*
  ge-brihtan, to brighten, make beautiful.
brim, brym, *st. m. m.* (brim), flood, sea, ocean, wave. (Icel. *brim*.)
brim-ceald, *adj.* cold as the seawater, very cold.
brim-clif, *st. n.* seacliff, cliff washed by the sea.
brim-faro, *st. f.* seaway, waves of the ocean. Dan. 322.
brim-flôd, *st. m.* seaflood, sea.
brim-fugol, *st. m.* seafowl, gull.
brim-gæst, -giest, *st. m.* seaguest, sailor.
brim-hengest, *st. m.* senhorse, ship.
brim-hlæst, *st. f.* seaburden, fishes.
brim-lâd, *st. f.* seaway, floodway, sea-journey.
brim-lidend, *part. & subs.* seafarer, sailor.
brim-man, *st. m.* seaman.
brim-nesen, *st. f.* safe sea-passage. El. 1004.
brim-râd, *st. f.* searoad, sea.
brim-stæd, *st. n.* seashore.
brim-strēam, *st. m.* 1. seastream, sea-flood, current, sea.— 2. a rapid river.
brim-þisa, *w. m.* a noisy rusher over the sea, ship.
brim-wisa, *w. m.* leader at sea, sea-king.
brim-wudu, *st. m.* seawood, sea.

brim-wylf, *st. f.* she seawolf.
brim-wylm, *st. m.* seawave, surge.
bringan, *st. abl. v.* I. to **bring,** bring forward, lead to, adduce, produce, bear, carry. (Ger. *bringen*.)
  ge-bringan, same as above.
brinnan, *st. abl. v.* I.
  on-brinnan, to influence, kindle.
brit = brided. See **brēdan.**
brittian. See **bryttian.**
brōc, *st. m.* **brook.** (Ger. *bruch.*)
brocen, *part.* See **brecan.**
brocen, *part.* See **brūcan.**
brōga, *w. m.* terror, fear, horror, (O. H. Ger. *brôgo.*)
brōhte. See **brengan.**
brōh-þrēa, *w. m.* terrific calamity, starvation.
brosnian, *w. v.* to crumble, become rotten, fall to pieces, disappear.
  ge-brosnian, to corrupt, spoil, destroy.
brosnung, *st. f.* corruption, decay, ruin.
brōðor, brōður, *irreg. w. dat. sg.* **brēðer,** *st. m.* **brother.** (Ger. *bruder.*)
brōðor-bana, *w. m.* brother-murderer, fratricide.
brōðor-cwealm, *st. m.* brother-murder, fratricide.
brōðor-gyld, *st. n.* brother-vengeance, vengeance for brothers. Exod. 199.
brōðor-lēas, *adj.* brotherless.
brōðor-sib, *st. f.* **1.** brotherhood, kinship of brothers.— **2.** brotherly love.
brū, brūn, *st. f.* eyebrow, **brow.** (Ger. *braue, braune.*)
brūcan, *st. abl. v.* VI. to use, make use of, enjoy, have, possess. (Ger. *brauchen.*)
  ge-brūcan, to enjoy fully.
brūn, *adj.* **brown,** having a metallic color, dark, black. (Ger. *braun.*)

brūn-ecg, *adj.* brown-edged, having a steel-colored or gleaming blade.
brūn-fāg, *adj.* gleaming like metal, brown-hued.
brūn-wann, *adj.* dark brown, dusky.
bryce, brice, *st. m.* break, injury.
bryce, brice, *adj.* liable to break, fragile, futile, fleeting.
brŷce, brice, *st. m.* advantage, gain, use, pains, labor. (Ger. *brauch.*)
brŷce, *adj.* useful, fit for use, serviceable.
bryced. See **brecan.**
brycg, bricg, *st. f.* **bridge.** (Ger. *brücke.*)
brycgan, -ian, *w. v.* to **bridge,** make a bridge.
brycg-weard, *st. m.* bridgewarder, keeper or defender of a bridge.
brŷd, *st. f.* **bride,** betrothed woman, young woman, woman, wife. (Ger. *braut.*)
brŷd-būr, *st. n.* woman's chamber, bedchamber.
bryddan, *w. v.*
  ge-bryddan, to frighten, terrify, stun.
brŷd-guma, *w. m.* betrothed man, **bridegroom.**
brŷd-lufe, *w. f.* a bride's love.
brygd. See **brigd.**
brygdan, *w. v.* to turn.
  on-brygdan, to lift, raise up.
brym. See **brim.**
bryne, *st. m.* burning, fire, conflagration. (Ger. *brunst;*—Goth. *brunsts*).
bryne-brōga, *w. m.* fear or dread of fire.
bryne-gield, *st. n.* burnt-offering.
bryne-hāt, *adj.* burning hot.
bryne-lēoma, *w. m.* fire-flame, flame.
bryne-tear, *st. m.* burning tear.
bryne-wylm, -welm, *st. m.* waves of a conflagration.

bryrdan, *w. v.* to prick, goad, incite, arouse, encourage.
  in-bryrdan, same as above.
  on-bryrdan, same as above.
bryta. See **brytta.**
bryten, breoton, *adj.* stretched out, broad, roomy.
bryten-grund, *st. m.* spacious land, earth.
bryten-rice, *st. n.* spacious kingdom.
bryten-wang, *st. m.* spacious plain, world.
brytnian, *w. v.* to dispense, distribute, administer.
brytta, bryta, *w. m.* dispenser, distributor, divider, governor;—appellation for king. (Icel. *bryti*.)
bryttian, brittian, *w. v.* to dispense, distribute, impart, administer, enjoy.
bryden, *st. f.* broth, drink.
bû. See **begen.**
bû, *st. m.? f.? n.? pl.* **bŷ**; dwelling, dwelling-place. (Ger. *bau*.)
bûan, bûwan, *st. abl.* VI. **1.** to stay, remain, dwell, live.— **2.** to inhabit, occupy. (Ger. *bauen*.)
  ge-bûan, to inhabit, occupy, to make habitable or comfortable.
bûend, *part. & subs.* dwelling, inhabiting;—dweller, inhabitant.
bûgan, *st. abl. v.* VI. to **bow,** bend, bow down, sink, curve, give way, turn, go, flee. (Ger. *biegen*.)
  â-bûgan, to bend off, curve away from, incline, bow down;—to be turned, turn one's self.
  be-, bi-bûgan, 1. to turn, hold one's self at a distance, shun, avoid.— **2.** to go or flow around, encircle, surround, shut in, inclose.— **3.** *intrans.* to reach, extend.
  for-bûgan, to turn away from, shun, avoid.
  ge-bûgan, *intrans.* or *w. acc.* of thing, to bend, bow, sink, submit.
  on-bûgan, 1. to escape, get off. — **2.** to invade, overwhelm.

bûian, bûgan, bûgian, bûwian, *w. v.* **1.** to stay, remain, dwell.— **2.** to inhabit, occupy.
bunden-stefna, *adj.* furnished with a bound or well-joined prow. Grein.
bunden-stefna, *w. m.* a bound prow. B.-T.
bune, *w. f.* can, cup, drinking-vessel.
bûr, *st. n.* bower, room, lady's chamber. (Ger. *bauer*.)
burg, burh, *irreg. st. f.; sg. gen.* **byrig, burge**;—*dat.* **byrig, byrg**; *—pl. nom. acc.* **byrig**;—*gen.* **burga, byrga**;— *dat.* **burgum** (-burgh, **borough**), city, castle, fortress, Heaven, hell. (Ger. *burg;* Goth. *baurgs*.)
burg-âgend, *part.* possessing or owning a fortress or palace.
burgent, *st. f.* city. El. 31.
burg-fæsten, *st. n.* fortified city, fortress, citadel.
bûr-geteld, *st. n.* tent, bedchamber.
burg-geat, *st. n.* city gate.
burg-hlid, -hleod, *st. n.* fortress or city height,—the height on which a fortress or city stands.
burg-land, *st. n.* city land, land on which the city stands, city.
burg-leode, *st. f. pl.* town-people, citizens. (Ger. *burg-leute*.)
burg-loca, *w. m.* city inclosure, barrier, city, castle-bar.
burg-ræced, *st. n.* city dwelling, fortress.
burg-sæl, *st. n.* castle-hall.
burg-sele, *st. m.* castle-hall, city dwelling.
burg-sittende, *part. & subs.* inhabitants of a city, citizens.
burg-stede, *st. m.* castle-place, place where castle or city stands, city, castle.
burg-steal, *st. m.* city-place, citadel.
burg-tûn, *st. m.* city-hedge, the quickset hedge around a town.
burg-þelu, *st. f.* castle-floor.

burg-wara, *w. m.* inhabitant of the city, citizen.
burg-waru, *st. f.* inhabitants of a city as a body, citizens.
burg-wela, *w. m.* city wealth, treasures.
burg-weall, *st. m.* city wall, wall.
burg-weard, *st. m.* castle warder, city defender.
burg-wigend, *part. & subs.* warrior of city, warrior.
burh. See **burg.**
burna, burne, *w. m. f.* (burn, bourn), fountain, spring, brook, water, river. (Ger. *brunnen, born.*)
burn-sele, *st. m.* spring or bathhouse.
bûr-þegn, *st. m.* bower-thane, chamberlain, page.
bûtan, bûton, I. *conj.* 1. *w. subj.* but, unless, except.— 2. *w. ind.* except, unless, save that.— 3. *without verb,* except.— II. *prep. w. dat.* 1. out of, against. An. 679.— 2. except, without.
bûte = **bûtan,** *conj. w. subj.* unless.
bûtû. See **begen** and **twegen.**
bycgan, bicgan, bycgean, *w. v.* buy, procure. (Goth. *bugjan.*)
    be-bycgan, to sell.
    ge-bycgan, to buy, procure.
byden, *st. f.* butt, tun, cask, barrel. (O. H. Ger. *butin.*)
bŷgan, bigan, -ean, *w. v.* to bow, bend, bow down, humiliate, abase.
    for-bigan, to bend in the wrong direction, bow down, humiliate, weaken, abase.
    ge-bŷgan, to bow, bend, bow down, curve, abase, break to pieces.
    on-bŷgan, to curve inward, curve.
byht, *st. m.* corner, bay, dwelling, abode, territory. (Ger. *bucht.*)
bylda, *w. m.* builder, householder, proprietor.

byldan, *w. v.* to embolden, incite, urge on, encourage, confirm.
    ge-byldan, same as above.
byldan, *w. v.*
    ge-byldan, to make sad, sadden.
byldo, *st. f.* toil, misery, hardship.
byled-brêost, *adj.* having a bill-like breast.
bylgan, *w. v.*
    â-bylgan, to insult, enrage, vex, anger.
bylgian, *w. v.*   [wrong.
    â-bylgian, to be wanting, do
bŷme, *w. f.* trumpet.
bylwit, bylywit. See **bilwit.**
byrdan, *w. v.*
    geed-byrdan, to regenerate.
byrd-scipe, *st. m.* birthship, childbearing.
byrdu-scrûd, *st. n.* shield ornament, design upon a shield.
byre, *st. m.* son, young man, youth. (Goth. *baur.*)
byre, *st. m.* opportunity, time.
byrele, *st. m.* steward, waiter, cupbearer.
byrelian, byrlian, *w. v.* to drink to one, to taste before, drink, serve.
byred. See **beran.**
byrg, byrig. See **burg.**
byrgan, byrgian, byrigan, *w. v.* to taste, feast, eat. (O. N. *byrgja.*)
    ge-byrgan, to taste, feast, eat.
    on-byrgan, same as above.
byrgan, byrigan, *w. v.* to hide, **bury,** inter. (Ger. *bergen.*)
    be-, bi- byrgan, to raise a mound to, bury, inter.
byrgen, *st. f.* mound, grave, tomb.
byrgend, *part. & subs.* burier, gravedigger.
byrged. See **beorgan.**
byrht, *adj.* bright, shining, clear, clear-toned, loud.
byrhtan, *w. v.* to shine.
    ge-byrhtan, to lighten, illumine, make celebrated.

byrhtm, *st. m.* breaking, crash, noise.
byrhtu, *st. f.* brightness, splendor.
byrht-word, *adj.* clear-voiced.
byrhđ. See **beorgan.**
byrian, *w. v.*
   ge-byrian, to happen, occur.
byrian, *w. v.*
   ge-byrian, to beseem, be becoming, fit, proper.
byrlian. See **byrelian.**
byrman, *w. v.*
   ge-byrman, to ferment, leaven; *part.* proud, swollen.
byrnan, *w. v.* to burn, consume.
byrne, *w. f.* burnie, corselet, shirt of mail. (Ger. *brünne.*)
byrne, *w. f.* burn, rushing brook, torrent. [mail.
byrn-hama, *w. m.* corselet, coat of
byrn-hom, *st. m.* corselet, coat of mail.
byrn-wiga, *w. m.* warrior clad in coat-of-mail. [above.
byrn-wigend, *part. & subs.* same as
byrst, *st. m.* loss, damage, defect.
byrđ. See **beran.**

byrđen, *st. f.* **burthen,** burden, load, weight. (Ger. *bürde.*)
bysen, bisen, *st. f.* **1.** pattern, example, similitude, resemblance, parable.— **2.** command, order, precept.
bysgian, bisgian, biesgian, bysigan, *w. v.* to be busy, engaged, occupy, afflict, vex, torment.
   â-bysgan, to occupy, engage.
   ge-bysgan, to be busy, occupy, master, seize, perfect, disquiet, vex, torment.
bysgu, bysigu, bisgu, *st. f.* work, labor, exertion, pains, trouble, affliction.
bysmer, bysmerian. See **bismer, bismerian.**
byst. See **beôn.**
bytla, *w. m.* builder? houseowner? Gû. 119, 705.
bytlian, *w. v.* to build, erect.
byđ. See **beôn.**
bŷwan, *w. v.* to arrange, adorn, ornament. (O. N. *búa.*)
   â-bŷwan, to clean, purify.

C

cǣg, cǣge, *st. & w. f.* **key.**
caf, *adj.* ready, quick, active, adroit, prompt.
cafe, *adv.* quickly, promptly.
cafer-tûn, *st. m.* court or vestibule of a temple or palace.
caf-lice, *adv.* quickly, manfully, valiantly.
calc-rand, -rond, *adj.* supplied with shoes, shod.
cald, caldu. See **ceald, cealdu.**
calend, *st. m.* **1.** month.— **2.** life, end of life? Sal. 479.
calic, *st. m.* **chalice,** cup.
calu, *adj.* bald, without hair, **callow.** (Ger. *kahl.*)

cambol, combol (= **cumbol**), *st. m.* sign, standard.
camp, *st. m.* fetter for the feet, fetter, chain.
camp, comp, *st. m.* battle, combat, fight, contest. (Ger. *kampf.*)
campian, compian, *w. v.* to fight, strive, contest. (Ger. *kämpfen.*)
camp-rǣden, *st. f.* military service, contest.
camp-stede, *st. m.* battlefield, place of battle. [weapon.
camp-wǣpen, *st. n.* war or battle-
camp-wig, *st. m. n.* battle, contest.
camp-wudu, *st. m.* war-wood, spear, shield?

can. See cunnan.
cân, *st. m.* germ, sprout? Ps. 79, 10. (Ms. *tánas.*)
candel, condel, *st. f.* candle, light.
cann, canst. See cunnan.
cantic, *st. m.* canticle, song.
carc-ern, *st. n.* prison-house, prison.
caru. See cearu.
câser-dôm, *st. m.* rule or sway of an emperor, imperial rule.
câsere, *st. m.* emperor.
ceder, *st. f.* cedar.
ceder-bêam, *st. m.* cedar-tree, cedar.
cêgan, cêgian, *w. v.* to call, invoke, name.
cêlan, *w. v.*
   â-cêlan, to cool off, still, quiet.
cêle, *st. m.* coldness, cold.
cêlod, cêllod, *adj.* keeled, in the form of a skiff, hollow.
cempa, *w. m.* warrior, fighter, hero, champion.
cên, *st. m.* pine, pine-torch; — name for the Rune c. (Ger. *kien.*)
cêne, *adj.* keen, bold, warlike. (Ger. *kühn.*)
cennan, *w. v.* 1. to beget, to bear, bring forth. — 2. to create, make, prove, attribute. (Ger. *kennen.*)
   â-cennan, to beget, conceive, bring forth, bear.
cennan, *w. v.* to confess, explain, show, proclaim, ascribe, impute. (cf. Ger. *bekennen.*)
   ge-cennan, to acknowledge, confess.
cêndu, *st. f.* keenness, boldness.
cêpa, *w. m.* chapman, merchant.
cêpan, *w. v.*
   ge-cêpan, to buy, purchase.
cerge, cerr. See cearig, cyrr.
cerran, *w. v.* 1. to turn, turn about. — 2. to turn one's self, return.
   â-cerran, to turn off or from; — turn one's self, go.
   be-cerran, to turn, turn round, convert.

   ge-cerran, 1. to turn, turn round, change. — 2. to turn one's self, turn one's self round, go, return.
   on-cerran, 1. to turn round or about, change, alter, transform. — 2. to turn off or away. — 3. to turn one's self, go.
   ymb-cerran, to turn round, wander about, make the circuit of.
cest, cester. See cist, ceaster.
ceafer-tûn. See cafer-tûn.
ceafl, *st. m.* beak, mouth, jaw, jawbone, snout. (Ger. *kiefel.*)
ceafor, *st. m.* beetle, chafer. (Ger. *käfer.*)
ceald, cald, *adj.* cold. (Ger. *kalt.*)
ceald, cald, *st. n.* coldness, cold.
ceald-heort, *adj.* cold-hearted, inhuman, cruel.
cealdian, *w. v.* to become cold. (Cf. Ger. *erkalten.*)
cealdu, caldu, *st. f.* coldness, cold.
cealf, calf, *st. m., n. pl.* cealfas and cealfru, calf. (Ger. *kalb.*)
ceallian, *w. v.* to call, call out, shout. (Scand. *kalla.*)
cêap, *st. m.* cattle; — purchase, transaction, price, sale, bargain, object of sale or price, possession, property, especially cattle. (Ger. *kauf.*)
cêap-êadig, *adj.* rich in cattle, goods, rich, wealthy.
cêapian, *w. v.* (to cheapen), 1. to buy, purchase. — 2. to endeavor to bribe. (Ger. *kaufen.*)
   ge-ceapian, to bargain, trade, buy, pay.
cêapung, *st. f.* buying and selling, trade, business.
cear, *adj.* anxious, careful, full of anxiety.
cearc, *st. m.? n.?* sorrow, care; — crex = cerx, cearces? El. 610. (*ms.* rex. *Zupitza.*)

ceare-lice, *adv.* sorrowfully, miserably.
cear-ful, *adj.* careful, sorrowful.
cear-gæst, -gest, *st. m.* care-guest, guest of sorrow, devil.
cear-gealdor, *st. n.* sorrowful song or speech.
cearian, *w. v.* to care, take care, trouble one's self.
cearig, *adj.* chary, sad, sorrowful, dire.
cear-léas, *adj.* careless, free from care or sorrow, reckless.
cear-seld, *st. n.* dwelling of sorrow, home of care.
cear-síd, *st. m.* sorrowful way, undertaking bringing sorrow, sad fortune, fate.
cear-sorg, *st. f.* careful, sorrowful anxiety.
cearu, caru, *st. f.* care, sorrow, lamentation, grief. (Goth. *kara.*)
cear-wylm, -wælm, -welm, *st. m.* waves of sorrow, anxious emotion.
céas, *st. f.* strife, quarrel, battle. (O. H. Ger. *kósa.*)
ceaster, cester, *st. f.* fortified place, castle, city;—heaven.
ceaster-búend, *part. & subs.* inhabitants of a fortress, town, or city.
ceaster-hlid, *st. n.* castle or city lid, gate.
ceaster-hof, *st. n.* house or building in the city.
ceaster-wara, *w. m.* inhabitant of a city, citizen.
céol, ciol, *st. m.* keel, ship. (Ger. *kiel.*)
ceolas, *st. m. pl.* cold winds, cold.
ceole, *w. f.* throat. (Ger. *kehle.*)
céol-þelu, *st. f.* keel-boarding, ship.
ceorfan, *st. abl. v.* I. to carve, cut, cut down, hew, engrave. (Ger. *kerben.*)
 á-ceorfan, to hew off, cut off.
 be-ceorfan, to cut off, separate.
 for-ceorfan, to cut apart, cut off.

ceorl, *st. m.* churl, a man of lower class, husbandman, countryman, freeman, man, husband, hero. (Ger. *kerl.*)
céosan, ciosan, *st. abl. v.* VI. 1. to choose, pick out, assume, elect, seek.— 2. to accept. (Ger. *kiesen.*)
 ge-céosan, to choose, select, elect, seek out, seek, attain, obtain, take up.
céowan, *st. abl. v.* VI. to chew, gnaw, eat, consume. (Ger. *kauen.*)
 be-céowan, bi-, to chew thoroughly, gnaw in pieces.
cídan, *w. v.* to chide, contend, strive, quarrel, rebuke, complain.
cigan, ciegan, -ean, cýgan, *w. v.* 1. to call, call upon, invoke.— 2. to name.— 3. to call, cry aloud.
 á-cígan, to call, call to one, or hither.
cild, *st. n.* child.
cild-geong, *adj.* young as a child.
cild-hád, *st. m.* childhood.
cildisc, *adj.* childish, puerile.
cile, cime, cimd. See **cýle, cyme, cuman.**
cin-berg, *st. f.* chin-defense, visor.
cing. See **cyning.**
cinnan, *st. abl. v.* I. to gape, yawn, bring forth? Reim. 52.
 for-cinnan, to deny, disown, repudiate. Sal. 107.
cir. See **cyrr.**
circe, cirice, cyrce, cyrice, *w. f.* church, temple. (Ger. *kirche.*)
circ-nyt, *st. f.* church-service.
circul, *st. m.* circle.
cire, cirice. See **cyre, circe.** [roar.
cirm, cyrm, *st. m.* noise, shout, uproar.
cirman, cyrman, *w. v.* to make a noise, shout.
cirran, *w. v.* to turn.
 on-cirran, to turn, change.
cist. See **cyst.**
cíð, *st. m.* germ, bud, sprout, something growing, grass.

cierr, ciegan, ciest. See cyrr, cigan, cyst (cist).
ciol, ciosan. See cêol, cêosan.
clâ, *st. f.* claw, nail, hoof. (Ger. *klaue.*)
clǽne, clêne, *adj.* clean, pure, chaste, innocent, just, whole; — noble, holy, shining, brilliant; — sagacious, ingenious, acute, intellectual. (Ger. *klein.*)
clǽne, clêne, *adv.* clean, entirely, fully.
clǽn-georn, *adj.* yearning after or desirous of purity.
clǽn-lic, *adj.* cleanly, pure, clean.
clǽn-nes, *st. f.* cleanness, purity.
clǽnsian, *w. v.* to cleanse, purify.
   ge-clǽnsian, same as above.
clam, clom, *st. m. f.* (*n.?*) fetter, chain; — figuratively, of a strong grip, net, fold, prison.
clânsian, *w. v.*
   ge-clânsian, to cleanse, purify.
clâð, *st. m.* cloth, dress, clothes, swaddling-cloth. (Ger. *kleid.*)
clâwe. See clâ.
clemman, *w. v.*
   be-clemman, to fetter, shut in, inclose. (Ger. *beklemmen.*)
clêne. See clǽne.
clengan = glengan, to adorn? or is clenged (Rä. 29, 8) a subst.? (Grein.)
clengan, *w. v.* to exhilarate. (B.-T.)
clêo, *st. f.* claw, hoof.
clêofa, *w. m.* cleft, hole, cell, chamber, tent, den.
clêofan, *st. abl. v.* VI. to cleave, split. (Ger. *klieben.*)
   tô-clêofan, to split, cleave asunder.
cleofian (clifian), *w. v.* to cleave, stick.
cleopian, *w. v.* to call, call out, cry.
cleowen, *st. n.* clew, ball of thread, ball.

clibbor, *adj.* sticky, adhesive. (O. H. Ger. *klebar.*)
clif, cleof, *st. n.* cliff, rock, promontory. (Ger. *klippe.*)
clifan, *st. abl. v.* V.
   ôð-clifan, to stick, cleave, adhere.
clingan, *st. abl. v.* I. to cling, shrink, draw up, pine, wither, become weak.
   be-clingan, to surround, bind.
   ge-clingan, to contract, draw up, shrivel.
clipian, *w. v.* to call.
clom. See clam.
clûs, *st. f.* cell, lockup, prison. (Ger. *klause.*)
clûstor, *st. n.* lock, bar, barrier, cell. (Ger. *kloster.*)
clûstor-clêofa, *w. m.* prison-chamber, cell.
clymmian, *w. v.* to climb, ascend.
clympre, *w. m.* clump or lump of metal, metal.
clynian, *w. v.* to clang, resound.
clypian, *w. v.* to call, cry. (Chaucer *clepe.* Cf. *y-clept.*)
clyppan, *w. v.* to clip, clasp, embrace. (Icel. *klippa.*)
   be-, bi- clyppan, same as above.
   ymb-clyppan, same as above.
clypung, *st. f.* calling, cry, prayer.
clŷsan, *w. v.*
   be-clŷsan, to close, shut to.
cnâwan, *st. red. v.*
   ge-cnâwan, to know, perceive, recognize. (O. H. Ger. *knâjan.*)
   on-cnâwan, to know, perceive, recognize; — distinguish, hear; — to look back upon, acknowledge, confess.
cnêa, *gen. pl.* of cnêo, race, relationship.
cnear, *st. m.* ship. (Icel. *knarri.*)
cnêo, cnêow, *st. n.* knee. (Ger. *knie.*)

cnêo, cnêow, *st. n.* generation, relationship, race.

cnêodan, *st. abl. v.* VI.
  ge-cnêodan, to join to, give, dedicate.

cnêo-mâgas, *st. m. pl.* kinsfolk of the same race or generation.

cnêo-rim, *st. m.* member of the tribe or kinsfolk, progeny, family.

cnêo-ris, *st. f.* generation, progeny, posterity, race, tribe, family, nation.

cnêo-sib, *st. f.* generation, race.

cnêow. See **cnêo**.

cniht, cnyht, *st. m.* 1. **knight,** boy, youth.—2. servant. Met. 26, 85. (Ger. *knecht*.)

cniht-geong, *adj.* young as a child.

cniht-wesende, *part.* still being a child or boy, while still a boy.

cnoll, *st. m.* **knoll,** hilltop, summit. (Ger. *knollen*.)

cnôsl, *st. n.* posterity, race, kin, family, tribe, progeny.

cnossian, *w. v.* to be struck or hit upon, to bound against.

cnyht. See **cniht**.

cnyssan, *w. v.* to strike, hit upon, dash against each other, press, excite, disquiet, vex, disturb.
  ge-cnyssan, to press, oppress, vex.
  on-cnyssan, same as above.

côc, *st. m.* **cook.** (Ger. *koch*.)

côcer-panna, *w. m. f.* cooking-pan, frying-pan.

cocor, *st. m.* 1. sword, spear.—2. quiver for arrows, case.

côfa, *w. m.* **cove**; hence, chamber, room, couch.

côfor-flôd, *st. m.* sea of Galilee.

cohhetan, *w. v.* to give forth a violent sound;—to cough, puff and blow (Grein); to bluster (B.-T.).

col, *st. n.* **coal.** (Ger. *kohle*.)

côl, *adj.* **cool.** (Ger. *kühl*.)

côlian, *w. v.* to become cool, **cool**; to be cold. (Ger. *kühlen*.)
  â-côlian, same as above.

collen- ferd, -ferhd, -fyrhd, *adj.* literally, of swollen mind or heart, in consequence of either sorrow or anger, high-minded, noble, bold, courageous.

côl-nes, *st. f.* **coolness**.

com. See **cuman**.

combol. See **cambol**.

cometa, *w. m.* **comet**.

comp, compian. See **camp, campian**.

con, conn, const. See **cunnan**.

corn, *st. n.* **corn,** grain, seed. (Ger. *korn*.)

cordor, *st. n.* herd, flock, troop, band, army, retinue, throng, crowd.

cost, *part.* tried, proved.

costian, *w. v.* to try, tempt, prove, test, examine;—to bring into danger, into temptation. (Ger. *kosten*.)
  ge-costian, the same as above.

costing, *st. f.* trial, temptation, tribulation.

costnung, *st. f.* same as above.

costung, *st. f.* same as above.

côda, côdu, *w. m. f. & st. f.* evil, disease, sickness.

côd-lice, *adv.* ill, miserably.

cræft, *st. m.* 1. **craft,** skill, art, talent, power, cunning, physical strength. —2. a great quantity. B. 2222.— 3. craft, vessel, ship. (Ger. *kraft*.)

cræftan, *w. v.*
  ge-cræftan, to effect, bring about.

cræftga. See **cræftiga**.

cræft-glêaw, *adj.* artful, skillful, wise.

cræftig, creaftig, *adj.* crafty, powerful, strong, mighty, skillful, artistic, cunning, virtuous. (Ger. *kräftig*.)

cræftiga, cræftga, *w. m.* craftsman, artist, workman, artificer, artist, architect.

cræt, *st. n.* **cart,** wagon, carriage. (Ger. *krätze*.)

crex = cerc. See cearc.
creaftig, *adj.* See cræftig.
creôdan, *st. abl. v.* VI. to crowd, press, drive.
creôpan, *st. abl. v.* VI. to creep, crawl. (Ger. *kriechen.*)
 be-creôpan, to creep into, crawl, slip into.
crib, cryb, *st. f.* crib. (Ger. *krippe.*)
crincan, *st. abl. v.* I. to become ill, fall.
 ge-crincan, same as above.
cringan, crincgan, *st. abl. v.* I. to cringe, become ill, fall, submit, sink in death.
 ge-cringan, same as above.
crist, *st. m.* anointed one, Christ.
cristallum, *acc. sg.* crystal. Ps. 147, 6.
cristen, *adj.* christian.
cristnian, *w. v.* to christen, christianize, baptize.
croda, gecrod, *w. m. & st. n.* crowd, throng.
cryb, crýded. See crib, creôdan.
cû, *pl.* cý, cýe, *st. f.* cow. (Ger. *kuh.*)
cuc. See cwic.
culfre, culufre, *w. f.* dove, pigeon.
culpe, *w. f.* fault, sin.
cuma, *w. m.* new-comer, guest.
cuman, *st. abl. v.* II. (*pret.* côm and cwôm), to come, go;—often used with inf. of a verb of motion, expressing various adverbial relations, manner, purpose, &c. (Ger. *kommen.*)
 â-cuman, to come, come out.
 an-cuman, to arrive. (Ger. *ankommen.*)
 be-, bi- cuman, to become, happen, befall, come, arrive, reach, approach, enter;—come into, come together.
 for-cuman, to come before, surprise, excel, conquer.
 fore-cuman, to come before, prevent.
 ofer-cuman, to overcome, withstand, fall upon, attack, compel, conquer;—*impers.* Deor. 26.
cumbol, *st. m.* sign,—especially a military standard, ensign, banner; —a cognizance or sign worn upon the helmet.
cumbol-gebrec, *st. n.* breaking or hewing helmet-signs in battle;— crash of helmets.
cumbol-gehnâd, *st. n.* conflict of banners, battle.
cumbol-gehnâst, *st. n.* same as above.
cumbol-haga, *w. m.* a protecting ornament on the helmet? Jul. 395 (Grein);—compact rank, phalanx (B.-T.)
cumbol-hete, *st. m.* hate signified by opposing standards, hate.
cumbol-wiga, *w. m.* warrior.
cumbor = cumbol.
cund, *adj.* derived or sprung from. (O. H. Ger. *-kund.*)
cunnan, *v. pret. pres., pres. sg.* 1. can, con, cann, conn.—2. canst, const; *pl.* cunnon; *pret.* cûde;—1. *w. acc.* to know, be acquainted with.— 2. *w. inf.* can, know how to. (Ger. *können.*)
 on-cunnan, *w. v.* to make known, accuse, attack.
cunnian, *w. v.* to investigate, inquire into, try, prove, experience.
 ge-cunnian, to inquire into, try, prove, seek for, search out, experience.
cunnung, *st. f.* trial, temptation.
cûsc, *adj.* chaste, modest, honorable. (Ger. *keusch.*)
cûd, *adj.* (cf. *uncouth*), 1. known, well known, celebrated, clear, evident, certain, sure.—2. familiar, friendly, affable, kind.—3. usual, customary.—4. having the praise of excellence, of being well known, famed, celebrated.—5. sure, safe, trustworthy. (Ger. *kund.*)

cûde, *adv.* clearly, plainly.
cûdice = cûd-lice, *adj.* the same as above.
cûd-lice, *adv.* 1. certainly, surely, plainly, evidently. — 2. therefore, to be sure (Cod. 141), hence (Bout. Ev.) 3. familiarly, friendly, kindly, affably. — 4. nobly (B. 244), openly, publicly (H.-S).
cwacian, *w. v.* to quake, tremble.
cwalu, *st. f.* murder, violent death, death, destruction. (Ger. *qual.*)
cwânian, *w. v.* to complain, lament, bemoan.
cweccan, *w. v.* to move, swing.
    â-cweccan, the same as above.
cwelan, *st. abl. v.* II. to die.
    â-cwelan, the same as above.
cwellan, *w. v.* (*pret.* cwealde), to quell, kill. (Ger. *quälen.*)
    â-cwellan, the same as above.
cwelm. See cwealm.
cwelman, *w. v.* to kill, put to death.
cwêman, *w. v.* to be agreeable, please, delight, satisfy, comply with, serve, be obedient to. (Ger. *bequemen.*)
    ge-cwêman, same as above.
cwên, *st. f.* 1. woman. — 2. wife. — 3. queen, empress.
cwêne, *w. f.* woman.
cwên-lic, *adj.* womanly, feminine, queenly.
cwedan, *st. abl. v.* III. quoth, to say, speak. (Goth. qiþan.)
    æfter-cwedan, to speak after;— *pres. part.* praising after death.
    â-cwedan, to speak out, say out, say.
    be-, bi- cwedan, 1. to say.— 2. to blame, reproach.
    for-cwedan, to boast, promise great things.
    ge-cwedan, to say, speak.
    on-cwedan, 1. to address, accost.— 2. answer.— 3. resound, to make or give an answer or reply to. Dôm. 144.

cwealde. See cwellan.
cwealm, cwelm, *st. m.* qualm, violent death, death, destruction, torment, pain. (Ger. *qualm.*)
cwealm-bealu, *st. n.* evil of murder, deadly evil.
cwealm-cuma, *w. m.* death-bringer, death-plotting guest.
cwealm-drêor, *st. m.* death's blood, bloodshed of death.
cwealm-þrêa, *indecl. m.?* deadly terror.
cwic, cwyc, cwuc, cuc, *adj.* quick, having life, alive. (Ger. *keck.*)
cwicen, *adj.* the same as above.
cwic-hrêrende, *part.* moving with life; moving the living? Sch. 5.
cwician, cwycian, *w. v.* to quicken, give life to.
    â-cwician, the same as above.
    ge-cwician, the same as above.
cwic-lifigende, *part.* living.
cwic-sûsl, *st. n.* eternal punishment, pains of hell.
cwicu, *adj.* alive, living.
cwicu-lice, *adv.* quickly vividly.
cwiddian, *w. v.*
    hearm-cwiddian, to lay hold of craftily, calumniate, reproach.
cwide, cwyde, *st. m.* saying, speech, thought, judgment, teaching.
cwide-gied, *st. n.* speech, news, (Grein);—song, ballad (B.-T.).
cwist, cwid. See cwedan.
cwidan, *st. abl. v.* V. to complain, bemoan, mourn, lament. (Icel. kwida.)
cwide. See cwide.
cwom. See cuman.
cwuc, cwyc, cwycian, cwyddian, cwyde. See cwic, cwiccan, cwiddian, cwide.
cwyld-rôf, *adj.* deadly bold, murderous, savage.
cwylman, *w. v.* to kill, slay.
cwŷst, cwyd. See cwedan.

cwyd, *st. f.* what is promised, curse? Gen. 1596.
cȳgan. See cigan.
cȳle, cile, *st. m.* chill, coldness, cold. (Ger. *kühle*.)
cȳle-gicel, *st. m.* cold icicles.
cyll, cylle, *st. f. m.* skin, bottle, flagon. (Icel. *kyllir*.)
cym. See cuman.
cyme, cime, *st. m.* coming, arrival.
cyme, *adj.* becoming, lovely, glorious, splendid.
cyme, cymest, cymed. See cuman.
cym-lic, *adj.* comely, lovely, splendid.
cym-lice, *adv.* conveniently, fitly, beautifully, splendidly, grandly.
cymd. See cuman.
cyn, *adj.* becoming, seeming, fit, proper; — in the *pl.* used as a *subs.* = the becoming, the suitable, that which is suitable or proper.
cyn, *st. n.* kin, race, genus (= all species of one kind), kind; — crowd, heap, multitude, folk, people, nation, tribe, family, offspring, progeny; — kind, nature, quality.
cynde, *adj.* natural, innate, inborn.
cynde-lic, the same as above.
cyne, *adj.* kinglike, noble.
cȳne = cêne, *adj.* keen, bold, brave.
cyne-beald, *adj.* remarkably brave (Grein); — cyning-balde, *ms.* nobly bold (Thorpe); — excellently brave (Heyne). B. 1634.
cyne-bearn, *st. n.* royal child, noble son, Christ.
cyne-cyn, *st. n.* royal race, kingly family.
cyne-dôm, *st. m.* kingdom, royal sway, power.
cyne-gerela, *w. m.* royal dress, kingly robe.
cyne-gôd, *adj.* of good family, noble, well-born.
cyne-gold, *st. n.* royal gold, crown, diadem.
cyne-lic, *adj.* kingly, noble.

cyne-lice, *adv.* in a kingly manner, nobly, royally.
cyne-rice, *st. n.* kingdom, rule, government.
cyne-rôf, *adj.* kingly bold, very brave.
cyne-stôl, *st. m.* royal seat, throne, dwelling, city.
cyne-þrym, *st. m.* royal glory, worth, renown, majesty.
cyne-word, *st. n.* a word by which the race or family is made known? proper, fitting. Rä. 44, 16.
cyning, cining, cyng, cing, kyning, kynincg, *st. m.* king, earthly king, God, Christ, — occasionally Satan. (Ger. *könig*.)
cyning-beald? See cynebeald.
cyning-dôm, *st. m.* kingdom, rule.
cyn-lice, *adv.* in a becoming, fit, proper manner.
cynn. See cyn.
cyn-ren, *st. n.* progeny, posterity, kind.
cȳpan, *w. v.* to sell, barter.
  ge-cȳpan, to purchase, buy.
cypera, *w. m.* kipper, kind of fish. Met. 19, 12.
cyrce, cyrice. See circe.
cyre, *st. m.* choice, option, free will, will. (Ger. *kur, kür*.)
cyre-beald, *adj.* bold in choosing, bold, firm.
cyrm, cyrman. See cirm, cirman.
cyrr, cierr, *st. m.* change, space of time; — æt sumum cyrre, at some time, once.
cyrran, *w. v.* 1. to turn. — 2. to turn one's self, go, return. (Ger. *kehren*.)
  â-cyrran, to turn away from, avert.
  ge-cyrran, 1. to turn, turn about. 2. to turn one's self, go, return. — 3. to go, *w. cognate acc.*
  mis-cyrran, to turn around, pervert.

on-cyrran, to turn, turn about, change.— 2. to turn away, avert. 3. to turn one's self, go.

ôd-cyrran, to turn one's self away from, be turned.

ymb-cyrran, to turn around, go around, make the circuit of.

cyrten, *adj.* chaste, beautiful.
cyspan, *w. v.* to bind, fetter.
cyssan, *w. v.* to **kiss**. (Ger. *küssen*.)
  ge-cyssan, to kiss.
cyst, *adj.* chosen, desirable.
cyst, *st. f.* 1. free will, choice.— 2. choice, election.— 3. *w. gen. pl.* what is chosen, best of its kind.— 4. virtue, excellence, goodness.— 5. generosity, munificence.
cyst, cist, cest, *st. f.* chosen body, cohort.
cystig, *adj.* just, upright, good.
cyte, *w. f.* cot, hut, den, cave, cell.

cŷd, cŷdd, *st. f.* 1. home.— 2. country, region, place. (Ger. *kunde*.)
cŷdan, *w. v.* to make known, announce, relate, tell, inform, to speak, utter, pronounce.— 2. to make celebrated, uncover, reveal, declare, manifest, prove, show, confess, do, perform. (Ger. *künden*.)
  â-cŷdan, to proclaim, manifest, let be known, strengthen, demonstrate, prove.
  for-cŷdan, to conquer in a dispute. Sal. 176, 206.
  ge-cŷdan, to make known, give information, announce, speak out, say out, tell, utter, inform.— 2. to make known, uncover, reveal, manifest, show, proclaim, effect.— 3. to make celebrated.
cŷddu, *st. f.* home.

D

dǽd, dêd, *st. f.* **deed**, action. (Ger. *that*.)
dǽd-cêne, *adj.* keen for action, active, bold.
dǽd-from, *adj.* vigorous in action, energetic.
dǽd-fruma, *w. m.* doer of deeds, doer, perpetrator.
dǽd-hata, *w. m.* he who hates or pursues through his deeds (Grein); deed-commander, instigating to deeds (Leo). B. 275.
dǽd-hwæt, *adj.* quick to do, ready, bold.
dǽd-lêan, *st. m.* reward for deeds, recompense.
dǽd-rôf, *adj.* bold in deeds, valiant.
dǽd-scûa, *w. m.* he who acts in darkness, devil.
dǽd-weorc, *st. n.* deed, work, great work.

dæg, *st. m.* **day**; and name for the Rune d;— **dæges**, *gen. sg., adv.* days, by day;— **dæges** and **nihtes**, days and nights;— on dæge (dæg), by day;— to-dæge, to-day;— of dæge on dæg, from day to day;— ofer midne dæg, afternoon;— on midne dæg, midday; *pl.* **dagas**, days, life, period of a man's life;— emnihtes dæg, equal day and night, equinox;— wintres dæg, the beginning of winter.
dæg-candel, *st. f.* day's candle, sun.
dæg-hluttre, *adj.* clear, bright as day.
dæg-hwam, *adv.* daily.
dæg-hwamlice(-hwæm-), *adv.* daily.
dæg-hwil, *st. f.* a day's time, space of one day.
dæg-long, *adj.* one day long, during one whole day.

dæg-rêd, *st. n.* daybreak, dawn.
dægrêd-wôma, *w. m.* the stir or rush accompanying daybreak, rush of early morning, dawn.
dæg-rim, *st. n.* number of days, course of days, fixed number of days.
dǽg-sceald, *st. m. n.* "day-ruler," sun; — **dǽgscealdes hléo**, pillar of cloud, lit. shade of the day-ruler.
dæg-tîd, *st. f.* daytime, time, epoch, period; — **dægtîdum**, *instr. pl.* by day, in the daytime.
dæg-weorc, *st. n.* a day's work, fixed, stated service.
dæg-weorðung, *st. f.* celebration of a day, feast, festival.
dæg-wôma, *w. m.* See **dægrêdwôma**.
dæl, *st. n.* **dale**, valley, den, gulf. (Ger. *thal*.)
dǽl, *st. m.* **deal**, part, portion. (Ger. *theil*.)
dǽlan, dêlan, *w. v.* 1. to deal, divide, separate. — 2. to separate from something. — 3. to share with. — 4. to distribute, deal, dole, impart, bestow. — 5. to take part in, be a sharer or partaker. — 6. to be divided. — 7. *w. instr.* **hilde (earfoðe) dǽlan**, to fight, contend. (Ger. *theilen*.)
  â-dǽlan, to divide, separate.
  be-, bi- dǽlan, to deprive, free from, release, bereave.
  efen-gedǽlan, to divide equally.
  ge-dǽlan, 1. to divide, separate. 2. to sunder, cut loose from, renounce. — 3. to be divided, separate, be divided from something, renounce, refuse, forego. — 4. to part, impart, distribute, bestow, share. — 5. to take part in, become partaker of. — 6. ordain, arrange, create.
  tô-dǽlan, 1. to divide, separate.

2. to dismember, destroy. — 3. to distribute. — 4. to be divided. — 5. to separate, distinguish.
dǽl-nimend, -neomend, *part. & subs.* partaking, sharing; — partaker, sharer, participator.
dæne. See **denu**.
dærste, *w. f.* dregs, lees.
dafenian, *w. v.*
  ge-dafenian, to suit, to be fit, becoming, behave aright.
daga, *w. m.* day.
dagian, *w. v.* to **dawn**, become day. (Ger. *tagen*.)
daroð (-að, -eð), deared, *st. m.* dart, spear; — figuratively, part of a loom; — **dareða lâf**, remainder of an army after a battle.
daroð-æsc, *st. m.* (*n.?*), ash spear.
daroð-hæbbend, *part. & subs.* spearbearer, spearman.
daroð-lâcend, *part. & subs.* fighter with a spear, spearman.
daru, *st. f.* hurt, harm, damage.
Decembris, *m.* December.
dêd. See **dǽd**.
dêgan, *w. v.*
  ge-dêgan, -digan, -dŷgan (-ean), to bear, stand, endure, overcome.
dêge-lîce, *adj.* secretly.
dêglian. See **dêaglian**.
dêgol, *st. n.* concealment, secrecy, mystery.
dêgol, *adj.* concealed, hidden, secret, obscure, dark.
dêgol-ful, *adj.* full of secrecy, mysterious.
dêhter. See **dôhtor**.
delan, *st. abl. v.* II. to fall, decay? fall into ruins? (Grein); — to be proud or arrogant, to boast one's self (Leo). Ps. 118, 63.
delfan, *st. abl. v.* I. to **delve**, dig, furrow, dig out.
  â-delfan, the same as above.
  be-delfan, to dig up, into; — to bury, inter.

ge-delfan, to dig.
þurh-delfan, to dig through.
dêlan. See **dǽlan.**
dêma, *w. m.* judge, umpire, ruler, lord, master.
dêman, *w. v.* 1. to deem, think, judge, decide, determine, prove, doom, condemn.— 2. to count, muster, estimate, reckon.— 3. to praise, laud, tell, narrate.
  â-deman, to bar or shut out from by a legal decision.
  ge-deman, to judge, doom, condemn.— 2. to decide, fix, appoint.
dêmend, *part. & subs.* judge, umpire.
dên, dênd. See **dôn.**
denn, *st. n.* den, cave.
dennian, *w.v.* to become firm, smooth, slippery? **Adelst.** 12.
denu, *st. f.* valley, vale, dale.
derian, *w. v.* to hurt, injure, damage.
derne, *adj.* concealed, hid, secret.
dêad, *adj.* dead;—also used as a *subst.*
dêaf, *adj.* deaf. (Ger. *taub.*)
dêag. See **dugan.**
dêagan, *st. red. v.* to color, tinge (Grein);— to conceal one's self, hide (Leo). B. 850.
dêaglian, dêglian, *w. v.*
  be-dêaglian, to hide, conceal, hold secret, keep close.
dêagol, *adj.* secret.
dêah. See **dûgan.**
deal, deall, *adj.* proud, confident, cautious, bold, renowned.
dear, deared. See **durran, darod.**
dearnenga, *adv.* secretly, clandestinely, insidiously.
dearninga, *adv.* the same as above.
dearnunga, *adv.* the same as above.
dêad, *st. m.* death, dying. (Ger. *tod.*)
dêad-bed, *st. n.* deathbed, grave.
dêad-berende, *part.* death-bringing.
dêad-bêam, *st. m.* death-tree, death-bringing tree.
dêad-cwalu, *st. f.* violent death, ruin and death, pains of death.

dêad-cwealm, *st. m.* violent death, murder.
dêad-dæg, *st. m.* dying, death-day, day of death.
dêad-denu, *st. f.* valley of death.
dêad-drepe, *st. m.* death-blow, death.
dêad-fǽge, *adj.* destined to die, doomed, given over to death.
dêad-firen, *st. f.* death sin, mortal sin, capital offense.
dêad-gedâl, *st. n.* separation of body and soul by death.
dêad-lêg, *st. m.* death-flame, deadly flame, Muspilli.
dêad-mægen, *st. n.* death-bringing troop, deadly band.
dêad-ræced, *st. n.* dwelling of the dead, grave.
dêad-rǽs, *st. m.* rush of death, sudden death.
dêad-rêow, *adj.* greedy of slaughter, murderous, savage.
dêad-scûa, *w. m.* death-bringing, deadly being, demon of death.
dêad-sele, *st. m.* death-hall, lower world, hell.
dêad-slege, *st. m.* death-stroke.
dêad-spere, *st. n.* death-spear, death-aiming spear.
dêad-stede, *st. m.* death-place, battlefield.
dêad-wang, *st. m.* same as above.
dêad-wêg, *st. n.* cup of death.
dêad-wêrig, *adj.* death-weary, dead.
dêad-wic, *st. n.* dwelling of death, home of death.
dêaw, *st. m.* dew. (Ger. *thau.*)
dêaw-drêas, -drias, *st. m.* dewfall.
dêawig, *adj.* dewy.
dêawig-federe, *adj.* dewy-feathered, having moist feathers.
dêoful, -ol, *st. m. n.* **devil.** (Ger. *teufel.*)
dêoful-cund, *adj.* of hellish origin, diabolical.
dêoful-dǽd, *st. f.* work of the devil, devilish deed.

dêoful-gild, -gield, -gyld, *st. n.* devil's sacrifice, idolatry, worship of the devil, idol, image of the devil.
dêoful-witga, *w. m.* devil's prophet, soothsayer, magician.
dêog. See dêagan.
dêogol, *adj.* hidden, secret, concealed, dark, unknown. [dark.
dêogol-lice, *adv.* secretly, in the
dêop, *st. n.* deep, abyss. (Ger. *tiefe.*)
dêop, *adj.* deep, abysmal, profound, solemn, earnest, grave. (Ger. *tief.*)
dêope, diope, *adv.* deeply, thoroughly, earnestly, solemnly.
dêop-hycgende, *part.* deeply meditating.
dêop-hŷdig, *adj.* the same as above.
dêop-lic, *adj.* deep.
dêop-lice, *adv.* deeply, profoundly, thoroughly.
dêop-nes, *st. f.* deepness, depth.
dêor, dior, *st. n.* (deer), animal, wild animal, beast;—most frequently in contrast to domestic animals. (Ger. *thier.*)
dêor, *adj.* 1. wild, bold, brave, skillful.—2. heavy, severe, terrible, vehement, violent.
dêoran, *w. v.* to glorify, prize, hold dear, love.
dêor-boren, *adj.* noble born.
deorc, *adj.* dark, obscure, gloomy, sad. (O. H. Ger. *tarni.*)
deorce, *adv.* darkly, obscurely, sadly.
dêore, diore, *adj.* 1. dear, beloved, cherished.—2. dear, costly, excellent.—3. glorious, noble, illustrious. (Ger. *theuer.*)
dêore, diore, *adv.* 1. dearly, at a high price.—2. friendly, kindly.
deored-sceaft, *st. m.* shaft of a dart, spear, lance.
dêor-lic, *adj.* wild, bold, brave.
dêor-lice, *adv.* gloriously. preciously, worthily.
dêor-ling, *st. m.* darling, favorite.

dêor-môd, *adj.* of daring mood, courageous, bold.
dêor-wyrde, *adj.* precious, costly, considerable, important.
digan (âdigan). See drygan.
digan. See dêgan.
digol, digle. See dŷgol, dŷgle. (O. H. Ger. *tougal.*)
dihtig. See dyhtig.
dilgian, *w. v.* (Ger. *tilgen.*)
â-dilgian, to destroy, blot out.
dim, *adj.* dim, dark, obscure, hidden. (O. H. Ger. *timbar.*)
dim, *st. m.* din, noise? Sat. 606, perhaps din.
dimman, *w. v.* to dim.
â-dimman, to be dim, darken.
dim-scûa, *w. m.* darkness, sin.
ding, *st. f.* prison, dungeon.
Dinges mere, proper name, Irish Sea (Grein);—on dinnes mere, on a stormy sea (B.-T).
disc, *st. m.* dish, plate, bowl. (Ger. *tisch.*)
disig. See dysig.
diacon, *st. m.* deacon.
dierne. See dyrne.
diope, dior, diore. See dêope, dêor, dêore.
dôgian, *w. v.* to suffer, bear. Rä. 1, 9.
dôgor, *st. m. n.* day. [Thorpe says 24 hours: others, 12.]
dôgor-gerim, *st. n.* number or series of days, allotted time of life.
dôgor-rim, *st. n.* same as above.
dohte. See dugan.
dohtor, *irreg. f. dat. sg.* dehter;—*nom. acc. pl.* dohtor, dohter, dohtra, dohtru,—daughter. (Ger. *tochter.*)
dol, *adj.* dull, foolish, silly;—proud, boastful, erring, heretical. (Ger. *toll.*)
dolg, *st. n.* wound. (O. H. Ger. *tolg.*)
dolg-ben, *st. f.* wound.
dolgian, *w. v.* to wound.
ge-dolgian, to wound.

dol-gilp, *st. m. n.* idle, foolish, boasting (Grein);— promise of bold deeds (II.-S.).
dolg-slege, *st. m.* wounding blow.
dolh-wund, *adj.* wounded.
dol-lic, -lig, *adj.* audacious, rash, foolish.
dol-lice, *adv.* foolishly, rashly.
dol-sceaða, *w. m.* foolhardy, audacious enemy; bold enemy.
dol-willen, *st. n.* rashness, madness.
dol-willen, *adj.* rash, bold.
dol-wite, *st. n.* punishment for rashness.
dôm, *st. m.* **1. doom,** judgment, judicial opinion.— 2. court, tribunal, assembly, council.— 3. judicial sentence, verdict, decision, decree. 4. statute, law, command, ordinance.— 5. justice.— 6. advice, counsel.— 7. rule, government, power, might, dominion.— 8. majesty, glory, honor, renown, worth, praise, dignity, authority.— 9. especially heavenly glory and majesty.— 10. might, power, free will, choice, pleasure, option.— 11. custom, what is becoming, customary. 12. meaning, signification, sense, interpretation. (Ger. *-tum*; O. H. Ger. *tuom*.)
dôm-dæg, *st. m.* **doomsday,** judgment-day.
dôm-êadig, *adj.* mighty, powerful, noble, happy, renowned.
dôm-fæst, *adj.* firm in judgment, just, mighty, famous.
dôm-georn, *adj.* striving for glory or for uprightness, ambitious, just.
dôm-hwæt, *adj.* eager for honor, renown.
dômian, *w. v.* to glorify, magnify.
dôm-lêas, *adj.* without reputation, inglorious, hapless.
dôm-lic, *adj.* glorious, praiseworthy.
dôm-lice, *adv.* judiciously, powerfully, gloriously.

dôm-setl, *st. n.* judgment-seat, throne, tribunal.
dôn, dên, *irreg. v. pres. sg.* **1. dô.**— 2. **dêst.**— 3. **dêd,** *pl.* **dôd;** *subj. sg.* **dô,** *pl.* **dôn;** *imper.* **dô, dôd;** *pret.* **dyde, dide, dæde;** *part. pret.* **dôn, dên,** to do, make, act, perform, cause. (Ger. *tun*.)
â-dôn, to do away, remove, free, set free.
be-dôn, to close, shut.
for-dôn, 1. to fordo, corrupt, destroy, kill.— 2. to seduce?— 3. *part. pret.* wicked, abandoned, defiled, corrupted.
ge-dôn, to do, make, cause.
un-dôn, to undo, open, loose, separate.
dor, *st. n.* door, gate. (Ger. *thor*.)
dorste. See **durran.**
draca, *w. m.* **1.** dragon.— 2. the devil. (Ger. *drache*.)
drædan, *st. red. v.* (*pret.* **drêord, drêd**), to dread. (O. H. Ger. *antrâtan*.)
an-, on-drædan, to fear, dread.
dræfan, *w. v.*
â-dræfan, to shut out, drive out.
ge-dræfan, to drive, push, urge, vex.
tô-dræfan, to drive or bring apart, separate, destroy.
dræfend, *part. & subs.* driver, hunter.
dragan, *st. abl. v.* IV. to draw, drag. (Ger. *tragen*.)
be-dragan, to draw away, seduce, deceive.
drapa. See **dropa.**
dreccan, *w. v.* to plague, vex, disquiet, oppress, burden, torture, torment.
ge-dreccan, the same as above.
drêfan, *w. v.* to disturb, vex, excite, move, agitate, stir up, afflict. (Ger. *trüben*.)
ge-drêfan, to disturb, bring into confusion, move, trouble.

drenc, *st. m.* **drench,** drink; drowning.
drencan, *w. v.* **1.** to **drench,** give to drink.— **2.** to drown.
   â-drencan, to drown.
   ge-drencan, to drown.
   ofer-drencan, to make drunk.
drenc-, drence-flôd, *st. m.* the flood, deluge.
dreng, *st. m.* young man, follower (of the comitatus), warrior.
drepan, *st. abl. v.* III. to hit, strike, beat. (Ger. *treffen.*)
drepe, *st. m.* blow, stroke.
drettan, *w. v.*
   ge-drettan, to consume.
drêam, perhaps *dat. pl.* of **drêa,** *w. m.* magician? Sal. 44.
drêam, *st. m.* **1. dream,** song, melody, harmony, joyous music.—**2.** crowd, throng.— **3.** joyous actions, rejoicing, joy, pleasure.—**4.** used especially of the joys of heaven. (Ger. *traum.*)
drêam-hæbbende, *part.* rejoicing, joyful.
drêam-healdende, *part.* the same.
drêam-lêas, *adj.* joyless, without rejoicing, sad.
drêarung, *st. f.* falling, distillation.
drêas, drias, *st. m.* falling, fall.
drêogan, *st. abl. v.* VI. **1.** to bear, suffer, endure, carry.— **2.** to bear, carry out, perfect, do, work, perform, lead (a life);—**wide drêogan,** to wander.—**3.** to enjoy.— **4.** *intrans.* to be busy, employed, to do. (Scotch, *dree.*)
   â-drêogan, **1.** to bear, suffer, endure.— **2.** to act, perform, complete, practice. [joy.
   ge-drêogan, to live through, en-
dreont? Rä. 4, 45.
drêopan, *st. abl. v.* VI. to drop. (Ger. *tropfen.*)
   â-drêopan, to pour out drop by drop.
drêopian, *w. v.* to drop, drip, trickle.

drêor, *st. m.* running or flowing blood, blood. (O. H. Ger. *trôr.*)
drêor-fâh, *adj.* spotted, stained with blood, bloody, gory.
drêorgian, *w. v.* to mourn? be dreary, fall.
drêorig, *adj.* **dreary,** sad, sorrowful. (Ger. *traurig.*)
drêorig, *adj.* bloody, bleeding.
drêorig-ferhd, *adj.* sad in heart, sorrowful.
drêorig-hlêor, *adj.* sad of countenance.
drêorig-lic, *adj.* bloody.
drêorig-môd, *adj.* sad in mind.
drêor-lic, *adj.* bloody.
drêor-sele, *st. m.* dreary, lonely hall.
drêorung, *st. f.* falling, dropping.
drêosan, *st. abl. v.* VI. to mourn, be sad, desolate.
drêosan, *st. abl. v.* VI. to fall, perish, be ready to fall, become weak. (Goth. *driusan.*)
   â-drêosan, to fall to pieces, decline, vanish, fail.
   be-, bi-drêosan, **1.** to deceive, seduce.— **2.** to deprive of, bereave.
   ge-drêosan, to fall down, sink, disappear, fail.
drifan, *st. abl. v.* V. **1.** to **drive,** drive away, drive back, impel, incite, strike.— **2.** to follow, practice. (Ger. *treiben.*)
   â-drifan, to drive out, expel.
   be-drifan, **1.** to drive, drive together, compel.—**2.** drive, beat, strike.
   for-drifan, to drive, expel, banish, force, compel, consume. (Ger. *vertreiben.*)
   in-drifan, to drive out, thrust out.
   tô-drifan, to drive apart, disperse, scatter, destroy, repel.
   þurh-drifan, **1.** to shove or push through.—**2.** perforate, bore through.— **3.** penetrate, imbue.
   wid-drifan, to repel, ward off.

drige, driht, drihten. See dryge, dryht, dryhten.
drinc, st. m. drink, a drink. (Ger. trunk, trunk.)
drincan, st. abl. v. I. to drink. (Ger. trinken.)
  â-drincan, to be plunged under water, immersed, drowned.
  ge-drincan, to drink, swallow, engulf.
  on-drincan, to drink.
drias. See drēas.
drōf-lic, adj. turbulent, troublesome, sad.
droht, st. m.? n.? condition of life.
drohtad, -od, st. m. condition of life, manner of life, calling, vocation, business, conduct, society.
drohtian, w. v. to have conversation; to live, pass life.
drohtnod, st. m. way or manner of life.
dropa, drapa, w. m. drop. (Ger. tropfen.)
dropen. See drepen, drēopan.
droppetan, w. v. to drop, drip, distil.
droppung, st. f. dropping, dripping, falling.
drucen? See druncen.
drugian, w. v. to become dry, wither.
  for-drugian, to become dry, wither.
  ge-drugian, to dry, dry up.
druh, st. m. dust? Seel. 17.
druncan, druncian, w. v. to suck out, drink.
druncen, st. f. drunkenness.
druncen, adj. drunken, besotted.
drunc-mennen, st. n. drunken maidservant.
drûsan, drûsian, w. v. to drowse, be in a state of decay, become lazy, weak, inactive; — to mourn, be sad.
drŷ, st. m. sorcerer, magician, wizard.
drŷ-cræft, st. m. magic art, sorcery, witchcraft.

drygan, drigan, w. v. to dry, dry up, wither.
  â-drigan, to dry up, wither.
dryge, drige, adj. dry, withered; — tô dryggum, even to decay, exhaustion. Met. 7, 16. (Ger. trocken.)
dryht, driht, st. f. company, troop, folk, people, band of warriors, comitatus, noble band; — in pl. men.
dryht-bearn, st. n. a noble youth, princely child.
dryht-cwên, st. f. queen.
dryhten, drihten, st. m. commander, leader, lord, prince, God, Christ. (O. H. Ger. truhtin.)
dryhten-bealo, st. n. extreme evil, great misfortune.
dryhten-dôm, st. m. rule, dominion, majesty, glory.
dryhten-hold, adj. friendly, well disposed to the prince, to the Lord.
dryhten-nes, st. f. ruler's glory, majesty? Gen. 17.
dryhten-weard, st. m. king, Lord.
dryht-folc, st. n. band, troop, folk, nation.
dryht-gesid, st. m. follower, attendant.
dryht-gestrêon, st. n. people's treasure.
dryht-guma, w. m. man of the warrior band, noble warrior, man.
dryht-lêod, st. n. popular or noble song.
dryht-lic, adj. lordly, noble, excellent.
dryht-lice, adv. nobly, excellently, in a lordly manner.
dryht-mâdum, st. m. people's treasure, splendid jewels.
dryht-nêas, st. m. pl. bodies of the slain belonging to the comitatus (on the battlefield), carcasses.
dryht-scype, st. m. warlike virtue, heroic deed, bravery, glory, rulership, domination, dignity.

dryht-sele, *st. m.* the hall for the comitatus, splendid dwelling.

dryht-sib, *st. f.* peace or friendship between troops of noble warriors, or between noble families.

dryht-weras, *st. m. pl.* attendants, men.

dryht-wuniende, *part.* living among the people, folk-dweller.

drȳman, *w. v.* to sing aloud, rejoice.

drymman, *w. v.* to be careful, solicitous.

drync, *st. m.* drink, draught, a drink.

drync-fæt, *st. n.* drinking-vessel, cup.

drype, *st. m.* blow, stroke.

dryre, *st. m.* fall, falling, ceasing, decline.

drysmian, *w. v.* to become obscure, gloomy.

dûfan, *st. abl.* VI. **1.** *intrans.* to **dive**, sink.—**2.** *trans.* to dip in, immerse.
   ge-dûfan, *intrans.* to dive, sink under, be submerged, sink in.
   in-dûfan, to dip in, immerse, submerge.
   þurh-dûfan, to swim through by diving, dive through.

dugan, *pret. pres., pres. sg.* **dêag, dêah;** *pl.* **dugon;** *pret.* **dohte,** to avail, be capable, be good, be of use, fit, strong, liberal, to present. (Ger. *taugen.*)

dugað, -oð, *st. f.* what avails; hence, **1.** manhood, and all that have reached manhood.—**2.** men capable of bearing arms, troops, multitude, army, folk, noble band of warriors, men in general.—**3.** the heavenly host.—**4.** glory, magnificence, majesty, might, power, virtue.—**5.** advantage, gain, riches, means, blessings, welfare, salvation.—**6.** benefit, gift.—**7.** what is becoming, fit, seemly, decorum.

dumb, *adj.* dumb, mute, speechless. (Ger. *dumm.*)

dûn, *st. f.* **down,** hill;—of dûne, downwards. (Ger. *düne.*)

dûn-scræf, *st. n.* mountain cave.

durran, *pret. pres., pres. sg.* dear; *pl.* **durron;** *subj.* **durre, dyrre;** *pret.* **dorste,** to **dare,** presume. (O. H. Ger. *turran.*)

duru, *st. f.* **door,** gate, wicket. (Ger. *thüre.*)

duru-þegn, *st. m.* doorkeeper.

dust, *st. n.* **dust.** (Ger. *dust.*)

dwælan, *w. v.*
   ge-dwælan, to mislead, lead astray.

dwæs. See **gedwæs.** [guish.

dwæscan, *w. v.* to put out, extinâ-dwæscan, the same as above.
   tô-dwæscan, same as above.

dwelan, *st. abl. v.* II. to be led into error, err. (O. H. Ger. *twelan.*)
   ge-dwelan, to wander, err.

dwellan, *w. v.* (to **dwell**), **1.** to prevent, hinder, delay.—**2.** to lead into error, mislead, deceive. (O. H. Ger. *twaljan.*)
   ge-dwellan, 1. to lead astray, seduce, deceive.—**2.** to err.

dwol-cræft, *st. m.* foolish or magic art, magic.

dwolema, dwolma, *w. m.* chaos.

dȳfan, *w. v.* (to **dive**), to make to dive, dip, immerse.

dȳgan. See **dêgan.**

dȳglan, *w. v.*
   ge-dȳglan, to hide, conceal, darken, cover.

dȳgle, dîgle, *adv.* secretly, covertly.

dȳgol, dîgol, *adj.* hidden, secret, concealed, inaccessible, dark, unknown.

dȳgol, dîgol, *st. n.* secrecy, darkness, what is hidden.

dyhtig, dihtig, *adj.* **doughty,** strong, useful, good for. (Ger. *tüchtig.*)

dyn, *st. m.* **din,** noise.

dyne, *st. m.* the same as above.

dyng. See **ding.**

dynnan, *w. v.* to sound, make a noise, resound.
dynt, *st. m.* **dint,** a blow causing or giving a sound, blow, stroke.
dȳp, *st. n.* the deep.
dȳran, *w. v.* to glorify, prize, love.
   ge-dȳran, the same as above.
dȳre, *adj.* dear, beloved, worthy, costly, glorious, noble, excellent.
dyreþran (Cri. 790), to be changed into þȳ reþran.
dyrling, *st. m.* darling, loved one.
dyrnan, *w. r.* to hide, secrete, conceal, restrain, obscure.
   be-, bi-dyrnan, the same as above.
   ge-dyrnan, the same as above.
dyrne, *st. n.* a secret.

dyrne, dierne, *adj.* **1.** hidden, secret, close, obscure, out of the way, remote. — **2.** secret, dark, deceitful, magical, malicious, evil. (O.H.Ger. *tarni.*)
dȳrsian, *w. v.*
   ge-dȳrsian, to prize, hold dear, honor, glorify. [bold.
dyrstig, *adj.* venturesome, daring.
dysegian, *w. v.* to be foolish, stupid, do foolishly, err.
dysig, *adj.* dizzy, silly, foolish, ignorant, stupid. (O. H. Ger. *tusig.*)
dysig, disig, *st. n.* foolishness, ignorance, stupidity, folly.
dys-lic, *adj.* foolish, silly, stupid.
dys-lice, *adv.* foolishly, stupidly.
dyttan, *w. v.* to close, shut up, stop.

E

ebba, *w. m.* **ebb.** (Ger. *ebbe* is a borrowed word; cf. Goth. *ibuks.*)
ebbian, *w. v.* to **ebb.**
êc, *adv.* eke, also.
êcan, *w. v.* to eke, increase, enlarge, add to, prolong.
êce, æce, *adj.* eternal, everlasting, perpetual. (Ger. *ewig.*)
êce, *adv.* eternally, ever, evermore, perpetually.
eced, *st. n.* **acid,** vinegar. (Ger. *essig;* Goth. *akeit;* Lat. *acetum.*)
êcen, *adj.* increased, great, weighty, important.
ecg, *st. f.* edge (of the sword), point, sword, battle-ax. (Ger. *ecke.*)
ecg-bana, *w. m.* murderer by the sword, sword-killer.
ecg-clif, false reading for **êg-clif,** sea-cliff. B. 2893.
ecg-hete, *st. m.* hate shown by the sword, sword-hate, enmity.
ecg-heard, *adj.* with hard, sharp edge.

ecg-plega, *w. m.* sword-play, battle.
ecg-þracu, *st. f.* sword-storm, hot fighting.
ecg-wæl, *st. n.* sword-slaughter, those slain in battle by the sword.
êc-nes, -nis, -nys, *st. f.* eternity, forever.
ed-cerr, -cir, -cyr, *st. m.* return.
eder-. See **edor.**
ed-geong, *adj.* made young again.
ed-hwyrft, *st. m.* return, change, going back (to a former state of things).
êdisc, *st. n.* edish, pasture, park, fishpond, vivary.
ed-lêan, *st. n.* retribution.
ed-neowe, -niowe, *adj.* renewed, new, again new, renewing itself ever.
ed-niowunga, *adv.* anew, again.
ed-niwe, *adj.* new, renewed.
ed-niwe, *adv.* anew, again.
ed-niwinga, *adv.* same as above.
edor, *st. m.* hedge, quickset fence, fold, inclosure, dwelling.

edor-gang, *st. m.* begging, the going around of mendicants from house to house.
edre, *adv.* forthwith, immediately.
êdre. See **ǣdre.**
edring, *st. f.* refuge? Seel. 107.
ed-sceaft, *st. f.* new creation, regeneration.
ed-wenden, *st. f.* turning, change, overturning, end.
ed-wendu, *st. f.* change, end.
ed-wiht, *st. n.* something, anything.
ed-wit, *st. n.* reproach, blame, disgrace, ignominy, contumely, scorn.
edwit-lif, *st. n.* disgraceful, shameful life.
edwit-scype, *st. m.* disgrace, ignominy, cowardice.
edwit-sprǣc, *st. f.* reproachful, defaming speech, scorn.
edwit-spreca, *w. m.* scorner, caviler, devil.
edwit-stæf, *st. m.* reproach, disgrace, dishonor.
êd-wylm = **ǣdwylm,** *st. m.* waves of fire, hell.
efe-long = **efen-long,** *adj.* just as long? oblong? Rä. 45, 7.
efen, efn, *adj.* even, equal, like; — **on efen,** *adv.* together; or *prep. w. dat.* upon the same level, near. (Ger. *eben.*)
efen, *adv.* evenly, just as, equally.
êfen. See **ǣfen.**
efen-behêfe, *adj.* equally useful, just as necessary.
efen-beorht, *adj.* equally bright, of like brilliancy.
efen-êce, *adj.* co-eternal.
efen-êđe, *adj.* just as easy.
efen-êadig, *adj.* equally happy, blessed.
efen-eald, *adj.* of the same age, equally old.
efen-eardigende, *part.* dwelling together.

efen-fela, *indecl. n.* just as much, so many.
efen-hlêođor, *st. m.* with equal voice or harmony, united voice.
efen-lic, *adj.* equal, of like age.
efen-lica, *w. m.* one of the same age.
efen-mǣre, *adj.* equally prized, or thought of.
efen-micel, *adj.* equally great.
efen-mid, *adj.* middle, in the middle, center of.
efen-nêah, *adj.* even nigh, equally near.
efen-niht. See **emniht.**
efen-scearp, *adj.* equally sharp.
efen-swiđ, *adj.* equally strong.
efen-wesende, *part.* contemporaneous, co-existent.
efn. See **efen.**
efnan, *w. v.* **1.** to carry out, perform, accomplish, do, make. — **2.** to prostrate, throw down. Rä. 28, 8.
 ge-efnan, 1. to accomplish, do, perform, carry out. — **2.** to hold, sustain.
efne, *adv.* even, just, exactly, alike, likewise; — **efne swâ,** even so, even as, just as if, when; — **efne swâ þêah,** even though; — **efne,** enclitic, indeed, just: — at the beginning of a sentence — lo! behold!
efnetan, *w. v.* to equal, emulate. Rä. 41, 63.
êfstan, *w. v.* to hasten, make haste, be in haste.
eft, æft, *adv.* (eft, cf. eft-soons). **1.** again, anew. — **2.** back, re- (retro, rursus). — **3.** thereupon, afterwards. — **4.** again, on the other side, likewise. (Goth. *afta.*)
eft-cyme, *st. m.* return.
eft-lêan, *st. n.* retribution, recompense.
eft-siđ, *st. m.* journey back, return.
eft-wyrd, *st. f.* future destiny.
êgan, *w. v.*
 on-êgan, to fear, dread.

êg-bûend, *part. & subs.* island or sea-dweller.
êg-clif, *st. n.* sea-cliff, shore.
ege, *st. m.* awe (cf. ôga), fear, fright, dread, horror. (Goth. *agei;* O. H. Ger. *egi.*)
êge = êage, *w. n.* eye.
ege-lâf, *st. f.* what has escaped horror, battle-remnant.
egesa, egsa, *w. m.* state of terror, frightfulness, terror, horror, dread, fear.
êgesa, êgsa, *w. m.* possessor, owner. Gn. Ex. 117; B. 1757.
eges-ful, *adj.* fearful, terrible, wonderful, awful.
egesful-lic, *adj.* the same as above.
egesig, eisig, *adj.* same as above.
eges-lic, *adj.* the same as above.
eges-lice, *adv.* fearfully, terribly, wonderfully.
ege-wylm, *st. m.* terrible wave.
egl, *st. f.* mote, beard (on wheat), point, claw, talon, beam. (Ger. *achel.*)
eglan, *w. v.* to ail, trouble, pain, grieve. (Ger. *ekeln.*)
    æt-eglan, to cause or bring about trouble, pain, grief.
    ge-eglan, to trouble, pain, grieve.
êg-land, -lond, *st. n.* island.
egle, *adj.* troublesome, grievous, hateful, hostile, disgraceful, loathsome. (Goth. *agls, aglus.*)
êgor-here, *st. m.* army of the ocean, waves of the sea, the deluge.
êgor-strêam, *st. m.* sea-stream, ocean.
egsa, êgsa. See egesa, êgesa.
egsian, *w. v.* to frighten, terrify (Grein & B.-T.); — to have terror, distress (Heyne).
êg-, êh-strêam, *st. m.* water-stream, sea, river.
eh, *st. n.* horse; and the Rune e. (Lat. *equus.*)
ehtan, *w. v.* to esteem, consider. Rü. 37, 4.

ehtan, *w. v., w. acc.,* and *gen.* of person, — to persecute, pursue, annoy, afflict.
êhtend, *part. & subs.* persecutor.
ehtian, *w. v.* to esteem, make prominent with praise, deem, consider.
êht-nes, *st. f.* persecution.
ehtung, *st. f.* deliberation, counsel.
eisig. See egesig.
eld, eldu, *st. f.* age, old age.
elde, *st. m. pl.* men.
eldra. See elra.
eldran, *adj. compar. pl.,* used as a *subs.* elders, parents, ancestors.
ele, *st. m.* oil.
ele-bêam, *st. m.* olive-tree.
ele-land, *st. n.* foreign land.
eleð, *st. m.* allodium, freehold. Gû. 38.
el-land, *st. n.* foreign country.
ellefne, *num.* eleven.
ellen, *st. m. n.* strength, heroic strength, bravery, courage, fortitude, zeal, heroic deeds. (Goth. *aljan.*)
ellen-cræft, *st. m.* strength, might, power.
ellen-dæd, *st. f.* heroic deed, deed of valor.
el-lende, *adj.* foreign, strange.
ellen-gæst, *st. m.* strength-spirit, demon with heroic strength.
ellen-heard, *adj.* mighty, brave, bold, courageous.
ellen-lêas, *adj.* strengthless, wanting courage.
ellen-lice, *adv.* strongly, with heroic strength.
ellen-mærðu, *st. f.* renown of heroic strength, heroic deed.
ellen-rôf, *adj.* renowned for heroic strength, daring, bold.
ellen-sêoc, *adj.* sick in strength, mortally wounded.
ellen-spræc, *st. f.* strong speech, brave word.
ellen-þrist, *adj.* energetic, bold.

ellen-weorc, *st. n.* heroic deed, achievement in battle.
ellen-wôd, *st. n.* zeal.
ellen-wôd, *adj.* furious, raging.
elles, *adv.* else, otherwise, in another manner. (Goth. *allis.*)
ellor, *adv.* else-whither, elsewhere, to some other place; — **ellor londes**, in another land.
ellor-fûs, *adj.* eager, ready for another place, ready to go elsewhere.
ellor-gâst, -gæst, *st. m.* spirit living elsewhere.
ellor-sid, *st. m.* departure, death.
el-mehtig, *adj.* almighty.
eln, *st. f.* elbow, ell. (Ger. *elle;* Goth. *aleina.*)
eln-gemet, *st. n.* ell-measure, ell.
elnian, *w. v.* **1.** to emulate, be zealous, exert one's self. — **2.** to strengthen, comfort. Gen. 48, 2.
elra, *adj. compar.* another.
el-reordig, *adj.* speaking another tongue, barbarous.
el-pêod, *st. f.* **1.** foreign people, enemy. — **2.** all peoples, all nations. Cri. 1084, 1337.
ol-pêodig, *adj.* belonging to another nation, foreign, strange, hostile.
emb, embe, *prep.* **1.** *w. acc.* about, round, around. — **2.** *w. dat.* after.
emn = efen, *adj.* even, equal, plain, level, just; — **on emn**, *w. dat.* by, near.
emn-ædele, *adj.* equally noble.
emne = efne, *adv.* evenly, equally, plainly, exactly, even, just.
emniht, efen-niht, *st. f. n.?* equinox.
ênd, *adv.* formerly, of old; at last.
ende, *st. m.* end. (Ger. *ende;* Goth. *andeis.*) [ment.
ende-byrd, *st. f. n.?* order, arrange-
ende-byrdes, *adv.* orderly, regularly, properly.
ende-dæg, *st. m.* last day, day of death.
ende-dêad, *st. m.* death.

ende-dôgor, *st. m. n.* last day, death.
ende-lâf, *st. f.* last remnant, the last.
ende-lêan, *st. n.* final reparation, reward.
ende-lêas, *adj.* endless, infinite.
ende-lif, *st. n.* life's end, death.
endemnes, *adv.* **1.** fully, entirely. — **2.** at the same time, together.
ende-rim, *st. m.* final number, number.
ende-sæta, *w. m.* one who sits on the border, boundary-guard.
ende-stæf, *st. m.* end.
endian, *w. v.* **1.** *trans.* to end, make an end, put an end to. — **2.** *intrans.* to end.
  ge-endian, to make an end, end.
endgum = êadgum. Sal. 345.
ênga = ænga, *w. adj.* alone, sole.
enge, *adj.* narrow, constrained, oppressed, anxious.
engel, ængel, *st. m.* angel.
engel-cund, *adj.* angelic, coming from an angel.
engel-cyn, *st. n.* angelic race, order.
engu, *st. f.* narrowness, confinement.
ent, *st. m.* giant; — **enta geweorc, ærgeweorc**, stronghold, statue, sword-hilt, dragon's cave, dragon's treasure.
ent-isc, *adj.* coming from giants.
er = ear, *st. n.* ear of corn. (Ger. *ähre.*)
erfe-weard, *st. m.* heir.
erian, *w. v.* to ear, plow. (Goth. *arjan;* Ger. *ären, eren.*)
erinaces (as ?), *pl.* hedgehog.
ermđu, *st. f.* misery, calamity.
ern, ærn, *st. n.* house.
erucan, erucam? Ps. 77, 46; — **eruca**, cabbage and cabbage-worm.
esl, *st. f.* shoulder.
esne, *st. m.* slave, servant; — also, man, young man.
esol, *st. m.* ass. (Ger. *esel.*)

êst, *st. m. f.* agreement, harmony, favor, grace, kindness, love, good-will, liberality. (Ger. *gunst;* O. H. Ger. *anst.*)

êstan. See êastan.

êste, *adj.* gracious, liberal, benevolent.

êstig, *adj.* the same as above.

êst-lice, *adv.* graciously, bountifully, gladly.

etan, *st. abl. v.* III. to **eat**, devour, consume. (Ger. *essen.*)

   þurh-etan, to eat through, consume.

   under-etan, to eat from below, underneath.

êd, *adv. compar.* more easily.

êdan, *w. v.*

   ge-êdan, to lighten, ease.

êdan, ǽdan, *w. v.* to lay waste, devastate.

   â-êdan, the same as above.

êd-begete, *adj.* easy to obtain, ready.

êde, *adj.* easy, pleasant, ready.

êde, *adj.* barren, waste, desolate.

êdel, œdel, ǽdel, *st. m.* hereditary estate, possessions, home, fatherland, dwelling-place, realm, land. (O. H. Ger. *uodal;* Icel. *ôdal.*)

êdel-boda, *w. m.* the land's apostle (Thorpe); — a native preacher (B.- T.); — ǽdelboda (Grein). Gû. 976.

êdel-cyning, *st. m.* king of the land.

êdel-drêam, *st. m.* domestic joy, happy life at home on the paternal estate in the fatherland.

edele. See ǽdele.

êdel-eard, *st. m.* inherited dwelling.

êdel-fæsten, *st. n.* fortified dwelling, fortress.

êde-lice, *adv.* easily.

êdel-land, *st. n.* fatherland, land, country.

êdel-lêas, *adj.* without a native country, exiled.

êdel-mearc, *st. f.* march or boundary of one's country, dwelling.

êdel-rice, *st. n.* fatherland, native country.

êdel-riht, *st. n.* inherited privileges, native right.

êdel-seld, *st. n.* hereditary estate, native dwelling, seat.

êdel-setl, *st. n.* the same as above.

êdel-stæf, *st. m.* staff of the hereditary estate, heir, successor.

êdel-stadol, *st. m.* hereditary estate, dwelling.

êdel-stôl, *st. m.* hereditary seat, fatherland, inherited throne, chief city, royal city.

êdel-stôw, *st. f.* hereditary dwelling-place, place of habitation.

êdel-turf, *st. f.* inherited ground, hereditary estate, native country, realm.

êdel-þrym, *st. m.* glory, renown of one's own land.

êdel-weard, *st. m.* master of the hereditary estate, lord of the realm, king.

êdel-wyn, *st. f.* joy in, or enjoyment of, hereditary possessions.

êd-fynde, *adj.* easy to find, easily found.

êd-gesŷne, *adj.* easily seen, visible.

êdian, *w. v.* 1. to breathe, to wave? float up? El. 1107. — 2. to smell.

êdm = ǽdm, *st. m.* breath, vapor, steam.

edda, *conj.* or.

êwan, *w. v.*

   ôd-êwan, 1. to manifest, make known, show. — 2. to seem, appear.

exl = eaxl, *st. f.* shoulder.

êa, êaw (ǽ), *interj.* oh! ah! alas! — joined with lâ.

êa, *st. f.* water, river.

êac, 1. *conj.* eke, also, likewise, moreover. — 2. *prep. w. dat.* with, in addition to, besides.

êaca, *w. m.* increase, addition;— tô êacan, besides, moreover.
êacen, *part. adj.* 1. increased, widespread, large, great, heavy, full, extended;—great, mighty, powerful. 2. heavy, pregnant.
êacen-cræftig, *adj.* immense, enormously great.
êacnian, âcnian, *w. v.* to increase, be enlarged, become pregnant, conceive.
    ge-êacnian, 1. to become pregnant, conceive.—2. to enrich, fructify.
êacnung, *st. f.* conception, childbearing.
êad, *adj.* rich, happy, blessed.
êad, *st. n.* possessions, riches, happiness, joy. (O. H. Ger. *ôt.*)
êaden, *part. adj.* given, granted, conceded.
êad-fruma, *w. m.* author of happiness, giver of joy.
êadgian, *w. v.* to make happy, enrich.
êad-gifa, -giefa, *w. m.* giver of happiness.
êad-gifu, -giefu, *st. f.* gift of happiness, blessedness.
êad-hrêdig, *adj.* blessed, happy.
êadig, *adj.* enriched, blessed with possessions, rich, happy, prosperous, blessed.
êadig-, êadi-lic, *adj.* having an abundance, happy, prosperous; others, êadiglice, *adv.* in abundance, in joyous plenty.
êadig-nes, *st. f.* riches, happiness, good fortune, blessedness.
êad-lufe, *w. f.* love, blessedness of love.
êad-mêde, *adj.* humble, modest, pious.
êad-mêdu, *st. n. pl.* 1. humility.— 2. good will, kindness.
êad-môd, *adj.* 1. humble, meek, pious.—2. benevolent, favorable, friendly, affectionate.
êad-môdlice, *adv.* kindly, graciously.

êad-nis, *st. f.* inner peace, joy, happiness.
eador = geador, *adj.* together.
eador-geard, *st. m.* house of the veins, body? An. 1183.
êad-wacer, *st. m.* watchman of the estate, property.
êad-wela, *w. m.* riches, abundance of wealth, happiness, blessedness.
êa-fisc, -fix, *st. m.* river-fish, fish.
eafod, *st. n.* strength, might, power.
eafor, *st. m.* wild boar, boar.
eafora, afora, -era, -ara, *w. m.* descendant, offspring, son, successor.
eafor-heafod-segn, *st. m.* a banner for the head with the picture of a wild boar upon it;—others take heafod-segn as apposition to eafor.
êage, êge, *w. n.* eye. (Ger. *auge.*)
êag-gebyrd, *st. f.* nature of the eye, power of sight.
êagor-strêam, *st. m.* sea-stream, sea.
êag-sŷne, *adj.* visible to the eye.
eah-strêam, *st. m.* sea.
eaht = æht, *st. f.* deliberation, council.
eahta, ahta, *num.* eight.
eahtan, *w. v.* 1. to consider, deem, judge, observe.—2. *w. gen.* to lie in wait for, ambush, pursue, persecute.
eahta-têoda, *num. adj.* eighteenth.
eahteda, -eada, -oda, *num. adj.* eighth.
eahtian, *w. v.* 1. to consider, deliberate.—2. to consult about, counsel, rule.—3. to mention with praise, speak of.
eaht-nis, *st. f.* persecution.
eahtoda. See eahteda.
eal, eal¹, al, *adj.* all, entire, whole, universal;—eal, *acc. n. adv.* all, quite, fully, entirely;—ealles, *gen. n. adv.* same as above. (Ger. *all.*)
êa-lâ. See êa, *interj.*
êa-lâd, *st. f.* seaway, voyage.
êa-land, *st. n.* island.

eal-beorht, *adj.* all-bright, very bright.
eald, ald, *adj.* old, ancient, antique, of yore, advanced in years, aged; — *compar.* **yldra**, elder, older; — *superl.* **yldest**: **1.** the oldest. — **2.** the most respected. (Ger. *alt.*)
eald-cȳd, -cȳddu, *st. f.* old home, former dwelling-place.
eald-dagas, *st. m. pl.* **old days**, former times.
eald-fæder, *st. m.* old father, father, ancestor.
eald-feond, *part. & subs. pl.* **find**, old enemy, one who has for a long time been a foe, devil.
eald-gecynd, *st. n.* old nature or endowments, original disposition.
eald-geneat, *st. m.* an old companion (*i. e.*, one who has been a companion for a long time), or an aged companion. [devil.
eald-genidla, *w. m.* ancient enemy,
eald-gesegen, *st. f.* old saying, traditions from old times.
eald-gesid, *st. m.* companion of many years, an old courtier.
eald-gestreon, *st. n.* treasure out of old times.
eald-geweorc, *st. n.* old, ancient work, the world.
eald-gewin, *st. n.* fight, conflict of the olden time.
eald-gewinna, *w. m.* old enemy, enemy for many years.
eald-gewyrht, *st. n.* **1.** old, long done deed. — **2.** merit for services rendered for many years, desert.
eald-hettend, *part. & subs.* old enemy, ancient foe.
eald-hlaford, *st. m.* possessor, lord since many years.
ealdian, *w. v.* to grow old. (Ger. *altern.*)
    ge-ealdian, to grow old.
eald-metod, *st. m.* God ruling ever since ancient times.

ealdor, aldor, *st. m.* **1.** elder, chief, prince, lord. — **2.** *pl.* ancestors. Ps. 108, 14. (Ger. *eltern, ältern.*)
ealdor, aldor, *st. n.* **1.** age, old age. **2.** life. — **3.** on **ealdre** and to **ealdre**, ever, forever, always. (Ger. *alter.*)
ealdor-bana, *w. m.* life-destroyer, murderer.
ealdor-bealu, *st. n.* life's evil, death.
ealdor-burg, *st. f.* prince's castle, royal city.
ealdor-cearu, *st. f.* life-care, great sorrow.
ealdor-dagas, *st. m. pl.* days of one's life, life.
ealdor-dema, *w. m.* supreme judge, prince.
ealdor-dom, *st. m.* **1.** principality, rule, dominion. — **2.** beginning? Jul. 190.
ealdor-dugud, *st. f.* nobles, highest officers.
ealdor-frea, *w. m.* over-lord, king.
ealdor-gedal, *st. n.* separation of life, end, death.
ealdor-gesceaft, *st. f.* situation, state, destiny of life.
ealdor-gewinna, *w. m.* life-enemy, one who strives to take his enemy's life.
ealdor-geard, *st. m.* life's protection, body.
ealdor-lagu, *st. f. dat. sg.* **-lege**. **1.** the appointed time of life, fortune. — **2.** death.
ealdor-lang, *adj.* lifelong, eternal, everlasting.
ealdor-leas, *adj.* lifeless, dead.
ealdor-leas, *adj.* without a lord, ruler.
ealdor-lic, *adj.* princely, excellent, holy.
ealdor-lice, *adv.* excellently, grandly.
ealdor-man, *st. m.* (**alderman**), prince, ruler, high officer of state, noble, official.

ealdor-naru, *st. f.* life's nourishment, safety, refuge.
ealdor-sacerd, *st. m.* high priest.
ealdor-stôl, *st. m.* lord's seat, throne.
ealdor-þegn, -þægn, *st. m.* king's servant, a principal nobleman of the court, courtier, servant, prince.
ealdor-wisa, *w. m.* principal leader.
eald-riht, *st. n.* old right or ancient privilege.
eald-spell, *st. n.* old saying, old story.
ealdur. See **ealdor.**
eal-dwêrig, *adj.* altogether perverse, depraved? Exod. 50. Others, **ealdwêrig,** vile of old.
eal-fela, *indecl. n.* very much.
eal-felo, *adj.* very destructive, deadly.
eal-gearo, *adj.* fully ready or prepared, equipped, ready, willing.
ealgian, algian, *w. v.* to shield, defend, protect.
    ge-ealgian, the same as above.
eal-grêne, *adj.* all green, entirely green.
eal-gylden, *adj.* all golden, entirely of gold.
ealh, alh, *st. m.* hall, palace, temple, shrine.
eal-hâlig, *adj.* all holy.
ealh-stede, *st. m.* palace, temple.
eal-iren, *adj.* entirely of iron.
eal-isig, *adj.* all icy, having the appearance of ice.
êa-lidende, *part. & subs.* seafaring, sailor.
eall, eall-. See **eal, eal-, æl-.**
eallenga, *adv.* fully, entirely, altogether, quite, indeed.
eallunga, *adv.* the same as above.
eal-, al-mægen, *st. n.* all might, power.
eal-meaht, -miht, *st. f.* the same as above.
eal-meahtig, -mihtig, *adj.* almighty.
ealneg, -nig, *adj.* always.
eal-nacod, *adj.* entirely naked.
ealo. See **ealu.**

eal-tela, *adv.* quite well.
eal-teaw, *adj.* altogether good.
ealu, *st. n.* ale, beer.
ealu-benc, *st. f.* ale-bench, bench for those drinking ale.
ealu-drincende, *part.* ale-drinking.
ealu-gâl, *adj.* drunk with ale.
ealu-wæ̂ge, *st. n.* ale-can, portable vessel out of which ale is poured into the cups.
ealu-wôsa, *w. m.* tippler, drunkard? Wy. 48.
eal-wealda, al-walda, *w. adj.* almighty, all-ruling (God).
eal-wealdend, al-waldend, *adj.* the same as above.
eal-wihte (al-, all-), *pl.* all creatures, all created things.
eal-wundor, *st. n.* an altogether wonderful thing.
eam, eom, 1. *sg. pres.* I am.—**2.** þu eart, þu eard (Dan. 609), eartþu, earttu;—*pl.* earon, earun. See **nearun.**
êam, *st. m.* uncle, mother's brother. (Ger. *oheim.*)
eaples, ear. See **æpl, er.**
ear (earh), *st. m.* sea, ocean.
êar, *st. m.* earth, ground, grave;—and name for the Rune êa.
earc, *st. f.* ark, chest, ark of the covenant.
earce, *w. f.* ark.
earcnan-stân, *st. m.* gem, precious stone.
eard, *st. m.* **1.** cultivated ground, estate, hereditary estate, fatherland, stopping-place, dwelling-place, dwelling, home.—**2.** place.—**3.** earth, land.—**4.** situation, condition, fate. Hy. 7, 97. (Ger. *art.*)
eard-fæst, *adj.* established, settled, abiding.
eard-geard, *st. m.* place of habitation, world.
eard-gif, *st. n.* gift from one's native place.

eardian, w. v. 1. *trans.* to inhabit.— **2.** *intrans.* to have a dwelling-place, live.
   ge-eardian, to take a dwelling, dwell.
earding, *st. f.* dwelling-place, house.
eard-land, *st. n.* native land.
eard-lufe, *w. f.* love of one's native land.
eard-rice, *st. n.* habitation, paradise.
eard-stapa, *w. m.* one wandering over the earth, wanderer.
eard-stede, *st. m.* place of habitation.
eardung, *st. f.* place of habitation, dwelling.
eardung-stôw, *st. f.* place of habitation, dwelling.
eard-wic, *st. n.* place of habitation, dwelling.
êare, *w. n.* ear. (Ger. *ohr;* Goth. *auso.*)
earendel, *st. m.* brightness, splendor, glory.
earfeðe, *adj.* difficult, troublesome.
earfeðe, *st. n.* labor, pains, trouble, difficulty, woe, torment.
earfoð, *st. n.* same as the above.
earfoð-cyn, *st. n.* depraved race, unworthy generation.
earfoð-dæg, *st. m.* day of tribulation, trouble.
earfoð-hâwe, *adj.* difficult to be seen.
earfoð-hwil, *st. f.* troublesome time, time of hardship.
earfoð-lic, *adj.* difficult, troublesome, full of labor and trouble.
earfoð-lice, *adv.* with trouble, with difficulty, with vexation, angrily, sorrowfully, scarcely.
earfoð-mæcg, *st. m.* unhappy, afflicted man, sufferer.
earfoð-sælig, *adj.* unhappy, unfortunate.
earfoð-sid, *st. m.* troublesome journey, misfortune, trouble, calamity.
earfoð-tæcne, *adj.* difficult to be shown.

earfoð-þrâg, *st. f.* time of trouble, sorrowful time.
earg, earh, *adj.* **1.** lazy, cowardly, timid.— **2.** depraved, wicked, abandoned, vile. (Ger. *arg.*)
earge, *adv.* inertly, vilely, ill.
ear-gebland, earh-geblond, *st. n.* tumult of the waves, mingling of the waves, sea.
earg-faru. See **earhfaru.**
ear-grund, *st. m.* bottom of the sea.
earh, *st. n.* arrow, dart. (Goth. *arhwazna.*)
earh-faru, *st. f.* **1.** the flying of an arrow, arrow-flight.— **2.** arriere ban, army of bowmen, archers.
earh-gebland. See **eargebland.**
earm, *st. m.* arm. (Ger. *arm.*)
earm, *adj.* poor, miserable, wretched, unhappy. (Ger. *arm.*)
earm-bêag, *st. m.* arm-ring, bracelet.
earm-cearig, *adj.* miserable, full of sorrows.
earme, *adj.* miserably, badly.
earm-hrêad, *st. f.* arm-ornament.
earming, *st. m.* miserable, unhappy being.
earm-lic, *adj.* miserable, unhappy, wretched, pitiable.
earm-lice, *adv.* miserably, wretchedly.
earm-sceapen, *part. adj.* wretched by the decree of fate, wretched.
earmung, *st. f.* misery? Rä. 81, 82.
earn. See **irnan.**
earn, *st. m.* eagle. (Ger. *aar.*)
earnian, arnian, *w. r.* to earn, deserve, get, labor for. (Ger. *ernten.*)
   ge-earnian, same as the above.
earning, *st. f.* earning, desert, merit, reward.
earnung, *st. f.* same as the above.
earp, *adj.* dusky, dark brown, dark.
eart, eard, earun. See **eam.**
earu, *adj.* quick, swift, ready.
earwunga, *adv.* gratuitously, for nothing.

êast, *adv.* in the east, east. (Ger. *ost, osten.*)
êasta, *w. m.* east. (Ger. *ost, osten.*)
êastan, -en, *adv.* from the east.
êa-stæd, *st. n.* seashore, river-bank.
êast-dǽl, *st. m.* eastern part of the earth, or of a country, east.
êasterne, *adj.* eastern, east.
êaste-weard, *adj.* eastward. •
êast-land, *st. n.* east land, the east.
êastor, *st. n.* easter. (Ger. *ostern.*)
êastor-mônad, *st. m.* easter month, April.
êastor-niht, *st. f.* easter-night, night before easter.
êastor-tîd, *st. f.* easter-time.
êa-strêam, *st. m.* water-stream, river.
êast-rodor, *st. m.* eastern part of the heavens.
êast-weg, *st. m.* east way, eastward, east.
eatol, *adj.* hostile, frightful, cruel, foul.
êad, *adv.* easily.
êad-bede, *adj.* easily entreated, entreatable.
êad-bêne, *adj.* exorable.
êade, *adj.* easy, smooth, pleasant.
êade, *adv.* easily, readily, lightly.
êad-fynde, *adj.* easy to find.
êad-hrêdig, *adj.* happy, blessed.
êad-mêde, *adj.* lowly, humble, gentle.
êad-mêdu, *st. n. pl.* 1. weakness, humility, impotency.— 2. light, joyous way of thinking, happy thoughts.— 3. humanity, affability, kindness.
êad-metto, *st. n. pl.* humility, weakness, impotency.
êad-môd, *adj.* 1. lowly, humble;— *w. dat.* obliging, obedient.— 2. favorable, kind, friendly. Cri. 255.
êaw. See êa, *interj.*
êawan, *w. v.* to show, disclose, prove.

ge-êawan, 1. to show, offer, present.— 2. *intrans.* appear.
ôd-êawan, the same as above.
êawunga, *adv.* openly, plainly.
eax, *st. f.* axis, axletree. (Ger. *achse, axe.*)
eaxe (-a)? Seel. 122. (êagan, Vercelli.)
eaxl, exl, *st. f.* shoulder. (Ger. *achsel.*)
eaxle-gespann, *st. n.* shoulder-span, *i. e.* the part of the cross where the beams intersect.
eaxl-gestella, *w. m.* one who has his position at the shoulder of his lord, trusty companion, counselor.
êoc. See gêoc.
eode, iode, eodon, *pret.* went, proceeded, walked. See gangan, gân. [Other forms of this verb are not found in Anglo-Saxon.]
   be-, bi-eode, committed, perfected, fulfilled, observed, cherished.
   ful-eode, followed after, served, assisted.
   ful-geode, -geeode, the same as above.
   ge-eode, 1. went.— 2. happened, occurred, took place.— 3. conquered, won by fighting, went under, submitted.— 4. obtained, reached, effected, accomplished.
   of-eode, went away, avoided.
   ofer-eode, 1. went over.— 2. overcame, fell upon.— 3. *imper. w. gen.* it passed by, it was withstood, overcome. Dêor. 7, &c.
   ôd-eode, went thither, escaped.
   ymb-eode, went around.
eodor, *st. m.* 1. fence, hedge, inclosure, house.— 2. limit, margin, coast, region. Jul. 113.— 3. protection, lord, prince. (O. H. Ger. *etar.*)
eodor-wîr, *st. m.* wire fence, inclosure made of wire.
eofod, *st. n.* strength, power.

eofor, -er, -ur, *st. m.* **1.** boar, wild boar.—**2.** boar-image (on the helmet).—**3.** bold hero, brave fighter. (Ger. *eber*.)
eofor-cumbol, *st. n.* boar-image on the helmet, helmet.
eofor-lic, *st. n.* image of a boar, boar-likeness.
eofor-sprêot, *st. m.* boar-spear.
eofot, *st. n.* debt, sin, crime.
eoful-sæc, *st. f. n.?* blasphemy.
eofur. See **eofor.**
êogod = **gêogud,** *st. f.* youth, young (warriors).
eoh, *st. m.* horse.
êoh (= **iw**), yew-(tree); and name for the Rune **êo.**
eolet, *st. n.* quick journey? B. 224; (Grein);—sea, ocean (B.-T.).
eolh, *st. m.* elk; and name for the Rune **x.** (O. H. Ger. *elaho*.)
eolh-stede, *st. m.* temple, sanctuary.
eom. See **eam.**
eorcan-, eorcnan-, eorclan-stân, *st. m.* precious stone. [dwell.
eordian = **eardian,** *w. v.* to inhabit,
êored, êorod, *st. n.* cavalry, troop, band, legion.
êored-cist, -ciest, -cyst, *st. f.* chosen band, picked legion, troop.
êored-geatwe, *st. f. pl.* warlike adornments, military trappings.
êored-mæcg, *st. m.* horseman.
êored-þrêat, *st. m.* band, troop.
eorl, *st. m.* earl, man of noble birth, nobleman, hero, leader, chief, courtier, attendant, man, human being.
eorl-gebyrd, -gebyrdo, *st. f.* noble birth, nobility.
eorl-gestrêon, *st. n.* riches, possessions, wealth of the nobles.
eorl-gewǣde, *st. n.* a hero's dress, armor.
eor-lic = **eorl-lic,** *adj.* knightly, noble, manly.
eorl-mægen, *st. n.* band, company of men, of noble warriors.

eorl-scipe, -scype, *st. m.* manhood, manliness, chivalrous nature, knightly bearing, knighthood, nobility.
eorl-weorod, *st. n.* band of warriors, a noble's followers.
eormen, yrmen, *adj.* immensely extended, whole, universal, entire.
eormen-cyn, *st. n.* the human race, mankind.
eormen-grund, *st. m.* an immeasurably wide surface, the whole earth.
eormen-lâf, *st. f.* enormous legacy.
eormen-strŷnd, *st. f.* widespread race, generation.
eormen-þêod, yrmen-, *st. f.* widespread folk, great nation.
eornad. See **irnan.**
eornest, *st. f.* earnest, earnestness, battle. (Ger. *ernst*.)
eorneste, *adj.* earnest, serious.
eorneste, eornoste, *adv.* earnestly, seriously, zealously, hastily.
eorp, *adj.* dark brown, dusky, dark, swarthy.
eorre, *adj.* angry, enraged, fierce.
eorringa, *adv.* angrily, fiercely.
eorð, *st. f.* seedtime, crop.
eorð-ærn, *st. n.* earth-house, grave.
eorð-bûend, -bûgend, *part. & subs.* earth-dweller, man.
eorð-cund, *adj.* sprung from the earth, earthy, earthly.
eorð-cynn, *st. n.* earth-kind, human race, man.
eorð-cyning, *st. m.* earthly king, king of the country.
eorð-draca, *w. m.* earth-dragon, dragon that dwells in the earth.
eorðe, *w. f.* **1. earth,** in contrast to heaven and hell, as a part of the world and dwelling-place of man.—**2.** plain, country.—**3.** earth, ground, soil.—**4.** land, in contrast to water.—**5.** earth as substance, material, matter. (Ger. *erde*.)

eord-fæt, *st. n.* earthen vessel, body.
eord-gesceaft, *st. f.* earthly creature.
eord-græf, *st. n.* ditch, well.
eord-grâp, *st. f.* earth's grip or hold, grave. Ruin. 6.
eord-lic, *adj.* earthly, terrestrial.
eord-mægen, *st. n.* earthly power, might, strength? Reim. 69.
eord-reced, *st. n.* hall in the earth, cave.
eord-rice, *st. n.* kingdom of earth, earth.
eord-scræf, *st. n.* hole in the earth, cave, cavern, grave.
eord-sele, *st. m.* earth-hall, dwelling in the earth, cave.
eord-stede, *st. m.* earth.
eord-tudor, *st. n.* earth's race, men.
eord-wæstm, *st. f.* fruit of the earth, plant.
eord-wara, *w. m.* earth-dweller, inhabitant of the earth.
eord-waru, *st. f.* earth-dwellers, mankind.
eord-weg, *st. m.* earthly way, earth.

eord-wela, *w. m.* earthly riches, wealth.
eord-weall, *st. m.* earth-wall.
eord-weard, *st. m.* land property, estate.
eoten, *st. m.* giant, harmful enemy. (O. N. *jötunn.*)
eoton. See etan.
eotonisc, *adj.* made by giants.
eoton-weard, *st. f.* protection against giants, safety from monsters.
êow. See ge, *pron.* (Chaucer *yow*, you.)
êowan, iowan, iewan, -ian, *w. r.* to let be seen, show, manifest, confer.
æt-êowan, 1. to show, make visible, manifest, disclose, declare.
2. to appear.
ge-êowan, to show, disclose.
ôd-êowan, 1. to show, disclose.
2. to appear.
eowde, *st. n.* herd, flock.
eowde-scêap, *st. n.* sheepfold, flock of sheep.
êower, 1. *pron. possessive,* your, yours.— 2. *gen. pl. pron. personal,* see ge, *pron.*
êowic. See ge, *pron.*

F

fâ. See fâh.
fâcen, *st. n.* fraud, stratagem, deceit, evil, malice, injustice, overstepping the bounds of duty, crime. (O. H. Ger. *feihan.*)
fâcen-dǽd, *st. f.* sin, crime.
fâcen-geswipere, *st. n.* cunning, crafty counsel, deceit.
fâcen-lice, *adv.* deceitfully, artfully.
fâcen-searu, *st. n.* cunning intrigue, treachery through deceit.
fâcen-stæf, *st. m.* wickedness, treachery, deceit.
fâcen-tâcen, *st. n.* wicked, treacherous sign, deceitful token.

fâcne, *adv.* very, greatly, exceedingly, hostilely.
fæc, *st. n.* space, interval of time, time. (Ger. *fach.*)
fǽcne, fâcne, *adj.* deceitful, cunning, vile, wicked, worthless, untrustworthy.
fǽcne, *adv.* deceitfully, maliciously; ignominiously, disgracefully.
fæder, feder, *st. m.* father. (Ger. *vater.*)
fædera, *w. m.* father's brother, uncle.
fæder-ædelo, *st. n. pl.* genealogy, ancestry, origin, paternal honors, noble nature and character of the father.

fæderen, *adj.* fatherly, paternal, from the father's side.
fæderen-brôðor, *st. m.* brother (from the same father).
fæderen-cynn, *st. n.* father's race or kin.
fæderen-mǣg, *st. m.* kinsman descended from the same father, co-descendant.
fæder-geard, *st. m.* father's dwelling, house.
fæder-lic, *adj.* **fatherly,** paternal. (Ger. *väterlich.*)
fædrunga, *w. f.* paternal relation, kinswoman? mother? B. 2128.
fǣge, *adj.* devoted to death, allotted to death by fate. — 2. dead. — 3. unhappy, accursed, condemned. — 4. fearful, timid, cowardly. (Ger. *feig.*)
fǣgen, *adj.* **fain,** glad, joyous, joyful, rejoicing.
fǣger, *adj.* **fair,** beautiful, lovely, joyous. (Goth. *fagrs.*)
fǣgere, fǣgre, fegere, *adv.* 1. fairly, beautifully, pleasantly, gently, excellently. — 2. well, becomingly, according to etiquette.
fǣger-wyrde, *adj.* becomingly, beautifully speaking, fair in word.
fǣgnian, *w. v.* to rejoice, be joyous, glad, exult.
  ge-fǣgnian, to rejoice, gladden, make glad.
fǣgon. See feohan, fêon.
fǣgrian, *w. v.* to become fair, beautiful
fǣgð, *st. f.* imminent death.
fǣhð, *st. f.* **feud,** enmity, revenge, hostile act, battle. (Ger. *fehde.*)
fǣhðe, *w. f.* the same as above.
fǣhðo, fǣhðu, *st. f.* same as above.
fǣle, *adj.* true, faithful, good, dear.
fǣle, *adv.* truly, aptly, well.
fǣlsian, *w. v.* to bring again into a good condition, cleanse.
  ge-fǣlsian, the same as above.
fǣman, *w. v.* [lently.
  â-fǣman, to breathe out vio-

fǣmig, *adj.* foamy.
fǣmne, fêmne, *w. f.* virgin, woman, young woman.
fǣr, *st. n.* vessel, ship.
fǣr, *st. n.* warlike expedition, war.
fǣr, fêr, *st. m.* **fear,** that which comes suddenly and unexpectedly; sudden, unexpected attack; fright, evil, destruction. (Ger. *ge-fahr.*)
fǣr (= **fǣger**), *adj.* fair, beautiful, lovely.
fǣran, *w. v.*
  â-fǣran, to make to fear, frighten, terrify, cause sudden fright.
fǣran (= **fêran**), *w. v.*
  ge-fǣran, to lead, bring. Sat. 92.
fǣr-bifongen, *part.* beset by dangers or terrors.
fǣr-bryne, *st. m.* terrible fire, great heat.
fǣrbu, *st. f.* color. (Ger. *farbe.*)
fǣr-cŷle, *st. m.* terrible cold, intense cold.
fǣr-drype, *st. m.* sudden or terrible blow.
fǣreld, fǣryld, *st. n.* way, course, journey, departure, expedition.
fǣr-gripe, *st. m.* sudden, treacherous gripe, attack.
fǣr-gryre, *st. m.* fright, horror caused by sudden attack.
fǣr-haga, *w. m.* hedge of dangers, peril. Gû. 933.
fǣringa, *adv.* suddenly, unexpectedly, quickly.
fǣr-lice, *adv.* suddenly.
fǣr-nið, *st. m.* deadly hostility, hostile attack.
fǣr-sceaða, *w. m.* enemy bringing sudden destruction.
fǣr-scyte, *st. m.* sudden or fatal shot.
fǣr-searo, *st. n.* treacherous plotting, sudden artifice.
fǣr-slide, *st. m.* sudden, unexpected fall.

fǽr-spell, *st. n.* news of an unexpected event, sudden tidings.
færd = **ferd**, thought? mind? Met. 27, 24.
fǽr-wundor, *st. n.* sudden wonder.
færyld. See **færeld.**
fǽs, *st. m.* terror, horror, dread. B. 2230.
fæsl, *st. n.? m.?* fetus, seed, offspring.
fæst, *st. f.* fastness, house, citadel? Gû. 192. (Ger. *feste*.)
fæst, fest, *adj.* fast, firm, fixed, steadfast. (Ger. *fest*.)
fæstan, *w. v.* to fasten, make fast or firm. (Ger. *festen, be-festigen*.)
 æt-fæstan, to fasten to something, affix, fasten, drive into, afflict.
 be-, bi-fæstan, 1. to give over for safe keeping, trust, intrust.— 2. to ground, fix, fasten, make fast, establish.
 geblǽd-fæstan, to establish in fruitfulness, in riches.
 gesige-fæstan, to strengthen, make triumphant, crown.
 ôd-fæstan, to fasten, make firm, affix, fix into, fix on or upon.
fæstan, *w. v.* 1. to fast.— 2. to expiate by fasting. (Ger. *fasten*.)
fæste, feste, *adv.* fast, firmly, fixedly.
fæsten, *st. n.* fasting, a fast. (Ger. *fasten*.)
fæsten, *st. n.* 1. firmament, sky.— 2. any well-inclosed or fortified place, fortress, city, castle, village.
fæsten-geat, *st. n.* castle-gate, city-gate.
fæsten-gangol, *adj.* steadfast, constant.
fæst-hŷdig, *adj.* of constant mind, steadfast, brave.
fæst-lic, *adj.* firm, fixed, steadfast.
fæst-lice, *adv.* firmly, steadfastly, fast.

fæstnian, *w. v.* to **fasten,** make firm, bind, fetter, confirm.
 â-fæstnian, to fasten, strengthen, fix on or upon, confirm.
 ge-fæstnian, to fasten, strengthen, fix on or upon, bind, confirm.
fæstnung, *st. f.* fastening, strengthening, confirmation.
fæst-rǽd, *adj.* having firm,fixed purpose, firmly resolved.
fæst-steall, *adj.* standing firmly, fixed.
fæt, *st. m.* step, going, way.
fæt, *st. n.* vat, vessel, vase, cup. (Ger. *fass*.)
fæt, *adj.* fat, fleshy. (Ger. *fett*.)
fæt, *st. n.* plate, sheet of metal;— especially gold plate. See **fatu.**
fæted, fætt, *part.* ornamented with gold beaten into plate-form, covered, gold-mounted, ornamented with gold plate; as attribute of gold, brought into the proper form (*i. e.* sheet or plate form), set in, beaten fine.
fæted-hlêor, *adj.* with golden spangles adorned cheek, with ornamented bridles.
fæted-sinc, *st. n.* beaten gold, fine treasure.
fætels, *st. m. n.* vessel, sack, pouch, wallet.
fæt-gold, *st. n.* gold in sheets or plates.
fæt-hengest, *st. m.* riding-horse, road-horse.
fætian, *w. v.*
 ge-fætian, to fetch, bring.
fætt. See **fæted.**
fædm, *st. m. f.* (**fathom**), 1. the outspread, encircling arms.— 2. embrace, encircling, encompassing. 3. power, sway, grasp, power of possession, possession, property. 4. protection, embrace, shield.— 5. bosom, lap, breast.—6. expanse, surface. (Ger. *faden*.)

fǽdman, *w. v.* (to **fathom**), to embrace, encircle, envelope.
   be-fǽdman, to embrace, encircle, envelope.
   ofer-fǽdman, to encompass, spread out over from above, overshadow.
fǽdmian, *w. v.* to embrace, take into itself, engulf.
fǽdm-rim, *st. n.* fathom-measure, cubit.
fág, fáh, *adj.* many-colored, variegated, of varying color, shining, dyed, colored. (Goth. *faihs*.)
fágian, *w. v.* to change, vary in color.
fáh, fá, fág, fêh, *adj.* (**foe**), 1. proscribed, without peace, outlawed, guilty.— 2. hostile, inimical.
fal, fallan. See **feal, feallan**.
fám, *st. n.* foam. (Ger. *feim*.)
fámgian, *w. v.* to **foam**, boil.
fámig, *adj.* **foamy**, foaming.
fámig-bord, *adj.* having foamy sides.
fámig-bósm, *adj.* having foamy bosom.
fámig-heals, *adj.* foamy-necked.
fana, *w. m.* flag, standard. (Ger. *fahne*.)
fandian, *w. v.* to search out, test, prove, try, examine, tempt. (Ger. *fahnden*.)
   á-fandian, to attempt, try.
   ge-fandian, to attempt, try, search for, investigate, find out, experience.
fandung, *st. f.* trying, investigating, finding out.
fangen. See **fón**.
fára, *gen. pl.* from **fáh**.
faran, *st. abl. v.* VI. (to **fare**), general expression for any kind of movement from one place to another; hence, to go, walk, travel, draw. ride, drive, march, sail, &c.; to practice, be versed in (Gen. 531); to be, fare. Ælf. N. T., p. 40. (Ger. *fahren*.)
   á-faran, to go out, away, depart, remove.
   be-faran, to go around, travel through, surround, flow around, encompass.
   ge-faran, 1. *intrans.* to go, wander, travel.— 2. to proceed, act. B. 738.— 3. to die. El. 872.— 4. *w. acc.* to travel to a place.
   geond-faran, to fare or go through, over, pervade, flow over.
   ofer-faran, 1. to go over, or across, cross, wander over or through.— 2. to overtake, take unawares.— 3. to overcome, withstand.
   ód-faran, to come off, escape, flee from.
   tó-faran, to go apart, be scattered, separate.
   wid-faran, to come off, escape.
farod, farad, *st. m.* stream, flood of the sea, shore.
farod-hengest, *st. m.* seahorse, ship.
farod-lácende, *part. & subs.* 1. swimming.— 2. sailing, sailor.
farod-ridende, *part.* sailing.
farod-strǽt, *st. f.* sea-street, sea.
faru, *st. f.* 1. way, going, passage. 2. movable possessions, family.— 3. expedition, line (of movers), host on the march.
Fastitocalon, whale.
fatu, *st. f.* plate, sheet of metal, especially gold plate. See **fæt**.
Februarius, February. Men. 18.
fec? B. 2246.
feccan, *w. v.* to **fetch**.
   ge-feccan, to fetch, bring, lead, draw.
fecgan, *st. abl. v.* III.
   ǽt-fecgan, to seize, lay hold of.
   ge-fecgan, to snatch, take to one's self.

fec-word, *st. n.* conjuring, adjuring word. B. 2246.
fêdan, *w. v.* 1. to feed, nourish, support.—2. to bear, bring forth, produce. (Ger. *füttern.*)
 â-fêdan, the same as above.
feder. See **fæder.**
fêgan, *w. v.* to join, unite, fix. (Ger. *fügen.*)
 ge-fêgan, to join, unite, fix, join together, compact.
fegere, fêh, fêhđ. See **fægere, fâh, fôn.**
fel, fell, *st. n.* fell, skin, hide, leather. (Ger. *fell.*)
fêl = **fêol,** *st. f.* file.
fela, feala, feola, feolo, 1. *indecl. n.* 2. *adj.*—3. *adv.* much; much, many; very. (Ger. *viel.*)
fela-fǽcne, *adj.* very treacherous, deceitful.
fela-frêcne, *adj.* very fierce, wild.
fela-geong, *adj.* very young.
fela-geonge, *adj.* much traveled.
fela-gêomor, *adj.* very sad, sorrowful.
fela-hrôr, *adj.* very active against the enemy, very warlike.
fela-lêof, *adj.* very dear, much loved.
fela-meahtig, *adj.* very powerful, mighty.
fela-môdig, *adj.* very courageous.
fêlan, *w. v.* to feel, perceive, touch. (Ger. *fühlen.*)
 ge-fêlan, to feel, perceive, touch.
fela-synnig, *adj.* much oppressed with sins, very sinful.
fela-wlanc, *adj.* very stately.
feld, *st. m.* field, plain, open country. (Ger. *feld.*)
feld-gangende, *part.* wandering about the field, field-going.
feld-hûs, *st. n.* field-house, tent.
fêle-lêas, *adj.* without feeling, dead. (Ger. *ge-fühllos.*)
felgan, *st. abl. v.* I. 1. *trans.* to get into something, undergo.— 2. to betake one's self into, enter, conceal. (Ger. *befehlen;* Goth. *filhan.*)

 æt-felgan, to hold to, hold fast, stick to.
 be-, bi-felgan, to stick, cling to, affix, deliver.
fell. See **fel.**
fell, *st. m.* falling, ruin, death.
fellan, *w. v.* to fell, cut down. (Ger. *fällen.*)
 be-fellan, 1. to fell, lay low, strike down.— 2. to deprive by killing, bereave.
fêmne. See **fǽmne.**
fen, *st. n.* fen, moor, marsh. (Ger. *fenne.*)
fen-freođo, *st. f.* asylum, refuge in the moors.
feng, *st. m.* 1. grasp, hold, gripe, embrace.— 2. handle? Exod. 246.
fêng. See **fôn.**
fengel, *st. m.* lord, prince, king.
fen-gelâd, *st. n.* fen-path, fen.
feng-net, *st. n.* catching-net, net.
fen-hliđ, *st. n.* precipice at the edge of a moor, marsh-precipice.
fen-hôp, *st. n.* a pool of water in the midst of a marsh, refuge in the fen.
fênix, *st. m.* 1. the bird phœnix.— 2. date-palm. Ph. 174.
fen-ýce, *w. f.* marsh-frog.
fêr. See **fǽr.**
fêran, *w. v.* to move one's self, make journey, go, travel, march, sail, &c.
 ge-fêran, 1. to fare, go, come (*intrans.* or *w.* cognate *acc.*)— 2. to undergo, endure, suffer, experience. 3. to attain, obtain, fulfill, effect, perfect.— 4. to behave one's self, conduct one's self.
 geond-fêran, to wander over or through.
feran (See f. 26), to be changed into **frêfran.**
fêr-blǽd, *st. m.* sudden, fearful blast of wind.
fêr-clam, *st. m.* sudden seizing, or unexpected, dangerous straits.
ferd-rinc, *st. m.* warrior.

fere, *acc.* of **faru,** *st. f.* bearing, bringing.
fêrend, *part. & subs.* farer, seafarer, sailor.
fergan. See **ferian.**
ferh, *st. m. n.* life.
ferh, fearh, *st. m.* (farrow), hog, boar; picture of a boar on a helmet. (Ger. *ferkel;* O. H. Ger. *farh.*)
ferht = ferhð, *st. n.* soul, mind, thought.
ferht-lic, *adj.* sensible, wise, just.
ferhð, *st. m. n.* **1.** soul, mind, heart. **2.** life.
ferhð-bana, *w. m.* soul, life-destroyer, murderer.
ferhð-cearig, *adj.* of anxious mind, sorrowful.
ferhð-cleofa, *w. m.* couch or seat of the soul, breast.
ferhð-côfa, *w. m.* same as above.
ferhð-freo, *adj.* having good courage, bold, brave.
ferhð-geniðla, *w. m.* life-enemy, mortal enemy.
ferhð-gleaw, *adj.* prudent, wise, sagacious.
ferhð-loca, *w. m.* inclosure of the soul, breast.
ferhð-sefa, *w. m.* life-spirit, mind, thought.
ferian, fergan, *w. v.* **1.** to bear, carry, bring, lead, conduct, bring forward.— **2.** *w. reflex. acc.* to betake one's self to, be versed in.— **3.** to set out, depart, go. (Ger. *führen.*)
feriend, *part. & subs.* leader, bringer.
fêring, *st. f.* journey, wandering.
fêr-nes, *st. f.* transition, passing away.
ferran. See **feorran.**
ferran, *w. v.*
  â-ferran, to remove.
fersn. See **fiersn.**
ferð, *st. m. n.* **1.** soul, heart, mind.— **2.** life.

ferð = ferd, fyrd, crowd? troop? Wand. 54.
ferð-fridende, *part.* life-keeping, life-preserving.
ferð-gewit, *st. n.* consciousness, understanding.
ferð-grim, *adj.* of a grim, cruel mind, savage.
ferð-loca, *w. m.* inclosure of the soul, heart, breast.
ferð-sefa, *w. m.* spirit of life, soul, thought.
ferð-wêrig, *adj.* life-weary, sad, sorrowful.
fest, feste. See **fæst, fæste.**
fêt. See **fôt,— feet.**
fetel, *st. m.* belt, girdle.
fetel-hilt, *st. n.* a sword-hilt, with gold chains fastened to it.
feter. See **fetor.**
feterian, fetran, fetrian, *w. v.* to fetter.
  ge-feterian, to fetter, tie.
fetian, fettan, *w. v.* to fetch, bring near, bring.
  ge-fetian, to fetch, bring near, bring.
fetor, feter, *st. f.* fetter, chain. (Ger. *fessel.*)
fetor-wrâsen, *st. f.* fetter, chain.
fêð. See **fôn.**
fêða, *w. m.* **1.** infantry-man, foot-soldier.— **2.** infantry, troop of warriors, line of battle, army.— **3.** battle. Jul. 389.
fêðe, *st. n.* going, gait, pace, power of going.
fêðe-cempa, *w. m.* foot-soldier.
fêðe-gang, *st. m.* journey on foot.
fêðe-gæst, -gast, *st. m.* guest coming on foot.
fêðe-georn, *adj.* desirous of going, willingly going.
fêðe-hwearf, *st. m.* band or troop of footmen, pedestrians.
fêðe-lâst, *st. m.* signs of going, footprint, going afoot.

fêde-lêas, *adj.* footless.
fêde-mund, *st. f.* going-hand, forefoot of the badger.
feder, fider, fyder, *num.* four,—only found in compounds.
feder, *st. f.* feather. (Ger. *feder.*)
feder-gearwe, *st. f. pl.* feather equipment, feathers of the shaft of the arrow.
feder-hama, *w. m.* feather-home, covering of birds, of angels, and of the devil; feathers, wings, plumage.
feder-scette, *adj.* quadrangular, extended in four directions.
feder-scêatas, *st. m. pl.* four sides, quarters.
fêde-spêdig, *adj.* speedy of foot, swift.
fêde-wig, *st. m.* battle on foot.
fedran, *w. v.* to feather.
    ge-fedran, to supply with feathers or wings, give wings to.
fex, fêo. See **feax, feoh**.
fêa, *adj.* few, little. (Goth. *faus, faws.*)
fêa, *adv.* a little, at all.
feal, feala. See **feall, fela.**
fealdan, *st. red. v.* to fold. (Ger. *falten.*)
    be-, bi-fealdan, to surround, encompass, embrace, grasp.
fealdian, *w. v.*
    gemænig-fealdian, to multiply.
feall, fall, *st. m.* fall, slaughter (*ms.* ful). Exod. 167.
feallan, *st. red. v.* **1.** to fall, fall headlong.—**2.** to befall, come upon, overtake.—**3.** to fall down, go to ruin. (Ger. *fallen.*)
    â-feallan, 1. to fall, fall down. **2.** to make to fall, kill.
    be-feallan, 1. to fall, fall into. **2.** *part.* **befeallen,** deprived of, robbed.
    ge-feallan, to fall, sink down;—

sometimes *w. acc.* (of place, whither), to fall to, overwhelm.
    of-feallan, to cut off.
fealo. See **fela.**
fêa-lôg, *adj.* helpless, destitute.
fealu, fealo, *adj.* fallow, pale red, pale yellow, dun-colored, tawny. (Ger. *fahl, falb.*)
fealu-hilt, *adj.* having a yellow, *i. e.* golden hilt or handle.
fealu-wian, feal-wian, *w. v.* (to fallow), to become fallow, grow yellow, ripen, wither.
fearh. See **ferh.**
fearm, *st. m.* freight, cargo.
fearn, *st. n.* fern. (Ger. *farn.*)
fearod. See **farod.**
fêa-sceaft, *adj.* abandoned, alone, lonely, miserable, unhappy, helpless.
fêa-sceaftig, *adj.* the same as above.
feax, fex, *st. n.* hair of the head, hair. (O. H. Ger. *fahs.*)
feax-hâr, *adj.* hoary, gray-haired.
fêo. See **feoh.**
fêogan, fiogan, fêon, *w. v.* to hate, be hostile to, persecute, disturb. (Goth. *fijan.*)
feoh, fêo, *st. n.* (fee), **1.** cattle, herd. **2.** hence, as cattle were used as exchange in buying and selling, money, possessions, property, treasure, riches.—**3.** name of the Rune f. (Ger. *vieh.*)
feohan, fêon, *st. abl. v.* III. to rejoice, enjoy one's self.
    ge-feohan, to enjoy one's self, take delight in; object of joy in *gen.* or *instr.*
feoh-gesteald, *st. n.* possession of riches.
feoh-gestrêon, *st. n.* treasure, possessions, riches.
feoh-gift, -gyft, *st. f.* bestowing of gifts or treasures.
feoh-gifu, -giefu, *st. f.* same as above.

feoh-gifre, *adj.* greedy of money, avaricious.
feoh-gitsere, *st. m.* miser.
feoh-lêas, *adj.* that can not be atoned for by gifts, inexpiable.
feoh-sceat, *st. m.* money, treasure.
feoht, *st. n.* fight, battle. (*ms.* **fohte,** By. 103.) (Ger. *gefecht.*)
feohtan, *st. abl. v.* I. to fight, contend, combat, strive, struggle. (Ger. *fechten.*)
 â-feohtan, 1. to fight against, overcome.— **2.** to tear out, destroy.
 æt-feohtan, to feel about with the hands (like a blind man), grope.
 bi-feohtan, to deprive of by fighting, rob. Rä. 4, 32.
 ge-feohtan, 1. to fight, combat, struggle.— **2.** to overcome by fighting, win, gain.
 ofer-feohtan, to overcome, conquer.
 on-feohtan, to attack, assault, fight with.
 wider-feohtan, to fight against, be an adversary, enemy.
fechte, *w. f.* combat, battle.
fêol, fêl, *st. f.* file. (Ger. *feile.*)
feola. See **fela.**
feolan, fiolan, *st. abl. v.* II. **1.** to stick, adhere.— **2.** to attain to, come, pass.
 æt-feolan, to stick to, hold on to, cleave, adhere, continue.
 be-, bi-feolan, to fix in, fasten, commit, deliver, command, grant.
 geond-feolan, to fill completely, envelope, surround.
feolde. See **folde.**
fêol-heard, *adj.* so hard that it withstands the file, exceedingly hard.
feolo. See **fela.**
fêon. See **fêohan** and **fêogan.**
fêond, fiond, *part. & subs.* fiend, enemy. (Ger. *feind.*)

fêond-æt, *st. n.* eating of sacrifice to an idol.
fêond-grâp, *st. f.* foe's clutch, enemy's gripe.
fêond-gyld, *st. n.* something consecrated to idolatry, an idol. Ps. 105, 25.
fêond-lice, *adv.* hostilely.
fêond-ræs, *st. m.* hostile attack.
fêond-sceaða, *w. m.* hurtful enemy, foe, robber.
fêond-scipe, -scype, *st. m.* enmity, hostility.
feor, feorr, *adj.* far, remote, at a distance.
feor, fior, fier, *adv.* **1.** far, far away, far off.— **2.** far back in the past. **3.** further, moreover. (Ger. *fern.*)
feor-bûend, *part.* dwelling far away.
feor-cund, *adj.* far-coming, foreign.
feor-cŷð, *st. f.* home of those living far away, foreign land.
feore, feores, *dat. gen.* of **feorh.**
feorh, feorg, *st. m. n.* **1.** life, vital principle, soul.— **2.** living being, individual.— **3.** body, corpse. (Ger. *ferch.*)
feorh-bana, *w. m.* destroyer of life, manslayer, murderer.
feorh-ben, *st. f.* wound that threatens life, deadly wound.
feorh-berend, *part.* life-bearing, living.
feorh-bealu, *st. n.* evil destroying life, violent death.
feorh-bold, *st. n.* life's dwelling, body.
feorh-cwalu, *st. f.* death.
feorh-cwealm, *st. m.* killing, murder, slaughter.
feorh-cyn, *st. n.* race of the living, mankind.
feorh-dagas, *st. m. pl.* life's days, life.
feorh-dolg, *st. n.* wound threatening life, deadly wound.
feorh-êacen, *adj.* living.

**feorh-gebeorh, ** *st. n.* life's protection, refuge.
feorh-gedâl, *st. n.* separation from life, death.
feorh-genidla, *w. m.* one who plots against life, life's enemy, mortal enemy.
feorh-giefa, *w. m.* giver of life.
feorh-gifu (Reim. 6). See **feohgifu.**
feorh-gôme, *w. f.* means of existence, or care for life? Cri. 1549. (Grein.)
feorh-gôma, *w. m.* fatal or deadly jaws. (B.-T.)
feorh-hirde, *st. m.* life's guardian.
feorh-hord, *st. n.* life's treasure, life.
feorh-hûs, *st. n.* life's house, body.
feorh-lagu, *st. f.* life's end, murder, death.
feorh-lâst, *st. m.* way taken for the preservation of life, flight (Grein); —trace of (vanishing) life, sign of death (Harrison & Sharp). B. 846.
feorh-lêan, *st. n.* revenge for bloodshed (Grein); life's gift (B.-T.). Exod. 150.
feorh-lif, *st. n.* life.
feorh-loca, *w. m.* life's inclosure, breast.
feorh-naru, *st. f.* life's nourishment; life's preservation, rescue, refuge.
feorh-ræd, *st. m.* counsel, action for preserving life.
feorh-sêoc, *adj.* life-sick, mortally wounded.
feorh-sweng, *st. m.* death-blow, stroke.
feorh-þearf, *st. f.* life's need, urgent need.
feorh-wund, *st. f.* deadly wound, fatal hurt.
feor-land, *st. n.* far-away land.
feorm, *st. f.* **(farm),** 1. meal, banquet. 2. sustenance, subsistence, entertainment, entertaining.— 3. food, provisions, goods, substance.— 4. use, benefit, profit, enjoyment.
feorma, *w. adj.* the first.

feormend, *part. & subs.* 1. one who hospitably entertains, an entertainer.— 2. cleanser, cleaner, polisher.
feormend-lêas, *adj.* wanting the cleanser or polisher.
feormian, feorman, *w. v.* (to **farm),** 1. to entertain, receive as guest.— 2. to come for, cherish, support. 3. to eat, devour, consume.— 4. to keep in a good condition, clean, cleanse, polish.
   ge-feormian, 1. to receive as guest, be hospitable.— 2. to care for, advise.— 3. to feast, eat, consume.
feorr. See **feor.**
feorran, *w. v.* to remove, free from.
feorran, *adv.* 1. from afar, afar, far off,— used both of space and of time.
feorran-cund, *adj.* having origin or birth far away, foreign-born.
feorsian, *w. v.* to proceed farther, go beyond.
feorsn. See **fiersn,** heel.
feor-weg, *st. m.* far, long way.
feorð, *st. n.* life, soul.
feorða, *w. adj.* the fourth.
feorum, *dat. pl.* of **feorh.**
fêoung, *st. f.* hate, enmity, hatred.
fêower, *num.* **four.**
fêowerða, *w. adj.* the **fourth.**
fêower-fête, fier-, *adj.* four-footed.
fêower-tig, *num.* **forty.**
fêower-týne, *num.* **fourteen.**
fîc-bêam, *st. m.* fig-tree.
fîf, *num.* **five.**
fîf = fîfel, sea-monster? B. 420.
fîfel, *st. n.* sea-monster, giant.
fîfel-cyn, *st. n.* giant race, race of sea-monsters.
Fîfel-dor, *st. n.* door of sea-monsters, river Eider.
fîfel-strêam, *st. m.* ocean, sea.
fîfel-wǣg, *st. m.* ocean, sea.
fîf-hund, *num.* **five hundred.**

fíf-mægen, *st. n.* magic power? Sal. 136.
fífta, *w. adj.* the fifth.
fíftêne, -týne, *num.* fifteen.
fíftig, *num.* fifty.
filed. See **feolan.**
findan, *st. abl. v.* I. (*pret.* **fand, funde**), to find, find out, invent, imagine, ascertain, attain, discover, seek out, visit, go to. (Ger. *finden.*)
  â-findan, to experience, feel.
  on-findan, 1. to find out, hit upon, observe, discover.— 2. to experience, feel.— 3. to be sensible of, perceive, notice.
finger, *st. m.* finger. (Ger. *finger.*)
finta, *w. m.* 1. tail.— 2. consequences of an action.
firas, fyras, *st. m. pl.* men, human beings.
firen, fyren, 1. *st. f.* going beyond usual or customary bounds.— *adv. instr. pl.* **firenum,** immoderately, excessively, extraordinarily, terribly, very.— 2. overstepping custom and law or right, wicked deed, sin, trespass, crime.— 3. extraordinary calamity or pain which one suffers or inflicts, cunning waylaying, insidious hostility, outrage, malice, torment, tribulation, suffering, pain. (Goth. *fairina.*)
firen, *adj.* 1. sinful, vicious, wicked, malicious.— 2. unnatural, monstrous.
firen-bealu, *st. n.* sinful, evil.
firen-cræft, *st. m.* sinful craft, wickedness, impiety.
firen-dǽd, -dêd, *st. f.* wicked deed.
firen-earfede, *st. n.* dire distress, sore affliction.
firen-fremmende, *part.* evil-doing, committing crimes.
firen-full, *adj.* sinful, wicked.
firen-georn, *adj.* inclined to sin, loving sin.

firenian, firnian, *w. v.* 1. to sin.— 2. to scold, upbraid.
  ge-fyrnian, to sin.
firen-lic, *adj.* 1. wicked, malicious.— 2. too great, vehement.
firen-lîce, *adv.* vehemently, rashly.
firen-lust, *st. m.* lust, sinful desire.
firen-synnig, *adj.* evil-minded, sinful.
firen-þearf, *st. f.* great need, terrible distress.
firen-weorc, *st. n.* evil, sinful work, sin, crime.
firen-wyrcend, *part. & subs.* evil-working, sinner.
firen-wyrhta, *w. m.* same as above.
firgen, fyrgen, *st. n.* mountain-;— used only in compounds.
firgen-bêam, *st. m.* tree of a mountain-forest.
firgen-holt, *st. n.* mountain-wood, mountain-forest.
firgen-strêam (**firigend-**), *st. m.* mountain-stream, sea.
firhd-sefa, *w. m.* spirit, mind.
firnian. See **firenian.**
firran, *w. v.*
  â-firran, to remove, take away.
first, *st. m.* space of time, time. (Ger. *frist.*)
firwet. See **fyrwet.**
fisc, fix, *st. m.* fish. (Ger. *fisch.*)
fisc-net, *st. n.* fish-net.
fit, *st. f.* fit, contest, fight. Gen. 2072. [See next word.]
fit, *st. f.* fit, song, poem. [Cf. Skeat's Etym. Dict., under **fit,** 2.]
fider. See **feder.**
fider-lêas, *adj.* featherless, without feathers.
fidrian, *w. v.* (Ger. *fiedern.*)
  ge-fidrian, to feather, furnish with wings.
fidru, *st. n. pl.* wings, plumage, feathers. (Ger. *gefieder.*)
fix. See **fisc.**
fíer. See **feor.**
fiersu, *st. f.* heel. (Ger. *ferse.*)

fier-, fierst, fiogan, fiolan, fiond, fior. See feower-, fyrst, feogan, feolan, feond, feor.
flâ, *w. f.* arrow, dart, javelin.
flacor, *adj.* flickering, flying.
flǽman. See flêman.
flǽsc, *st. n.* flesh,—in contrast partly with bones and skin and partly with the soul: in the latter sense, also, as seat of sensuous feelings or desires; finally, the general term for any living corporeal creature. (Ger. *fleisch.*)
flǽsc-hama, -homa, *w. m.* flesh-dress, body, carcass.
flâh, flâ, *adj.* tricky, deceitful, crafty, hostile.
flâh, *st.n.* deceit, cunning, wickedness.
flân, *st. m. f.* arrow, dart, javelin.
flân-boga, *w. m.* bow adapted to arrows, bow.
flân-geweorc, *st. n.* apparatus suited for hurling or shooting, arrow-work.
flân-hred, *adj.* arrow-equipped.
flân-þracu, *st. f.* force or impetus of darts or arrows, onset, attack.
flêma, *w. m.* fugitive.
flêman, *w. v.* to make to flee, put to flight.
    ge-flêman, -flǽman, the same.
flet, *st. n.* (Scotch flet), 1. ground, floor of a hall.—2. hall, mansion.
flet-gesteald, *st.n.* household wealth, riches, adornment of the hall.
flet-pæd, *st. m.* hall-path, floor of the house.
flet-ræst, *st. f.* resting-place in the hall, night-couch.
flet-sittende, *part.* sitting in the hall.
flet-werod, *st. n.* troop of the hall, comitatus, body-guard.
flêam, *st. m.* flight.
flêogan = flêohan, to flee. See flêon.
flêogan, *st. abl. v.* VI. to **fly**. (Ger. *fliegen.*)

ge-flêogan, 1. to fly.— 2. to fly over; reach by flying.
ôđ-flêogan, to fly away from, escape.
flêoge, *w. f.* fly.
flêohan. See flêon.
flêoh-cyn, *st. n.* a kind of flies.
flêoh-net, *st. n.* fly-net, net for keeping off insects.
flêon, flêohan, flêogan, flion, *st. abl.v.* VI. 1.*intrans.* to **flee**, fly.— 2.*w.acc.* to flee, avoid, escape. (Ger. *flichen.*)
    â-flêon, to flee from, escape.
    be-flêon, to flee from, escape, avoid.
    in-flêon, to flee from, escape.
    ofer-flêon, to flee from, yield.
flêos. See flŷs.
flêot, *st. n.* (fleet), raft, ship, float. (Ger. *fliesz, flosz.*)
flêotan, *st. abl. v.* VI. (to fleet), float upon the water, swim, navigate, sail. (Ger. *fliessen.*)
flêotig, *adj.* fleet, swift.
fliht. See flyht.
flihđ. See flêogan.
flint, *st. m.* flint, flintstone.
flint-græg, *adj.* gray like flintstone.
flit, *st. n.* strife, contention. (Ger. *fleiss.*)
flita, *w. m.* striver, fighter.
flitan, *st. abl. v.* V. to exert one's self, strive, contend, emulate, fight, quarrel.
    ofer-flitan, to surpass in a contest, overcome, conquer.
flion, flius. See flêon, flŷs.
floccan, *w. v.* to clap, applaud? Rä. 21, 34.
flôd, *st. m. n.* flood, stream, wave, tide, sea-stream, current of the sea, overflow, inundation, river. (Ger. *flut.*)
flôd-blâc, *adj.* flood-pale, made pale by the waters through fear of drowning.

flôd-egsa, w. m. fear of water, flood-terror.
flôd-græg, adj. water-gray.
flôd-weg, st. m. waterway, sea.
flôd-weard, st. f. flood-guard, i. e. the walls caused by dividing the Red Sea. Exod. 493.
flôd-wudu, st. m. flood-wood, ship.
flôd-wylm, st. m. billows, raging sea.
flôd-ŷd, st. f. flood-wave.
flôr, st. f. m. floor, stone floor, plain, field. (Ger. *flur*.)
flot, st. n. water deep enough to float a ship, sea.
flota, w. m. 1. ship.—2. sailor, sea-robber.
flot-here, st. m. fleet, naval force.
flot-man, st. m. sailor, pirate.
flot-weg, st. m. seaway, sea.
flôwan, st. red. v. to flow, stream. (O. H. Ger. *flawjan*.)
  be-flôwan, to flow around, wash.
  geond-flôwan, to flow over or through.
  tô-flôwan, 1. to flow down, away, or apart.—2. to flow or stream to, pour in.
  under-flôwan, to flow under.
flyge, st. m. flying, flight.
flyge-rêow, adj. wild-flying, fierce in flight.
flyge-wil, st. n. flying wile, Satan's dart.
flyht, fliht, st. m. flight, flying. (Ger. *flucht*.)
flyht-hwæt, adj. quick in flight, ready for flight.
flŷhd. See flêon.
flŷma, w. m. fugitive.
flŷman, w. v. to put to flight, rout.
  â-flŷman, the same as above.
  ge-flŷman, the same as above.
flŷs, flius, st. n. fleece, wool. (Ger. *vliess, fliesz*.)
fnæd, st. n. fringe, border.
fnæst, st. m. strong or violent breath of air, blast, breathing, breath.

fôdor, fôddor, -ur, st. n. fodder, food, nourishment, victuals. (Ger. *futter*.)
fôdor-þegu, st. f. feeding, eating, nourishment, food.
fôdor-wela, w. m. wealth of food, provisions.
fôh. See fôn.
folc, st. n. folk, people, nation, crowd, throng; a people, tribe, family, band of warriors;—pl. fighting-men, warriors, people, men. (Ger. *volk*.)
folc-âgend, part. & subs. leading a band of warriors, ruling over a people;—leader, ruler.
folc-bealu, st. n. great evil, horrible torment.
folc-bearn, st. n. child of the people, fellow-man.
folc-biorn, st. m. man of the multitude, common man.
folc-cû, st. f. folk-cow, cow of the herd.
folc-cûd, adj. known to the people, celebrated, popular.
folc-cwên, st. f. folk-queen, queen of a warlike host.
folc-cyning, st. m. folk-king, king of a warlike host.
folc-dryht, -driht, st. f. multitude of people, followers.
folc-egsa, w. m. folk-fright, terror, fear
folc-firen, st. f. crime of the people.
folc-frêa, w. m. lord of the people, leader of the host.
folc-gesid, st. m. one of the same country, countryman, one of the leader's chief attendants, thane, warrior.
folc-gestealla, w. m. same as above.
folc-gestrêon, st. n. riches, possessions of a people.
folc-getæl, st. n. number of the people, number, tale.
folc-getrum, st. n. army, host.
folc-gewin, st. n. war.

folc-land, *st. n.* folk-land, land held in common by freemen of all ranks.
folc-mægen, *st. n.* people's force, multitude, people.
folc-mægd, *st. f.* tribe, nation.
folc-mǣre, *adj.* celebrated.
folc-nêd, *st. f.* care for the people. Ps. 77, 16.
folc-rǣd, *st. m.* what best serves a warlike host, public benefit.
folc-rǣden, *st. f.* decree or ordinance of the people.
folc-riht, *st. n.* **folk-right,** common privilege, the rights of every freeman, public right, rightful share in the possessions of the community.
folc-sæl, *st. n.* people's hall, hall in which the leader entertains his personal followers.
folc-scearu, *st. f.* part of a host of warriors, nation, province;—folk-share? folk-land? B. 73. [lain.
folc-sceada, *w. m.* people's foe, villain.
folc-scipe, *st. m.* nation, people.
folc-stede, -styde, *st. m.* place or habitation of the people, place where a band of warriors is quartered; fortress, city, land.
folc-swêot, *st. m.* multitude, host.
folc-talu, *st. f.* numbering of the people, genealogy.
folc-toga, *w. m.* leader of the host, commander of an army, prince, duke.
folcû. See **folc-cû.**
folc-weras, *st. m. pl.* men of the people, people.
folc-wiga, *w. m.* warrior, fighter.
folc-wita, *w. m.* public counselor, senator.
fold-ærn, *st. n.* earth-house, grave.
fold-bold, *st. n.* earthly dwelling, castle.
fold-bûend, -bûende, *part. pl.* & *subs.* earth-dwellers, men.

folde, *w. f.* 1. earth, firm land,—in contrast with water, heaven and hell, the dwelling-place of man and the producer of fruits, &c.— 2. land, country, district, region. 3. soil, ground, crust.— 4. earth, dust of the earth. Gû. 795.
fold-græf, *st. n.* earth-grave.
fold-græg, *adj.* earth-gray, earth-colored.
fold-hrêrend, *part.* earth-touching, walking on the earth.
fold-ræst, *st. f.* rest in the earth, in the grave.
fold-wang, *st. m.* plain, earth.
fold-wæstm, *st. m.* fruits of the earth.
fold-weg, *st. m.* 1. path over the earth, way by land.— 2. earth.
fold-wela, *w. m.* earthly riches.
folgad, -od, *st. m.* 1. office, service of a follower, service, attendance. 2. situation or condition of life, destiny.
folgere, *st. m.* follower.
folgian, *w. v.* 1. to **follow.**— 2. to pursue, follow after.— 3. to follow, obey.— 4. to perform vassal-duty, serve, follow. (Ger. *folgen*.)
folm, *st. f.* palm of the hand, hand.
folme, *w. f.* the same as above.
fôn, *st. red. v.* to catch, grasp, take hold of, take, receive. (Ger. *fangen*.)
â-fôn, to lay hold of, seize;—
forht âfangen, invaded with fear.
an-fôn, to accept, receive.
be-fôn, bi-fôn, to surround, ensnare, encompass, embrace; to lay hold of, seize; conceive, receive;
—**wordum befôn,** to tell, relate.
for-fôn, 1. to seize, lay hold of, take away.— 2. to arrest.
ge-fôn, *w. acc.* to seize, grasp.
ofer-fôn, to capture, take prisoner.
on-fôn, to receive, accept, take, hear, perceive.

þurh-fôn, to grasp through, break through with a gripe.

wid-fôn, to seize or grasp at, clutch, seize.

ymb-, ymbe-fôn, to surround, encompass, encircle, embrace.

for, *prep.* (for), I. *w. dat.* **1.** local: before, in the presence of.— **2.** causal: (*a.*) to denote a subjective motive, on account of, through, from.— (*b.*) to denote an objective cause, through, from, for, by reason of, on account of.— (*c.*) after verbs denoting fear, anxiety, care, &c., as well as those protecting, defending, freeing from, &c.— for, by reason of, of, against, from, about.— (*d.*) *w. dat.* of person: for or on account of whom something is done or suffered.— (*e.*) to show agreement or fitness, according to, in accordance with, on account of. (*f.*) to denote purpose: to, for.— (*g.*) with verbs of begging, swearing, promising—for the sake of, by: **for dryhtne**, by God.— (*h.*) to denote that for which or against which something is done for.— (*i.*) as to, considering, about.— **3.** temporal: before, sooner than.— II. *w. acc.* (*a.*) local: before, in the sight of.— (*b.*) temporal: before, sooner than.— (*c.*) before, above.— (*d.*) for, instead of, as: **for þæt**, for that, thereof, therefrom, &c.— III. *w. instr.* = **for**, *w. dat.* (Ger. *vor*.)

for-, (Ger. *ver-*, Goth. *fair-, fra-, faur-*.)

fôr, *st. f.* a going, departing, course, trip, journey; way, behavior, manner of life.

foran, I. *adv.* before, among the first, forward, in front.— II. *prep. w. dat.* before.

ford, *st. m.* ford. (Dan. *fjord;* Ger. *furt*.)

fore, I. *prep.* **1.** *w. dat.* (*a.*) local: before, in the presence of, in sight of, in hearing of.— (*b.*) causal: on account of, by reason of, for the sake of, from, for, through, because of.— (*c.*) temporal: before. Cri. 1031; El. 637.— (*d.*) for, instead of, Cri. 1292; Gû. 373: by, Jul. 540.— **2.** *w. acc.* (*a.*) local and temporal: before, for.— (*b.*) for, instead of. See f. 21, 22.— II. *adv.* before, aforetime, formerly, once.

fore-beacen, *st. n.* prodigy, wonder.

fore-genga, *w. m.* **1.** ancestor.— **2.** forerunner.

fore-genga, *w. f.* female servant. Jud. 127. [others.

fore-glêaw, *adj.* prudent, wise above

fore-mǣre, *adj.* illustrious, very celebrated, renowned above others.

fore-meahtig, -mihtig, *adj.* very potent, exceedingly powerful, most mighty.

fore-scyttels, *st. m.* bolt or bar, crossbeam.

fore-snotor, *adj.* beyond others wise, very wise, sagacious.

fore-spreca, *w. m.* advocate. (Ger. *fürsprecher*.)

fore-tâcen, *st. n.* foretoken, prodigy.

fore-þanc, -þonc, *st. m.* forethought, consideration, deliberation.

fore-þancol, -þoncol, *adj.* provident, prudent, considerate.

fore-weall, *st. m.* forewall, rampart.

fore-weard, *adj.* **1. forward**, inclined to the front.— **2.** denoting the first part or the beginning of anything, fore, early, new, former.

fore-weard geâr, new year.

for-gefenes, *st. f.* **forgiveness**. [cft.

for-gifnes, *st. f.* present, largess, bon-

for-heard, *adj.* very hard.

for-hogednes, *st. f.* contempt.

forht, *adj.* **1.** timid, frightened, fearful, cowardly.— **2.** frightful, terrible, dreadful.

forhtian, *w. v.* **1.** *intrans.* to be timid, be afraid, fear.— **2.** *trans.* to fear, stand in fear of. (Ger. *fürchten.*) **on-forhtian**, to be timid, be afraid, fear. Deut. 31, 6.

forht-lic, *adj.* **1.** fearful, cowardly. **2.** frightful, terrible. [fully.

forht-lice, *adv.* tremblingly, fearfully.

forht-môd, *adj.* of a fearful mind, timid. [loss.

for-lor, *st. m.* perdition, destruction,

forma, *w. adj.* the first.

for-manig, *adj.* very many.

for-nêan, *adv.* very nearly, almost, about.

forod, *part. & adj.* broken, without strength, worn out, useless.

for-rynel, *st. m.* forerunner, precursor.

for-sceap, *st. n.* evil deed, crime.

forst, *st. m.* frost, cold. (Ger. *frost.*)

for-strang, *adj.* very strong.

for-swid, *adj.* the same as above.

for-swide, *adv.* very strongly, very .... indeed.

ford, *adv.* **forth, 1.** local: (*a.*) hither, near, in the presence of.—(*b.*) forward, further thence.—(*c.*) to denote motion toward.—(*d.*) to denote the going beyond a limit, or superiority.—(*e.*) forth, away, hence. **2.** temporal: (*a.*) forth, from now on.—(*b.*) from now on as formerly, yet further.—(*c.*) uninterruptedly, continually.—(*d.*) to denote the immediate necessary consequence or result. Rä. 21, 24.— **4.** very. Ps. 68, 5. (Ger. *fort.*)

ford-bǽro, *st. f.* creation.

ford-gang, *st. m.* going forth, progress.

ford-gesceaft, *st. f.* **1.** creature, created being or thing, world.— **2.** fate, destiny,—especially the future condition or state of the soul.

ford-gesýne, *adj.* visible, conspicuous.

ford-georn, *adj.* desirous of going away, or of proceeding.

ford-here, *st. m.* front line of an army, van.

fordian, *w. v.* **ge-fordian**, to promote, complete, fulfill.

ford-mǽre, *adj.* very glorious, exceedingly bright.

ford-ryne, *st. m.* running forward, course.

ford-sid, *st. m.* **1.** going away, departure.— **2.** death.

ford-snotter, *adj.* very wise.

ford-spell, *st. n.* saying, declaration, word.

fordum. See **furdum.**

ford-weg, *st. m.* onward way, journey, departure, death.

ford-weard, *adj.* **1.** inclined forward, forward, situated in front.— **2.** tending toward.— **3.** everlasting, unceasing, continual.

ford-weard, *st. m.* pilot in the front part of the ship.

for-wel, *adv.* very.

for-weard, *adj.* forward, in front.

for-weard, *adv.* further, continually.

for-wyrd, *st. f.* destruction, ruin, loss, perdition, death.

for-wyrht, *st. n.* sin.

fôstur, *st. n.* nourishment, pasture.

fôstur-lêan, *st. n.* reward or pay for fostering.

fôt, *st. m. dat.* **fêt, fôte;** — *nom. acc. pl.* **fêt, fôtas,** — foot. (Ger. *fusz.*)

fôt-gemearc, *st. n.* measurement by feet, number of feet.

fôt-lâst, *st. m.* footprint.

fôt-mǽl, *st. n.* foot-measure, foot;— **fôtmǽl landes**, a foot's length, space of a foot.

fox, *st. m.* **fox.** (Ger. *fuchs.*)

fracod, -ed, *st. n.* baseness, insult, contumely, disgrace.

fracedu, *st. f.* the same as above.

fracod, fracod, *adj.* vile, base, detestable, objectionable, useless, unworthy, impious.
fracode, fracude, *adv.* disgracefully, shamefully.
fracod-lic, *adj.* base, shameful.
fracod-lice, *adv.* basely, shamefully.
fracud. See **fracod.**
fræ-, fræcne. See **frêa-, frêcne.**
frægn, question? An. 255.
fræm-sum. See **fremsum.**
fræt, *adj.* perverse, proud, obstinate.
frætig, *adj.* the same as above.
frætuwe, frætwe, *st. f. pl.* ornament, anything costly;—originally, carved object.
frætwan, *w. v.* (to fret), to ornament, adorn.
   ge-frætwan, the same as above.
frætwian, *w. v.* the same as above.
   ge-frætwian, same as above.
fragan, *st. abl. v.* IV. (Ger. *fragen?*)
   ge-fragan, to ask, find out by hearsay, learn.
fram, from, I. *prep.* **1.** *w. dat.* **from,** (*a.*) local: (1.) from, away from something. (2.) from, hither, from something. (3.) from, at a distance from.—(*b.*) causal: (1.) from w. passive verbs. (2.) w. verbs of speaking, saying, &c., of, about, concerning.—(*c.*) temporal: from, since: frequently found after the dative.— **2.** *w. instr.* away from.— II. *adv.* away, thence, forth, out. (O. H. Ger. *fram.*)
fram, *adj.* strong, stout, excellent, splendid.
framde, *adj.* foreign, strange.
franca, *w. m.* lance, dart, javelin.
frâsian, frêasian, *w. v.* to question, tempt, try. (Goth. *fraisan.*)
fratu. See **frætuwe.**
frec, *adj.* bold, rash, daring, greedy. (Ger. *frech.*)
freca, *w. m.* wolf; hence, warrior, hero.

frêcen, *st. n.* danger, dangerous situation.
frêcen-lic, *adj.* dangerous, perilous.
frêcne, fræcne, *adj.* dangerous, bold, daring, terrible, horrible, savage, hard, provoking.
frêcne, fræcne, *adv.* boldly, audaciously, fiercely, harshly, dangerously, savagely.
frêcnen-spræc, *st. f.* provoking, bitter, hostile speech.
frêcnes (= **frêcennes**), *st. f.* danger, peril; deed boldly or rashly done? Gû. 81.
frêcnian, *w. v.*
   ge-frêcnian, to make cruel or proud, corrupt.
frêfran, *w. v.* to comfort, console, make glad.
   â-frêfran, same as the above.
frêfrend, *part. & subs.* comforted;—consoler.
frêfrian, *w. v.* to comfort, console.
fremde, fremede, fremde, *adj.* **1.** foreign, strange, belonging to another country, distant.— **2.** *w. dat.* strange, estranged, hostile, remote.— **3.** *w. gen.* without, devoid of. (Ger. *fremd.*) [gain.
freme, *w. f.* advantage, good, benefit,
freme, *adj.* good, excellent, splendid.
fremed, *st. f.* glory, renown, honor, virtue, uprightness? B. 1701. (Grein.)
fremed, performs, practises; *3d sg. pres.* of **fremman.** B. 1701. (B.-T.)
fremman, *w. v.* to press forward, further, help on, support.— **2.** to frame, make, do, perform, accomplish, perpetrate, effect, commit.
   ge-fremman, 1. to bring forward, further. B. 1718.— **2.** to do, make, render, effect, accomplish.
fremme, *w. f.* brave deed? See f. 75.
frem-sum, fræm-, *adj.* benevolent, benignant, kind, gracious. [ness.
fremsum-nes, *st. f.* benignity, kind-
fremde. See **fremde.**

fremu, *st. f.* advantage, gain, fruit, benefit, safety.
fretan, *st. abl. v.* III. 1. to fret, eat, consume, devour.— 2. to break. Exod. 147. (Ger. *fressen.*).
frettan, *w. v.* to eat up, devastate, consume. Ps. 79, 13; 82, 10.
fredo. See **frido.**
frêa, *adj.* joyful. (Ger. *froh.*)
frêa, *w. m.* 1. master, ruler, lord,— especially God, Christ.— 2. husband. (Goth. *frauja.*)
frêa, *f.* mistress. See **âgendfrêa.**
frêa-, fræ̂-beorht, *adj.* very celebrated, illustrious. [band.
frêa-, freah-drihten, *st. m.* lord, husfrêa-glêaw, *adj.* very wise, prudent, skillful.
frêa-mǣre, *adj.* very celebrated, renowned.
freasian. See **frâsian.**
frêa-wine, *st. m.* lord and friend, dear lord, friendly ruler.
frêa-wrâsen, *st. f.* encircling ornament like a diadem.
frêo, *adj.* free, freeborn, one's own master, well-born, noble, excellent, illustrious. (Ger. *frei.*)
frêo = frêa, master, lord.
frêo, *st. f.* mistress, lady.
frêo, *st. m.* free man, man.
frêo-bearn, *st. n.* freeborn chief, noble child.
frêo-brôdor, *st. m.* an own brother.
frêo-burg, *st. f.* city of a freeman, noble city.
frêod, *st. f.* love, friendship, peace, favor, gratitude.
frêo-dôm (frio-), *st. m.* freedom.
frêo-dryhten, *st. m.* freeborn or noble lord, ruler.
frêogan, frêon, *w. v.* to love, think of lovingly. (Ger. *freien,* to woo.)
frêogan, frêon, *w. v.* to free, liberate. (Ger. *befreien.*)
    be-frêogan, to free, liberate.
    ge-frêogan, to free, liberate.

frêo-lîc, *adj.* free, freeborn, glorious, stately, illustrious, comely, lovely.
frêo-lîce, *adv.* freely, unhesitatingly, becomingly, nobly, liberally.
freom, *adj.* strong, firm, prompt, ready, powerful.
frêo-mǣg, *st. m.* cousin-german, kinsman.
frêo-man, *st. m.* freeman, freeborn man.
frêon. See **frêogan.**
frêo-nama, *w. m.* surname.
freond, *part. & subs. nom. acc. pl.* **frŷnd, frêondas,**— friend. (Ger. *freund.*)
frêond-lâr, *st. f.* friendly advice, counsel.
frêond-ladu, *st. f.* friendly invitation, challenge.
frêond-lêas, *adj.* friendless.
frêond-lîce, *adv.* in a friendly manner, kindly.
frêond-lufu, *st. f.* friendship, love.
frêond-mynd, *st. f.* friendly, loving thoughts.
frêond-rǣden, *st. f.* friendship, conjugal love.
frêond-scipe, *st. m.* **friendship,** intimacy;— used often of the relationship of husband and wife.
frêond-spêd, *st. f.* good fortune in respect to friends, abundance of friends.
frêorig, *adj.* 1. cold, shivering, freezing.— 2. stiff with fright, fear, or sorrow, sad, mournful.
frêorig-ferd, *adj.* of a sad mind, mournful.
frêorig-môd, *adj.* the same as above.
frêos? Dan. 66.
frêosan, *st. abl. v.* VI. to **freeze.** (Ger. *frieren.*)
freoda, *w. m.* protector, refuge.
freodian, *w. v.* to have a care for, support, cherish, favor, protect; observe.

ge-freodian, 1. *w. dat.* or *acc.* to watch, guard, protect.—2. to quiet, pacify? Gû. 123.—3. to strengthen? Gû. 382.
freodo, friodo, -du, *st. f.* peace, safety, protection, asylum, security; grace, blessing, liberty, pardon. (Ger. *friede.*)
freodo-bêacen, *st. n.* peace-token, sign of peace.
freodo-burg, *st. f.* castle or city affording protection.
freodo-lêas, *adj.* peaceless, pitiless.
freodo-scealc, *st. m.* minister of peace, angel.
freodo-spêd, *st. f.* abundance of peace, peaceful protection.
freodo-þêaw, *st. m.* pacific manner, habit of peace.
freodo-wǽr, *st. f.* covenant or agreement of peace.
freodo-wang, *st. m.* field of peace, field of protection.
freodo-waru, *st. f.* protection, safety.
freodu. See **freodo.**
freodu-webbe, *w. f.* peace-weaver, bond of peace, queen.
freodu-weard, *st. m.* peace-guardian.
frêo-wine, *st. m.* noble friend, friendly lord, ruler.
fri (frig), *adj.* free, freeborn, noble.
fricca, *w. m.* herald.
fricgan, -ean, *st. abl. v.* III. 1. to ask, inquire into, investigate.—2. to learn, find out by inquiry.—3. to ask, beg, demand.
   ge-fricgan, to learn, learn by inquiry, hear of. [for.
friclan, *w. v.* to seek, desire, strive
fridan, *st. abl. v.* V. to guard. (*ms.* fudon.)
frid-hengest, *st. m.* stately horse.
frige, *st. m. pl.* freeborn men, freemen, nobles.
frignan, *st. abl. v.* I. to ask, inquire. (Ger. *fragen.*)

ge-frignan, *part.* **gefrægen, gefrægn,** 1. to ask, inquire.—2. to find out by inquiry, learn by narration.
frigu, *st. f.* love.
frimdig. See **frymdig.**
frinan, *st. abl. v.* I. to ask, inquire.
   ge-frinan, to learn by hearsay, hear of.
fringan, *st. abl. v.* I. same as above.
   ge-fringan, the same as above.
frise, fryse, *adj.* crisp, curly.
frid, fryd, *st. m. n.* peace, protection, safety. (Ger. *friede.*)
frid, *adj.* stately, beautiful.
frid-candel, *st. f.* candle of peace.
frid-candel, *st. f.* beautiful light, sun.
fride-lêas, *adj.* peaceless.
fride-mǽg = **sêo fride mǽg.** Rä. 10, 9.
frid-gedâl, *st. n.* separation from peace, destruction, death.
frid-geard, *st. m.* seat of peace, asylum.
fridian, *w. v.* to protect, defend.
   ge-fridian, the same as above.
frido, fridu, frydo, fredo, *st. f.* peace.
frido-sib, *st. f.* peace-giving kin, peace-bringer, queen.
frido-spêd, *st. f.* good fortune of peace.
frido-tâcen, *st. n.* peace-token, sign of peace.
frido-wǽr, *st. f.* peace-covenant, agreement.
frido-webba, *w. m.* peace-weaver, angel.
frid-stôl, *st. m.* peace-stool, asylum, refuge.
frid-stôw, *st. f.* peace-place, asylum, refuge.
fridu. See **frido.**
frio, frío, friodu. See **freo, frêo, freodu.**

frôd, *adj.* 1. intelligent, experienced, wise, prudent, skillful.— 2. having experience; hence, aged, old, ancient. (Goth. **froþs**.)

frôdian, *w. v.* to be wise, to have understanding, insight.

frôfor, -er, -ur, *st. f.* solace, consolation, compensation, help.

from, I. *prep. w. dat.* 1. local: (*a.*) **from**, away from something. (*b.*) hither, from something.— 2. temporal: from—on, since.—3. causal: (*a.*) *w.* the passive form. (*b.*) *w.* verbs of saying and hearing—of, about, concerning. — II. *adv.* 1. away, thence.— 2. forth, out.

from = **fram**, *adj.* pressing forward, striving forward, firm, bold, brave, skillful; excellent, splendid, abundant, rich. (Ger. *fromm*.)

from-cyme, *st. m.* progeny, offspring.

from-cynn, *st. n.* 1. progeny, posterity, offspring.— 2. the race from which one springs, ancestors, origin, parentage.

from-lâd, *st. f.* going away, departure, death? flight?

from-lîce, *adv.* boldly, courageously, stoutly, readily, quickly.

from-sîd, *st. m.* going away, departure.

from-weard, *adj.* about to go away, destined to die, striving forward.

frum, *adj.* skillful, brave, bold, rapid, quick.

fruma, *w. m.* 1. beginning, origin, commencement.— 2. originator, inventor, author. — 3. the prince standing first or at the head, prince first in rank, king, chief, ruler.— 4. the first. Gen. 1277. (Goth. *frums*, from *fruma*, first; Lat. *primus*.)

frum-bearn, *st. n.* firstborn.

frum-cnêow, *st. n.* primitive race or kind, first generation.

frum-cyn, *st. n.* 1. ancestry, offspring, descent, origin.— 2. race, tribe, family.

frum-gâr, *st. m.* duke, prince, patriarch, chieftain, nobleman.

frum-gâra, *w. m.* the same as above.

frum-gesceap, *st. n.* creation of the world, beginning.

frum-hrægl, *st. n.* first dress, garment.

frum-ræden, *st. f.* previous arrangement, former agreement, predetermination.

frum-sceaft, *st. f.* 1. first creation, in contrast to **edsceaft**, after the destruction of the world by fire, beginning.— 2. creature.— 3. original state or condition, predetermination, origin, beginning, past? B. 91.

frum-scyld, *st. f.* original sin, chief sin.

frum-slǽp, *st. f.* first sleep.

frum-sprǽc, *st. f.* former speech, promise.

frum-stadol, *st. m.* original seat, first dwelling-place.

frum-stôl, *st. m.* earlier seat, principal seat, place of honor, first seat.

frumd, *st. m. f.* beginning.

frum-wæstm, *st. f.* first fruits.

frum-weorc, *st. n.* work done in the beginning, creation.

frymdig, frimdig, *adj.* seeking after, demanding, asking for, desirous, suppliant.

frymd, *st. m. f.* origin, beginning, first fruits.

fryse. See **frise**.

fryd, frydo. See **frid, frido**.

fugol, *st. m.* **fowl**, bird. (Ger. *vogel*.)

fugol-bana, *w. m.* bird-killer, fowler.

fugol-timber, *st. n.* young bird, young.

ful, *st. n.* cup, beaker; any receptacle of fluids, cloud, sea.

ful, full, *adj.* full, filled, stuffed, complete, perfect, entire. (Ger. *voll*.)
ful, *adv.* fully, entirely, very, full.
fûl, *adj.* foul, dirty, unclean, bad, vile, corrupt, putrid. (Ger. *faul*.)
fûl, *st. n.* foulness, impurity, crime.
full. See **ful**.
ful-lǽst, -lêst, *st. m.* help, support.
fullian, *w. v.* to fill, fulfill, perfect.
    ge-fullian, the same as above.
    un-gefullian, ungefullod, *part.* unfulfilled.
fulluht, fullwiht, fullwon. See **fulwiht, fulwon**.
fûl-nes, *st. f.* **foulness,** uncleanness, impurity.
fultum, *st. m.* help, support, protection.
fultuman, -ian, *w. v.* to help, aid, support, stand by, assist.
    ge-fultuman, *w. v.* **1.** to help, aid, assist.— **2.** to be propitious, make allowance for, overlook.
fulwian, *w. v.* to baptize.
    ge-fulwian, the same as above.
fulwiht, fulluht, *st. f. n. (m.?)* baptism.
fulwiht-tîd, *st. f.* time for baptism (6th Jan.).
fulwiht-þeaw, *st. m.* rite of baptism.
fulwon, *st. f.* baptism.
funde. See **findan**.
fundian, *w. v.* to strive, have in view, wish, intend, tend to, hasten. (O. H. Ger. *fundjan*.)
furdor. See **furdur**.
furdum, furdon, fordum, *adv.* **1.** at first, first, just, exactly, even, perhaps.— **2.** also, indeed, too, surely, at least.— **3.** further, before, previously.
furdur, furdor, *adv.* local and temporal: further, forward, more distant, more, past, later. (Ger. *fürder*.)
furum, Rä. 59, 15, perhaps **fultum**.
fûs, *adj.* striving forward, inclined to, favorable, ready, prompt, quick, desirous, prepared for death, ready to die;— *w. gen.* longing for, expecting. B. 1916.
fûs, *st. n.* hastening, pressing forward? B. 1916.
fûs-léod, *st. n.* song of the dying, death-song, dirge.
fûs-lic, *adj.* prepared, ready, ready for the journey.
fýf, *num.* five.
fyhte-horn, *st. m.* fighting-horn, horn.
fyl, fyll, *st. m.* fall, decay, defeat, ruin, destruction, slaughter, death.
fylce, *st. n.* tribe, race, province. (Icel. *fylki*.)
fylgean, fylgian, fyligan, *w. v.* to follow after, persecute, set upon, add to. (Ger. *folgen*.)
    æt-fyligan, to adhere, cling to.
    ge-fylgan, to follow, persist in.
fyllan, *w. v.* to fell, cut down, make to fall, throw away, give up, destroy.
    â-fyllan, to throw down, demolish, destroy.
    be-fyllan, 1. to fell, cast down, strike down, kill.— **2. befylled,** bereaved.
    ge-fyllan, 1. to fell, slay in battle.— **2. gefylled,** bereaved.
    tô-fyllan, to divide, tear asunder.
fyllan, *w. v.* to fill, replenish, finish, complete, fulfill.
    â-fyllan, the same as above.
    ge-fyllan, the same as above.
fyllað, *st. m.* filling, filling up.
fyllo, *st. f.* **1.** fullness, abundance, supply.— **2.** especially an abundance of food; rich, abundant meat. (Ger. *fülle*.)
fýlnes. See **fûlnes**.
fylst, *st. f.* help, aid.
fylstan, *w. v.* to aid, assist, help.
    ge-fylstan, the same as above.
fyl-wêrig, *adj.* weary enough to fall, faint to death, dying.
fýnd. See **féond**.

fyr, fyrr, *adv.* for, afar off, far away, farther, more distant.
fȳr, fir, *st. n.* fire. (Ger. *feuer.*)
fyras. See **firas.**
fȳr-bæđ, *st. n.* fire-bath, hell-fire.
fȳr-bend, *st. m.* band forged in the fire.
fȳr-clam, -clom, *st. m.* fetter forged in the fire.
fyrd, *st. f.* 1. journey, trip, undertaking, expedition, warlike expedition.—2. army.—3. camp. (Ger. *fahrt.*)
fyrd-gestealla, *w. m.* comrade in a warlike expedition, companion in battle.
fyrd-getrum, *st. n.* battle-array, company, martial band or host.
fyrd-geatwe, *st. f. pl.* war-equipments, arms.
fyrd-hom, *st. m.* war-dress, coat-of-mail.
fyrd-hrægl, *st. n.* same as above.
fyrd-hwæt, *adj.* sharp, bold in war, brave in war, warlike.
fyrd-lēođ, *st. n.* war-song.
fȳr-draca, *w. m.* fire-dragon, fire-spitting dragon.
fyrd-rinc, *st. m.* warrior.
fyrd-sceorp, *st. n.* warlike adornment, war-vest.
fyrd-searu, *st. n.* equipment for an expedition, war-equipment.
fyrd-wic, *st. n.* camp.
fyrd-wisa, *w. m.* leader of a warlike expedition, leader.
fyrd-wyrđe, *adj.* renowned in warlike expeditions, famous.
fyren. See **firen.**
fȳren, *adj.* fiery, burning, flaming.
fȳr-gebræc, *st. n.* noise or crash of fire.
fyrgen. See **firgen.**
fȳr-gnâst, *st. m.* spark of fire.
fȳr-hât, *adj.* hot as fire, burning.
fȳr-heard, *adj.* hardened by fire.
fyrht, *adj.* timid.

fyrhtan, *w. v.* to frighten. (Ger. *fürchten.*)
â-fyrhtan, to frighten, affect with fear, terrify.
fyrhto, -u, *st. f.* fright, fear, dread, terror.
fyrhđ = ferhđ, *st. m. n.* 1. soul, mind, spirit.— 2. life.
fyrhđ-glēaw, *adj.* wise in mind, prudent.
fyrhđ-loca, *w. m.* soul or mind inclosure, breast.
fyrhđ-lufe, *w. m.* soul-love; intense, heartfelt love.
fyrhđ-sefa, *w. m.* spirit of life, mind.
fyrhđ-wêrig, *adj.* sad at heart, sorrowful.
fȳr-lēoht, *st. n.* firelight.
fȳr-lēoma, *w. m.* splendor or brilliancy of fire.
fȳr-loca, *w. m.* fiery inclosure.
fȳr-mǣl, *st. n.* fire-marks, mark burnt in with fire.
fyrmest, *adv.* 1. foremost, first.— 2. first of all, in the first place.— 3. most, especially, best.
fyrn, *adj.* old, ancient. (Ger. *firn.*)
fyrn, *adv.* formerly, long ago, of old, once.
fyrn-dagas, *st. m. pl.* former days, olden time, yore, days of yore;— **frôd fyrndagum,** old, aged.
fyrn-geflit, *st. n.* old quarrel or strife.
fyrn-geflita, *w. m.* ancient enemy.
fyrn-gemynd, *st. n.* recollection of former deeds, history.
fyrn-gesceap, *st. n.* what was formerly created, fixed, or determined; ancient decree.
fyrn-gesetu, *st. n. pl.* former dwelling-place.
fyrn-gestrêon, *st. n.* treasure handed down from the olden time.
fyrn-geweorc, *st. n.* ancient work, work done in old times (statue, world, sun, treasure).

fyrn-gewinn, *st. n.* battle in the days of yore.
fyrn-gewrit, *st. n.* old or former writings, ancient scripture.
fyrn-gewyrht, *st. n.* what was formerly wrought or decreed.
fyrn-gêar, *st. n. pl.* years gone by.
fyrn-gid, *st. n.* ancient prophecy.
fyrn-man, *st. m.* man of ancient times.
fyrnian. See **firenian.**
fyrn-sægen, *st. f.* old saying, ancient tradition.
fyrn-sceada, *w. m.* old friend, devil.
fyrn-strêamas, *st. m. pl.* old streams, ocean.
fyrn-syn, *st. f.* old sin.
fyrn-weorc, *st. n.* work of old, creation, creature.
fyrn-wita, -weota, *w. m.* old counselor, or wise man, prophet; one who lived formerly, or one who has had long experience.
fyrn-wited, *adj.* rendered wise by long experience? Gen. 1154.
fyrr. See **fyr.**
fyrran, *w. v.*
 â-fyrran, to remove, withdraw, turn off or away.
fyrs, *st. m.* furze, furze-bush, bramble, blackberry.
fyrst, fierst, *st. m.* portion of time, definite space of time, time.

fyrst-gemearc, *st. n.* definite, fixed time; appointed time.
fŷrst, *adj.* first. (Ger. *fürst.*)
fyrst-mearc, *st. f.* definite, fixed time; appointed time; interval.
fŷr-sweart, *adj.* fire-swart, blackened by thick smoke.
fyrdran, *w. v.* to **further,** advance, promote.
 ge-fyrdran, to bring forward, further.
fyr-wit, -wet, -wyt (fîr), *st. n.* curiosity, prying spirit. (O. H. Ger. *firiwizzi.*)
fyrwit-georn, *adj.* curious, inquisitive.
fŷr-wylm, *st. m.* wave of fire, flamewave.
fŷsan, *w. v.* **1.** to hasten.—**2.** to make or get one's self ready, prepared, make haste.—**3.** to stimulate, incite, urge on, drive away.
 â-fŷsan, 1. to hasten.—**2.** to make ready, prepare, urge on, accelerate, hasten away.
 ge-fŷsan, to urge on, accelerate, hasten away, make ready, prepare, provide with;—*w. gen.* to be ready for, determined.
fŷst, *st. f.* fist. (Ger. *faust.*)
fyorh. See **feorh.**

G

gâd, gǽd, *st. n.* want, need; desire. (Goth. *gaidw.*)
gader-tang, *adj.* hanging together, associated with, united.
gadorian, gadrian, gædrian, *w. v.* to **gather,** collect, unite, store up. (Ger. *gattern.*)
 ge-gadorian, ge-gædrian, to bring together, collect, unite, join; —*w. dat.* to associate.

gadu, *st. f.* gad, point, sting, goad, sword. (Goth. *gazds.*)
gæd, *st. n.* state or condition of being brought together, society, fellowship.
gǽd. See **gâd.**
gædsling, *st. m.* companion, comrade, relation.
gædrian. See **gadrian.**
gǽlan, *w. v.* **1.** *w. acc.* to retard, hold back.—**2.** *intrans.* to delay, linger.

â-gǽlan, 1. to hinder, hold back, retard.— **2.** to delay, be negligent, neglect.

gǽlsa, w. m. wantonness, extravagance, luxury. [*gras.*)

gærs, st. n. grass, herb, hay. (Ger.

gærs-bed, st. n. grass-bed, grave.

gærs-hoppa, w. m. grasshopper, locust.

gærwan. See **gerwan.**

gǽsne, gêsne, geâsne, adj. unfruitful, barren, destitute, empty, poor in, not partaking of, without, lifeless.

gæst, gast, gest, gist, giest, gyst, st. m. **1. guest.**—**2.** hostile stranger, enemy. (Ger. *gast.*)

gǽst. See **gâst.**

gǽstan, w. v. to afflict, torment. (Cf. Goth. *us-gaisjan.*)

gæst-ærn, st. n. guest-house, inn, guest-chamber.

gæst-hof, st. n. the same as above. (Ger. *gasthof.*)

gæst-hûs, st. n. the same as above.

gæst-lic, adj. hospitable, ready for guests.

gǽst-lic, adj. ghastly, strange, foreign, hostile, frightful, terrible.

gæst-lidnes, st. f. hospitality.

gǽst-mǽgen, st. n. company of guests, guests.

gǽst-sele, st. m. guest-hall, hall in which the guests spend their time.

gǽd. See **gân.**

gafol, gaful, st. n. tribute, recompense, tax; sacrifice.

gaful-rǽden, st. f. same as above.

gâl, adj. joyful, gay, light, wanton, wicked. (Ger. *geil.*) [folly.

gâl, st. n. lasciviousness, lust, luxury,

galan, st. abl. v. IV. to sing, resound, sound, cry aloud, cry, call, strike up. Cf. **nightingale.**

â-**galan,** to sing, resound, ring out.

galdor, galg-, galga. See **gealdor, gealg, gealga.**

gâl-ferhd, adj. wanton, licentious.

gâl-môd, adj. wanton, licentious.

gâl-scipe, st. m. excess, extravagance, wantonness.

gamban, gomban, st. f., or, according to Bouterwerk, **gombe,** w. f. tribute, interest.

gamelian, gomelian, w. v. to age, grow old.

gamen, gomen, st. n. game, social pleasure, rejoicing, joyous doings, joke, play, sport, joy, pleasure.

gamen-wâd, st. f. journey in joyous society, joyous journey.

gamen-wudu, st. m. joy-giving wood, harp.

gamol, gomel, adj. **1.** old, aged, gray. **2.** of things,— old, from old time. **3.** pl. late, belonging to the former time, ancestors.

gamol-ferhd, adj. aged.

gamol-feax, adj. with gray hair, gray-haired.

gân, to go, come, walk, happen. Cf. **gangan.** (Ger. *gehen.*)

â-**gân, 1.** to pass, come to pass, befall.— **2.** to come forth, grow.— **3. bearnum âgân,** to approach with children.

be-, bi-gân, to commit, exercise, practice, celebrate, cherish.

ful-gân, 1. to bring to an end, fulfill, accomplish.—**2.** to follow, comply with, carry out.

ge-gân, 1. to go.— **2.** to come to pass, happen, befall.—**3.** to pass, go by.—**4.** to attain through going, overcome, conquer, occupy.—**5.** to observe exercise, practice.

ymb-gân, to go around.

gancgan. See **gangan.**

gang, pret. of **geongan.**

gang, gong, st. m. **1.** going, gait, way, course.— **2.** step, footstep.— **3.** way, extent, course, going, space. **4.** force, assault, attack.— **5.** outpouring, passage. Kr. 23.

gangan, gongan, *st. red. v.* **1.** to go, come, walk, march.—**2.** to happen, turn out, take place.
  â-gangan, to pass over, pass by, go out, forth, befall, happen.
  æt-gangan, to go to, approach.
  be-, bi-gangan, to commit, exercise, fulfil, perform, practice, cherish, observe, worship.
  for-gangan, to go before.
  fore-gangan, to go before.
  ful-gangan, to go through to the end, perfect, finish, suffer, endure.
  ge-gangan, **1.** to go, approach. **2.** to keep, observe.—**3.** to occur, happen, befall, fall to one's share. **4.** to take possession of, obtain, acquire, overcome, become partaker of, possess.—**5.** to effect, attain, reach, bring about.
  ofer-gangan, **1.** to go or pass over.—**2.** to overcome.—**3.** to come upon, overtake.
  on-gangan, to come toward, approach.
  tô-gangan, **1.** to go into.—**2.** *impers. w. gen.* to pass, happen.
  þurh-, þuruh-gangan, to go through, press through, penetrate, perforate.
  wið-gangan, **1.** to go against, ("to prosper," Thorpe).—**2.** to pass away, vanish, disappear.
  ymbe-gangan, to go around.
gânian, *w. v.* **to yawn**, gape, open. (Ger. *gähnen*.) [fowl.
ganot, ganet, *st. m.* diver, water-
gâr, *st. m.* point of an arrow or spear, arrow, spear, dart, javelin, missile. (Ger. *ger*.)
gâr, *st. m.* biting, cutting cold. Gen. 316.
gâr-berend, *part. & subs.* spear-bearer, warrior.
gâr-beam, *st. m.* spear-shaft.
gâr-cêne, *adj.* spear-bold.

gâr-cwealm, *st. m.* death by the spear.
gâr-faru, *st. f.* **1.** spear-bearing host. **2.** shower of darts, flying missiles.
gâr-getrum, *st. n.* thick mass of spears, many spears.
gâr-gewinn, *st. n.* battle of spears, battle.
gâr-hêap, *st. m.* spear-heap, band of spearmen.
gâr-holt, *st. n.* wood of the spear, shaft, spear.
gâr-mitting, *st. f.* spear-meeting, battle.
gâr-nið, *st. m.* spear-battle, fight fought with spears.
gâr-ræs, *st. m.* spear-rush, battle.
gâr-secg, -sæcg, *st. m.* sea, ocean.
gâr-torn, *st. n.* anger shown by spears.
gâr-þracu, *st. f.* storm or attack of spears, battle.
gâr-þrist, *adj.* bold with the spear, daring.
gâr-wiga, *w. m.* one who fights with the spear, spearman.
gâr-wigend, *part. & subs.* same as above.
gâr-wudu, *st. m.* spear-wood, lance, dart, spear.
gast. See **gæst**.
gâst, gæst, *st. m.* **1. ghost**, breath, spirit, soul; spirit as principle of life, thought, &c.; souls of the dead.—**2.** man, human being.—**3.** angel.—**4.** Holy Ghost.—**5.** devil, demon.—**6.** sprite, fairy, elf. (Ger. *geist*.)
gâst-bana, *w. m.* soul-murderer, devil.
gâst-berend, *part. & subs.* soul-bearer, man.
gâst-côfa, *w. m.* chamber of the soul, breast.
gâst-cund, *adj.* coming from the soul, spiritual.

gâst-cwalu, *st. f.* soul-torment, pains of hell. [God.
gâst-cyning, *st. m.* king of the soul,
gâst-gedâl, *st. n.* separation of soul and body, death.
gâst-gehygd, *st. f. n.* thought of the mind, thought.
gâst-gemynd, *st. n.* same as above.
gâst-genidla, *w. m.* enemy of souls, devil.
gâst-gerŷne, *st. n.* 1. spiritual mystery.— 2. thought, consideration, reflection, deliberation.
gâst-gewinn, *st. n.* torment of the soul, pains of hell.
gâst-hâlig, *adj.* holy in spirit, holy.
gâst-lêas, *adj.* soulless, dead.
gâst-lic, *adj.* ghostly, spiritual.
gâst-lice, *adv.* spiritually.
gâst-lufe, *w. f.* love of the soul, spiritual love.
gâst-sunu, *st. m.* spiritual son, Christ.
gât, *st. m. f.* goat, she-goat. (Ger. *geisz.*)
ge, *conj.* and; ge—ge, both—and, not only—but also.
ge, *pron. nom. pl.* ye; *gen.* êower; *dat.* êow, iow; *acc.* êowic, êow.
ge-aru, ge-arnung. See geearu, geearnung.
ge-ædele, *adj.* ancestral, hereditary, natural.
ge-æhtla, *w. m.* persecutor? warrior? B. 369. (Grein.)
ge-æhtle, *w. f.* estimation, consideration. (B.-T.) [tion.
ge-æhtung, *st. f.* counsel, delibera-
ge-bæru, *st. n. pl.* behavior, manner, conduct, doing, demeanor; address, bearing, manners.
ge-ban, -bann, *st. n.* commission, order, command.
ge-bed, *st. n.* prayer, petition, supplication. (Ger. *gebet.*)
ge-bedda, *w. m. f.* bedfellow, wife.
gebed-scipe, *st. m.* a lying together, bedfellowship, marriage.

gebed-stôw, *st. f.* place of prayer, oratory.
ge-beorg, -beorh, *st. n.* mountain, chain of mountains? Ps. 67, 15.
ge-beorg, -beorh, *st. n.* place of refuge, protection, defense, safety.
ge-bêot, *st. n.* oath, promise, agreement.
ge-bihd, *st. f.* dwelling-place, village, region (abode, Thorpe). Gû. 846.
ge-bind, *st. n.* band, fetter, chain.
ge-bland, -blond, *st. n.* blending, mingling, turmoil, commotion, uproar.
ge-blêod, *part.* colored, variegated, appearing colored, beautiful in appearance.
ge-bod, *st. n.* command, order. (Ger. *gebot.*)
gebod-scipe, *st. m.* command, order.
ge-bræc, *st. n.* breaking, noise, crash, sound.
ge-brec, *st. n.* the same as above.
ge-bregd, *st. n.* vibration, movement, agitation, tossing to and fro.
gebregd-stafas, *st. m. pl.* arts, artifices? Sal. 2.
ge-brôđor, -brôđru, *st. m. pl.* brothers, brethren. (Ger. *gebrüder.*)
ge-byrd, *st. f.* 1. birth.— 2. kind, nature, quality.
ge-byrd, *st. n. f.* fate, destiny? B. 1074.
ge-byrde, *adj.* by birth, natural, innate, inborn.
gebyrd-tid, *st. f.* birthtime.
ge-byrdu, *st. f.* 1. birth.— 2. race, origin.— 3. nature, quality. (Ger. *geburt.*)
ge-byre, *st. m.* (favorable) opportunity, occasion.
ge-byrmed, *st. n.* leavened bread.
ge-camp, *st. n.* soldiery, army; contest, fight, battle.
ge-corenes, *st. f.* election, choice.
ge-cost, *adj.* proved, chosen, tried.
ge-crod, *st. n.* crowd, throng.

ge-cwême, *adj.* agreeable, dear, pleasant, acceptable, obedient. (Ger. *bequem.*)
ge-cynd, *st. f.* nature, natural disposition, kind, spirit, quality, peculiarity, condition.— 2. birth, origin, generation. Hy. 9, 11, 52.— 3. sum-total of beings of one kind, genus.
ge-cynde, *adj.* inborn, innate, natural, belonging by birth.
ge-cynde, -cynd, *st. n.* 1. nature, spirit, natural disposition, kind, quality, peculiarity, original condition.— 2. manner, way.— 3. destiny, fate. (Ger. *kind.*)
ged, *st. n.* song, poem.
ge-dafen, *part. & adj.* becoming, suitable, fit.
ge-dafen-lic, *adj.* same as above.
ge-dâl, *st. n.* 1. separation, parting. 2. distribution. Wíd. 73.
ge-dêfe, *adj.* 1. fit, proper, appropriate, seemly, agreeable, decent; respectable, mild, gentle, good, kind, friendly. (Goth. *gadobs.*)
ge-dêfe, *adv.* fitly, decently.
ge-dræg. See **gedreag.**
ge-dræfnes, *st. f.* perturbation, unrest, disquiet.
ge-drêfednes, *st. f.* same as above.
ge-drême, -drŷme, *adj.* harmonious, joyous, cheerful.
ge-drep, *st. n.* stroke, blow.
ge-dreag, -dræg, *st. n.* dragging hither and thither, driving, tumult, noise, disturbance.
ge-driht. See **gedryht.**
ge-drinc, *st. n.* drinking, carouse.
ge-dryht, -driht, *st. f.* crowd, host, multitude.
ge-drŷme. See **gedrême.**
ge-dwǣs, *adj.* foolish, silly, stupid.
ge-dweola, *w. m.* godlessness, error, heresy.
ge-dwild, -dwield, -dwyld, *st. n.* the same as above.
ge-dwola, *w. m.* the same as above.

gedwol-mist, *st. m.* mist, obscurity of error.
ge-dyn, *st. n.* din, noise.
ge-dyrst, *st. f.* unrest, excitement, anxiety? Hö. 108.
ge-drystig, *adj.* bold, rash, daring.
ge-earnung, -arnung, *st. f.* merit, desert, benefit.
ge-earu, -aru, *adj.* unimpeded, quick, ready.
ge-fædran, *w. m. pl.* godfathers.
ge-fǣgra. See **gefêge.** B. 915.
ge-fǣr, *st. n.* journey, expedition, warlike expedition.
ge-fora, *w. m.* traveling companion, companion.
ge-fêge, *adj.* agreeable, pleasant, useful.
ge-fêra, *w. m.* companion, associate, comrade.
ge-fêre, *adj.* easy of access, accessible.
gefêr-scipe, *st. m.* companionship, company, society.
gefest. See **geaf.**
ge-fêa, *w. m.* joy.
ge-feald, *st. n.* fold, region, abode.
ge-fêalic, *adj.* joyous, refreshing, delightful.
ge-feoht, -feht, *st. n.* fight, combat, warlike deed.
gefeoht-dæg, *st. m.* day of battle.
ge-fic, *st. n.* fraud, deceit.
ge-flit, *st. n.* contention, dispute, quarrel, contest, emulation, rivalry.
ge-flota, *w. m.* swimming-companion, floater, whale.
ge-fôg, *st. n.* juncture, joining, joint.
ge-frǣge, -frêge, *adj.* what is asked after or talked about; hence, well-known, famous, celebrated, notorious, renowned.
ge-frǣge, -frêge, *st. n.* information through hearsay:—**mine gefrǣge,** as I have learned from others.
ge-frige, *st. n.* hearsay, inquiry, investigation.

ge-fyrn, *adv.* once, formerly, of old, in ancient days.
gegen. See gegn.
ge-genge, *adj.* becoming, fit.
gegn, geagn, gêan, gên, *prep.* against, again.
gegn-cwide, *st. m.* reply, answer, response.
gegninga, geagninga, *adv.* fully, entirely, plainly, evidently, openly, directly, straightway.
gegn-pæd, *st. m.* opposite, hostile path.
gegn-, gêan-ryne, *st. m.* running against, meeting.
gegn-slege, *st. m.* return blow, exchange of blows, battle.
gegnum, *adv.* forward, against, thither, toward, away.
gegnunga, gênunga, *adv.* 1. openly, plainly, evidently, directly, fully, entirely, surely.— 2. straightway. Gû. 785.
ge-grind, *st. n.* rubbing or grinding, crash, war, commotion.
ge-hange, -honge, *adj.* having the hang of, disposed, inclined to.
ge-hât, *st. n.* stipulation, agreement, vow, promise. (Ger. *geheisz;* O. H. Ger. *kiheiz*.)
ge-hende, *adj.* neighboring, near, next.
ge-hende, *adv.* near, at hand.
ge-hêrnes. See gehýrnes.
ge-heald, *st. m.* keeper, guardian.
ge-healt, *st. f. n.* watch, guard.
ge-hêaw, *st. n.* hewing, striking together, gnashing.
ge-heort, *adj.* courageous, stouthearted.
ge-higd. See gehygd.
ge-hilt, *st. n.* hilt, handle.
ge-hlǽg, *st. n.* derision, mockery, scorn.
ge-hlêða, *w. m.* companion, comrade, inhabitant.

ge-hlid, -hlid, *st. n.* lid, covering, inclosure, gate, portal.
ge-hlýde, *st. n.* cry, calling aloud.
ge-hlyn, *st. n.* noise, din, disturbance.
ge-hnǽst, -hnâst, *st. n.* collision, battle.
ge-hola, *w. m.* protector, defender.
ge-hrêow, *st. n.* lamentation.
gehdu, geohdu, giohdu, gihdu, geodu, gidu, *st. f.* care, sorrow, anxiety, sadness.
ge-hwâ, *pron.* every one, whoever.
ge-hwǽr, *adv.* 1. everywhere.— 2. whithersoever, in all directions.
ge-hwæder, *pron.* each of two, either, other, both.
ge-hwædre, *adv.* nevertheless, however.
ge-hwelc. See gehwilc.
ge-hweorf, *adj.* tractable, obedient.
ge-hwider, *adv.* in every direction, everywhere.
ge-hwylc, -hwilc, -hwelc, *pron.* each, every, any, whoever, whatever.
ge-hýd = gehygd, *st. n.* thought, reflection. Dan. 732.
ge-hygd, -higd, *st. f. n.* reflection, consideration, sentiment, thought, endeavor, counsel, consultation.
ge-hyld, *st. n.* 1. custody, keeping, protection.— 2. preservation. Az. 169.
ge-hyld, *st. n.* recess, vault; what is brought into safe keeping.
ge-hýrnes, -hêrnes, *st. f.* hearing, report, praise.
ge-hyrst, *st. f.* ornament.
ge-lâc, *st. n.* 1. play, sport;— ecga gelâc, battle.— 2. fortune, destiny? An. 1094.— 3. crowd, multitude. Cri. 896.
ge-lâd, *st. n.* way, path, course.
ge-lagu, *st. f. n.?* sea;— holma gelagu, stormy, tempestuous sea.

ge-lang, -long, *adj.* along of, dependent, extending, reaching to something or somebody, ready, prepared, at hand; — gelang on, long of, owing to. Bed. 3, 10.
ge-lâd, *adj.* hostile.
geldan. See gildan.
ge-lenge, *adj.* belonging to, pertaining to, given up to, addicted to.
ge-lêafa, *w. m.* belief, faith. [true.
gelêaf-ful, *adj.* believing, faithful,
gelêaf-sum, *adj.* credible, sure.
ge-leoren, *part.* gone hence, dead.
ge-lîc, *adj.* 1. like, similar, equal. — 2. likely, probable. Met. 19, 12. (Ger. *gleich*.)
ge-lîc, *st. n.* likeness, similarity.
ge-lîca, *w. m.* like, equal.
ge-lîce, *adv.* equally, alike, as, in like manner.
ge-lîcnes, *st. f.* likeness, image, resemblance.
ge-limp, *st. n.* occurrence, event, favorable situation, good fortune.
ge-list. See gelysted.
gellan, giellan, gyllan, *st. abl. v.* I. to yell, cry out; sound, ring, war, sing, cry, call. (Ger. *gellen*.)
  bi-gellan, to sing, celebrate.
ge-lôme, *adv.* continually, frequently, often, always, repeatedly.
gelp. See gilp.
ge-lynd, *st. f.* fat, grease.
ge-mæc, *adj.* becoming, fit, suitable, companionable.
ge-mæcca, *w. m.* comrade, companion, spouse, husband or wife.
gemæc-scipe, *st. m.* companionship, cohabitation, marriage.
ge-mæl, *adj.* tinctured, colored, dyed. (Cf. Ger. *malen;* Goth. *maljan*.)
ge-mæne, *adj.* common, in common, general, mutual. (Ger. *gemein*.)
gemǽn-nes, *st. f.* communion, fellowship.
gemǽn-scipe, *st. m.* same as above.

ge-mǽre, *st. n.* border, boundary, end, limit.
ge-mâgas, *st. m. pl.* kindred by blood, relations.
ge-mâh, *adj.* unsuitable, silly, impious.
gêman. See gŷman.
ge-mâna, *w. m.* communion, fellowship, commerce, company, society, union, companionship, community.
ge-mang, -mong, *st. n.* mixture, crowd, troop, mass, congregation, company.
ge-mêde, *adj.* agreeable, pleasant.
ge-mêde, *st. n.* consent, agreement, approval, permission.
gêmen. See gŷmen.
ge-met, *st. n.* 1. measure, bounds, limit. — 2. portion, share. — 3. boundary, limit, end. — 4. regulation, rule, law. — 5. capacity, ability, might, strength, power.
ge-met, *adj.* measured, fit, becoming, suitable, good, meet.
ge-mete, *adv.* aptly, fitly, meetly.
ge-mête, *adj.* meeting, lighting upon (Grein); — *part.* met. (B.-T.) Jul. 334.
gemet-fæst, *adj.* moderate, modest.
ge-mêting, *st. f.* 1. meeting, assembly, congregation. — 2. hostile meeting, battle.
gemet-lîce, *adv.* in a proper manner, meetly.
ge-mearc, *st. n.* what is marked off, boundary, limit.
ge-meotu, *st. n. pl.* See gemet.
ge-môt, *st. n.* 1. moot, coming together, meeting, assembly, society, council. — 2. running together, meeting, conflict.
gemôt-stede, *st. m.* place of meeting.
ge-mynd, *st. f. n.* 1. memory, recollection, remembrance. — 2. mind, thought, intention, meaning, consideration. (Goth. *ga-munds*.)

ge-mynde, *adj.* mindful, heedful, remembering.
ge-myndig, *adj.* the same as above.
gên, gien, 1. denoting the continuance of an action or a condition; again, yet, still.— 2. further, besides, also.— 3. yet (what is near, impending, not done yet, for which there is just time, &c.)—4. again, moreover, once more, once again. 5. hitherto, up to this time, in past time.— 6. *w. compar.* yet, even.— 7. *w. negative,* not yet, no more, no longer.
gên-. See gegn-.
gêna, giena, gêno = gên, yet, still.
ge-nægled, *part. & adj.* nailed.
ge-namne, *pl.* of like name, of the same name (Grein);—ge-numne(?) See ge-niman (B.-T.). Rä. 53, 3.
ge-nâg,*adj.* stemming, striking, pressing? Reim. 57, 58.
ge-nehe, -nehhe, -nehhige. See geneahhe, -neahhige.
ge-ner, *st. n.* refuge.
ge-nêahe, *st. pl.* neighbors? near relations? Lêas. 36.
ge-neahhe, -neahe, -nehhe, -nehe, *adv.* enough, sufficiently, in the highest degree, very, much, frequently, immediately.
ge-neahhie, -neahhige, nehhige, *adv.* the same as above.
ge-nêahsen, *adj.* neighboring, near.
ge-nêat, *st. m.* comrade, companion. (Ger. *genoss.*)
genêat-scolu, *st. f.* crowd, band of comrades.
geng, gêng. See geong, gangan.
gengan, *w. v.* to go, run, travel, pass.
    tô-gengan, to separate, depart.
genge, *adj.* customary, current, usual, weighty, successful.
ge-niht, *st. f. n.* abundance, plenty, fruitfulness, sufficiency, fullness.

geniht-sum,*adj.* 1. plentiful, copious, abundant, sufficient.— 2. easily satisfied, contented.
ge-nip, *st. n.* enveloping darkness, mist, cloud, darkness, obscurity.
ge-nîdla, *w. m.* enemy, hostility, enmity, hate.
gennan, *w. v.* to gallop, dash forward.
gêno. See gêna.
genôg, -nôh, *adv.* enough, abundantly, sufficiently. (Ger. *genug.*)
gênunga. See gegnunga.
ge-râd, -ræd, *adj.* advised, informed. experienced, prudent, skillful, ready, prepared, tasteful, elegant.
gerâd-scipe, *st. m.* wisdom, prudence, reason.
ge-rædan? Gn. Ex. 178.
ge-ræde, *st. n.* trappings for the breast, housings, equipage, harness, household furniture (Grein); arrangement, adjustment, mediation, interposition (Zupitza).
ge-ræf, *st. n.* what is decided, fixed. (*ms.* græf.) Reim. 71.
ge-ræswa, *w. m.* comrade, leader.
gêr. See geâr.
gere. See geare. [ment.
ge-rec, *st. n.* rule, direction, government.
gerec-lîce, *adv.* straightway, immediately, directly.
ge-rêfa, *w. m.* an officer appointed by the king, officer, prefect. (Cf. sheriff = scir-gerêfa.)
gerela, gierela, *w. m.* clothes, garment, covering.
ge-rên, *st. n.* ornament.
ge-rêne. See gerŷne.
ge-reord, -reorde, *st. n.* tongue, speech, language, speaking, voice.
ge-reord, -reorde, *st. n.* refreshment, meal, feast, supper, hospitality.
ge-riht, -ryht, *st. n.* direction, right path.
ge-rim, *st. n.* number, count, reckoning.

ge-rísne, -rýsne, *st. n.* what is appropriate, proper, becoming, seeming, convenient;—appropriate, becoming manner, propriety, convenience.

ger-scipe, *st. m.* joke, polish, culture, cleverness, dexterity (Leo). Reim. 11.

ge-rúm, *st. n.* room, space;—on gerúm, at large, farther = far and wide. Rä. 21, 14;—away, apart. El. 320.

ge-rúma, *w. m.* wide, extended space.

ge-rúme, *adj.* roomy, extended, ample, spacious, great, lying open. (Ger. *geraum*.)

gerwan, gærwian, girwan, gierwan, gyrwan, gearwian, *w. v.* **1.** to equip, clothe.—**2.** to equip, make ready for battle, prepare beforehand.—**3.** to adorn, decorate.—**4.** to prepare, make ready, put in condition, make, build, erect.

ge-gerwan, &c., **1.** to put on, array, bind about, clothe.—**2.** to adorn, ornament.—**3.** to equip, provide with, endow.—**4.** to make ready, prepare, fit out.

on-gyrwan, to unclothe.

ge-ryde, *adj.* convenient, opportune, fit, suitable.

ge-ryht. See **geriht.**

ge-rýne, -réne, *st. n.* secret, mystery, wonder.

ge-rysne. See **gerisne.**

ge-saca, *w. m.* adversary, enemy, opponent, foe.

ge-sǽlig, *adj.* happy, fortunate, favored by fortune, prosperous, rich, powerful.

gesǽlig-lic, *adj.* the same as above.

gesǽlig-nes, *st. f.* happiness.

gesǽl-lic, *adj.* favored, fortunate, happy.

ge-sǽld, *st. f.* good fortune, success, prosperity, good, wealth.

ge-samning, -somning, *st. f.* congregation, assembly.

ge-samnung, *st. f.* same as above.

ge-scád, -sceád, *st. n.* **1.** distinction, discrimination, difference, reason. —**2.** distinction, separation.

gescád-lice (-sceád-), *w. v.* in a reasonable manner, rationally.

gescád-wis (-sceád-), *adj.* intelligent, wise, discriminating, prudent.

gescádwis-nes (-sceád-), *st. f.* discrimination, intelligence, prudence, discretion.

ge-scæp-hwíl, *st. f.* fated hour, death-hour.

ge-scentu, *st. f.* confusion, disturbance? Seel. 49.

ge-sceád. See **gescád.**

ge-sceaft, -scæft, -sceft, *st. f.* **1.** creature, creation, what is created; —in the *sg.* it is used to denote partly the whole creation, partly the earth or the heavens, and sometimes a single creature.—**2.** what is sent by God; lot, fate, destiny.

ge-sceap, *st. n.* **1.** creature, creation, world.—**2.** fate, destiny, what is fixed or appointed by destiny, a gift of destiny, nature, natural disposition, form, shape, manner, appearance. (Ger. *geschöpf*.)

ge-scildend, -scyldend, *part. & subs.* protection, protector.

ge-scip, *st. n.* fate, destiny, fortune. B. 2570. (Groschopp.)

ge-scife, *adj.* advancing. B. 2571. (Harrison & Sharp.) [dress.

ge-scirpla, *w. m.* clothing, apparel,

ge-scot, *st. n.* dart, thunderbolt.

gescot-feoht, *st. f.* fighting with darts or arrows, battle. [ders.

ge-sculdre, -sculdru, *st. n. pl.* shoul-

ge-scý, *st. n.* covering for the feet, shoes.

ge-scyldend. See **gescildend.**

ge-scyldru, *st. n. pl.* shoulders.

ge-sêft, *part.* & *adj.* softened, mild, gentle, pleasant.
ge-segen, *st. f.* saying, tradition.
ge-selda, *w. m.* companion, comrade.
ge-seld, *st. f.* dwelling-place, house, mansion.
ge-sêne. See **gesŷne.**
ge-set, *st. n.* seat, dwelling, domicile, house.
geset-nes, *st. f.* place, station.
gesewen-lic, *adj.* visible.
geseotu, *st. n. pl.* See **geset.**
ge-sib, -syb, *adj.* belonging to the same race; kin, related, near, intimate.
gesib-lice, *adv.* peacefully, harmoniously.
ge-sihđ, -siehđ, -syhđ, *st. f.* sight, power of seeing, eyes, face, appearance, aspect, view.
ge-sine. See **gesŷne.**
ge-singe, *w. f.* wife.
ge-sid, *st. m.* companion, comrade, follower, associate.
gesid-mægen, *st. n.* crowd or concourse of followers.
ge-sidd, *st. n.* companionship, fellowship, company. (Ger. *gesinde.*)
ge-siehđ, -siene. See **gesihđ, -sŷne.**
ge-sleht, -sliht, -slyht, *st. n.* battle, conflict.
gêsne. See **gǽsne.**
ge-som, *adj.* concordant, unanimous, united, friendly.
ge-span, -spon, *st. n.* joining, plaiting, fastening together, web, clasp.
ge-span, -spon, *st. n.* enticement, seduction, wile. [clasp.
ge-spang, -spong, *st. n.* fastening,
ge-sprec, *st. n.* ability to speak, power of speech.
ge-spreca, *w. m.* one that speaks with another, counselor.
ge-spring, *st. n.* surge, eddy, stream.
gest. See **gǽst.**
ge-stæddig, *adj.* stable, fixed, firm.

ge-steal, *st. n.* foundation, ground, space.
ge-steald, *st. n.* place, dwelling, abode.
ge-stealla, *w. m.* comrade, companion.
ge-strêon, *st. n. pl.* collected or acquired treasures, possessions, jewels, property, riches, gain, treasure.
ge-stun, *st. n.* war, crash.
ge-sund, *adj.* whole, unhurt, safe, well, healthy, happy, prosperous. (Ger. *gesund.*)
ge-swǽs, *adj.* dear, pleasant.
ge-sweorc, *st. n.* darkness, mist, cloud.
ge-sweoru, -swiru, -swyru, *st. n. pl.* hills.
ge-sweoster, *pl.* sisters. (Ger. *geschwister.*)
ge-swin. See **geswins.**
ge-swinc, *st. n.* labor, pains, tribulation.
geswinc-dagas, *st. m. pl.* days of tribulation.
ge-swing, *st. n.* vibration, fluctuation, tossing.
ge-swins, *st. n.* modulation of the voice in singing, song, melody.
ge-swiru. See **gesweoru.**
ge-swyru, -syb, -syhđ. See **gesweoru, -sib, -sihđ.**
ge-sŷne, -sêne, -sine, -siene, *adj.* visible, seen, plain, evident, open, clear.
ge-synto, *st. f.* health, unchanged condition, fruit, prosperity, safety. (Ger. *gesundheit.*)
get, geta. See **git, gita.**
ge-tæl, -tel, *st. n.* **1.** tale, number, series, count, reckoning.—**2.** race, mass, company, tribe, hundred.
getæl-rim, *st. n.* the computed number, full number.
ge-tǽse, *adj.* quiet, still, gentle, peaceful, comfortable, suitable.
ge-tâh, *st. n.* teaching, doctrine, discipline? Reim. 2.

ge-tal, *adj.* quick, swift, ready, expeditious.

getan, *w. v.* (to get, see gitan,) to hurt, injure, destroy, kill.

â-getan, the same as the above.

ge-tang, -tong, *adj.* given up to.

ge-tang, -tong, *st. n.* quick movement, haste? Reim. 8.

ge-tawa, *st. f. pl.* equipment, instruments.

ge-tel. See getæl.

ge-tenge, *adj.* near, reaching to, attached to, lying on or by, pressing on, heavy, oppressive; in short, showing immediate nearness.

ce-têoh, *st. n.* matter, material (universe). Reim. 2.

ce-timbru, *st. n. pl.* building, edifice, structure. (Ger. *gezimmer*.) [tle.

ge-toht, *st. n.* warlike expedition, battle.

ge-trêowe, *adj.* true, faithful.

ge-trum, *st. n.* band, crowd, host, army.

ge-trym, *st. m.* firmament, canopy.

ge-trŷwe, *adj.* true, faithful.

ge-twinnas, *st. m. pl.* twins. (Ger. *zwillinge*.)

ge-tŷne, *st. n.* entrance, court.

ge-tynge, *adj.* speaking fluently, loquacious.

ge-þaca, *w. m.* one that covers or overlays anything, coverer, covering.

ge-þafa, *w. m.* favorer, helper, supporter, promoter.

ge-þanc, -þonc, *st. m. n.* thought, thinking, intention, mind, opinion.

ge-þancol, *adj.* thoughtful, mindful.

ge-þeaht, *st. f. n.* reflection, consideration, counsel, advice.

ge-þeahting, -þeahtung, *st. f.* counsel, determination, consent, agreement.

ge-þêawe. See geþŷwe.

ge-þêode, *st. pl.* nations, peoples. Sat. 19.

ge-þêode, *st. n.* speech, language.

ge-þing, *st. n.* 1. council, assembly. 2. agreement, terms, covenant. B. 1085. — 3. fate, providence, issue, destiny.

ge-þingdu, *st. f.* worth, honor, dignity.

ge-þoht, *st. m.* thought, mind, manner of thinking; plan, determination.

ge-þræc, -þrec, *st. n.* press, crush, throng, crowd, stir, tumult.

ge-þrang, *st. n.* throng, tumult. (Ger. *gedränge*.)

ge-þring, *st. n.* tumult, throng, crush, whirlpool.

ge-þrûen, *adj.* brought together, pressed, compact.

ge-þwǣre, *adj.* united, willing, harmonious, gentle, mild, peaceful, quiet, complaisant.

ge-þŷde, *adj.* good, liberal.

ge-þyht, *adj.* suitable, pleasing.

ge-þyld, *st. f.* patience, endurance, steadfastness. (Ger. *geduld*.)

ge-þyldig, *adj.* patient, long-suffering, even-minded, quiet. (Ger. *geduldig*.)

ge-þyncdu = geþingdu, *st. f.* honor, dignity, worth.

ge-þŷwe, -þêawe, *adj.* wont, accustomed, customary, usual.

ge-un-wendnes, *st. f.* unchangeableness, immutability.

ge-wǣde, -wêde, *st. n.* weeds, clothing, garment, battle-dress, shirt-of-mail.

ge-wêd, *st. n.* fury, rage.

ge-wêde. See gewǣde.

ge-wef, *st. n.* woof, weaving, web.

ge-wel-hwǣr, *adv.* everywhere.

ge-wealc, *st. n.* rolling, motion (of the wave); attack. Chron. Sax. a. 1100.

ge-weald, -wald, *st. f. n.* might, power. (Ger. *gewalt*.)

ge-wealdend, *part. & adj.* mighty, strong, powerful.

gewealdend-lice, *adv.* mightily, powerfully.
gewealden-môd, *adj.* of a brave mind, bold, courageous.
geweald-leder, *st. n.* leather for guiding, rein.
ge-weoldum. See **gewild.**
ge-weorc, *st. n.* work, deed, labor.
ge-weorht. See **gewyrht.**
ge-weorp, *st. n.* throwing, tossing, dashing.
ge-widor, *st. n.* storm, tempest, weather. (Ger. *gewitter.*)
ge-wil, -will, *st. n.* will, decision, wish.
ge-wild, *st. n.* will, free will.
ge-wilt? El. 938 = **gewitt.**
ge-win, -winn, *st. n.* **1.** fight, contest, strife, war, attack, disturbance, uproar, tumult.— **2.** pains, trouble, sorrow, oppression, agony. **3.** gain, profit. (Ger. *gewinn.*)
gewin-dæg, *st. m.* day of battle or of labor, pains, oppression, day of battle.
ge-winna, *w. m.* enemy, oppressor, rival, foe.
gewin-woruld, *st. f.* world full of pain and misery, world of care.
ge-wiȝ, *adj.* certain, sure, trustworthy. (Ger. *gewiss.*)
gêwiȝ, *st. f.* distress, tribulation, need.
ge-wislice, *adv.* truly, surely, certainly.
ge-wit, *st. n.* wits, understanding, mind, thought, insight, consciousness, knowledge, breast, soul, heart.
ge-wita, *w. m.* witness, accessory.
ge-wita, *w. m.* comrade, companion.
gewit-lêaȝ, *adj.* thoughtless, foolish, silly.
gewit-loca, *w. m.* the inclosure of intelligence, mind, thought, breast.
gewit-nes, *st. f.* witness, testimony, joint knowledge; knowledge, cognizance; a witness (testis).

ge-witod, *st. m.* condition of life fixed for any one by destiny? Reim. 44. (*ms.* **gewited.**)
ge-witt. See **gewit.**
ge-wittig, *adj.* having intelligence, knowing, conscious.
ge-wlô, *adj.* decorated, adorned.
ge-worf. See **geweorf.**
ge-writ, *st. n.* writing, letter, book, especially the Scriptures.
ge-wrixle, *st. n.* change, exchange, barter, arrangement, bargain.
ge-wun, *adj.* wont, accustomed.
ge-wuna, *w. m.* use, custom, manner, rite.
ge-wydor. See **gewidor.**
ge-wyrd, *st. f.* **1.** event, occurrence. **2.** destiny, lot assigned by fate. Men. 66.
ge-wyrht, -weorht, *st. n.* **1.** deed, work, labor, service.— **2.** fate's decree, lot fixed by destiny. Dôm. 61.
ge-wyrhta, *w. m.* worker, doer, author.
gêac, *st. m.* (**gawk**), cuckoo. (Ger. *kuckuk, gauch.*)
gêacnung. See **ge-êacnung.**
geador, gador, *adv.* together, at the same time, altogether, jointly.
geaf, *adj.* serving for pastime, jocose.
geafe, *w. f.* gift, present.
geaflas, *st. m. pl.* beak, jaws, (**gaffles**).
geafol, *st. n.* tribute, gift.
geagl, *st. m.* throat, gullet; jaws.
geagn-, geagninga, gêahd. See **gegn-, gegninga, gêad.**
gealdor, galdor, *st. n.* sound, tone, song, magic song, incantation, spell, excommunication, speech.
gealdor-cræft, *st. m.* magic art, incantation, excommunication.
gealdor-cwide, *st. m.* song, speech, incantation.
gealdor-word, *st. n.* word of a song, magic word.
gealga, galga, *w. m.* **gallows**, cross. (Ger. *galgen.*)

gealg-, gealh-, galg-môd, *adj.* bilious, choleric, furious, wroth, angry;—melancholy, sad, gloomy.

gealg-trêow, *st. n.* gallows-tree, gallows, cross. [*galle.*]

gealla, ealla, *w. m.* gall, bile. (Ger.

gêan, gêanes. See **gegn, gegnes.**

geap, gate? Ruin. 11, 31. (Grein.)

gêap, gêapu, *st. f.* expanse, room. (B.-T.)

gêap, *adj.* **1.** broad, wide, spread out, roomy.—**2.** experienced, astute, sly, crafty, cunning.

gêap-neb, *adj.* an epithet of the coat-of-mail;—into gêap-neb? to be changed. Wald. 2, 18. (Grein.) **geap-neb,** crooked-nibbed, with a bent beak, arched. (B.-T.)

gear, sport? jest? Reim. 25.

geâr, gér, *st. n.* **1.** year.—**2.** yearly tribute. (Ger. *jahr.*)

geâra, *adv. gen. pl.* of **geâr,**—yore, of yore, in former times, once, formerly.

geara, *adv.* fully, entirely, very well, enough, satisfactorily, sufficiently.

gearo, *adj.* ready, prompt.

geard, *st. m.* yard, hedge, inclosed space, dwelling-place, house. (Ger. *garten.*)

geâr-dagas, *st. m. pl.* **1.** days of the year or of life.—**2.** former time, days of yore, former days;—**geârdagum,** *adv. instr.* formerly, in ancient days, once.

geare, gere, *adv.* complete, entirely, thoroughly, very well, sufficiently.

gearewe. See **gearwe.**

geâr-gemearc, *st. n.* mark or boundary of years; a year's time.

geâr-gerim, *st. n.* number of the years, years in number.

geâr-mǽl, *st. n.* time of years, in course of time, year by year.

gearnung. See **ge-earnung.**

gearo. See **ge-earu.**

geâr-rim, *st. n.* number of years.

geâr-torht, *adj.* splendid, bright in years, illustrious on account of yearly revenue.

gearu. See **ge-earu.**

gearu, gearo, *adj.* yare, ready, prepared, prompt, finished, equipped; complete.

gearu, gearo, *adv.* promptly, readily, fully, entirely, altogether, thoroughly, very well, richly.

gearu-brygd, *st. f.* prompt, complete vibration. Crä. 50.

gearu-folm, *adj.* with ready hand.

gearu-gangende, *part.* going unimpeded, swiftly.

gearu-lice, *adv.* completely, fully, very well.

gearu-snotor, -snottor, *adj.* very wise, prudent.

gearu-þancol, *adj.* very thoughtful, prudent.

gearuwian. See **gerwan.**

gearu-wyrdig, *adj.* ready with words, ready to strike, eloquent.

gearwe, gearuwe, gearewe, *adv.* completely, entirely, altogether, well, very well, safely, satisfactorily. (Ger. *gar.*)

gearwe, *st. f. pl.* equipment, clothing, ornaments, gear.

gearwe, *w. f.* the same as above.

gearwian. See **gerwan.**

geâsne. See **gǽsne.**

geat, gat, *st. n.* gate, door. (Ger. *gasse.*)

geato-lic, *adj.* ready, well-prepared, handsome, splendid.

geatwan, *w. v.* to make ready, prepare, adorn.

geatwe, *st. f. pl.* equipment, adornment.

gêad, gêahd, *st. f.* foolishness, lasciviousness, wantonness, luxury, mockery.

gêo, gio, *adv.* once, formerly. (Goth. *ju.*)

geoc, gioc, *st. n.* yoke.

gêoc, êoc, gioc, *st. f.* help, support, rescue, safety, consolation, alleviation.
gêocend, *part. & subs.* helper, rescuer, Savior.
gêocian, *w. v., w. gen.,* or *dat.* to help, preserve, rescue, save.
gêocor, *adj.* strong, brave, wild, wicked, bad, ill, perilous, oppressive, bitter, dire, sad.
gêocre, *adv.* harshly, roughly, severely, angrily.
geocsa, geohsa, gihsa, *w. m.* sobbing, rattling in the throat. Met. 2, 5.
geofa, geofan, geofe. See gifa, gifan, gife, gifu.
geofian, *w. v.* to give, present.
geofon, gifen, gyfen, *st. n.* sea, flood.
geofon-flôd, *st. m.* flood of the sea.
geofon-hûs, *st. n.* sea-house, ship.
geofen-ýd, *st. n.* sea-wave, billow.
geofu. See gifu.
geoguđ, gioguđ, *st. f.* **1. youth,** age or state of youth, time of youth.— **2.** youth, young persons, young men, young warriors. (Ger. *jugend*.)
geoguđ-cnôsl, *st. n.* young family, children.
geoguđ-feorh, *st. n.* age of youth, youth.
geoguđ-hâd, *st. m.* state of youth, time of youth, youth.
geoguđ-myru, *st. f.* joy of youth? Rä. 39, 2.
geohsa, geohđu. See geocsa, gehđu.
geoleca, geolca, gioleca, *w. m.* yolk.
geolo, -u, *adj.* yellow.
geolo-rand, *st. m.* yellow shield (shield with a covering of interlaced linden-bark).
gêomǣr? Ps, 77, 39:—perhaps to be changed into gêon-, gêan-cer. Cf. geoncyr occursus. (Lye.)
gêo-man, *st. m.* man of former times.

gêomor, giomor, *adj.* sorrowful, sad, troubled, miserable, depressed in spirits, wretched. (Cf. Ger. *jammer*.)
gêomor-frôd, *adj.* old in sorrows, sage, wise, very old.
gêomor-gid, -gyd, *st. n.* dirge, funeral song, elegy, lamentation.
gêomor-lic, *adj.* sad, sorrowful, painful.
gêomor-lice, *adv.* sadly, sorrowfully, mournfully. [mind.
gêomor-môd, *adj.* sad, sorrowful in
gêomran, -rian, *w. v.* to mourn, lament, be sorrowful, be sad, complain. (Ger. *jammern*.)
gêoncer. See gêomǣr.
geond, giond, *prep. w. acc.* through, throughout, along, over, as far as. beyond, between;—used in general to denote extension in space.
geong, geng, ging, iung, giung, *adj.* **1. young,** youthful.— **2. recent.** new, fresh.— **3.** *superl.* the last. B. 2817. (Ger. *jung*.)
geong, *st. m.* going, course, journey.
gêong, *pret.* of gangan.
geongan, *st. abl. v.* I. to go.
geonge-wifre, *w. f.* a weaver in going, spider.
geongor-dôm, *st. m.* discipleship, obedience, service.
geongor-scipe, *st. m.* same as above.
geongra, giongra, gingra, *w. m.* disciple, follower, dependant, vassal, servant. (Ger. *jünger*.)
geongre, gingre, *w. f.* female servant.
gêopan, *st. abl. v.* VI. to take up into one's self. swallow.
georn, *adj.* diligent, studious, desirous of seeking after, striving, eager, ardent, zealous. (Ger. *gerne*.)
georne, *adv.* **1. willingly,** obligingly, gladly, readily, diligently, zealously, carefully, eagerly, anxiously.— **2.** completely, fully, exactly, safely, surely. (Ger. *gern*.)

georn-ful, *adj.* solicitous, eager, desirous, zealous.
georn-líce, *adv.* eagerly, zealously, carefully, diligently, willingly.
georran, *st. abl. v.* I. to sound, creak, grate.
gêo-sceaft, *st. f.* long-fixed destiny, fate.
gêosceaft-gâst, *st. m.* spirit of remote antiquity, having his origin in the beginning of the world?— demon sent by fate? B. 1266.
geostra, giestra, gystra, *adj.* yester-, of yesterday. (Ger. *gestern*.)
geotan. See **gitan**.
gêotan, *st. abl. v.* VI. **1**. to pour, pour out, pour forth, shed.—**2**. *intrans.* to pour, empty, stream, flow. (Ger. *giessen*.)
 â-gêotan, **1.** to pour out, shed.— **2.** to empty.—**3.** to stream out or forth, flow.
 be-gêotan, **1.** to pour upon or over.— **2.** to pour into.
 ge-gêotan, to pour.
 þurh-gêotan, to pour through, fill entirely, imbue.
geodu. See **gehdu**.
gicel, *st. m.* icicle (= ice-icel).
gid, gidd, gied, gyd, *st. n.* song, solemn alliterative song, speech, lay, poem, riddle.
giddian, gieddian, gyddian, *w. v.* to sing, speak, recite (in alliterative verse).
gidding, giedding, *st. f.* song, earnest discourse, saying, prophecy.
gif, gyf, *conj.* **1.** *w. indic.* & *subj.* if.— **2.** *w. indic.* or *subj.* although, even if. Gen. 661.—**3.** *w. indic.* or *subj.* whether.
gif, gyf, *st. n.* gift, favor, grace.
gifa, giefa, geofa, gyfa, *w. m.* giver, distributer.
gifan, giefan, gefan, geofan, giofan, gyfan, *st. abl. v.* III. to give. (Ger. *geben*.)
 â-gifan, **1.** to give, deliver, give or send forth, impart, return.— **2.** to restore, give back again.— **3.** to give up, abandon, lose.
 æt-gifan, to render, bring to the help of, afford help to.
 for-gifan, **1.** to give, grant, concede, allow, deliver.—**2.** to forgive. **3.** to give up, leave, cease.
 of-gifan, to give up, resign, lose, leave, send away, give away, set out.
gifen. See **geofon**.
gifer, *st. m.* eater, glutton? See l. 118.
gifed, sea, ocean? An. 489. (Grein.) But see **gifede**, *st. n.*
gifede, gyfede, *adj.* given, granted.
gifede, *st. n.* what is given by destiny, fate. B. 3085.
gif-fæst, *adj.* endowed, gifted.
gif-heal, *st. f.* hall in which gifts are distributed, throne-hall.
gifl, gifel, giefl, gyfl, *st. n.* food, bit, morsel.
gif-nes, *st. f.* kindness, grace, favor.
gifre, *adj.* greedy, ravenous, rapacious, eager, desirous.
gifre, *adj.* salutary, useful.
gif-sceat, *st. m.* gift of value, present, tribute. B. 378.
gif-stôl, *st. m.* seat from which gifts are distributed, royal seat, throne.
gift, gyft, *st. f. n.* gift, dowry, marriage. (O. H. Ger. *gift*.)
gifu, giefu, geofu, giofu, gyfu, *st. f.* gift, present, benefit, grant, fief, grace, favor, talent, virtue, capacity, ability. (Ger. *gabe*.)
gigant, *st. m.* giant.
gigant-mæcg, *st. m.* son of a giant.
gihsa, gihdu. See **geocsa, gehdu**.
gild, gield, gyld, *st. n.* **1.** reparation, reward, requital, retribution.— **2.** amends for something, compensation, substitute.— **3.** worship, cult, service, sacrifice.—**4.** divinity, deity.—**5.** idol.

gildan, gieldan, gyldan, geldan, *st. abl. v.* I. (to **yield**), **1.** to make reparation, restore, requite, repay, reward, pay.— **2.** to vow, sacrifice. (Ger. *gelten.*)
   â-gildan, 1. to give back, pay.— **2.** to offer one's self.
   an-gildan, to pay for.
   for-gildan, 1. to requite, pay.— **2.** to reward one with something. B. 956.— **3.** to give, pay, reward.— **4.** to pay, fulfill. (Ger. *vergelten.*)
   ge-gildan, to grant, give.
   on-gildan, 1. to atone for, expiate.— **2.** to pay, give up.— **3.** to receive as punishment. Fä. 71.
gilp, gelp, gielp, gylp, *st. m. n.* glory, glorious renown, boasting, boastful speech, big talking, arrogance, promise of great deeds.
gilpan, gielpan, gylpan, *st. abl. v.* I. (to **yelp**), to praise one's self, boast, be haughty, exult insolently, triumph, rejoice, exult.
   â-gilpan, to boast, rejoice.
gilp-cwide, *st. m.* boastful speech, defiant speech.
gilpen, *adj.* vainglorious, boastful.
gilp-hlæden, *adj.* laden with boasts of defiance; he who has many such boasts, and consequently has been victorious in many combats; covered with glory. B. 868.
gilp-lic, *adj.* boastful, splendid.
gilp-plega, *w. m.* play in which defiance or boasts are hurled back and forth, war.
gilp-sceada, *w. m.* boastful, big-talking, arrogant enemy.
gilp-spræc, *st. f.* speech of defiance, boastful speech.
gilp-word, *st. n.* proud, boastful word (speech).
gilt. See **gylt.**
giltan. See **gyltan.**

gim, *st. m.* **1. gem,** jewel.— **2.** eye.— **3.** sun, constellation, star. (O. H. Ger. *gimma.*)
gim-cyn (gym), *st. n.* kind of gems, precious stones.
gim-reced, *st. n.* hall adorned with precious stones, or in which precious stones are distributed.
gin, *adj.* gaping, wide, extended.
gin, gyn, *st. n.* gaping abyss, chasm, expanse, deep, bottom.
ginan, *st. abl. v.* V.
   be-ginan, to yawn at, stare at any one yawning.
   tô-ginan, to be opened, be cleft, to split, gape.
gin-fæst, *adj.* firm on all sides, strong, mighty, powerful.
ging, gingra, gingre. See **geong, geongra, geongre.**
ginnan, gynnan, *st. abl. v.* I. (to **gin.**)
   an-ginnan, to begin, commence.
   be-ginnan, to **begin,** commence.
   on-ginnan, 1. *w. inf.* to begin;— often used as a periphrastic way of denoting the simple action of the verb.— **2.** *w. acc.* to begin, undertake.— **3.** to make an attack upon any one, attack, rush upon, assail, assault, storm.
ginne. See **gin.**
gin-, ginn-wîsed, *adj.* very wise.
girran, girwan, gist. See **georran, gerwan, gæst.**
gisel, gŷsel, *st. m.* hostage. (Ger. *geissel.*)
git, gyt, *nom. voc.* dual of the *pers. pron.* of the second person, ye two;
   —**git Johannis,** thou and John;— *gen.* incer; *dat.* inc; *acc.* incit, inc.
git, get, giet, gyt, *adv.* **yet,** now, still, again, moreover, hitherto, up to this time;— *w. negative,* not yet, never before.
gita, geta, gieta, gyta, *adv.* hitherto, as yet.

gitan, gietan, gytan, geotan, *st.abl.v.* III. to get.
    â-gitan, to destroy, put out, overturn, hurt.
    an-gitan, to take hold of, grasp, seize.
  be-, bi-gitan, 1. to take, grasp, seize, reach, gain, attain, receive, befall. **2.** to seize, attack. See f. 24.
    for-gitan, *w. acc. & gen.* to forget. (Ger. *vergessen.*)
    ofer-gitan, to neglect, forget.
    on-gitan, to take hold of, grasp; especially to grasp intellectually; comprehend, perceive, distinguish, behold, recognize.
gitsian, gŷtsian, *w. v.* to desire ardently, be avaricious, be greedy. (Ger. *geizen.*)
gitsung, *st. f.* concupiscence, lust, desire, avarice, covetousness.
gied, gieddian, giedding. See **gid, giddian, gidding.**
giefa, giefan, giefl, giefu. See **gifa, gifan, gifl, gifu.**
gield, gieldan, giellan, gielp, gielpan, gielt. See **gild, gildan, gellan, gilp, gilpan, gylt.**
gieman, gien, giena. See **gŷman, gên, gêna.**
gieng, *pret.* from **gangan.**
gierd, gierela, gierwan. See **gyrd, gerela, gerwan.**
giest, giestra. See **gæst, geostra.**
giet, gieta, gietan. See **git, gita, gitan.**
gio (gio-), gioc, gioc, giofu, giofan, giogud, giohdu, gioleca, gioman, giomor, giond, giong, giong, giongor, giongra, giotan. See **geo, geoc, geoc, gifu, gifan, geogud, gehdu, geoleca, geoman, geomor, geond, geong, gangan, geongor, geongra, geotan.**
giong, *pret.* from **gangan.**
giung. See **geong.**

gladian, *w. v.* **1.** to gleam, shimmer. **2.** to cheer up, make glad;—*intrans.* to be glad, rejoice.
glæd, *adj.* **1.** bright, gleaming, shining, beaming.—**2. glad,** joyful.—**3.** agreeable, pleasant, gracious, friendly, kind, obliging. (Ger. *glatt.*)
glæd, *st. n.* hilarity, joyousness, joy, gladness;—(**glade,** cheer. Halliwell).
glæde, *adv.* gladly, in a friendly, gracious way.
glæd-lic, *adj.* bright, shining, pleasant, agreeable, friendly.
glæd-lice, *adv.* gladly, willingly; in a gracious, pleasant manner.
glæd-môd, *adj.* **1.** glad of mind, joyous, cheerful.—**2.** friendly, kind, courteous, gracious.
glæde-stede. See **glêdstede.**
glæm, *st. m.* gleam, brightness, splendor, beauty.
glæs, *st. n.* glass. (Ger. *glas.*)
glæs-hluttor, glas-hluþor, *adj.* clear as glass, transparent.
glêd, *st. f.* heat, coals, fire, flame. (Ger. *gluth.*)
glêdan, *w. v.*
    ge-glêdan, to make hot, kindle, light up.
    þurh-glêdan, to heat through.
glêd-egesa, *w. m.* terror on account of fire, fire-terror.
glêd-stede, -styde, *st. m.* place for fire, hearth, altar.
glendran, *w. v.*
    for-glendran, to devour greedily, swallow up.
gleng, *st. f.* ornament, honor.
glengan, *w. v.* to adorn, decorate.
    ge-glengan, the same as above.
glêam, *st. n.* joy, jubilation, loud rejoicing.
glêaw, *adj.* **1.** penetrating, acute, sly, skilled, sagacious, wise: knowing, having knowledge of any-

thing.—2. good.—3. cowardly,neglectful, economical, considerate, avaricious. (Ger. *glau.*)
glêawe, *adv.* wisely, considerately, prudently, carefully; — exactly, well.
glêaw-ferhđ, *adj.* prudent, good in disposition or mind, sagacious.
glêaw-hycgende, *part.* thoughtful, prudent, wise.
glêaw-hŷdig, *adj.* same as above.
glêaw-lice, *adv.* prudently, wisely, diligently, carefully, well.
glêaw-môd, *adj.* of a wise mind, sagacious, good.
glêaw-nes, *st. f.* wisdom, prudence.
glêo. See **gleow**.
glêo-bêam, *st. m.* tree of music, wood for giving joy, harp.
glêo-drêam, *st. m.* joyous diversion, social gayety, mirth.
glêo-man, *st. m.* glee-man, singer, musician, harper, player, jester.
gleomu, glimu, *st. f.* splendor, adornment.
gleow, glêo, glio, glig, *st. n.* social entertainment, joyful diversion, joy, music, play, jest, song, glee.
gleow-stôl, *st. m.* seat of joy.
glêo-, glio-word, *st. n.* word of joy, song, poem.
glida, *w. m.* glede, kite.
glidan, *st. abl. v.* V. **1.** to glide.— **2.** to glide away, vanish. (Ger. *gleiten.*)
  be-glidan (bi-), to glide away, vanish, leave.
  ge-glidan, to glide, fall.
  ôđ-glidan, to glide away, escape.
  tô-glidan, to glide apart or asunder, fall asunder, separate, vanish.
glig. See **gleow**.
glimu. See **gleomu**.
glisnian, glissian, *w. v.* to **glisten**, shine, glitter, gleam.

glitinian, *w. v.* to glisten, glitter, light, gleam.
gliw. See **gleow**.
gliwian, *w. v.* to make joyful? to adorn? Rä. 27, 13.
gliw-stæf, *st. m.* sign of joy, melody.
glio. See **glêo**.
glof, *st. n.* cliff, rock.
glôf, *st. f.* glove.
glôm, *st. m.?* (gloom, glum), twilight, morning or evening splendor. Sch. 71. Cf. **gloaming**.
gnæt, *st. m.* gnat, midge.
gnêađ, *adj.* niggardly, sparing, stingy.
gnorn, *adj.* sad, gloomy, mournful, depressed.
gnorn, *st. m.* sorrow, sadness.
gnornian, *w. v.* to be sad or sorrowful, to complain, to have sorrow.
  be-gnornian, to bemoan, mourn for.
gnorn-cearig, *adj.* sad, troubled.
gnorn-hof, *st. n.* dwelling of sorrow, prison, cell.
gnorn-scendende, *part.* hastening away in sadness.
gnorn-sorg, *st. f.* sadness, tribulation, anxiety, sorrow.
gnornung, *st. f.* sadness, sorrow, complaining, mourning.
gnorn-word, *st. n.* word of sorrow, wailing, lamentation.
gnyrn, *st. f.* **1.** sadness, mourning, calamity.— **2.** wrong, insult, fault.
gnŷde. See **gnêađ**.
god, *st. m.* God, deity, divinity. (Ger. *Gott.*)
gôd, *adj.* good, fit, liberal. (Ger. *gut.*)
gôd, *st. n.* **1.** good, good thing, good deed, the good. — **2.** goodness shown, benefit, favor, kindness, gift, present, liberality.— **3.** good, blessing, welfare, goodness, ability.
goda, *w. m.* God, deity.
god-bearn, *st. n.* God's Son, Christ.

god-cund, *adj.* coming from God, divine.

gôd-dǣd, *st. f.* 1. good deed, good work.— 2. benefit.

gôd-dônd, -dôend, *part. & subs.* 1. one that does good.—2. benefactor.

god-drēam, *st. m.* joys of heaven.

gode-gyld, *st. n.* idol.

gode-web. See **godweb**.

god-fæder, *st. m.* God the Father.

god-ferht, -fyrht, *adj.* God-fearing.

gôd-fremmend, *part. & subs.* one that does good.

god-gim, *st. n.* divine gem, heavenly jewel.

gôdian, *w. v.* to become good, make good, better.
    ge-gôdian, to assist, enrich.

gôd-lic, *adj.* goodly, good.

gôd-nes, *st. f.* goodness, compassion.

god-sǣd, *st. n.* God's seed, piety.

god-scyld, *st. f.* sin committed against God.

god-scyldig, *adj.* criminal, guilty.

gôd-spêdig, *adj.* rich in blessings, rich, happy.

god-spel, *st. n.* the story of God, gospel.

god-þrym, *st. m.* divine majesty or glory.

god-web, gode-web, *st. n.* divine, very costly texture, purple cloth, silk, tapestry.

gold, *st. n.* gold. (Ger. *gold*.)

gold-ǣht, *st. f.* possessions in gold, treasure.

gold-beorht, *adj.* bright with gold.

gold-burg, *st. f.* castle adorned, decorated with gold.

gold-fæt, *st. n.* golden vessel.

gold-fæt (-fatu?), *st. f.* golden bracelet. Ph. 303.

gold-fâh, *adj.* variegated with gold, shining with gold.

gold-frætwe, *st. f. pl.* golden ornaments.

gold-gifa, -gyfa, -giefa, *w. m.* gold-giver, prince, lord.

gold-hama, *w. m.* garment ornamented with gold, coat-of-mail.

gold-hilted, *adj.* gold-hilted, having a golden hilt.

gold-hladen, *part.* gold-laden, adorned with gold.

gold-hord, *st. n.* treasure of gold, treasure.

gold-hroden, *part.* covered with gold, adorned with gold.

gold-hwæt, *adj.* rich in gold (Grein); greedy for gold, striving after gold (B.-T.).

gold-mâđm, *st. m.* treasure of gold, treasure.

gold-sele, *st. m.* gold-hall, hall in which gold is distributed, ruler's hall.

gold-smid, *st. m.* **goldsmith**, worker in gold.

gold-smiđu, *st. f.* art of working in gold.

gold-spêdig, *adj.* rich in gold.

gold-torht, *adj.* shining like gold.

gold-weard, *st. m.* keeper, defender of the gold.

gold-wine, *st. m.* friend who distributes gold, ruler, king, prince.

gold-wlanc, -wlonc, *adj.* elegantly adorned with gold, rich in gold.

gôma, *w. m.* **gums**, palate, jaws. (Ger. *gaum, gaumen*.)

gombon. See **gamban**.

gomel, gomelian, gomen. See **gamol, gamelian, gamen**.

gong, gongan. See **gang, gangan**.

gop, *st. m.* slave, servant. Rä. 50, 3.

gor, *st. n.* dung, dirt, filth.

gôs, *st. f.* goose. (Ger. *gans*.)

grǣd, *st. m.* **greed**, desire, hunger.

grǣdan, *w. v.* to cry, call out.

grǣdig, grêdig, *adj.* **greedy**, voracious, hungry, covetous.

græf, *st. n.* grave. (Ger. *grab*.)

græf-hús, *st. n.* grave-house, grave, place of torment, hall.
græft, *st. m. f. n.* carving, sculpture, a graven image.
grǣg, *adj.* gray. (Ger. *grau.*)
grǣg-hama, *w. m.* gray garment, shirt-of-mail.
grǣg-mǣl, *adj.* marked with gray, having a gray color.
græs, *st. n.* grass.
græs-molde,*w.f.*grass-plot,meadow.
græs-wang, *st. m.* same as above.
grǣtan, grêtan, *st. red. v.* (to greet), weep, lament, bemoan, deplore. (Goth. *gretan, greitan.*)
  be-grêtan, to bemoan, deplore.
gráf, *st. m. n.* grove.
grafan, *st. abl. v.* VI. 1. to dig, dig up.— 2. to grave, carve, chisel, engrave. (Ger. *graben.*)
  á-grafan, to cut, engrave.
  be-, bi-grafan, to bury, inter.
gram, grom, *adj.* hostile, enraged, furious, fierce, dire, cruel, wild, terrible. (Ger. *gram.*)
grame, grome, *adv.* hostilely, inimically, fiercely, terribly, cruelly.
gram-heort, *adj.* evil-minded, of a hostile heart.
gram-hycgende, *part.* evil-minded, having a hostile purpose.
gram-hýdig, *adj.* same as above.
gram-hygdig, -hegdig, *adj.* same as above.
gram-lic, *adj.* hostile, fierce, cruel.
gram-lice, *adv.* hostilely, fiercely, cruelly.
gram-word, *st. n.* hostile or evil word (speech).
grandor-léas, grondor-léas, *adj.* faultless.
gránian, *w. v.* to lament, murmur, complain.
gráp, *st. f.* the hand ready to grasp, hand, claw, clutch.
grápian, *w. v.* to seize, lay hold of, grasp, grope.

ge-grápian, to feel with the hands, touch.
grêdig. See grǣdig.
gregg, *adj.* gray.
gremian, gremman, *w. v.*
  ge-gremian, to exasperate, embitter, enrage.
grêne, *adj.* green. (Ger. *grün.*)
grênian, *w. v.* to become green. (Ger. *grünen.*)
grennian, *w. v.* to grin, show the teeth. (Ger. *greinen.*)
grêtan. See grǣtan.
grêtan, *w. v.* 1. to greet, salute, address, accost, call upon, take leave of.— 2. to approach, come near, seek out, touch, take hold of, assail, go in, visit. (Ger. *grüszen.*)
  ge-grêtan, the same as above.
great, *adj.* great, immense, grand. (Ger. *gross.*)
grêosan, *st. abl. v.* VI.
  be-grêosan, to be seized with fright. Sat. 52.
grêot, *st. m.* grit, sand, earth, dust. (Ger. *gries.*)
grêotan, *st. abl. v.* VI. to cry, weep, lament, mourn.
grêot-hord, *st. n.* earth-treasure, *i. e.* human body, because it is buried in the earth.
grim, *adj.* grim, fierce, wild, furious, enraged, angry, hostile, severe, cruel, savage, horrible. (Ger. *grimm.*)
grima, grimma, *w. m.* mask, visor, ghost, helmet.
grimetan, grymetan, -ian, *w. v.* to give forth a sound of rage, to rage, gnash with the teeth, roar, grunt.
grim-helm, *st. m.* mask-helm, helmet with visor.
grim-lic, *adj.* grim, terrible.
grim-lice, *adv.* grimly, terribly, harshly, cruelly.
grimman, *st. abl. v.* I. 1. to snort, roar, rage.— 2. to go forward hastily, to hasten. B. 306.

grimme, grymme, *adv.* grimly, fiercely, cruelly, in a hostile manner, sharply, bitterly, sternly.

grim-nes, -nys, *st. f.* grimness, ferocity, cruelty.

grin, gryn, *st. f.* noose, snare, trap, gin.

grindan, *st. abl. v.* I. to grind, rub together, strike, clash, collide.
    be-grindan, 1. to grind off, polish, sharpen.—**2.** to deprive of, rob.
    for-grindan, to grind up, grind to pieces, destroy, ruin.— **2.** to destroy, kill? or to stop, put a stop to a person's proceedings. B. 424.
    ge-grindan, to grind off, sharpen; *part.* **gegrunden.** Ruin. 14?

grindel, *st. m.* bar, bolt, clog.

gring, *st. f. n.?* slaughter, downfall.

gringan, *st. abl. v.* I. to fall, sink down, perish.

gring-wracu, *st. f.* death-torment.

gripan, *st. abl. v.* V. to gripe, seize, lay hold of, grasp. (Ger. *greifen*.)
    for-gripan, 1. to lay hold of, apprehend, grasp, snatch away.— **2.** to lay hands on violently, do violence to, kill by the gripe.
    ge-gripan, to gripe, seize, grasp, lay hold of.
    wið-gripan, *w. dat.* to strike against (Grein);— to seize at, oppose a thing, restrain it (Groschopp);— to maintain, hold erect (H. & S.). B. 2522.

gripe, *st. m.* gripe, attack, hold, grasp, seizure, clutch;— **gūðbilla gripe,** shield. Wald. 2, 13.

gripu, *st. f.* kettle, vessel (Leo) Sal. 46.

grist-bitung, *st. f.* gnashing of teeth.

grið, *st. n.* peace.

grom, grondor. See **gram, grandor.**

grorn, *st. m.?* sorrow, sadness, mourning. (*ms.* **grom.** Reim. 66.)

grorne, *adv.* sorrowfully, miserably, sadly.

grorn-hof, *st. n.* house of sorrow, hell.

grornian, *w. v.* to mourn.
    be-grornian, to mourn for, bemoan.

grorn-torn? *st. m.?* sadness, mourning? Reim. 66.

grōwan, *st. red. v.* to grow, sprout, bud, become green, spring up.
    for-grōwan, in the expression **in forgrōwan,** to grow into something. Reim. 46.

grund, *st. m.* (literally, the thing ground, from **grindan**), **1.** ground, bottom, the lowest part of a body, the bottom or foundation of anything.— **2.** ground, earth, plain, fields, land.— **3.** depth, abyss, hell, sea, ocean. (Ger. *grund*.)

grund-bedd, *st. n.* ground, soil.

grund-būend, *part. & subs.* earth-dweller.

grund-fūs, *adj.* inclined to the abyss, to the lower world.

grund-hirde, -hyrde, *st. m. f.* keeper or defender of the bottom of the sea. B. 2136.

grund-lēas, *adj.* **1.** groundless, bottomless, very deep.— **2.** homeless, banished, exiled.

grund-scēat, *st. m.* lap of the earth, earth.

grund-sele, *st. m.* hall at the bottom of the sea.

grund-wæg, *st. m.* foundation-wall, earth.

grund-wang, *st. m.* ground surface, lowest surface, bottom.

grund-wela, *w. m.* possession of the ground (earth).

grund-weall, *st. m.* foundation-wall, ground-wall.

grund-wyrgen, *st. f.* she-wolf of the bottom of the moor, Grendel's mother. B. 1518.

gryn, grymetan, grymme, gryn. See **grim, grimetan, grimme, grin.**

gryn, *st. f.* sorrow, care, evil (Grein); net, noose, snare (H. & S.).

gryndan, *w. v.* to be deep, or to be in the deep? Dan. 324. (Ger. *gründen.*)
 â-gryndan, to come to the ground, to descend.

grynde, *st. n.* abyss. (Cf. Goth. *afgrundipa;* Ger. *abgrund.*)

gryn-smid, *st. m.* originator of evil, pain, or sorrow; plotter of mischief.

gryre, *st. m.* dread, terror, horror, fright; what is horrible or terrible.

gryre-brôga, *w. m.* terror and horror, amazement.

gryre-fæst, *adj.* terribly firm, strongly fixed.

gryre-fâh, *adj.* horribly gleaming? terribly hostile.

gryre-gæst, *st. m.* terror-bringing stranger, terror-guest.

gryre-geatwe, *st. f. pl.* equipments against the terror of battle, warlike equipments.

gryre-hwîl, *st. f.* time of terror.

gryre-leôd, *st. n.* terror-song, fearful song.

gryre-lic, *adj.* terrible, horrible.

gryre-sid, *st. m.* way of terror, terrible journey.

gu-dǽd. See **iudǽd.**

guma, *w. m.* (bride-groom), man, human being. (Goth. *guma;* Lat. *homo.*)

gum-cyn, *st. n.* human race, people; a people, nation.

gum-cyst, *st. f.* man's excellence, man's virtue, bravery, piety, liberality, &c.

gum-drêam, *st. m.* joyous doings of men.

gum-dryhten, *st. m.* lord of men.

gum-fêda, *w. m.* troop of men going on foot.

gum-frêa, *w. m.* lord of men, king.

gum-man, *st. m.* man, human being.

gum-rîce, *st. n.* kingdom of men, kingdom, earth.

gum-rinc, *st. m.* man, warrior.

gum-stôl, *st. m.* seat of man, castle (Grein); — throne (B.-T.).

gum-þegen, *st. m.* man.

gum-þeod, *st. f.* a folk, people.

gûd, *st. f.* war, battle, combat, conflict.

gûd-beorn, *st. m.* hero of the fight, warrior.

gûd-bill, *st. n.* battle-sword.

gûd-bord, *st. n.* war-shield.

gûd-byrne, *w. f.* coat-of-mail, battle-corselet.

gûd-cearu, *st. f.* care or sorrow which battle brings.

gûd-cræft, *st. m.* strength in battle, warlike strength.

gûd-cwên, *st. f.* battle-queen.

gûd-cyning, *st. m.* king in battle, king directing the battle.

gûd-cyst, *st. f.* battle-host? chosen warriors? bravery? Exod. 343.

gûd-dêad, *st. m.* death in battle.

gûd-fana, *w. m.* battle-flag, military standard.

gûd-flâ, *w. f.* battle-arrow.

gûd-floga, *w. m.* flying fighter, dragon.

gûd-frec, *adj.* bold, ready for battle, warlike.

gûd-fremmend, *part. & subs.* warrior, fighter.

gûd-frêa, *w. m.* lord of the battle, prince, chieftain.

gûd-fruma, *w. m.* a warlike chief.

gûd-fugol, *st. m.* warlike bird, eagle.

gûd-gelâca, -gelǽca, *w. m.* comrade in war, warrior.

gûd-gemôt, *st. n.* meeting in battle, battle. [ments.

gûd-getawa, *st. f. pl.* battle equip-

gûd-geþingu, *st. n. pl.* imminent or expected battle (Grein); — the lot to be expected from impending war (B.-T.).

gûd-gewǽde, *st. n.* war-dress, armor.
gûd-geweorc, *st. n.* battle-work, warlike deed.
gûd-gewinn, *st. n.* contest of battle, battle.
gûd-geatwe, *st. f. pl.* war-equipments, weapons.
gûd-hafoc, *st. m.* war-hawk, eagle.
gûd-helm, *st. m.* battle-helmet.
gûd-here, *st. m.* warlike host, army.
gûd-heard, *adj.* bold, excellent in battle.
gûd-horn, *st. n.* battle-horn, trumpet.
gûd-hrêd, *st. m.* battle-fame, warlike glory.
gûd-hring? *st. m.* noise, wail? B. 1118. (*ms.* -rinc. See gudrinc.)
gûd-hwæt, *adj.* quick, fierce in battle.
gûd-lêod, *st. n.* war-song.
gûd-mæcga, *w. m.* warrior.
gûd-maga, *w. m.* warrior.
gûd-môd, *adj.* courageous in battle, disposed to battle.
Gûd-myrce, *st. pl.* the blacks accustomed to battle, warlike Ethiopians.
gûd-plega, *w. m.* war-play, battle.
gûd-rǽs, *st. m.* rush, onset of battle, attack, battle.
gûd-rêaf, *st. n.* battle-dress, arms.
gûd-rêow, *adj.* fierce in battle.
gûd-rinc, *st. m.* fighter, warrior, hero.
gûd-rôf, *adj.* bold, skillful in battle, renowned.
gûd-scear, *st. m.* slaughter in battle, defeat.
gûd-sceada, *w. m.* he who injures through battle, foe.
gûd-sceorp, *st. n.* warlike ornament or clothing.
gûd-scrûd, *st. n.* battle-dress.
gûd-sele, *st. m.* battle-hall, *i. e.* the hall in which a battle takes place.
gûd-searo, *st. n.* battle-equipment, arms, armor.
gûd-spell, *st. n.* report of the battle, tidings from the war.
gûd-swecrd, *st. n.* battle-sword.

gûd-þracu, *st. f.* warlike force, power, hostile attack.
gûd-þrêat, *st. m.* war-band, warlike host.
gûd-wêrig, *adj.* wearied by battle, death-weary.
gûd-weard, *st. m.* keeper of the battle, leader.
gûd-weorc, *st. n.* warlike work or deed.
gûd-wiga, *w. m.* warrior, fighter of battles.
gûd-wine, *st. m.* battle-friend, comrade in battle.
gûd-wudu, *st. m.* battle-wood, spear.
gyd, gyddian. See gid, giddian.
gyden, *st. f.* goddess. (Ger. *göttinn*.)
gyf, gyfa, gyfan, gyfen, gyfede, gyfl, gyft, gyfu. See gif, gifa, gifan, geofon or gifen, gifede, gifl, gift, gifu.
gŷlan, *w. v.* to exult, shout, yell.
gyld, gyldan. See gild, gildan.
gylden, *adj.* golden.
gyllan, gylp, gylpan. See gellan, gilp, gilpan.
gylt, gelt, gielt, *st. m.* guilt, trespass, sin, wrong.
gyltan, giltan, *w. v.*
  â-gyltan, to commit a sin, do wrong.
gŷman, gêman, giman, gieman, *w. v.* to bear sorrow for, to sorrow, care for, to be careful about, observe, watch, keep.
  for-gŷman, to neglect, slight, not to care for.
  ofer-gŷman, the same as above.
gym-cyn. See gim-cyn.
gŷme-lêas, *adj.* careless, negligent, heedless, improvident.
gŷmen, gêmen, *st. f.* care, solicitude.
gyn (gynn), gyman. See gin, ginnan.
gyrd, gierd, *st. f.* rod, twig. (Ger. *gerte*.)

gyrdan, *w. v.* to **gird,** lace, encircle, surround. (Ger. *gürten.*)
    be-gyrdan, to encircle, gird, strengthen.
    embe-gyrdan, same as above.
    ge-gyrdan, the same as above.
gyrdels, *st. m.* girdle, belt, zone. (Ger. *gürtel.*)
gyrd-wite, *st. n.* punishment brought upon the Egyptians by the rod of Moses, afflictions.
gyren, *st. f.* noose, snare, gin.
gyrn, *st. m. n.* sorrow, mourning, sadness, ill, trouble, disquiet, unhappiness, injury, calamity.

gyrnan, *w. v.* to **yearn,** desire, demand, long for.
    ge-gyrnan, the same as above.
gyrn-stæf, *st. m.* injury, affliction.
gyrn-wracu, *st. f.* revenge for harm or for trouble.
gyrwan, gŷsel, gyst, gystra, gyt, gyta, gytan. See **gerwan, gisel, gæst, geostra, git, gita, gitan.**
gyte, *st. m.* outstreaming flood. (Ger. *guss.*)
gyte-sæl, *st. m.* joy produced by wine.
gŷtsian. See **gitsian.**

H

habban, *w. v., pres. ind. sg.* **1. hæbbe, hafa, hafo, hafu.** — **2. hæfst, hafast, hafest.** — **3. hafað, hæfeð, hæfð;** — *pl.* **habbað, hæbbað;** — *subj. sg.* **hæbbe, hæbben;** — *imper.* **hafa, habbað;** — *pret.* **hæfde;** — *part.* **hæfed.** — **1.** to have, possess, occupy, comprehend, hold, keep, hold together, assert, maintain. — **2.** *auxiliary vb.* have. (Ger. *haben.*)
    be-habban, 1. to surround, encompass, inclose. — **2.** to seize hold of, apprehend, understand.
    for-habban, to hold, hold together, hold back, restrain, avoid; to keep one's self, restrain one's self, contain, refrain, abstain from.
    ge-habban, *intrans.* to hold, keep firm ground, resist.
    on-habban, to abstain from, hold one's self far from.
    wið-habban, *w. dat.* to resist, offer resistance, hold out against one.
    wiðer-habban, to remain, be.

hâd, *st. m.* **1.** person. — **2.** sex. — **3.** age, degree, rank, order, condition, dignity; especially ecclesiastical degree, rank, or order. — **4.** race, family, tribe, kind. — **5.** general designation for beings of one genus or species. — **6.** choir; — **on hâde,** in the choir. — **7.** shape, form, appearance, nature, kind. — **8.** manner. Wald. 2, 21., perhaps to be changed into **hand.** (Ger. *-heit.*)
hador. See **heador.**
hâdor, *adj.* bright, clear, fresh, loud, brilliant. (Ger. *heiter.*)
hâdre, *adv.* clearly, brightly, loudly.
hæbbað, hæbbe, hæbben, hæbbende, hædre (*adj.*). See **habban** and **hebban, hâdor.**   [iously.
hædre, *adv.* straitly, narrowly, anxhædre, *adv.* brightly, clearly, loudly, serenely.
hæf, heaf, *st. n.* sea. (Icel. *haf;* Dan. *hav.*)
hæfde, hæfed, hæfeð, hæfst, hæfen. See **habban, hebban.**
hæft, *st. n.* haft, handle.

hæft, *st. m.* 1. prisoner, captive.— 2. slave, servant.

hæft, *st. m.* 1. fetter, bond.— 2. captivity, bondage, imprisonment.— 3. pressure, distress, affliction. (Ger. *haft*.)

hæftan, heftan, *w. v.* to make captive, bind, fetter. (Ger. *heften*.)
   ge-hæftan, to fetter, bind, take prisoner.

hæfte-clom, *st. m.* fetter.

hæfte-dôm, *st. m.* servitude, slavery.

hæfte-nêod, *st. f.* desire of vexing or of binding (Grein); — custody, prison? (B.-T.).

hæft-ling, *st. m.* captive. See **helle-hæftling**.

hæft-mêce, *st. m.* sword with a handle or hilt.

hæftnan, -ian, *w. v.* to capture, seize, take prisoner.
   ge-hæftnan, to fetter, bind.

hæft-nêd, -nŷd, *st. f.* necessity of captivity, thraldom, oppression.

hæfd. See **habban**.

hægan, *w. v.*
   ge-hægan, to fight, vex, disturb (Grein):— to surround as with a hedge (B.-T.).

hægel, hægl, *st. m.* **hail**;—name for the Rune **h**.

hæge-steald. See **hagusteald**.

hægl-faru, *st. f.* hailstorm. [storm.

hægl-scûr, *st. m.* **hail-shower**, hail-

hæl, *st. n.* favorable omen, token of favorable omen. (O. H. Ger. *heil*.)

hæl, *st. f.* health, happiness, welfare, luck. (O. H. Ger. *heili*.)

hæl, *adj.* whole, full, complete.

hæla. See **hêla**.

hælan, hêlan, *w. v.* to **heal**, make whole, cure. (Ger. *heilen*.)
   ge-hælan, the same as above.

hæle, *st. m.* man.

hæle, *w. f.* health, welfare, safety.

hælend, hêland, hælynd, *part. & subs.* healer, Savior. (Ger. *heiland*.)

hæled, heled, *st. m.* **hero**, warrior, man, human being. (Ger. *held*.)

hæled-helm, *st. m.* a helmet rendering the wearer invisible. Gen. 444.

hæls-man (hêls-), *st. m.* enchanter? B. 3056 (Grein). (*ms.* he is manna.)

hælu, hælo, hêlo, *st. f.* health, healing, safety, welfare, luck.

hælu-bearn, *st. n.* child of healing, Christ.

hæman, *w. v.* to live with, go in unto, to be guilty of or commit sodomy.

hæmed, *st. n.* sexual intercourse.

hæmed-lâc, *st. n.* sexual intercourse.

hæn, hen, *st. f.* **hen**. (Ger. *henne*.)

hændu. See **hŷndu**.

hær, hêr, *st. n.* **hair**. (Ger. *haar*.)

hær-fest, *st. m.* **harvest**, time of harvest, autumn. (Ger. *herbst*.)

hær-lic, hærian. See **hêrlic, hêrian**.

hærn, *st. f.* sea, ocean, flood, wave.

hærn-flota, *w. m.* ship.

hæs, *st. f.* behest, command, order, commission.

hæst, hêst, *st. f.* zeal, violence, exertion, fury, contention.

hæste, *adj.* hasty, violent, vehement.

hæst-lice, *adv.* vehemently, hotly, fiercely.

hætan, *w. v.* to **heat**, make hot. (Ger. *heizen*.)
   on-hætan, to heat, set afire, kindle, enflame, make hot.

hætsan, *w. v.* to strike, hurl? throw? Rä. 4, 5.

hætte, hæted. See **hâtan**.

hættian, *w. v.* to sculp.

hætu, hæto, *st. f.* **heat**, warmth. (Ger. *hitze*.)

hæd, *st. f.* **heath**, hedge, waste, untilled land. (Ger. *heide*.)

hæden, *adj. & subs.* **heathen**, pagan, gentile, heathenish.

hæden-cyning, *st. m.* heathen king.

hæden-cynn, *st. n.* heathen race.

hæden-dôm, *st. m.* **heathendom**.

hǣden-feoh, *st. n.* heathen sacrifice.
hǣden-gild, -gield, *st. n.* idol, idolatry.
hǣden-styrc, *st. m.* heathen steer, the golden calf.
hǣđ-stapa, *w. m.* that which goes about on the heath, wolf, stag.
hǣwen, *adj.* blue, azure.
hafa, hafast, hafađ, hafo, hafu. See habban.
hafenian, *w. v.* to hold, hold firm, to raise, uplift.
hafoc, hafola. See heafoc, heafola.
haga, *w. m.* (haw), inclosed piece of ground, hedge, farm-inclosure, small farm, court, house.
hagal, hagol, *st. m.* hail. (Ger. *hagel.*)
hagol-scûr, *st. m.* hail-shower.
hagu-, hæg-, hæge-steald, *st. m.* one who lives in another's inclosure, liegeman, servant, vassal; youth, bachelor.
hago-stealdman(hægstealdman)= hagusteald.
hagu-steald, *st. n.* celibacy.
hâl, *adj.* whole, sound, healthy, unhurt, hale. (Ger. *heil.*)
haldan, half. See healdan, healf.
hâlgian, *w. v.* to hallow, sanctify, make holy, consecrate. (Ger. *heiligen.*)
   ge-hâlgian, 1. to consecrate.— 2. to sanctify, keep holy.
hâlig, *adj.* holy. (Ger. *heilig.*)
hâlig-mônđ, *st. m.* holy month, September. Men. 164.
hâlig-nes, *st. f.* 1. holiness.— 2. sacred thing, sanctuary.
hâlor, *st. m.? n.?* safety, salvation.
hals. See heals.
hâls, heâls, *st. f.* health, safety, salvation.
hâlsian, heâlsian, *w. v.* to entreat earnestly, beseech, implore, conjure, exorcise.
halsre. See healsre.
hâlsung, *st. f.* entreaty, request.

hâls-wurđung, -weorđung, *st. f.* praise and thanksgiving for a blessing received.
hâl-wende, *adj.* healthy, salutary.
ham, hom, *st. m.* dress, garment.
hâm, *st. m.* home, dwelling-place;— *acc.=adv.* home, homeward. (Ger. *heim.*)
hama, homa, *w. m.* dress, garment.
hamelian, *w. v.* to hamble, hamstring, mutilate.
hâm-fæst, *adj.* resident, permanently at home.
hâm-lêas, *adj.* homeless.
hamor, homer, *st. m.* hammer. (Ger. *hammer.*)
hâm-sittende, *part. & subs.* sitting at home, home-dwellers.
hâm-weorđung, *st. f.* honor or ornament of the home, or of the house.
hana, *w. m.* cock. (Ger. *hahn.*)
han-crêd, *st. m.* cock-crow, crowing of the cock.
hand, hond, *st. f.* hand. (Ger. *hand.*)
hand-bana, *w. m.* hand-killer, murderer with the hand.
hand-gemôt, *st. n.* hand-to-hand conflict, battle.
hand-gesceaft, *st. f.* a creature formed or fashioned by the hand, Adam.
hand-gesella, *w. m.* hand-companion, a comrade close by one.
hand-, heand-gestealla, *w. m.* same as above.
hand-geswing, *st. n.* swing of the hand, battle.
hand-geweald, *st. f. n.* power of the hand, power.
hand-geweorc, *st. n.* handiwork, work or deed of the hands.
hand-gewinn, *st. n.* fight, labor, pains, contest.
hand-gewriđen, *part.* wreathed or woven with the hands, hand-wreathed, hand-twisted.
hand-gift, *st. f. n.* bridal gift.

hand-hrine, *st. n.* hand-touch, touch with the hand.
hand-lean, *st. n.* reward through the hand, recompense, retribution.
hand-locen, *part.* joined, united by the hand. [hand.
hand-mægen, *st. n.* strength of the hand-plega, *w. m.* hand-play, contest with the hands, fighting, encounter.
hand-ræs, *st. m.* rush of battle, onset.
hand-rôf, *adj.* strong with the hand, renowned for strength.
hand-scâlu, -scôlu, *st. f.* hand-attendance, retinue.
hand-scio, *st. m.* an attack made with the hands; or a proper name. B. 2076 (Grein); — a glove (B.-T.).
hand-slyht, *st. m.* stroke or blow with the hand.
hand-spor, *st. n.* hand-spur, claw.
hand-þegen, *st. m.* immediate attendant, servant.
hand-weorc, *st. n.* handwork, work or deed of the hands.
hand-wundor, *st. n.* wonder done by the hand, wonderful handwork.
hand-wyrm, *st. m.* handworm, a kind of worm attending the itch.
hangen. See hôn.
hangelle, *w. f.* pendulum.
hangian, hongian, *w. v.* to hang, be suspended.
hâr, heâr, *adj.* hoar, gray, old.
hâr. See hær.
hard. See heard.
hâs, *adj.* hoarse. (Ger. *heiser*.)
hasu, heasu, *adj.* gray, ashen, tawny.
hasu-fâg, *adj.* ash-colored, grayish.
hasu-pâd, *adj.* having gray feathers, gray-coated.
haswig-federe, *adj.* same as above.
hât, *adj.* 1. hot, burning, glowing, flaming, fervent, fervid, fierce.— 2. warm, dear. (Ger. *heiss*.)
hât, *st. n.* heat, fire.

hâta, *w. m.* commander, orderer, ruler, summoner. [Used only in compounds.]
hâtan, *st. red. v. pret.* heht, hêt.
1. to order, bid, command, direct.
2. to promise, vow. Jul. 53.— 3. to call, name, give a name to. (Ger. *heissen*.)
 be-hâtan, to promise, vow, threaten.
 for-hâtan, to despise, hate;— *part.* weak form forhâtena, the arch-fiend, devil.
 ge-hâtan, 1. to promise, give one's word, vow.— 2. to order, bid; to call near.— 3. to call, be called.
 on-hâtan, to promise, vow.
hâtan, *w. v.* to be named or called. (Ger. *heissen*.)
hâte, *adv.* hotly, fervidly, warmly.
hât-heort, *adj.* hot-hearted, wroth, furious, ardent.
hât-heortnes, *st. f.* wrath, anger, fury, zeal.
hât-hige, *st. m.* hot-headed thought, fury, rage.
hatian, *w. v.* to hate, be an enemy to, hurt. (Ger. *hassen*.)
hât-wende, *adj.* hot, burning.
hâwe, *adj.* in appearance. [Used only in compounds.]
hê, *m.*, heô, *f.*, hit, *n.; pers. pron.* he, she, it; in oblique cases reflexive;—*sg. nom. m.* hê; *f.* heô, hio, hie, hi; *n.* hit, hyt; *gen. m.* his, hys; *f.* hire, hyre, hiere; *n.* his; *dat. m.* him, hym; *f.* hire, hyre; *n.* him; *acc. m.* hine, hyne, hiene; *f.* hi, hŷ, hie, heô; *n.* hit, hyt; *pl. nom. acc. m. f. n.* hi, hŷ, hie, heô, hio, hig; *gen. m. f. n.* hyra, heora, hiora, hiera; *dat. m. f. n.* him, hym, heom, hiom.
hebban, hæbban, *st. abl. v.* IV. to heave, lift up, raise, erect exalt. (Ger. *heben*.)

á-hebban, to raise, lift from, take away, elevate, exalt, erect, lift up.
 in-hebban, to lift away from, lift up and away.
 on-hebban, to erect, lift up.
hédan, *w. v.* to heed, guard, protect; to get possession of, obtain. See also hýdan. (Ger. *hüten*.)
 ge-hédan, to get possession of, give, acquire, win.
hefe, hefed. See hebban.
hefgan. See hefigian.
hefig, *adj.* heavy, weighty, troublesome.
hefig, *adv.* heavily, weightily.
hefigian, hefigan, hefgan, *w. v.* 1. to molest, afflict.— 2. to become heavy, depressed, weakened.
 ge-hefigian, to burden, oppress, vex, afflict, disquiet, molest.
hefig-nes, *st. f.* heaviness, burden, slowness.
hefon, heftan. See heofon, hæftan.
hég. See hig.
hégan, *w. v.* to hedge. (Ger. *hegen*.)
 ge-hégan, to foster, cherish, entertain, practise, do, effect, perfect, carry out.
hégan, *w. v.* to exalt, celebrate? Dan. 207.
hegdig. See hygdig.
héh, heht, héhd, héhdu. See héah, hyht, hátan, héahdu.
hel, hell, helle, hyll, *st. f.* hell. (Ger. *hölle*.)
héla, hǽla, *w. m.* heel.
helan, *st. abl. v.* II. to conceal, hide, cover. (Ger. *hehlen*.)
 .be-, bi-helan, to cover.
 for-helan, to hide, cover, conceal.
hélan. See hǽlan.
hell-bend, *st. m. f.* bond or chain of hell.
hell-cræft, *st. m.* hellish strength or power, hellish art.

hel-cwalu, *st. f.* pains of hell, torment.
held. See hyld.
heldan (= healdan?), cf. hyldan.
 be-heldan, to give heed to, observe.
hel-dor, *st. n.* gate of hell.
hélend, heled. See hǽlend, hǽled.
hel-firen, *st. f.* crime of hell.
hel-fús, *adj.* hellward inclined, bound for hell.
hel-geþwing, *st. n.* restraint of hell.
hel-héodo, *st. f.* hall or vault of hell, hell.
helian, *w. v.*
 be-, bi-helian, to cover, bury.
hell, hell-, helle. See hel and hel-.
helle-bealu, *st. n.* evil, sorrow of hell.
helle-bryne, *st. m.* brand of hell, hell-fire.
helle-ceafl, *st. m.* jaws of hell, gulf of hell.
helle-clam, *st. m.* chain or bond of hell.
helle-cynn, -cinn, *st. n.* hellish race.
helle-déoful, *st. m. n.* devil of hell, devil.
helle-dor, *st. n.* gate of hell.
helle-duru, *st. f.* same as above.
helle-flór, *st. m.* floor of hell, courts of hell.
helle-fýr, *st. n.* hell-fire.
helle-gást, -gǽst, *st. m.* spirit of hell.
helle-grund, *st. m.* abyss, gulf of hell.
helle-gryre (hylle-), *st. m.* hellish horror.
helle-hæft, *st. m.* captive or servant of hell.
helle-hæfta, *w. m.* same as above.
helle-hæftling, *st. m.* captive or servant of hell, devil.
helle-héaf, *st. m.* wailings or howlings of hell.

helle-hinca, *w. m.* hell-limper, devil.
helle-hûs, *st. n.* hell-house.
helle-nið, *st. m.* torments of hell.
helle-scealc, *st. m.* servant, slave of hell.
helle-sceaða, *w. m.* hellish enemy, devil.
helle-sêað, *st. m.* hell-pit or pool, hell.
helle-þegen, *st. m.* devil.
helle-wite, *st. m.* torment of hell.
helm, *st. m.* 1. protection, guard, covering affording protection.— 2. helm, helmet.— 3. crown, diadem.— 4. protection, protector, defender, shield (God, Christ, and earthly lord), covering. (Ger. *helm*.)
helman, *w. v.* cf. hylman.
    be-helman, to cover over, cover.
    ofer-helman, to cover over, overshadow.
helm-berend, *part. & subs.* helmet-wearer, warrior.
helmian, *w. v.* to draw over, cover.
    bi-helmian, to cover over, cover.
helo, *st. f.* covering, equipment. B. 2723. (Leo.)
hêlo. See hǽlo.
help, *st. f.* help, succor, aid, support. (Ger. *hülfe*.)
helpan, *st. abl. v.* I. to help, aid, assist, support. (Ger. *helfen*.)
    â-helpan, the same as above.
helpe, *w. f.* help.
helpend, *part. & subs.* helper.
hel-rûna, *w. m.* sorcerer, hellish monster.
hêls-. See hǽlsman.
hel-sceaða, *w. m.* hellish enemy, fiend, devil.
hel-træf, *st. n.* devil's temple. An. 1693.
hel-trega, *w. m.* torment of hell.
hel-waran, *w. m. pl.* inhabitants of hell.

hel-waru, *st. f.* hell's population.
hen, hênan. See hǽn, hŷnan.
hendan, *w. v.*
    ge-hendan, to seize, hold.
hêng. See hôn.
hengest, *st. m.* stallion, horse. (Ger. *hengst*.)
hentan, *w. v.* to follow anything vigorously in order to get it again, to seek after, follow, pursue.
    ge-hentan, to get by hunting after, to seize, lay hold of.
hênd, hêndu. See hŷnd, hŷndu.
hêr, *adv.* 1. here (that is, in this world, in this land).— 2. hither, to this place.— 3. in this year. (Ger. *hier*.)
hêr. See hǽr.
hêr, *adj.* noble, elevated, sacred. (Ger. *hehr*.)
hêra, *w. m.* one who belongs to another, servant, vassal, follower.
hêran. See hêrian and hŷran.
hêr-bûend, *part. & subs.* here (in this world) dwelling, inhabitant of earth.
hêr-cyme, *st. m.* hither-coming, advent.
herd. See heord.
herdan, *w. v.* to harden, make hard. Cf. hyrdan.
herde. See hirde.
here, *st. m.* army, troops, band, host, multitude. (Ger. *heer*.)
hêre, hǽre, *st. f.* dignity, majesty. (O. H. Ger. *hêre*.)
here-blêað, *adj.* timid, cowardly, panic-stricken.
here-broga, *w. m.* terror of the army, fear of war.
here-bŷme, *w. f.* war-trumpet, sackbut.   [let.
here-byrne, *w. f.* coat-of-mail, corseere-combol, *st. n.* army-standard, battle-flag (Grein);— war-signal, battle-cry (B.-T.).

here-cirm, *st. m.* noise of battle, war-cry.
here-cist, -cyst, *st. f.* division of an army, cohort.
here-fèda, *w. m.* a troop on foot, infantry.
here-feld, *st. m.* battlefield, field.
here-flyma, *w. m.* a fleeing warrior, deserter from battle.
here-folc, *st. n.* army-folk, army.
here-fugol, *st. m.* any bird that follows an army, eagle, vulture, raven.
here-geatu, *st. f.* war-equipments.
here-grima, *w. m.* battle-mask, helmet with visor.
here-hlôd, *st. f.* war-host, troop.
here-hûd, *st. f.* booty taken in war, spoil, plunder.
here-lâf, *st. f.* remains of an army.
here-mæcg, *st. m.* warrior, fighter.
here-mægen, *st. n.* a warlike force, multitude, assembly of the people.
here-medel, *st. n.* council, assembly of the people.
here-nes, -nis, -nys, *st. f.* praise.
here-net, *st. n.* war-net, coat-of-mail.
here-nid, *st. m.* battle-enmity, battle.
here-pâd, *st. f.* battle-dress, coat-of-mail, armor.
here-pað, *st. m.* military road, way, road.
here-ræswa, *w. m.* warrior.
here-rêaf, *st. n.* booty, plunder.
here-rinc, *st. m.* warrior, fighter, hero.
here-sceaft, *st. m.* battle-shaft, shaft of a spear, spear.
here-sceorp, *st. n.* warlike ornament.
here-sið, *st. m.* warlike expedition, march.
here-spêd, *st. f.* success in war.
here-stræl, *st. m.* arrow, missile.
here-stræt, *st. f.* public way, military road.
here-swêg, *st. m.* noise or rejoicing of the armed host.
here-syrce, *w. f.* battle-sark, shirt-of-mail.

here-têma, -tŷma, *w. m.* army-leader, general, king, emperor.
here-têam, *st. m.* 1. plunder, spoils of war.—2. warlike expedition, plundering, predatory excursion. An. 1553.
here-toga, *w. m.* duke, leader of an army, general. (Ger. *herzog.*)
here-þrêat, *st. m.* company, cohort, band.
here-wǣd, *st. f.* war-weed, coat-of-mail.
here-wǣpen, *st. n.* war-weapon.
here-wǣsma, *w. m.* fierce strength in war. B. 667.
here-wǣða, *w. m.* warlike hunter.
here-weorc, *st. n.* war-work, battle.
here-wic, *st. n.* camp, encampment.
here-wisa, *w. m.* leader of the army.
here-wôp, *st. m.* weeping or cries of the army.
here-wôsa, *w. m.* army-leader (Grein); one who is fierce in fight, warrior? (B.-T.)
here-wulf, *st. m.* war-wolf; warlike, cruel enemy, warrior.
herga, hergas. See here, hearg.
herge, hergea, hergeas, hergum See here.
hergian, *w. v.* to harry, lay waste, devastate. (Ger. *verheeren.*)
herh-eard. See heargeard. [pise.
herian, herigean, *w. v.* to mock, des-
herian, hergan, hergian, hærian, heran, *w. v.* to praise, give praise to, glorify, commend;—with reference to God, to adore.
â-herian, to praise fully? Hy. 3, 10.
ge-herian, to praise, laud, glorify.
herige, heriges, herigum, herigweard. See here, hearg, heargweard.
her-lic (hær-), *adj.* praiseworthy, glorious, excellent. (Ger. *herrlich.*)
herm, herra. See hearm, hearra.
herstan. See hyrstan.

herwan, hyrwan, hirwan, *w. v.* to neglect, scorn, despise, blaspheme.
ge-hyrwan, the same as above.
hêst, hêt. See **hǽst, hátan.**
hêtan, *w. v.*
and-hêtan, to confess.
hete, *st. m.* hate, enmity, hostility, envy, malice, spite. (Ger. *hass.*)
hete-grim, *adj.* cruel, fierce.
hete-lic, *adj.* hateful, hated. (Ger. *hässlich.*)
hetend. See **hettend.**
hete-nid, *st. m.* enmity full of hate, hostility.
hete-rôf, *adj.* skilled in hating, very hateful.
hete-rûn, *st. f.* a Rune which produces hate. Rä. 34, 7.
hete-sprǽc, *st. f.* malicious speech, hostile talk.
hete-sweng, *st. m.* hostile blow, chastisement.
hete-þanc, *st. m.* hostile thought or design.
hete-þoncol, *adj.* hostilely disposed.
hetlen, *adj.* full of hate, hostile, malignant.
hettend, hetend, *part. & subs.* enemy.
hêa (= **hêo, hie**), *nom. pl.* of **hê.**
hêa, hêa-burg. See **hêah, hêahburg.**
hêa-dûn. See **hêah** and **dûn.**
heador. See **heador.**
hêaf, *st. m.* wailing, mourning, lamentation.
hêafan, *st. red. v.* to weep, mourn, lament, wail.
hêa-fæder. See **hêahfæder.**
heafdian, *w. v.*
be-heafdian, to behead. (Cf. Ger. *enthaupten.*)
heafo. See **hæf.**
heafoc, hafoc, hafuc, *st. m.* hawk. (Ger. *habicht.*)
heafod, heafud, *st. m. n.* head. (Ger. *haupt.*)

heafod-beorh, *st. f.* head-defense, protection for the head.
heafod-beorht, *adj.* with a splendid, shining head.
heafod-gerim, *st. n.* (certain) number of persons.
heafod-gim, *st. m.* gem of the head, eye.
heafod-gold, *st. n.* head-gold, diadem, crown.
heafod-lêas, *adj.* headless.
heafod-mǽg, *st. m.* head kinsman, very near relation.
heafod-maga, *w. m.* same as above.
heafod-swima, *w. m.* swimming of the head, drunkenness.
heafod-sŷn, -sien, *st. f.* sight of the head, eyes.
heafod-weard, *st. m.* head-warder, chief watch or lord.
heafod-wisa, *w. m.* head-leader, chief director.
heafod-wôd, *st. f.* voice of the head.
heafod-wylm, *st. m.* tears.
heafola, hafola, -ela, -ala, *w. m.* head.
hêah, hêa, hêh, *adj.* 1. high, tall, sublime, lofty. — 2. high, lofty, noble, excellent, illustrious, important, weighty, heavy. — 3. high-minded, proud. (Ger. *hoch.*)
hêah, hêa, *adv.* high.
hêah-beorh, *st. m.* a high hill or mountain.
hêah-bliss, *st. f.* exultation, rejoicing.
hêah-boda, *w. m.* archangel.
hêah-, hêa-burh, *st. f.* high city, first city of a country, metropolis.
hêah-câsere, *st. m.* high ruler, highest emperor.
hêah-clif (*pl.* **cleofu**), *st. n.* high cliff, lofty rack.
hêah-cræft, *st. m.* superior art, excellent skill.
hêah-cyning, *st. m.* **high king,** most noble of kings, king of kings.
hêah-, hêh-engel, *st. m.* archangel.

hêah-, hêa-, hêh-fæder, *st. m.* patriarch.
hêah-fæst, *adj.* immutable, unchangeable, fixed.
hêah-flôd, *st. m.* high tide, the deep (of the flood).
hêah-frêa, *w. m.* highest, most noble lord.
hêah-fýr, *st. n.* lofty flame.
hêah-gæst, *st. m.* Holy Ghost.
hêah-gesceaft, *st. f.* high creature.
hêah-gesceap, *st. n.* destiny fixed by the Highest; fate, destiny.
hêah-gestrêon, *st. n.* excellent, splendid treasure, rich jewels.
hêah-getimbrad, *part.-adj.* nobly, magnificently built.
hêah-getimbru, *st. n. pl.* lofty edifice, grand building.
hêah-geþring, *st. n.* force or press of the lofty waves, flood, breakers.
hêah-geweorc, *st. n.* noble, excellent work.
hêah-gealdor, *st. n.* incantation, magic word.
hêah-gnornung, *st. f.* great sighing or groaning.
hêah-god, *st. m.* the high God, Most High.
hêah-heort, *adj.* high-minded, proud.
hêah-hlid, -hleod, -hliod, *st. n.* high, lofty hill.
hêah-land, *st. n.* high land, mountainous country.
hêah-lic. See hêalic.
hêah-lufe, *w. f.* high love, great love.
hêah-mægen, *st. n.* high strength, power, virtue.
hêah-miht, *st. f.* supreme power.
hêah-môd, *adj.* 1. of high spirits, joyous, courageous, lofty-minded. 2. high-minded, proud.
hêah-nama, *w. m.* most excellent name.
hêah-, hêa-nes, -nis, hêan-nes, *st. f.* hight, highest point, sublimity, excellence.

hêah-ræced, *st. n.* high house, temple.
hêah-rodor, *st. m.* lofty sky, high firmament.
hêah-sæ, *st. f.* high sea, deep sea.
hêah-sæl. *st. f.* favorable opportunity, good fortune, luck.
hêah-seld (hêh-), *st. n.* high seat, throne.
hêah-sele, *st. m.* high hall, first hall in the land, hall of the ruler.
hêah-setl, *st. n.* high seat, throne.
hêah-stede, *st. m.* high place, ruler's place.
hêah-stefn, *adj.* having a high prow, high-prowed.
hêah-stêap, *adj.* very high, steep.
hêah-strengdu, *st. f.* strength, bravery.
hêah-timber, *st. n.* lofty building.
hêah-trêow, *st. f.* high compact, solemn league.
hêah-, hêh-þegen, *st. m.* angel.
hêah-þegnung, *st. f.* high service, illustrious office.
hêah-þearf, *st. f.* great need, necessity.
hêah-þrêa, *w. m.* great terror, affliction, punishment.
hêah-þrym, *st. m.* great glory.
hêah-þrymnes, *st. f.* great glory.
hêahdu, hêhdu, hêhd, hiehdo, *st. f.* hight, point, top, summit.
hêah-þungen, *part. adj.* noble, well-born, illustrious.
hêah-weorc, *st. n.* high, lofty work.
heal, heall, *st. f.* hall, main apartment, large building.
heal-ærn, *st. n.* hall-building, castle.
healdan, haldan, *st. red. v.* 1. to hold, hold fast, uphold, support, have in custody.— 2. to have in one's power, hold, have, own, possess, occupy, inhabit.— 3. to watch over, protect, guard, defend; keep, preserve, observe, fulfill, perform, hold, assert, retain; to celebrate, observe; to hold, cherish.— 4. to

rule, direct.— **5.** to reach forth, offer, furnish, give. — **6.** to hold out, last. (Ger. *halten*.)

an-healdan, to preserve, hold, maintain.

be-, bi-healdan, 1. to hold, have, possess, occupy, inhabit. — **2.** to hold upright, preserve, protect, defend, guard, take care of, attend to, cherish. — **3.** to look at, behold, consider, observe, view.

for-healdan, to hold in dishonor, disregard, treat slightingly, despise, fall away from, rebel.

ge-healdan, 1. to hold with the hands, hold fast.— **2.** to hold, maintain, preserve, watch over, guard. — **3.** to hold, possess, occupy, rule.— **4.** to hold, keep, observe, hold on, persist in.— **5.** *w. predicate adj.* or *part.* to hold, keep, preserve.— **6.** *reflex.* to hold one's self to, guard one's self.

ymb-healdan, to hold on all sides, contain.

healdend, *part.* & *subs.* holder, watch, keeper, dweller, inhabitant, king, lord, God.

healf, half, *adj.* half. (Ger. *halb*.)

healf, *st. f.* **1.** the half, a part.— **2.** side. (Ger. *halbe*.)

healf-cwic, *adj.* half-quick, half-dead.

healf-weard, *st. m.* sharer in rule or in possession.

heal-gamen, *st. n.* hall-joy, social enjoyment in the hall.

hêa-lic, *adj.* **1.** high.— **2.** noble, excellent, distinguished. — **3.** high-flown, proud, haughty.

hêa-lice, *adv.* highly, loftily, excellently.

heall, heall-. See **heal, heal-**.

healm, *st. m.* haulm, straw, stalk of grass, stem. (Ger. *halm*.)

heal-reced, *st. n.* hall-building, hall.

heals, hals, *st. m.* **1.** neck.— **2.** prow of a ship. (Ger. *hals*.)

heâls. See **hâls**.

heals-bêag, *st. m.* neck-ring, collar.

heals-fæst, *adj.* stiff-necked, obstinate.

heals-gebedda, *w. f.* beloved bed-fellow, wife.

heâlsian. See **hâlsian**.

heal-sittende, *part.* sitting in the hall.

heals-mæged, *st. f.* maid whose neck a man embraces, beloved maid.

healsre-, halsre-feder, *st. f.* neck-feather, down.

heals-wrida, *w. m.* chain for the neck, necklace.

healt, *adj.* halt, limping.

heal-þegen, *st. m.* hall-thane, one who is acquainted with or occupies the hall.

heal-wudu, *st. m.* hall-wood, frame, woodwork, paneling, &c., of a hall.

hêan, *w. v.* to lift up, magnify, exalt. (Ger. *erhöhen*.)

hêan, *adj.* depressed, downcast, poor, miserable, abject, low, despised, rejected. (Goth. *hauns*.) [la.

heand-gestealla. See **handgestealla**.

hêane, *adv.* lowly, basely, ignominiously.

hêa-nes, -nis. See **hêahnis**.

hêan-lic, *adj.* base, ignominious.

hêan-lice, *adv.* lowly, basely, miserably, disgracefully.

hêan-môd, *adj.* downcast or depressed in spirits, sad, sorrowful.

hêanne, hêannes. See **hêah, hêan, hêahnis**.

hêan-spêdig, *adj.* having poor success, poor.

heap. See **hæp**.

hêap, *st. m. f.* (Sat. 87), heap, multitude, crowd, troop, band, army; body of men, assembly. (Ger. *haufe*.)

hêar, hêara, *gen. pl.* See **hâr, hêah**.

heard, *adj.* **1. hard,** of natural hardness.— **2.** bold, brave, able, skillful, strong, efficient in war.— **3.** hard, hardened; hard-hearted, unmerciful.— **4.** hard, harsh, severe, stern, rough, obstinate, cruel, impetuous, terrible; hard to bear. (Ger. *hart.*)

heard-cwide, *st. m.* sharp word, abuse.

hearde, *adv.* **1.** hardly, severely, vigorously, vehemently, rashly, fiercely.— **2.** firmly, closely, narrowly.— **3.** very, very much, exceedingly.

heard-ecg, *adj.* sharp-edged, hard of edge.

heard-fyrde, *adj.* hard to bear away, heavy.

heard-hycgende, *part. & adj.* of a bold disposition, brave, warlike.

hearding, *st. m.* bold man, hero.

heard-lic, *adj.* hard, severe, rash, impetuous, dire, terrible, heavy.

heard-lice, *adv.* hardly, severely, sharply, vehemently, very, very much.

heard-môd, *adj.* of a brave or bold mind, stout-hearted.

heard-rǽd, *adj.* firm of counsel, constant.

heard-sǽlig, *adj.* unhappy.

hearg, hearh, herg, herig, *st. m.* **1.** grove, wood.— **2.** grove sacred to the gods, temple, idol. (Icel. *hörgr;* O. H. Ger. *haruc, haruch.*)

hearh-, herh-eard, *st. m.* a dwelling in the wood.

hearh-træf, *st. n.* a temple for idols, heathen temple.

hearh-, herig-weard, *st. m.* guardian of the temple.

hearm, herm, *st. m.* **1.** harm, sorrow, affliction.— **2.** loss, hurt, injury, misfortune, misery, evil.—**3.** harmful, biting speech, insult. (Ger. *harm.*)

hearm, herm, *adj.* causing harm or sorrow, hurtful, sharp, biting, malignant, malicious.

hearm-cwalu, *st. f.* great suffering.

hearm-cwedend (herm-), *part. & subs.* calumniator, evil-speaker.

hearm-cwide, -cwyde, *st. m.* hurtful speech, calumny, blasphemy, curse.

hearm-edwit, *st. n.* grievous, cutting reproach.

hearm-lêoð, *st. n.* elegy, lamentation, song of sorrow.

hearm-loca, *w. m.* place of sadness, hell, prison.

hearm-plega, *w. m.* painful play, fight, strife.

hearm-scearu, *st. f.* what is imposed as a punishment or penalty.

hearm-sceaða, -scaða, *w. m.* sorrow or injury bringing enemy, grievous enemy.

hearm-slege, *st. m.* hurtful, grievous blows.

hearm-stæf, *st. m.* the cause of sorrow, loss, affliction, tribulation.

hearm-tân, *st. m.* twig of sorrow, germ of misfortune.

hearpe, *w. f.* harp, cittern. (Ger. *harfe.*)

hearpere, *st. m.* harper.

hearra, herra, hierra, heorra, *w. m.* lord, master.

hêarsum. See **hŷrsum.**

heaðor, heador, hador, *st. n.* place of deposit, safe-keeping, receptacle, warehouse, depot.

heaðorian, *w. v.*
    ge-heaðorian, to shut in, force, press in, confine, control, compress.

heaðu, heaðo, battle, fight. [Used only in compounds.]

hêaðu (= **hêahðu?**), *st. f.* deep sea, high waves.

heaðu-byrne, *w. f.* battle-mail, coat-of-mail.

heaðu-ðeor, *adj.* daring, brave in battle.
heaðu-fremmende, *part.* giving battle, fighting.
heaðu-fȳr, *st. n.* battle-fire, fiery breath.
heaðu-geong, *adj.* young and warlike.
heaðu-glem, *st. m.* wound in battle, wound.
heaðu-grim, *adj.* grim, fierce in battle.
heaðu-helm, *st. m.* battle-helmet.
heaðu-lâc, *st. n.* war-play, battle.
hêaðu-liðend, *part. & subs.* seafarer, sailor.
heaðu-lind, *st. f.* shield of lindenwood, war-shield.
heaðu-mǣre, *adj.* renowned in war.
heaðu-rǣs, *st. m.* rush of battle, attack.
heaðu-rêaf, *st. n.* battle-dress, coat-of-mail.
heaðu-rinc, *st. m.* battle-hero, warrior. [tle.
heaðu-rôf, *adj.* bold, skillful in battle-
heaðu-sceard, *adj.* scarred in battle, cut to pieces in battle.
heaðu-sêoc, -sioc, *adj.* battle-sick, wounded.
hêaðu-sigel, *st. m.* sun rising out of the sea. Rä. 72, 16.
heaðu-stêap, *adj.* high in battle, commanding in battle, lofty.
heaðu-swât, *st. m.* blood shed in battle.
heaðu-sweng, *st. m.* battle-stroke, blow of the sword. [tle.
heaðu-torht, *adj.* loud, clear in bat-
heaðu-wǣd, *st. f.* battle-dress, shirt-of-mail.
heaðu-wælm, -welm, -wylm, *st. m.* battle-wave; fierce, deadly flame-wave, surging flames.
heaðu-wêrig, *adj.* battle-weary.
heaðu-weorc, *st. n.* battle-work, battle.

hêawan, *st. red. v.* to **hew,** cut, strike, smite. (Ger. *hauen.*)
 â-hêawan, to hew off, cut off.
 be-, bi-hêawan, to cut off, rob or deprive of by cutting off.
 for-hêawan, to hew or cut in pieces, cut down, kill by hacking.
 ge-hêawan, to hew, cut, cleave.
hêo. See **hê, hiw.**
hêo-dæg, *adv.* to-day. (Ger. *heute.*)
hêof, *st. m.* lamentation, wailing, mourning.
hêofan, hiofan, *w. v.* to lament, wail, howl, mourn.
heofod? = **heafod?** Gn. Ex. 68.
heofon, hiofon, hefon, -un, -en, *st. m.* **heaven.** (Goth. *himins*; Ger. *himmel.*)
hêofon, *st. f.* lamentation, mourning.
heofon-bêacen, *st. n.* heavenly sign, token.
heofon-beorht, *adj.* heavenly bright, glorious.
heofon-bȳme, *w. f.* heaven's trumpet.
heofon-candel, -condel, *st. f.* heaven's candle, heavenly light, column of fire, sun and moon, stars.
heofon-col, *st. n.* a heavenly coal, heat of the sun.
heofon-cund, *adj.* celestial, heavenly.
heofon-cyning, *st. m.* heaven's king.
heofon-dêma, *w. m.* heaven's ruler.
heofon-drêam, *st. m.* heaven's joys.
heofon-dugud, *st. f.* heavenly host.
heofon-engel, *st. m.* angel of heaven.
heofon-fugol, *st. m.* bird under heaven, bird, fowl of the air.
heofon-hâlig, *adj.* holy and heavenly.
heofon-hâm, *st. m.* heavenly home.
heofon-hêah, *adj.* high as heaven, sublime.
heofon-hlâf, *st. m.* bread of heaven.
heofon-hrôf, *st. m.* heaven's roof, heaven.
heofon-hwealf, *st. f.* heaven's vault.
heofon-lêoht, *st. n.* heaven's light.

heofon-lêoma, *w. m.* heaven's splendor, sun.
heofon-lic, *adj.* **heavenly.** (Cf. Ger. *himmlisch.*)
heofon-mægen, *st. n.* heavenly strength;—used with reference both to God and to the heavenly hosts.
heofon-rice, *st. n.* heavenly kingdom. (Cf. Ger. *himmelreich.*)
heofon-steorra, *w. m.* star of heaven.
heofon-stôl, *st. m.* heaven's throne.
heofon-timber, *st. n.* heavenly building, heaven.
heofon-torht, *adj.* heavenly bright, glorious.
heofon-tungol, *st. n.* star of heaven, constellation, heavenly body.
heofon-þrêat, *st. m.* heaven's army.
heofon-þrym, *st. m.* heavenly glory, heavenly majesty.
heofon-waru, *st. f.* inhabitants of heaven.
heofon-weard, *st. m.* heaven's keeper, God.
heofon-wolcen, *st. n.* cloud of heaven, heaven's welkin.
heofon-wôma, *w. m.* resounding crash of heaven.
heofon-wuldor, *st. n.* heavenly glory.
hêof-, hêow-sid, *st. m.* sorrowful, mournful fate; sad condition.
heofun, hêofun. See **heofon, hiofon.**
heolfor, *st. n.* blood, gore, putrid or festering blood.
heolfrig, *adj.* bloody.
heolod-cyn, *st. n.* inhabitants of the lower world.
heolod-helm, *st. m.* helmet rendering the wearer invisible. Wal. 45.
heolstor, *adj.* dark, shadowy.
heolstor, *st. n.* covering, hiding-place, lurking-place, cavern, darkness. (Goth. *hulistr.*)
heolstor-côfa, *w. m.* covered resting-place, grave.

heolstor-hof, *st. n.* dark dwelling, hell.
heolstor-loca, *w. m.* prison, cell.
heolstor-sceadu, *st. f.* darkness.
heolstor-scuwa, *w. m.* darkness.
heona, hiona, *adv.* hence, from here.
heonan, hionan, -on, -un, *adv.* hence, from here, from now on.
heonane, heonone, *adv.* from here, hence.
heonan-sid, *st. m.* departure from here, death.
heonan-weard, *adj.* receding, passing away.
heopian, *w. v.*
 be-heopian, to rob, deprive of. Gen. 2644.
heor, *st. m. f.* hinge of a door.
heordan, *w. v.*
 â-heordan, to free from captivity? B. 2930.
heord, herd, hyrd, *st. f.* 1. guard, protection, keeping. — 2. flock, herd.— 3. family, household. (Ger. *heerde.*)
heorde. See **hirde.**
hêore, hiore, hýre, hire, *adj.* 1. pleasant. not haunted, secure.— 2. gentle, mild, obedient.—3. pure, clean, spotless.
heoro. See **heoru.**
heorot, heort, *st. m.* stag, hart, Heorot. (Ger. *hirsch.*)
heorra. See **hearra.**
heort, *adj.* high-minded, judicious? Ps. 118, 2.
heorte, hiorte, *w. f.* **heart.** (Ger. *herz.*)
heort-lufe, *w. f.* **heart-love,** hearty love.
heord, *st. m.* **hearth.** (Ger. *herd.*)
heord-genêat, *st. m.* hearth-companion, follower who shares the hearth of his lord.
heord-weorud, -werod, *st. n.* household sharing the same hearth, family, servants, retainers.

heoru, heoro, hioro, *st. m.* sword. (Goth. *hairus.*)
heoru-blâc, *adj.* pale from sword-strokes, mortally wounded.
heoru-cumbol, *st. n.* standard of war, ensign.
heoru-dolg, *st. n.* sword-wound, deadly wound.
heoru-drêor, *st. m.* sword-blood, gore.
heoru-drêorig, *adj.* bloody.
heoru-drync, *st. m.* the sword's drink, blood which follows the sword out of the wound.
heoru-fædm, *st. m.* sword's embrace, death-bringing embrace.
heoru-gifre, *adj.* greedy to destroy, eager for hostile inroads.
heoru-grædig, *adj.* bloodthirsty, greedy for blood.
heoru-grim, *adj.* very fierce or cruel, savage.
heoru-hôciht, *adj.* sharp like a sword, supplied with sharp, cutting hooks, barbed.
heoru-scearp, *adj.* exceedingly sharp.
heoru-sceorp, *st. n.* war equipments.
heoru-serce, *w. f.* coat-of-mail, war-shirt.
heoru-sweng, *st. m.* blow of the sword, sword-stroke.
heoru-swealwe, *w. f.* falcon, hawk.
heoru-wǣpen, *st. n.* war-weapon, sword.
heoru-weallende, *part.* fiercely boiling, raging.
heoru-wearh, *st. m.* bloodthirsty wolf (Grein); — he who is sword-cursed, who is destined to die by the sword (H.-S.).
heoru-word, *st. n.* cutting word, hurtful speech.
heoru-wulf, *st. m.* sword-wolf, warrior.
hêod, *st. f.* vaulted part of the hall where the dais sits (Grein); — room, hall (B.-T.).
hêow. See **hiw**

hêowan. See **hêofan.**
hêowian. See **hiwian.**
hêow-sid. See **hêofsid.**
hi, hie, hicgean, hidan. See **hê, hycgan, hŷdan.**
hider, hider, hyder, *adv.* hither.
hider-cyme, *st. m.* arrival, coming, advent.
hig. See **hê.**
hig, hêg, hio, *st. n.* hay. (Ger. *heu.*)
hige. See **hyge.**
hi-, hŷ-gedriht, *st. f.* band of household retainers.
higian, *w.v.* to hie, heed, strive, hasten.
  ofer-higian, to strive to surpass, to surpass, excel, exceed.
higora, *w. m.* jay, woodpecker. (O.H. Ger. *hehara.*)
hiht, hihtan, hild. See **hyht, hyhtan, hyld.**
hild, *st. f.* battle, fight, combat. (O. H. Ger. *hilt.*)
hild-bedd, *st. n.* war-bed, deathbed.
hilde-bill, *st. n.* battle-sword.
hilde-bord, *st. n.* battle-shield.
hilde-calla, *w. m.* war-herald, one who calls the troops to battle.
hilde-cordor, *st. n.* war-host, war-like band.
hilde-cyst, *st. f.* excellence in war, warlike valor.
hilde-dêoful, *st. n.* demon, devil.
hilde-dêor, *adj.* daring in battle, brave in war.
hilde-freca. See **hildfreca.**
hilde-frôfor, *st. f.* help for battle, weapon? sword?
hilde-gæst, -giest, *st. m.* battle-guest, enemy.
hild-egesa, *w. m.* terror of battle.
hilde-geatwe, *st. f. pl.* equipment for battle, adornment for combat, armor.
hilde-gicel, *st. m.* battle-icicle, blood dripping from the sword.
hilde-grâp, *st. f.* battle-gripe, hostile hand.

hilde-hlǣm, -hlem, *st. m.* rage, noise, tumult of battle.
hilde-lêoma, *w. m.* battle-light, gleam of battle.
hilde-lêoð, *st. n.* battle-song.
hilde-mæcg, *st. m.* man of battle, warrior.
hilde-mêce, *st. m.* war-sword.
hilde-nædre, *st. f.* battle-adder, dart, arrow, lance.
hilde-pil, *st. m.* warlike missile, dart.
hilde-rǣs, *st. m.* rush of battle, onset, attack.
hilde-rand, *st. m.* battle-shield.
hilde-rinc, *st. m.* hero of battle, warrior.
hilde-sǣd, *adj.* satiated with battle, tired of battle, mortally wounded.
hilde-sceorp, *st. n.* battle-adornment, armor, coat-of-mail.
hilde-scûr, *st. m.* battle-shower, darts (of disease).
hilde-segese, *w. f.* battle-scythe, sword (Grein); — others print **hildes-egesan.** B. 3155.
hilde-serce, *w. f.* battle-sark, shirt-of-mail.
hilde-setl, *st. n.* battle-seat, saddle.
hilde-spell, *st. n.* news of the battle, story of the fight.
hilde-strengo, *st. f.* battle-strength, bravery in battle.
hilde-swât, *st. m.* battle-sweat; hot, damp breath of the dragon. B. 2558.
hilde-swêg, *st. m.* din of battle, sound of battle.
hilde-torht, *adj.* having warlike splendor.
hilde-tusc, -tux, *st. m.* battle-tusk, tusk, fang.
hilde-þremma, *w. m.* warrior.
hilde-þrym, *st. m.* warlike strength or vigor.
hilde-þryð, *st. f.* the same as above.
hilde-wǣpen, *st. n* war-weapon.
hilde-wisa, *w. m.* leader in war, general.

hilde-wôma, *w. m.* tumult or crash of battle, terror of battle.
hilde-wrǣsn, *st. f.* warlike chain, fetter for captives.
hilde-wulf, *st. m.* battle-wolf, hero, warrior.
hild-, hilde-freca, *w. m.* battle-wolf, hero, warrior.
hild-from, *adj.* strong in battle, valiant in war. [peror.
hild-fruma, *w. m.* battle-chief, em-
hild-lǣt, *adj.* sluggish in battle, cowardly. (Grein.)
hild-lata, *w. m.* one sluggish in war, slow to fight, coward. (B.-T.)
hild-stapa, *w. m.* one who approaches as an enemy, warrior.
hild-þracu, *st. f.* onset of battle, power in war.
hilt, *st. m. n.* hilt, sword-hilt, handle.
hilte-cumbor, *st. n.* banner with a hilt.
hilted, *part. & adj.* furnished with a handle or hilt.
hina. See **hine, hiwan.**
hind, *st. f.* hind, female of the hart. (Ger. *hinde.*)
hindan, *adv.* behind, in the rear. (Ger. *hinten.*)
hindan-weard, *adv.* at the hinder or farther side.
hindema, *w. adj.* the last, hindmost.
hinder, *adv.* behind, back, after, in the farthest part. (Ger. *hinter.*)
hinder-hôc, *st. m.* trick, snare.
hinderling,—used only in the phrase **on hinderling,** backwards.
hinder-þeostru, *st. n. pl.* the farther part of hell's darkness; hence, the darkest part.
hinder-weard, *adj.* tending backward, artful.
hinde-weard, *adj.* backward, behind.
hine, *adv.* hence, away.
hine. See **hê.**
hin-fûs, *adj.* hastening to depart, ready to die.

hin-gang, *st. m.* departure, going away, death.
hingran. See **hyngran**.
hin-, hinn-sið, *st. m.* going away, departure, death.
hinsið-gryre, *st. m.* dread of death, fear of going away, of dying.
hiran. See **hȳran**.
hirde, hierde, heorde, hiorde, hyrde, *st. m.* (herd), keeper, guardian, protector, lord, possessor. (Ger. *hirte*.)
hire. See **hē**.
hire. See **hēore**.
hi-, hȳ-rēd, *st. m.* household, family, assembly.
hirēd-man, *st. m.* follower.
hirwan See **herwan**.
his, hit. See **hē**.
hitsian, *w. v.* to be heated, warm, hot (Grein);—others print **hyt sȳ**. B. 2649.
hidan, hider. See **hȳdan, hider**.
hiw, hēow, hēo, *st. n.* appearance, form, figure, look, color, **hue**. (Goth. *hiwi*.)
hiwan, *w. m. pl.* domestics, servants.
hiw-, hiow-beorht, *adj.* of exceeding beauty, of striking figure.
hiw-cūð, *adj.* familiar, well-known.
hiwe, *adj.* of perfect form, beautiful.
hiwian, hēowian, *w. v.*
  ge-hiwian, to form, fashion, shape.
hie, hiedan, hiehðu, hiene, hiendo, hieran, hierde, hierra, hiedan. See **hē, hȳdan, hēahðu, hē, hȳnð, hȳran, hirde, hearra, hȳdan**.
hio, hiofon, hiold, hiom, hiona, hionan, hiorde, hiore, hioro, hiorte, hiow. See **hē** and **hig, heofon, healdan, hē, heona, heonan, hirde, hēore, heoru, heorte, hiwbeorht**.
hladan, *st. abl. v.* IV. 1. to lade, load, heap up, bring together, pile up in layers.—2. to load, lay, place upon, place in.—3. to load, burden. 4. to draw. (Ger. *laden*.)
  ā-hladan, to draw out, lead out.
  ge-hladan, 1. to load, heap up. 2. to load, burden, freight.
  tō-hladan, to scatter, disperse.
hlǣder, *st. f.* ladder, flight of steps. (Ger. *leiter*.)
hlǣfdige, *w. f.* lady, mistress of a house.
hlǣman, *w. v.*
  bi-hlǣman, to resound, strike with noise.
hlǣnan, *w. v.* to lean, incline.
  ā-hlǣnan, to rise up against.
  be-hlǣnan, to surround or beset by leaning.
hlæst, *st. n.* burden, load;—holmes hlæst, fishes. (Ger. *last*.)
hlæstan, *w. v.*
  ge-hlæstan, to load, burden, freight, adorn.
hlǣw, hlāw, *st. m.* 1. hill, mound,—especially a grave-hill.—2. grave-dwelling, hole, cave.
hlāf, *st. m.* loaf, bread. (Goth. *hlaifs*.)
hlāf-gebrece, *st. n.* bit of bread, morsel.
hlāf-mæsse, *w. f.* **Lammas**, the first of August.
hlāf-ord, -urd, *st. m.* lord, ruler, master.
hlāford-lēas, *adj.* lordless.
hlanc, *adj.* lank, lean, thin, gaunt.
hlāw. See **hlǣw**.
hlēgan. See **hligan**.
hlehhan, hlihhan, hlihan, hlyhhan, *st. abl. v.* IV. to laugh, rejoice, deride. (Ger. *lachen*.)
  ā-hlehhan, 1. to laugh out, laugh at, deride.—**2.** to laugh out loud, shout, exult, rejoice.
  bi-hlehhan, to laugh at, deride, exult over.
hlem, *st. m.* noise, sound, crash. [Used only in compounds.]

hlemman, *w. v.* to cause to sound, clash; — **hlemman togædre**, to strike together.
  bi-hlemman, the same as above.
hlence, hlenca, *w. f. m.* link, chain, coat-of-mail.
hleahtor, *st. m.* 1. noise, din.— 2. laughter, unrestrained laughter. 3. laughter, derision.—4. exultation, rejoicing.—5. joy, merriment.
hleahtor-smid, *st. m.* causer of laughter.
hleapan, *st. red. v.* to leap, run, spring, dance. (Ger. *laufen*.)
  â-hleapan, to leap up, jump, exult.
  ge-hleapan, *w. acc.* to overtake by running, get by leaping, leap upon, run or leap to.
hleo, hleow, *st. m.* 1. shelter, protection, roof.— 2. shelter, defense. 3. protector, defender.
hleo-bord, *st. n.* protecting board, book-cover. Rä. 27, 12.
hleo-burh, *st. f.* fortress or city giving protection, ruler's castle or city.
hleo-dryhten, *st. m.* protector, defender.
hleo-fæst, *adj.* firm or mighty in protecting or consoling.
hleo-leas, *adj.* 1. without shelter.— 2. affording no shelter, roofless, cheerless.
hleo-mæg, *st. m.* a kinsman whose duty it is to afford right and lawful protection.
hleon, hleowan, *w. v.* 1. to warm, make warm, cherish.— 2. to become warm or hot.
hleonad, *st. m.* place of safety, couch, dwelling.
hleonian, hlinian, *w. v.* to incline, hang over, recline, lie down.
hleor, *st. n.* cheek, face. (Icel. *hlyr*.)
hleor-bere, *w. f.* what is worn on the cheek, visor (of the helmet?) B. 304.

hleor-bolster, *st. m.* cheek-bolster, pillow.
hleor-dropa, *w. m.* drop running down the cheek, tear.
hleor-sceamu, *st. f.* shame shown on the cheek, blush.
hleor-torht, *adj.* having bright, beautiful cheeks.
hleo-sceorp, *st. n.* protecting ornament.
hleotan, *st. abl. v.* VI. 1. to cast lots. 2. to obtain by lots, share in, participate, attain, get. (Cf. Ger. *erlösen*.)
  ge-hleotan, to obtain by lot, attain, get. [ing.
hleod, hleowd, *st. f.* shelter, cover-**hleodian**. See **lidian**.
hleodor, *st. n.* 1. hearing.— 2. sound, tone, clang.— 3. voice, speech, cry, song.— 4. oracle, response.
hleodor-cwide, -cwyde, *st. m.* 1. speech, saying, vocal utterance.— 2. narration, narrative.— 3. prophecy, revelation, oracular utterance.
hleodor-stede, *st. m.* oracle, place for prophesying.
hleodrian, *w. v.* 1. *intrans.* to speak, talk earnestly, exclaim.— 2. *w. acc.* to say.— 3. to sound, resound, cry aloud, sing.
hleodu. See **hlid**.
hleow, hleow, hleowan. See **hleo, hlowan, hleon**.
hleow-fedre, *st. f. pl.* wings affording protection, sheltering wings.
hleow-lora, *w. m.* one who has lost a protector.
hleow-stôl, *st. m.* safe seat, asylum.
hleowd. See **hleod**.
hlid, *st. n.* lid, covering, protection, door, gate. (O. H. Ger. *hlit*.)
hlidan, *st. abl. v.* V. 1. to cover, shut, close.— 2. to come forth, spring up.
  be-hlidan, to cover, shut up, close.

on-hlīdan, 1. to unlock, open.— 2. to rise.
tō-hlīdan, to spring apart, open, burst, gape, spring to pieces, break.
hlīfian, w. v. to rise up, be prominent, tower up.
ofer-hlīfian, to rise over, overtop.
hlīgan, st. abl. v. V. to call, call upon; to praise.
be-, bi-hlīgan, to speak ill of, defame. Gn. Ex. 65.
hlihhan. See hlehhan.
hlim, st. f. stream, torrent. Ps. 82, 8.
hlimman, hlymman, st. abl. v. I. to sound, roar, resound, rage.
hlimme, w. f. stream, torrent.
hlin. See hlyn.
hlin, name of a tree, ash? Rä. 56, 9.
hlin- (lean-. (Ger. lehn-.) Cf. hleonan. [Used only in compounds.]
hlin-bed, st. n. bed for reclining, resting-place.
hlinc, st. m. hill, rising ground. (link, linch. Cf. Halliwell.)
hlin-duru, st. f. the leaned to or closed door.
hlinian, hlingan. See hleonian.
hlin-ræced, st. n. a closed house, prison.
hlin-scūa, -scūwa, w. m. the darkness of a closed room.
hlinsian, hlisa, hlistan. See hlynsian, hlȳsa, hlystan.
hlīosa. See hlȳsa.
hlīd, st. n. cliff, precipice of a mountain. (Ger.-leite.)
hlosnian, w. v. to listen, be on the lookout.
hlōd, st. f. troop, band, crowd, multitude, people. [mass.
hlōd-gecrod, st. n. crowded, dense
hlōwan, st. red. v. to low, roar, blow loudly.
hlūd, adj. loud. (Ger. laut.)
hlūde, adv. loudly.

hlutor, hluttor, adj. clear, pure, clean, bright. (Ger. lauter.)
hlutre, hluttre, adv. clearly, brightly.
hluttran, w. v. to clear, purify, make bright.
ā-hluttran, the same as above.
Hlȳda, w. m. sounding, stormy month; March; —so called on account of equinoctial storms.
hlȳdan, w. v. to strike up, cry aloud, make a great noise. (Ger. lauten.)
hlȳgan, hlyhhan, hlymman. See hligan, hlehhan, hlimman.
hlyn, hlin, hlynn, st. m. sound, din, noise, clatter, clamor.
hlynian, w. v. to sound, resound, roar, shout.
hlynnan, w. v. to sound, resound, groan, roar, cry aloud, make a noise or din.
hlynsian, hlinsian, w. v. the same as above.
hlȳp, st. m. leap, jump, spring.
hlȳsa, hlīosa, hlisa, w. m. what is heard. — 1. sound. — 2. report, fame, rumor, renown.
hlyst, st. f. 1. hearing.— 2. listening with eager attention.
hlystan, hlistan, w. v. to list, listen to, hear, attend.
ge-hlystan, the same as above.
hlyt, st. m. lot, portion.
hlytm, st. m. lot, portion.
hlȳdan, w. v.
be-hlȳdan, to rob, deprive of.
hnǣcan, w. v. to kill.
ge-hnǣcan, to push, rub against, strike on, bruise.
hnægan, hnēgan, w. v. to bend, humiliate.
ge-hnægan, to bow, humble, bring down, strike down, fell, subdue.
hnǣgan (= nǣgan), w. v. to speak to, greet. B. 1320.
hnæsc, hnesc, adj. weak, tender, soft.

hnâg, hnâh, *adj.* **1.** low, inferior, miserable, poor.— **2.** of a low way of thinking, mean, niggardly.

hnappung, *st. f.* **napping,** slumbering, slumber.

hnâtan, *st. red. v.* to strike together, clash.

hnecca, *w. m.* **neck.** (Ger. *nacken.*)

hnêgan, hnesc. See **hnǣgan, hnǣsc.**

hnêapan, *st. red. v.*
  â-hnêapan, to pluck off.

hnêaw, *adj.* avaricious, stingy, close. (Ger. *genau.*)

hnêaw-lîce, *adv.* stingily, sparingly.

hnigan, *st. abl. v.* V. **1.** to bend, bow one's self.— **2.** to make a bow, prostrate one's self (in greeting or in making a request, &c.)— **3.** to descend, fall.
  ge-hnigan, to bow down, be humble.
  on-hnigan, to bow down, incline one's self, worship.
  under-hnigan, to bow down, go down under or into.

hnipian, *w. v.* to incline, bow down. (Ger. *nippen.*)

hnitan, *st. abl. v.* V. to strike, dash against, encounter.

hnossian, *w. v.* to strike.

hnyssan, *w. v.*
  ge-hnyssan, to frighten;—*part.* affrighted.

hô. See **hôh.**

hôc, *st. m.* **hook,** hinge, snare, trap.

hôciht, *adj.* having hooks, barbed, hooked.

hôf. See **hebban.**

hof, *st. n.* inclosed space, courtyard, estate, house, dwelling. (Ger. *hof.*)

hôf, *st. m.* **hoof.** (Ger. *huf.*)

hôfian, *w. v.*
  be-, bi-hôfian (behoove), to need, require, want.

hogde. See **hycgan.**

hogian, *w. v.* to think.

hogede, hogode, hogade. See **hycgan.**

hôh, hô, *st. m.* **hough,** heel;—on hôh, behind, back.

hohsnian, *w. v.*
  on-hohsnian, to scold, mock, scorn (Grein). B. 1944.
  on-hôhsnian, *w. v.* to hinder (H.-S.). (*ms.* on hoh snod.)

hol, *st. n.* **hole,** cave, cavern, den.

hôl, *st. n.* silly talk, foolish speech, calumny.

hold, *adj.* inclined to, attached to.—
  1. used of a lord or ruler to his subjects: friendly, kind, gracious, good.— **2.** of subjects to their lord: obedient, true, loyal, devoted, faithful.— **3.** in general: true, kind, friendly, favorable, faithful, loyal. **4.** pleasant, dear, agreeable. (Ger. *hold.*)

holde, *adv.* graciously, devotedly.

holde-lîce, *adv.* devotedly.

hold-lîce, *adv.* graciously, pleasantly, kindly, devotedly.

holen, holegn, *st. m.* **holly.**

hôlinga, hôlunge, *adv.* in vain, without reason.

holm, *st. m.* literally, a rounded hight.— **1.** high-going sea-waves. **2.** deep sea, ebb, wave, sea, water. **3.** helm of the ship. An. 396.

holm-ærn, *st. n.* sea-house, ship.

holm-clif, *st. n.* sea-cliff, rocky shore, promontory.

holmeg, *adj.* stormy as on the sea? misty. Exod. 396.

holm-mægen, *st. n.* strength of the waves or fullness of the deep.

holm-þracu, *st. f.* tumult of the waves or sea, storm at sea, tossing of the sea, violence of the waves.

holm-weg, *st. m.* seaway. [waves.

holm-weall, *st. m.* sea-wall, wall of

holm-weard, *st. m.* sea-warder, governor of the ship. [cross.

holm-wudu, *st. m.* mountain-wood,

holm-wylm, *st. m.* waves of the sea, billows.
holt, *st. n.* **1. holt,** wood, forest, hedge.—**2.** wood. (Ger. *holz.*)
holt-wudu, *st. m.* **1.** forest-wood, grove, forest.—**2.** wood.
hôlunge, hom, homa, honcer. See **hôlinga, ham, hama, hamer.**
hôn, *st. rcd. v.* to hang, suspend. (Ger. *hangen.*)
    â-hôn, to hang, suspend, crucify.
    be-, bi-hôn, to behang, hang round.
    ge-hôn, to hang with, adorn.
hond, hongian. See **hand, hangian.**
hôp, *st. n.* (hoop); hence, something round, hope, bay, moor, marsh; extended in meaning, sea.
hôp-gehnâst, *st. n.* dashing of the waves;—used of the sea-beaten cliffs.
hopian, *w. v.* to hope. (Ger. *hoffen.*)
hôpig, *adj.* in ring-shaped waves, eddying. Ps. 68, 2.
hord, *st. n. m.* the guarded treasure, hoard, treasure; the thoughts shut up in the breast, the spirit dwelling in the body; secrets; and finally whatever is collected or brought together, fullness, abundance. (Ger. *hort;* Goth. *huzd.*)
hord-ærn, *st. n.* treasure-house, treasure-room.
hord-burh, *st. f.* city or castle in which the ruler's (king's) treasure is kept, royal city.
hord-côfa, *w. m.* chamber or closet of the secret thoughts, breast, heart.
hord-fæt, *st. n.* treasure-vessel, (sc. in utero Mariæ).
hord-gestrêon, *st. n.* treasure-hoard, precious treasure.
hord-geat, *st. n.* door to the secret treasure.
hord-loca, *w. m.* treasure-chest, coffer; secret thoughts.

hord-mægen, *st. n.* abundance of treasure, riches.
hord-mâddum, *st. m.* treasure-jewel, costly jewel.
hord-wela, *w. m.* wealth of treasures, abundance of riches.
hord-weard, *st. m.* warder of the treasure, keeper of treasure.
hord-weordung, *st. f.* gift out of the treasure.
hord-wyn, *st. f.* treasure-joy, joy-giving treasure.
horn, *st. n.* horn. **1.** of an animal. **2.** horn, trumpet.—**3.** pinnacle, horn-shaped gable-end. (Ger. *horn.*)
horn-boga, *w. m.* horn-bow, bow made of horn, bow with the ends curved like a horn.
horn-bora, *w. m.* horn-bearer, trumpeter.
horn-fisc, *st. m.* hornfish, a kind of pike.
horn-gestrêon, *st. n.* all the pinnacles of a house.
horn-gêap, *adj.* rich in pinnacles (Grein);—having a wide extent between the "horns," (B.-T.)
horn-reced, *st. n.* pinnacled house, building having pinnacles (Grein & B.-T.);—building whose two gables are crowned by the halves of a stag's antler (?) (Heyne).
horn-sæl, *st. n.* the same as above.
horn-scip, *st. n.* ship with beak, or horn-shaped prow.
horn-sele, *st. m.* hall, house having pinnacles.
hors, *st. n.* horse. (Ger. *ross.*)
horsc, *adj.* **1.** quick, swift, expeditious.—**2.** quick in thought, ready, active, wary, prudent.
hors-lice, *adv.* promptly, prudently, wisely.
horu, *st. m.* dirt, filth, spittle. (O.H. Ger. *horo.*)

hôs, *st. f.* accompanying troop, escort. (Goth. *hansa.*)
hosp, *st. m.* reproach, blasphemy, insult, contumely, disgrace.
hosp-cwide, *st. m.* contemptuous, insulting words.
hosp-word, *st. n.* same as above.
hodma, *w. m.* place of concealment, cave, grave.
hrâ, hrâw, hreâ, hreâw, hrǽw, hrǽ, *st. n.* 1. body of a living human being.—2. corpse.
hraca, *w. m.* throat, jaws, gullet. (Ger. *rachen.*)
hræd, hred, *adj.* quick, active, nimble, ready, busy.
hræder. See hreder.
hræd-lice, *adv.* quickly, immediately, straightway, soon, forthwith.
hræd-tæfle, *adj.* skilled in the game at draughts.
hræd-wægn, -wǽn, *st. m.* swift wain or wagon.
hræd-wyrde, *adj.* quick speaking, rash in speech.
hræfn, hrefn, hræm, hrem, *st. m.* raven. (Ger. *rabe.*)
hrægl, *st. n.* covering, dress, garment, armor.
hrægn-loca (Rä. 72, 21). See brægnloca.
hræd, hred, *adj.* quick. swift, sudden.
hræde, hræder. See hrade, hreder.
hrǽw. See hrâ.
hrâ-fyl, *st. m.* fall of bodies in battle, slaughter.
hragan, *st. abl. v.* IV. [spread.
ofer-hragan, to cover, over-
hran, hron, *st. m.* whale.
hran-fisc, *st. m.* whale.
hran-mere, *st. m.* whale-mere, ocean.
hran-râd, *st. n.* whale's road, sea.
hrade, hræde, hrede, *adv.*(rathe,*adj.* Milton), quickly, immediately, at once, forthwith, soon, straightway.
hrader. See hreder.
hrâw. See hrâ.

hrâ-wêrig, *adj.* body-weary, tired of life.
hrâ-wic (hreâ-), *st. n.* place of corpses, battle-field.
hred. See hræd.
hreddan, *w. v.* to rid, snatch away, rescue, deliver. (Ger. *retten.*)
â-hreddan, to take away, rescue, free from.
hreddan, *w. v.*
â-hreddan, to move, shake, make to tremble.
hrêfan, *w. v.*
ge-hrêfan, to cover, cover over, roof.
hrefn, hrem. See hræfn.
hrêman, *w. v.* to make a noise over, boast of. (Ger. *rühmen.*)
hrêmig, *adj.* 1. lamenting (Seel, 9). 2. rejoicing, boasting, exulting.
hreppan, *w. v.* to touch, lay hold of, afflict.
hrêran, *w. v.* to touch, move.—2. to be moved. (Ger. *rühren.*)
on-hrêran, to move, excite, agitate, disturb.
hrêrnes, *st. f.* excitement, commotion.
hrest (*pres.* 3 *sig.*), withers. Met. 11, 58.
hred. See hræd.
hrêd, *st. f.* honor, renown, glory, triumph, joy. (Cf. ruhm, Kluge, Etym. Wbh. p. 277.)
hrêdan, *w. v.* to glory in, exult, rejoice.
hrede. See hrade.
hrêde, *adj.* rough, savage, wild.
hrêd-eadig, *adj.* glorious, joyful.
hreder, hredor, hræder, hrader, *st. m.* 1. the inner parts of the body, entrails, heart, bosom, breast, —especially as seat of life, thought, and feeling.— 2. in general, the inside of anything.
hreder-bealo, *st. n.* evil that takes hold on the heart, sore evil.
hreder-côfa, *w. m.* breast.

hreðer-gléaw, *adj.* prudent, wise.
hreðer-loca, *w. m.* inclosure of the breast, breast.
hréðig, *adj.* triumphant, exulting.
hréd-léas, *adj.* joyless, or without renown.
hréd-sigor, *st. m.* glorious victory, triumph.
hreá, hreáw. See hrá.
hreám, *st. m.* cry, outcry, din, noise, tumult.
hreámig. See hrémig.
hréo. See hréoh.
hréof, *adj.* rough, scabby, leprous. (O. H. Ger. *riob.*)
hréofan, *st. abl. v.* V.
    be-hréofan? Ruin. 4.
hréoh, *st. n.* rough, stormy weather, tempest.
hréoh, hrioh, hréo, hréow, *adj.* 1. rough, wild, angry, raging, stormy, excited.— 2. sad, troubled.
hréoh-móð, *adj.* 1. angry at heart, enraged.— 2. sad at heart, troubled.
hréorig, *adj.* falling to decay, in ruins. Ruin. 3.
hréosan, *st. abl. v.* VI. to rush, fall headlong, break forth, fall, sink.
be-, bi-hréosan, 1. to cover over.— 2. *part.* behroren, divested of, fallen away from.
    ge-hréosan, to fall down, rush headlong, sink, disappear, fail.
    of-hréosan, to fall down, fall headlong.
    tó-hréosan, to fall asunder.
hréoðan, *st. abl. v.* VI. to draw over, cover, clothe, adorn, decorate.
    ge-hréoðan, the same as above.
    on-hréoðan, the same as above.
hréow. See hréoh.
hréow, *st. f.* sadness, distress, sorrow, regret, penitence. (Ger. *reue.*)
hréowan, *st. abl. v.* VI. *impers.* to rue, repent, be sorry for, grieve. (Ger. *reuen.*)
    ge-hréowan, same as above.

hréow-cearig, *adj.* sorrowful, sad.
hréowig, *adj.* the same as above.
hréowig-móð, *adj.* sad of heart, sorrowful.
hréow-lic, *adj.* the same as above.
hréow-lice, *adv.* miserably, cruelly.
hricg. See hrycg.
hrif, *st. f.* (-riff), belly, womb.
hrim? hrim on lime. Ruin. 4.
hrim, *st. m.* rime, hoar-frost. (O. H. Ger. *rime.*)
hriman, *w. v.*
    be-hriman, to cover with hoar-frost.
hrim-ceald, *adj.* icy cold.
hrim-gicel, *st. m.* icicle.
hrimig, *adj.* frosty, covered with frost.
hrimig-heard, *adj.* hard with frost.
hrinan, *st. abl. v.* V. to touch, lay hold of, grasp, strike. (O. H. Ger. *hrinan.*)
    ge-hrinan, the same as above.
    on-hrinan, the same as above.
hrind, *part.* dead (Grein); — rustling (Heyne);— barky (Thorpe);— rinded (Kemble); — placed in a ring or circle? (B.-T.). B. 1363.
hrindan, *st. abl. v.* I. to strike, push, thrust.
hring, *st. m.* 1. ring, gold ring as ornament.— 2. ring as a fetter.— 3. shirt-of-mail (of interlaced rings).— 4. circle formed by a number of men.— 5. circle of the year, circuit.— 6. orb or circumference of the earth.— 7. ban, extent of the ban, territory over which one's power extends.— 8. circle, circuit, territory, influence. (Ger. *ring.*)
hring, *st. m.* ring, sound.
hringan, *w. v.* to ring, clash, give forth a sound, rattle.
hring-boga, *w. m.* one who bends himself into a ring, bowed or bent dragon.

hringed, *adj.* supplied with rings, made of rings.
hringed-stefna, *w. m.* ship whose prow is provided with iron rings for making it fast to the land.
hring-iren, *st. n.* ring-iron, iron rings of a coat-of-mail (Grein);—sword ornamented with rings (H.-S.).
hring-loca, *w. m.* shirt-of-mail.
hring-mǽl, *st. n.* sword marked with rings, *i.e.* marked with ring-shaped characters, or ornamented with inlaid rings.
hring-mǽled, *adj.* marked with rings. See above.
hring-mere, *st. n.* water-basin in a bath-house, bath.
hring-naca, *w. m.* ship provided with iron rings in the prow.
hring-net, *st. n.* coat-of-mail made of iron rings.
hring-sele, *st. m.* ring-hall;—1. hall in which rings are distributed.— 2. the cave or hole of the dragon guarding the treasure consisting mainly of rings. B. 2840, 3053.
hring-þegu, *st. f.* the receiving of rings when distributed by one's lord.
hring-weorðung, *st. f.* donation of rings (Grein); — ring-ornament. (H.-S.) B. 3017.
hrisil, *st. f.* shuttle; bone of the lower arm, radius.
hrid, *st. f.* snowstorm? Wand. 102.
hrioh. See **hrech.**
hrôf, *st. m.* 1. roof, rafters, vault, chamber.— 2. top, the highest part of an object, point, summit.
hrôf-fæst, *adj.* with a firm roof, well-covered.
hrôf-sele, *st. m.* covered hall.
hron. See **hran.**
hrôpan, *st. red. v.* to call, cry out, scream, howl. (Ger. *rufen.*)
hrôr, *adj.* stirring, moving, strong, stout, valiant, skillful.
hrôst-béag, *st. m.* woodwork of the roof. Ruin. 32.

hrôdor, *st. m.* joy, delight, consolation, solace, benefit, advantage, gain.
hrôdor-léas, *adj.* joyless.
hrung, *st. f.* rung, staff, beam, pole (of a wagon-cover). (Ger. *runge.*)
hrungeat-torr, *st. m.* tower with a grate-door. (Ruin. 4.)
hruse, *w. f.* earth, soil, ground.
hrûtan, *st. abl. v.* VI. to make a noise, whiz, snore.
hrycg, hricg, *st. m.* back, height, surface, ridge. (Ger. *rücken.*)
hryre, *st. m.* fall, downfall, ruin, destruction, death.
hrysian, *w. v.* to shake, move.
hrystan, *w. v.* to adorn, ornament.
hrydig, *adj.* fallen to decay, in ruins.
hû (= **hwî**), *instr.* of **hwæt,** *adv.* how, why, wherefore; *w.* the *compar.* the.
hugod, hugende. See **hycgan.**
huilpa, *w. m.* name of a sea-animal (Wülcker), Seef. 21;—name of a bird,—so called from its note (B.-T.).
hû-lic, *adj.* of what sort.
hund, *st. m.* dog, hound. (Ger. *hund.*)
hund, *num.* one hundred.
hund-nigontig, *num.* ninety.
hundred, *num.* hundred.
hund-seofontig, *num.* seventy.
hund-teontig, *num.* hundred.
hund-twelftig, *num.* one hundred and twenty.
hungor, hungur, *st. m.* hunger, famine. (Ger. *hunger.*)
hungrig, *adj.* hungry, famishing. (Ger. *hungrig.*)
hunig, *st. n.* honey. (Ger. *honig.*)
hunig-flôwend, *part.* flowing with honey.
hunig-smæc, *st. m.* honey-smack, words sweet as honey.
hunta, *w. m.* hunter.
huntod, *st. m.* hunt, hunting. [hip.
hup-seax, *st. n.* knife worn on the

hûru, *adv.* at least, surely, yet, notwithstanding, however, indeed;— and **huru,** and especially. Sat.523.

hûs, *st. n.* house,—used collectively for household, family, race. (Ger. *haus.*)

husc, hux, *st. n.* mockery, derision, scorn, insult.

husc-word, *st. n.* insulting word, scornful speech.

hûsel, hûsl, *st. n.* insulting word, scornful speech.

hûsel, hûsl, *st. n.* housel, sacrifice, eucharist, consecrated bread and wine. (Goth. *hunsl;* Icel. *húsl.*)

hûsel-bearn, *st. n.* son (man) worthy of the eucharist.

hûsel-fæt, *st. n.* vessel for sacrifice.

hûsel-wer, *st. m.* man worthy of the eucharist.

hûđ, *st. f.* booty, spoil, plunder.

hûđan, *st. abl. v.* VI.
  â-hûđan, to rob, plunder.

hux. See **husc.**

hux-lic, *adj.* scornful, insulting, ignominious.

hwâ, *nom. n.* **hwæt;** *gen. m. n.* **hwæs;** *dat. m. n.* **hwâm, hwǣm,** *acc. m.* **hwone, hwane, hwǣne;** *n.* **hwæt;** *instr. n.* **hwî, hwig, hwŷ, hwan, hwon.**—I. *pron. interrog.* who, what, how,—in dependent clauses with indic. & subjunc.— II. *pron. indef.* any one, some one; any thing, some thing; **swâ hwâ (hwæt) swâ,** whosoever, whatsoever, whatever. (Ger. *wer.*)

hwæl, *st. m.*? wheel, circuit. Exod. 161. (Icel. *hvel.*)

hwæl, *st. m.* whale. (Icel. *hvalr.*)

hwæla, *w. m.* whale.

hwæl-mere, *st. m.* whale-mere, sea.

hwǣm, hwǣne. See **hwâ, hwêne.**

hwænne, hwonne, *adv. & conj.* when, as long as, until:—**hwonne ǣr,** how soon, when first.

hwǣr, hwâr, *w. v.* **where,** whither, anywhere, somewhere; when. B. 3062.

hwærfed, hwærgen. See **hwearfan, hwergen.**

hwæs, *adj.* sharp, piercing.

hwæt (= *neut.* of **hwâ**), 1. why.— 2. how! what! lo! ah! indeed!— 3. indeed, surely, verily, for, truly, not. (Ger. *was.*)

hwæt, *adj.* sharp, bold, valiant, brave, courageous.

hwǣte, *st. m.* **wheat.** (Ger. *weizen.*)

hwǣte-cyn, *st. n.* kind of corn, corn.

hwǣten, *adj.* **wheaten.**

hwæt-ĕadig, *adj.* rich in courage, very brave.

hwæt-hwega, -hwiga, -hwyga, hwugu, *n.* (used as noun or as adverb), somewhat, a little.

hwæt-lice, *adv.* quickly, promptly.

hwæt-môd, *adj.* courageous, bold in mind.

hwæt-rǣd, -rêd, *adj.* firm, determined.

hwæđer, *pron.* 1. **whether,** which of two.— 2. one of two, either (Met. 5, 41).— 3. each of two, both (Sat. 132).— 4. **swâ hwæđer,** whoever of two.

hwæđer, *conj. w. subjunc.* **whether.**

hwæđer = hwider, whither. B.1331.

hwæđere, hwæđre, hweđere, 1. *adv.* yet, however, nevertheless.— 2. *conj.* whether. B. 1314, Gû. 323.

hwam, hwom, *st. m.* corner, angle.

hwan. See **hwâ.**

hwanan, hwanon, hwonan, *adv.* whence.

hwanne, hwâr. See **hwænne, hwǣr.**

hwelan, *st. abl. v.* II. to roar, rage.

hwelc. See **hwilc.**

hwelp, *st. m.* **whelp,** a young dog; the young of an animal. (O. H. Ger. *hwelf.*)

hwêne, *adv. w. compar.* (*instr. sg.* of **hwôn**), a little.
hwer, *st. m.* kettle, caldron.
hwerfan, *w. v.* to turn one's self around, be turned, revolve.
  â-hwerfan, to turn from, avert.
  be-hwerfan, to roll, turn.
  for-hwerfan, to change into, to transform.
  ymb-hwerfan, to go about or around, travel or march round.
hwergen, hwærgen, *adv.* anywhere; —**elles hwergen,** elsewhere.
hwetan, *st. abl. v.* III. to whet, to sharpen.
hwettan, *w. v.* to **whet,** excite, incite, urge on, encourage. (Ger. *wetzen.*)
  â-hwettan, 1. to excite, kindle. **2.** to hold out to, provide.— **3.** to drive away, cast out.
hweder (Seef. 63), **hwedere.** See **hreder, hwædere.**
hwealf, *adj.* arched, convex. (Ger. *gewölbt.*)
hwealf, *st. m.* vault, arch. (Cf. Ger. *gewölbe.*)
hwearf, *st. m.* crowd, congregation.
hwearf, *adj.* violent, gusty, turning rapidly, changeable (Grein);—**and-hwearf,** *pret.* of **and-hweorfan,** to move against, come against, blow into one's face. (Thorpe, Kemble, & Heyne). B. 548.
hwearfan, *w. v.* to turn, go, revolve, roll, change.
  ymb-hwearfan, to go around, make the circumference of.
hwearfian, *w. v.* to turn, go, flit about, wander about, roll on, pass by. (Goth. & O. H. Ger. *hwarbon.*)
hwearft, *st. m.* going around, circuit, circle, revolution.
hweôl, *st. n.* **wheel.**
hweorfan, hworfan, hwurfan, *st. abl. v.* I. **1.** to turn. Cri. 485.— **2.** to turn one's self, be turned, turn around, change, return, depart, be converted.— **3.** to go, wander, go about, hover over.— **4.** to go to or from a place, die. (Goth. *hwairban.*)
  â-hweorfan, 1. to turn away, turn about, convert.— **2.** to turn away from, turn, move.
  æt-hweorfan, to enter, to go to.
  be-hweorfan, to change, turn.
  ge-hweorfan, 1. to turn, turn about, go, wander, go over, come. **2.** to turn, change, convert.
  geond-hweorfan, to wander about in, go through from end to end.
  on-hweorfan, 1. to turn, change. **2.** to turn.
  tô-hweorfan, to go away, separate, scatter.
  ymbe-hweorfan, to go around, wander about.
hweodu, *st. f.* air, breeze. Ps. 106, 28.
hwi, hwig, *instr.* of **hwæt.** Cf. **hû.**
hwider, hwyder, *adv.* whither; — at times like **hwær,** *w. gen.*
hwil, *st. f.* **while,** time, space of time; —*acc.* þâ hwile þâ, as long as, until;—**hwile,** for a time, a while, long;—**hwile-hwile,** sometimes—sometimes, now—now;— *dat. pl.* **hwilum (whilom), hwilon,** at times, many times, often; — **hwilum—hwilum,** now—now, at one time, at another. (Ger. *weile.*)
hwilc, hwelc, hwylc, *pron. interrog.* **which,** of what sort, who, what;— *indef.* some, any, every, of any kind. (Ger. *welcher.*)
hwilen, *adj.* temporary.
hwiled (An. 495). See **hwelan.**
hwinan, *w. v.* to whizz, whirr; later, to whistle (of the wind).
hwit, *adj.* **white,** brilliant, shining, glistening, flashing, clear. (Ger. *weiss.*)

hwitan, to whiten, polish (Reim.62); perhaps **hwitan** (akin to **hwæt**), to sharpen (cf. **hwetan**) would be better. Cf. **sweord-hwita.**

hwit-loc, *adj.* having white locks, fair-haired, blonde. Rä. 43, 3.

hwit-locced, *part.* same as above.

hwom, hwon. See **hwam, hwâ.**

hwôn, *st. n.* a little, very little.

hwonan. See **hwanan.**

hwôn-lice, *adv.* a little, very little.

hwonne. See **hwanne.**

hwôpan, *st. red. v.* to **whoop,** cry aloud, threaten.

hworfan, hwurfan, hwŷ, hwyder, hwylc. See **hweorfan, hwî, hwider, hwilc.**

hwylfan, *w. v.*
  â-hwylfan, to cover over, subvert, submerge.
  be-hwylfan, same as above.

hwyrfan, *w. v.* 1. to turn, change.—2. to turn, be changed.—3. to go hither and thither, wander about. 4. to fall.
  â-hwyrfan, to turn away, cast off.
  for-hwyrfan, to turn about, pervert.
  ge-hwyrfan, to avert, to turn aside; to turn around, pervert, change.
  on-hwyrfan, to turn, to turn around, to invert.
  ymb-hwyrfan, to go around or about, to travel or march about.

hwyrfe (Dan. 221). See **hweorfan.**

hwyrft, *st. m.* 1. way out, outlet, issue.—2. circuit, space.—3. going, descent, turn.—4. crowd, mob.—(Others make **hwyrftum,** *adv.* to and fro. See above — circling movement, turn, under 3).—5. circle, orb.

hwyrft-weg, *st. m.* turning-way, way out.

hŷ. See **hê.**

hycgan, hicgan, -ean, *w. v.* (*pret. hogade, hogode, hogede, hogde*). 1. to think.—2. to meditate, think about.—3. to think of, be mindful of, study.—4. to determine, resolve, purpose.—5. to remember, consider.—6. to hope. (See Sievers, Ags. Gram. §§ 415, 416. Aum. 3.)
  â-hycgan, to think out, devise, seek after, search, invent.
  be-hycgan, *w. acc.* to be solicitous about, to have great anxiety on account of.
  for-hycgan, to despise, scorn, reject with contempt.
  ge-hycgan, 1. to think.—2. to consider, take to heart, deliberate. 3. to devise.—4. to think of, determine upon, resolve, purpose.—5. to be mindful of, care for.—6. to hope.—7. to be disposed, inclined; *part.* **gehugod,** disposed, minded, inclined.
  • **ofer-hycgan,** to contemn, despise, give up, renounce.
  on-hycgan, to weigh, consider.
  wid-hycgan, to withstand in mind, contemn, despise.

hŷd, *st. f.* **hide,** skin. (Ger. *haut.*)

hŷdan, hidan, hiedan, hêdan, *w. v.* to **hide,** conceal, protect, preserve.
  â-hŷdan, to hide away, conceal.
  be-, bi-hŷdan, to cover up, hide away, conceal.
  for-hŷdan, the same as above.
  ge-hŷdan, 1. to hide, protect, preserve.—2. to bring into safety, fasten (Wal. 13).—3. to hide, conceal.—4. to obtain, get.

hyder. See **hider.**

hŷdig, *adj.* heedful, thoughtful, attentive.

hygd, *st. f.* thought, mind.

hyge, hige, *st. m.* manner of thinking, thought, mind, soul, heart, courage, disposition.

hyge-bend, *st. m. f.* mind-fetter, heart-band.
hyge-blind, *adj.* blind of soul.
hyge-blíðe, *adj.* blithe of heart, gay, joyful.
hyge-clǽne, *adj.* clean in heart.
hyge-cræft, *st. m.* strength of mind, power of thinking, knowledge, wisdom.
hyge-cræftig, *adj.* wise, prudent, sagacious.
hȳ-gedryht. See **hi-gedriht.**
hyge-fæst, *adj.* firm, shut up in mind, concealed.
hyge-frôd, *adj.* wise, prudent.
hyge-frôfor, *st. f.* consolation for the heart, solace of the soul.
hyge-gǽlsa, *w. adj.* proud, haughty. Ph. 314.
hyge-gâl, *adj.* loose, unbridled, lascivious.
hyge-gâr, *st. m.* mind's dart.
hyge-geômor, -giomor, *adj.* of sad mind, mournful, complaining. •
hyge-gleaw, *adj.* prudent, wise, skillful.
hyge-grim, *adj.* savage, cruel.
hyge-leás, *adj.* thoughtless, rash, heedless.
hyge-leást, *st. f.* heedlessness, rashness.
hyge-mǽd, *st. f.* becoming, careful attention, due respect.
hyge-méðe, *adj.* soul-crushing, sorrowful.
hyge-rôf, *adj.* vigorous-minded, bold, valiant.
hyge-rûn, *st. f.* secret of the heart.
hyge-sceaft, *st. f.* thought, mind, soul.
hyge-snottor, *adj.* sagacious, wise.
hyge-sorg, *st. f.* heart-sorrow.
hyge-strang, *adj.* strong-minded, firm, bold, brave.
hyge-teôna, *w. m.* soul-injury, insult.
hyge-treôw, *st. f.* fidelity.

hyge-þanc, -þonc, *st. m.* thoughts of the mind, mind, thought.
hyge-þancol, -þoncol, *adj.* thinking, reflecting, weighing, considering, mindful, thoughtful.
hyge-þrym, *st. m.* strength of mind, fortitude.
hyge-þrýd, *st. f.* impetuosity of mind, pride, insolence.
hyge-þyhtig, -þihtig, *adj.* doughty, courageous.
hyge-wælm, *st. m.* boiling of the mind, anger.
hyge-wlanc, -wlonc, *adj.* haughty, proud.
hȳhst, *superl.* See **heáh.**
hyht, hiht, heht, *st. m.* (*f.*), 1. hope. 2. intention of the mind, desire, striving.— 3. joyful thinking, joy, exultation, rejoicing.
hyhtan, hihtan, *w. v.* 1. to hope.— 2. to rejoice, exult, be glad.
hyht-ful (heht-), *adj.* 1. full of joy or hope, mirthful, pleasant.— 2. joyful, joyous.
hyht-gifa, *w. m.* giver of joy.
hyht-giefu, *st. f.* pleasure-giving gift.
hyht-leás, *adj.* hopeless, distrustful, unbelieving.
hyht-lic, *adj.* joyful, pleasant, agreeable, sweet.
hyht-lice, *adv.* joyfully, pleasantly, sweetly.
hyht-plega, *w. m.* refreshing, pleasant play.
hyht-willa, *w. m.* hoped-for good, expected joy.
hyht-wyn, *st. f.* hoped-for joy.
hyld, hild, held, *st. m.* protection, favor, grace, observance, reverence.
hyldan, *w. v.* to protect, guard, keep, sustain.
    ge-hyldan, to preserve, keep, hold.

hyldan, heldan, w. v. to incline, incline one's self, lie down.
   â-hyldan, 1. to incline, bend, bow down.—**2.** to avert from, turn away from. Jul. 171.
   on-hyldan, 1. to incline.—**2.** to incline one's self, descend, go down.
hylde-léas, adj. defenseless.
hylde-mǽg, st. m. near kinsman.
hyldo, hyldu, st. f. grace, favor, inclination. (Ger. huld.)
hylest, hyll. See **helan, hell.**
hyll, st. m. hill. (Cf. Ger. hügel.)
hylman, w. v.
   for-hylman, to transgress.
   ofer-hylman, to transgress.
hylt, 3d sig. of **hyldan.**
hyltan, w. v.
   â-hyltan, to block the way of, supplant.
hym. See **hê.**
hýnan, hênan, w. v. to bring low, humiliate, crush, afflict, injure.
   ge-hýnan, the same as above.
hyne. See **hê.**
hyngran, hingran, w. v. to hunger, to be hungry. (Ger. hungern.)
hýnd, hýndo, -u, hêndo, hǽndo, hiendo, st. f. oppression, humiliation, damage, injury, affliction.
hýra. See **hêra.**
hýran, hêran, hieran, w. v. **1.** to hear, perceive, learn by hearsay. **2.** to hear, hearken, obey.—**3.** to belong to, be subject to. (Ger. hören.)
   ge-hýran, 1. to hear, perceive. **2.** to grant.—**3.** to obey.
   ofer-hýran, not to hear, neglect.
hýran, w. v. to honor, adore.
hyrcnian, w. v. to hearken, listen. (Ger. horchen.)
hyrd (Gen. 2695). See **heord.**
hyrdan, w. v. to harden, make hard; encourage, animate, exhort. (Cf. Ger. verhärten.)
   â-hyrdan, the same as above.

   for-hyrdan, to harden against, hold out against.
   ge-hyrdan, to harden, make hard.
   on-hyrdan, to strengthen, encourage.
hyrde. See **hirde.**
hyrd-nes, st. f. watch.
hyre, hýre, hýrêd. See **hê, hêore, hirêd.**
hyrgan, w. v.
   on-hyrgan, to imitate, emulate.
hyrned, part. horned.
hyrned-neb, adj. having a horned neb or beak.
hýrra, compar. of **hêah.**
hyrst, st. f. equipment, ornament, accoutrements, armor, costly object, jewel, treasure. (O. H. Ger. rust; Ger. rüstung.)
hyrstan, w. v. to equip, deck, adorn, decorate. (Ger. rüsten.)
   ge-hyrstan, the same as above.
hyrstan, w. v. to roast. (Cf. Ger. rösten; Middle Eng. rosten, from O. Fr. rostir.)
hýr-sum, hêar-sum, adj. obedient.
hyrtan, w. v. to hearten; w. reflex. to take heart, be emboldened. B. 2593. (Ger. herzen.)
hyrwan. See **herwan.**
hys. See **hê.**
hyscan, w. v.
   on-hyscan, to curse, abhor, abominate.
hyse, hysse, st. m. youth, young man, boy.
hyse-beordor, st. m. boy? An. 1144.
hyspan, w. v. to mock, laugh at, deride, upbraid, reproach.
hyt. See **hê.**
hýd, st. f. haven, harbor.
hýdan, hidan, hiedan, w. v. to make booty, plunder.
   â-hýdan, to plunder, lay waste, destroy, kill.
hyde-lic, adj. suitable, proper.
hýd-weard, st. m. haven-warder, keeper of the harbor.

I

ic, *pron.* **I;** *gen.* **min;** *dat.* **mê;** *acc.* **mec, mê.** (Ger. *ich.*)

ican. See **ŷcan.**

ioge-gold, *st. n.* treasure-gold, rich gold? (Heyne); — **sword,** edge (Körner). B. 1107.

idel, *adj.* **1. idle,** worthless, useless, empty, bare.—**2.** deprived of. B. 2888. (Ger. *citel.*)

idel-hende, *adj.* with empty hands, empty-handed.

idel-nes, *st. f.* **idleness,** vanity, emptiness; idle, vain existence.

ides, *st. f.* woman, wife, lady, queen.

idig, *adj.* greedy for, desirous of. Ph. 407.

idlian, *w. v.* to become idle or useless.

ig, ieg, *st. f.* island.

ig-bûend, *part. & subs.* islander, dweller on an island.

ig-land, *st. n.* island.

ilca, ylca, *w. pron.* the same, idem.

ilde. See **ylde.**

in, *prep.* I. *w. dat.* **1.** denoting place, condition, situation: in, on, upon, —often equivalent to *into*, w. acc. **2.** temporal: in, at, during.—II. *w. acc.* **1.** local: in, into, upon, up to,—sometimes equivalent to **in,** *w. dat.* in German.—**2.** denoting purpose: in, to, for.—**3.** temporal: in, at, about, toward.—III. *w. instr.* **in.** Jud. 2.

in, inn, *adv.* **1.** in, within, inside of.— **2.** into.

in, inn, *st. n.* chamber, tent, inn, house.

in-bend, *st. m. f.* inner bond or chain.

inc. See **git.**

inca, incga, *w. m.* disquieting doubt, suspicion, ground, cause, inducement, complaint, grievance.

inca-þeode=in-geþeode. Exod. 443.

incer, 1. *pron. pers.* you two, both, belonging to both of you.—**2.** *gen.* see **git.**

incg, *adj.* costly? mighty? or **Incges?** B. 2577 (Grein); — edge (Körner).

incit. See **git.**

in-côfa, *w. m.* inner place, breast, heart.

in-dryhten, *adj.* very noble, most illustrious. [bility.

in-dryhto, *st. f.* noble followers, no-

in-flêde, *adj.* very watery or billowy.

in-frôd, *adj.* very aged, very experienced.

ing = ging, geong, *adj.* young. Exod. 190.

in-, inn-gang, *st. m.* entrance, access to. (Ger. *eingang.*)

in-gebed, *st. n.* earnest, inward prayer.

in-gefolc, *st. n.* native, home people.

in-, inn-gehygd, *st. n.* innermost, most secret thinking, intention.

in-gemynd, *st. n.* inward thought, consideration, memory.

in-gemynde, *adj.* fixed in the mind, well-remembered.

in-genga, *w. m.* ingoer, visitor.

in-gesteald, *st. n.* house-property, possessions in the house.

in-geþanc, -geþonc, *st. m. n.* inner thinking, earnest thought, mind.

in-geþeode, *st. n. pl.* people, nation.

in-lende, *adj.* inland, domestic, native. (Cf. Ger. *inländisch.*)

in-locast, *adv.* innermost, most heartily.

inn. See **in,** *subs. & adv.*

innan, I. *adv.* within, inside, in.— often used with **in, on, geond;— þær on innan,** therein, thereinto. II. *prep. w. gen. & dat.* in.—**3.** *w. acc.* into. (Ger. *innen.*)

innan-cund, *adj.* inner, entire, whole.
innan-weard, *adj.* within, inward, intrinsic.
innad, innod, *st. m. f.* inner parts, contents, entrails, belly, womb, breast.
inne, *adv.* 1. inside, within.—2. into, within.—3. still further, besides. B. 1867. (Ger. *inne.*)
innera, *w. adj.* the inner, inward.
inne-weard, *adj.* inward, within.
inn-gang, inn-gehygd. See ingang, ingehygd.
innian, *w. v.*
 ge-innian, to fill.
innod. See innad.
inn-weorud, *st. n.* retainers, followers, house-companions.
inn-wit. See inwid, inwit.
in-sittende, *part.* sitting in.
in-stæpes, *adv.* immediately, on the spot.
in-tinga, *w. m.* cause, ground, reason.
inweard-líce, *adv.* inwardly, in soul.
in-weorud. See innweorud.
in-wid, in-wit (inn-), *st. n.* iniquity, injustice, malice, evil, fraud, deceit, cunning, hostility.
in-wid, in-wit, *adj.* unjust, bad, wicked, malicious.
in-wid-. See inwit-.
inwit-feng, *st. m.* malicious grasp, hostile attack.
inwit-flâ, *w. f.* hostile dart, a missile of malice.
inwit-full, *adj.* wicked, crafty, cunning.
inwit-gæst, *st. m.* evil guest, hostile stranger.
inwit-gecynde, *st. n.* wicked nature, evil kind.
inwit-gyren, *st. f.* treacherous snare, trap.
inwit-hlem (inwid-), *st. m.* malicious wound, wound inflicted through malice.

inwit-hróf, *st. m.* hostile roof, lair.
inwit-net, *st. n.* net of malice, cunning snare.
inwit-nid, *st. m.* cunning hostility, hostility through secret attacks.
inwit-rún, *st. f.* evil, crafty counsel.
inwit-scear, *st. m.* massacre through cunning; murderous contest.
inwit-searo, *st. n.* cunning, artful intrigue.
inwit-sorh (inwid-), *st. f.* sorrow caused by malice or treachery; grief, misfortune.
inwit-spell, *st. n.* tale of woe, tidings of misfortune.
inwit-stæf, *st. m.* wickedness, evil, malice.
inwit-þanc (inwid-), *st. m.* wicked, deceitful thought; malicious, hostile disposition.
inwit-þanc, *adj.* malicious, hostile, ill-disposed, crafty, cunning.
inwit-wrâsen, *st. f.* deceitful band, hostile fetter.
íren, *st. n.* iron, sword. (Ger. *eisen.*)
íren, *adj.* of iron, iron.
íren-bend, *st. m. f.* iron band, bond, rivet.
íren-byrne, *w. f.* iron coat-of-mail.
íren-heard, *adj.* hard as iron, of hard iron.
íren-þreát, *st. m.* troop in iron armor.
irnan, yrnan, *st. abl. v.* I. to run, leap, flow. (Ger. *rinnen.*)
 â-irnan, to go or pass by, run out.
 be-irnan, to run up to or into, to occur, happen.
 on-irnan, to run back, open, give way.
 tô-irnan, to run hither and thither, wander about.
irre, irsung. See yrre, yrsung.
is, ys, *3d pers. sg.* of eam, is;—used either absolutely—is, exists, endures, &c.; or with *adj.* or *subs.* predicate, or *w. pret. part.* (Ger. *ist.*)

ís, *st. n.* ice, name of the Rune í. (Ger. *eis.*)
ís-ceald, *adj.* ice-cold, cold as ice.
ísen, *st. n.* iron.
ísen, *adj.* of iron, iron.
ísern, *st. n.* iron, sword.
ísern, *adj.* of iron, iron.
ísern-byrne, *w. f.* iron corselet.
ísern-here, *st. m.* iron army, host in iron armor.
ís-gebind, *st. n.* ice-fetters.
ísig, *adj.* icy, shining, brilliant.
ísig-federa, *adj.* with ice-covered wings.
ís-mere, *st. m.* ice-sea, frozen sea.
istoria, history.
it, ited, itst. See etan (to eat).
íw, *st. m.* yew, yew-tree. (Ger. *eibe.*)
íecan, ieg. See êcan, ȳcan, íg.
ieht, *st. f.* increase, strength, size.
ierne, ieted, iewan. See yrre, etan, eowan.

iode, iogod. See eode, geogod, youth.
ior, *st. m.* name of a fish, and of the Rune io.
iorne, iowian. See yrre, êowan.
iu, *adv.* still, yet. Sol. 249.
iu, *adv.* once, formerly, ever, of old.
iu-dǣd, gu-dǣd, *st. f.* former deed, deed done formerly.
iu-lêan, *st. n.* reward for a former deed.
iu-man, *st. m.* man of old, of the former times.
iu-mêowle, *w. f.* formerly a virgin, aged woman.
iung. See geong. (Ger. *jung.*)
iu-wine, *st. m.* former, dead friend.
Januarius, January. Men. 10.
Jula, *w. m.* Yule, December and January. Men. 221.
Julius mônað. Men. 132.
Junius mônað. Men. 109.

L

lâ, *interj.* O, lo. See êa.
lâ, *enclitic.* yes, indeed, certainly, undoubtedly (= ecce, certe).
lâc, *st. n.* 1. play, sport, strife, contest.— 2. booty, spoils.— 3. gift, present.— 4. offering, sacrifice.— 5. message. Gû. 1317.
lâcan, *st. red. v.* 1. to spring, jump, fly, swoop, swing, take ship, flutter, waver.— 2. to fight, contend.— 3. to change the voice, modulate. Rid. 32, 19.
    be-lâcan, to flow around.
    for-lâcan, to mislead, betray, deceive.
    geond-lâcan, to flow through.
lâc-geofa, *w. m.* giver of gifts. Cf. wedlock.
lâcnian, *w. v.* to heal, to cure. Cf. to leech.
    ge-lâcnian, same as the above.

lâd, *st. f.* 1. road, way, journey.— 2. nourishment, maintenance, support. Gû. 360.
lâdian, lâdigan, *w. v.* 1. to cleanse, purify, free from guilt. — 2. to excuse.
lâd-têow. See lâttêow.
lǣc, *adj.* wounded? Fin. 34?
lǣcan, *w. v.* to spring up, rise, strike upward.
    nêah-lǣcan (nêa-), to bring near, approach.
    ge-nêalǣcan, same as above.
lǣccan, *w. v.* to seize, take, grasp. Cf. latch.
lǣce, *st. m.* leech, physician.
lǣce-cynn, *st. n.* the leechkin, profession of physician, physician's way or manner.
lǣcedôm, *st. m.* leech-craft, healing art.

lǽdan, lêdan, *w. v.* 1. to lead, conduct, bring.— 2. to move (Kr. 5). 3. to produce (Gen. 1298).— 4. to sprout forth, grow.

   â-lǽdan, 1. to lead, lead forth, produce.— 2. to come forth, creep out, sprout forth or up.

   on-lǽdan, to lead on or to, bring up, draw forward, conduct to.

   for-lǽdan, 1. to mislead, lead astray.— 2. to fail in leading, lead unsuccessfully.

   ge-lǽdan, 1. to lead, conduct, bring.— 2. to go, journey? An. 43.

   on-lǽdan, to lead on, conduct to.

   ôd-lǽdan, to lead away or out; deprive of, carry off, snatch from.

   wið-lǽdan, the same as above.

lǽdan, to excuse. Ps. 140, 5.

lǽfan, *w. v.* to leave, leave behind or over, have left.

lǽgdon. See lecgan (to lay).

lǽht. See lǽccan (to seize).

lǽl, *st. f.* 1. rod, whip.— 2. spot, bruise, boil.

lǽlan, lǽlian, *w. v.* to be or become blue or bruised.

lǽmen, *adj.* loamy, clayey.

lǽn, *st. n.* what is left over, remnant, gift, present, benefit.

lǽnan, *w. v.* to lend, give, grant.

   on-lǽnan, to lend (as a loan).

lǽn-dagas, *st. m. pl.* transitory days, one's (brief) lifetime, loan-days.

lǽne, lêne, *adj.* transitory, temporary, lent, perishable, evanescent, liable to death or destruction.

lǽran, *w. v.* (cf. learn), to teach, instruct, advise, admonish, command.

   â-lǽran, to teach, instruct.

   for-lǽran, to mis-teach, mislead by teaching, seduce.

   ge-lǽran, 1. to teach, instruct. 2. to bring before (Sat. 413: 9); to advise to do, persuade, convince.

lǽr-gedêfe, *adj.* fitted to teach, for teaching, adapted for instruction.

lǽrig, *st. m.* rim or edge of a shield.

lǽs, *adv.* 1. less, lest;— þý, þê lǽs, *conj.* lest.— 2. *n.* the less;— þý lǽs, so much the less.

lǽssa, *w. adj.* (*superl.* lǽsast, -est), less, smaller, slighter.

lǽst, *st. f.* performance, fulfillment.

lǽstan, lêstan, *w. v.* 1. to perform, follow out, hold, fulfil, execute, accomplish.— 2. to follow (as a retainer). Met. 1, 27.— 3. to last, continue, remain.

   ge-lǽstan, 1. to perform, make, carry out, accomplish.— 2. to hold, perform, fulfil.— 3. to stand by, follow (as a retainer).— 4. to last, continue, remain.

   ful-lǽstan, to help, stand by, assist.

   ge-fullǽstan, same as above.

lǽt, *adj.* 1. (cf. late), slack, lax, negligent, hesitating.— 2. slow (of time).— 3. patient? Cri. 436.

lǽtan, lêtan, *st. red. v.* 1. to let be done, cause, occasion, permit, endure.— 2. to leave (behind), abandon.— 3. to hand over. Chr. Sax. 852.

   â-lǽtan, 1. to let, permit, endure.— 2. to pardon.— 3. to liberate, free.— 4. to let go, give up, leave behind.

   for-lǽtan, 1. to let, permit, cause;— ân, ânne, âne forlǽtan, to let alone, leave to one's self, give up, abandon.— 2. to release, pardon.— 3. to leave, abandon, avoid, leave behind.— 4. to pass over, indulge, conceal.

   ge-lǽtan, to let.

   of-lǽtan, to abandon, leave behind.

   on-lǽtan, to release, liberate.

lǽt-hydig, *adj.* lazy, slow-minded.

lǽt-lice, *adv.* slowly, negligently.

lǽddu, *st. f.* suffering, insult, offense.

lâf, *st. f.* **leaving**, remnant, remains, relic, heritage, inheritance; *w. gen.* following: **1.** that of which something is left.— **2.** the leaver or bequeather.— **3.** a thing from which something has escaped.

lafian, *w. v.* in.
   ge-lafian, to refresh, cheer. Cf. Ger. *laben*.

lago, lagu, *st. m.* lake, sea, ocean;— name for the Rune l.

lagu, *st. f.* law.

lagu-cræftig, *adj.* acquainted with the sea, skilled in seafaring (**lake-crafty**).

lagu-fæsten, *st. n.* water-fastness, sea, ocean.

lagu-fædam, *st. m.* water-embrace, enveloping waves.

lagu-flôd, *st. m.* water-flood, sea, stream (**lake-flood**).

lagu-lâd, *st. f.* seaway, sea-path or journey.

lagu-mearg, *st. m.* seahorse, ship.

lagu-sid, *st. m.* sea-journey, navigation, ship's path.

lagu-strǽt, *st. f.* watery way, sea-path.

lagu-strêam, *st. m.* sea-stream, sea-current, sea, ocean, river.

lagu-swimmende, *part.* sea-swimming.

lâm, *st. m.* loam, clay, muck, filth.

lama, *w. adj.* lame, weakly.

lamb, *st. n.* lamb.

lambor, lomber, *st. n.* same as above.

lâm-fæt, *st. n.* vessel of clay (**loam-vat**).

lâm-rindum? Ruin. 17.

land, lond, *st. n.* **1. land** in contrast to water.— **2.** land in contrast to air.— **3.** tillable land, field, real estate, soil.— **4.** land, territory, dominion, realm.

land-bûend, *part. & subs.* land-dweller, inhabitant, native.

land-fruma, *w. m.* land prince.

land-gemyrcu, -gemercu, *st. n. pl.* landmarks, frontier, territory marked out.

land-gesceaft, *st. f.* earthly creature, mortal.

land-geweorc, *st. n.* working of the land? fortification? earthwork?

land-man, *st. m.* land-inhabiter, native.

land-mearc, *st. f.* landmark, limit of the land, frontier.

land-rest, *st. f.* rest in the grave.

land-riht, *st. n.* right to landed estate; hence, landed estate.

land-sceap, *st. n.* land, landscape.

land-scearu, *st. f.* land, province, domain.

land-scipe, *st. m.* land, landscape, landskip.

land-sôcn, *st. f.* land-seeking.

land-stede, *st. m.* place or position on the land, location.

land-waru, *st. f.* (total) land-population.

land-wela, *w. m.* earthly wealth, riches, possessions (**land-wealth**).

land-weard, *st. m.* land-warden, shore-guard.

lang, long, *adj.* long (space and time); *compar.* **lengra**; *superl.* **lengest**.

langad. See **langod**.

lange, longe, *adv.* long, a long time; *compar.* **leng** and **lenge**; *superl.* **lengest**.

lang-fyrst, *st. m.* long space of time, long time.

langian, longian, *w. v.* to long, long after; *impers. w. acc.* of person who longs.
   â-langian, *impers.* to last too long, to demand? Seel. 154.

langod, langad, longad, *st. m.* longing.

langsum, longsum, *adj.* longsome, long-lasting, lasting, tedious, long.

lang-twidig, *adj.* **long granted, lent for a long time.**
langung, longung, *st. f.* **1. longing. 2.** disgust, ennui. Ps. 118, 28.
langung-hwil, *st. f.* time of disgust, ennui.
lann, lonn, *st. f.* chain, fetter? Sal. 265, 278.
lâr, *st. f.* **1.** (lore), teaching, instruction, learning, preaching.—**2.**counsel, exhortation, encouragement, command, commission.—**3.** example (Exod. 405).—**4.** cunning (Gen. 2693).—**5.** history (An. 1480).
lâr-cræft, *st. m.* **lore-craft,** teaching, knowledge. Sal. 3.
lâr-cwide, *st. m.* teaching, speech, sermon, discourse.
lâreow, lâriow, *st. m.* teacher.
lâr-smid (*pl.* **-smeodas**), *st. m.* **loresmith,** teacher, leader, counselor.
lâst, leâst, *st. m.* **1.** trace, a track left behind, footstep, trail. Cf. shoe-last.— **2.** on **lâste,** behind, following behind.— **3.** gait, step.
lâst-weard, *st. m.* track-guarder; hence, **1.** successor, heir.— **2.** persecutor, pursuer.
lâst-word, *st. n.* fame after death, posthumous glory.
late, *adv.* laxly, slowly.
latian, leatian, *w. v.* to be slack, late, indolent; to hesitate.
lâttêow, lâtþeow, *st. m.* leader, guide.
latu, *st. f.* hesitation, tarrying.
lâd, *st. n.* suffering, harm, evil, injury,difficulty, injustice, insult,sin.
lâd, *adj.* **loath,** loathing.— **1.** causing pain,sorrow,death; painful,bitter, bad.— **2.** hateful, hated, **loathsome.— 3.** hostile.—*subs.* enemy.
lâd-bite, *st. m.* hostile bite, wound.
lâde, *adv.* hostilely. Ps. 118, 87.
lâd-genîdla, *w. m.* one that thinks, strives after, hostility; persecutor, enemy.

lâd-getêona, *w. m.* harm-doer,enemy.
lâd-gewinna, *w. m.* enemy.
ladian, *w. v.* to invite, ask. (Ger. *laden.*)
 ge-ladian, the same as above.
lâd-lic, *adj.* **loathly,** hateful, unpleasant, troublesome, painful.
lâd-lice, *adv.* hatefully,disgustingly.
lâd-scipe, *st. m.* **loath**someness, suffering, misfortune, unhappiness.
lâd-searo, *st. n.* hateful cunning, intrigue.
lâd-sîd,*st. m.* hateful journey,death, destruction.
lâd-spell, *st. n.* sad or evil tidings, **loathly spell.** Cf. **good-spell** (gospel).
lâd-trêow, *st. n.* **loathly tree,** tree of death or destruction.
lâd-wende, *adj.* hostile, hateful, troublesome, bad.
lâd-wendemôd, *adj.* hostile-minded.
lâd-weorc, *st. n.* **loathly work,** evil deed.
leccan, *w. v.* (*pret.* **leohte**), to wet, moisten.
 ge-leccan, the same as above.
leccan, *w. v.?*
 ô-leccan,-liccan,to flatter,make advances, honor, revere, adore.
lecgan, *w. v.* to lay, set, place.
 â-lecgan, 1. to lay, lay down.— **2.** to lay upon, impose (Gen. 2684). **3.** to lay down, resign, give up, abandon.— **4.** to diminish, lessen.
 be-, bi-lecgan,to belay,surround.
 ge-lecgan, to lay, place.
 of-lecgan, to lay down or off.
lêdan, lêde. See **læ̂dan, lecgan.**
lef, *adj.* weak, feeble.
lêfan, lêft. See **lŷfan, lŷft.**
lêg, *st. m.* flame, fire. Cf. **low.**
lêgan, *w. v.* to break out in flames, to ignite.
 be-, bi-lêgan, to flame about, surround with fire.
lêg-bryne, *st. m.* burning fire.

lêg-draca, *w. m.* fiery dragon.
legen, *part.* Cf. licgan (to lie).
lêgen, *adj.* flaming, fiery.
leger, *st. m.* lying-place, bed. Cf. lair.
leger-bed, *st. n.* the same as above.
lêh, *pret.* Cf. lêogan (to speak falsely).
lehtor. See leahtor (laughter).
lemian (lemman?), *w. v.* to lame, hinder, oppress, crush.
lencten, *st. m.* spring, springtime (lent).
lencten-tid, *st. f.* same as above.
lendan, *w. v.* to land.
lêne. See lǣne (lent).
leng. See lange.
lengan, *w. v.* 1. to lengthen out, prolong, procrastinate, put off.— 2. *intr.* to extend to, reach, attain.
 ge-lengan, to lengthen, prolong.
lenge, lengest. See lange, lang.
lenge, *adj.* at hand, near, extending along.
lengian, *w. v.* to long for, demand; *impers. w. acc.* of person who longs. Sal. 270.
lengra, lengust. See lang.
lengu, *st. f.* length.
leppan, *w. v.* to weaken, exhaust, render languid.
lesan, *st. abl. v.* III. to pick, select, collect. [choose.
 â-lesan, to pick out, select,
lêsan. See lȳsan.
lêst. See lêast.
lêstan. See lǣstan.
lêtan. See lǣtan.
lettan, *w. v.* (*w. acc.* of person, and *gen.* of thing), to let or hinder one in a matter.
 ge-lettan, to hinder, detain, prevent, injure.
leðer, *st. n.* leather, hide.
leðre. See lyðre.
lêad, *st. n.* lead.
lêaf, *st. f.* leave, permission.
lêaf, *st. n.* leaf, foliage.

lêafnes-word, *st. n.* leave, permission.
lêaf-scæd, *st. n.* leaf-shadow, tree-shadow.
leáh. See lihan (to lend).
leahan. See lêan (to lend).
leahtor, leahter, *st. m.* 1. reproach. 2. sin, crime, misdoing.
leahtor-cwide, *st. m.* reproachful talk, blasphemy.
leahtor-lêas, *adj.* 1. blameless, free from reproach.— 2. sinless, crimeless.
lêan, *st. abl. v.* IV. to scold, blame, censure.
 be-lêan (*w. dat.* of person, and *gen.* of thing), to censure one out of a thing, to dissuade by blame or reproach.
lêan, *st. n.* loan, reward, restitution, compensation, advantage, profit.
lêan, *st. n.* loan, partial gift.
lêanian, *w. v.* to reward, compensate.
 ge-lêanian, the same as above.
lêap, *st. m.* 1. basket.— 2. carcass. (Jud. 111), lap?
lêas, *adj.* loose, free, empty, bare, bereft.
lêas, *adj.* loose, false, deceitful, faithless, inconstant, disgraceful.
lêas, *st. n.* falsehood, lie.
lêasing, lêasung, *st. f.* leasing, falsehood, lie, deceit, delusion.
lêas-lic, *adj.* false, deceitful.
lêast. See lâst (track).
leatian. See latian (to be slack).
lêaw-finger, *st. m.* index-finger.
leax, *st. m.* salmon. (Ger. *lachs*.)
leo, *w. m. & f.* lion, lioness.
lêod, *st. m.* prince, leader.
lêod, liod, *st. f.* folk, people;— *n. pl.* one's race; people, men.
leoda. See lida.
lêodan, liodan, *st. abl. v.* VI. to spring up, grow.
 â-lêodan, the same as above.
 ge-lêodan, to grow, increase.

lêod-bealu, *st. n.* folk-bale, injury to the people or nation.
lêod-burg, *st. f.* folk-burg, princely castle, capital, metropolis.
lêod-cyning, *st. m.* folk-king, ruler.
lêod-fruma, *w. m.* prince of the people, ruler.
lêod-geborga, *w. m.* people's protector, influential man.
lêod-gebyrga, -gea, *w. m.* the same.
lêod-gewin, *st. n.* popular strife, struggle.
lêod-geard, *st. m.* national or urban inclosure or limits; town, state, domain.
lêod-gryre, *st. m.* people's terror, horror seizing and afflicting the people.
lêod-hata, *w. m.* people-hater, tyrant, despot.
lêod-hete, *st. m.* hate from the people, popular hatred.
lêod-hryre, *st. m.* defeat, downfall, death of the people or prince.
lêod-hwæte, *adj.* very valiant.
lêod-mǽg, *st. m.* relation from the same people, one of the people, people's companion, comrade.
lêod-mægen, *st. n.* might of the people, multitude, host.
lêod-mearc, *st. f.* people's mark, domain, territory.
lêod-riht, *st. n.* law of the land.
lêod-sceaða, *w. m.* folk-scather, destroyer of the people.
lêod-scearu, *st. f.* division of the people, tribe, nation, country, province.
lêod-scipe, *st. m.* same as above.
lêod-stefn, *st. m.* race, tribe.
lêod-þeow, *st. m.* people's custom, popular usage.
lêod-weras, *st. m. pl.* men, human beings.
lêod-werod, *st. n.* host, collection of people.
lêod-weard, *st. f.* guardianship of the people, government, territory.
lêod-wyn, *st. f.* people's joy, joy from living together with one's people.
lêof, liof, *adj.* dear, valued (lief).
lêofan, *st. abl. v.* VI. to love, enjoy, choose, prefer? value? Dan. 56.
leofon, lifen, *st. f.* food, nourishment.
leofian. See **lifian** (to live).
lêofian, *w. v.* to be or become dear. Gû. 110.
lêoflic, *adj.* lovely, dear, valued, amiable.
lêoflice, *adv.* in a loving, friendly manner.
lêof-spell, *st. n.* love-spell, loving or precious knowledge.
lêof-tǽl (-tǽle), *adj.* kind, friendly.
lêof-wende, *adj.* loving, friendly, courteous.
lêof-wendum, *adv. instr. pl.* same as above.
lêogan, *st. abl. v.* VI. to lie, deceive, betray.
  â-lêogan, to lie, belie, leave unfulfilled.
  ge-lêogan, to lie, deceive, betray.
leoht. See **leccan** (to wet).
lêoht, *adj.* light.
lêoht, *adj.* bright, flashing, clear.
lêoht, lioht, liht, *st. n.* light, daylight.
lêohtan, *w. v.* to lighten, shine forth, illumine.
  in-lêohtan, the same as above.
  on-lêohtan, the same as above.
lêoht-bǽre, *adj.* light-bearing, brilliant.
lêoht-berende, *part.* light-bearing, Lucifer.
leohte, *pret.* of **leccan** (to wet).
lêohte, *adv.* brightly, clearly, brilliantly.

lêoht-fǣt, *st. n.* light-vessel, lantern, candelabrum, torch.
lêoht-fruma, *w. m.* creator, prince of light.
lêohtian, *w. v.* to give light, illumine.
lêoht-lic, *adj.* brilliant, flashing, light-like. [going.
lêoht-môd, *adj.* light-minded, easy-
lêolc, *pret.* of lâcan (to play).
lêoma, *w. m.* light, brightness.
leomu, *pl.* of lim (limb).
leoran, *w. v.* to go, move off or by, pass away, vanish.
    ge-leoran, to go, wander, roam.
    ofer-leoran, to pass over or beyond.
leornere, *st. m.* scholar, one taught, learner.
leornian, *w. v.* to learn, estimate, reflect over, think out, conceive.
    ge-leornian, to learn.
leorning, leornung, *st. f.* learning, teaching.
leornung-cræft, *st. m.* learning, science, knowledge.
lêort, *pret.* of lǣtan.
lêosan, *st. abl. v.* VI. in
    be-lêosan, bi-, 1. to rob of, deprive.— 2. to be robbed, lose.
    for-lêosan, 1. *w. acc.* to destroy, ruin.— 2. *w. acc. & instr.* to lose something.
lêot, *pret.* of lǣtan.
lêod, liod, *st. n.* lay, song, poem.
lêod-cræftig, *adj.* skilled in song, acquainted with song.
lêod-gidding, *st. f.* lay, song, poem.
leodian. See liðian.
lêodian, *w. v.* to sing, sound (forth), resound.
leodu, *st. f.* retinue, followers. Reim. 14.
leoðo, *pl.* of lið, or leoðu.
lêoðor = hlêoðor, sound, tone?— or leoðor, leather?
lêoðu-bend, *st. m. & f.* limb-band, fetter. (Ger. *glied.*)

lêoðu-cǣge, *st. f.* limb-key (?), limbs serving for a key? Cri. 334.
lêoðu-cræft, *st. m.* skill of limb, sleight-of-hand.
lêoðu-cræft, *st. m.* lay-craft, poesy, *ars poetica.*
lêoðu-cræftig, *adj.* skilled with one's limbs, alert.
leoðu-fæst, *adj.* well-skilled in.
lêoðu-lic, *adj.* appertaining to the limbs.
lêoðu-rûn, *st. f.* song-secret, secret instruction or message given in song.
lêoðu-syrce, *w. f.* limb-sark, corselet woven of links.
lêoðu-wâc, *adj.* (limb-weak), with supple limbs.
lêoð-word, *st. n.* song-word, poetic word, words of a song.
lêoð-wyrht, *st. f.* poetry, something wrought in song.
libban, lybban, *w. v.* to live.
    â-libban, the same as above.
    be-libban, *part.* belifd, deprived of life, dead.
lic, *st. n.* body. Cf. M. E. lyche. (Ger. *leiche.*)
lican, *v.* to please, like (*impers*).
lic-bysig, *adj.* ready of body, active of limb.
liccan. See leccan (to hurt).
liccian, *w. v.* to lick.
licend-lic, lŷcend-, *adj.* likable, agreeable, pleasant.
licettan, *w. v.* to pretend, be hypocritical, delude, dissemble.
lic-fæt, *st. n.* (body-vat), body.
licgan, licgean, *st. abl. v.* III. 1. to lie, lie down.— 2. to lay one's self, succumb, lie prostrate, rest, fail
    â-licgan, to lie, succumb, lie prostrate, rest, cease, fail, give up.
    be-, bi-licgan, to lie about, surround, inclose. (Cf. beleaguer.)
    for-licgan, to lie unlawfully, lie with, cohabit.

lic-hama, -homa, *w. m.* body (as the soul's home).
lic-hord, *st. n.* body-hoard, body's contents or interior.
lic-hryre, *st. m.* decay, destruction of the body.
lician, *w. v.* to like (*impers.*) please. **ge-lician,** same as above. Hy. 11, 17.
liciend-lic, *adj.* agreeable, pleasant.
lic-sâr, *st. n.* wound, bodily pain. Cf. **sore**.
lic-syrce, *w. f.* body-sark, body-corselet.
lic-wund, *st. f.* **wound**.
lic-wyrde, -werde, *adj.* worthy of applause or liking, agreeable.
lid, lid, *st. n.* vehicle, means of getting about, boat.
lida, leoda, *w. m.* sailor.
lidan, *st. abl. v.* V. to grow. Ps. 91: 11; Rid. 34: 11).
lidon. See **lidan**.
lid-man, *st. m.* sailor, seafarer.
lid-wêrig, *adj.* sea-**weary**.
lid-weard, *st. m.* ship-**warden**.
lif, *st. n.* life.
lif, *adj.* weak? Wy. 18.
lifan. See **lýfan** (to allow).
lifan, to leave, leave over (Gen. 1916), concede, relinquish.
lif-bysig, *adj.* toiling for life, struggling with death.
lif-cearu, *st. f.* life-care, grief.
lif-dæg, *st. m.* life-day, life.
lifde, *pret.* of **libban** (to live).
lifen. See **leofen**.
lifer, *st. f.* **1.** liver.— **2.** the liver-mass, together with its blood. An. 1278.
lif-fæst, *adj.* vigorous.
lif-frêa, *w. m.* lord of life.
lif-fruma, *w. m.* originator or author of life.
lifgan. See **lifian**.
lif-gedâl, *st. n.* separation from life, death.

lif-gesceaft, *st. f.* life-fate, destiny.
lif-getwinnan, *w. m. pl.* **twins**.
lifian, liffian, lifgan, leofian, *w. v.* to live.
lif-naru, *st. f.* (*dat.* **nere**), food, nourishment, that which preserves life.
lift. See **lyft** (air).
lif-weg, *st. m.* life-path, **way** of life.
lif-wela, *w. m.* **1.** life-weal, life's blessings; glorious, heavenly life. **2. wealth**.
lif-weard, *st. m.* life-warden, guardian of life.
lif-wradu, *st. f.* life-protection, personal safety.
lif-wyn, *st. f.* enjoyment of life, pleasure, joy.
lig, ligg, *st. m. & n.* flame, fire.
lig-bryne, *st. m.* burning fire.
lig-cwalu, *st. f.* fiery torment.
lig-draca, *w. m.* fiery **dragon**.
lige. See **lyge** (lie).
lig-egesa, *w. m.* fiery horror or terror (of the dragon).
ligen. See **lygen** (lie).
liget, *st. f. & n.* flash, lightning-flash.
lig-fýr, *st. n.* flame of fire.
lignian. See **lýgnian** (to deny).
lig-þracu, *st. f.* fiery onset or impetus.
lig-ýð, *st. f.* wave of fire.
lihan, lýhan, *st. abl. v.* V. to lend, give. **on-lihan,** the same as above.
liht. See **lêoht** (light).
lihtan, *w. v.* to alight, light, descend. **ge-lihtan,** to descend to (Sat. 431); also, **gelýhtan,** to shine forth, illumine.
lihtan. See **lýhtan**.
lilie, *f.* lily.
lim, *st. n.* **1.** limb.— **2.** branch.
lim, *st. m.* **lime,** gluten, mortar, cement.
lim-hâl, *adj.* **limb-whole,** sound of limb.

lim-nacod, *adj.* naked of limb, stark naked.

limpan, *st. abl. v.* I. (*impers. w. dat.*), to happen, occur, take place, happen to, befall, succeed.
   â-limpan, to occur, take place, befall, fall to one's lot.
   be-limpan, *w. dat.* to come upon, befall.
   ge-limpan = limpan.

lim-sêoc, *adj.* limb-sick, lame, paralytic.

lim-wǽde, *st. n.* limb-weeds, clothing, covering for the limbs.

lim-wæstm, *st. m.* growth of limb, stature.

lim-wêrig, *adj.* limb-weary, weary of limb.

linan, *w. v.* to follow line by line, examine critically, learn. Sol. 86.

lind, *st. f.* linden, lime; — in the poets=shield, linden-shield (shield covered with linden-bast).

lind-croda, *w. m.* shield-crowding, collision of shields, battle-clash, battle.

linden, *adj.* linden, of lime-wood.

lind-gebora, *w. m.* shielded protector.

lind-gecrod, *st. n.* shielded crowd, troop with shields.

lind-gelâc, *st. n.* shield-sport, battle between shield-bearers (soldiers).

lind-gestealla, *w. m.* shield-comrade, battle-companion, squire.

lind-hæbbend, *part. & subs.* shield-bearer, warrior with shield.

lind-hwæt, *adj.* shield-brave, valiant shield-bearer. El. 11.

lind-plega, *w. m.* shield-play, conflict of shield-bearers.

lind-wered, *st. n.* troop armed with shields.

lind-wiga, *w. m.* shield-warrior.

lind-wigen, -wiggend, *part. & subs.* the same as above.

line, *w. f.* line, cable, hawser; line, series, row; discipline, directing, direction.

linnan, lynnan, *st. abl. v.* I. to yield, go off, desist; — *w. instr.* or *gen.* to be deprived of, lose.
   â-lynnan, to free, liberate.

lis, liss, *st. f.* indulgence, favor, grace, softness, rest, pleasure.

lisne? Ps. 52, 6.

lissan? Sol. 294.

list, *st. m. & f.* art, experience, wisdom, skill, cunning; — *instr. pl.* listum, artfully, thoughtfully, heedfully. (Ger. *list.*)

list-hendig, *adj.* cunning-handed, skilled.

listan. See lystan (to lust after).

lit (Met. 26: 119). See lýtan (to bow).

litel. See lytel.

lid. See lid.

lid = liged. See licgan (to lie).

lid, *st. n.* limb, limbs. (Scotch, lith.)

lid, *st. m.* a drink; beaker, cup.

lid, *adj.* gentle, soft, mild. Cf. lithe. (Ger. *lind.*)

Lida, *w. m.* the months June and July. Men. 108.

lidan, *st. abl. v.* V. 1. to go, move, travel, voyage, fly. — 2. to be deprived of, lose. Gn. Ex. 26.
   be-lidan, to flee away, escape, abandon; to rob of.
   ge-lidan, to move, journey, go, come, reach; to pass away.
   ofer-lidan, to stride over, pass over or beyond.

lide, *adj.* gentle, mild, soft, kind, agreeable, peaceful, friendly, benevolent.

lide, *adv.* gently, softly.

lidian, leodian, *w. v.* in
   â-leodian, to remove a limb, take out, extract.
   tô-lidian, to dismember, separate.

lidigan, *w. v.* to soften.
   on-lidigan, to indulge, become indulgent.

liðre, *w. f.* sling, slinging-pouch.
liðs, *st. f.* mildness, gentleness, repose.
lið-wǣge, *st. n.* drinking-cup containing lið (a fermented, wine-like drink). B. 1982.
linan = linnan. Sol. 86.
lixan, liexan, *w. v.* to flash, shine forth.
líod, líodan, líof, lioht, liod, liodu. See léod, léodan, léof, léoht, léod, leodu.
loc, *st. m.* lock (of hair).
loc, *st. n.* lock, bolt, bar.
loca, *w. m.* lock, bolt, bar; locking up, captivity, imprisonment.
locen, *st. n.* lock.
locen, *part.* of lúcan (to lock).
lócian, *w. v.* to look, see, behold.
lof, *st. n.* (*m.*) praise, laudation. (Ger. *lob.*)
lof, *st. n.* shady spot, protection, help, favor, grace.
lof-dǣd, *st. f.* deed of praise.
lof-georn, *adj.* desirous of praise.
lofian, *w. v.* to praise, exalt, celebrate, magnify.
lof-mǣgen, *st. n.* numerous manifestations of praise; laudation.
lof-sang, *st. m.* song of praise, eulogy, hymn.
lof-sum, *adj.* praiseworthy.
lóg, *pret.* of léan (to blame).
loga, *w. m.* liar. [Used only in compounds.]
lomber, lond, long, longad, longe, longian, lonn. See lamber, land, &c.
losian, *w. v.* to be loosed from, taken out; to escape, get away.
lot, *st. n.* cunning, fraud, deceit, betrayal.
lóda, *w. m.* mantle, garment.
lúcan, *st. abl. v.* VI. 1. to lock, close, inclose.—2. to unite, link together, interweave.—3. *intr.* close.

be-, bi-lúcan, to close, inclose, embrace, preserve, protect.
ge-lúcan (to close together), to unite, weave together.
on-lúcan, to unlock, open.
tó-lúcan, to open, dissolve, break to pieces, destroy.
lufe, *w. f.* love.
lufen, *st. f.* hope, comfort! B. 2886, Dan. 73.
lufian, *w. v.* to love, exhibit love by word or deed.
ge-lufian, to love, cherish.
luf-sum, *adj.* lovesome, loving, friendly.
luf-tácen, *st. n.* love-token.
lufu, *st. f.* love.
lungre, *adv.* hastily, quickly, soon, immediately.
lust, *st. m.* pleasure, joy, lust, longing, desire.
lust-gryn, -grin, *st. f.* pleasure-trap. Seel. 23.
lustice, *adv.* merrily, gayly, lustily.
lust-lice, the same as above.
lútan, *st. abl. v.* VI. to lout, bow, bend, fall down.
on-lútan, to bend, bow, incline, strive.
under-lútan, to bow or bend beneath or under.
lutian, *w. v.* in.
ge-lutian, to be concealed, hide one's self.
lybban. See libban (to live).
lyccan, *w. v.* to snatch out, pluck out. Met. 12, 28.
lýcend-líc. See lícendlíc.
lýf. See líf.
lýfan, *w. v.* (léof), in.
ge-lýfan, to render dear, endear. Cf. lief.
lýfan, léfan, lífan, *w. v.* to leave, allow, let, permit, grant, concede.
á-lýfan, to allow, grant, concede, hand over.
ge-lýfan, to allow, grant.

lýfan, lêfan, lifan, *w. v.* to **believe**, trust (in).
  ge-lýfan, to **believe**, trust, hope.
lyfian. See lifian.
lyft, *st. m. & f.* air. Cf. M. E. **lift**. (Ger. *luft*.)
lýft, lêft, *st. n.* vow, promise, gift.
lyft-edor, *st. n.* air-region, space of the sky.
lyft-fæt, *st. n.* air-vessel (the moon).
lyft-fêogende, *part.* flying in air, air-traversing.
lyft-floga, *w. m.* flier in air.
lyft-gelâc, *st. n.* air-sport, flight.
lyft-geswenced, *part.* air-rocked, wind-tossed (of a ship in harbor). B. 1913.
lyft-helm, *st. m.* air-**helm**, atmosphere, cloud, mist.
lyft-lâcende, *part.* sporting in the air, flying.
lyft-sceada, *w. m.* air-**scather**, foe living in the air (crow).
lyft-wundor, *st. n.* air-**wonder**, meteor.
lyft-wyn, *st. f.* revel in the air, joy in the air (of the dragon).
lyge, lige, *st. m.* **lie**.
lygen, ligen, *st. f.* same as above.
lygen-word, *st. n.* **lie-word**, falsehood.
lyge-searu, *st. n.* lying deception, machination, cunning.
lyge-synnig, *adj.* **sinning by lies**, liar.
lyge-torn, *st. n.* hypocritical or pretended wrath.
lyge-word, *st. n.* **lie-word**, lie.
lyge-wyrhta, *w. m.* **lie-wright**, manufacturer of lies.
lýgnian, lignian, *w. v.* to deny. Cf. Ger. *läugnen*.
lýhan. See lîhan (to lend).

lýhtan, lihtan, *w. v.* to **lighten**, flash, shine.
  geond-lýhtan, to flash or shine through.
  in-lýhtan, to flash forth, illumine.
  on-lýhtan, the same as above.
lyhd, lýhd. See lêan, lêogan.
lynd, *st. f.* fat, grease.
lynnan. See linnan (to cease).
lyre, *st. m.* loss, destruction.
lýsan, lêsan, *w. v.* to **loose**, redeem, liberate.
  â-lýsan, to let **loose**, release, ransom, liberate.
  on-lýsan, 1. to loose, **unloose**. 2. to redeem, ransom.
  tô-lýsan, 1. to dissolve.—2. to separate.
lystan, *w. v., impers. w. acc.* of person, and *gen.* of thing; or *w. inf.* to **lust** after, long for, long;—*part.* gelysted, longing for, desirous of.
lysu, *adj.* base, false, faithless.
lysu, *st. n.* falsehood.
lyt, *adj.* little.
lyt, *n. adj.* few, not many.
lýt, 3*d pers. sg. pres.* of **lûtan** (to bow).
lýtan, litan, *w. v.* to **lout**, bow, bend, turn.
lytegian, *w. v.* to be hypocritical, dissimulate, pretend, dissemble.
lytel, litel, *adj.* little, small.
lytel-hýdig, *adj.* little-minded, pusillanimous.
lytes-nâ, *adv.* within a little, nearly, almost.
lyt-hwôn, *n. & adv.* little, but little.
lytlian, *w. v.* to lessen, decrease.
  ge-lytlian, to diminish, depreciate, **belittle**, degrade.
lydre, ledre, *adj.* **lewd**, bad, base, corrupt, unworthy.

M

mâ, 1. *n. subs. & adj.* **more.**—**2.** *adv.* more, longer (quantitative or temporal or frequentative), = *plus, magis,* and *amplius.*

macian, *w. v.* in.
   ge-macian, to **make,** prepare.

mâ-cræftig, *adj.* having more vigor or power than others, highly skilled.

mâd-môd, *st. n.* **madness,** weak-mindedness.

mǽ, *adv.* **more.**

mæc, *adj.* comrade-like, companionable.—*subs.* comrade.

mæcg, mecg, *st. m.* man.

mæcga, *w. m.* the same as above.*

mǽdan, *w. v.* in [fatuate.
   ge-mǽdan, to fool, **madden,** in-

mæg. See **magan.**

mǽg, *st. m.* blood relation of any kind; son, nephew, cousin, brother, grandson, kinsman, &c.

mǽg, *st. f.* female blood-relation; wife, woman, maiden.

mǽg-burg, *st. f.* **1.** kindred in general; family, tribe, race, people, nation.—**2.** genealogy, family tree.

mægden, *st. n.* **maiden,** girl, young woman (unmarried).

mægden-hâd, *st. m.* **maidenhood.**

mǽge. See **magan.**

mǽge, *w. f.* female (blood) relation.

mǽgen. See **magan** (may).

mægen, mægn, mægyn, *st. n.* **1.** power, main-strength, bodily vigor, might, ability, virtue.—**2.** forces, multitude, army.

mægen-âgend, *part.* possessing strength, valiant, heroic.

mægen-byrden, *st. f.* immense burthen.

mægen-cordor, *st. n.* strong troop, large force.

mægen-cræft, *st. m.* great strength, power.

mægen-cyning, *st. m.* mighty king, virtuous king.

mægen-dǽd, *st. f.* **deed** of strength or power.

mægen-ellen, *st. n.* great strength, heroic vigor.

mægen-êaca, *w. m.* increase of power or strength, strengthening.

mægen-êacen, *adj.* vigorous, sturdy, able-bodied.

mægen-earfede, *st. n.* great misery or trial.

mægen-fæst, *adj.* steadfast, strong.

mægen-folc, *st. n.* powerful nation or people.

mægen-fultum, *st. m.* vigorous support.

mægen-hæp, -heap, *adj.* vigorous, powerful.

mægen-rǽs, *st. m.* violent onslaught.

mægen-rôf, *adj.* powerful.

mægen-scype, *st. m.* might, power.

mægen-spêd, *st. f.* abundant power, strength, **main-speed.**

mægen-stân, *st. m.* immense **stone,** rock.

mægen-strang, *adj.* strong, energetic.

mægen-strenge, *adj.* same as above.

mægen-strengdu, -strengu, *st. f.* **main strength,** great strength, power.

mægen-þegen, *st. m.* powerful thane.

mægen-þise, *w. f.* attack? Rid. 28, 10.

mægen-þrêat, *st. m.* host, large troop

mægen-þrym, *st. m.* **1.** glory.—**2.** vigor, strength, power.—**3.** noise, tumult (Exod. 540).—**4.** heavenly host or glory.

mægen-þrymnes, *st. f.* great glory, majesty.
mægen-weorc, *st. n.* immense work.
mægen-wiaa, *w. m.* (powerful) leader, general.
mægen-wudu, *st. m.* might-wood, spear.
mægen-wundor, *st. n.* (great) marvel of glory, striking wonder.
mæged. See mægđ.
mæg-lufe, *w. f.* love between kindred; connubial love.
mægn. See mægen.
mægnian, *w. v.* to be strong, mighty, possess strength.
mægon. See magan (may).
mæg-ræden, *st. f.* relationship, kinship.
mægđ, mæged, *st. f.* maid, virgin, wife, woman.
mægđ, *st. f.* tribe, folk, nation, family.
mægđ-hâd, *st. m.* maidenhood, virginity.
mæg-wine, *st. m.* blood-friend, kinsman.
mæg-wlite, mâg-, *st. m.* family likeness, aspect, appearance, form, figure.
mægyn, mæht, mæhtig. See mægen, meaht, meahtig.
mæl, *st. n.* 1. measure.— 2. what is measured: time, point of time.— 3. meal, meals.— 4. mole, spot.— 5. in compounds, meal, in piecemeal, &c.
mæl, *st. f.* speech.
mælan, *w. v.* to speak, talk.
    ge-mælan, the same as above.
    on-mælan, to address, speak to.
mælan, *w. v.* to fleck, spoil, soil, mark. Cf. mildew (?).
    ge-mælan, the same as above.
mæl-cearu, *st. f.* time-care, trouble from (evil) times? B. 189.
mæl-dæg, *st. m.* a day's time, day.

mældan. See meldan.
mǽl-gesceaft, *st. f.* time allotted by fate, lifetime, destiny.
mæn. See man.
mǽnan, *w. v.* to share; communicate, announce, pronounce, speak of.
    ge-mǽnan, to pronounce, speak out, inform.
mǽnan, *w. v.* 1. *intr.* to moan, complain, sorrow, grieve.— 2. *w. acc.* to bemoan, mourn over.
    bi-mǽnan, to bewail, mourn over.
mǽnan, *w. v.* to think. (Ger. *meinen*.)
mǽnan, *w. v.* in.
    ge-mǽnan, to injure maliciously, break. B. 1101.
mǽne, *adj.* mean, inimical, infamous, godless.
mængan, mæni, mænig, mænieo, mænigeo. See mengan, manig, menigo.
mǽran, *w. v.* to spread, divulge, disseminate, make known, mention, magnify, eulogize, praise.
mǽran, *w. v.* in.
    ge-mǽran, to define, mark off; increase. Wîd. 42.
mǽre, mêre, *adj.* 1. bright, clear, mere.— 2. sublime, illustrious, famous, well-known, distinguished.
mǽre-, mêre-torht, *adj.* bright-shining.
mǽr-lice, *adv.* nobly, illustriously.
mǽrsian, *w. v.* 1. to make known, celebrate, narrate.— 2. to distinguish (Met. 1, 6), render famous.
    ge-mǽrsian, to distinguish, celebrate, render famous.
mǽrđ, mǽrđu, *st. f.* 1. glory, repute, fame.— 2. glorious deed.
mǽr-weorc, *st. n.* noble work or deed.
mæsse, *w. f.* mass; fair (day on which the annual fair is held, 2d February). Men. 20.

mæssere, *st. m.* priest who conducts mass.

mæst, most, *st. m.* 1. trunk of a tree, branch.—2. mast (of a vessel).

mæst, *st. f.* mast (vegetable matter).

mæst, *adj. superl.* 1. greatest, most. 2. *subs. n.* most.—3. *adv.* most, in the greatest degree.

mæstan, *w. v.* to feed with mast, fatten.

â-**mæstan,** the same as above.

mæst-râp, *st. m.* mast-rope, halyard.

mætan, *w. v.* in.

ge-**mætan,** *impers. w. dat.* or *acc.* of person, to dream.

mæte, *adj.* moderate, small, slight, modest.

mætgan, *w. v.* in

ge-**mætgan,** to lessen, diminish.

mæting, *st. f.* dream.

mæð, *st. f.* (= gemet) (right) measure, limit; one's due, honor, right.

mæð, *st. n.* dishonor? disgrace? Dêor. 14.

mædel, medel, *st. n.* 1. place of assembly.—2. assembly.—3. speech, interview.

mædel-, medel-cwide, *st. m.* speech.

mædel-, medel-hêgend, *part.* holding conclave, deliberating.

mædel-hergend, *part.* the same.

mædel-, medel-stede, *st. m.* place of assembly where a court is held, negotiations take place, &c.

mædel-, medel-word, *st. n.* word, speech.

mædlan, medlan, *w. v.* to speak, talk.

mæw, *st. m.* sea-mew, gull.

maga, *w. m.* son, young man, man.

mâga, *w. m.* relation. [Used only in compounds.]

magan (mugan), *pret. pres. v.* may, can;—*pres. indic. sg.* 1st & 3d *pers.* mæg; 2d meaht, miht; *pl.* mâgon, mægon (Gen. 2013); mâgan (An.

760, 1349); **mâgum** (Cri. 1179); mâgun (Cri. 862); *subj. sg.* 1, 3, mæge; *pl.* mægen, mæge (Exod. 428, Hy. 3, 13); *pret. indic. sg.* 1, 3, meahte, mehte, mihte; 2, meahtes; *pl.* meahtum (Jul. 599); meahton, meahtan, mihton, mihten (Jud. 24); *subj. sg.* 1, 3, meahte, mihte; 2, meahte, meahtes (Met. 24, 8, 11); meahtest (Met. 24, 15); *pl.* meahton, mihton (An. 132), meahtan (Az. 164), meahten (Ph. 573), mihten (Sat. 500), meahte (Gû. 404), mihte (Ps. 77, 1);— the *indic.* mæg, may, is used in a hortative, semi-imperative sense.

mâgas. See mæg.

mâge, *w. f.* female relation.

magister, *st. m.* master.

magon. See magan.

magu, mago, *st. m.* 1. son.—2. servant.—3. man.

magu-dryht, -driht, *st. f.* troop, band (of young men).

magu-geoguð, *st. f.* youth, young man.

mâgum, mâgun. See magan.

magu-rædend, *part.* & *subs.* troop-adviser, counselor.

magu-ræswa, *w. m.* leader of men.

magu-rinc, *st. m.* man.

magu-timber, *st. n.* 1. son.—2. growth, increase (of family relationships or connections).

magu-tudor, *st. n.* (*f?*), descendant, scion.

magu-þegn, *st. m.* liegeman, vassal, knightly follower, man.

mâg-wlite. See mæg-wlite.

mâh, *adj.* regardless, unfortunate, stubborn, hard, bad.

Maius, *m.* May. Men. 79.

mânrian, *w. v.* to think out, elicit by thought, scrutinize.

man. See munan.

man, mann, mon, monn, *irreg. m.;* *gen.* **mannes;** *dat.* **mænn, men, menn;** *nom. & acc. pl.* **mæn, men, menn;** *gen.* **manna;** *dat. instr.* **mannum;** — 1. **man,** person. — 2. *indef.* one, they, anybody. (Ger. **man.**

mân, *adj.* bad, godless, criminal, mean.

mân, *st. n.* unright, badness, meanness, injustice, crime, sin, evil deed.

mân-bealu, *st. n.* crime, cruelty, detestable deed.

mân-cwealm, *st. m.* destruction, death.

man-cyn, -cynn, *st. n.* mankind, men.

mand. See **mond.**

mân-dǽd, *st. f.* evil deed, crime, evil. Cf. **main-swear.**

man-drêam, *st. m.* human joy, revelry, festivity.

mân-drinc, *st. m.* deadly drink, potion.

man-dryhten, -drihten, *st. m.* lord of men, prince of the people, prince, lord.

manegu, manetian. See **mengo, monetian.**

mân-fǽhđu, *st. f.* deadly hostility, feud, enmity.

man-faru, *st. f.* army, host (in motion?) Cf. **agmen.**

mân-folm, *st. f.* criminal hand, deadly hand.

mân-fordǽdla, *w. m.* evil-doer, criminal.

mân-forwyrht, *st. n.* evil deed, sin.

mân-fremmende, *part.* crime-doing, sinning, criminal, vicious.

mân-frêa, *w. m.* evil, criminal lord; ruler, devil.

mân-ful, *adj.* full of evil, infamous, mean, degraded.

mân-genidla, *w. m.* evil foe, persecutor.

mân-gewyrhta, *w. m.* evil-doer, sinner.

mân-hûs, *st. n.* evil house, house of crime or criminals.

manian, monian, *w. v.* to admonish, challenge, warn, remind.

ge-manian, the same as above.

mân-idel, *adj.* mean and idle, vain and bad.

manig, mænig, monig, *adj.* many a, many.

manigeo. See **mengu.**

manig-feald, *adj.* many-fold.

manig-, mæni-fealdlice, *adv.* the same as above.

man-lica, *w. m.* man-likeness, statue, effigy.

man-lice, *adv.* like a man.

man-lufe, *w. f.* love for men.

mann. See **man.**

manna, monna, *w. m.* man, person. (*vir* and *homo.*)

manna, *n.* manna (Hebrew). Ps. 77, 25.

man-rim, *st. n.* multitude of men.

mân-sceađa, maan-scađa, *w. m.* evil injurer, malicious foe, robber, sinner.

mân-sceat, *st. m.* usury, iniquitous demand or exaction.

mân-scyld, -scild, *st. f.* guilt, crime, fault.

mân-scyldig, *adj.* criminal, guilty.

mân-slagu, *st. f.* sinful torture, cruel torment, scourging.

mân-swara, -swora, *w. m.* main swearer, perjurer.

man-þêaw, *st. m.* men's habit, custom.

man-þwǽre, *adj.* philanthropic, benevolent, gentle, mild.

man-þwǽrnes, *st. f.* philanthropy, kindness, gentleness, mildness.

mân-wam, -wom, *st. m.* evil stain, crime.

mân-weorc, *st. n.* evil work, crime.

mân-weorc, *adj.* sinful.

man-weorud, *st. n.* collection of men, multitude, congregation.

man-wise, *w. f.* men's wise, custom, habit.

mân-word, *st. n.* **mean word**; base, evil word.

mân-wyrhta, *w. m.* evil-doer, sinner.

mâra, *compar. adj.* 1. greater. — 2. more. — *acc. sg. n. adv.* more, further.

marmor-stân, *st. m.* marble.

Martius, *m.* March. Men. 36.

martyr-dôm, *st. m.* **martyrdom,** martyr's death.

martyre, *st. m.* **martyr.**

martyr-hâd, *st. m.* martyrdom, **martyrhood.**

madelian, madolian, *w. v.* to speak, utter words.

mâdum, mâddum, mâdm, mâdum, *st. m.* gift; jewel, valuable.

mâdum-æht, *st. f.* possessions in jewels, jewel.

mâdum-fæt, *st. n.* treasure vessel, casket, costly vessel.

mâdum-ge-steald, *st. n.* possessions in jewels, treasure, wealth.

mâdum-ge-strêon, *st. n.* jewel-treasure, costly jewels.

mâdum-gyfa, *w. m.* jewel-**giver**, dispenser of treasure or jewels.

mâdum-gifu, *st. f.* dispensing of jewels or treasure.

mâdum-hord, *st. n.* treasure-**hoard**.

mâdum-sele, *st. m.* treasure-hall, hall where treasure is dispensed.

mâdum-sigle, *st. n.* costly jewel, precious treasure or gem.

mâdum-sweord, *st. n.* costly **sword**.

mâdum-wela, *w. m.* **wealth** in jewels, treasure.

mâwan, *st. red. v.* to **mow**.
    â-mâwan, to mow down.

me, mec. See **ic** (I).

mêce, *st. m.* sword.

mecg. See **mæcg** (kinsman).

mecgan (Gu. C. 24, for **mencgan?**).

mêd, *st. f.* **meed,** reward, compensation, price.

mêdan, *w. v. impers.* to suppose, occur to one's mind.
    ge-êad-mêdan, to humble.

mêde, *adj.* of a (certain) mind or **mood,** minded.

mêder, medo, medo-. See **môdor, meodu.**

mêdren-cyn, *st. n.* **mother's kindred,** female line.

med-spêdig, *adj.* moderately happy or fortunate, middling fortunate.

med-, met-trymnes, *st. f.* weakness, infirmity.

medu, medu-, medum. See **modu, meodum.**

med-wis, *adj.* moderately or middling **wise**.

meht, mehte, mehtig. See **meaht, magan, meahtig.**

meld, *st. f.* announcement, information, news, power to explain or announce.

melda, *w. m.* announcer, indicator, informer, betrayer.

meldan, mældan, *w. v.* to announce, speak, inform. (Ger. *melden*.)
    tô-mældan, to announce in twain, destroy or break up by words.

meldian, meldigan, *w. v.* to announce, speak, inform, show, reveal.
    ge-meldian, to announce, make known.

mele-dêaw, *st. m.* **mildew,** honey-dew.

meltan, *st. abl. v.* I. to **melt,** become fluid, dissolve, burn up.
    for-meltan, to melt to pieces, melt up.
    ge-meltan, to melt, dissolve, burn up, pass away.

meltan, *w. v.* to smelt, free, liberate.
    on-meltan, to soften.
men, mencgan. See **man, mengan.**
mene, *st. m.* necklace.
mengan, mencgan, mængan, *w. v.*
    1. to **mingle,** mix with (Sat. 132).
    2. to **mix.** — **3.** to mix among, associate, unite with.
    ge-mengan, to mix, **mingle,** confuse, unite, compound, saturate with.
    geond-mengan, to confuse, bewilder.
mengu (-go, -geo), menigo (-ego, -igeo (-ego, -igeo), menio, mænigo (-ego, -igeo, -egeo), mænieo, manegu (-igeo), *st. f.* **many,** multitude, folk, people.
menn. See **man.**
mennen, *st. n.* maid, maid-servant.
mennisc, *adj.* manlike, human, natural.
mennisc, *st. m.* **man,** human being. (Ger. *mensch.*)
menniscnis, *st. f.* humanity, human nature, incarnation. Hö. 123.
merce. See **mearc.**
merced = myrced, darkened? **murky?** Sat. 710.
mercels, *st. m.* **mark,** goal, aim.
mere, *st. m.* mere, sea, marsh.
mêre. See **mǣre.**
mere-bât, *st. m.* sea-boat.
mere-candel, -condel, *st. f.* sea-candle, sea-lamp, sun.
mere-ciest, *st. f.* sea-**chest,** ship, ark.
mere-dêad, *st. m.* death at sea; drowning.
mere-dêor, *st. n.* sea-animal.
mere-fara, *w. m.* sea-**farer,** sailor.
mere-farod, *st. m.* billowing of the sea, fluctuation of the waves.
mere-fisc, *st. m.* sea-fish.
mere-flôd, *st. m.* sea-flood.
mere-grund, *st. m.* sea-bottom, depth of the sea.
mere-hengest, *st. m.* seahorse, ship.

mere-hrægl, *st. n.* sea-garment, sail. (M. E. *rail.*)
mere-hûs, *st. n.* sea-**house,** ship, ark.
mere-hwearf, *st. m.* seashore. Cf. **wharf.**
mere-lâd, *st. f.* seaway.
mere-lidende, *part.* sea-traversing, seafarer, skipper, sailor.
mere-smylte, *adj.* sea-still, quiet as the sea.
mere-stræt, *st. f.* sea-**street,** seaway.
mere-strengo, *st. f.* **strength** exerted in the sea. B. 533. (*vis maris?*)
mere-strêam, *st. m.* sea-current, sea-flood.
mere-tor, *st. m.* sea-tower, sea-rampart.
mere-torht, *adj.* sea-bright, bright like the sea.
mere-þissa, -þyssa, *w. m.* sea-traverser, ship.
mere-weard, *st. m.* sea-**warden,** guardian of the sea.
mere-wêrig(e), *adj.* sea-weary.
mere-wif, *st. n.* sea-woman, titaness of the sea.
merg, *adj.* gay, **merry,** delightful.
mergan. See **merian** (to cleanse).
mergen, *st. m.* **morning, morn.**
mergen-tid, *st. f.* **morning tide.**
merian, mergan, *w. v.* to purify, cleanse, render mere.
    â-merian, to test, cleanse, purify.
merran, *w. v.* in.
    â-merran, to provoke, disquiet, disturb.
mersc, *w. m.* **marsh,** swamp.
merwe. See **mearu.**
mêsan, *w. v.* to breakfast, eat.
metan, *st. abl. v.* III. **1.** to measure or traverse a space. — **2.** to **mete,** measure, measure out. — **3.** to measure, mark off (Exod. 92). — **4.** esteem, estimate.
    â-metan, 1. to measure out. — **2.** to deal, give to. — **3.** to get, procure. El. 730.

ge-metan, to traverse (a space).
métan, *w. v.* to meet, find, encounter.
ge-mētan, the same as above.
mete, *st. m.* meat, food.
mête, *adj.* meeting, encountering, coming toward.
metend, *part. & subs.* measuring (one), creator, God.
metegian, metigean, *w. v.* to reflect over, consider, meditate upon.
ge-metgian, the same as above.
ge-þanc-metian, to think over, meditate upon.
metegung, *st. f.* reflection, meditation.
mete-lêas, *adj.* meatless, without food.
mete-lêast, -list, *st. f.* lack of food.
mete-þegn, *st. m.* meat-thane, steward.
mete-þearfende, *part.* needing food, destitute.
metgian, *w. v.* to moderate, control, guide, govern.
ge-metgian, 1. to moderate, control, guide, govern.— 2. to restrain or control one's self, soften.
metod, metud, mettrymnes. See meotud, med-trymnes.
mêđe, *adj.* 1. tired, weary.— 2. troubled, sad. (Ger. *müde.*)
medel. See mæđel.
mēdgian, *w. v.* in.
ge-mêđgian, to exhaust, tire.
medlan. See mædlan.
meagol, *adj.* mighty, strong, powerful, able, emphatic.
meagol-lice, *adv.* powerfully, vigorously, emphatically.
meaht, mæht, meht, miht, mieht, myht, *st. f.* might, power.
meaht, *adj.* mighty, powerful.
meaht, meahte, meahtan, meahten, meahtes, meahtest, meahton, meahtum. See magan.
meahte-lice, *adv.* mightily.

meahtig, mæhtig, mehtig, mihtig, *adj.* mighty, powerful.
meaht-môd (miht-), *st. n.* strong mind, violent temper.
mear. See mearg (horse).
mearc, merc, *st. f.* 1. definite point of time, goal, mark, end.— 2. limit, boundary marked off.— 3. domain, district marked off.— 4. province.
mearcan, *w. v.* in.
ge-mearcan, to remark, note, observe.
mearc-hof, *st. n.* place, court, or house lying within a district, mark, or limit.
mearcian, *w. v.* 1. to note, mark distinctly.— 2. to indicate, characterize.— 3. to dwell? put up? B. 450.
â-mearcian, to indicate, characterize.
ge-mearcian, to draw, indicate, determine, mark off, deal out, close.
mearc-land, *st. n.* march-land, border-land; domain, province, land, march.
mearc-pæd, *st. m. n.* march-path, road through a province.
mearc-stapa, *w. m.* march-stepper, one that strides through a land or province.
mearc-stede, *st. m.* place in a district or province.
mearc-þrêat, *st. m.* army that crosses a frontier.
mearc-wâdu (El. 233). See mearc-pæd.
mearc-weard, *st. m.* march-warden, forest-watch, wolf.
mearg, mearh, mear, *st. m.* horse. Cf. mare.
mearh-côfa, *w. m.* marrow-coffer, bone (?).
mearm-stân, *st. m.* marble.
mearu, meru, *adj.* tender, soft.

meodu, meoð, medu, medo, *st. m.* **mead,** honey-drink, hydromel.
meodu-ærn, *st. n.* **mead-**hall.
meodu-benc, *st. f.* **mead-bench,** bench in the mead-hall.
meodu-burg, *st. f.* **mead** palace or castle.
meodu-drêam, *st. m.* **mead-joy,** revelry, joyous doings over mead.
meodu-drinc, *st. m.* **drink of mead,** mead-drinking.
meodu-ful, *st. n.* **mead-cup.**
meodu-gâl, *adj.* mad with **mead,** joyous, tipsy.
meodu-heal, *st. f.* **mead-hall.**
meodum, medum, *adj.* **1. middling,** moderate, mediocre, small.— **2.** respectable, considerable.
meodu-ræden, *st. f.* providing with **mead,** dealing out mead.
meodu-scenc, *st. m.* **mead-skinker,** mead-pourer.
meodu-seld, *st. n.* **mead-**dwelling, mead house or hall.
meodu-setl, *st. n.* same as above.
meodu-stig, *st. m.* **mead-**path, path to the mead-hall.
meodu-wang, *st. m.* **mead-**field, field surrounding the mead-palace.
meodu-wêrig, *adj.* **mead-weary,** drunk.
meohx, meox, *st. m.* dung, filth, dirt.
meolc, meoluc, *st. f.* **milk.**
meord, meorð, *st. f.* reward, compensation, pay.
meoring, *st. f.* hindrance, danger? Exod. 62.
meornan, *st. abl. v.* I. **1.** to be apprehensive, anxious.— **2.** to shrink from. [over.
    be-meornan, to bemoan, grieve
meorð. See **meord** (pay).
meoto, *st. f.* thought, reflection.
meotud, meotod, metod, metud, *st. m.* **1.** fate (Wald. 1,19).— **2.** creator, God, Christ.

meotud-ge-sceaft, *st. f.* fate, allotment; fate after death.
meotud-sceaft, *st. f.* same as above.
meotud-wang, *st. m.* field of battle, battlefield.
mêowle, *w. f.* maiden, woman, wife.
meox. See **meohx** (filth).
micel, mycel, *adj.* **mickle,** great;— *instr. sg.* **micle;** — *w. compar. & superl.* by much, by far; — *gen. sg.* **micles,** and *instr. pl.* **miclum;** — *adv.* by much, by far, much, very.
micel-lic, *adj.* great, magnificent.
micel-môd, *adj.* great-minded, magnanimous.
micelnes, *st. f.* greatness, magnanimity.
miclian, *w. v.* **1.** to render large, magnify, increase.— **2.** to become great, large; to increase in size, grow.
    ge-miclian, to render large, to make larger.
mid, I. *prep., w. dat., instr., & acc.* **1.** with: expresses accompaniment, community, accompanying circumstances, simultaneity.— **2.** with, among, in (with plural or a collective), among (a number). **3.** means by which, with, by means or help of, through, by.— **mid** often follows the governed word.— II. *adv.* with, at the same time, simultaneously.
mid, midd, *adj.* **middle,** midway, in the middle.
mid, *st. n.* **middle;** — **tô-middes,** in or into the middle or midst of.
middan-eard, *st. m.* **mid-earth,** earth.
middan-geard, *st. m.* same as above.
midde, *w. f.* middle, center.
middel, *st. m.* **middle,** middle part.
middel-ge-mǽru, *st. n. pl.* middle district, mid-province.
middel-neaht, -niht, *st. f.* **midnight.**

midl, *st. n.* iron **middle-piece**, bit of a bridle.
midor, *compar.* of **mid**, *adj.*
mid-wist, *st. f.* presence, being present.
miht, mihte, mihten, mihton. See **magan.**
miht, mihtig, miht-môd. See **meaht, meahtig, meaht-môd.**
mil, *st. f.* mile.
milde, *adj.* mild, kind, friendly.
milde, *adv.* the same as above.
mild-heort, *adj.* mild-hearted.
mild-heortnes, -hiortnys, *st. f.* sympathy, pity, mercy.
milds, milts, *st. f.* 1. mildness, sympathy, favor, grace.—2. joy, gayety.
mildsian, miltsian, *w. v.* 1. to pity, sympathize with, feel favorably toward.—2. to act mildly or kindly toward, to render gentle or mild.
mildsung, miltsung, *st. f.* sympathy, compassion.
mil-ge-mearc, *st. n.* mile's distance, mile.
mil-pæđ, *st. m.* mile-path, distance or road reckoned by miles.
miltan, myltan, *w. v.* 1. to melt, dissolve, vanish.—2. to free, liberate. Sol. 55.
 ge-miltan, to melt, dissolve; relax.
milts, miltsian, miltsung. See **milds, mildsian, mildsung.**
min, *adj.* 1. small.—2. low, common, vulgar, vile.
min, 1. *poss. pron.* mine.—2. *gen.* of **ic.** See **ic.**
min-dôm, *st. m.* powerlessness, feebleness.
mine. See **myne.**
minsian, *w. v.* to grow less, decrease, dwindle.
mirc, mirce, mirhđ, mirigđ. See **myrc, myrce, myrgđ.**
mis-dǽd, -dêd, *st. f.* misdeed, evil deed.

mis-ge-dwield, *st. n.* distortion, error, wrong, perversion.
mis-ge-hyd, *st. f. n.* misthought, wrong mode of thinking.
mis-ge-mynd, *st. f.* same as above.
mis-lic, *adj.* various, manifold, diverse.
mis-lice, *adv.* the same as above.
mis-micel, *adj.* of varying size.
missan, *w. v.* to miss, fail in or of.
missen-lic, *adj.* various, manifold, diverse.
missen-lice, *adv.* same as above.
missere, *st. n.* semester, half-year. Cf. the counting by half-years with the counting by nights, winters, &c.
mist, *st. m.* mist, vapor.
mist-glôm, *st. m.?* mist-gloom, darkness, cloud. Wal. 47.
mist-helm, *st. m.* mist-helm, enveloping cloud (blindness).
mist-hlid, -hleod, *st. n.* misty slope, hillside covered with cloud.
mistig, *adj.* misty.
mittan, *w. v.* to find, encounter, meet.
 ge-mittan, the same as above.
midan, *st. abl. v.* V. 1. to hide, conceal, keep to one's self.—2. *w. instr.* to avoid, shun.—3. to dissemble. 4. *intr.* to conceal one's self.
 be-, bi-midan, to hide, conceal, keep secret.
mieht. See **meaht.**
môd, *st. n.* 1. mood, spirit, soul, heart (as seat of thought, feeling, passion, sensibility).—2. courage. 3. arrogance, pride, moodiness.— 4. greatness, power (Ps. 144, 5; 150, 2); violence (Exod. 488).
môd-blind, *adj.* mood-blind, spiritually blind.
môd-blissiende, *adj.* mood-joyful, exultant of mind.
môd-bysgung, *st. f.* mood-depression, sorrow, mental affliction.
môd-cearig, *adj.* sorrowful.

môd-cearu, *st. f.* mood-care, sorrow, grief of heart.
môd-cræft, *st. m.* mood-craft, power of mind, wisdom, shrewdness, cleverness.
môd-cræftig, *adj.* judicious, possessing judgment, skillful.
môd-cwânig, *adj.* sad at heart, sorrowful, querulous.
môddor, môder. See **môdur.**
môde-lice, *adj.* valiantly, bravely.
môde-wǽg, *st. m.* rushing wave, current.
môd-earfod, *st. f.* grief, sorrow, misery of mind.
môd-ge-hygd, *st. f.* mood-thought, mind, thought.
môd-ge-mynd, *st. f. n.* sentiment, thought, reflection, memory.
môd-ge-þanc (-ge-þonc), *st. m. n.* mood-thought, thought, mind.
môd-ge-þoht, *st. m.* same as above.
môd-ge-þyldig, *adj.* patient of mind, enduring with courage.
môd-ge-winna, *w. m.* mood-foe, sorrow, grief.
môd-gêomor, -giomor, *adj.* sorrowful-minded.
môdgian, -igan, *w. v.* **1.** to rage, roar, become excited or **moody.** (Exod. 458).— **2.** to show bravery, boldness.
    ofer-môdgian, to be arrogant, proud, presumptuous. [ous.
    môd-glæd, *adj.* glad-minded, joy-
môd-glêaw, *adj.* wise, clear-minded, quick-witted, clever.
môd-hæp, -heap, *adj.* rich in courage, brave.
môd-hete, *st. m.* hate, hatred.
môd-hord, *st. n.* heart's treasure, secret thoughts.
môd-hwæt, *adj.* bold, energetic, valiant.
môdig, *adj.* **1.** spirited, courageous. **2.** roused, excited, angry.
môdigan. See **môdgian** (to rage).

môdig-lic (-môdi-), *adj.* courageous, brave, high-spirited.
môd-lêof, *adj.* dear, precious.
môd-lufe, *w. f.* love.
môdor. See **môdur** (mother).
môd-rôf, *adj.* vigorous-spirited, valiant-hearted.
môd-sefa, *w. m.* mood-thought, mind, spirit.
môd-sêoc, *adj.* mind-sick, sad.
môd-snottor (-snotor), *adj.* shrewd, sharp-minded, wise.
môd-sorg, *st. f.* heart-sorrow, sadness, grief.
môd-swið, *adj.* brave, valiant.
môd-þracu, *w. f.* bold-mindedness, courage, valor, fortitude.
môd-þrêa, *w. m.* uneasiness of mind, terror, vexation.
môd-þrydu, *st. f.* strength of mind or soul, energy, vigor? B. 1931.
môdur, môdor, môddor, môder, *irreg. f. gen. sg.* **môdur, môdor, môddor;** — *dat. sg.* **mêder, mêder** = mother. [son.
môdur-cild, *st. n.* mother's child,
môd-wên, *st. f.* thought, opinion? Rid. 87, 7.
môd-wlanc, *adj.* haughty, arrogant.
mold-ærn (-ern), *st. n.* house of mold, earthy house, grave.
molde, *w. f.* **1.** dust, earth as material.— **2.** soil, **mold.**— **3.** earth as habitation of men,— opposed to water, air, sky.— **4.** province, district.
mold-græf, *st. n.* **grave,** grave in the earth.
mold-hrêrende, *part.* earth-touching, moving in or on the earth.
mold-weg, *st. m.* earthway, earth.
mold-wyrm, *st. m.* earthworm.
molsian, *w. v.* to molder, rot, decay.
    ge-molsian, to wither, fade.
mon, môn. See **man** and **manan** (*vb.*), **mân.**
môna, *w. m.* **moon.**

mônađ, mond, *st. m.* (**moonth**), month.
mond, *st. n.?* Gû. 514.
monetian, *w. v.* to despise, contemn? An. 747.
monian, monig, monn, monna. See **manian, manig, man, manna.**
môr, *st. m.* **1.** moor, morass, swamp. **2.** mountain, wooded mountains.
morgen, *st. m.* morn, morning, forenoon.
morgen-ceald, *adj.* morn-cold, cold as at early morn.
morgen-colla, *w. m.* terror at morn? Jud. 245.
morgen-lang, *adj.* morning-long, lasting through the morning.
morgen-lêoht, *st. n.* morning light.
morgen-regn, -rên, *st. m.* morning rain.
morgen-sêoc, *adj.* sick, ill, or sad in the morning.
morgen-spell, *st. n.* morning news, news spreading in the morning.
morgen-steorra, -stiorra, *w. m.* morning star.
morgen-swêg, *st. m.* morn-sound, cry at morn.
morgen-tid, *st. f.* morning-tide, time.
morgen-torht, *adj.* morn-bright, bright at morn or in the morning.
môr-hǣđ, *st. f.* moor-heath; swampy, mountainous heath.
môr-heald, *adj.* surrounded by moors, marshy? Ex. 61.
môr-hôp, *st. n.* moor-bight, hiding-place in the moor?
môr-land, *st. n.* moorland, mountain-land.
morna, *gen. pl.* of **morgen.**
môr-stapa, *w. m.* moor-stepper, traverser of moors and mountains.
morđ, *st. n.* **1.** murder, death.—**2.** deadly sin. Gen. 691.
morđ-bealu, *st. n.* murder-bale, murder, violent death.

morđor, morđur, *st. n.* **1.** violent death, murder.— **2.** punishment by death, death-torment, martyrdom.— **3.** crime, deadly sin.
morđer-bed, *st. n.* murder-bed, bed of death.
morđor-bealu, *st. n.* murder, baleful death.
morđor-côfa, *w. m.* murder-cell, prison, torture-house.
morđor-cræft, *st. m.* murderous craft or might.
morđor-cwealm, *st. m.* murder, death.
morđor-hete, *st. m.* murderous hate, deadly hostility, bloody feud.
morđor-hof, *st. n.* murder-house, place of punishment (hell).
morđor-hûs, *st. n.* same as above.
morđor-hycgende, *part.* with murderous thoughts.
morđor-lêan, *st. n.* reward for murder or crime.
morđor-scyldig, *adj.* guilty of murder, crime.
morđor-sleaht, -sleht, *st. m.* slaughter, defeat.
morđur. See **morđor** (murder).
môs, *st. n.* food, feed, victuals.
môt. See **môtan** (must).
môtan, *pret.-pres.; pres. ind. sg.* **1, 3,** môt.— **2.** môst; *pl.* môtan (Gû. 786), môtun (Ph. 668), môton, môtan (An. 109), môten (Sat. 297); *subj. sg.* môte; *pl.* môtan (Reb. 16), môten (El. 433), môte (Cri. 1327); *pret.* môste, to be in a position adapted to, to have an opportunity or leisure for; hence, **1.** to be permitted, to be able.— **2.** must (B. 1939, 2886. Sat. 108.)
modde, *w. f.* moth, book-worm or moth.
mugan. See **magan** (may).
munan, *pret.-pres.; pres. ind. sg.* **1, 3,** man, mon.— **2.** manst; *pl.* munon; *subj.* mune; *pret.* munde.— **1.** to

think of or about, be mindful of, remember.— **2.** to esteem, appreciate, value.

    ge-munan, to remember, be mindful of, recollect.

    on-munan, 1. to provide with, deem worthy of.— **2.** to remind, admonish? B. 2640.

mund, *st. m.* **1.** hand.— **2.** protection, guardianship.

mund, *st. m.* bridal gift, dower. Cri. 93.

mund-beorg, *st. m.* hill of refuge or protection, mountain refuge.

mund-bora, *w. m.* protection-bearer, protector, guardian, tutor.

mund-byrd, -berd, *st. f.* protection, patronage, aid, help.

mund-gripe, *st. m.* hand-grip.

mund-heáls, -háls, *st. n.* protection? guardianship? *salus tutelæ?* Cri. 446.

mundian, *w. v.* to protect, to watch over.

mund-róf, *adj.* strong-handed.

munec, *st. m.* **monk.**

munt, *st. m.* mount, mountain.

munt-gióp = **munt-giôf,** Jupiter's mountain, **Mons Jovis,** Alps? Met. 1: 8–14.

múr, *st. m.* wall. (Ger. *mauer.*)

murc, *adj.* murky, gloomy.

murge, *adv.* cheerfully, brightly, merrily.

murnan, *w. v.* to mourn, sorrow, long after; bemoan.

    be-, bi-murnan, to mourn, mourn over, sorrow for.

must, *st. m.* must (of grapes).

mútian, *w. v.* in
    bi-mútian, to change, exchange for.

múd, *st. m.* **1.** mouth.— **2.** opening, door.

múda, *w. m.* mouth, opening, entrance.

múd-bana, *w. m.* mouth-murderer, one that kills with the mouth.

múd-hǽl, *st. n.* mouth-"hail," "hail" spoken with the mouth.

múd-léas, *adj.* mouthless.

mycel, myclian, myht. See **micel, miclian, meaht.**

mylen-scearp, *adj.* whetted on the grindstone.

myltan. See **miltan** (melt).

myndgian, *w. v.* to remind, recall to mind, remember, be mindful of.

    ge-myndgian, same as above.

myne, mine, *st. m.* **1.** spirit, soul.— **2.** feeling, sentiment.— **3.** mind. **4.** intention, aim, demand.— **5.** love, affection.

myne-lic, *adj.* desirable, loveworthy, noble, splendid.

myngian, *w. v.* **1.** to warn, admonish, suggest.— **2.** to remember.

    ge-mynegian, to remember.

mynian, mynnan, *w. v.* to be mindful of, have one's mind on; to strive for, long for, demand.

    ge-mynian, to be mindful of, intent on, heedful; to see to, see.

mynle, *w. f.* mind, spirit; demand, desire.

mynster, *st. n.* **minster,** monastery, cloister.

myntan, *w. v.* to have one's mind on, intend, be mindful of, think.

    ge-myntan, the same as above.

myrc, mirc, *st. n.* murk, darkness, disaster, mischief.

myrce, mirce, *adj.* murky, dark, uncanny.

myrce, *adv.* the same as above.

myrcels, *st. f.* peril, disaster, mischief. Gú. 429.

myrgan, *w. v.* to be merry, rejoice.

    á-myrgan, to delight, cheer. Sol. 240.

myrgen, *st. f.* mirth, joy, pleasure.

myrgđ, myrđ, mirđ, mirigđ, *st. f.* the same as above.

myrran, *w. v.* to mar, disturb, confuse, render uneasy.
  â-myrran, to disquiet, hinder, oppose, prevent.
  ge-myrran, to provoke, irritate, disquiet, hinder, prevent.

myrrelse, *w. f.* offense, provocation, scandal, irritation.
myrđ. See **myrgđ**.
myrđ, *st. f.* sorrow? grief? marring? B. 810.
mysci, *pl.* mosses.

N

nâ (= ne & â), *adv.* never, not by any means.
nabban (= ne & habban), *pres. ind. sg.* 1. næbbe. — 2. nafast, næfst. 3. nafađ, næfđ; — *pl.* nabbađ; — *subj. pres.* næbbe; — *pret.* næfde, not to have.
naca, *w. m.* boat, vessel.
nacod, nacud, *adj.* naked, nude.
nǽdl, *st. f.* needle.
nædre, næddre, nedre, *w. f.* adder (*w. n.* dropped); viper, snake.
næfne. See **nefne**.
nǽfre (ne & ǽfre), *adv.* never.
nǽgan, nēgan, *w. v.* to approach, attack, assail; — wordum nǽgan, to address, speak to.
  ge-nǽgan, to attack, assail, oppress, disquiet; to call, address.
nægel, *st. m.* 1. nail. — 2. plectrum (in harp-playing: Wy. 84). — 3. nail (of fingers and toes).
nægled, *part.* nailed.
nægled-bord, *adj.* with nailed sides.
nægled-cnear, *st. m.* nailed vessel.
nǽh, nællæs. See **nēah, nealles**.
nǽman, *w. v.* in
  be-nǽman, to deprive of, rob of, take away. (Ger. *benehmen*.)
nǽnne, *acc.* of **nân** (none).
nǽnig (= ne & ǽnig), *pron.* none (often strengthened by ne).
nǽrende. See **neam** (am not).
næs (= ne & wæs), was not; — *pl.* nǽron (= ne & wǣron); — *subj.* nǣre (= ne & wǣre).
næs, *adv.* not, not at all.

næs, nes, *st. m.* 1. stratum, layer, portion or crust of earth. — 2. naze (cf. nose), cape, sea-cliff, promontory, precipitous bank.
næs-hliđ, -hleođ, *st. n.* naze-slope, precipice of a promontory.
næssa, *w. m.* promontory.
nǽstan, *w. v.* in
  ge-nǽstan, to push, urge, vex, fight with? Rid. 28, 16.
nǽtan, *w. v.* to afflict, press upon, vex, attack.
nâgan (= ne & âgan), *pres. ind. sg.* nâh; — *pl.* nâgon; — *pret.* nâhte, not to have, not to own.
nâht. See **nâwiht** (naught).
nahte, *pret.* did not grant? Dan. 454.
nâht-fremmende, *part.* nought-doing, useless.
nâ-hwǽr, -hwar, *adv.* nowhere.
nâ-hwǽđer, *pron.* neither, nothing.
nalas, nalǽs, nales, nalles. See **nealles**.
nâm, *st. f.* taking; rapine, appropriation, deprivation, robbery.
nama, noma, *w. m.* name.
namian, nomian, *w. v.* in
  ge-namian, to name, mention.
nân (= ne & ân), none; — *neut.* nothing.
nâpan, *st. red. v.* in
  ge-nâpan, to attack? to overwhelm? to destroy? Exod. 475.
nard, *st. m.* nard (perfume).
nâst, nât. See **nitan** (ne & witan).

nât-hwǽr (=ne & wât), *adv.* I know not where, somewhere or other.
nât-hwæt, *pron.* I know not what, something or other.
nât-hwilc, -hywlc, *pron.* I know not which, some one or other.
nâuht. See nâwiht.
nâ-wiht, nâwuht, nâuht, nâht, *neut. pron.* naught, not a whit.
nâwðer (= ne & âwðer), neither.
ne, *adv.* not; ne—ne, neither—nor. [ne is often doubled to strengthen the negative.]
nê, nêo, *st. m.* corpse, cadaver, dead human body.
neb, nebb, *st. n.* face, countenance, mouth, nib, beak.
neð, nêðan, neðre. See nŷð, nêoð, nŷðan, nædre.
nefa, *w. m.* nephew, grandson.
nefne, næfne, nemne (= ne & gif & ne), 1. *conj.* if not, unless.— 2. *prep. w. dat.* except, with exception of.
nefre, *adj.* weak (Gn. Ex. 38), infirm.
nê-fugol, *st. m.* corpse-bird, carrion fowl.
nêgan, nêh, neht, nellan, nêman, nemde (*prct*). See nǽgan, nǽah, neaht, nillan, nǽman, nemnan.
nemnan, *w. v.* 1. to name, give a name to.— 2. to address, speak to.— 3. to mention by name, make mention of.— 4. to relate, narrate. Gû. 64.
   â-nemnan, to pronounce, inform, tell.
   be-nemnan, to pronounce solemnly, affirm, asseverate, confirm.
   ge-nemnan, to name.
nemne. See nefne.
nemned (Ps. 106, 41, = hemned?) hemnan, to stop up, close, shut.
nemðe, nimðe, nymðe, *conj. w. subj.* if not, unless, except.
nep? neþ? = neap-tide? Exod. 469.

nerian, nerigan, nergan, *w. v.* to nourish, preserve, save, heal, redeem, liberate.
   ge-nerian, to ransom, redeem, liberate; to preserve, save, protect.
neriend, nerigend, nergend, *part. & subs.* savior, redeemer, God, Christ.
nes. See næs (was not).
nesan, *st. abl. v.* III. to endure successfully, survive, be freed from, be saved.
   ge-nesan, 1. *intr.* to remain safe, survive uninjured, be preserved.— 2. *w. acc.* to endure successfully, be fortunate, be freed from, be saved.
nest, *st. n.* nest.
nest, nyst, *st. n.* nourishment, food, means of traveling, *viaticum.*
net, *st. n.* net.
netan. See nitan (ne & witan).
nêten, nieten, nŷten, *st. n.* neatcattle, beast of burden, cattle.
nêðan, *w. v.* to dare, venture, display valor.
   ge-nêðan, to dare, venture, risk one's self, strive to.
nêðing, *st. f.* daring, valor.
nêad. See nŷð (effort).
nêad-côfa, *w. m.* prison.
neafola, *w. m.* nable.
nêah, nêh, *adj., adv., & prep. w. dat.* near, nigh;—*compar.* neâr, niôr;—*superl.* neâhst, nêhst, nŷhst, nihst, niehst.— 1. next, nearest. 2. latest, last.— 3. *adv.* in the next place, at last.
neah. See nugan.
neah, *adv.* enough, sufficiently.
nêah-bûend, *part. & subs.* near-dwelling, neighbor.
neahhige, *adv.* enough.
nêah-man, *st. m.* neighbor.
neaht, neht, niht, nyht, *st. f.* night, (often used in enumerations, where

Mod. Eng. uses *days);—adv. gen.*
nihtes (*n.? m.?*), of a night, nights,
by night;—**dæges and nihtes**, by
day and by night, day and night.
neaht-, niht-bealu, *st. n.* night-
bale, destruction that comes by
night.
neaht-, niht-egesa, *w. m.* night
horror, nocturnal terror.
neaht-, niht-feormung, *st. f.* night-
haven or refuge, place of protection for the night.
neaht-, niht-ge-rim, *st. n.* night-
number (numbering by "nights");
reckoning of time (Gen. 1193),
chronology.
neaht-, niht-glôm, *st. m.?* night-
gloom, morning or evening twilight, darkness.
neaht-, niht-helm, *st. m.* helm or
veil of night.
neaht-hræfn, niht-hrefen, *st. m.*
night-raven.
neaht-, niht-lang, *adj.* lasting the
livelong night.
neaht-, niht-rest, *st. f.* night-rest.
neaht-, niht-rim, *st. n.* number of
nights.
neaht-scûa, niht-scuwa, *w. m.*
night-shadow.
neaht-, niht-weard, *st. m.* night-
warden, watchman by night.
neaht-, niht-weorc, *st. n.* night-
work, deed or doings done at
night.
nêah-, nêa-west, *st. f.* being near;
vicinity, neighborhood; cohabitation.
**nealles, nalles, nallas, nællæs, nales,
nalas, nalæs**, *adv.* not at all, by
no means, least of all.
neam, neom (= ne & eam), I am
not; 3d *sg.* **nis, nys**; *pl.* **nearon**
(Seaf. 82); *pres.-part.* **nǽrende**.
neân, *adv.* 1. from near.— 2. near,
near by.— 3. almost, nearly.
neâr, nearon. See **nêah, neam**.

nearu, nearo, *adj.* narrow, near together, close, confining, producing
misery or oppression.
nearu, nearo, *st. f.* narrowness,
closeness, straitness, oppression.
nearu-bregd, *st. f.* oppression, com-
pression, crushing.
nearu-cræft, *st. m.* narrowness, art
of rendering difficult of access?
inaccessibility. B. 2243.
nearu-grâp, *adj.* close-clutching.
Rid. 81, 6.
nearu-lic, *adj.* oppressing, clutching
closely.
nearu-nêd, *st. f.?* close quarters, captivity.
nearunes, *st. f.* narrowness, oppression.
nearu-searu, *st. f.* dark cunning,
secret fraud or intrigue, misery-
bringing quarrel.
nearu-sorg, *st. f.* crushing sorrow,
anxiety.
nearu-þearf, *st. f.* crushing need,
distress.
nearu-wrence, *st. m.* crushing cunning, guile.
nearwe, *adv.* narrowly, tightly,
closely, precisely.
nearwian, *w. v.* 1. to force in, con-
fine.— 2. to force one's self in, become smaller, shrink.
  ge-nearwian, to force in, drive
to close quarters, oppress.
nêat, *st. n.* neat cattle, beast of
burden, cattle, ox.
nêa-west. See **nêahwest**.
nêo. See **nê** (corpse).
nêo-, nio-bed, *st. n.* deathbed, dying
bed.
nêod, niod, nied, nýd, nêd, *st. f.?*
effort, eagerness, zeal, longing,
desire, pleasure:—*instr. sg.* eagerly, zealously, carefully, diligently,
violently.
nêod-fracu, *st. f.* effort, striving,
longing, yearning.

nêod-ful, *adj.* eager, zealous, careful, sedulous.
nêod-laðu, *st. f.* polite invitation, hospitable pledging at drink. B. 1320.
nêod-lice, *adv.* eagerly, carefully.
nêod-lof, *st. n.* eager praise, eulogy.
nêod-spearuwa, *w. m.* sparrow.
nêod-weorðung, *st. f.* eager appreciation, exalted praise.
nêol. See **neowol** (chasm).
neom. See **neam** (I am not).
neoman. See **niman** (to take).
nêomian, *w. v.* to sing (Wy. 84).
nêon. See **niwan** (lately).
neorxna-, neorxena-wang, *st. m.* Paradise.
nêosan, niosan, *w. v.* **1.** to search, acquaint one's self with, spy out, seek to learn.—**2.** to seek, hunt for, visit, attack.
nêosian, niosian, *w. v.* **1.** to search out, investigate.—**2.** to hunt for, visit, seek (with hostile intent), to attack.
   ge-nêosian, to visit.
nêo-sið, *st. m.* death.
nêotan, niotan, *st. abl. v.* VI. to enjoy, use.
   be-, bi-nêotan, to deprive of, to rob.
neoðan, nioðan, *adv.* from beneath, beneath, below.
neoðane, -one, *adv.* same as above.
neoðe-mest, *adj. superl.* (be)neathmost, farthest beneath, lowest.
neoðor. See **niðer** (below).
neoðo-, nioðo-weard, *adj.* underward, **beneath.**
neowan, neowe, neowinga. See **niwan, niwe, niwinga.**
neowol, nêol, nywol, *adj.* inclined, steep, precipitous, deep.
neowol-, nêol-, nywolnes, *st. f.* abyss, chasm.
nicor, *st. m.* nixie, water-sprite, marine monster.

nicor-hûs, *st. n.* nixie-house, dwelling of water-sprites.
nifol, *adj.* nebulous, cloudy, dark, gloomy.
nigan? Rid. 9: 8, 9.
nigen, nigon, *num.* **nine.**
nigeða, nigoða, *ord. num.* **ninth.**
nigon-tig, *num.* ninety. See **hund-nigontig.**
nigon-tyne, *num.* nineteen.
nihst, riht. See **nêah, neaht.**
nillan, nellan, nyllan (= **ne & willan**), *pres. ind. sg.* **1, 3, nelle, nele, nylle, nyle;** *pl.* **nellað;** *pret.* **nolde,**—will not. Cf. **nolo = ne & volo.**
niman, nyman, neoman, nioman, *st. abl. v.* II. **1.** to take, assume, accept, receive; occupy, seize, grasp.—**2.** to take away, take from.—**3.** to suffer, tolerate, endure, attain, obtain.
   â-niman, to take, take from, rob.
   æt-niman, to take away, take from.
   be-, bi-niman, to take away, deprive of. (Ger. *benehmen*).
   for-niman, to take away, deprive of.
   ge-niman, 1. to take, appropriate, seize, receive, occupy.—**2.** to take, take away, remove.—**3.** to attain, endure.—**4.** to enter? take? obtain? Dan. 313.
nimðe. See **nemðe** (except).
nipan, *st. abl. v.* V. to spread gloom or darkness, veil over, cover.
   ge-nipan, 1. to be or become dark or gloomy.—**2.** to come upon, cover over, veil.
nis. See **neam** (am not).
nistlan, nystlan, *w. v.* to **nestle,** build **nests** (in).
nitan, nytan, netan (= **ne & witan**), *pres. ind. sg.* **1, 3, nât.**—**2. nâst;** *pl.* **nyton, neton;** *pret.* **nyste, nysse,** not to know, **wit, wot.**

nid, *st. m.* creature, human being, person. [Used in the plural only.]
nid, *st. n.* abyss. Sat. 634.
nid, *st. m.* **1.** striving, effort, exertion, violence.—**2.** deed of valor, battle, strife.—**3.** hostile onslaught, attack, pursuit, oppression, misery. **4.** hate, envy, hostility.—**5.** meanness, badness, unworthiness.
nid, *adj.* intended? Môd. 44.
nid-cwalu, *st. f.* miserable death, destruction.
nid-cwealm, *st. m.* murder, violent death.
nid-draca, *w. m.* battle-dragon, hostile dragon.
nide, *adv.* below, beneath. B. 2243.
nider, nyder, nydor, niodor, *adv.* nether, downward, down, below.
nider-dǽl, *st. m.* **nether part.**
nider-heald, *adj.* downward inclined, downward, prone.
niderian, nyderian, *w. v.* in ge-nyderian, to degrade, humble, cast down.
nider-weard, *adj.* **netherward,** downward tending, prone.
'nid-gǽst (-gyst), *st. m.* hostile stranger, mischief-making alien.
nid-ge-teon, *st. n.* (cf. **teen**), battle-effort, exertion in battle, battle.
nid-ge-weorc, *st. n.* foe's work, battle deed, fierce deed.
nid-grim, *adj.* furious in battle, fierce.
nid-gripe, *st. m.* furious grip, fierce assault.
nid-hete, *st. m.* **1.** fierce hate, hostility.—**2.** torment, misfortune.
nid-hete, *st. m.* fierce hater, foe.
nid-heard, *adj.* hardened to battle, bold, valiant.
nid-hycgende, *part.* hate-cherishing, hostile-minded.
nid-hydig, *adj.* in mood for battle, brave-minded.

nid-loca, *w. m.* dungeon, place of torment.
nid-plega, *w. m.* battle-sport, battle, fight.
nidre, *adv.* below, beneath.
nid-sceada, *w. m.* foe, persecutor.
nid-sele, *st. m.* hall below, submarine hall, cavern in the deep.
nid-syn, *st. f.* heavy sin. [tle.
nid-weorc, *st. n.* battle-**work**, bat-
nid-wracu, *st. f.* torture, punishment, death penalty, mischief.
nid-wundor, *st. n.* **wonder** below, wonder of the deep.
niwan, neowan, nêon, *adj.* **1.** newly, lately.—**2.** anew, again. B.3104.
niwe, neowe, niowe, *adv.* **newly.**
niwian, niowian, *w. v.* to **renew.**
  ed-niwian, same as above.
  ge-ed-niwian, same as above.
  ge-niwian, same as above.
niwinga, neowinga, *adv.* **anew,** again.
niwlice, *adv.* **newly,** lately.
niw-tyrwed (-tyrwyd), *part.* newly tarred.
nied, niehst, nieten. See **nýd, nêod, nêah, nêten.**
niobed, niod, nioman, nior, niosan, niosian, niotan, niodan, niodor, niodoweard, niowe, niowian. See **nêobed, nêod, niman, nêah, nêotan, nêosan, nêosian, neodan, nider, neodoweard, niowe, niwian.**
nô (= **ne & ô**), *adv.* never, not at all, by no means, not.
nôht, nohte. See **nôwiht, nugan.**
nolde, noma, nomian. See **nillan, nama, namian.**
nôn, *st. f.* (**noon**), **hora, nona,** ninth hour of the day (3 o'clock in the afternoon).
nord, *st. m.* **north;** *adv.* northward, in the north.
nordan, *adv.* from the **north.**

nord-dǽl, *st. m.* northern region, north wind (*aquilo*).
nord-ende, *st. m.* northern end.
nordern, *adj.* northern, northerly.
nord-healf, *st. f.* northern side or quarter.
nord-man (-mon), *st. m.* inhabitant of the north.
nord-mest, *adj.* northernmost.
nord-rôdor, *st. m.* northern sky.
nord-weg, *st. m.* way to the north.
nôse, *w. f.* noselike projection, promontory, naze.
nosu, *st. f.* nose.
nôd, *st. f.* 1. boldness, daring, valiant deed.— 2. booty, plunder. Wal. 28.
Nowembris, November. Men. 196.
nôwiht, nôht, 1. *neut.* naught, nothing.— 2. *adv.* not, not at all.
nu, 1. *adv.* now.— 2. *conj.* inasmuch as, since, because, as.
nugan, *pret.-pres.*, *pres.ind.sg.* neah; *pl.* nugon; *pret.* nohte, in
 be-nugan, to have in one's power, at one's disposal, enjoy.
 ge-nugan, to suffice, satisfy. (Ger. *genügen*.)
nŷd. See **nêod** (effort).
nŷd, nied, nêad, nêd, *st. f.* need, necessity, violence, force;— name of the Rune n.
nŷdan, nêdan, *w. v.* to force, compel.
 ge-nŷdan, to force, compel, force upon.
nŷdan, *w. v.* to be eager for, exert one's self to, strive to.
 ge-nŷdan, the same as above.
nŷd-bâd, *st. f.* forced pledge, extorted pledge.
nŷd-bi-bod, *st. n.* compelling or binding command.
nŷd-boda, *w. m.* boder of evil, messenger of ill.
nŷd-bysgu, *st. f.* labor, effort, toil, wretchedness.
nŷd-bysig, *adj.* forced to labor, working from necessity, self-exhausting.

nŷd-clâfa, *w. m.* prison, dungeon, torture-chamber.
nŷd-, nêd-cleofa, *w. m.* the same.
nŷd-costing, *st. f.* misery, oppression, disquietude.
nŷd-fara, *w. m.* need-farer, fugitive from necessity. [death.
nŷd-ge-dâl, *st. n.* forced separation,
nid-genga, *w. m.* wanderer in misery or need.
nid-ge-stealla, *w. m.* companion in misery.
nŷd-ge-weald (-gewald), *st. f. & n.* tyranny, violence, force.
nŷd-grâp, *st. f.* compelling hand, compelling grasp.
nŷd-, nêd-þearf, *st. f.* 1. need, distress.— 2. want, thing needed.
nŷd-þeow, nied-þiow, *st. m.* servant or server from necessity, poor servant.
nŷd-, nied-wǽdla, *w. m.* needy one, person in need.
nŷd-wracu, *st. f.* violent persecution, oppression, vexation.
nŷhst, nyht, nyllan, nyman, nymde. See **nêah, neaht, nillan, niman, nemde**.
nyrwian, *w. v.* in
 ge-nyrwian (cf. **narrow**), to force in, press upon, drive into a corner, oppress.
nys, nyst, nyste, nystlan, nytan. See **neam, nest, nitan, nistlan, nitan**.
nyt, *adj.* useful, of use, helpful.
nyt, *st. f.* 1. use, advantage, profit. 2. duty, service, office.
nytan, nŷten. See **nitan, nêten**.
nyttian, *w. v.* to enjoy, to use.
 ge-nyttian, the same as above.
nyd = nŷd, *st. f.* zeal, eagerness, desire? Gn. Ex. 38.
nyder, nydor. See **nider**.
nyderian. See **niderian**.
nywol, nywolnes. See **neowol, neowolnes**.

O

ô, *adv.* ever, at any time.

October, October. Men. 183.

of, I. *prep. w. dat.* **of,** out of, from, from — to, since (sometimes postponed).— II. *adv.* **off,** away, absent.

ofæt. See **ofet** (fruit).

of-dæl, *st. n.* abyss, chasm.

ofen, ofn, *st. m.* **oven.**

ofer, *prep.* **over.—1.** *w. acc.* (*a*) with verbs of motion, seeing, &c.,—direction, tendency (above, below, toward,&c.)— **2.** indicating motion from below upward, above something.—**3.** the end or aim or object of motion.—**4.** extent over a space. **5.** like German *auf, über, w. dat.* indicating rest. — **6.** indicating power or sway over.—**7.** preference, excellence, transgression.— **8.** contrariety, opposition to one's wish, command, desire.— **9.** without (Dan. 73, B. 685).— **10.** the cause of joy or object of conversation (B. 2724; Ps. 118, 162).—**11.** temporal: after, through. Jud. 20. II. *w. dat.* **1.** above a thing.— **2.** upon a thing.— **3.** preference, excellence, superiority over (Ps. C. 75).— **4.** over (of rule, sway, dominion).—the preposition is sometimes separated from its case).

ôfer, *st. m.* shore, bank, beach, edge. (Ger. *ufer.*)

ofer-ceald, *adj.* excessively **cold.**

ofer-geatu, *st. f.* negligence, forgetfulness. [above.

ofer-gitnes (-gytnes), *st. f.* same as

ofer-gitol, -gittol, -gyttol, -geotul, -geottul, *adj.* **forgetful.**

ofer-gitolnes, -gytolnes, -gittolnes, *st. f.* forgetfulness.

ofer-hêah, *adj.* extremely **high,** lofty.

ofer-hidig (-higd). See **oferhydig (-hygd).**

ofer-hige, *st. m.* elevation, highmindedness, exaltation.

ofer-hlêoður, *adj.* failing to hear or perceive.

ofer-holt, *st.* **·** *n.* over-wood, cover, shield.

ofer-hyd, *st. n.* haughtiness, pride, arrogance, assumption.

ofer-hydig, *adj.* haughty, proud, arrogant.

ofer-hydig, *st. n.* pride, over-mindedness.

ofer-hygd (-higd), *st. n.* the same.

ofer-hyrned, *part.* strong-**horned,** with large horns.

ofer-lêof, *adj.* over-dear, very dear.

ofer-mæcga, *w. m.* one over-mighty, superior in might, very powerful. Gû. 664.

ofer-mægen, *st. n.* over-might, superiority.

ofer-mæte, *adj.* immoderate, beyond bounds.

ofer-mâdmas, *st. m. pl.* precious jewels.

ofer-mêde, *st. n.* haughtiness, pride.

ofer-medla, *w. m.* same as above.

ofer-met, *st. n.* extravagance, pride, haughtiness.

ofer-mihtig, *adj.* very **mighty,** powerful.

ofer-môd, *st. m.* **over-mood,** pride, insolence.

ofer-môd, *adj.* puffed up, proud, insolent.

ofer-môdig, *adj.* same as above.

ofer-sæld, *st. f.* false happiness.

ofer-þearf, *st. f.* great need, extreme distress.

ofer-þrym, *st. m.* excessive strength, power.

ofer-wealdend, *part. & subs.* highest lord, sovereign.

ofer-wlenca, *st. f. pl.* great wealth, riches.
ôfest. See **ôfost** (haste).
ofet, ofæt, *st. n.* fruit. (Ger. *obst.*)
of-hende, *adj.* lost, misplaced. Cf. **off-hand.**
of-longod, *part.* seized with longing, yearning.
of-lysted, -lyst, *part.* very lustful, voluptuous.
ofn. See **ofen** (oven).
ôfost, ôfest, *st. f.* haste.
ôfost-lîce, ôfest-, ôfst-, ôfes-, *adv.* hastily, in haste, quickly.
oft, *adv.* often.
of-pyrsted, *part.* very **thirsty,** greedy
ôht. See **ôwiht** (aught).
ôht, *st. f.* persecution, oppression, disquietude.
ôht-nýd, -nied, *st. f.* same as above.
ô-hwǽr, ô-wer, *adv.* anywhere, anywhither.
ô-hwǽder. See **ôwðer** (either).
ô-hwonan, *adv.* anywhence, from any source.
ôl, *pret.* of **alan**, to grow, spring up, beget, arise. Rim. 23.
ôm, *st. m.* rust, corruption; eruption.
om-beht, -biht, -bieht. See **am-beht.**
ômig, *adj.* rusty, rust-eaten.
on. See **unnan** (to grant).
on, *prep.* I. *w. dat.* or *instr.* **1. on,** upon, besides, in; on (of musical instruments accompanied by singing).— **2.** from, of (*w.* verbs of taking, receiving; and expressions of material).— **3.** in, on, upon (often *w.* verbs of placing, motion, &c).— **4.** temporal: in, on, during.— II. *w. acc.* **1.** on, upon, in, to, toward, to one side (*w.* verbs of hoping, trusting, believing, thinking, seeing, looking, hearing, making, becoming, changing).— **2.** into.— **3.** according to, in accordance with.

4. toward. — **5.** temporal: to, at, for, on, in. [The preposition often follows its case, or is separated from it.]
on-ǽdele, *adj.* innate, natural.
on-bǽru, *st. f.* renunciation? abstinence? self-denial? Gû. 1027.
on-heht, -hyht. See **amheht.**
on-bîd, *st. n.* abiding, expectation, hope; lingering, wasting.
oncer, oncyr. See **ancor** (anchor).
on-cýð, *st. f.* pain, suffering.
on-cýð-dǽd, *st. f.* **deed** causing pain or suffering.
on-cýðig, *adj.* suffering; painful.
ond, ond-, onda. See **and, anda.**
on-drysne, *adj.* frightful, terrible, awe-inspiring, awful, venerable.
on-drýsnlic, *adj.* terrible, frightful. Ps. Th. 46, 2.
on-ettan, *w. v.* to hasten, hurry, eagerly set to work.
on-eardiend, *part. & subs.* indweller, inhabitant.
on-feng, *st. m.* **1.** seizing on, grasping (Run. 44).— **2.** hostile seizure, attack.
on-foran, *adv.* afore, in front of.
on-forht, onga, onge. See **anforht, anga, ange.**
on-gegn, -gegen, -geán, -gân, -gên, *prep. w. dat. & acc. & adv.* **against,** opposite.
on-gend, *prep.* beyond? on yonder side? Wîd. 85.
on-gin, *st. n.* **1.** beginning, commencement (Ph. 638).— **2.** something begun, enterprise, undertaking.— **3.** onrush, attack. An. 466.
on-hǽl, *adj.* **whole, hale,** entire.
on-hǽle, *adj.* secret, concealed.
on-hinden, *adv.* behind.
on-hrêrnes, *st. f.* confusion, uproar, excitement.
on-lang, *adj.* continuous, extended, along. Exod. 53.

on-lic, *adj.* like, resembling, similar.
on-lice, *adv.* the same as above.
on-licnes, *st. f.* 1. likeness, resemblance, similarity.— 2. image, effigy, likeness.
on-medla, -mædla, *w. m.* haughtiness, pride.
on-môd, *adj.* valiant, brave.
onn. See unnan (to grant).
on-riht, *adj.* 1. lawful, proper, true. 2. partaking of? clinging to? Exod. 358.
on-sǣge, *adj.* tending to fall, falling.
on-scêoniendlic, *adj.* to be shunned, abominable.
on-segednes, *st. f.* offering, sacrifice.
on-sêon, -sien, -sion. See onsŷn (sight).
on-stæl, *st. m.* arrangement, destination, determination.
on-stealle? Dan. 247.
on-sund, *adj.* sound, hale, whole, uninjured.
on-sŷn, -synn, -sêon, -sien, -sion, *st. f.* sight, glance, face, aspect, appearance.
on-sŷn, -sien, *st. f.* lack, deficiency.
on-sŷne, *adj.* visible, evident, prominent.
on-wald, -walg, -walh. See onweald, onwealh.
on-weg, *adv.* away, off.
on-wendednes, *st. f.* change, exchange.
on-weald, -wald, *st. m.* might, power.
on-weald, *adj.* mighty, powerful.
on-wealda, *w. m.* prince, lord.
on-wealh, -walg, *adj.* sound, whole, uninjured.
on-wille, *adj.* agreeable, pleasant, dear.
on-wist, *st. f.* presence at, on, or in a place; presence.
on-wunung, *st. f.* dwelling, house.
open, *adj.* open, evident, clear, well-known.

openian, *w. v.* to open, open up, declare, reveal.
ge-openian, the same as above.
open-lice, *adv.* openly, publicly.
ôr, *st. n.* 1. origin, beginning.— 2. vanguard of an army, front rank in battle, front. (Ger. ur-.)
ôra, *w. m.* edge, brink, margin.
orad. See ord (breath).
orc, *st. m.* vessel, beaker, can.
or-cnâwe, -cnǣwe, *adj.* evident, noticeable, well-known.
orc-nê, *st. m.* sea-monster, larva.
ord, *st. n.* (cf. odd), point— 1. sword-point, spear-point, sword, spear.— 2. beginning.—3. head of an army, foremost rank, line of battle.—4. head, prince, chief.
ord-bana, *w. m.* spear-slayer, one who kills with a spear.
ord-fruma, *w. m.* 1. originator, author, creator.—2. sovereign, prince.
ord-stapu, *st. f.* spear-ingress or entrance, entrance of a spear.
ord-wiga, -wŷga, *w. m.* forefighter in battle.
oret, *st. m.* & *n.?* battle, labor. Ps. 127, 2.
oreta. See oretta.
oret-mæcg, -mæg, -mecg, *st. m.* warrior, soldier, hero, champion.
oretta, *w. m.* the same as above.
orettan, *w. v.* to exert one's self, fight or contend for, pursue eagerly.
ge-orettan, to confuse, confound, put out of countenance.
ored. See ord (breath).
or-feorme, *adj.* naked, bare, empty, aimless, useless, without means.
organ, -gana, -ganon, *st.* & *w. m.* 1. organ.— 2. song, canticle.
or-gete, -geate, *adj.* known from the beginning, well known.
or-hlyte, *adj.* without lot or part, unpossessed of, destitute of.
or-læg, *st. n.* ancient, primitive, or primeval law, fate.

or-læg-gifre, *adj.* greedy for war, fond of war.

or-leg, *st. n.* destruction, evil, effort, trouble, torture.

or-leg-cêap, *st. m.* prize of war, booty, spoil.

or-lege, *st. n.* lawlessness, war, conflict, hostility. — 2. contradiction (Jul. 97).— 3. martyrdom, torture, misery.

or-lege, *adj.* hostile, inimical.

or-leg-from, *adj.* fitted or able for war or battle, strenuous.

or-leg-hwîl, *st. f.* time of battle, war-time.

or-leg-nid, *st. m.* battle-rage, hostility, war.

or-leg-sceaft, *st. f.* death-penalty or punishment.

or-leg-stund, *st. f.* time of battle, decision of battle.

or-leg-weorc, *st. n.* war-deed, **work** of war.

or-leahtre, *adj.* blameless, unblemished.

or-mǽte, *adj.* immeasurable, measureless, immense.

or-mete, *adj.* the same as above.

or-môd, *adj.* despairing, hopeless.

orod. See ord (breath).

or-sâwle, *adj.* soulless, lifeless.

or-sorg, *adj.* careless, free from care or sorrow.

or-sorgnes, *st. f.* carelessness, freedom from care or sorrow.

or-trȳwe, *adj.* without trust, mistrustful, distrustful.

ord, orad, ored, orod, orud, *st. n.* breath, spirits, snorting.

or-þanc, -þonc, *adj.* artistic, ingenious. Ruin. 16.

or-þanc, -þonc, *st. m. & n.* 1. original thought, genius, spirit, skill, art.— 2. thoughtlessness, negligence. Sol. 164. [bond.

or-þonc-bend, *st. f.* artistic band or

or-þonc-pil, *st. n.* artistic staff, rod? stylus?

orud. See ord (breath).

or-wêna, *w. adj.* hopeless, despairing, mistrustful. Cf. ween.

or-wênnys, *st. f.* despair, hopelessness.

or-wearde, *adv.* without a **guard,** keeper, or guardian.

or-wige, *adj.* unwarlike, cowardly.

or-wyrdu, *st.f.* unworthiness, shame.

or-yldu, *st. f.* great age, weakness of old age, senility. Cf. Ger. *uralt.*

ôs, *st. m.* 1. God.— 2. name of the Rune o. Run. 10.

otor, *prep.* over, beyond, beside, apart from, outside of. Dan. 73.

ôđ, I. *prep. w. acc.* until, to, up to, as far as;— ôđ þæt, *conj. w. ind. & subj.* until, till; so long as (An. 827);— ôđ þe, *conj.* until, till.— II. *conj.* till, until.

ôđel, *st. m.* home.

ôđer, *pron.* 1. (the) **other,** (the) second;— ôđer— ôđer, the one— the other;— *pl.* the rest, the others.— 2. one of two.— 3. another.

ôđer. See ôwđer (either).

ođđe, *conj.* or

ô-wiht, ôht, *neut.* aught, a whit, something.

ôwđer, ôđer (= ôhwæđer), *pron.* either, one of two.

ô-wer. See ôhwǽr (anywhere).

oxa, *w. m.* ox (bos).

P

pâd, *st. f.* covering, garment. Cf. pea-jacket?
pæd, pad, *st. m.* **path**.
pæddan, peddan, *w. v.* to traverse, penetrate, travel over.
palma, *w. m.* **palm-tree**.
palm-trêow, *st. m.* same as above.
panna, panne, *w. m.* & *f.* **pan**.
pandher, *st. m.* **panther**.
pater-noster, *m. n.* paternoster (our Father).
pad. See pæd.
pentecosten, *n.* **pentecost**.
pernex, *st. m.* a bird? Rid. 41: 66.
peddan. See pæddan (to traverse).
pêa, *w. m.* **peacock**.
peord, name for the Rune p. Run. 38.
pil, *st. m.* arrow, dart, pilum.
plega, *w. m.* **1.** quick motion, journey, movement.— **2.** battle-**play**, battle.— **3. play**, jest, sport, pastime, joy.
plegan, plegian, *w. v.* **1.** to put one's self in rapid motion, to move rapidly.— **2.** to clap the hands.— **3.** to play, sport, jest.
porte, *w. f.* portal, gate, door.
portic, *st. m.* portico, colonnade, porch.
prass? (By. 68), **press?** throng?
prêost, *st. m.* **priest**, presbyter.
psalterium,— psalter.
pund, *st. n.* **pound**.
pynd? pond? cistern? lake? Rim. 49.
pyndan, *w. v.* in for-pyndan, to crush, suppress, remove.
pyt, *st. m.* **pit**.

R

racente, *w. f.* chain, fetter.
racentêag, *st. f.* the same as above.
racian, *w. v., w. dat.* to rule, guide, control.
racu, *st. f.* course of a thing, evolution, unfolding, representation, recounting, narration, cause.
râd, *st. f.* **1.** riding, raid (Run. 13). **2.** journey (El. 982).— **3.** road, way.— **4.** rhythm, time.— **5.** name of the Rune r. Run 13.
râdor. See rôdor (sky).
râd-pyt, *st. m.* riding-pit, *i. e.* well with drawing-pole attachment. Rid. 59: 14, 15.
râd-wêrig, *adj.* **road-weary**, footsore.
ræcan, ræcean, *w. v.* to reach, stretch out, extend, run along.
ge-ræcan, **1.** to reach, attain, strike, hit, take.— **2.** reach after, extend to, reach to (Ps. 137: 7).— **3.** to reach to, extend, stretch out (Gn. Ex. 92).— **4.** to attain, win.— **5.** *intr.* to reach. Wid. 16: 27.
ræced, reced, recyd, *st. m.* & *n.* building, house, room, hall.
ræd, rêd, *st. m.* **1.** counsel, good advice, **rede**.— **2.** advantage, gain, profit.— **3.** power, might.
rædan, *st. red. v.* **1.** to advise, counsel, persuade.— **2.** to advise for, care for.— **3.** to rule, govern, reign. **4.** to have power over, possess.— **5.** to guess, forebode. (Ger. *rathen*.)
rædan, *w. v.* **1.** to advise, counsel, **2.** to rule, guide.— **3.** to **read**.
â-rædan, to unriddle, decipher.

be-rǽdan, to betray, withdraw, take away, rob of.
rǽdan, w. v. in
 â-rǽdan, to make ready? prepare? Wand. 5; Gn. Ex. 192.
 ge-rǽdan, to start, get ready, prepare, execute, resolve.
rǽd-bora, w. m. rede-bearer, adviser.
rǽde, adj. ready, complete.
rǽdelle, w. f. riddle (something to read, or guess.)
rǽdend, part. & subs. adviser, guide, ruler, commander.
rǽd-fæst, -fest, adj. resolute, resolved, steadfast, determined.
rǽd-ge-þeaht, st. n. deliberation, counsel, consultation.
rǽd-hycgende, part. acquainted with, cognizant of.
rǽd-léas, adj. 1. redeless, ill-advised. 2. abandoned, bad.
rǽd-snottor, adj. wise in counsel, clever, sage.
rǽd-þeahtende, part. that deliberates, wise, sagacious.
rǽd-þeahtere, st. m. deliberator, adviser.
rǽfnan, refnan, rǽfnian, w. v. 1. to do, execute, accomplish.— 2. to endure, sustain, tolerate. Ph. 643.
 â-rǽfnan, to endure, suffer, carry out, accomplish, do.
ræft, mold, decay? Rim. 66. (Eng. raft = fusty smell?)
rǽg-hǽr, adj. hoar, roe-colored.
rǽgn, rǽgol-fæst. See regn, regol-fæst.
rǽman, w. v. in
 â-rǽman, to rise, stand up.
rǽndan, w. v. in
 tô-rǽndan, to rend, to tear in pieces.
rǽpan, w. v. to bind, tie with ropes.
 ge-rǽpan, the same as above.
rǽping, st. m. one bound, prisoner.

rǽran, w. v. to rear, rise up, lift up, erect, arrange, elevate, promote; arouse, set in motion.
 â-rǽran, the same as above.
rǽs, st. m. 1. attack, onslaught, onrush.— 2. leap, jump, rush.
rǽsan, w. v. 1. to rush on or at, attack, press.— 2. to send. Rid. 26: 8.
 ge-rǽsan, the same as above.
 þurh-rǽsan, to rush through.
rǽs-bora, w. m. rusher-on, leader, deliberator, provider, adviser, king.
ræst, rǽstan. See rest, rěstan.
rǽsu, st. f. foresight? Az. 126.
rǽswa, w. m. prince, ruler, adviser, guide.
rafan, st. abl. v. IV. in
 be-rafan, to rob of, despoil.
rahte, pret. of reccan (to rule).
ram, rom, st. m. ram.
ranc-strǽt, st. f. street through the foe, gap in hostile ranks. Gen. 2112.
rand, rond, st. m. rim, margin, edge. 1. edge of a rock (B. 2538).— 2. edge or rim of a shield.— 3. shield.
randa, w. m. shield. By. 20.
rand-burg, st. f. 1. fortress or castle provided or decked with shields? shield-wall? defense? Jul. 19.— 2. shield-wall of waves, upheaved Red Sea. Exod. 463.
rand-ge-beorh, st. n. shield-defense, protecting shield (wave).
rand-hæbbende, part. shield-holder, shield-warrior.
rand-wiga, w. m. shield-warrior, warrior.
rand-wigend, -wiggend, part. & subs. the same as above.
râp, st. m. rope.
râsettan, w. v. to rage.
râsian, w. v. to search out, explore, discover,
 â-râsian, to search out, discover, uncover, seize.

rade, *adv.* instantly, at once, quickly. Cf. **rathe.**
rêc, *st. m.* **reek,** smoke, steam.
rêcan, *w. v.* to smoke, **reek.**
rêcan, rêccan, *w. v.* to **reck,** care about, seek after, examine, long for, demand.
reccan, recan, reccean, *w. v. (pret.* **reahte).**—**1.** to rule, guide, direct, govern.—**2.** to stretch out, extend (Met. 29: 63).—**3.** to recount, inform, narrate, say, speak.
    â-reccan, 1. to spread out, strike out (Cri. 1125).—**2.** to put in order, build up, complete (Rim. 10).—**3.** to erect, build up.—**4.** to explicate, explain, clear up.—**5.** to say, pronounce, announce, **inform,** narrate.
    and-reccan, to narrate, inform, bring forward.
    ge-reccan, 1. to guide, arrange, set up, establish.—**2.** to explicate, represent, explain.—**3.** to narrate, inform.—**4.** to blame, reprimand, scold.
reccend, *part. & subs.* ruler, regent, guide, leader.
rêce-lêast, -lêst, *st. f.* **recklessness,** carelessness.
reced, rêcels. See **ræced, rŷcels.**
recen, recon, *adj.* ready, prompt, quick.
rêcen, *adj.* smoky, smoked, **reeking,** filthy.
recene, ricene, ricone, rycene, *adv.* immediately, instantly, at once.
recenian, *w. v.* in
    ge-recenian, to explain, represent clearly.
recon, recyd. See **recen, ræced.**
rêd. See **ræd** (advice).
rede, *adj.* **ready.**
redian, *w. v.* in
    â-redian, *trans. & intrans.* to find one's way, attain, reach; to do, execute, effect.

refnan. See **ræfnan** (to perform).
regn, rên, *st. m.* **rain.**
regn-heard, *adj.* very hard, firm.
regnian, rênian, *w. v.* to arrange, prepare, plan.
    be-rênian, the same as above.
    ge-regnian, to prepare, provide, furnish, deck.
regnig, rênig, *adj.* **rainy.**
regol, regul, *st. m.* **rule,** regulation, canon, guidance.
regol-fæst, *adj.* rigid, strict, adhering to monastic **rules.**
regn-þêof, *w. m.* arrant **thief.**
regn-, rên-weard, *st. m.* preëminent ruler, excellent **guardian.**
regn-wyrm, *st. m.* **rainworm.**
reliquias *(acc. pl.* Latin), **relics.**
rên, rên-, rene, rênian, rênig. See **regn, ryne, regnian, regnig.**
rêran. See **ræran** (to rear).
rêsele, *w. f.* **riddle,** solution of a riddle. (Ger. *räthsel.*)
rest, ræst, *st. f.* **1. rest.**—**2.** resting-place, bed, grave.
restan, *w. v.* to **rest,** repose, celebrate holy days or holiday; to succumb;—often reflexive.
    ge-restan, the same as above.
rêstan, ræstan, *w. v.* to rejoice, exult, cry out. Ps. 113: 4.
rest-bedd, *st. n.* **bed of rest.**
rêtan, *w. v.* to delight, give pleasure to, cheer up.
    â-rêtan, the same as above.
rede, *adj.* intended, calculated; fixed, valid.
rêde, *adj.* rude, rough, wild, severe, furious, savage, **wroth.**
rêde, *adv.* the same as above.
rêde-hydig, *adj.* ready-minded, easy-tempered.
rêde-man, *st. m.* money-lender, capitalist.
rêde-môd, *adj.* savage, wroth, cruel.
redian, *w. v.* to arrange, dispose, fix, establish.

rêdig-môd, *adj.* savage, fierce-spirited.
rex (Latin), king.
rex genidlan (El. 609). See under cearc.
rêad, *adj.* red.
rêade, *adv.* the same as above.
rêad-fâg, *adj.* red, red-colored.
rêaf, *st. n.* robe, garment, corselet.
• 2. booty, plunder, spoil (in war).
rêafere, *st. m.* robber, rover.
rêafian, *w. v.* to rob, plunder, despoil, ravage.
   â-rêafian, to take away, deprive of, destroy.
   be-, bi-rêafian, to bereave, rob of, plunder.
rêaf-lâc, *st. n.* plunder, booty, spoil, rapine.
reahte, *pret.* of reccan (to rule).
rêoc, *adj.* tumultuous, wild, rough, raging.
rêocan, *st. abl. v.* VI. to reek, smoke.
rêod, *adj.* red, ruddy.
rêodan, *st. abl. v.* VI. 1. to redden, stain with blood. — 2. to kill, slay.
reoden, *st. f.* shaking? shaking up? sieve, dresser? Rid. 26: 8.
reodian, *w. v.* to pass through a sieve.
rêofan, *st. abl. v.* VI. to break up, split, reave, break through.
be-, bi-rêofan, to rob of, deprive of.
reomig-môd, *adj.* genial, generous-minded, cheerful in spirit.
rêon (?) lament, lamentation. Hö. 6.
rêon (*pret.*), rêone. See rôwan, rêow.
rêonig, *adj.* sad.
rêonig-môd, *adj.* sorrowful-minded.
reord, *st. f.* (*n.*), speech, talk, language, voice.
reord, *st. f.* means of subsistence, food. Gen. 1344.
rêord, *pret.* of rǣdan (to advise).
reord-berend, *part. & subs.* endowed with speech; human being.

reordian, *w. v.* to speak, talk, say.
   un-reordian, to dishonor, disagree. Sat. 66.
reordian, *w. v.* in
   ge-reordian, to sustain with food, satisfy, prepare food, entertain.
reot, *st. m.? f.?* noise? tumult? riot? noisy joy? B. 2457.
rêotan, *st. abl. v.* VI. to weep, wail, lament, sorrow.
   be-rêotan, to bewail, grieve over.
   wid-rêotan, to contend against, resist, frighten off.
rêotend, *adj.* weeping.
rêow, *adj.* rough, savage, furious.
rib, *st. n.* rib.
rice, *adj.* mighty, powerful, wealthy, rich.
rice, *st. n.* (cf. -rick), might, superior might, supremacy, rule. — 2. realm, domain.
ricels, ricene, ricone. See rȳcels, recene.
ricsian, rixian, *w. v.* to be mighty, powerful; to rule, govern.
ricu, *st. f.* direction? Rid. 4: 31; — 21: 16.
ridan, *st. abl. v.* V. 1. to ride. — 2. to move (in general). — 3. to lie upon, sit. Gen. 372.
   ge-ridan, to ride over (a place or spot).
   od-ridan, to ride to, go to.
ridan, *st. abl. v.* V. in
   ge-ridan, to prepare, get ready.
ridend, *part. & subs.* rider.
rift, ryft, *st. f.* linen cloth, sack, bag, veil, covering.
rignan, *st. abl. v.* I. to rain.
rihde (B. 2239). See wyscan.
riht, ryht, *adj.* 1. right, straight. — 2. right, correct, just, righteous. — 3. allowable, fitting.

riht, **st. n. 1.** right.—**2.** first=part, portion, possession.—**3.** duty, obligation, debt.—**4.** true state of a thing, correctness.—**4.** account.
rihtan, w. v. **1. to direct,** prepare, arrange.—**2. to set up,** erect.
    ge-rihtan, to direct.
riht-ædlo, st. n. pl. true natural disposition.
rihte, ryhte, adv. **rightly, correctly,** outright.
rihtend, ryhtend, part. & subs. director, leader, guide.
riht-fremmende, part. right-acting, right-doing.
riht-heort, adj. right-hearted, honest.
riht-lice, adv. rightly, correctly, justly.
rihtnes, -nys, st. f. **rightness,** rectitude, justness.
riht-ryne, st. m. right or straight course.
riht-scytte, st. m. good and true protection or defense? true shot?
riht-, ryht-wis, adj. **righteous,** just.
riht-wislice, adv. **righteously,** wisely.
riht-wisnes, st. f. **righteousness,** rectitude; justness, straightness.
rim, st. n. **(rime),** number, multitude.
riman, w. v. **1. to count.**—**2.** reckon up, number.—**3.** to count among, reckon as belonging to.
    â-riman, to count out, through, up.
    ge-riman, to count.
rim-cræft, st. m. art of reckoning, calculation, numeration, arithmetic.
rim-, rym-cræftig, adj. good at reckoning.
rim-ge-tæl, -getel, st. n. number.
rim-talu, st. f. the same as above.
rinc, st. m. man (vir).
rinc-ge-tæl, st. n. number of men.
rind. See **lamrindum.**

rinnan, st. abl. v. **I. to run,** flow.
    â-rinnan, to run out, off, or away; to pass away.
    be-, bi-rinnan, to run upon, run over, overflow.
    ge-rinnan, to run together, coagulate.
    od-rinnan, to run off, out, away, escape.
rip, rȳp, st. n. **ripeness, harvest.**
rip, adj. **ripe,** mature.
ripan, w. v. **to reap,** harvest.
risan, st. abl. v. V. **to rise,** stand up.
    â-risan, to arise, rise up, originate, spring up or from.
    ge-risan, to fit, be fitting, appropriate, become, belong to.
rid, ryd, st. m. brook, stream.
rixian. See **ricsian** (to rule).
rocettan, w. v. to eructate, belch forth, throw up.
rôd, st. f. **rood,** cross, holyrood.
rôdor, râdor, st. m. (radiant?), sky, firmament, ether.
rôdor-beorht, adj. heaven-bright.
rôdor-, râdor-cyning, st. m. king of heaven.
rôdor-stôl, st. m. heaven-stool, throne of heaven.
rôdor-torht, adj. heaven-bright, with celestial brightness.
rôdor-tungol, st. n. heaven-star, star, constellation.
rôf, adj. able, strong, valiant.
rôf-word, adj. strong of speech, vigorous in word.
rogian, w. v. to thrive, grow, advance, go forward. (Ger. *rücken.*)
rom. See **ram** (male sheep).
rômian, rômigan, w. v. to strive for, seek to attain.
rond, rôp? (Rid. 58: 3). See **rand, rôf.**
rôrend, part. & subs. **rower.**
rôse, w. f. **rose.**
rôt, adj. cheerful, bright, lively.

rôw, *st. f.* repose, quiet. (Ger. *ruhe.* Cf. un-ruly.)

rôwan, *st. red. v.* to row, steer, swim, take ship.

rûh, rûw, *adj.* rough, rude; hirsute, hairy.

rûm, *st. m.* room, space.

rûm, *adj.* 1. roomy, spacious, wide, comprehensive.— 2. same meanings applied to the mind.— 3. of great weight, bearing, or effect (Hy. 7: 15).—4. extreme, far reaching (Gû. 460).

rûme, *adv.* 1. far.— 2. richly, plenteously, numerously.— 3. light-heartedly (Jud. 97).— 4. openly, publicly (Jul. 314).— 5. temporal: *compar.* rûmor, still further, further yet.

rûm-gâl, *adj.* exulting in space? much elated? Gen. 1466.

rûm-heort, *adj.* big-hearted, generous.

rûm-lice, *adv.* 1. richly, abundantly. 2. far, afar. B. 139.

rûm-môd, *adj.* great-minded, generous, big-hearted.

rûn, *st. f.* 1. secret conclave, council, deliberation.—2. secret.— 3. secret writing, runic writing, rune.

rûn-côfa, *w. m.* secret-holder, breast, bosom.

rûn-cræftig, *adj.* acquainted with runes.

rûn-stæf, *st. m.* rune-stave, rune, runic letter.

rûn-wita, *w. m.* 1. rune-wit, knower of secrets.— 2. privy councilor, private adviser.

rûw. See rûh (rough).

rŷcels, rêcels, ricels, *st. n.* incense, perfume.

rycene. See recene (quickly).

rŷfan, *w. v.* in
   be-rŷfan, to rob of, deprive, take away.

ryft, ryht, ryht-, ryhte, ryhtend. See rift, riht, rihte, rihtend.

rŷman, *w. v.* 1. to make room or place, spread, prepare.—2. to clear away, remove. Ex. 479.
   ge-rŷman, to make room or place, spread, grant, permit, allow.

rŷm-cræftig. See rimcræftig.

rŷn (?) roaring, roar.

rŷnan, *w. v.* to roar.

ryne, rene, *st. m.* 1. course, path.— 2. running (of fluids), rain. Gen. 1416.

rŷne, *st. n.* secret.

ryne-gæst, -giest, *st. m.* rain-spirit, lightning.

rynel, *st. m.* runner, courier, messenger.

rŷne-man, *st. m.* rune-man, one initiated into mysteries, cherisher or keeper of secrets.

ryne-strong, *adj.* strong in running.

ryne-swift, *adj.* swift in running, swift.

ryne-þragu, *st. f.* running.

rynig, *adj.* able to run, a good runner.

rŷp. See rîp (ripe).

rŷpan, *w. v.* in
   â-rŷpan, to separate, tear off or away, rip.
   be-rŷpan, to rob of, deprive of.

ryd. See rid (brook).

S

sacan, *st. abl. v.* IV. 1. to fight, contend, struggle.— 2. to attack, rush on, curse.

an-sacan, to repel, deny, refuse, contradict.

    for-sacan, to forsake, renounce (what is forbidden), repel.

    ge-sacan, to effect by contention, win, conquer, occupy.

    on-sacan, 1. to contest, strive with or against.— 2. to oppose, contend for.— 3. to deny.

    wid-sacan, to oppose, contend against, refuse, scorn, abandon, renounce.

sacerd, *st. m.* priest. Cf. sacerdos.

sacerd-hâd, *st. m.* priestly condition, rank, priesthood.

sacu, *st. f.* strife, controversy, hostility, feud, conflict.

sâda, *w. m.* sling.

sadian, *w. v.* in

    ge-sadian, to satisfy, satiate.

sadol, *st. m.* saddle.

sadol-beorht, *adj.* with bright saddle, finely caparisoned.

sǣ, *st. m. & f.* sea, ocean.

sǣ-bât, *st. m.* sea-boat.

sǣ-beorg, *st. m.* sea mountain or wall, shore, mountain of waves.

sæc, *st. n.* strife; controversy.

sǣcan. See sêcan (to seek).

sǣccan, to fight? Rid. 172.

sǣcie, sǣce. See sacu (strife).

sǣcgen, *st. f.* saying, announcement, utterance.

sǣcgan. See secgan (to say).

sǣ-cir, -cyr, *st. m.* sea-turning, ebb, backflow of the sea.

sǣcra = sǣtra, *gen. pl.* of sǣtere, ambuscade? plot? Rim. 65.

sǣ-cyning, *st. m.* sea-king.

sæd, *adj.* satisfied, satiated. Cf. sad = settled.

sǣd, *st. n.* 1. seed, sowing.— 2. seed. 3. seed, scion, descendant.— 4. seed, seed-field.— 5. growth.

sǣd-berende, *part.* seed-bearing; having increase in God? God-fearing? Gen. 1145.

sǣ-dêor, *st. n.* sea-beast.

sǣ-draca, *w. m.* sea-dragon.

sǣ-farod, -fearod, *st. m.* beating of the wave, wave-beat, wave.

sǣ-fæsten, *st. n.* sea-fastness, ocean.

sǣ-fisc, *st. m.* sea-fish.

sǣ-flôd, *st. m.* sea-flood.

sǣ-flota, *w. m.* sea-float, ship.

sǣ-fôr, *st. f.* seafaring, sea-journey.

sǣgan, *w. v.* to sink (*trans.*), cause to sink.

    ge-sǣgan, to fell, strike down, bend.

    on-sǣgan, to fell, cast down.

sǣgen, *st. f.* legend, tale, saga.

sǣ-genga, *w. m.* seagoer, seafaring ship.

sǣ-gêap, *adj.* sea-broad, broad enough for sea-navigation, spacious.

sægl, segl, *st. n.* sun (eye).

sǣgon. See sêon (to see).

sǣ-grund, *st. m.* sea-bottom, ocean depth.

sǣ-hengest, *st. m.* seahorse, ship.

sǣ-holm, *st. m.* ocean.

sæl, *st. n.* room, house, hall. (Ger. *saal*.)

sǣl, *st. m. & f.* 1. good fortune, happiness, well-being, bliss, joy.— 2. position, place, condition.— 3. auspicious opportunity, favorable time.

sǣl. See sêl.

sǣ-lâc, *st. n.* sea-spoil.

sǣ-lâd, *st. f.* seaway, path, sea-journey.

sǽ-lâf, *st. f.* left or saved from the sea; sea-leaving (s).
sǽlan, *w. v.* to take place, happen auspiciously, occur (to).
    ge-sǽlan, 1. to take place, happen luckily, occur to.—2. to effect, execute successfully. Gû. 318.
    tô-sǽlan, *impers.* 1. to be unsuccessful, fail.— 2. to fail, lack, want.
sǽlan, *w. v.* to tie, bind, fetter, fasten. (Ger. *seilen.*)
    â-sǽlan, the same as above.
    ge-sǽlan, the same as above.
    on-sǽlan, to untie, loosen, release.
sǽle. See sellan (to give).
sǽld. See seld (house).
sǽ-lida, -leoda, *w. m.* seafarer, sailor.
sǽ-lidend, *part. & subs.* the same.
sǽld, *st. f.* dwelling, house, hall, mansion.
sǽld, *st. f.* good fortune, auspicious fate, prosperity.
sæl-wǽg, *st. m.* house, wall.
sæl-wong, *st. m.* fertile and pleasant field.
sǽ-man, *st. m.* seaman.
sǽ-mêde, *adj.* sea-weary, exhausted from sea-travel. (Ger. *müde.*)
sǽmest. See sǽmra. [ship.
sǽ-mearh, -mear, *st. m.* seahorse,
sǽmra, *compar. adj.* weaker, smaller, slighter, meaner, worse; *superl.* sǽmest.
sǽ-naca, *w. m.* vessel, ship.
sǽ-nǽs, *st. m.* sea-promontory, cape, naze.
sǽne, *adj.* slow, slack, lazy, negligent (*segnis*).
sǽp, *st. m.* sap, juice. [sea.
sǽ-rinc, *st. m.* seaman, hero of the
sǽ-rôf, *adj.* brave at sea, bold on the sea.
sǽ-rýric, *st. m.* sea-reed. [sea.
sǽ-sid, *st. m.* sea-journey, trip by
sǽ-strêam, *st. m.* sea-current.

sǽt, *st. f.* ambush, ambuscade. Cf. sitting.
sǽta, *w. m.* settler.
sǽtan, sǽtian, *w. v.* to lurk in ambush, lie in wait for, plot against.
sǽtere, *st. m.* lurker in ambush, lier in wait.
sǽ-tilcas (Met. 8: 31) = sccalcas.
sǽtnian, *w. v.* to lie in wait for, cherish designs against.
sǽ-wǽg, *st. m.* sea-wave.
sǽ-wang, *st. m.* expanse along the sea, seashore.
sǽ-warod, *st. m.* seashore, bank, beach.
sǽ-wêrig, *adj.* sea-weary, tired of or by the sea.
sǽ-weall, *st. m.* sea-wall.— 1. seashore, beach.— 2. walls of divided water in the Red Sea.
sǽ-wicing, *st. m.* wicking, sea-robber, pirate.
sǽ-wudu, *st. m.* sea-wood, vessel, ship.
sǽ-wylm, *st. m.* surf, billowing of the sea.
sǽ-ýd, *st. f.* sea-wave.
sâg (?) bundle, load, (sack?)
sagian, *w. v.* (*defect.*), to say.
    ge-sagian, the same as above.
sagu, *st. f.* saw, saying, utterance, tradition (Gen. 535), narrative, saga.
sâl, *st. m.* rope, cord. (Ger. *seil.*)
salig, salh, *st. f.* willow, willow-tree (*salix*).
salletan, *w. v.* to sing to the psalter (*psallere*).
salt. See sealt (salt).
salor, *st. n.?* hall, room, royal hall.
salu, *pl.* of sǽl (room).
salu, salo, *adj.* sallow, darkish, dark brown.
salu-, sealo-brûn, *adj.* sallow-brown, dark-brown.
salu-neb, *adj.* sallow-beaked, with darkish beak.

salu-pâd, *adj.* dark-clad.
sâl-wang. See **sǽl-wang.**
salwed, *part.* darkened, colored dark, tarred.
salwig-federe, *adj.* sallow-feathered, dark-feathered.
salwig-, saluwig-pâd, *adj.* the same.
same, some, *adv.* similarly, in like manner; — **swâ some** = just as, equally as.
sam-heort, *adj.* of the **same heart,** one in mind, harmonious.
samnian, somnian, *w. v.* **1.** to collect, assemble, summon together. — **2.** to collect one's self, assemble, come together, meet.
 ge-samnian, 1. to collect, assemble, summon together, unite. — **2.** to unite, put together, associate. **3.** to gather, assemble, come together, meet.
samnunga, *adv.* suddenly.
samod, samed, somod, somud, somed, *adv.* **1.** together, simultaneously. — **2.** *prep., w. dat.* with, at the same time with. B. 1311 & 2942.
samode, *adv.* together. (Ger. *sammt.*)
samod-eard, *st. m.* dwelling-place in common.
samod-fæst, *adj.* established together, fixed together.
sam-râd, -rǽd, *adj.* of the same mind, accordant.
sam-tenges, *adv.* instantly, at once.
sâm-wis, *adj.* **semi-wise,** not clever, dull.
sam-, som-wist, *st. f.* living together, community.
sâm-worht, *adj.* **semi-wrought,** half-complete.
sanc. See **sang** (song).
sanct, *adj.* holy, **sainted.**
sand, sond, *st. m.* one **sent,** messenger. Run. 74.
sand, sond, *st. n.* **1. sand.** — **2.** sandy shore, beach, bank.

sand-beorg, *st. m.* **sand-mountain,** sandhill, sand-dune.
sand-corn, *st. n.* grain of sand, **sandkernel.**
sand-grot, *st. n.* sand-**grit,** grain of sand.
sand-hlid (*pl.* **hleodu**), *st. n.* sand slope, sandy declivity.
sand-hof, *st. n.* sand house, gravemound, grave.
sand-lond, *st. n.* sandy shore.
sang, song (**sanc**), *st. m.* **song,** lay, cry.
sang-cræft, *st. m.* **songcraft,** art of song or singing.
sangere, *st. m.* **singer.**
sânian, *w. v.* in
 â-sânian, to become slack, slow, negligent, lazy.
sâr, *st. n.* (**sore**), pain, dolor.
sâr, *adj.* **sore,** painful.
sâr-ben, *st. f.* painful wound or sore.
sâr-cwide, *st. m.* **1. sore speech;** insulting, wounding speech. — **2.** words of sorrow or pain. Met. 2: 4.
sâre, *adv.* sorely, painfully, bitterly. (Scotch *sair.*)
sâr-ferhđ, *adj.* sore in spirit, sorrowful.
sârgian, *w. v.* to cause pain, injure, wound.
 ge-sârgian, the same as above.
sârig, *adj.* **sorry,** sad.
sârig-ferhđ, *adj.* sorrowful-minded.
sârig-môd, *adj.* the same as above.
sârlic, *adj.* painful, sad, bitter.
sârlice, *adv.* the same as above.
sâr-slege, *st. m.* painful blow, chastisement.
sâr-spell, *st. n.* piteous story, lament, lamentation.
sâr-stæf, *st. m.* sore story, painful speech, abuse, insult, attack.
sâr-wracu, *st. f.* sore exile, painful exile, misery.
sâr-wylm, *st. m.* upwelling pain, illness, disease.

Satan, m. Satan.
sául. See sáwel (soul).
sáwan, st. red. v. to sow, strew (seed).
   á-sáwan, to sow, sow with.
   geond-sáwan, to strew, sow, scatter, disseminate.
   on-sáwan, to sow.
   tô-sáwan, to strew, scatter, spread.
sáwel, sáwol, sáwul, sáwl, sául, sáwle, st. f. soul.
sáwl-berend, part. & subs. soul-bearing, mortal.
sáwel-cund, adj. spiritual.
sáwel-dréor, st. m. soul-gore, life's blood, heart's blood.
sáwel-ge-dâl, st. n. soul-separation, death.
sáwel-hord, st. n. soul-hoard, life-treasure.
sáwel-hús, st. n. soul-house, body.
sáwel-léas, adj. soulless, lifeless.
sáwl, sáwle, sáwol, sáwul. See sáwel.
sáwon. See séon (to see).
scacan. See sceacan (to shake).
scádan, sceádan, st. red. v. 1. to divide, separate (as in water-shed). 2. to decide (Cri. 1233).—3. to be separated from, lose (Ruin. 31). (Ger. scheiden.)
   á-scádan, to divide off, separate, hold asunder, eliminate, cleanse.
   for-scádan, 1. to scatter, dissipate.—2. to damn, condemn. Gú. 449.
   ge-scádan, to separate, decide, arrange.
   tô-scádan, 1. to part, separate. 2. to distinguish, discriminate.
scáde, w. f. crown (of the head), vertex, apex. (Ger. scheitel.)
scadu-helm. See sceadu-helm.
scæcen, scæced. See sceacan (to shake).

scæd, scead, sced, st. n. shadow, shade.
scǽnan, scênan, w. v. in
   ge-scǽnan, to break, break in pieces, rub to pieces, graze, wound.
scǽnan, w. v. in
   ge-scǽnan, to cause to shine, to render brilliant.
scǽd, scêd, scead, sceâd, st. f. sheath, scabbard.
scal, scalc, scâlu, scamian, scamu. See sculan, scealc, scôlu, scamian, scamu.
scânan, st. red. v. to shine, flash.
scanca, sconca, w. m. shank, leg.
scand, sceand, scond, sceond, st. f. shame, disgrace. (Ger. schande.)
scand-, sceandlic, adj. shameful, disgraceful.
scada. See sceada (evil-doer).
sced, scêd (pret.). See scæd, scâdan (to divide).
sceddan, sceadian, w. v. in
   be-sceddan, to beshadow, overshadow.
sceft. See sceaft (shaft).
scehdun (Cri. 980), for scêndun, spared; or sceldun = scildun, shielded.
scel, sceld, sceldburg, sceldig, scell. See sculan, scild, scyld, scyldburg, scyldig, sculan.
scell, scyll, st. f. shell.
scênan. See scǽnan (to make shine).
scenc, st. m. cup-bearer, skinker. (Ger. schenke.)
scencan, w. v. to pour out or present wine.
   bi-scencan, to bepour, pour on, overflow.
scendan, scyndan, w. v. to disgrace, bring to shame.
   ge-scendan, to disgrace, confound, confuse.
scendan, scêne. See scyndan, scŷne.

scenne, *w. f.* thin sheet, plate, or blade of metal; part of a sword-hilt? lamina? (on a sword-hilt). B. 1694.

scêp. See **sceâp** (sheep).

sceppan, scyppan, sceappan, *st. abl. v.* IV. to **shape,** do, get done, effect, arrange, destine, fix, establish, conclude. (Ger. *schaffen.*)

   â-sceppan, to do, get done, fix, destine, determine.

   for-sceppan, to shape or form over, change, transform.

   ge-sceppan, to shape, form, arrange.

sceppend, scippend, scyppend, scypend, *part. & subs.* **shaper,** creator; — *adj.* in Hy. 4: 15.

sceran, sceoran, *st. abl. v.* II. to **shear,** cut, shave, cut through, break in pieces, erase.

   bi-sceran, to cut off, beshear, trim, remove.

   ge-sceran, to cut up, hew to pieces.

scerian, scirian, scyrian, *w. v.* to arrange in parts or sections, form in troops, arrange, depute, destine, refer, present.

   â-scyrian, to arrange, destine, determine; to remove, separate, free.

   be-, bi-scerian, to deprive of, rob of, separate from.

   ge-scerian, 1. to shear off, trim, deal out, allot, assign.—**2.** to count.

scerpen. See **scyrpan** (to adorn).

scerwan, *st. abl. v.* III. to squander, waste, dissipate.

   be-scerwan, to rob of, to deprive of.

scêt, *pret.* of **scêotan** (to shoot).

scêd. See **scæd** (sheath).

sceddan, scyddan, *w. v.* to scathe, injure, harm, oppress, disturb.

   ge-sceddan, the same as above.

sceacan, scacan, *st. abl. v.* IV. **1.** *intrans.* to **shake,** move violently, hurry, rush, jump, fly, escape, &c. **2.** *trans.* to shake (Exod. 176).

   â-sceacan, 1. to swing, set or be in motion, strike.— **2.** to become shattered, shaken, tottering.

   on-sceacan, to swing, set or be in motion.

scead, sceâdan, sceadian. See **scæd, scâdan, sceddan.**

sceaden-mæl, *adj.* inlaid with arabesque, or ornamental work? deadly weapon? B. 1939.

sceadu, *st. f.* **shadow.**

sceadu-genga, *w. m.* shadow-goer, twilight-stalker.

sceadu-helm, *st. m.* veil of shadow, veil of darkness.

sceâf, *st. m.* **sheaf,** bundle.

sceaft, sceft, *st. m.* **shaft** (of arrow or spear), spear, bolt; grain-straw.

sceal, *n.* (?) troop, band? Sat. 268.

sceal, sceall, scealt. See **sculan.**

scealc, *st. m.* slave, servant, lad, warrior, man.

sceâm, *st. m.* gray or gray-white horse. (Ger. *schimmel.*)

sceamian, scamian, scomian, sceomian, *w. v.* to **shame.**—**1.** to be ashamed, blush.—**2.** *impers.*= Lat. *pudet,* it shames me, &c.

   â-scamian, to shame, make ashamed.

   ge-sceamian, 1. to be ashamed, blush. — **2.** *impers. w. acc.*= Lat. *pudet,* it shames me, &c.

sceamu, scamu, scomu, sceomu, *st. f.* **1.** shame, disgrace, confusion.— **2.** shame-parts, *pudenda.*

sceamul, *st. m.* cushion. (Ger. *schemel.*)

sceand, sceandlic. See **scand.**

sceap, *st. n.* shape, vat, vessel, holder.

sceâp, scêp, *st. n.* **sheep.**

sceapen, *part.* of **sceppan** (to shape).

scear(u?), *st. f.* troop? band? B. 3171.
sceard, *part.* 1. notched.— 2. *w. gen.* robbed of, deprived of.
scearp, *adj.* 1. **sharp**, pointed.— 2. sharp, shrewd.
scearpe, *adv.* sharply.
scearplice, *adv.* sharply, quickly.
scearpnes, *st. f.* **sharpness**.
scearu, *st. m.* stylus? plectrum? pencil? Wy. 83.
sceat, *st. m.* (**scat**), coin, money.
scêat, *st. m.* 1. projecting corner, edge.— 2. part of the earth, locality, neighborhood.— 3. lap (of a garment and of the body).— 4. lap or surface of the earth.— 5. hiding-place (El. 583). (Ger. *schoos*.)
sceâd. See **scǣd** (sheath).
sceada, scada, *w. m.* 1. **scather**, injurer, robber, foe, antagonist, evil-doer (especially, the *devil*).— 2. hero, warrior.
sceadan, *st. abl. v.* IV. *w. dat.* to **scathe**, injure, hurt, oppress, disquiet.
   ge-sceadan, the same as above.
sceaden, *st. f.* scathing, injury, harm.
scêawend-wis, *w. f.* scenic song, theatrical song.
scêawere, *st. m.* observer, spy.
scêawian, *w. v.* 1. (**show**), *intrans.* to see, look, gaze.— 2. *trans.* to see, look at, behold, inspect, contemplate.— 3. *trans.* to see, go to see, visit. B. 308. (Ger. *schauen*.)
   be-sceawian, to behold, contemplate, inspect, foresee, care for.
   ge-sceâwian, 1. *intrans.* to see, look around, survey, reflect (Ps. 93:9).— 2. to see, behold, look at or on.— 3. to show, point out.
   geond-sceâwian, look through, to review (mentally).
sceâwung, *st. f.* contemplation, beholding, inspection.
scêo? Rid. 4:41.
scêoh, *adj.* **shy**, timid.

scêoh-môd, *adj.* timid, timorous.
sceoldan, sceolde, sceole (sceolon), sceôlu, sceomian, sceomu. See **scildan, sculan, scôlu, sceamian, sceamu**.
sceon, *w. v.* 1. to fall to, devolve upon, occur to.— 2. to turn suddenly.
   ge-sceon, to occur, happen, devolve upon; allot, assign.
sceond, sceône, sceop, sceoppan, scêor, sceoran. See **scand, scŷne, scop, sceppan, scûr, sceran**.
sceorp, *st. n.* ornament, clothing.
sceort, *adj.* **short**; *compar.* **scyrtra**.
scêot, *st. m.* quick movement or motion.
scêotan, sciotan, *st. abl. v.* VI. 1. *intrans.* to move violently, leap up, **shoot** forth.— 2. *intrans.* to shoot, hurl missiles.— 3. *trans.* to shoot, hurl missiles at.— 4. *w. acc.* to press upon, urge.— 5. *w. acc.* to push forward.
   ge-scêotan, *w. acc.* to shoot toward, to move precipitously toward.
   of-scêotan, to shoot dead, kill with missiles.
   tô-scêotan, to bring up or near violently? Met. 27:19.
scêotend, *part. & subs.* shooter (of javelins, &c.), warrior.
sceucca. See **scucca** (devil).
scild, sceld, scyld, *st. m.* 1. **shield**. 2. protection, defense (Ph. 463; Sol. 79).— 3. part of a bird's plumage (Ph. 308).
scildan, scyldan, sceoldan, *w. v.* to **shield**, protect, defend.
   ge-scildan, the same as above.
scildend, scyldend, *part. & subs.* shielder, protector.
scild-, sceld-burg, *st. f.* 1. shield-wall or fortress, roof of shields, defense, *testudo*.— 2. castle, fortress.

scild-, scyld-freca, *w. m.* shielded warrior.
scild-hreada, *w. m.* shield.
scild-hreoda, *w. m.* same as above.
scildig. See **scyldig** (guilty).
scild-weall, *st. m.* **wall** of shields.
scild-, scyld-wiga, *w. m.* shielded or shield-bearing warrior.
scyle. See **sculan** (shall).
scilling, *st. m.* **shilling,** silver coin.
scilling-rim, *st. n.* number or computation of shillings.
scima, *w. m.* **shimmer,** twilight, dim light.
scima, *w. m.* light, splendor, brightness, twinkling, coruscation.
scimian, *w. v.* to grow dusky or dim.
scin, *adj.* shining, brilliant. [tom.
scin, *st. n.* apparition, ghost, phanscinan, scȳnan, *st. abl. v.* V. to **shine,** flash, grow bright.
   â-scinan, to flash or shine forth, to beam, radiate.
   be-scinan, to beshine, shine upon, light up.
   ge-scinan, the same as above.
   geond-scinan, to shine through or upon, to illuminate.
   ymb-scinan, to shine around or about.
scin-ge-lâc, *st. n.* deceptive play, jugglery, magical practices, delusion, mockery.
scin-lâc, the same as above.
scinna, *w. m.* demon, devil; injurer, seducer.
scin-sceaða, -scaða, *w. m.* demonic foe, devil.
scip, scyp, *st. n.* **ship,** vessel, boat.
scip-fêrend, *part. & subs.* shipper, sailor.
scip-flota, *w. m.* same as above.
scip-here, *st. m.* ship-host or army.
scippend. See **sceppend** (creator).
scip-weard, *st. m.* ship-warden or guard, sailor.
scir, *adj.* **sheer,** bright, clear, pure.

sciran, scȳran, *w. v.* to render clear, brighten up, bring to the light, disclose; — *intrans.* to speak. Ps. 118: 23.
scire, *adj.* brightly, clearly, resonantly.
scir-ham, *adj.* with bright corselet or breastplate.
scirian. See **scerian** (to shear).
scir-mǽled, *part.* brightly marked.
scir-wered, *part.* brightly ornamented, decked. Gû. 1262.
sciene, scierpan, scio, scioide, scionan, scionon, sciotan. See **scȳne, scyrpan, sceon, sculan, scinan, scânan, sceotan.**
scôd, *pret.* of **sceadan** (to scathe).
scolde. See **sculan** (shall).
scôlu, sceôlu, scâlu, *st. f.* **1.** school (Boeth. 3: 1).— **2.** troop, number, shoal, multitude.
scomian, scomu, sconca, scond. See **sceamian, sceamu, scanca, scand.**
scop, sceop, *st. m.* singer, shaper, poet.
scotere, *st. m.* **shooter,** warrior, hurler of the javelin.
scotian, *w. v.* to **shoot,** hurl the javelin.
scrâd (?), ship? vessel? Reim. 13.
scrǽf, scref, *st. n.* hole, pit, excavation, grave, lair.
scralletan, *w. v.* to resound loudly or shrilly.
scrid, screod, *st. m.* wagon, chariot, vehicle.
scrid, *adj.* advancing, quick.
scrifan, *st. abl. v.* V. **1.** to hear confession, **shrive.**— **2.** to impose or exact penance after confession.— **3.** to judge, condemn, impose judicial or penal condemnation.— **4.** to grant, admit, allow, lavish, expend.— **5.** to impose, command. **6.** *w. gen.* or *dat.* to have regard to, to be troubled about.

for-scrifan, 1. to bewitch, cast under a spell (by written or incised magical characters).— 2. *w. acc.* or *dat.* to condemn, damn.

ge-scrifan, to ascribe to, impose upon, prescribe, assign, lend.

scrifen (?). Reim. 13.

scrift, *st. m.* confessor.

scrind, *st. f.* swift course? Ps. 103: 24.

scriđan, *st. abl. v.* V. to stride, go, roam, move.

   tô-scriđan, to stride or go asunder, apart.

   ymb-scriđan, to stride, to wander about or around.

scriđe, *st. m.* striding, running, course.

scrûd, *st. n.* (**shroud**), clothing, cloth, garment.

scûa, scûwa, *w. m.* shade? injury, harm, malice.

scucca, sceucca, *w. m.* seducer, devil, demon.

scucc-, sceucc-gyld, *st. n.* idol, demon-figure.

scûdan, *st. abl. v.* VI. to **scud**, run, hurry, flee.

scûfan, *st. abl. v.* VI. 1. *trans.* to shove, push, push forward.— 2. *intrans.* the same (By. 136).— 3. *intrans.* to shove one's self, move, go.

   â-scûfan, to shove off or away, to drive out, remove.

   be-scûfan, to push, to shove or push in, rush in.

   for-scûfan, to push away, reject, remove, scatter.

   ôd-scûfan, *w. reflex. dat.* to remove one's self, take one's self off.

   tô-scûfan, to shove asunder or apart, to scatter.

sculan, *pret.-pres., pres. sg. indic.* 1, 3. sceal, sceall (Sol. 159), scal (Gen. 663), scel (B. 2804), scell (An. 1483).— 2. scealt, scealtû (=

þû, An. 220); *pl.* sculon, sculun (Run. 64), sculan (Men. 68), sceolon, sceolun (Sat. 41), sceolan (Jul. 195); *subj. sg.* scyle, scile (B. 3177); *pl.* scylen, scyian (Ps. 139: 13); scyle (Ps. Th. 4: 5); sceole (By. 59); *pret.* sceolde, scolde, sciolde (Met. 26: 82), shall (especially in present tense often serving almost as a circumlocution of the future = shall, will), is said to.

scûnian, *w. v.* in

   on-scûnian, to shun, abhor, avoid, scorn.

scunnian, *w. v.* to urge on, incite against.

scûr, scêor, *st. m.* 1. **shower**, storm (of weather or missiles).— 2. quick, sudden movement (Hy. 11: 7).— 3. blow? shock? (Jud. 79).

scûra, *w. m.* shower, sudden rain-shower.

scûr-beorg, *st. f.* shower-defense, roof.

scûr-boga, *w. m.* rainbow.

scûr-heard, *adj.* hard or hardened in the storm of battle or strife, hardened by blows.

scûr-sceadu, *st. f.* protection or defense against weather (**shower-shade**).

scûwa. See scûa (harm).

scycoan, *w. v.* (*pret.* scyhte), to seduce, mislead, (incite?).

scyde, *pret.* of sceon (to befall).

scŷft, 3*d sig. pres.* of scûfan (to shove).

scyl, *adj.* resonant, resounding. Cf. schallen.

scyld, sceld, *st. f.* debt, obligation, crime, guilt, sin. (Ger. *schuld.*)

scyld, scyldan, scyldend, scyldfreca, -wiga. See scild, scildan, scildend, scild-freca, -wiga.

scyld-fracu, *st. f.* (*dat.* frece), guilty shamelessness, wanton guilt, audacity, impudence.

scyld-full, *adj.* full of guilt, guilt-laden, criminal.
scyld-hata, *w. m.* collector, exacter, lictor, tribune, executor.
scyld-hete, *st. m.* foe.
scyldig, sceldig, scildig, *adj.* guilty, in debt.
scyld-wreccende, *part.* debt or guilt avenger.
scyld-wyrcende, *part.* guilt, sin-worker, sinner.
scyle. See **sculan** (shall).
scylfe, *w. f.* **shelf,** covering of boards.
scyll, scŷnan, scyndan. See **scell, scinan, scendan.**
scyndan, *w. v.* to hurry, hasten, flee away or off, escape.
 ge-scyndan, the same as above.
scŷne, scēone, sciore, scēne, *adj.* sheen, brilliant, light, beautiful, well-formed.
scyp, scype, scyppan, scyppend, scŷran. See **scip, scipe, sceppan, sceppend, sciran.**
scyrdan, *w. v.* in
 ge-scyrdan (?). An. 1315.
scyrian. See **scerian** (to shear).
scyrpan, scierpan, scerpan, *w. v.* to deck, ornament, clothe (with).
 ge-scyrpan, the same as above.
scyrpan, *w. v.* to **sharpen.**
 â-scyrpan, to sharpen, put a point to.
scyrtan, *w. v.* in
 ge-scyrtan, to **shorten,** lessen, decrease, render smaller.
scyrtra, *compar.* of **sceort** (short).
scŷt, *3d pers. sg. indic.,* **scŷte,** *subj. pres.* of **scēotan** (to shoot).
scyte, *st. m.* **shot,** shooting, hurling the javelin.
scytel, *st. m.* arrow, dart, missile. Cf. **skittle.**
scyððan. See **sceððan** (to scathe).
se, sêo, sîo, *pron.* 1. *article* & *demons.* the, he, she.—2. *relative:* who, that (often connected with inde- clinable þe: se þe = who, he who; —se þe his = whose (by attraction: Sat. 253);—se þe him (whom). Wid. 132-33. See þæt, for the other cases and the neuter.
sê (= **swâ**), so;—**sê þêah,** nevertheless, yet, notwithstanding. Cf. **swâ.**
sêcan, sêcean, sêccan, seôccan, sǣcan, *w. v.* **1.** to **seek,** search for or through, hunt, try.—**2.** to hunt up, look for, come or go to (person or place), visit.—**3.** to hunt, seek with hostile intent, attack, wage war on.
 â-sêcan, 1. to seek out, pick out, select.—**2.** to search out, examine (into).—**3.** to demand, ask from.
 for-sêcan, to follow up closely, visit, requite, punish.
 ge-sêcan, 1. to seek.—**2.** to hunt up or for, come or go to, attain.—**3.** to seek with hostile intent, attack, surprise.—**4.** *intrans.* to go, travel.—**5.** to demand, determine, resolve, conclude. An. 1134; Ps. 104: 9.
 geond-sêcan, to seek or search through.
 ofer-sêcan, to overseek; to vanquish, overcome, conquer; to overreach.
 on-sêcan, to contest something with another person, demand from.
secg, *st. m.* **sedge,** reed, rush.
secg, *st. f.* **sword.**
secg, *st. m.* (**secgan?**), man, hero, (speaker?).
secgan, seccgan, secgean, sǣcgean, *w. v.* to **say,** speak.
 â-secgan, to speak out, say, deliver, narrate, announce.
 fore-secgan, to speak out, announce, predict.   [rate.
 ge-secgan, to say, address, narron-**secgan,** to vow a sacrifice or offering, to offer.

secge, *w. f.* speech? language? Cri. 190.
secg-hwæt, *adj.* bold with the sword.
secg-plega, *w. m.* sword-play, fighting with swords.
secg-róf, *st. n.* activity, fortitude, vigor? Ruin. 27.
sedian, *w. v.* in
  ge-sedian, to satisfy, satiate.
sefa, seofa, siofa, *w. m.* mind, soul, spirit.
sefian? Sol. 267.
sêft, sêftan. See **sôfte.**
sêfte, *adj.* soft, gentle, mild, sweet, pleasant.
sêft-êadig, *adj.* comfortable, luxurious.
segel. See **sægl** (sun).
segel, segl, *st. m. & n.* sail.
segel-gyrd, *part.* sail-girt.
segel-râd, *st. f.* sail-road, sea, ocean.
segel-rôd, *st. f.* sail-rod, pole, spar.
segen, segn, *st. m. & n.* token, field ensign, banner;—sign or token on shield and helmet.
segen-berend, *part. & subs.* sign-bearer, bearer of shield or helm-token, warrior.
segen-cyning (Exod. 172). See **sige-cyning**.
segel, segn. See **segel, sægl, segen.**
seglan, *w. v.* in
  ge-seglan, to equip with a sail.
segne, *w. f.* seine, drag-net.
segnian, sênian, *w. v.* to sign (with the cross), bless. (Ger. *segnen.*)
  ge-segnian, the same as above.
segning, *st. f.* blessing, benediction.
sêgon. See **sêon** (to see).
sel, *st. n.* hall (saloon), room, house.
sêl, sæl, *adv. compar.* better; *superl.* **sêlost.**
sêl, *adj.* good;—*compar.* **sêlra, sêlla, sÿlla;**—*superl.* **sêlost.**
seld, sæld, *st. n.* 1. hall, room, house. 2. seat, dwelling.—3. throne, dais.
selda, *w. m.* courtier.

seldan, seldon, seldum, *adv.* seldom.
seld-cyme, *st. m.* infrequent (seldom) coming.
seld-guma, *w. m.* houseman, room-haunter, stay-at-home.
seldlic, *adj.* singular, strange. (Ger. *selt*sam.)
seldon, seldum. See **seldan.**
sele, *st. m.* hall (saloon), room, house.
sêle, *acc.* of **sæl?** B. 1135.
sele-drêam, *st. m.* hall-joy, feasting in the hall, revelry.
sele-ful, *st. n.* hall beaker or cup.
sele-gæst, -gyst, *st. m.* hall-stranger, hall-guest, stranger received in the hall.
sele-ge-scot, -ge-sceot, *st. n.* house-floor, storey; timber-work, hut, tent. (Ger. *geschoss.*)
sele-rædend, *part. & subs.* hall-possessor, administrator, occupier.
sele-rest, *st. f.* resting-place in the hall.
sele-secg, *st. m.* hallman, courtier, attendant in the hall. [ant.
sele-þegen, *st. m.* hall-thane, attend-
sele-weard, *st. m.* hall-warden, guardian of the hall.
self, seolf, siolf, silf, sylf, *st. & w. pron.* self;—w. declension with art.= the same;—**þæt sylfe**, *adv.* that same (way); just so.
self-, sylf-æta, *w. m.* eater of his like, eater of his fellow-men, cannibal.
self-, sylf-cwalu, *st. f.* self-murder, suicide.
self-lic, *adj.* selfish.
self-sceaft, *st. f.* immediate creation as opposed to generation or procreation.
self-will, *st. n.* self-will.
selian. See **sylian** (to pollute).
sellan, sillan, syllan, *w. v.* (*pret.* **sealde**), to give, give up or over, lend, present, spend, expend, (sell).

â-sellan, to expel, drive away or off.
 be-sellan, to surround, cover (over).
 ge-sellan, to give, give over or up.
 ymb-sellan, to surround, envelop.
sellend, syllend, *part. & subs.* giver, spender, lavisher.
sellic, syllic, *adj.* strange, odd, singular, admirable.
sellice, syllice, *adv.* same as above.
seld. See **sæld** (good fortune).
sêman, *w. v.* 1. to smooth over, lay aside.— 2. to satisfy, pacify, content.
 ge-sêman, to satisfy, content.
semian, semle. See **seomian, simle**.
semninga, *adv.* at once, immediately, suddenly.
sencan, *w. v.* to sink, cause to sink.
 be-, bi-sencan, to cause to sink, send to the bottom.
sendan, *w. v.* 1. to send.— 2. to set on the table, prepare a meal? (B. 600), feast? banquet?
 â-sendan, to send forth or off.
 an-sendan, to send, send away or out.
 for-sendan, to send away, drive off, send to destruction.
 geond-sendan, to send through, send in all directions? suffuse.
 on-sendan, to send; send away, or out, or forth; to transmit.
sêngan. See **sênian** (to sign).
sênian. See **segnian** (to sign).
sênian, *w. v.* to see, behold. Az. 175.
 â-sêngan = â-sênian, to make distinct or plain. Jul. 313.
senn. See **syn** (sin).
senst = sendest; sent = sended.
Septembris, September. Men. 167.
serce, syrce, *w. f.* **sark**, corselet, shirt of mail.

serwan, serian, syrwan, *w. v.* to devise cunningly, machinate, plot, think out, accomplish; intrigue, conspire maliciously.
 be-serwan, to devise cunningly, effect, think out, plot; beguile, betray, deceive, rob.
 ge-serwan, 1. to devise cunningly, machinate, think or plot out.— 2. to fit out, equip, arm, prepare.
sess, *st. m.* seat, settle, place for sitting.
sessian, *w. v.* to sit, be quiet.
set, *st. n.* seat, place.
setl, sitl, *st. n.* settle, seat.
setlan, *w. v.* to settle, place, put.
setl-gang, *st. m.* settling, sinking.
setl-râd, *st. f.* the same as above.
sêton, *pref. pl.* of **sittan** (to sit).
settan, *w. v.* to set, place;—*w. reflex. pron.* to set or seat one's self. Ps. 117: 25.
 â-settan, 1. to set, set down, put down, lay down, set up or in. 2. sid âsettan, to accomplish or get over a journey.
 be-, bi-settan, to beset, occupy, surround.
 for-settan, to set, or place, or bring before.
 ge-settan, 1. to set, place, put, put down or in, destine, mark out. 2. to set, arrange, found, get, procure.— 3. to occupy, fill up, populate, people.— 4. to occupy, possess.— 5. to lay aside, smooth over, appease (B. 2029).— 6. to compose, set side by side (Met. 6: 7).— 7. *intrans.* to seat or set one's self. Gen. 1469.
 ymb-settan, to set around or about, surround, inclose.
settend, *part. & subs.* setter, founder, creator.
sêdan, *w. v.* in

ge-sêdan, to verify, confirm, testify, prove. Cf. sooth.
seddan, syddan, *w. v.* to punish, avenge.
sewian, *w. v.* to teach, instruct, show.
sewen (*part.*), sewenian (?). See sêon (to see), sênian.
sealcan, in
â-sealcan, to render slack, negligent, lazy, (sulky?). Gen. 2167.
seald (*part.*), sealde (*pret.*) of sellan (to give, &c.).
sealm, *st. m.* psalm.
sealma, *w. m.* sleeping-place or room.
sealm-fæt, *st. n.* psalm-vessel or vase (?).
sealo. See salu (dark).
sealt, *st. n.* salt, salt sea or flood.
sealt, salt, *adj.* salt, salty.
sealt-stân, *st. m.* salt-stone, pillar of salt.
sealt-ŷd, *st. f.* salt wave, sea-wave.
searian, *w. v.* to become sere, to wither.
searo, seara, *st. n.* 1. trappings, armor, weapons, war-gear. — 2. hostile cunning, machination, plot, controversy, deceit. — 3. cunning, skill, art, care, circumspection. — 4. work of art (Rid. 33: 3).
searo-bend, *st. f.* artistic band or bond.
searo-bunden, *part.* artistically bound.
searo-cǽg, *st. f.* artistic (complicated?) key.
searo-cêap, *st. m.* artistic ware or object.
searo-, siaro-cræft, *st. m.* artistic skill, art. — 2. cunning skill, guile, dissimulation, plotting, machination.
searo-cræftig, *adj.* skilled in art.
searo-cŷne, *adj.* very bold, valiant in arms. Cf. keen.

searo-fâh, *adj.* cunningly inlaid, variegated.
searo-fearo, *st. n.* hostile intrigue, plot, conspiracy? Rim. 65.
searo-ge-þræc, *st. n.* multitude of objects of art.
searo-gim, *st. m.* cunningly set gem.
searo-grim, *adj.* cunning and fierce, bold in battle.
searo-hæbbend, *part.* armed, weaponed, in arms.
searo-lic, *adj.* artistic, wonderful, admirable.
searo-lice, *adv.* the same as above.
searo-net, *st. n.* 1. armor-net, shirt of mail, corselet. — 2. fetter for the feet, fetter.
searo-nid, *st. m.* cunning hostility, malicious cunning, plotting. — 2. hostility, enmity, feud, battle.
searo-pil, *st. n.* artistically wrought javelin or dart.
searo-rûn, *st. f.* secret, mystery, (rune).
searo-sǽled, *part.* carefully or artistically tied, bound.
searo-þanc, -þonc, *st. m.* shrewdness, wisdom, sagacity, thought, ingenuity; —(in good and bad sense).
searo-þancol, -þoncol, *adj.* cunning-minded, sharp-sighted, shrewd, sly.
searo-wundor, *st. n.* wondrous object, rare wonder.
searwian (?). Rim. 37.
sêað, *st. m.* spring, cistern, pit, abyss, lake, pond.
sêaw, *st. n.* sap, juice.
seax, *st. n.* short sword, hip-knife, knife, dagger; coulter.
seax-, siex-ben, *st. f.* wound with a seax.
sêo. See se, si.
sêo, *st. f.* pupil (of the eye).
sêoc, *adj.* 1. sick, ill, frail, diseased, weak, relaxed, dying. — 2. sad, troubled.

sêocan. See **sêcan** (to seek).
sêocen, *adj.* **sick,** ill.
seofa. See **sefa** (soul, &c.).
sêofian, siofian, *w. v.* **1.** *intrans.* to **sigh.**— **3.** *w. acc.* to sigh over, utter with sighs.
seofon, seofone, syfone, *num.* **seven.**
seofon-feald, *adj.* **sevenfold.**
seofon-tig. See **hund-seofontig.**
seofon-tyne, *num.* **seventeen.**
seofon-, syfan-wintre, *adj.* seven winters (or years) old.
seofoða, *num. adj.* **seventh.**
sêofung, siofung, *st. f.* sighing, lamentation, lament.
seohon. See **sêon** (to see).
seolf. See **self.**
seolfer, silofer, sylfor, *st. n.* **silver.**
seolfren, seolofren, silfren, sylofren, *adj.* of silver, silvern.
seolh, *st. m.* seal, seadog.
seolh-bæð, *st. n.* seal's **bath,** sea, ocean.
seolh-wâðu, *st. f.* seal's path, sea, ocean.
seoloc, sioloc, *st. n.* **silk.**
seolofren. See **seolfren** (of silver).
sêoloð, sioloð, *st. m.* bight, bay, sea.
seomian, siomian, semian, *w. v.* to linger, tarry, abide.
sêon, sion, *st. abl. v.* III. (*pret.* **sâwon, sǣgon, sêgon**).— **1.** *intrans.* to see, look, behold.— **2.** *trans.* to see, look at, inspect, behold, gaze upon, find, visit.
   be-, bi-sêon, *intrans.* to see, look, gaze, look forth.— **2.** *trans.* to behold, inspect, visit, experience.
   for-sêon, to despise, scorn, abhor, depreciate.
   fore-sêon, to **foresee.**
   ge-sêon, to see, look, behold, look at, inspect, look into, recognize.
   geond-sêon, to look through or over, to inspect.
   of-sêon, to see, **look at or on,** behold.
   ofer-sêon, to oversee, observe, see, behold.
   on-sêon, to look on, glance at, gaze upon.
   þurh-sêon, to look through, examine.
   ymb-sêon, to see or look around, about, gaze about.
sêon, *st. abl. v.* V. in
   bi-sêon, to strain, filter, pour over.
sêon, sien, sŷn, *st. f.* seeing, sight, vision, eye.
sêon, seondan. See **si, sind.**
seonoð, sionoð, sinoð, *st. m.* **synod,** meeting.
seonoð-dôm, *st. m.* synodal resolution, enactment.
seonu, sionu, sinu, synu, *st. f.* sinew.
seonu-ben, *st. f.* sinew-wound, wound hurting the sinews.
seonu-dolg, *st. n.* same as above.
sêoslig, *adj.* tortured with pain.
sêoðan, *st. abl. v.* VI. to **seethe,** boil.
   â-sêoðan, the same as above.
seoððan. See **siððan** (since).
seowian, siowian, *w. v.* to **sew,** sew together, unite, weave together.
si, sŷ, sig, sie, sêo, sio; *pl.* **sien, sie, sŷn, sin, sêon,** = subj. forms of verb *to be.*
sib, syb, *st. f.* **1.** peace.— **2.** friendship, friendly union, bond of relationship.— **3.** love, affection, friendliness.
sib, syb, *adj.* united by friendship.
sib-æðeling, *st. m.* related **atheling,** noble kinsman.
sibbian, *w. v.* in
   ge-sibbian, to appease, satisfy, delight, please.
sib-, syb-cwide, *st. m.* word of peace, pacific speech.

sib-ge-byrd, *st. f.* relationship, blood-relationship, consanguinity.
sib-ge-dryht, ge-driht, *st. f.* peaceful troop, pacific band.
sib-ge-mâgas, *st. m. pl.* blood-relations.
sib-lufe, (sibb-), *w. f.* friendship, benevolence, love.
sib-spræc, *st. f.* peaceful and pleasant speech, talk.
sibsum, *adj.* peaceful, pacific.
siccetung, sicetung, *st. f.* sigh, groan, lamentation.
sid, sŷd, *adj.* wide, broad, ample, roomy, spacious.
side, *adv.* widely, far and wide, far.
side, *w. f.* side.
sid-fædme, *adj.* wide-bosomed, commodious, spacious.
sid-fædmed, *part.* same as above.
sid-folc, *st. n.* widespread folk, nation.
sidian, *w. v.* to extend, spread, lie open.
sid-land, *st. n.* wide-extended land, spacious land.
sid-rand, *st. m.* broad-rimmed shield.
sido, siodo, *st. m.* custom, habit. (Ger. *sitte*.)
sid-weg, *st. m.* wide or broad way, road.
sig. See si.
sigan, *st. abl. v.* V. 1. to sink, sink down, cause to sink, go down, fall, incline, bow, lay down.— 2. (general), to move, advance, go.
   â-sigan, to sink, sink down, cause to sink.
   ge-sigan, 1. to sink, fall.— 2. to cause to fall? Gn. Ex. 118.
sige, *st. m.* victory, success. (Ger. *sieg*.)
sige-bêacen, *st. n.* beacon or token of victory; cross of Christ.
sige-bêam, *st. m.* tree of victory, triumph; cross of Christ.

sige-bearn, *st. n.* (bairn), victorious son (Christ).
sige-beorn, *st. m.* victorious man.
sige-brôdor, *st. m.* victorious brother.
sige-bŷme, *w. f.* trump of triumph, victory.
sige-cempa, *w. m.* victorious champion, warrior.
sige-cwên, *st. f.* victorious queen.
sige-cyning, *st. m.* victorious king.
sige-dêma, *w. m.* judge or lender of victory.
sige-dryhten, -drihten, *st. m.* lord of victory, victorious lord.
sige-êadig, *adj.* victorious, triumphant.
sige-fæst, -fest, *adj.* victorious, triumphant.
sige-folc, *st. n.* victor-folk.
sige-hrêmig, *adj.* boastful of victory.
sige-hrêd-secg, *st. m.* hero of triumphant glory or repute.
sige-hrêdig, *adj.* famed for victory, rejoicing in victory.
sige-hwîl, *st. f.* time of victory. Cf. while.
sigel, *st. m.* 1. sun.— 2. name of Rune s.
sigel-beorht, *adj.* sun-bright, brilliant.
sige-lêan, *st. n.* reward of victory.
sige-lêas, *adj.* without victory.
sige-lêod, *st. n.* lay of victory, poem.
Sigel-hearwa, *w. m.* Ethiopian.
sigel-torht, *adj.* sun-bright, radiant.
Sigel-waras, *st. m. pl.* Ethiopians (sun-men).
sige-mêce, *st. m.* victorious sword.
sige-rîce, *adj.* victorious, triumphant.
sige-rôf, *adj.* famous for victory, able to win victory.
sige-sceorp, *st. n.* ornament of victory.
sige-spêd, *st. f.* victory, good fortune in the field.

sige-tâcen, *st. n.* token or evidence of victory.
sige-tiber, *st. n.* offering of or for victory.
sige-torht, *adj.* brilliant in victory.
sige-tudor, *st. n.* victorious descendants, posterity.
sige-þeod, *st. f.* victorious people or nation.
sige-þreat, *st. m.* victorious troop or band.
sige-þûf, *st. m.* flag of victory.
sige-wæpen, *st. n.* victorious weapon, sword.
sige-wang, -wong, *st. m.* field of victory.
sigle, *st. n.* sun-shaped, flashing ornament, jewel, necklace.
sigor, sygor, *st. m.* victory, triumph.
sigor-beacen, *st. n.* beacon or token of triumph, victory.
sigor-beorht, *adj.* brilliant in victory.
sigor-cynn, *st. n.* victorious kin or race.
sigor-eadig, *adj.* triumphant, victorious.
sigor-fæst, *adj.* the same as above.
sigor-lean, *st. n.* recompense or reward of victory.
sigor-spêd, *st. f.* victory, good fortune in the field.
sigor-tâcen, *st. n.* token or evidence of victory.
sigor-tiber, *st. n.* offering of or for victory.
sigor-weorc, *st. n.* work or deed of victory.
sigor-wuldor, *st. n.* glory of victory.
sigu, *st. f.* sinking, descending, decadence. Met. 13: 56.
sihan, sihsta, sihd, silf, silfren, sillan, silofer, silofren. See **seon, sixta, self, seon, seolfren, sellan, seolfor, seolfren.**
sima, *w. m.* fetter, knot, loop, snare.

simle, semle, symle, *adv.* continuously, continually, ever, always.
simles, symles, *adv.* ever, always.
sin. See **si** (be).
sin, *possess. pron.* his, their (Ger. *sein*);—used in the pl.? Dan. 393.
sin-byrnende, *part.* ever-burning.
sinc, sync, *st. n.* treasure, riches, valuables, jewels, property.
sin-cald, *adj.* very cold, icy cold.
sin-caldu, *st. f.* extreme cold, rigor.
sincan, *st. abl. v.* I. to **sink**.
  be-sincan, to submerge, immerse, dip, plunge.
  ge-sincan, to sink, fall.
sinc-fæt, -sync, *st. n.* costly vessel, jewel-casket, jewel.
sinc-fâg, *adj.* sparkling with jewels or with costly ornaments.
sinc-ge-strêon, *st. n.* treasure, jewel.
sinc-ge-wæge, *n.* allotment or distribution of treasure.
sinc-gifa, -giefa, -gyfa, *w. m.* treasure-giver, king.
sinc-gifu, *st. f.* **gift** of treasure.
sinc-gim, *st. m.* valuable gem, jewel.
sinc-hroden, *part.* jewel-laden, ornamented.
sinc-mâððum, *st. m.* jewel, treasure.
sinc-stân, *st. m.* precious stone.
sinc-þegu, *st. f.* reception or acceptance of jewels or treasure.
sinc-weordung, *st. f.* presentation or gift of jewels or treasure.
sind = sid, *st. m.* -time? (as a multiplicative suffix: one time, &c. Jul. 354.)
sind, sint, synd, synt, sindon, syndan, seondon, siendon, *indic. pres. pl.* of verb *to be.* Cf. **si**.
sinder, *st. m.? n.?* slag, iron-dross, scoria. (Ger. *sinter*.)
sin-, syn-dolg, *st. n.* huge wound, gash.
sin-drêam, *st. m.* everlasting joy, rejoicing.

sin-frêa, *w. m.* wedded lord, husband.
singal, *adj.* continuous, continuing, ever-during, constant.
singala, -e, -es, *adv.* constantly, ever, always.
singal-lice, *adv.* the same as above.
singan, *st. abl. v.* I. to sing, resound, trill; sing of, celebrate in song. Ps. 58: 16; 100: 1.
    â-singan, to sing, sing out or to the end.
    be-singan, to besing, sing of, celebrate in song.
    ge-singan, to sing.
singian. See **syngian** (to sin).
sin-grim, *adj.* exceeding fierce, cruel, grim.
sin-here, *st. m.* immense host, army.
sin-hiwan, *w. m. pl.* wedded couple (ever-united members of a family).
sinnan, *st. abl. v.* I. (Ger. *sinnen*), 1. to meditate on, think of, care about.— 2. to make mention of? Gen. 1853.
sin-, sien-, syn-neaht, -niht, -neht, *st. f.* eternal night.
sin-nid, *st. m.* perpetual misery, wretchedness, uneasiness.
sinod. See **seonod** (synod).
sin-scipe, *st. m.* perpetual association, marriage.
sin-, syn-snæd, *st. f.* great bite(s), bits, ravenous biting.
sin-sorh, *st. f.* perpetual grief, constant sorrow.
sint, sinu, sitlu. See **sind, seonu, setl.**
sit, 3d *pers. sg.* of **sittan** (to sit).
sittan, *st. abl. v.* III. to sit.
    be-sittan, *w. acc.* 1. to sit by, beside.— 2. to occupy, surround, envelop, beleaguer.
    for-sittan, 1. *w. acc.* or *instr.* to spend or lose by sitting, sit away, neglect.— 2. *intrans.* to grow inactive from sitting, neglect; to vanish.
    ge-sittan, 1. to sit, sit down, seat one's self.— 2. *trans.* to seat one's self on or in (B. 633).— 3. *trans.* to possess, inhabit.
    of-sittan, *w. acc.* to sit upon, rest one's self upon; surround, besiege.
    ofer-sittan, to leave off, leave undone, omit, forbear to do.
    on-sittan, *w. acc.* 1. to seat one's self in (Bo. 26).— 2. to be shocked or frightened at, to fear, to dread. (Ger. *entsetzen*.)
    ymb-sittan, to sit around or about, surround, besiege; sit over, reflect upon.
sið, 3d *pers. sg. pres.* of **séon** (to see).
sið, *st. m.* 1. going, way, journey, trip, war-expedition, course.— 2. arrival (B. 501).— 3. way, road (Gen. 733; Exod. 478).— 4. enterprise, undertaking.— 5. lot, fate, destiny, condition of life, experience.— 6. object or aim of travel, wooing, enlisting, message (B. 353). 7. -time (as multiplicative suffix).
sið, *adj.* late; *superl.* **sidast**, last; **æt sidestan**, at last, finally.
sið, *adv. compar.* 1. later, afterward. 2. late.
sið, *prep.* (sith), since (in sið þâm = since). Cf. **siddan.**
sid-boda, *w. m.* herald announcing a start; departure, or decamping.
sid-dagas, *st. m. pl.* later days or times.
sidd, *st. f.* company, accompaniment, escort. (Gen. 2401.)
siddan, siddon, syddan, seoddan, sioddan.— 1. *adv.* since, henceforth, hereafter, subsequently, consequently.— 2. *conj.* since, after, as soon as.
sid-fæt, *st. n.* 1. going, way, journey, expedition, trip, course.— 2. aim or object of travel, destination, enlisting.— 3. experience, fact. Jul. 537.

sid-from, *adj.* forward-striving, onward-tending, hastening forward.
sid-geomor, *adj.* travel-weary, sad from travel, footsore.
sidian, *w. v.* to make a journey, set out; travel, go, voyage, wander.
    for-sidian, to go or move to one's destruction, or to perdition.
sid-nese, *st. f.* happily accomplished journey.
sid-weg, *st. m.* path of travel, route.
sid-werod, *st. n.* traveling troop, marching band.
six, siex, syx, *num.* **six**.
sixta, syxta, siexta, sihsta, *num. adj.* **sixth**.
six-tig, syx-tig, *num.* **sixty**.
six-tyne, *num.* **sixteen**.
siaro. See **searo**.
sien, sie, sien, siendon, siex, siexta. See **sinneaht, seon, si, sind, six, sixta**.
sio, siodo, siofa, siofian, siofung, siolf, sioloc, siolod, siomian, sion, sionod, sionu, siow, siowian. See **se, si, sidu, sefa, siofian, seofung, self, seoloc, seolod, seomian, seon, seonod, seonu, sâwan, seowian**.
slæhte, *pret.* of **sleccan** (to weaken).
slæp, *st. m.* **sleep**.
slæpan, slâpan, slêpan, *st. red. v.* to **sleep**.
    â-slâpan, to be sleepy, slumber, dream.
slæp-werig, *adj.* **weary of sleep**.
slaga, *w. m.* striker, **slayer**, killer, murderer.
slagan. See **slêan** (to slay).
slagu, *st. f.* striking, blow.
slâpan. See **slæpan** (to sleep).
slâw, *adj.* **slow**, lazy.
sleccan, *w. v.* in
    ge-sleccan, to grow or make **slack**; to weaken, lame, disable. Cri. 149.
slege, *st. m.* blow, striking. Cf. **sledge-hammer**.

slege-fæge, *adj.* about to die from blows, death, slaying.
slegen (*part.*), **sleht, slêpan**. See **slêan, sleaht, slæpan, slûpan**.
slêpan, *w. v.* to cover, draw a slip over, impose.
    be-slêpan, the same as above.
sleac, *adj.* **slack**, relaxed, lazy.
slêan, slagan, *st. abl. v.* IV. **1**. *intrans.* to strike.— **2**. *trans.* to strike, flog. **3**. *trans.* to **slay**, kill.
    be-slêan, to rob of, plunder (in slaying).
    for-slêan, to slay, kill.
    ge-slêan, **1**. to slay, kill.— **2**. to strike, knock, tap (Gen. 383).— **3**. to win, gain, conquer.— **4**. to fight a battle (B. 459).— **5**. *intrans.* to strike up, leap up (Dan. 249).
    of-slêan, to slay, kill.
slidan, *st. abl. v.* V. to **slide**, slip, fall, fall down.
    â-slidan, the same as above.
slide, *st. m.* **slide**, sliding, fall.
slidor, *adj.* **slippery**.
sliht. See **sleaht** (blow).
slitan, *st. abl. v.* V. **1**. *trans.* to **slit**, slice, rend, tear in pieces, shiver. **2**. *intrans.* to be torn in pieces; to be broken up.
    be-slitan, to rob of (in rending to pieces).
    for-slitan, to tear with the teeth, consume.
slite, *st. m.* **slitting**, biting, rending, lacerating.
slidan, *st. abl. v.* V. to injure, wound, hurt.
slide, *adj.* injuring, injurious, bad, fierce, cruel, dangerous.
slide, *adv.* the same as above.
sliden, *adj.* the same as above.
slid-heard, -herd, *adj.* furious, savage, crushing.
sluma, *w. m.* **slumber**.
slûpan, slêpan, *st. abl. v.* VI. to **slip**, slide, fall.

â-slûpan, to slip off, to escape.
tô-slûpan, to slip asunder, go to pieces, become relaxed, dissolve, open.
smæc, *st. m.* smack, taste.
smæl, *adj.* small, narrow, weak, tender.
smǣte, *adj.* pure (of gold).
smêc, smêoc, *st. m.* smoke, vapor.
smêde, *adj.* smooth, soft, agreeable.
smêagan, smêan, *w. v.* to examine, search into, explore, reflect upon, look at closely, scrutinize.
smealice, *adj.* subtly, accurately, penetratingly.
smêoc. See smêc (smoke).
smêocan, *st. abl. v.* VI. to smoke, give off vapor.
smeolt. See smolt (serene).
smeoru, *st. n.* (smear), grease.
smicere, *adj. & adv.* smuck, choice, tasteful, trim.
smilte. See smylte (serene).
smitan, *st. abl. v.* V. to smite, strike, soil, pollute, debauch, dishonor.
be-, bi-smitan, to soil, debauch, fleck, dishonor.
smið, *st. m.* smith, armorer.
smið-cræftega, *w. m.* artist-smith, armorer.
smiðian (cf. smite?), *w. v.* in
be-smiðian, to besmith, to surround or cover with smithwork.
smiðde, *w. f.* smithy, forge.
smolt, smeolt, *adj.* serene, bright, cheerful, gentle, quiet, still.
smûgan, *st. abl. v.* VI. in
þurh-smûgan, to pierce, bore through, eat through.
smȳhd, 3d *pers. sg.* of smûgan.
smylte, smilte, *adj.* serene, cheerful, bright, gentle, quiet, still.
smyrian, *w. v.* to smear, anoint, salve.
ge-smyrian, the same as above.
snadan, *st. abl. v.* IV.; — snôd on hôh? = he drove out, expelled,
that? or = on-hôhsnôde = he hindered? B. 1944.
snǣd, *st. f.* bite, bit, snip. Cf. schnitt-chen.
snǣdan, *st. red. v.* in
be-snǣdan, to besnip, circumcise.
snægl, snæl, *st. m.* snail.
snâw, *st. m.* snow.
snâw-ceald, *st. n.* snowy, icy, cold.
snel, snell, *adj.* snell, quick, lively, brisk, vigorous, combative.
snellic, *adj.* the same as above.
snellice, *adv.* the same as above.
sneteru, sner. See snytru, snear.
snear, *st. f.* (snare), chord, cord, noose, string, harpstring.
snêome, sniome, *adv.* quickly, immediately, at once.
sneowan. See snowan (to hasten).
snican (?), to sneak, creep. Met. 31: 6.
snidan, *st. abl. v.* V. 1. (Ger. *schneiden*), to snip, cut.— 2. to mow, reap, harvest.
of-snidan, to snip or cut off.
sniwan, *w. impers. v.* to snow.
sniome. See snêome (quickly).
snotor, snottor, *adj.* shrewd, wise, clever, sensible.
snotorlice, *adv.* the same as above.
snowan, sneowan, *w. v.* to hurry, hasten.
snûd, *st. m.* quickness, swiftness, haste.
snûd, *adj.* quick, swift, soon at hand.
snûde, *adv.* the same as above.
snȳrian, snyrgan, *w. v.* to hasten, hurry, move forward quickly.
snytre, *adj.* clever, wise, ingenious.
snytrian, snyttrian, *w.v.* to be clever, wise, ingenious.
snytru, snyttru, snyteru, *st. f.* shrewdness, sagacity, wisdom, cleverness.
snytru-cræft, *st. m.* same as above.

snytru-hús, *st. n.* house of wisdom, tabernacle of testimony, ark of the covenant.
snydian, *w. v.* to hasten, hurry.
    be-snydian, to rob, deprive of.
sôcen, *st. f.* **1.** seeking, searching after.— **2.** visitation, hostile surprise, seeking, attack.— **3.** asylum, house of refuge, sanctuary.
sôfte, *adv. (compar.* **sêft),** softly, gently, quietly, lightly.
sôhte, *pret.* of **sêcan** (to seek).
sol, *st. n.* mud-puddle? water in general? bight? bog? B. 302.
sôl, *st. f.* sun.
solere, *st. m.* upper room, garret, balcony.
solian, *w. v.* to soil, become soiled or defiled.
Sol-mônad, *st. m.* February. Men. 16.
sôm, *st. f.* peace, reconciliation. (Icel. *som.*)
some, somnian, somod. See **same, samnian, samod.**
sôna, *adv.* soon, at once, forthwith; **sôna swâ—swâ** = so soon as.
sond, song. See **sand, sang.**
sorg, sorh, *st. f.* sorrow, grief, pain.
sorg-byrden, *st. f.* burden of sorrow.
sorg-cearig, sorhg-cearig, *adj.* sorrowful, grieved, sad.
sorg-cearu, *st. f.* sorrow, anxiety, grief.
sorgen. See **sorg.**
sorg-ful, *adj.* sorrowful, causing or enduring sorrow.
sorgian, *w. v.* to sorrow, grieve, be anxious.
    bi-sorgian, to fear, apprehend, dread, shrink from. [care.
sorg-lêas, *adj.* without sorrow or
sorg-lêod, *st. n.* song of sorrow, lament. [ed.
sorglic, *adj.* sad, distressful, wretch-
sorg-lufa, *st. f.* anxious love, love that awakens sorrow or apprehension.

sorg-stæf, *st. m.* something that brings sorrow, anxiety.
sorg-word, *st. n.* word of sorrow, lament.
sorg-wælm, -wylm, *st. m.* welling up of sorrow, grief.
sorh, sorh-. See **sorg** (sorrow).
sotel, *st. m.* settle, stool, chair, armchair.
sôd, *adj.* sooth, true, genuine, reliable, just.
sôd, *adv.* truly, indeed; but, yet.
sôd, *st. n.* **1.** sooth, truth.— **2.** justice, righteousness; rectitude.
sôd-cwide, -cwyde, *st. m.* true speech, true saying.
sôd-cyning, *st. m.* true king, or king of truth and justice; God.
sôde, *adv.* in sooth, in truth, indeed, really, rightly.
sôd-fæder, *st. m.* true father, God.
sôd-fæst, *adj.* **1.** firm or established in truth and justice, true, genuine, credible, pious, honest, just.— **2.** firm, unchangeable, unchanging, continuing.
sôd-fæstlic, *adj.* imperishable, durable, unceasing.
sôd-fæstnes, -festnys, *st. f.* truth, truthfulness, justice, piety.
sôd-gid, -gied, *st. n.* true speech, saying, report.
sôd-lic, *adj.* true, truthful, real.
sôdlice, *adv.* **1.** truly, truthfully, indeed, in sooth.— **2.** but, yet. Ps. 54: 16.
sôd-word, *st. n.* true word, word of justification.
spâdl, *st. n.* spittle, saliva.
spæc. See **spræc** (speech).
spætan, *w. v.* to spit, spew, spit upon or out.
spanan, *st. red. v.* to draw on, irritate, incite, lure, mislead, seduce, persuade.
    bi-spanan, to lead astray, seduce, persuade.

for-spanan, to mislead, lead astray, seduce.
spange, w. f. clasp, buckle, brooch, fibula. (Ger. *spange.*)
spannan, *st. red. v.* (span), to stretch, fasten, make fast, attach.
   ge-spannan, the same as above.
   on-spannan, to unspan, unloose, unbind, release, open.
sparian, w. v. to spare, indulge.
spâtl, *st. n.* spittle, saliva.
specan. See sprecan (to speak).
spêd, *st. f.* 1. speed, haste.—2. progress, success, fulfillment, luck, good fortune.—3. scion, descendant, lad (Ps. 103: 16).—4. substance, power, might, ability, multitude, abundance.
spêdan, w. v. to speed, hasten, hurry.
   â-spêdan, to come out of a matter successfully.
   ge-spêdan, to succeed, speed well.
spêd-dropa, w. m. wholesome and healing drop.
spêdig, *adj.* lucky, fortunate, rich, powerful.
spêdlice, *adv.* hastily, quickly, speedily, successfully.
spel, spell, *st. n.* (spell), speech, utterance, narrative, legend, account, news, message.
spel-, spell-boda, w. m. messenger, apostle, prophet, angel.
spellian, spellan, w. v. 1. to speak, talk, utter.—2. to announce, relate, deliver.
   god-spellian, to preach the godspel (good tidings, gospel).
spellung, *st. f.* speech, utterance, narrative.
spere, *st. n.* spear, javelin, lance.
spere-brôga, w. m. spear-terror, terrible javelin.
spere-nid, *st. m.* spear-battle.
spearca, w. m. spark.

spearcian, w. v. to throw out sparks, to sparkle.
spearuwa, spearwa, w. m. sparrow.
speornan, spornan, *st. abl. v.* I. to spur on, urge on, push against, spurn, tread, step.
   ge-speornan, same as above.
speowian. See spiwian (to spew).
spild, *st. m.* destruction, annihilation, waste, ruin.
spildan, w. v. to ruin, destroy.
   for-spildan, 1. to destroy, ruin. 2. to accomplish fully. Wy. 59.
spild-sid, *st. m.* destructive journey, expedition with intent to destroy foes.
spillan, w. v. to destroy, ruin, kill.
spiwan, *st. abl. v.* V. to spew, spit out, vomit.
spiwian, speowian, spiowian, w. v. to spew, spit.
splot (?), blot, spot (splotch?)
spor, *st. n.* trace, footstep. (Ger. *spur.*)
spora, w. m. spur.
spornan. See speornan (to spurn).
spôwan, *st. red. v.* to succeed, enjoy success, speed well, thrive.
   ge-spôwan, the same as above.
spôwendlice, *adv.* happily, fortunately, quickly, speedily.
spræcan. See sprecan (to speak).
spræc, spǣc, *st. f.* speech, word, talk, eloquence.—2. narrative, fable, material (Met. 26: 2).—3. conversation, dialogue.—4. court, judicial negotiation or investigation, judgment, decision.
sprec, *st. n.* speech, word. Gû. 225.
spreca, w. m. speaker.
sprecan, sprǣcan, specan, *st. abl. v.* II. to speak.
   â-sprecan, to speak out, speak.
   ge-sprecan, to speak.
spreccan, w. v. in
   on-spreccan, to become bushy, bud, burgeon, put out shoots.

sprengan, *w. v.* to cause to **spring,** burst, break open; to **sprinkle.**
    geond-sprengan, to besprinkle, to dash with water.
spreaht, *part.* of **spreccan** (to bud).
sprêatan, *st. red. v.* in
    geond-sprêatan, to **sprout** through, pervade.
spreocan. See **sprecan** (to speak).
sprêotan, *st. abl. v.* VI. cf. **sprŷtan** to sprout.
    â-sprêotan, to **sprout** out or up, come up or out.
spricest, spriced. See **sprecan** (to speak).
springan, *st. abl. v.* I. to **spring,** jump.
    â-springan, to spring up or forth; to dwindle, diminish, fail.
    æt-springan, *w. dat.* to spring forth, out, or up.
    ge-springan, 1. to spring forth or up; to originate, arise, grow up. 2. to befall, happen to, attack (Gn. Ex. 65).
    on-springan, 1. to spring or jump in two; to burst.— 2. to spring up, arise, originate.
sprycst. See **sprecan** (to speak).
sprŷtan, *w. v.* to **sprout,** come forth, germinate.
spryttan, *w. v.* the same as above.
spyrcan, *w. v.* in
    for-spyrcan, to squirt away, spill, shed, exhaust by spilling, dry up, &c. Ps. 101: 3.
spyrian, *w. v.* (to **speer,** Scotch), to track, trace, seek, examine, search through, reflect upon or about.
    â-spyrian, to track or trace out, to explore, fathom, find out.
stæde, stêde, *st. f.* **steadiness,** steadfastness, firmness, fixity.
stæde-, stêde-fæst, *adj.* **steadfast,** constant, firm.
stæde-, stêde-heard, *adj.* firm, hard, consistent.

stæf, *st. m.* 1. **staff, stave.**— 2. bookstave, letter.— 3. in compounds, **stæf** usually marks an abstract idea or conception.
stæfn, stæfna. See **stefn, stefna.**
stæl, *st. m.* place, spot. (Ger. *stelle.*)
stælan, *w. v.* to place, put down; to impose, cast blame or guilt on; to accuse, avenge on.
    ge-stælan, the same as above.
stælg = stægl, *adj.* steep. Cri. 679.
stæl-gæst, -giest, *st. m.* **stealing guest,** thievish guest.
stænan, stenan, *w. v.* to adorn, decorate with stones or gems.
    â-stænan, the same as above.
stænen, *adj.* of stone.
stæpe, *st. m.* 1. going, gait, pace, step, tread.— 2. step, stair.
stæppan, stærced-. See **steppan, sterced-.**
stæd, *st. n. (m.),* beach, shore.
stæddan, *w. v.* to support, establish, fix, fortify.
stæd-fæst, *adj.* steadfast, constant.
stæd-weall, *st. m.* shore-wall, sea or water rampart.
stalde, *pret.* of **stellan** (to place).
stalian, *w. v.* in
    ge-stalian, to found, establish, fix, confirm.
stal-gang, -gong, *st. m.* stealthy going, secret journey, course, step.
stân, *st. m.* **stone,** rock.
stân-beorh, *st. m.* stony mountain, mountain of rock.
stân-boga, *w. m.* arch or cavern of stone or rock, vaulted chamber in the rock.
stân-burg, *st. f.* town, castle, or fortress of stone or rock.
stân-clif, *st. n.* (*pl.* **cleofu**), crag, cliff.
standan, stondan, *st. abl. v.* IV. (*pret.* **stôd**), 1. to **stand.**— 2. to stand, step forward, appear, come in suddenly, disseminate.

â-standan, to stand forth or up, to arise, originate, reinstate.
  æt-standan, to stand at or beside.
  be-standan, to stand around, by, or about.
  for-standan, 1. *w. acc.* to stand before, place one's self before (toward off something, prevent: person or thing against which in the dat. or with **wið**; or to defend, protect: "from" = dat.).— 2. to understand. (Gen.769; Boeth. 5,3).
  ge-standan, 1. *intrans.* to stand. 2. *trans.* to attack, come on or in suddenly, press on.— 3. to resist, oppose, stop. Sol. 97.
  of-standan, to arise, originate.
  oð-standan, to escape, withdraw, get away.
  wið-standan, *w. dat.* to **withstand**, resist, oppose.
  ymb-, ymbe-standan, to stand about or around.
stân-fæt, *st. n.* **stone-vat**; vessel, trough, or chest of stone.
stân-fâh, *adj.* varied, inlaid, or paved with stone (?).
stân-ge-fôg, *st. n.* stone structure, stone-fitting.
stân-gripe, -greope, *st. m.* handful of stones.
stân-hlið, -hleoð, *st. n.* rocky slope, cliff, rock.
stân-hof, *st. n.* building or structure of stone.
stân-torr, *st. m.* **tower** of stone.
stân-wong, *st. m.* stony field, stone-strewn plain.
stapa, *w. m.* **stepper**, marcher. [Used only in compounds.]
stapan, *st. abl. v.* IV. to **step**, stride, go, advance, move.
  æt-stapan, to step or stride up to.
  ge-stapan, to step, go, move, stride.

stapu, *st. f.* stepping, striding, going about.
stapul, *st. m.* (**staple**), support, stay, pillar, column.
starian, *w. v.* to **stare**, fix the eyes on, gaze at.
  ge-starian, same as above. [lish).
staðelian. See **staðolian** (to establish.
staðol, -ul, *st. m.* 1. foundation, basis, ground, pedestal, place.— 2. sky, heaven. Edg. 50.
staðol-æht, *st. f.* stationary possessions (real estate?).
staðol-fæst, *adj.* fixed, firm, well-established, steadfast.
staðolian, -elian, *w. v.* to found, fix, establish, strengthen.
  ge-staðolian, the same as above.
staðol-wang, -wong, *st. m.* standing place, place, position.
stede, *st. m.* **stead**, place, spot, position, locality.
stêde, stêde-. See **stæde**.
stede-wang, -wong, *st. m.* field, space of ground.
stefn, stæfn, stemn, *st. f.* voice. (Ger. *stimme.*)
stefn, stæfn, stemn, *st. m.* 1. **stem**, trunk, stock, stick.— 2. stem, prow of ship; ship.— 3. stem, race, tribe (Sol. 51).— 4. -time (in multiplicatives); **nîvan stefne** = anew, again.
stefna, stæfna, *w. m.* **stem** or prow of a ship.
stefnan, *w. v.* in
  ge-stefnan, to support, prop, arrange, set in order.
stefn-byrd, *st. f.* hereditary quality, innate disposition, nature.
stefne, *w. f.* voice. (Ger. *stimme.*)
stelan, *st. abl. v.* II. in
  be-, bi-stelan, to **besteal**, rob, steal from.
  for-stelan, to steal, steal from.
stellan, *w. v.* (*pret.* **stealde**), in
  â-stellan, to place, put, erect, display. (Ger. *stellen.*)

on-stellan, to put in place; to devise, think out.
on-stellan, to put in place, effect, accomplish.
stêman, stemn. See stŷman, stefn.
stemnettan, *w. v.* to resist, stem, oppose, stand out, be steadfast.
stênan. See stǣnan.
stenc, *st. m.* stink, stench, odor; perfume, fragrance.
stencan, *w. v.* to press upon, afflict, trouble, disturb, weaken.
    tô-stencan, to drive apart or asunder, to scatter, disperse.
steng, *st. m.* pole, stake, rod. (Ger. *stange.*)
stent, *3d pers. sg.* of **standan** (to stand).
stêpan, *w. v.* 1. *w. acc.* (steep), to erect, raise (Gen. 1676). — 2. to elevate, raise up, distinguish, adorn, enrich.
    ge-stêpan, 1. to erect, raise. — 2. to elevate, support, help.
    on-stepan, to erect, raise up.
stepe-gang, *st. m.* stepping, going? Rim. 22.
steppan, stæppan, *w. v.* to step, stride, go, move.
    ge-stæppan, the same as above.
    ofer-stæppan, to overstep, stride over.
sterced-, stærced-ferhd, -fyrhd, *adj.* strong-minded, brave.
steal, *st. m.* place, spot. (Ger. *stelle?*)
stealc, *adj.* steep, precipitous, arduous.
stealdan, *st. red. v.* to possess, own.
steallian, *w. v.* to have room or place, to remain standing or in existence.
stêam, *st. m.* 1. steam, vapor, smoke, odor. — 2. steaming fluid, blood. Cr. 62.
stêap, *st. m.* (stoup), tall cup, beaker, flagon.
stêap, *adj.* steep, high.

stearc, *adj.* strong, vigorous; stark, stiff, hard, violent.
stearc-ferd, *adj.* strong-minded, courageous.
stearc-heort, *adj.* strong-hearted, valiant.
stearn, *st. m.* sea-swallow (*sterna*).
stêop-cild, *st. n.* stepchild.
stêor, *st. f.* governing, steering, restraint, check.
stêora, *w. m.* steersman, guide, pilot.
stêoran, *st. abl. v.* VI. 1. to steer, guide, govern. — 2. to restrain, check. Met. 4: 49.
    ge-stêoran, to steer, guide, control, restrain, check.
stêor-lêas, *adj.* steerless, without guidance or control, uncontrollable.
steorra, stiorra, *w. m.* star.
steort, *st. m.* tail. (Ger. *sterte.*)
sticce. See stycce (piece).
stician, *w. v.* 1. to stick, prick. — 2. to stick, inhere.
sticol, *adj.* sticking, pricking.
stig, *st. m.* (sty), path (up), way, ascent.
stig, *st. f.* path, way. (Ger. *steig.*)
stigan, *st. abl. v.* V. 1. to step, rise, mount, go, move (in general). 2. to mount, climb, ascend. — 3. to descend (Dan. 510). — 4. to scale, mount upon, ascend.
    â-stigan, 1. *intrans.* to ascend, mount up, scale, rise. — 2. *intrans.* to descend, come down. — 3. *w. acc.* to ascend, ascend to, mount.
    ge-stigan, to ascend, rise, mount up, scale; to descend.
    ofer-stigan, to overstep, overstride, excel, surpass.
stige, *st. m.* ascent, mounting.
stig-, sti-wita, *w. m.* steward, overseer of household matters.
stihtan, *w. v.* to destine, determine, dispose, govern, incite, instigate.

stihtend, *part.* & *subs.* instigator, inciter, guide.
stihtung, *st. f.* arrangement, direction, preparation, caution, foresight, discipline.
stillan, *w. v.* **1.** to be **still,** rest.— 2. *w. dat.* or *acc.* to still, quiet.
  ge-stillan, the same as above.
stille, *adj.* still, quiet, silent, stilly.
stille, *adv.* the same as above.
stincan, *st. abl. v.* I. **1.** to **stink,** smell, reek.— 2. to whirl up (Rid. 30: 12); to move about or around? inhale? snuff along? B. 2288.
  ge-stincan, to smell something.
stingan, *st. abl. v.* I. to **sting.**
stirian, stirgan. See **styrian.**
stið, *adj.* firm, fixed, strong; hard, stiff, severe, cruel.
stiðe, *adv.* **1.** firmly, steadfastly.— 2. harshly, bitterly.
stið-ecg, *adj.* stiff-**edged,** strongbladed.
stið-ferhð, -frihð, *adj.* stout-hearted, strong-minded, of valiant spirit.
stið-hugende, *adj.* same as above.
stið-hycgende, the same as above.
stið-hydig, *adj.* the same as above.
stið-hygd, *adj.* the same as above.
stiðlic, *adj.* firm, strong, stout.
stiðlice, *adv.* the same as above.
stið-mod, *adj.* strong, firm, stout, severe (of mind).
stið-weg, *st. m.* rough **way.**
sti-wita, stiell. See **stigwita, styll.**
stiep, *st. m.* downfall? fall? Gen. 60.
stieran, stiorra. See **styran, steorra.**
stód- (?), column, support, post? (B. 2545;—rather **stód an = stondan.**
stód, stódon, *pret.* of **standan** (to stand).
stofn (?), trunk, stem, pillar. (E.
stovin = stump?)
stol, *st. m.* **stool,** seat, chair, throne.

stondan, stówum. See **standan, stów** (place).
storm, *st. m.* **1. storm,** tempest.— 2. noise, uproar, tumult.— **3.** noisy onrush or attack. Hy. 4: 58.
stów, *st. f.* **stow,** place, spot, locality.
strâdan (?), to tread upon, **stride** over. B. 3073.
stræl, strêl, streâl, *st. m.* & *f.;* **stræle,** *w. f.* arrow. (Ger. *strahl.*)
stræt, *st. f.* **street.**
strang, strong, *adj.* **1. strong,** violent, hard, vigorous, valiant.— 2. *w. instr.* firmly inhering. Sat. 427.
strange, *adv.* violently, furiously.
strangian, *w. v.* in
  ge-strangian, to **strengthen,** invigorate.
strang-, strong-lic, *adj.* firm, strong, unchangeable; — hideous, cruel, dreadful.
strang-, strong-lice, *adv.* strongly, bravely, vigorously, actively.
streccan, *w. v.* in
  â-streccan, to **stretch** out, extend; to prostrate, fell.
stredan, *st. abl. v.* I. **1.** to scatter, sprinkle.— 2. to fall down, fall.
  tô-stredan, to scatter, dissipate.
strêgan, *w. v.* to strew, spread down, bestrew. [ter.
stregdan, *st. abl. v.* I. to strew, scatstrêl, strencð. See **stræl, strengð.**
streng, *st. m.* **string,** cord, rope, sinew.
strenge, *adj.* **strong,** brave; harsh, violent, strict, cruel.
strengel, *st. m.* ruler, lord, (**strength-ener?)**
strenglic, *adj.* strong, firm.
strengð, strengðu, *st. f.* **strength,** power, vigor, ability.
strengu, *st. f.* power, strength, ability, valor.
streðan, stryðan, *w. v.* in
  be-streðan, to bring to, draw over, cover, conceal.

streac, *adj.* strong, stiff, hard. (stark?)

streaht, (*part.*), streâl. See streccan (to stretch), and stræl.

strêam, *st. m.* stream, current, flow of the sea, river, ocean, — especially in the plural.

strêam-faru, *st. f.* motion or flowing of water(s), current.

strêam-ge-win,*st.n.*battling of or uproar on the water; stream-struggle.

strêam-racu, *st. f.* stream-course, stream.

strêam-râd, *st. f.* road or path of the stream or sea.

strêam-stæd, *st. n.* (stream-stead), shore, beach.

strêam-welm, *st. m.* billowing of the sea or water, fluctuation of tides.

strêam-weall, *st. m.* stream-wall, shore, beach.

strêon, *st. f.* cover.

strêonan, strienan, strŷnan, *w. v.*
1. to heap on or up, accumulate, amass. — 2. to strain, beget children.

â-strêonan, to strain forth, procreate, create.

ge-strêonan, 1. to amass, gain. 2. to procreate, create. Gen. 1220.

strican, *st. abl. v.* V. to move, go; to enter on or begin a course.

strid, *st. m.* strife, conflict. (Ger. *streit*.)

strienan, strong. See strêonan, strang.

strûdan, *st. abl. v.* VI. to ravage, devastate, plunder, rob, carry off.

be-strûdan, to plunder, rob.

ge-strûdan, to plunder, rob, ravage, waste.

strynan, *w. v.* in
ge-strynan, to stir up, torture? Secl. 45.

strŷnan, strydan. See strêonan, stredan.

stund, *st. f.* (Ger. *stunde*). — 1. point, particle. — 2. moment, hour, time; *instr. pl.* stundum, at times, meanwhile, sometimes; eagerly.

stunian, *w. v.* 1. to groan, roar, sound, resound. — 2. (stun), to strike violently, impinge.

stycce, sticce, *st. n.* bit, piece, fragment. (Ger. *stück*.)

stŷlan, *w. v.* to harden (like steel).

stŷle, *st. n.* steel.

stŷl-ecg, *adj.* steel-edged.

stŷlen, *adj.* of steel, hard as steel.

styll, stiell, *st. m.* leap, jump, running.

styllan, *w. v.* to leap, jump, run.

ge-styllan, to leap, jump, descend, reach by leaping, overtake by running.

stŷman, stêman, *w. v.* to steam, give forth an odor, smell of (from).

be-stŷman, to foam over, on, around.

stynt, *3d pers. sg.* of standan (to stand).

stŷpel, stêpel, *st. m.* steeple, tower.

stŷr, *st. f.* steering, directing, guiding.

stŷran, stieran, *w. v.* 1. *w. acc.* to steer, guide, direct, govern. — 2. to arrange, dispose, destine, determine (An. 1094). — 3. *w. dat.* to restrain, check, hinder.

ge-stŷran, *w. dat.* to steer, guide; to restrain, check.

styrfan, *w. v.* in
â-styrfan, to kill, slay.

styrian, styrgan, stirian, stirgan, *w. v.* 1. to stir, move, rouse, excite. 2. to be moved, roused, set in motion. — 3. to urge, incite, admonish (Fin. 18). — 4. to move against, attack, disturb (B. 2840). — 5. to deliver, narrate, sing of, celebrate (B. 872). — 6. cause to resound (Mct. 13: 49).

â-styrian, to stir up, excite, move forward or forth, remove.
　ge-styrian, to arouse, excite, stir up.
　geond-styrian, to stir through, to stir on all sides.
　on-styrian, to move, rouse, stir up.
styrman, *w. v.* to storm, roar, rage, cry out.
styrnan, *w. v.* to be stern, strict, severe.
styrne, *adj.* stern, grave, harsh, cruel, savage, furious.
styrnenga, *adv.* sternly, severely.
styrn-môd, *adj.* stern-minded, rigid, severe.
sû, sugu, *st. f.* sow.
sûcan, *st. abl. v.* VI. to suck.
　â-sûcan, to suck out, drain.
sûgan, *st. abl. v.* VI. in
　â-sûgan, to suck out, drain.
sugu. See sû (sow).
suht, *st. f.* malady, disease, illness.
suhtor-fædran, -ge-fædran, *w. m.* uncle and nephew.
suhtria, suhtriga, suhterga, *w. m.* brother's son.
sulh-ge-weorc, *st. n.* ploughing or field implement.
sum, *pron.* (= *aliquis, quidam, unus ex pluribus*), one, a certain, any, one of several, many a; — *neut.* something; — *adv., acc. n.* partly; — *gen. n.* sumes = in a certain degree or measure.
sumor, *st. m.* summer.
sumor-hât, *st. n.* summer heat.
sumor-lang, -long, *adj.* lasting through the summer.
sumsend, *part.* (Ger. *summen*), buzzing, rustling, humming? Rid.4:47.
sun-bearo, *st. m.* sunny grove (barrow).
sun-beorht, *adj.* sun-bright, sunshiny.
sund, *adj.* sound, uninjured, whole.

sund, *st. m.* 1. swimming.— 2. capacity or ability to swim.— 3. sound, sea-strait, sea, ocean (that which sunders?)
sund-bûend, *part. & subs.* sea-dweller, man, human being.
sund-flit, *st. f.* struggle in the water, swimming-match.
sund-ge-bland, *st. n.* tumult of waters, billowing of the sea.
sund-helm, *st. m.* sea-helmet, covering sea.
sund-hengest, *st. m.* 1. seahorse, ship.— 2. power that moves the ship.
sund-hwæt, *adj.* accomplished in swimming.
sund-liden, *st. f.* sea-journey? B. 223.
sund-nytt, *st. f.* employment, gift, or utilization of swimming; ability to swim.
sundor, sundur, *adv.* especially, apart, separately, aside, asunder.
sundor-cræft, *st. m.* special power, capacity, capability.
sundor-cræftig, *adj.* specially endowed, gifted.
sundor-ge-cynd, *st. n.* special endowment, natural gift, structure, quality.
sundor-gifu, *st. f.* special gift, privilege, distinction, quality.
sundor-nytt, *st. f.* special service or prerogative.
sundor-wine, *st. m.* special friend, bosom friend.
sundor-wis, *adj.* specially wise.
sundor-wundor, *st. n.* special wonder, peculiar marvel.
sundor-yrfe, *st. n.* special heritage.
sund-plega, *w. m.* sea-play, swimming, boating, bathing, sea-journey.
sundre, *w. f.* separateness, sundering, isolation.
sund-reced, *st. n.* sea-house, ship.
sundrian, *w. v.* in

â-sundrian, to separate, isolate, sunder.
ge-sundrian, the same as above.
sundur. See sundor.
sund-wudu, *st. m.* sea-wood, ship.
sunna. See sunnu (sun).
sunne, *w. f.* sun.
sunnu, -a, *st. f.* the same as above.
sun-sciene, *adj.* sunshiny, brilliant.
sunu, *irreg. m. sg. gen.* suna; *dat.* suna, sunu; *acc.* sunu; *pl. nom. acc.* suna, suno, sunu; *gen.* suna, sunena; *dat.* sunum,—son.
sun-wlitig, *adj.* lovely with sunshine; beautiful and bright.
sûpan, *st. abl. v.* VI. to sop up, absorb, swallow (greedily).
ge-sûpan, the same as above.
sûsl, *st. n.* misery, torture, torment, punishment, death-penalty.
sûsl-bana, -bona, *w. m.* devil.
sûsl-hof, *st. n.* house of misery, hell.
sutol. See sweotol (plain).
sûd, *adv.* south, southward, in the south.
sûda, *w. m.* south.
sûdan, *adv.* from the south.
sûdan-êastan, *adv.* from the southeast.
sûderne, *adj.* southern, southerly.
sûd-êast, *adv.* southeast, in the southeast.
sûd-folc, *st. n.* south-folk, folk from the south.
sûd-heald, *adj.* inclining southward, southward.
sûd-man, -mon, *st. m.* southern man, man from the south.
sûd-portic, *st. m.* south portico.
sûd-rôdor, *st. m.* southern sky.
sûd-weg, *st. m.* southway, way or path southward.
sûd-weardes, *adv.* southwards.
sûd-wind, *st. m.* south wind.
swâ, I. *adv. & conj.* so, as. 1. (referring back), so, consequently, in such wise, under such circumstances, therefore.— 2. *emphatically:* so, thus, indeed, even.— 3. *w. comparatives*, the.— 4. swâ þêah, nevertheless, yet.— 5. *relative:* as, so far as, how, where.— 6. *w. subj.* as if, us though.— 7. *w. indic.* (of time), so soon, as soon, as, when; though, unless, so that not (*w. neg.*)— 8. supplies place of relative pronoun.— 9. that, so that, in such manner that.
swæc, swec, *st. m.* 1. smell, odor; exhalation, breath.— 2. smack, taste.
swæfan, *w. v.* to stagger, reel, hesitate.
swægl. See swegl (ether).
swælan, *w. v.* in
be-swælan, to sweal, singe, parch, scorch.
swæman, *w. v.* in
â-swæman, to roam about, round, wander.
swær, *adj.* heavy, difficult. (Ger. *schwer.*)
swære, *adv.* the same as above.
swæs, *adj.* one's own, domestic, intimate; dear, precious, agreeable, benevolent.
swæsendu, *st. n. pl.* a meal. [able.
swæslic, *adj.* kind, friendly, agreeswæslice, *adv.* the same as above.
swætan, *w. v.* 1. to sweat.— 2. to bleed.
swæder = swâ hwæder, *pron.* whichever, whosoever (of two).
swædorian, swadrian, *w. v.* to decrease, diminish; become quiet, lie down, lie low or down.
swâfan, *st. red. v.* in
for-swâfan, to sweep away or off; to drive out, expel, frighten away.
swâmian, *w. v.* to become dark or obscure; to vanish.
â-swâmian, the same as above.
swan, swon, *st. m.* swan.

swân, *st. m.* swain, youth, young man. Fin. 39.

swancur, swancor, *adj.* 1. unsteady, pliant; languishing (Ps. 118: 81). 2. slender, supple-bodied (B. 2175). 3. causing to reel, limp, stagger (Dêor. 6). (Ger. *schwanken.*)

swangor, swongor, *adj.* heavy, weighty, torpid, inert. (Ger. *schwanger.*)

swan-râd, *st. f.* swan-road, path of swans, sea.

swâpan, *st. red. v.* 1. to sweep, swing.— 2. to blow, waft.
â-swâpan, to sweep off or away, to remove.
for-swâpan, to sweep aside, or away; to drive off, or out.
to-swâpan, to sweep in two, apart, or asunder.

swâr, *adj.* heavy. (Ger. *schwer.*)

swarian, swerian, sweorian, *w. v.* to talk, speak, utter.
and-swarian, ond-, to speak back, answer.

swart, swâs. See sweart, swǽs.

swât, *st. m.* 1. sweat.— 2. blood from wounds, blood, gore.

swât-fâg, *adj.* blood-stained, bloody.

swâtig, *adj.* 1. sweaty, sweating. 2. bloody.

swâtig-hlêor, *adj.* with sweating cheek or face.

swât-swadu, *st. f.* bloody trace or track.

swadrian. See swædorian.

swadu, *st. f.* trace, track.

swadul, *st. m.* smoke-reek, flame and smoke together.

swebban, *w. v.* to lull or put to sleep; to kill.
â-swebban, the same as above.

swec. See swæc (odor).

swefan, *st. abl. v.* III. to sleep, slumber; to sleep the death-sleep; rest, cease from. Exod. 36.

swefed, *part.* of swebban (to put to sleep).

swefel, *st. m.* sulphur. (Ger. *schwefel.*)

swefen, *st. n.* (swoon?)— 1. sleep, stupor (Gen. 720).— 2. dream.

swefed, 3d *pers. sg.* of swebban (to put to sleep).

swefnan, -ian, *w. v.* to dream.

swefot. See sweofot (sleep).

swêg, *st. m.* (swough), sound, tone, voice; noise, crash, tumult.

swêg-dyn, *st. m.* din, din of noise.

swêg-hlêodor, *st. n.* detonation, clamor, explosion, sound, resonance.

swegl, swegel, *st. m.* 1. ether, sky. 2. sun.— 3. song, chorus, symphony.

swegl-befalden, *adj.* ether-covered.

swegl-beorht, *adj.* ether-bright, radiant.

swegl-bôsm, *st. m.* bosom of heaven, the sky.

swegl-candel, -condel, *st. f.* sky-candle; light of heaven, or ether.

swegl-cyning, *st. m.* king of heaven or glory.

swegl-drêam, *st. m.* heavenly joy.

swegle, *adj.* clear (of sight or sound), luminous, resounding.

swegle, *adv.* clearly, brilliantly.

swêg-leder, -leoder, *st. n.* sound leather, bagpipe?

swegl-râd, *st. f.* change of tone(s), modulation. [zling.

swegl-torht, *adj.* heaven-bright, daz-

swegl-wered, *part.* ether-clad.

swegl-wuldor, *st. n.* heavenly glory.

swegl-wundor, *st. n.* heavenly wonder.

swelan, *w. v.* to (sweal), burn, glow, ignite, consume with heat.
for-swelan, to burn up.

swelc. See swilc (such).

swelgan, sweolgan, *st. abl. v.* I. to swallow, take in, absorb, imbibe.
for-swelgan, same as above.
ge-swelgan, same as above.

swelgian, *w. v.* in
ge-swelgian, to cause to **swell** up, inflate, be swollen? Pa. 41.
swellan, *st. abl. v.* I. to **swell,** swell up.
swelling, *st. m.* **swelling** sail.
sweltan, *st. abl. v.* I. to die.
swencan, *w. v.* to (**swink**), disturb, oppress, plague, torment.
ge-swencan, to confuse, disturb, oppress, exhaust, plague, chastise, crush.
swendan, *w. v.* in
tô-swendan, to cause to go asunder, destroy. (Ger. *schwinden*.)
sweng, *st. m.* (**swing**), blow, castigation, cut, thrust.
swengan, *w. v.* in
tô-swengan, to **swing** in pieces, drive asunder, destroy.
swer, swyr, *st. m. & f.* pillar, column.
swerian, *st. abl. v.* IV. to **swear.**
â-swerian, the same as above.
for-swerian, 1. to put one's self under a spell; to render invulnerable by magical utterance.— 2. to forswear, perjure, commit perjury.
ge-swerian, to swear.
swerian. See **swarian** (to speak).
swêtan, *w. v.* to **sweeten,** make sweet.
ge-swêtan, the same as above.
swête, *adj.* **sweet;**—*subs.* sweet(s). Seaf. 95.
swêt-met, *st. m.* **sweetmeat.**
swêtnes, *st. f.* sweetness.
swetole. See **sweotule** (plainly).
swedian, *w. v.* in
bi-swedian, to beswathe, wrap up, fold in.
swedrian, *w. v.* to diminish, decrease, neglect, yield, dwindle.
ge-swedrian, same as above.
swealg, *pret.* of **swelgan** (to swallow).
swealwe, *w. f.* **swallow** (bird).

sweart, swart, *adj.* **swart, swarthy.**
1. dark, obscure, black.— 2. mischievous, hurtful, infamous.
swearte, *adv.* mischievously, hurtfully, infamously.
sweart-läst, *adj.* leaving black tracks or traces. Rid. 27: 11.
sweofot, swefot, *st. m.* sleep.
sweolce, sweolgan. See **swylce, swelgan** (to swallow).
sweôlod, swôlod, *st. m.* glow, fire, flame (swealing).
sweon (Rid. 16: 4), **sweopa, sweopian, sweopu** (*pl*). See **sû, swipa, swipian, swip.**
sweor, *st. m.* father-in-law. (Ger. *schwäher*).
sweora, swiora, swira, swyra, *w. m.* neck, nape.
sweorcan, *st. abl. v.* I. to be or become gloomy, dark, sad.
for-sweorcan, to darken, grow dark.
ge-sweorcan, to darken, obscure, grow dark; to become sad, gloomy.
sweorcend-ferhd, *adj.* gloomy of spirit, sad.
sweord, swurd, swyrd, *st. n.* **sword.**
sweord-berend, *part. & subs.* swordbearer.
sweord-bealo, *st. n.* sword-bale, injury or destruction through the sword.
sweord-bite, *st. m.* sword-bite, wound with the sword.
sweord-freca, *w. m.* sword-wolf, sworded warrior.
sweord-ge-nidla, *w. m.* sworded foe, foe armed with a sword.
sweord-, swyrd-ge-swing, *st. n.* sword-**swinging**, combat, slaughter
sweord-gifu, *st. f.* sword-**giving,** gift of swords.
sweord-gripe, *st. m.* sword attack, onslaught with swords.

sweord-, swurd-léoma, *w. m.* sword-gleam, coruscation of swords.
sweord-plega, *w. m.* sword-play, conflict.
sweord-ræs, *st. m.* sword-rush; attack.
sweord-slege, *st. m.* sword-thrust, blow.
sweord-wigend, *part. & subs.* sworded warrior.
sweord-wund, *adj.* sword-wounded.
sweorfan, *st. abl. v.* I. to wipe off, cleanse, file, polish.
sweorian. See **swarian** (to speak).
sweostor, swuster, *st. f.* sister.
sweot, *st. n.* band, troop;—*instr. pl.* **sweotum,** in troops.
sweotol, swutol, sutol, *adj.* **1.** visible, distinct, plain, evident.—**2.** audible, clear, distinct. B. 90.
sweotule, swetole, *adv.* visibly, clearly, plainly, precisely.
sweotulian, swutulian, *w. v.* to be plain, visible, evident.
   ge-sweotulian, to render plain, distinct, visible.
sweotul-, swutollice, *adv.* plainly, visibly, distinctly, precisely.
sweodrian. See **swidrian** (to lessen).
swian. See **swigian** (to be silent).
swic, *st. m.* odor, smell.
swican, *st. abl. v.* V. **1.** (absolutely) to go, move about, yield, give way, evade, escape, get away.—**2.** ût **swican,** to go out or forth.—**3.** from **swican,** or **swican** from, to decline, fall off, revolt, desist, cease from.—**4.** *w. dat.* to desist, leave in the lurch, abandon, renounce.
   â-swican, to fall off, desert, abandon; to irritate, provoke.
   be-swican, to beguile, deceive, betray, mislead.
   ge-swican, to omit, intermit, desist, cease to help, abandon, deceive, renounce, betray.

swice, swyce, *st. m.* **1.** issue, result, success.—**2.** procrastination, delay (Gû. 1007).—**3.** offense, provocation, insult.
swice, *adj.* renouncing, deserting, abandoning.
swician, swycian, *w. v.* **1.** to err, wander, wander about.—**2.** to decline, fall off from, deviate (Ps. 118: 102).—**3.** to exert, weary one's self (Gen. 607).
swicol, *adj.* guileful, deceitful, false.
swifan, *st. abl. v.* V. to roam, ramble about. (Ger. *schweifen.*)
   on-swifan, 1. *w. acc.* to swing, to move against or toward.—**2.** to push off, put aside, turn away.
swift, *adj.* swift, quick.
swiftu, *st. f.* swiftness.
swige, *w. f.* silence, stillness, rest. (Ger. *schweigen.*)
swige, *adj.* silent, taciturn, quiet.
swigian, swŷgian, *w. v.* to be silent, quiet, still. (Ger. *schweigen.*)
   ge-swigian, 1. to be silent, quiet. **2.** to silence.
swilc, swylc, swulc, swelc, *pron.* **1.** each, every (B. 299).—**2.** who, whoever, whichever (Ps. Ben. 19: 9). **3.** such, such a.—**4.** which.—**5.** **swylc—swylc,** such—as, so—as.
swilce, swylce, swelce, sweolce, *adv.* **1.** also, moreover, and further, furthermore.—**2.** *w. subs.* as, so as. **3.** in like manner, likewise, after the same fashion, so, thus.—**4.** as (how).—**5.** *w. subj.* as if, as though.
swilt. See **swylt** (death).
swima, *w. m.* giddiness, vertigo, dizziness, swimming of the head.
swimman, swymman, *st. abl. v.* I. to swim.
   ofer-swimman, *w. acc.* to swim over, across, through.
swin, *st. n.* swine, hog, boar.—**2.** boar-figure or ornament on the helmet.

swincan, *st. abl. v.* I. to **swink,** labor hard, toil, exhaust one's self.
swingan, *st. abl. v.* I. 1. to flog, strike, scourge, whip, chastise.— 2. **swingan on twâ** = strike in two, divide by a blow.— 3. *intrans.* to swing, fly, flutter.
    be-swingan, to flog, beat, strike, scourge.
    ge-swingan, the same as above.
swingel, *st. f.* blow, beating, whipping; dejection, affliction.
swingela, swingla, *w. m.* whip, scourge.
swingere, *st. m.* swinger, striker, scourger.
swin-lica, *w. m.* **swine-likeness,** boar-figure on the helmet.
swinsian, swynsian, *w. v.* to sound, resound, sing, rustle.
swip, *st. n.* (*pl.* **sweopu**), whip, scourge.
swipa, sweopa, *w. m.* same as above.
swipian, swippan, sweopian, *w. v.* to whip, scourge, beat.
swira. See **sweora** (neck).
swid, swŷd, *adj.* 1. strong, vigorous, valiant, powerful, violent.— 2. in *compar.* right (or strong) hand (as opposed to left).
swidan, swŷdan, *w. v.* to strengthen, establish, assist, enrich.
    for-swidan, to crush, press upon, repel, push back.
    ge-swidan, to strengthen, render strong, invigorate, reënforce.
    ofer-swidan, *w. acc.* to excel, surpass, conquer, overwhelm, vanquish.
swide, swŷde, *adv.* strongly, very, much, violently;—*compar.* **swidor** = more, rather, more strongly, violently;—*superl.* most, very, exceedingly.
swid-ferd, -ferhd, *adj.* strong of mind, bold, brave.

swid-feorm, *adj.* strong, powerful, rich.
swid-, swŷd-ge-neahhe, *adv.* quite enough, very often, frequently.
swid-ge-neahhige, *adv.* the same as above. [quick.
swid-hwæt, *adj.* very prompt, agile,
swid-, swŷd-hycgende, *part.* strong-minded, bold, brave.
swidlic, *adj.* immense, great, violent.
swid-mihtig, *adj.* very powerful, mighty.
swid-môd, *adj.* of strong or impetuous mind, bold, brave, insolent.
swidrian, sweodrian, *w. v.* to increase, diminish, dwindle, give way, vanish, weaken, rest.
    ge-swidrian, to lessen, diminish, weaken; to effect, accomplish.
swid-snel, *adj.* very quick, agile, prompt.
swiora, swiodol. See **sweora, swadol.**
swôgan, *st. red. v.* (to **sough**), to rustle, whistle, hum, buzz, roar, rattle.
swôl? glow, fire, flame. (Ger. *schwül.*)
swôlod, swon, swoncor, swongor, swor (Exod. 239), **sworcan.** See **sweôlod, swan, swancor, swangor, spor, sweorcan.**
sworcen-ferd, *adj.* somber, sad. Wy. 25.
swulc, swurd, swuster, swutol, swutulian. See **swilc, sweord, sweostor, sweotol, sweotulian.**
swyce, swycian, swŷgian, swylc, swylce. See **swice, swician, swigian, swilc, swilce.**
swŷld, *st. f.* pain? Ps. 114:3.
swylian, *w. v.* in
    be-swylian, to soil, fleck, befoul.
swylt, swilt, *st. m.* death.
swylt-cwalu, *st. f.* death-torment, death.
swylt-dæg, *st. m.* **day** of death.

swylt-dêad, *st. m.* death, perishing.
swyttend. See **sweltan** (to die).
swylt-hwil, *st. f.* death-hour.
swymman, swynsian, swyr, swyra, swyrd, swŷd, swŷdan, swŷde. See **swimman, swinsian, swer, sweora, sweord, swid, swidan, swide.**
sŷ, syb, sŷd. See **si, sêon, sib, sid.**
syfon-. See **seofon-wintre.**
sŷfer, *adj.* sober, self-denying, pure, clean. (Ger. *sauber.*)
syflan, *w. v.* in
 ge-syflan, to provide or supply with relishes or stimulants to appetite.
syfone. See **seofan** (seven).
syge (?), sight, aspect.
sygor, syhd, sylf, sylfor. See **sigor, sêon, self, seolfor.**
sylian, selian, *w. v.* to sully, spot, fleck, pollute.
 be-sylian, the same as above.
syll, *st. f.* sill, doorsill, threshold, dais whereon benches stand.
sŷlla, syllan, syllend, syllic, sylofren. See **sêl, sellan, sellend, sellic, seolfren.**
symbel, *st. n.* banquet, drinking-bout, feast, carouse, meal, festivity.
symbel, *st. n.* duration, continuance.
symbel-dæg, *st. m.* day of feasts or feasting, holidays.
symbel-gâl, *adj.* merry or riotous in feasting, intoxicated, drunk.
symbel-ge-fêra, *w. m.* constant companion.
symbel-ge-reordu, *st. n. pl.* banquetings, feastings, carousings.
symbel-gifa, *w. m.* giver of feasts or meals.
symbel-wêrig, *adj.* weary of the carouse or feast.
symbel-wlonc, *adj.* insolent or elated from feasting.
symbel-wyn, *st. f.* joy of feasting, social delight.

symble, *adv.* ever, forever, always.
symblian, symblan, *w. v.* to feast, carouse, enjoy one's self.
symle, symles, syn-, sŷn. See **simle, simles, sin-, si, sêon.**
syn, sinn, senn, *st. f.* 1. sin, guilt. 2. hostility, enmity, feud.
syn-byrden, *st. f.* burden of sin.
sync, synd. See **sinc, sind.**
syn-dǽd, *st. f.* deed or act of sin.
syndig, *adj.* skilled in swimming? Crä. 58.
syndon. See **sindon** (are).
syndrian, *w. v.* in
 â-syndrian, to sunder, separate, divide.
 tô-syndrian, the same as above.
syndrig, *adj.* special, apart, alone, unique.
syn-fâh, -fâ, *adj.* sin-stained.
syn-full, *adj.* sinful, guilty.
syngian, singian, *w. v.* to sin.
 ge-syngian, the same as above.
syn-gryn, *st. f.* sin, harm, mischief of sin.
syn-lêasig, *adj.* sinless, guiltless, innocent.
synlice, *adv.* sinfully, foully, infamously.
syn-lust, *st. m.* pleasure in sin, desire to sin.
synn. See **syn** (sin).
synnig, *adj.* sinful, guilty, punishable, criminal.
syn-rust, *st. m.* sin-rust, filth of sin.
syn-sceada, -scada, *w. m.* sinful scather, unjust criminal.
synt, symu. See **sind, seonu.**
syn-wracu, *st. f.* punishment for sin.
syn-wund, *st. f.* wound of sin.
syn-wyrcende, *part.* sin-worker.
sŷp, *st. m.* sip, sup, sipping, drinking in.
syrce, syrwan. See **serce, serwan.**
syddam. See **siddan** (since).
syddan, *w. v.* to surrender, deliver up, cast down? Ps. 73:18.

T

tâcen, tâcn, *st. n.* 1. token, mark. 2. suggestion, indication, symbol. 3. wonder, marvelous deed, act, heroic deed. — 4. proof, ground, demonstration, subject.

tâcnian, *w. v.* in
    ge-tâcnian, to sign, mark, characterize, betoken, designate, destine, determine, establish.

tǽcan, tǽcean, *w. v.* to show, point out, exhibit. (Ger. *zeigen.*)
    be-tǽcan, to show, point out, characterize, make over, assign, deliver.
    ge-tǽcan, to show, point out, reveal, designate, refer, make over, arraign.

tǽcnan, *w. v.* to mark by a token, to denote, designate, trace out.
    ge-tǽcnan, to show, point out.

tǽcne, *adj.* (in compounds), to be shown or pointed out.

tǽfel, *st. f. & n.* die, cube, game at dice, dice-playing.

tǽfle, *adj.* acquainted with or devoted to dice-playing.

tægel, *st. m.* tail.

tæl. See talu (number).

tǽlan, *w. v.* to slander, calumniate, accuse, blame, scold.

tǽle, tǽled, (*part.*), tǽlian. See tâlu, tellan, talian.

tæl-met, *st. n.* tale, number, computation.

tæl-mearc, *st. f.* counting over, calculation.

tǽl-, tělnis, *st. f.* removal, deprivation, depreciation, degradation, blame, censure, transgression of duty, breach of official fidelity.

tǽsan, *w. v.* 1. to touse, tease, tug, pluck. — 2. to wound, injure.

tǽse, *adj.* mild, gentle.

tǽsu, *st. f.* harm, injury, destruction.

tǽtan (?), to caress. Wy. 4.

talian, tælian, *w. v.* to count, calculate, value, consider (as), mention, believe, think.

talu, *st. f.* 1. tale, number, calculation. — 2. speech, telling, narrative.

tâl, *st. f.* calumny, false witness, abuse, malicious accusation.

tam, tom, *adj.* tame.

tama, *w. m.* tameness.

tân, *st. m.* 1. rod, switch, bush, sprout, twig, branch. — 2. staff, rod used in divination, magic, or prophecy; fate, destiny.

tân, *adj.* (tined?), branched, furnished with branches.

tapur, *st. m.* taper, wax taper.

tedre. See tydre (soft).

têgan, *w. v.* in
    ge-têgan, to make. Met. 13: 14.

tela, teala, *adv.* fitly, fittingly, well, rightly.

teldan, *st. abl. v.* I. in
    be-, bi-teldan, to cover, cover over, screen, protect, envelop, surround. (Ger. *celt.*)
    ofer-teldan, the same as above.

telg, *st. m.* fluid, infusion, tincture.

telga, *w. m.* branch, twig, vine-shoot.

telge (B. 2067). See talian (to count).

telgian, *w. v.* to put forth branches, or twigs.

tellan, *w. v.* (*pret.* tealde), 1. to tell, count. — 2. to reckon up, calculate, count out. — 3. to esteem, reckon (as), mention, believe, think.
    ge-tellan, to count, count out or over, compute, consider, weigh.
    tô-tellan, to separate in counting, arrange, distinguish.

telnys. See tǽlnis (blame).

temian, *w. v.* in

â-temian, to **tame**, to render gentle or quiet.

têman, týman, *w. v.* to bear, bring forth, **teem** with.

tempel, *st. n.* temple.

ten, tene, tyn, tyne, *num.* ten.

tênan. See týnan (to injure).

tengan, *w. v.* to press toward, hurry, hasten.

ge-tengan, to press; to devote, dedicate.

tennan, *w. v.* to lure, allure? Wy. 4.

teran, *st. abl. v.* II. to **tear**.

tergan, tyrgan, *w. v.* to pull or pluck hither and thither, torment, tease; to scorn.

tesu, teswian. See teosu, teoswian.

têđ. See tôđ (tooth).

têafor, *st. n.* foundation, place for building (with external walls of a house). Ruin. 31.

têag, *st. f.* thong, rope, band, fetter, towline.

teagor, *st. m.* **tear**, teardrop.

teala. See tela, til, talu.

tealde, *pret.* of tellan (to count).

tealt, *adj.* tilting, unsteady, tottering.

tealtrian, *w. v.* to tilt, totter, vacillate, be in peril. [ant.

têam, *st. m.* sprout, scion, descendant.

teâr, tǽr, *st. m.* 1. drop.— 2. **tear**.

teârig-hleôr, *adj.* with tearful cheeks.

teôfenian, *w. v.* to join, put together, unite.

teôfrian, *w. v.* the same as above.

teoh, teohh, *st. f. & m. (n.?)* race, company, number, band, troop, society.

teôhan. See teôn (to accuse).

teohhian, tiohhian, tihhian, tyhhian, *w. v.* to fix, establish, show, direct, determine, resolve, believe.

teolian, teolum. See tilian, til.

teôn, tion, *st. abl. v.* VI. (Ger. *ziehen*.) 1. *w. acc.* to draw, lead.— 2. educate, rear (Ps. 79: 5).— 3. *intrans.* to move, go, roam.— 4. *w. acc.* to create, procreate, beget. Gen. 980.

â-teôn, 1. to draw out, off, from. 2. to handle, treat.— 3. to move, journey, roam. — 4. *intrans.* up âteôn, to ascend, draw up, move away (Exod. 490).

for-teôn, 1. to draw away, distort, mislead.— 2. to draw or put over; to obstruct, cover.

ge-teôn, 1. to draw.— 2. to give, lend, put at the disposal of.

of-teôn, 1. to draw off, withdraw, take away.— 2. to refuse, withhold, deny, deprive of.

ofer-teôn, to draw over, cover.

tô-teôn, to draw in two, draw in pieces.

þurh-teôn, to draw or put through, to execute, carry out.

teôn. See tihan (to accuse).

teôn, tion, *w. v.* 1. to make, produce, work, set, fix, establish, constitute. 2. to furnish with or out, to deck. B. 43.

fore-teôn, to make beforehand, establish, exhibit, arrange, dispose, ordain.

ge-teôn, to make, work, set, establish, conclude.

teôn, *st. n.* teen, harm, hurt, hostility.

teôna, *w. m.* reproach, accusation, insult, offense, discord, enmity, injury.

teôn-cwide, *st. m.* hurtful speech, calumny, reproach, blasphemy.

teône, *w. f.* calumny, injustice.

teôn-ful, *adj.* teenful, injurious, unworthy, malicious.

teôn-hete, *st. m.* malicious hate.

teôn-lêg, *st. m.* destroying flame, fire of perdition, burning of the world.

teônlic, *adj.* destructive, hurtful, shameful.

teônlice, *adv.* the same as above.

teôn-smiđ, *st. m.* calumniator, doer of injustice, evil-doer.

teon-tig, *num.* (ten-ty), hundred.
têon-wærgdu, *st. f.* punishment.
têon-wit, *st. m.* quarrel, strife.
têon-word, *st. n.* abuse, calumny.
teorian, *w. v.* **1.** *intrans.* to dwindle, vanish, become weary, yield.— **2.** *w. acc.* to exhaust, tire. Ps.141: 3.
    ge-teorian, to dwindle, vanish, weary, yield.
teosel, *st. m.* die (dice).
teosu, tesu, *st. f.* harm, injury, destruction.
teosu-spræc, *st. f.* calumny, harmful speech.
teoswian, teswian, *w. v.* to offend, insult.
têoda, *num. adj.* tenth.
tiber, tifer, *st. n.* offering, victim, sacrifice, sacrificial animal.
ticlum (?). (Rid. 40: 2. = tidum?)
tid, *st. f.* **1.** tide, time; —*instr. pl.* tidum, timely, at the right time (Gn. Ex. 125).— **2.** feast-day, festal tide.— **3.** hour.
tid-dæg, *st. m.* lifetime, death.
tid-ege, *st. m.* dread of one's appointed time, death.
tid-fara, *w. m.* timely traveler, opportune journeyer. Cri. 1674.
tidlice, *adv.* timely, in time.
tifer, tigan. See tiber, týgan.
tigol, *st. f.;* tigele, *w. f.* tile.
tigel-fâg, *adj.* with colored tiles.
tigdian. See tidian (to grant).
tihan, têon, *st. abl. v.* V. to accuse, accuse of. (Ger. *zeihen.*)
    of-tihan, to deny, refuse.
tihhian, tiht, tihtan, tihd. See teohhian, tyht, tyhtan, têon, tihan.
til, till, *adj.* adapted, suitable, fitting, good, useful.
til, *st. n.* goodness, fitness.
tila, tela, *adv.* fitly, well. Rid. 49: 2.
Tile, the isle of Thule (Met. 16: 15); —usually þyle.
til-, till-fremmend, *part.* well-doing, well-acting.

tilian, tiligan, tiligean, tilgan, teolian, tiolian, *w. v.* (*w. inf.*), **1.** to aim, have in view, strive for, seek, exert one's self.— **2.** *w. gen.* to attain, seek to attain, effect by effort, win, deserve.
    ge-tilian, to win, give.
till,*st.n.* fixed standing-place, station, place. Met. 20: 172.
tillic, *adj.* fit, good.
tillice, *adv.* the same as above.
til-môd, *adj.* well-disposed, kind, good.
til-môdig, *adj.* the same as above.
tima, *w. m.* time.
timber, *st. n.* material (timber), structure, building.
timbran, timbrian, *w. v.* to build, construct, erect, form, forge.
    • â-timbran, to build up, erect.
    be-timbran, to cover with timber, construct, build up. [struct.
    ge-timbran, to build, erect, contimpanum. See tympanum.
tingan, *st. abl. v.* I. in
    ge-tingan, to join, add one's self to, associate with, unite with, press upon.
tinnan (?). Rim. 54.
tintreg, tinterg, *st. n.* torture, torment, punishment.
tin-trega, *w. m.* the same as above.
tir, týr, *st. m.* **1.** glory, honor, ornament, brilliancy.— **2.** name of the Rune t.— **3.** name of a constellation that does not set. Run. 48.
tir-, týr-êadig, *adj.* glorious.
tir-fæst, *adj.* established in reputation, famous.
tir-fruma, *w. m.* prince of glory.
tir-lêas, *adj.* without fame, shamefully vanquished. B. 843.
tir-meahtig, *adj.* glorious, powerful.
tid, týd, *st. f.* assent, permission: gift, favor.
tida, *w. m.* (with gen. of thing), in possession of, participant in.

tídian, tigdian, týdian, *w. v.* to grant a request, grant, perform, hold, keep.
    ge-tídian, the same as above.
tiedran. See tydran (to beget).
tier (?), tier, series, mass. Met. 20: 81.
tiohhian, tiolian, tion, tion-lêg. See teohhian, tilian, têon, têon-lêg.
tô, I. *prep.* 1. *w. dat.* to. — (*a.*) answers to question *whither?* (aim, object, end of motion; person spoken to or addressed). — (*b.*) to, for, into, answers to questions *wherefore?* to, or *for*, or *into* what? (end or aim; to make *into*, change to or *into*, become). — (*c.*) at, by, near, from, answers to questions *where?* (from w. verbs of asking, receiving, &c.). — (*d.*) phrases: ne tô wuhte, by no means, under no circumstances (Gen. 839); tô him, next to or nearest to him (Gen. 254); tô hwænes willan, in accordance with some one's will (Gen. 717. — (*e.*) in temporal relations, *for:* tô langre hwíle (Gen. 489; *up to, till:* næs long tô þon þæt, until (B. 2591); *to, during:* tô dæge, to-day (Hy. 5: 6). — 2. *w. gen.* phrases: tô þæs, to him (Gn. Ex. 35); tô þæs, thither, to that point (An. 1125); tô þæs þe, thither where (An. 1061); tô þæs, whither, where (An. 1072); tô hwæs, whither (Exod. 192); tô þæs (before adjectives and adverbs), to that degree, so, so very; tô middes dæges, at midday. — 3. *w. acc.* to, toward, at, in; tô dæg, to-day. — 4. to, *w. inf.* (*a.*) uninflected inf. (Az. 37). — (*b.*) w. inflected inf. = Latin, *gerund, supine,* ut and *subj. & fut. act. part.* (Gen. 243; B. 257). — II. adverb: two, in two. — 1. w. verbs in improper compounds. — 2. thereto (?) (Gen. 1224). — 3. before adjectives and adverbs too, too much, very.

tô-gadere, -gædere, -gædre, *adv.* together.
tô-gegnes, -gênes, -geânes, *adv.* towards, against.
tô-heald, *adv.* forward, in advance.
tô-hiht. See tôhyht (hope).
tô-hopa, *w. m.* hope, expectation.
tohte, *w. f.* expedition, march, campaign, battle, conflict.
tô-hyht, tô-hiht, *st. m.* (?). Cf. hyhtes, (Jul. 442; Cri. 58, &c.), hope.
tom. See tam (tame).
tôme, *adv.* (*w. gen.*), free of, empty of, vacant.
tor, torr, *st. m.* 1. tower. — 2. mountain top, summit, rock. (Met. 5: 17.)
tord, *st. m.* turd, dung, filth.
torht, *adj.* bright, luminous, illustrious, famous.
torhte, *adv.* brightly, luminously, clearly.
torhtlíc, *adj.* brilliant, clear.
torhtlíce, *adv.* the same as above.
torht-môd, *adj.* of brilliant mind or spirit.
torn, *st. n.* (Ger. *zorn*), offense, insult, misery, suffering, pain, grief, wrath. [bad.
torn, *adj.* grievous, saddening, bitter,
torn-cwide, *st. m.* offensive or insulting speech.
torne, *adv.* insultingly, bitterly, grievously.
torn-ge-môt, *st. n.* angry collision, hostile meeting.
torn-ge-nídla, *w. m.* wrath-provoking foe, angry opponent.
tornlíc, *adj.* sorrowful, grievous.
torn-môd, *adj.* wrathful-minded, angry.
torn-sorg, *st. f.* heartfelt sorrow, care, or anxiety. [ous word.
torn-word, *st. n.* insulting or grievtorn-wracu, *st. f.* outburst of wrath.
torr. See tor (tower).
tô-samne, -somne, *adv.* together.
toste, *w. f.* toad, paddock.

tôđ, m. tocth: *irreg. dat.* teđ (Exod. 2124); *nom. & acc. pl.* tôđas (Ph. 407); têđ (Deut. 32: 24); tôđ (Ps. Stev 57: 7).

tôđ-mægen, *st. n.* tooth-power, strength or firmness in the teeth.

tô-weard, *adj.* 1. impending, imminent, future.— 2. toward, against. Met. 28: 7.

tô-wiđere, -wiđre, *prep., w. dat.,* or *acc.* toward, against.

trǽdan (?), (to tread?), to roam through, roam about. Rid. 58: 5.

træf, *st. n.* 1. tent.— 2. building, structure? An. 844.

trag, *adj.* evil, mean, bad, unfavorable, disgusting.

trage, *adv.* the same as above.

trag-mǽl, *st. n.* disturbance, disquietude, misery, oppression, torment.

tragu, *st. f.* the same as above.

trahtian. See treahtian (to think).

tredan, *st. abl. v.* III. 1. to tread, trample, mistreat.— 2. to enter, enter upon, go upon, roam through.

treddan, *w. v.* to search out, scrutinize, think over, reflect upon.

â-treddan, the same as above.

treddian, tryđđian, *w. v.* to tread, tramp, stride, go, go about.

trede, *adj.* current, customary, possible, practicable.

trega, *w. m.* oppression, grievance, disturbance, uneasiness, pain.

trem, tremman. See trym, trymman (to strengthen).

trendlian, *w. v.* in
â-trendlian, to fly forth or up, to unroll.

treaflic, *adj.* oppressing, grieving, crushing.

treahtere, *st. m.* interpreter, expounder, meditator (on, over).

treahtian, trahtian, *w. v.* in
ge-trahtian, to think over or upon, reflect upon, consider.

trêo, treow, *st. n.* 1. tree.— 2. wood, grove (Ph. 200).— 3. wood, material (Rid. 57: 9).— 4. tree of the cross, cross.

trêo-cynn, *st. n.* sort or kind of wood, wood species.

trêo-fugol, *st. m.* tree-fowl, forest bird.

treow. See trêo (tree).

trêow, trŷw, *st. f.* 1. firmness, reliability (Run. 25).— 2. fidelity to a promise, covenantal faith.— 3. plighted troth, vow of fidelity.— 4. favor, grace, kindness.— 5. confidence, belief.

trêowan, trûwan, trŷwan, *w. v.* to trust, intrust, have confidence in, believe confidently. (Ger. *trauen.*)
ge-trêowan, 1. to trust, believe, hope.— 2. to confirm, authenticate, render certain or credible, vow solemnly. (B. 1095; Ps. 92: 6.)
ge-or-trêowan, to mistrust, lose faith in.
on-trêowan, to intrust, confide.

trêo-, trêow-wæstm, *st. f.* tree.

trêowe, trŷwe, *adj.* true, faithful.

trêow-, triow-fæst, *adj.* the same.

trêow-ge-þofta, *w. m.* faithful comrade, plighted companion, confederate.

trêowian, trûwian, trŷwian, *w. v.* 1. *w. gen.* or *dat.* to trust, intrust, confide in, have confidence in, trust to.— 2. *w. dat.* to be faithful. (Gen. 2324.)
ge-trêowian, to trust, intrust, confide in, hope.

trêow-lôga, *w. m.* troth-breaker, pledge-breaker.

trêow-lufu, *st. f.* true love.

trêow-rǽden, *st. f.* true covenant, treaty, compact.

trêowđ, *st. f.* truth, fidelity, veracity.

trêow-þrâg, *st. f.* time of or for faithfulness, fidelity.

treow-wæstm. See trêow-wæstm.

trided, trieded, 3*d pers. sg. pres.* of **tredan** (to tread).

trio, triow. See **trêo, trêow.**

trodu, *st. f.* step, treading, pace, track, vestige.

trum, *adj.* firm, fixed, vigorous, active, cheerful.

trumlic, *adj.* the same as above.

trumnad, *st. m.* confirmation, assurance.

trûwan, trûwian. See **trêowan, trêowian** (to trust).

tryddian. See **treddian** (to tread).

tryded, 3*d pers. sg. prcs.* of **tredan** (to tread).

trym, trem, (Ger. *trümmer*), *st. n.* fragment, part, piece; — **fôtes trym,** foot's length.

trymian, *w. v.* to strengthen, exhort, encourage, incite.

    ge-trymian, the same as above.

trymman, tremman, *w. v.* **1.** to invigorate, strengthen, fortify, build firmly. — **2.** to strengthen, encourage, exhort, incite, comfort. — **3.** to storm, rage, roar, whirr (El. 35; Exod, 159).

    ge-trymman, to invigorate, strengthen, fortify, encourage; to get, procure. (Gen. 248.)

trymnes, *st. f.* firmness, solidity.

trŷw, trŷwan, trŷwe, trŷwian. See **trêow, trêowan, trêowe, trêowian.**

tû. See **þû** and **twegen** (two).

tucian, *w. v.* (Ger. *zucken*, **twitch**), to cause to quiver, palpitate, shake, convulse, disturb.

tuddor, tudor, *st. n.* scion, descendant, progeny, growth, posterity.

tuddor-spêd, *st. f.* fertility, fruitfulness.

tuddor-têonde, *part.* begetting posterity.

tûn, *st. m.* hedge, fence, inclosed dwelling, place, **town.**

tunece, *w. f.* **tunic,** undergarment, garment.

tunge, *w. f.* **tongue.**

tungol, tungel, tungl, *st. m. & n.* constellation, star, planet.

tungol-gim, *st. m.* star-gem, constellation.

turf, *st. f.* (*dat. sg.* **tyrf**), **turf,** soil, grass.

turf-haga, *w. m.* turf-cover, turf, covering of grass.

turtle, *w. f.* **turtle-dove.**

twâ. See **twegen** (two).

twǣfan, *w. v.* in

    ge-twǣfan, 1. to separate from, deprive of, hinder in, incapacitate for. — **2.** to confuse, bewilder (Gen. 53; Exod. 119).

twǣman, *w. v.* in

    ge-twǣman, to incapacitate for, to render incapable of.

    tô-twǣman, to dissever, break up or in pieces, to dissolve.

    ge-tô-twǣman, to sever, part, hinder in, incapacitate for.

twegen, twâ, tû, *num.* **two, twain;** *nom. & acc.* **twegen,** *f.* **twâ,** *n.* **tû, twâ;** (**twâ** is also of common gender: **wit Adam twâ,** Adam and I: Sat. 411); *gen. m., f., & n.* **twegra, twega;** — *dat. m., f., & n.* **twâm, twǣm.**

twelf, *num.* **twelve.**

twelfta, *num. adj.* **twelfth.**

twelf-tig (**twelve-ty** = 120). See **hund-twelftig.**

twen-tig, *num.* **twenty.**

twêo, *st. m.* **1. twoness,** doubt. — **2.** difference, distinction (El. 668).

twêogan, twêon, *w. m.* **1.** to be of **two minds,** doubt, doubt of. — **2.** *impers. w. acc.* of person: to seem or appear doubtful.

    ge-twêogan, to doubt, hesitate, vacillate, be irresolute.

tweoh. See **twih** (both).

twêone, *num.* **bini,** two.

twêo-spræce, *adj.* two-spoken, ambiguous, double-minded.
tweox. See **twih** (both).
twidig, *adj.* granted, allowed, permitted.
twi-ecg, *adj.* two-edged.
twig, *st. n.* twig, branch, vine-shoot.
twiga, *w. m.* the same as above.
twigan, *w. v.* in
    ge-palm-twigan, to deck or ornament with **palm-branches.**
twih, *acc.* both, two; **mid unc twih,** between us two. (Gen. 2253.)
twŷ-. See **twi-ecg.**
tŷan, *w. v.* to draw, pull, rear, instruct, teach.
    ge-tŷan, the same as above.
tydernes, *st. f.* (?). Sol. 47.
tydran, tyddran, tiedran, *w. v.* 1. *intrans.* to get children.— 2. *w. acc.* to beget, produce, bear, bring forth.
    â-tydran, to beget.
tydere, tedre, *adj.* weak, tender, feeble, cowardly.
tydrian, *w. v.* to weaken, soften, become feeble, fall to pieces.
tŷgan. See **têag** (rope).
tŷgan, tigan, *w. v.* in
    ge-tigan, to **tie,** bind together, to fetter. [lish).
tyhhian. See **teohhian** (to establish).
tŷhst, *2d pers. st. pres.* of **tihan, têon** (to accuse).

tyht, tiht, *st. m.* 1. training, discipline, instruction.— 2. movement, motion.
tyhtan, tihtan, *w. v.* to train, breed, educate, instruct, goad, incite.
    â-tyhtan, 1. to beget.— 2. to lead? lure in? Met. 1: 8.
    for-tyhtan, to mislead, lead astray.
    ge-tyhtan, to educate, teach, instruct.
    on-tyhtan, to urge on, incite.
tŷhd, *3d pers. sg. pres.* of **tihan, têon.**
tyllan, *w. v.* in
    for-tyllan, to lead astray, mislead. Cri. 270.
tyllan. See **til** (fit).
tŷma, tŷman. See **têma, têman.**
tympanum, *n.* tympanum.
tyn. See **ten.**
tŷnan, *w. v.* in
    â-tŷnan, to shut off or out.
    be-, bi-tŷnan, to hedge about, inclose, close up, bury.
    ge-tŷnan, to shut or close in, to bury.
    on-tŷnan, to unclose, open, reveal, unveil.
    un-tŷnan, the same as above.
tŷnan, *w. v.* to grieve, insult, trouble.
tyne, tŷr, tyrf. See **ten, tir, turf.**
tŷtan, *w. v.* to sparkle, shine.
tŷd, tŷda, tŷdian. See **tid, tida, tidian.**

Þ

þâ, 1. *adv.* there, then.— 2. *conj.* as, inasmuch as, if, when, since.
þa, þâ. See **þæt** (*pron.*), **þâw.**
þæc, *st. n.* thatch, roof. (Ger. *dach.*)
þæh, þæm, þænne. See **þeah, þæt,** (*pron.*), **þeam, þanne.**
þær, þar, þer, 1. *adv. & conj.* of place: there, yonder.— 2. where, there. 3. thither.— 4. whither.— 5. thitherwhere.— II. represents demonstratives and relative pronouns in union with (postponed) prepositions.— III. *conj.* with *subj. & indic.* if, though.
þæra, þære, þæs, þæs. See **þæt,** (*pron.*), **þes.**
þæt (*m.* **se,** *f.* **sêo, sio**), that: *gen. m. & n.* **þæs, þes;** *dat. m. & n.* **þâm, þæm, þân, þon;** *gen. & dat. f.* **þære, þâre, þâra** (Ps. C. 34), **þêre;**

acc. m. þane, þæne, þone, f. þâ, n. þæt; instr. m. & n. þŷ, þi, þê; pl. nom. & acc. m. & f. þâ, n. þa; gen. m. & f. þâra, þǽra, þeara; dat. m. & f. & n. þâm, þǽm, þêm, þân, þon.— I. adj. before a noun (as unaccented demons. or article: a relative in subordinate clause may refer to it).— II. subs. 1. demonstrative: phrases: gen. sg. n. þæs, on this account, therefore, for this, since; þæs, þe, see þe; þæs (before adj. & adv.), to that degree, that, so; tô þæs, see tô, w. gen.; dat. sg. n. bi (be) þâm, þon, thereon, therein; êac þâm (þân, þon), in addition to this, besides this, as also, moreover; ǽr þon þe (conj.), ere, before; æfter þâm (þân, þon), after, later, next, in or after that fashion; for þâm (þǽm, þân, þon), therefore, on that or this account, for this reason; for þâm þe, for, because; ful nêah þon, almost, nearly; on þâm, in or on that, therein, thereon; on þân þe, in this, in that; sid-dâm,— sithence, since, see sid-dan; instr. n. æfter þŷ, after (that), later; þŷ, on this account, by that, therefore; the (with comparatives, the more, &c.)— 2. relative: by attraction or ellipsis of þe, þæt becomes both relative and conj.: (a.) ellipsis of the relative þe; gen. sg. þæs (for þæs þe: Gen. 456); dat. þâm (= þâm þe: Sch. 9); gen. pl. þâra (= þâra þe: Hy. 4: 23); acc. pl. þâ (= þâ (= þâ þe: Dan. 125).— (b.) ellipsis of the conj.: þæs = þæs þe, for this, for that, because (Wald. 1: 26); as far as, as (Dan. 648); tô þæs (= tô þæs þe), thither where (whither); for þâm (= for þâm þe), for this reason that, for, because; ǽr þâm (= ǽr þâm þe), ere, before; sid-

dam (= siddan þe), after, when; þŷ (= þŷ þe), by this, by that, because (Rid. 10: 12); that, in order that (B. 242), because, as if; þŷ læs (conj.), that not, lest: see læs; for þŷ (= for þŷ þe), for this reason that, for, because.

þæt, conj. that, so that, in order that; þæt þe, that.

þætte=þæt þe: I. pron. that which. II. conj. that, so that, in order that.

þafian, w. v. to submit to, yield, accede, agree, permit.

ge-þafian, to allow, permit, grant, approve, effect; endure.

þâm, þân. See þæt (pron.).

þan, þon, adv. 1. thence, from that point or time (B. 2423).— 2. in neg. clauses w. comparative = in comparison with, beginning from that point.— 3. inasmuch as, when (Seel. Ex. 42; Gen. Ex. 42, 108).

þanan, þanon, þonan, þonon, adv. 1. thence, from there, from that time.— 2. from where, whence.— 3. of that, though that, thereof, therethrough (Ps. 67: 3).— 4. temporal: than, thereupon, henceforth.

þananne, þanonne, adv. from thence, thence. Jud. 13.

þanc, þonc, st. m. 1. thought, reflection, sentiment.— 2. grace, favor, pardon (Gen. 796; Ps. 101: 15).— 3. satisfaction with or pleasure in something.— 4. thanks.— 5. reward, recompense (Gû. 442).

þanc-hycgende, part. thoughtful, full of thought, considerate.

þancian, þoncian, w. v. to thank, recompense, reward. (Gen. 2689.) ge-þancian, to thank.

þancol, þoncol, adj. thoughtful, considerate, cautious, wise.

þancol-, þoncol-môd, adj. the same as above.

þanc-, þonc-snottor, *adj.* wise, prudent, ingenious.

þancung, *st. f.* thanking, thanksgiving.

þanc-, þonc-wyrðe, *adj.* thankworthy (worthy of thought), agreeable.

þanne, þænne, þonne, **1.** *adv.* then, there, thereupon, thereafter, henceforth; but, then, on the contrary, to be sure; — in the main clause the adv. þonne (then) corresponds to the conj. þonne (if) or gif in the subord. clause: it is sometimes found in broken discourse (anacolouthon); in questions, þonne = then (Lat. *nam.*)— II. *conj.* **1.** temporal: *w. indic. & subj.* when (quum), as, when (quando), how long, so long as, as. — **2.** in comparative clauses — than; often þonne þæt (*w. subj.*) than that; or þonne þonne, þonne gif (*w. indic.* or *subj.*), than when, than if; so after **gelice, ungelice,** &c. Sometimes the compar. is wanting in main clause. (B. 70; Exod. 337, &c.)

þanon, þanonne, þar, þâra, þâs (*pl*). See þanan, þananne, þær, þæt, (*pron.*), þes, þâw.

þâw, *st. m.* slave, servant.

þawenian, *w. v.* in
ge-þawenian, (to **thaw**), to moisten, bedew, water.

þe, *indecl. rel. particle.*—I. represents rel. pron. in all cases, sg. & pl., alone or with a demons.; verb is usually in sg. after þâra þe, of those that.—þe is often associated by attraction with pers. pron.: þe ic, I (Cri. 792); þe wê, we (Cri. 25); þe he ûsic, us that he (B. 2638); þe þû, thou (Hö. 126); þû þe, thou that (Ps. 79: 1); þe he (Ps. 67: 4); þe hêo (Jud. 6); þe his, whose, of whom (Ps. Th. 39: 4); þe þû his, whose, of whom, than (Ps. 79: 14); se þe his, he, whose, of whom (Sat. 283); þe him, to whom (Sch. 66); þe ic him, to whom I (Wîd. 133), &c.—Pronouns of 1st and 2d pers. sometimes fall out: thus, þe = þe ic (Kid. 28: 16); þe = þe þû (Hy. 10: 2); þe = þe ge (El. 577).—II. *conj.* **1.** that, because.— Phrases: þæs þe, that (Gen. 1469), for that that, because (Gen. 77); in so far, as (Cri. 74); since, after (Jud. 13); on þân þe, in this that (Ps. 118: 7); wið þân þe, against this that, in opposition to (Ps. 118: 59); ær þon þe, ere, before (Jud. 252); for þâm þe, for this reason that, for, because (Dan. 226); þŷ þe, because (Dan. 85).—**2.** or (Cri. 1307); þe — þe, either — or.— **3.** than (after comparatives: Dan. 264); the (=Ger. *je*), (Met. 10: 20). **4.** stands for þær (where), in El. 717); tô þæs þe, thither where (B. 714); ôð þe, up to, until (B. 649); þeah þe. See þeah.

þe, þec, þê. See þû, þæt (*pron.*).

þeccan, -ean, *w. v.* (to cover up?), to eat, consume.

þeccan, *w. v.* (*pret.* þehte, þeahte; *part.* þeaht), to **thatch**, bedeck, cover, cover over.
be-, bi-þeccan, same as above.
ge-þeccan, the same as above.
ofer-þeccan, the same as above.

þeccend, *part. & subs.* protector, defender.

þecele, *w. f.* torch. [roof.

þecen, *st. f.* thatch, cover, covering,

þecgan, *w. v.* in
â-þecgan, to take up or in.
ge-þecgan, to use up, consume.
of-þecgan, to snatch or take off or away.

þegan (?), to accept, take? (Gû. 140).

þêgan, *w. v.* in
ge-þêgan, to use up, consume. (Cri. 1510.)

þegen, þegn, þên, *st. m.* thane, man, liegeman, feudal vassal, knight.

þegenlice, *adv.* in knightly or manly fashion, valiantly.

þegn-scipe, *st. m.* 1. thaneship, feudal service, service.— 2. manliness. Gen. 836.

þegn-sorg, *st. f.* thane-sorrow, grief for the loss of one's men.

þegn-weorud, *st. n.* thane-troop, followers.

þegn. See þegen (thane).

þegnian, þênian, *w. v.* to serve, attend, wait on.

ge-þegnian, the same as above.

þegnung, *st. f.* serving, service.

þêgon, *pret. pl.* of þicgan (to take).

þegu, *st. f.* reception. [Used only in compounds.]

þeh. See þeah (though, yet).

þehte. See þeccan (to deck).

þel, *st. n.;* þelu, *st. f.* deal-(boards). [Used only in compounds.]

þell-fæsten, *st. n.* fastness made of deal-boards, ship, ark.

þel-trêow, *st. n.* tree? Hy. 11: 4.

þên. See þegen (thane).

þencan, -ean, *w. v.* (*pret.* þohte), to think, be of a mind, remember, intend, fancy, opine, recollect, reflect upon.

â-þencan, 1. to think out, invent, conceive.— 2. to remember, intend, wish. B. 2643.

bi-þencan, to think upon or over, ponder, remember, be minded about; to care, be apprehensive, anxious.

for-þencan, to mistrust.

ge-þencan, 1. to think.— 2. to think upon, ponder, take to heart. 3. to remember, be mindful.— 4. to think out, invent.— 5. to intend, wish.

geond-þencan, to think through or over.

ymbe-þencan, to think about, consider. Met. 10: 4.

þencan (?): Wy. 43.

þenden, þendan, þendon, þynden, I. *conj., w. indic., & subj.* during, whilst, so long as, until.— II. *adv.* meanwhile, in the interval.

þengel, *st. m.* prince, lord.

þênian. See þegnian (to serve).

þênian, þennan, *w. v.* (cf. thin), to stretch, extend, draw out, stretch forth.

â-þenian, the same as above.

be-þennan, to span, stretch on or upon.

þer. See þær (there).

þerscan, *st. abl. v.* 1. to thresh, beat, strike.

þersc-wald. See þyrsc-wold.

þes, þeos (þios), þis, *adj. & subs. pron.* this; *nom. sg. m.* þes; *f.* þêos, þios; *n.* þis, þys; *gen. m. & n.* þisses, þysses, þises; *dat. m. & n.* þissum, þyssum, þeossum, þisum, þysum, þisson, þysson, þisan, þyssan; *gen. & dat. f.* þisse, þysse; *acc. m.* þisne, þysne; *f.* þâs; *n.* þis; *instr. m. & n.* þŷs, þis; *nom. & acc. pl. m. & f.* þâs, þæs; *gen.* þissa, þyssa; *dat.* þissum, þyssum, þŷsum, þiossum.

þêwan. See þêowan (to crush).

þêah, þæh, þêh, 1. *adv.* though, yet, nevertheless, notwithstanding; swâ, sê þêah, nevertheless, however.— 2. *conj., w. indic., & subj.* though, although: (so þêah þe).

þeaht, *st. f.* 1. afterthought, reflection, thought (El. 1242).— 2. advice, counsel.

þeahtian, *w. v.* to think over, weigh, ponder.

þêam, þæm, *st. m.* steam, vapor? Sat. 179.

þêana, *adv.* nevertheless, yet;— swâ þêana, yet though, however.

þeâra, þearf. See þæt, þurfan (to need).

þearf, *st. f.* 1. need; necessaries.— 2. use, utility, profit, advantage. 3. privation, need, want (Gen.503). 4. need, distress, misery.

þearfa, *w. m.* needy one, pauper, beggar.

þearfende, *part.* the same as above.

þearfendlic, *adj.* needy, miserable.

þearfian, *w. v.* to starve, be in need, want.

    ge-þearfian, to impose compulsion, necessity, or force upon.

þearflice, *adv.* according to need or necessity? carefully? Met. 1: 60.

þearl, *adj.* violent, strict, harsh, vigorous, bold.

þearle, *adv.* violently, very, extremely.

þearlic, *adv.* harsh, violent, grievous.

þearl-môd, *adj.* harsh-minded, of violent spirit.

þeaw, *st. m.* (thew), custom, habit, usage.

þeaw-fæst, *adj.* virtuous, moral, honorable.

þeo. See þeod, þeoh, þeow.

þeod, þiod, *st. f.* folk, population, nation;—in *pl.* also people.

þeod, *st. f.* training, rearing, chastisement? Az. 171; Gn. Ex. 18.

þeodan, þiodan, þiedan, þýdan, *w. v.* in

    ge-þeodan, to associate with, join; to give up or away.

    ôd-þeodan, to separate, sever.

    under-þeodan, to subjugate, to subject.

þeod-bealu, *st. n.* misfortune affecting a whole people; general misfortune.

þeod-bûend, *part. & subs.* earth-inhabiter, human being.

þeod-cwên, *st. f.* people's queen.

þeod-cyning, *st. m.* people's king, king of nations, God. Seel. 12.

þeod-egsa, *w. m.* people's terror, general or great terror.

þeoden, þioden, *st. m.* people's lord, king (temporal and eternal).

þeoden-ge-dâl, *st. n.* separation from one's lord (through his death).

þeoden-hold, *adj.* pleasing to or well-disposed toward one's lord.

þeoden-lêas, *adj.* lordless, bereft of one's lord.

þeoden-mâdum, -mâdm, *st. m.* jewel or gift given by the chief to his men.

þeoden-stôl, *st. m.* prince's stool, throne.

þeod-fruma, *w. m.* prince of the people or of nations.

þeod-ge-strêon, *st. n.* people's treasure, great treasure.

þeod-guma, *w. m.* man of the people.

þeod-here, *st. m.* host, army of the people.

þeodisc, *st. n.* speech, language. Cf. *Deutsch.*

þeod-land, *st. n.* folk's land, neighborhood, province.

þeod-mægen, *st. n.* folk's might, power, host, cohort, division.

þeod-mearc, *st. m.* folk's march, section, division of land, land.

þeod-sceada, *w. m.* folk-scather, foe of the people, robber.

þeod-scipe, *st. m.* 1. folk, population. 2. assembly, company, community (Jul. 178).—3. discipline, training, administration, constitution, law.

þeod-stefn, *st. m.* tribe, nation.

þeod-þrea, *st. m. & n.* misery of the people, general distress.

þeod-wiga, *w. m.* popular hero.

þeod-wundor, *st. n.* people's wonder, great marvel.

þeof, *st. m.* thief, robber.

þeoh, þêo, *st. n.* thigh, hip.

þeon, þion, *st. abl. v.* VI. to thrive, grow, grow up, prosper, be profitable, advantageous, able.

ge-þeon, to thrive, prosper, grow (up), increase, grow in power and influence. [cessful.
   mis-þeon, to thrive ill, be unsuc-
   on-þeon, to grow forth, grow, escape, thrive, stand successfully.
þeon, *w. v.* to commit, perform, execute.
   ge-þeon, the same as above.
þeon, þeo-nŷd. See **þeowan, þeownŷd.**
þeos. See **þes** (this).
þeoster, þŷster, þeostru, þiostru, (cf. Ger. *düster*), *st. n. & f.* darkness, gloom, obscurity.
þeoster-côfa, *w. m.* dark space or room.
þeoster-loca, *w. m.* dark lock-up, hold; custody.
þeostre, þŷstre, *adj.* dark, gloomy, obscure; sad, mournful.
þeossum. See **þes** (this).
þeotan, *st. abl. v.* VI. **1.** to howl.— **2.** to be noisy, rave, rage, roar. Rid. 39: 4.
þeow, þeo, *st. m.* slave, servant; arranger, disposer.
þeow, *adj.* slavish, servile.
þeowa, þiowa, *w. m.* slave, servant.
þeowan, þeon, þŷwan, þŷan, þewan, þiwan, *w. v.* to crush, push, urge, oppress, check.
   for-þeon, to press out, crush, suppress, oppress.
   ge-þeowan, to press, crush, push, oppress, overwhelm, check, crush down.
þeowan, *w. v.* to serve, wait on.
þeow-dôm, *st. m.* service, servitude, slavery.
þeowe, *w. f.* maid, female servant.
þeowen, *st. f.* the same as above.
þeowene, *w. f.* the same as above.
þeowet, þeowot, *st. m. & n.* service (general or menial).
þeowian, þiowian, *w. v.* to serve, minister, help, assist.

þeow-mennen, *st. n.* maid, female servant.
þeow-nêd, -nŷd, *st. f.* slavery, servitude.
þicce, *adj.* **thick,** close, dense.
þicce, *adv.* **1.** thickly, closely, richly. **2.** frequently. Gen. 684.
þicgan, -ean, *st. abl. v.* III. to take, touch, appropriate, eat, accept, receive.
   ge-þicgan, the same as above.
   ôd-þicgan, to withdraw, snatch or take away.
þicgan, þycgan, *w. v.* to take, accept, appropriate, eat.
þiclice, *adv.* frequently.
þider, þyder, *adv.* thither.
þider-weard, *adv.* thitherward.
þigde, *pret.* of *w. v.* **þicgan** (to take).
þigen, þin, *st. f.* **1.** eating, consumption of food.— **2.** food.
þignen, þinen, *st. f.* maid, female servant.
þihan, *st. abl. v.* V. to thrive, grow, increase, progress, succeed, help, benefit. (Ger. *deihen*.)
   ge-þihan, the same as above.
   on-þihan, *w. gen.* to derive benefit from.
þihtig, þin. See **þyhtig, þû, þigen.**
þin, þŷn, *poss. pron.* thy, thine. Cf. **þû.**
þinc, þincg, þincan. See **þing, þyncan.**
þindan, *st. abl. v.* I. to swell, swell up; melt, pass away (wrongly,— through confusion between *tabescere* and *tumescere.* Ps. 111: 9; 118: 158.
   â-þindan, to swell (up), increase; melt, pass away.
þinen. See **þignen** (maid).
þing, þincg, þinc, *st. n.* **1. thing,** object, venture, deed, enterprise, event; one's affairs, condition, circumstances;— **ælces þinges,** entirely, in every regard;— **nænige**

þinga, in no regard, by no means. 2. thing, assembly, judicial assembly.—3. *instr. pl.* þingum, powerfully, violently.

þingan, *st. abl. v.* I. to thrive, prosper, have repute.

   ge-þingan, to wax, grow, thrive, increase (in power, authority, &c.)

   ofer-þingan (?), to outwit, overcome, vanquish.

   on-þingan, to grow out of or forth from, to escape, endure successfully.

þingan, *w. v.* in

   ge-þingan, 1. to negotiate, treat (for), to seek help and support (tô, at, from. B. 1837).—2. to prescribe, institute, appoint.—3. to resolve, include, design, purpose, undertake. Dôm. 5.

þing-ge-mearc, *st. n.* marking off or characterizing a certain thing;—reckoning of time, chronology.

þingian, *w. v.* 1. *w. dat.* (Ger. *dingen*), to beg, pray, ask, intercede for.—2. *w. acc.* to conciliate, smooth over, lay aside, expiate, atone for; feo (compound with money. B. 156, 470).—3. to speak, make a public speech.— 4. to sojourn, dwell? Sat. 447.

   ge-þingian, 1. *intrans.* to beg, ask, supplicate pardon or grace (Jul. 198).— 2. *w. dat.* to pray, beg, ask, intercede for (Cri. 342).— 3. to reconcile (Jul. 717).—4. to smooth over or appease a quarrel (Cri. 616). 5. to unite, conclude a treaty (Gn. Ex. 57).— 6. to conclude, purpose, design. Sat. 598.

þing-ræden, *st. f.* 1. mediation, intercession, intervention.—2. bride-wooing? Jul. 126.

þing-stede, *st. m.* thing-place, assembly or place of parliament.

þinne. See þynne (thin).

þinra? Met. 16: 8.

þirel, þirsced, þirst, þis, þís, þisa, þisan, þises. See þyrel, þerscan, þyrst, þes.

þisla, *w. m.* pole (of a wagon), thill, shaft. Met. 28: 10. (Ger. *deichsel.*)

þisne, þissa, þissan, þisse, þisses, þisson, þissum, þisum, þislic, þistrian, þiwan. See þes, þyslic, þýstrian, þeowan.

þiedan. See þeodan.

þiod, þiodan, þioden, þiodisc, þion, þios, þiestro, þiotan, þiowa, þiowian. See þeod, þeodan, þeoden, þeodisc, þeon, þes, þeostor, þeotan, þeowa, þeowian.

þohte, *pret.* of þencan (to think).

þolian, *w. v.* 1. *w. acc.* to thole, endure, suffer, bear;—to grant, allow, admit, permit (Gen. 597).— 2. *w. gen.* to do without, dispense with.—3. *intrans.* to persevere, persist, stand out.

   â-þolian, to vanish, pass away.

   for-þolian, to dispense with, do without.

   ge-þolian, 1. to thole, endure, suffer, fear.— 2. to await patiently, persevere.—3. *w. gen.* to do without, dispense with. Sat. 237.

þon, þonan, þonon, þonc, þonc-, þoncian, þoncol, þonne. See þan, þanan, þanc, þancian, þancol, þanne.

þorn, *st. m.* thorn;—also, name for the Rune þ.

þracu, *st. f.* onrush, attack, pressure, fury, conflict.

þræc-heard, *adj.* valiant in combat, strong in battle.

þræc-hwil, *st. f.* time of combat or misery.

þræc-rôf, *adj.* able or strenuous in fight.

þræc-wig, *st. m.* violent combat.

þræc-, þrec-wudu, *st. m.* battle-wand, spear.

þræd, *st. m.* thread.

þræft, *st. n.* loquacity, garrulousness;—eagerness to contend or quarrel.

þrægan, *w. v.* to run, move swiftly, race.

þræstan, *w. v.* in
ge-þræstan, to trouble, grieve, oppress.

þráfian, *w. v.* to shove, crowd, press, urge.

þrág, þráh, *st. f.* 1. course, running, race (Rid. 82: 4; Ph. 68).—2. course or space of time, time; order or condition of things, fate; bad time(s), (B. 2883).—Phrases: *acc. sg.* þráge, some time, long time; ealle þráge, all the time, continually;—lytle þráge, for a little time;—*instr. pl.* þrágum, some time, at times, sometimes.

þrág-bysig, *adj.* busy with, engaged in, fond of running (?).

þrág-mǽlum, *adv.* from time to time, at times.

þrec, þremma, þresc-wald. See þræcwudu, þyrmma, þyrscwold.

þréa, *st. m., f., & n.* menace, threat, invective, attack, oppression, disturbance, terror, evil, need, misfortune.

þréagan, þréan, *w. v.* to threaten, menace, attack, scold, chastise, torture.
ge-þréan, to torture, torment, chastise, oppress, press.

þréalic, *adj.* terrible, threatening, calamitous.

þréa-nýd, -nied, -néd, *st. f.* (*n.?*), crushing necessity, misery, need, distress, calamity, danger.

þréa-nýdlic, -niedlic, *adj.* the same as above.

þréa-nýdla, -niedla, -nédla, *w. m.* misery, violence, distress, opposition.

þrét, *st. f.* the same as above. Cf. threat.

þréat, *st. m.* crowd, troop, band, force.

þréat (?), part of a loom. Rid. 36: 6.

þréatian, *w. v.* to fall upon, attack, press, press forward, oppress, cause misery to, force.
ge-þréatian, the same as above.

þréa-weorc, *st. n.* tribulation, misery, deed of oppression.

þréo. See þri (three).

þreodian, þrydian, *w. v.* to think over, reflect upon, cogitate, ponder.

þreohtig, *adj.* persistent, persevering, laborious.

þréo-niht, *st. f.* period of three nights. Cf. fortnight.

þréora, *gen.* of þri (three).

þreostru, þriostru, þrystru, *st. f.* or *st. n. pl.* (Lat. *tristis?*), gloom, darkness.

þréotan, *st. abl. v.* VI. in
á-þréotan, 1. *impers.* to produce annoyance or disgust; to be weary or disgusted.—2. *pers.* to be weary of or disgusted with something.

þréo-tene, -tyne, *num.* thirteen.

þréo-téoða, þréot-téoða, *num. adj.* thirteenth.

þréowan, *st. abl. v.* VI. in
á-þréowan, to excite, stir up, press out, spill, shed? An. 1427.

þreowian. See þrowian.

þri, þrie, þrio, þria, þréo, þrý, *num.* three;—*nom. & acc. m.* þri, þrý; *f.* þréo; *n.* þréo, þrio, þria;—*gen.* þriora, þréora; *dat.* þrim, þrým.

þriccan. See þryccan (to crush).

þridda, *num. adj.* third.

þri-, þrie-feald, *adj.* threefold.

þrim, þrim. See þrym, þri (three).

þrindan, þrintan, *st. abl. v.* I. to be swelled, swollen up.
á-þrintan, the same as above.

þri-, þrý-nes, *st. f.* threeness, trinity.

þringan, *st. abl. v.* I. to **throng**, press, press on, move violently; to hurry, hasten, break forth;— also *w. acc.* to urge, crowd, crowd upon. Luc. 8: 45; Marc. 5: 24–31.

 â-þringan, 1. to crowd or throng out, push out.— 2. to rush forth, break out.

 æt-þringan, to snatch or take away, extort from.

 be-, bi-þringan, to crowd, urge, press on from all sides, surround.

 for-þringan, to extort, press out of, take from, defend against.

 ge-þringan, 1. *intrans.* to throng, press, press one's self, hurry.— 2. *w. acc.* to press, oppress, press out of, extort, overcome.— 3. to swell up (Wid. 84: 2).

 on-þringan, 1. to press on or forward. — 2. to be or become moved, to move. Gû. 1300.

 ôd-þringan, to force or press out of, from, take away.

 tô-þringan, to press in two or to pieces, to drive asunder.

 ymb-þringan, to press around, throng about.

þrintan. See þrindan (to swell).

þri-rêdre-cêol, *st. m.* galley with three banks of oars, trireme.

þrist, þriste, *adj.* bold, daring, rash, confident, resolute, audacious.

þriste, *adv.* the same as above.

þrist-hycgende, *part.* bold of spirit, valiant-minded.

þrist-hydig, *adj.* the same as above.

þristlíce, *adv.* boldly, daringly.

þri-tig, þrit-tig, *num.* **thirty**.

þrid, þridu. See þryd (strength).

þriwa, *adv.* thrice.

þria, þrie, þrio, þriostru. See þri, þreostru.

þroht, *st. m.* effort, exertion, trouble, difficulty.

þroht, *adj.* difficult, dire, troublesome, tormenting.

þroht-heard, *adj.* 1. strong in enduring, able to bear torture, patient. 2. hard to bear. An. 1141.

þrosm, *st. m.* steam, fume, vapor, smoke.

þrowere, *st. m.* endurer, martyr.

þrowian, þreowian, *w. v.* to endure, bear, suffer.

 ge-þrowian, the same as above.

þrowing, þrowung, *st. f.* suffering, passion, **throe**, endurance.

þrý. See þri (three).

þryccan, þriccan, (Ger. *drücken*), *w. v.* 1. *trans.* to crush (Met. 4: 38). 2. *intrans.* to press, urge (Gû. 256).

 bi-þryccan, to becrush, crush down, oppress.

 for-þryccan, the same as above.

 of-þryccan, the same as above.

þrydian. See þreodian (to reflect on)

þrydig, *adj.* heedful, thoughtful, considerate.

þrym, prim, *st. m.* 1. (properly) noisy troop, band, multitude, host, chorus. — 2. noise, uproar, tumult, storm, violence. — 3. might, power, strength, ability.— 4. glory, beauty, majesty, brilliancy.— 5. the Glorious (epithet of God).

þrym-cyme, *st. m.* glorious **coming**, arrival.

þrym-cyning, *st. m.* **king** of glory, God.

þrym-fæst, *adj.* glorious, illustrious, noble, mighty, able.

þrym-ful, *adj.* the same as above.

þrymlic, *adj.* the same as above.

þrymlíce, *adv.* the same as above.

þrymma, *w. m.* brave man, hero.

þrym-sittende, *pret.* throned in glory, dwelling in heaven.

þrýnes. See þrínes (trinity).

þrysman, *w. v.* in

 â-þrysman, to suffocate, stifle with smoke; to cover over.

þrystru. See þreostru (darkness).

þrýd, þríd, þrýdu, þrídu, *st. f.* strength, power, might, abundance, excellence, glory, splendor.

þrýd-ærn, *st. n.* glorious house, king's palace.

þrýd-bearn, *st. n.* strong son, youth.

þrýd-bord, *st. n.* strong shield.

þrýd-cyning, *st. m.* king of glory.

þrýd-full, *adj.* strong, brave.

þrýd-ge-steald, *st. n.* great wealth, splendid dwelling.

þrýdian, *w. v.* in
ge-þrýdian, to invigorate, to strengthen, harden, temper? Ph. 486.

þrýdlíc, *adj.* noble, excellent, valiant.

þrýd-swíd, -swýd, *adj.* strong and powerful.—["great pain or grief." Grein.]

þrýdu, -þrýdo. See þrýd (might).

þrýd-weorc, *st. n.* strong or firm piece of work, fortification.

þrýd-word, *st. n.* chosen word, excellent speech.

þú, *pron.* thou; *gen.* þín; *dat.* þé; *acc.* þec, þé.

þúf, *st. m.* flag, pennant, field-ensign.

þúhte, *pret.* of þyncan (to seem).

þuncan, *w. v.* in
be-þuncan, to trouble one's self about, to care.

þunian, *w. v.* 1. (cf. Ger. *dehnen*), to stretch, extend, swell, strut.— 2. to thunder, roar, groan, crash.
on-þunian, to swell up, move around? Rid. 41:91.

þunor, *st. m.* thunder. [der.

þunor-rád-stefn, *st. f.* voice of thun-

þunrian, *w. v.* to thunder.

þun-wang, -wange, -wenge, *st. n.* (the) temples of the head.

þuren. See þweran (to hammer, &c.)

þurfan (Ger. *dürfen*), *pret. pres., indic.* 1, 3. þearf.— 2. þearft; *pl.* þurfon; *subj. sg.* þurfe; *pl.* þurfe, þyrfen; *pret.* þorfte.— 1. *w. inf.* in neg. clauses = not to need, not to require.— 2. *w. inf.* in affirm. clauses = to need, require, have reason.— 3. *w. gen.* or *acc.* = to be in need of, to require.— 4. absolutely = to need (Dan. 430).
be-, bi-þurfan, to need, require, be in need of.

þurh, þurg, þuruh, I. *prep.* through.
1. *space:* through.— 2. *time:* through, during.— 3. *means:* through, by means of.— 4. *effective cause:* in consequence of, in conformity with.— 5. accompanying circumstances.— 6. for the sake of, in the name of (w. verbs of begging, asking, conjuring, swearing, &c.)— 7. *end or aim:* with a view to, in behalf of.—
II. *adv.* through, throughout.

þurh-hát, *adj.* hot through and through.

þurst, *st. m.* thirst.

þurstig, *adj.* thirsty, greedy, desirous.

þus, *adv.* thus, so.

þúsend, *num.* thousand.

þúsend-ge-rím, *st. n.* calculation by thousands.

þúsend-mælum, *adv.* thousand-meal or fold; in thousands.

þweran, *st. abl. v.* II. to thicken, to render compact by blows; to forge, to render malleable, make tractable.
ge-þweran, the same as above.

þwerian, þweorian, *w. v.* in
ge-þwerian, to soften, reconcile, to render accordant, make harmonious.

þweahan, þwéan, *st. abl. v.* IV. to wash, wash off, cleanse.
á-þwéan, the same as above.

þweorh, *adj.* thwart, bent, crooked, twisted, cross.

þweorh-téme, -týme, -time, *adj.* crooked, twisted;— cross, savage, truculent, defiant.

þweorian. See þwerian (to soften).

þwitan, *st. abl. v.* V. to cut out or off, to excise.
þý = þeow, *st. m.* slave, servant? Gn. Ex. 50.
þý, þy, þýan, þycgan, þýdan, þyder. See þæt (*pron.*), þe, þeowan, þicgan, þeodan, þider.
þyhtig, þihtig, *adj.* doughty, strong, able.
þyle, *st. m.* speaker, spokesman, leader of the conversation at court.
þylman, *w. v.* in
  for-þylman, to surround, shut in, inclose.
þýn. See þin (thine).
þyncan, þyncean, þincan, (Ger. *dünken*), *w. v.* (*pret.* þúhte), to seem, appear. Cf. methinks.
  ge-þyncan, the same as above.
  of-þyncan, to displease, wound, insult.
þynden. See þenden (while, &c.)
þynne, þinne, *adj.* thin.
þyr, *adj.* dry, arid. (Ger. *dürr*.)
þyrel, þyrl, *adj.* perforated, pierced with holes. Cf. nos-tril = nose-thyrel.
þyrel, *st. n.* perforation, opening, aperture.
þyrel-wamb, *adj.* with pierced belly.
þyrl. See þyrel (pierced).
þyrnen, *adj.* thorny.
þyrran, *w. v.* to dry, render dry. (Ger. *dürren*.)
þyrs, *st. m.* giant.
þyrsc-wold, þersc-, þerx-, þrescwald, *st. m.* threshing-wood, threshold.
þyrst, þirst, *st. m.* thirst.
þyrstan, *w. v.* to thirst.
þys, þýs. See þes (this).
þyslic, *adj.* thus-like, in this manner.
þysne, þyssa, þyssan, þysse, þysses, þysson, þyssum, þysum. See þes. [tre.
þýster, þýstre. See þeoster, þeos-
þýstrian, þistrian, *w. v.* in
  á-þistrian, to darken, obscure.
þýtan, *w. v.* in
  á-þýtan, to toot, blow the horn.
þýwan. See þeowan (to serve).

U

ufan, ufon, *adv.* 1. from above.— 2. above.
ufan-cund, *adj.* coming or originating from above.
ufane, *adv.* above.
ufera, *compar. adj.* later, posterior.
ufe-weard, *adj.* upward, ascending.
ufor, *adv.* higher; later in time, subsequent, posterior.
uht-cearu, *st. f.* night-grief, sorrow at morn or night.
uhte, *w. f.* early morn, morning twilight, dawn.
uht-floga, *w. m.* flying in the twilight (dawn or dusk).
uht-hlem, *st. m.* cry at morn, tumult or conflict at dawn.
uht-sceaða, *w. m.* twilight foe, robber in the dark.
uht-tid, *st. f.* twilight tide, dawn tide.
umbor, *st. n.* young child, babe newborn.
un-ædele, *adj.* not noble, not famous.
un-âga, *w. m.* unowning, one that owns nothing, poor.
un-âr, *st. f.* unhonor, lack of honor, dishonor.
un-ârlic, *adj.* dishonorable, dishonest.
un-ârlice, *adv.* 1. dishonorably, dishonestly.— 2. unmercifully.
un-â-secgendlic, *adj.* unspeakable, unutterable.

un-â-þreotend, *part.* unwearied, assiduous, persistent.
un-â-wendend, *part.* unchangeable, unceasing.
un-â-wendendlic, same as above.
un-be-fohten, *part.* undisputed, unimpeached.
un-bêted, *part.* unexpiated (bootless), uncompensated.
un-beald, *adj.* unbold, distrustful, cowardly.
un-bealu, *st. n.* innocence.
un-bi-þyrfe, *adj.* inactive, useless, idle, vain.
un-blîde, *adj.* 1. unblithe, joyless. 2. unfriendly, unkind.
un-bræce, *adj.* that can not be broken, infrangible, imperishable.
un-bryce, -brice, *adj.* same as above.
un-brŷce, *adj.* that can not be used, useless, worthless. Cf. Ger. *brauchen*
un-bunden, *part.* unbound.
un-byrnende, *part.* not burning.
unc, uncer. See wit (we two).
uncer, *possess. pron.* of or belonging to us two.
un-cêapunga, *adv.* gratuitously, gratis, without pay.
un-clǣne, *adj.* unclean, impure.
un-clǣnnis, *st. f.* uncleanness.
un-cûd, *adj.* 1. unknown, strange.— 2. unheard of, unusual (B. 876).— 3. uncertain, undetermined (Hy. 11: 4).— 4. unfriendly, unkind, rough, uncouth, unwieldy.
un-cyst, *st. f.* mistake, error, crime, loathsomeness.
un-cŷddu, *st. f.* unknown land, foreign land.
un-cŷdig, *adj.* 1. ignorant, unacquainted with (El. 961).—2. strange, alien, without participation in (Gû. 1199).
under, I. *prep., w. dat. & acc.* under, below, beneath.— II. *adv.* below, underneath.

un-derne, -dyrne, *adj.* unconcealed, not hidden, well known.
un-derne, -dyrne, *adv.* the same as above.
undern-mǣl, *st. n.* noontide, midday.
under-nîdemest, *adj. superl. adj.* lowest of all.
under-stadol-fæst, *adj.* unsteady, inconstant, vacillating.
un-dearninga, -nunga, *adv.* without concealment, openly.
un-dyrne. See underne (well known)
un-efen, *adj.* uneven, unlike.
un-efne, *adv.* same as above. [*arg.*]
un-earg, *adj.* uncowardly, bold. (Ger.
un-êade, *adj.* uneasy, not easy, with difficulty, hard.
un-fǣcne, *adj.* without cunning or fraud, sincere, honest.
un-fǣge, *adj.* not "fey," not near to death.
un-fæger, *adj.* unfair, unlovely, unlovable.
un-fǣgre, *adv.* the same as above.
un-fǣle, *adj.* uncanny, unlovely, not good.
un-feor, *adj.* unfar, not far.
un-flitme, *adj.* without rival, invincible, not to be opposed (B. 1097, 1129).
un-for-cûd, *adj.* not to be despised, not wrong, honorable, noble.
un-for-cûdlice, *adv.* same as above.
un-forht, *adj.* fearless, bold, unterrified.
un-fremu, *st. f.* something deadly or pernicious.
un-frêondlice, *adv.* unkindly, in an unfriendly manner.
un-fricgende, *part.* uninquiring, not questioning.
un-frôd, *adj.* not aged, young.
un-from, *adj.* unfit, unambitious, inactive, not brave.
un-fyrn, *adv.* unfar off, soon.
un-ge-bletsod, *part.* unblessed.
un-ge-blŷged, *part.* unterrified.

un-ge-dêfelice, *adv.* unduly, unfittingly, contrary to right and custom.
un-ge-fullod, *part.* unfulfilled.
un-ge-lêaf, *adj.* unbelieving.
un-ge-lic, *adj.* unlike.
un-ge-lice, *adv.* the same as above.
un-ge-mêde, *adj.* incompatible, intolerant.
un-ge-met, *st.* over-measure, excess, superfluity; — *adv. gen. sg.* ungemetes, and *instr. pl.* ungemetum, excessively, extremely, very. [ive.
un-ge-met, *adj.* immoderate, excess-
un-ge-met, -gemete, *adv.* the same as above.
un-ge-myndig, *adj.* unmindful, heedless of.
un-ge-sǽlig, *adj.* unhappy, wretched.
un-ge-sceâd, *adv.* undauntedly, intrepidly, exceedingly. (Ger. *ungescheidt.*)
un-ge-sewenlic, *adj.* unseen, invisible.
un-ge-sib, *adj.* unrelated, not trusted, not intimate, not befriended, not familiar.
un-ge-trêow, *adj.* untrue, faithless.
un-ge-þêod, -þeoded, *part.* un-united, disunited.
un-ge-wemmed, *part.* unspotted, uninjured, unblemished.
un-ge-wyrded, *part.* uninjured, unhurt.
un-geâra, *adv.* 1. not long ago, lately. Cf. yore.— 2. without delay or procrastination: shortly, soon.
un-gearu, *adj.* unready, unprepared.
un-gifede, -gyfede, *adj.* ungiven, not lent, not belonging to.
un-gifre, *adj.* mischievous, destructive, pernicious.
un-gin, *adj.* not great or broad (Gû. Ex. 206).
un-glêaw, *adj.* not loitering or dilatory (from reflection), not quick, regardless, reckless? B. 2564.

un-glêawlice, *adv.* unwisely, ignorantly.
un-gnyde, *adj.* not niggardly or economical, not sparing.
un-gôd, *adj.* not good.
un-grêne, *adj.* ungreen, not green.
un-grund, *adj.* without ground or bottom, unfathomable, unmeasurable. [less.
un-grynde, *adj.* groundless, bottom-
un-gyfede. See ungifede (ungiven).
un-hǽlu, *st. f.* unwholesomeness, mischief, destruction.
un-hâl, *adj.* unhale, unwhole, weak, unsound.
un-hâr, *adj.* hairless, bald.
un-heore, -hiore, -hŷre, *adj.* (Ger. *ungeheuer*), monstrous, unlovely, uncanny, horrible.
un-heore, -hiore, *adv.* same as above.
un-hlêow, *adj.* offering no protection or defense.
un-hlitme (B. 1129, for unflitme).
un-hnêaw, *adj.* not sparing, generous, liberal.
unhold, *adj.* ungracious, unfavorable. (Ger. *unhold.*)
unholda, *w. m.* monster, devil.
un-hwilen, *adj.* untemporary, eternal
un-hydig, *adj.* unwise, unheedful, ignorant.
un-hyldo, *st. f.* disfavor, disgrace. (Ger. *unhuld.*)
un-hŷre. See unheore (horrible).
un-hydig, *adj.* profitless, unlucky, unhappy.
un-lǽd, -lǽde, *adj.* poor, wretched, unhappy.
un-lǽred, *part.* unlearned, untaught.
un-lǽt, *adj.* unwearied, indefatigable, restive.
un-land, -lond, *st. n.* unland, no land; — falsely taken (for land). Wal. 14.
un-lêof, *adj.* unlief, not dear.
un-lide, *adj.* harsh, hard. (Ger. *lind.*)

un-lifigende, -lifgende, -lyfigende, *part.* unliving, lifeless, dead.
un-lust, *st. m.* disgust, displeasure, disinclination.
un-lyt, *n.* not or no little.
un-lytel, *adj.* unlittle, not little, very large.
un-mǽg, *st. m.* (a) non-relation, stranger, alien.
un-mǽge, *adj.* unrelated, not akin.
un-mǽle, *adj.* unspotted, unblemished, immaculate.
un-mǽne, *adj.* unmean, not criminal, innocent, pure.
un-mǽte, *adj.* unmeasured, excessive, immense, great.
un-mendlinga, -myndlinga, *adv.* unexpectedly.
un-meaht, -miht, *st. f.* unmight, weakness.
un-meahtig, -mehtig, *adj.* unmighty, weak.
un-murn, *adj.* careless, untroubled.
un-murnlice, *adv.* untroubled, unmourning, careless, fearless.
unnan, *pret. pres. sg.* 1, 3. an, ann, onn.— 2. unne; *pl.* unnon; *pret.* ûde.— 1. (Ger. *gönnen*), to grant, give, present, lend.— 2. to be glad to see, to wish, to desire.
 ge-unnan, the same as above.
 of-unnan, to begrudge, grudge, envy.
un-neah, *adj.* unnear, far.
un-nyt, -net, *adj.* useless, worthless, idle, vain, (Ger. *unnütz.*)
un-ofer-swided, *part.* unvanquished, unconquered.
un-orne, *adj.* old, obsolete, wornout, decrepid.
un-rǽd, *st. m.* bad counsel, ill-advised or injurious act, folly.
un-rǽden, *adj.* the same as above.
un-rǽd-sid, *st. m.* act of folly, foolish enterprise.
un-riht, *adj.* unright, unjust, wrong.

un-riht, -ryht, *st. n.* unright, injustice, badness, evil, sin.
un-riht-dôm, *st. m.* unrighteousness, wrong.
un-riht-feoung, -fioung, *st. f.* unrighteous hate, hatred.
un-riht-hæmed, *st. n.* unrighteous connection, adultery, fornication.
un-rihtlice, *adj.* unjustly, partially, unrightly.
un-riht-wis, *adj.* unrighteous, unwise, ignorant.
un-riht-wyrhta, *w. m.* worker of unright, injustice, sinner.
un-rim, *st. n.* immense number.
un-rim, *adj.* numberless, innumerable
un-rôt, *adj.* joyless, sad.
un-rôtnes, *st. f.* sadness.
un-ryht. See unriht (unright).
un-sǽd, *adj.* unsated, insatiable.
un-sǽlig, *adj.* 1. unhappy, wretched. 2. mischievous, pernicious. Gen. 637.
un-scende, -scynde, *adj.* not injuring, blameless, not to be ashamed of or despised.
un-sceamig, -scamig, *adj.* without shame, disgrace, or crime.
un-sceamlice, -scomlice, *adv.* unchastely, dissolutely.
un-scyldig, *adj.* innocent, guiltless, debtless. (Ger. *unschuldig.*) [less.)
un-scynde. See unscende (blame-
un-slâw, *adj.* unslow, stirring, active.
un-smêde, *adj.* unsmooth, rough.
un-snyttro, *st. f.* unwisdom, folly. ignorance.
un-soden, *part.* unsodden, not boiled or cooked.
un-sôfte, 1. *adv.* unsoftly, ungently, harshly, bitterly.— 2. with effort, hardly, scarcely.
un-sôd-fæst, *adj.* unjust, unrighteous.
un-sôd-fæst-nes, -nys, *st. f.* injustice, unrighteousness.

un-spêdig, *adj.* unfruitful, infertile.
un-stille,*adj.*unstill,unquiet,uneasy.
un-swǽse, *adj.* unpleasant, disagreeable, ungenial.
un-swǽslic,*adj.*ungentle,not sweet, wretched.
un-swête, *adj.* unsweet.
un-sweotule, *adj.* invisible, unrecognizable, indistinct.
un-swiciende, *part.* imperishable, untransitory. [ly.
un-swidor, *compar. adv.* less violent-
un-sȳfre, *adj.* unclean, untidy, dirty. (Ger. *unsauber*.)
un-sȳfre, *adv.* the same as above.
un-syn, *adj.* unsinning, innocent.
unsynnig, *adj.* the same as above.
un-tǽle, *adj.* blameless.
un-teorig, -tiorig, *adj.* untiring, unceasing.
un-traglice, *adj.* without reserve or fraud.
un-trêow, *st. f.* untruth, unfaithfulness.
un-trêowđ, -trȳowđ, *st. f.* same as above.
un-trum, *adj.* not strong, weak, infirm.
un-trymnes, *st. f.* weakness, feebleness, infirmity.
un-twêo, *adj.* undoubted.
un-twêod, *part.* unwavering, unvacillating.
un-twêo-feald, *adj.* sincere, without duplicity.
un-twêonde, *part.* not doubting, unwavering.
untyddre, *adj.* not pliant or flexible, firm, unbending.
un-tyder, *st. m.* evil race, race of monsters. B. 111.
un-þanc, *st. m.* disinclination, aversion.
un-þêaw, *st. m.* immorality, wickedness.
un-þinged, *part.* uncalled, unsummoned, unchallenged.

un-wâclic, *adj.* unweakly, strong, firm, unyielding.
un-wâclice, *adv.* the same as above.
un-wǽr, *adj.* unwary, incautious, careless.
un-wǽrlice,*adv.* the same as above.
un-wǣstm-bǣre, *adj.* unfruitful.
un-wemme, *adj.* unblemished, without spot, uninjured.
un-wên, *adj.* unweening, hopeless.
un-wered, *part.* unprotected, uncovered, unclothed.
un-wearnum, *adv.* irresistibly.
un-weaxen, *part.* unwaxen, not grown up or full grown.
un-weord,*adj.* unworth, not valued, not dear.
un-willa, *w. m.* unwillingness.
un-wis, *adj.* unwise, ignorant, uninformed.
un-wislice, *adv.* the same as above.
un-wita, *w. m.* unwit, iguoramus.
un-wiotod, *part.* unallotted, not determined.
un-wrecen, *part.* unwreaked, unavenged.
un-wundod, *part.* unwounded, not wounded.
un-wurdlice, *adv.* unworthily.
un-wyrđe, *adj.* the same as above.
up, upp, *adv.* 1. up, upward.— 2. above.—(ûp, ûpp?)
up-cund, *adj.* originating above, celestial, supernal.
up-cyme, *st. m.* upcome, rising, origin, source.
up-ende, *st. m.* upper-end; vertex; polar region.
up-engel, *st. m.* angel above, angel of heaven.
up-eard, *st. m.* upper yard, mansion above, heaven.
up-gang, *st. m.* up-going, origin, beginning.
up-ganga, *st. m.* the same as above.
up-ge-mynd, *st. n.* upward-thinking, contemplation of things above.

up-hebbe, w. f. wáter-hen, coot, fulica chloropus.
up-hêah, adj. uplifted, high, elevated.
up-heofon, st. m. heaven above.
up-lang, adj. uplong, upright, erect.
up-, upplic, adj. above, upper, uplifted, celestial, supreme.
up-lyft, st. f. (the lift), upper air, ether.
upon, adv. from above.
upp. See up.
uppan, adv. & prep. upon, over, above; moreover, besides.
uppe, adj. above, atop, high up, exalted.
uppe, adv. above.
up-, upp-riht, adj. upright.
up-rôdor, -râdor, st. m. upper heaven, ether, firmament.
up-stige, st. m. upgoing, ascent, ascension to heaven.
up-weg, st. m. way up, ascent.
up-weard, adj. upward.
up-weardes, adv. upwards.
ur, adv. once, formerly? Cri. 806; El. 1266.
ûr, st. m. aur, aurochs; also, name of Rune û.
ûre, possess. pron. our, ours. Cf. wê.
ûrig-feđera, adj. dewy-feathered.
ûrig-lâst, adj. leaving moist tracks.
ûs, ûsic, ussic, ûser, usser. See wê (we).

ûser, usser, possess. pron. of us, our, ours.
ût, adv. 1. out (hither or thither). 2. outside, without.
utan. See wutan (let us [go]).
ûtan, ûton, adv. outside, without, from without.
ûtan-weard, adj. outward.
ûte, adv. out, without (motion hence. Gen. 369; 415).
ût-fûs, adj. ready to depart, ready to sail.
ût-gang, st. m. outgoing, exit, issue.
ût-garsecg, st. m. outermost ocean, farthest sea.
ût-ge-mǣru, st. n. pl. extreme or outermost limits.
ût-land, st. n. (the) outland, foreign land(s).
ût-myne, st. m. striving outward, toward the outside (?).
uton. See wutan (let us [go]).
ûtor, uttor, adj. & adv. outer, without, outside.
ût-sið, st. m. outgoing, departure, going away, going to destruction.
ût-weard, adj. outward-striving, trying to get out.
ûđe. See unnan (to grant).
ûđ-genge, adj. vanishing, departing, fleeing. Cf. Icel. ôđfluga.
ûđ-wita, -weota, w. m. philosopher, sage, scholar.

W

wâ, 1. adv. woe. — 2. interj. woe! oh, woe! oh, terror!
wâc, adj. weak, soft, pliant, vacillating, cowardly, timid, lazy.
wacan, st. abl. v. IV. (to wake), arise, originate, descend, be born.
  â-wacan, 1. to awake, wake from sleep. — 2. to arise, originate, be born.
  on-wacan, the same as above.

wâce, adv. weakly, slowly, negligently, poorly.
wacian, w. v. to watch, wake.
wâcian, w. v. to weaken, languish, vacillate, yield.
  â-wâcian, to desist from, abstain.
wacnian, w. v. in
  on-wacnian, to awaken, wake (from sleep).

wadan, *st. abl. v.* IV. (to **wade**), press through, stride, go, move.
    an-wadan, to invade, attack, come at or on, seize.
    be-wadan, *part.* **wombe bewaden,** disemboweled? Kid.88:24.
    ge-wadan, to go, stride, advance, reach, press, press in.
    on-wadan, to invade, attack, come at or on, seize, occupy, employ.
    þurh-wadan, to **wade through,** penetrate, go or strike through.

wǽcan, *w. v.* to render **weak,** soft, ripe; to exhaust, enervate; to trouble, grieve.
    ge-wǽcan, the same as above.
    on-wǽcan, to soften, debilitate.

wǽcce, *w. f.* **watching, watch.**
wǽccende, *part.* **watching,** watchful, awake.
wǽcnan, wǽcnian, wecnian, *w. v.* to (a)**waken,** arise, originate, proceed from.
    â-wǽcnan, the same as above.
    on-wǽcnan, the same as above.

wǽd, *st. n.* **wading-place;** — cf. **vadum,** ford; sea, ocean, water.
wǽd, *st. f.;* **wǽde,** *st. n.* **weeds,** clothing, garment, covering.
wǽdl, *st. f.* poverty, beggary, need, want.
wǽdla, *w. m.* beggar, needy person, pauper.
wǽfan, *w. v.* in
    be-wǽfan, to be**woof,** cover over or around.
wǽfer-sŷn, *adj.* **wavering** (?) scene, vision, play, spectacle, example.
wǽfre, *adj.* **wavering,** unsteady, unquiet.
wǽg, wag, wah, *st. m.* wall, partition, side (*paries* and *murus*).
wǽg, wêg, *st. m.* **wave,** billow, flood, sea.
wǽg, *st. f.* **weighing-instrument,** scales.

wǽgan, *w. v.* to cause to move, to trouble, afflict, grieve, disturb.
    ge-wǽgan, to drive forth, expel, afflict, trouble, weary.
wǽgan, *w. v.* to play, sport, jest, deceive (**wag?**).
    â-wǽgan, to frustrate, destroy.
    ge-wǽgan, the same as above.
wǽg-bora, *w. m.* **wave-bearer:** *i. e.* either dwelling under the waves, on the sea-bottom, or = wave-bringer, wave-rouser, swimmer. B. 1440.
wǽg-bord, *st. n.* **wave-board,** ship, vessel.
wǽg-dêor, *st. n.* **wave-deer,** sea-beast.
wǽg-dropa, *w. m.* **wave-drop,** water-drop, tear.
wǽge, wêge, *st. n.* cup, drinking-vessel.
wǽg-faru, *st. f.* **wave-faring,** sea-path, journey by sea.
wǽg-fæt, *st. n.* **wave-vat,** water-jar; clouds.
wǽg-, wêg-flota, *w. m.* **wave-float,** ship.
wǽg-hengest, *st. m.* **wave-horse,** ship. (Ger. *hingst.*)
wǽg-holm, *st. m.* the **wave-filled** sea, deep sea.
wǽg-lîðend, *part. & subs.* **wave-**traversing, seafarer, sailor.
wǽgn, wǽn, *st. m.* **wain,** wagon, vehicle.
wǽgnan, *w. v.* in
    be-wǽgnan, to offer, proffer, tender.
wǽg-stǽð, *st. n.* **wave-stead,** sea-shore, bank.
wǽg-strêam, *st. m.* **wave-stream,** sea-current.
wǽg-sweord, *st. n.* **weighty sword.**
wǽg-þel, *st. n.* **wave-deal** (board), ship, vessel.
wǽg-þrêa, *st. m.* terror or danger on or of or from the sea.

wǽg-þreát, *st. m.* inundation (of waves), deluge.

wæl, *st. n.* **1.** sum-total of fallen warriors chosen by the **Walkyrie** to be carried from the battlefield to **Walhalla.**— **2.** body of an individual warrior.— **3.** corpse-strewn battlefield.

wǽl, *st. m. & n.* welling of water, mælstrom, whirlpool (weel).

wǽlan, *w. v.* to oppress, press upon, vex, torture, torment.
 be-wǽlan, the same as above.
 ge-wǽlan, the same as above.

wæl-bed, *st. n.* deathbed, bier.

wæl-ben, *st. f.* deadly wound.

wæl-bend, *st. f.* death-bond.

wæl-blát, -bleát, *adj.* death-blue, deadly pale.

wæl-ceald, *adj.* death-cold, cold as a corpse.

wæl-ceásig, *adj.* corpse-choosing, carrion-picker (the raven).

wæl-clam, -clom, *st. m.* death-clamp, deadly fetter, bond of death.

wæl-cræft, *st. m.* killing (craft) power, deadly force.

wæl-cwealm, *st. m.* death in battle or on the battlefield, violent death.

wæl-deád, *st. m.* the same as above.

wæl-dreór, *st. m.* battle-gore, blood of the slain.

wǽl-fáh, *adj.* hostile to the whirlpool or the sea? *i. e.* ice that covers the water; or **wæl-fáh**, *adj.* bloodstained? B. 1128.

wæl-fǽhð, *st. f.* deadly feud, destructive hostility.

wæl-fædm, *st. m.* deadly embrace.

wæl-fel, *adj.* bloodthirsty, greedy for corpses.

wæl-feld, *st. m.* battle-field, field of the slain.

wæl-feall, wæll-fyll, *st. m.* fall of warrior-bodies, bloody death, defeat, carnage.

wæl-fús, *adj.* bringing to or ready for death.

wæl-fyllo, *st. f.* abundance of the slain, carnage.

wæl-fýr, *st. n.* **1.** deadly fire, flames of the dragon (B. 2582).— **2.** funeral pyre, flames of the pyre (B. 1119).

wæl-gár, *st. m.* deadly spear.

wæl-gæst, *st. m.* deadly or death-bringing guest.

wæl-gifre, *adj.* greedy for the dead (bodies), murderous.

wæl-gim, *st. m.* death-bringing gem? Rid. 21:4.

wæl-grǽdig, *adj.* greedy for the dead (bodies), flesh-eating.

wæl-, wæll-grim, *adj.* full of deadly fury, cruel, fateful, dire.

wæl-gryre, *st. m.* deadly horror or dread.

wæl-here, *st. m.* army doomed to death or destruction; or intent on slaughter (?).

wæl-hlem, *st. m.* death-stroke, deadly blow.

wæl-hlence, *w. f.* battle-link, chain-armor, shirt of mail.

wæl-hreów, -hriow, *adj.* savage in battle, cruel.

wæl-hwelp, *st. m.* deadly whelp, destroying hound.

Wǽlisc, *adj.* **Welsh.**

wæll-. See **wæl-.**

wælm, welm, *st. m.* tossing sea, tumbling flood, tide, current.

wælm-fýr, *st. n.* tossing or billowing fire.

wæl-mist, *st. m.* deadly mist, mist of death.

wæl-net, *st. n.* death-net.

wæl-nið, *st. m.* deadly hostility, enmity, war.

wæl-, wæll-notu, *st. f.* death sign or token, fatal mark.

wæl-pil, *st. m.* deadly dart, arrow.

wæl-ræs, *st. m.* deadly attack, onrush, bloody battle.
wæl-râp, *st. m.* wave-fetter or bond, *i. e.* covering of ice.
wæl-rêc, *st. m.* death-bringing reek, suffocating smoke.
wæl-, wæll-regn, *st. m.* deadly rain, shower (deluge).
wæl-rest, -ræst, *st. f.* death-rest, deathbed, grave.
wæl-reâf, *st. n.* battle-plunder, spoil of the slain.
wæl-reôw, *adj.* savage in battle, furious.
wæl-rûn, *st. f.* battle-rune, secret, mystery or secret of carnage.
wæl-scel (?), slaughter, defeat (Jud. 313).
wæl-sceaft, *st. m.* deadly shaft, spear.
wæl-seax, *st. n.* deadly hip-sword, dagger.
wæl-sleaht, -sliht, *st. m. n.?* slaughter, massacre.
wæl-spere, *st. n.* deadly spear.
wæl-steng, *st. m.* death-pole, stake, spear-shaft. (Ger. *stange.*)
wæl-stôw, *st. f.* battlefield.
wæl-stræl, *st. m. & f.* deadly arrow, dart. (Ger. *strahl.*)
wæl-streâm, *st. m.* deadly stream, deluge.
wæl-sweng, *st. m.* deadly blow, thrust.
wæl-wang, *st. m.* field of battle, field of the slain.
wæl-weg, *st. m.* fateful journey, way of slaughter.
wæl-wulf, *st. m.* battle-wolf, warrior, cannibal.
wæn. See wægen (wagon).
wæpen, *st. n.* **1.** weapon (shield, sword, spear).— **2.** *membrum virile, penis.*
wæpen-ge-wrixle, *st. n.* exchange of arms, hostilities, contest, battle.

wæpen-hete, *st. m.* weapon-hate, hostility shown by use of weapons.
wæpen-stræl, *st. m.* arrow, dart.
wæpen-þracu, *st. f.* storm of weapons, conflict.
wæpen-þræge (?), weapon, equipment? Crü. 61.
wæpen-wiga, *w. m.* weaponed warrior.
wæpned, *part.* weaponed, armed with a *penis;* male, man.
wæpned-cyn, *st. n.* male kin, tribe, race.
wæpned-man, *st. m.* man, male.
wær, *adj.* wary, cautious.
wær, *st. n.* sea, ocean:—old Norse *ver* and *vör*.
wær, *st. f.* covenant, treaty, compact, promise, vow, troth.
wær, *adj.* true, correct. Gen. 681. (Ger. *wahr.*)
wærc, *st. n.* wark, pain.
wær-fest, *adj.* covenant-keeping, holding fast to a promise, faithful, true.
wærgan. See wergan (to curse).
wær-genga, wer-genga, *w. m.* one seeking protection, wanderer, stranger, immigrant.
wærgdu. See wergdu (curse).
wær-leâs, *adj.* treaty-breaking, faithless, perfidious.
wærlic, *adj.* wary, cautious, circumspect.
wærlice, *adv.* the same as above.
wærlice, *adv.* truly, verily.
wær-, wêr-loga, *w. m.* warlock, covenant-breaker, faithless one, devil.
wærnis, -nys, *st. f.* curse, damnation.
wæron. See wesan (to be).
wærdo, *st. f.* something uncommon, (a) wonder, monster? Met. 28: 82.
wær-wyrde, *adj.* wary-worded, cautious in speech.

wæstm, wæstum, westem, *st. m., f.,* & *n.* **1.** growth, stature, bodily structure.— **2.** a growth, plant.— **3.** fruit.— **4.** abundance.
wæstm-bǽre, *adj.* fruitful, fertile.
wǽt, *adj.* wet, moist.
wǽta, *w. m.* wetness, moisture, water.
wǽtan, *w. v.* to wet, moisten, water.
  ge-wǽtan, the same as above.
wæter, wætter, *st. n.* water.
wæter-ǽdr, *st. f.* vein of water, waterfall.
wæter-bróga, *w. m.* water-horror, tumult of waters, frightful flood.
wæter-egesa, *w. m.* same as above.
wæter-flód, *st. m.* water-flood.
wæter-grund, *st. m.* sea-bottom, depth.
wæter-helm, *st. m.* water-helm, covering or floor of ice.
wæter-scipe, *st. m.* collection of waters, water-floods.
wæter-spring, -sprync, *st. m.* water-spring, whirlpool, eddy.
wæter-stefn, *st. f.* voice of the waters.
wæter-stréam, *st. m.* water-stream, river.
wæter-þisa, -þiswa, *w. m.* water-traverser; whale (Wal. 50); ship (Gû. 1303).
wæter-þryð, *st. f.* noise of water(s).
wæter-ȳð, *st. f.* wave, billow.
wǽdan, *w. v.* to hunt, roam around.
wáfian, *w. v.* to waver, hesitate; to stare, be astounded.
wag, wah. See **wæg** (wall).
wagian, *w. v.* to wag, vacillate, totter, move.
wála, *w. m.* **(wale),** part of the helmet through which the plume is fastened. B. 1031.
Valas, walca, waldan, wall. See **Wealh, wealca, wealdan, weall.**
Wale, *w. f.* **Welshwoman,** slave.
wálian, *w. v.* in

â-wyrt-wâlian, to root up, extirpate.
wélic, *adj.* woful, pitiful.
wam, wom, *st. m.* & *n.* **1.** spot, blemish, disgrace, ignominy, crime, sin. **2.** injury, loss, hurt, misfortune.
wam, wom, *adj.* shameful, ignominious, mean, bad.
wamb, womb, *st. f.* womb, belly.
wamb-, womb-hord, *st. n.* womb-hoard, contents of the belly.
wam-, wom-cwide, *st. m.* shameful or blasphemous speech, curse.
wam-, wom-dǽd, *st. f.* deed of shame, crime.
wam-, wom-ful, *adj.* full of spots or blemishes; shameful, sinful, bad.
wam-, wom-sceaða, *w. m.* sin-stained foe, devil.
wam-, wom-scyldig, *adj.* sinful, criminal.
wam-, wom-wyrcende, *part.* worker of sin or shame.
wan, won, *st. n.* want, lack.
wan, won, *adj.* (*w. gen.* of thing), in want of, deficient in.
wan, wann, won, wonn, *adj.* wan, wanting color, dark, black, lurid.
wana, *w. m.* want, decrease.
wan-, won-ǽht, *st. f.* want, poverty.
wandian, *w. v.* to desist, cease from, hesitate, tarry.
wandrian, *w. v.* to wander, roam, fly around.
wan-fâg, won-fâh, *adj.* wan-colored, dark-hued.
wan-, won-feax, *adj.* dark-haired.
wan-, won-fȳr, *st. n.* lurid flame, flame mingled with smoke.
wang, wong, *st. m.* field, mead, place, plain.
wange, wonge, *w. n.* (cf. **wang-tooth,** cheek, jaw. (Ger. *wange.*)
wang-, wong-stede, *st. m.* field, place, locality.
wan-, wann-, won-hâl, *adj.* unsound, sick, ill.

wan-hoga, *w. m.* thoughtless one, fool; — *adj.* thoughtless, foolish.

wan-hyd, won-hygd, *st. f.* want of sense or foresight; carelessness, senselessness, audacity, heedlessness.

wan-, won-hydig, *adj.* heedless, audacious, ignorant.

wanian, wonian, *w. v.* **1.** *intrans.* to **wane**, lessen, decrease, dwindle. **2.** *trans.* to diminish, cause to decrease.

 ge-wanian, the same as above.

wânian, wânigean, *w. v.* to **whine**, weep, complain, lament, bemoan.

wann. See **wan** (dark).

wan-, won-sǽlig, *adj.* unhappy, miserable.

wan-, wonn-sceaft, *st. f.* condition of want, misery, misfortune, mishap.

wan-, won-spêdig, *adj.* unhappy, miserable.

wâr, *st. n.* alga, seaweed (**waur**).

waran, *w. m. pl.* inhabitants, burghers, citizens.

warenian, *w. v.* in
 be-warenian, (*refl.*), to guard one's self, to be on one's guard.

warian, *w. v.* **1.** to guard, heed, hold, possess, inhabit. — **2.** to be on one's guard against (Gen. 236, 801).
 be-warian, 1. to keep from, preserve from. — **2.** to defend, guard, protect.

wârig, *adj.* covered with seaweed, slimy, dirty, squalid.

warnian, warnung, warod, wârod. See **wearnian, wearnung, warud, wârud.**

waru, *st. f.* citizenship, citizen. [Used only in compounds.]

waru, *st. f.* cave, shelter, protection, guarding.

warud, warod, wearod, *st. m.* shore, bank, margin.

wârud, wârod, *st. n.* alga, sea-grass, fucus.

warod-farud, *st. m.* surf, shore-surge.

warud-ge-winn, *st. n.* same as above.

wascan, *st. abl. v.* IV. to **wash**.

wadol, *st. m.* full moon.

wâd, *st. f.* **1.** wandering, journey. — **2.** hunt, hunting, chase (Met. 27: 13).

wadum, *st. m.* water, flood, stream.

waduma, wadema, *w. m.* flood, stream, sea.

wâwa, *w. m.* **woe**, misery.

wâwan, *st. red. v.* to **blow**.
 bi-wâwan, to blow around or about.

wê, *pron.* **we**; *gen.* ûser, usserûre; *dat.* ûs; *acc.* ûsic, ussic, ûs.

web, *st. n.* **web**, weaving, tapestry.

webban, webbian, *w. v.* to **weave**, work, think, continue, project.

weccan, weccean, *w. v.* **1.** to **wake**, wake up. — **2.** to waken, rouse, call up, bring forth. — **3.** to exhort, encourage, raise, rouse one's energies. — **4.** to move, to set in motion.
 â-weccan, to **awaken**, wake up, rouse, incite, get.
 tô-weccan, to arouse, excite.

wecgan, *w. v.* **1.** (Ger. *wegen*), to move, drive hither and thither. — **2.** to be moved (Met. 27: 4).
 â-wecgan, to move, rouse up, excite.

wecnian. See **wæcnian** (to be born).

wed, *st. n.* (**wedding**), pledge, security.

wêdan, *w. v.* (Ger. *wüthen*), to rage, to be insane or mad. (Old Eng. *wood*.)

weddian, *w. v.* in
 bi-weddian, to bind by a wed or pledge; to affiance, engage.

wêde-hund, *st. m.* (**wood-** [mad] **hound**), mad dog.

weder, *st. n.* **weather**, air.

weder-burg, *st. f.* **burgh** (castle, town) exposed to the wind and weather (?).

weder-candel, -condel, *st. f.* **weather-candle,** sun.
weder-dæg, *st. m.* **weather-day,** day distinguished for its weather; (breezy day?)
weder-tâcen, *st. n.* **weather-token** or sign in the air, sun.
weder-wolcen, *st. n.* **weather-welkin,** cloud in the air.
wefan, *st. abl. v.* III. to **weave,** contrive, project, dispose.
   â-wefan, to **weave** out, to weave.
   ge-wefan, the same as above.
wefl, *st. f.* tuft, panicle? *cladica?* Rid. 36: 3.
weg, wêg. See **wig, wǣg.**
weg, *st. m.* **way,** path.
weg (in connection with **lâ: weg lâ),** quite right, *euge.* Ps. 69: 4.
wegan, *st. abl. v.* III. 1. to **bear,** carry.— 2. to be moved, to move (Exod. 180; Rim. 6).
   â-wegan, to bear away, remove, destroy.
     æt-wegan, to bear to or away.
     be-wegan, 1. to slay, kill (By. 183).— 2. to surround, envelop, cover.
     for-wegan, to slay, kill.
     ge-wegan, to fight, contend.
     tô-wegan, to scatter, dissipate.
wêge, wehte, *pret.* See **wǣge, weccan** (to wake).
wel, well, *adv.* **well.**
wêl, *st. f.* trinket, jewels. Wy. 74.
wela, weala, weola, *w. m.* **wealth,** riches, abundance.
wel-dǣd, *st. f.* **deed of weal,** good deed.
weleras, weoloras, *st. m. pl.* lips.
welgian, weligian, *w. v.* 1. to enrich. 2. *intrans.* to be wealthy, affluent; to abound.
wel-hwâ, *pron.* each, every;—*adv. gen. n.* **wel-hwæs,** in general, altogether (Met. 2: 10).
wel-hwǣr, *adv.* everywhere.

wel-hwilc, *pron.* each, every.
welig, *adj.* **wealthy,** opulent.
well. See **wel** (well).
well, *st. m.* **well,** spring.
wella, *w. m.* the same as above.
wellan, *w. v.* iu
   â-wellan, to bring into commotion.
   on-wellan, to bring into violent excitement or commotion.
welm. See **wælm** (flood, &c.)
wel-þungen, *part.* well-thriven, prosperous, able; holy, honorable.
wêman, *w. v.* 1. to sound forth, resound (Icel. *wóma*), call, cry (An. 741).— 2. to strike up, begin to sing, to announce (An. 1482).— 3. to advise, persuade, convince, allow, lead astray.— 4. to address kindly, console, comfort? (Wand. 29).
wemman, *w. v.* to abuse, revile, calumniate.
   ge-wemman, to render odious, to spoil, befoul, pollute, mistreat, injure.
wen, wenn. See **wynn** (joy).
wên, *st. f.* 1. belief, opinion, fancy. 2. probability.— 3. **weening,** hope, expectation of something.— 4. name of the Rune **w.** Cf. **wynn.**
wêna, *w. m.* 1. belief, opinion, fancy. 2. weening, hope, expectation.
wênan, *w. v.* to believe, think, fancy, **ween,** hope, reckon upon, look for.
   ge-wênan, to **ween,** hope, expect.
wencel, wencele, *adj.* vacillating, unsteady, weak. (Ger. *wanken.*)
wendan, *w. v.* 1. to **wend,** turn, turn round, change.— 2. to bound, limit? (Gen. 2209).— 3. to turn one's self; become connected, turn about, alter, change, go.— 4. to change, vary, be different (?), to show one's self different or altered (?).

â-wendan, 1. to avert, turn aside.—**2.** to turn, alter, change (Gen. 259).—**3.** to turn one's self away or aside (Ps. 77: 57).

ed-wendan, to turn one's self away or aside again; to yield, give way, cease.

ge-wendan, 1. to turn, turn round.—**2.** to turn one's self, turn round, alter, change.

on-wendan, 1. *trans.* to turn, turn round, avert, put aside, alter. **2.** *intrans.* to turn about or around, to return (Ps. 1452).

ôd-wendan, to remove, pilfer, purloin, steal.

wendig, *st. f.* turning, change, alteration.

wenian, *w. v.* to accustom, habituate, inure; to entertain.

be-wenian, to entertain, care for.

ge-wenian, to accustom, habituate, inure.

wêninga, *adv.* by a wee bit, little, almost. (Ger. *wenig?*).

wenn. See **wynn.**

wenna (?). Rim. 7.

wêpan, *st. red. v.* **1.** *intrans.* to weep, moan aloud, complain.—**2.** to bewail, mourn over, deplore.

wer, *st. m.* man, person (*vir* & *homo*).

wer-bêam, *st. m.* tree of defense, warrior; man strong as a **beam?** Exod. 486.

werc, wercan. See **weorc, wyrcan.**

wer-cyn, *st. n.* kin of men, human race, tribe.

werdan, wered. See **wyrdan, weorud** (troop).

wered, *st. n.* sweet drink, mead.

werg, wergan. See **wearg, werig, wergian, werian.**

wergend, *part. & subs.* envier, begrudger, rogue.

wergend, *part. & subs.* defender, protector.

wer-genga. See **wær-genga** (alien).

wêrgian, *w. v.* in

ge-wêrgian, to **weary,** exhaust.

wergian, wergan, *w. v.* to outlaw, condemn, curse.

wergdu, werhdu, wærgdu, *st. f.* curse, imprecation, condemnation, punishment.

wergun, *st. f.* curse, condemnation. Sat. 42.

werian, werigean, wergan, *w. v.* **1.** to defend, protect.—**2.** to guard, hold, occupy, inhabit (Gû. 322).—**3.** to cover over, clothe, envelop. **4.** to ward off, hinder, prevent.

â-werian, 1. to defend, protect. **2.** to ward off, hinder (Ps. 105: 24). **3.** to surround, inclose (Rid. 41: 47).

be-, bi-werian, 1. to defend, protect, hinder, prohibit.—**2.** to hold in check, within limits, in order.

ge-werian, to cover over, clothe, envelop.

werig, *adj.* accursed, outlawed, execrable, damned.

wêrig, *adj.* weary, tired, unnerved, dejected, wretched, unhappy, sad.

werigean, werigend. See **werian, wergend.**

wêrig-ferd, -ferhd, *adj.* weary of spirit, cast down; exhausted. Wal. 19.

wêrig-môd, *adj.* the same as above.

wêr-loga. See **wǣrloga** (warlock).

wer-mǣgd, *st. f.* human race, tribe, nation.

wermôd, *st. m.* **wormwood,** absinthe.

werod. See **weorud** (troop).

wêron. See **wǣron** (were).

wer-þeod, -þiod, *st. f.* men-folk, folk, population;—in *pl.* people.

wesan, *st. abl. v.* III. (*pret.* **wæs, wǣron**), to be;—*w. past part.* forms the passive voice.

for-wesan, to pass away, rot. Ruin. 7.

ge-wesan, to be. Sol. 181.

west, *adv.* **westerly,** toward the west.
westan, *adv.* from the west.
wêstan, *w. v.* to **waste,** devastate.
west-dǽl, *st. m.* **western** part.
wêste, *adj.* **waste,** uninhabited, abandoned, desolate.
westem. See **wǽstm** (fruit).
wêsten, *st. m. & n.* **waste,** desert, solitude.
west-ende, *st. m.* **west end.**
wêsten-gryre, *st. m.* horror of the waste, dread of the desert.
wêsten-stadol, *st. m.* **waste** place.
west-mest, *adj.* **westmost.**
west-rôdor, *st. m.* **western** sky.
west-weg, *st. m.* **western** way.
wedan, *st. abl. v.* III. to tie, bind? (Ps. 106: 28);—assuage? gladden?
wêde, *adj.* sweet, mild, agreeable.
wedel, *st. f.* poverty, want, need.
wêd-nes, *st. f.* agreeability, grace, sweetness.
wexe. See **weax** (wax).
wêa, *w. m.* **woe,** trouble, misery, misfortune.
wêa-dǽd, *st. f.* **woe-deed.**
wêa-ge-sid, *st. m.* companion in misery.
weaht, *part.* from **weccan;**—*pret.* **weahte,** to wake.
weal, weala. See **weall, wela.**
wêa-lâf, *st. f.* woful remnant, relic left by misfortune.
wea-land, wealh-land, *st. n.* **Welshland,** foreign country.
Wealas. See **wealh** (Welshman).
wealca, walca, *w. m.* **1.** billow, rolling wave.—**2.** light, floating garment.
wealcan, *st. red. v.* (cf. **walk?**), to move (around or about), roll, toss.
    ge-wealcan, the same as above.
    on-wealcan, to roll around, wallow.

weald, wald, *st. m.* **weald, wold,** wood;—bushes, foliage, branch. Gen. 846.
wealdan, waldan, *st. red. v.* to **wield,** exercise, or possess authority; to possess, rule, guide.
    ge-wealdan, to **wield,** rule, command, guard;—*part.* **ge-wealden, 1.** strong, vigorous, active.—**2.** subject, submissive (B. 1732).
wealdend, *part.* wielding authority, powerful.
wealdend, waldend, *part. & subs.* **wielder,** guide, ruler, lord, king.
wealdend-god, *st. m.* **wielding God,** Lord God.
weald-, wald-swadu, *st. f.* track or trail in the wood(s); forest path.
wealh, *st. m.* **Welshman,** stranger, slave.
wealh-stôd, *st. m.* interpreter. Cf. **Wealh.**
wêalic, *adj.* woful.
weall, weal, *st. m.* **1. wall,** earthwall, dam, hill, mountain.—**2.** bank, shore, wall of rock.—**3.** (ordinary) wall.
weallan, *st. red. v.* (Ger. *wallen*), to **well** up, to billow, undulate, rock (as waves do);—*w. acc.* to scourge, lash (Sol. 143).
    â-weallan, 1. to **well** forth, flow out, spring up.—**2.** *part.* **âweallen?** Cri. 625.
weall-, weal-clif, *st. n.* **wall-cliff,** cliff on the shore.
weall-dor, *st. n.* **door** in the **wall.**
weall-, weal-fæsten, *st. n.* **wallfastness,** rampart of defense, castle, fortress.
weall-, weal-geat, *st. n.* **wall-gate,** postern, exit.
weallian, *w. v.* to roam, ramble, sojourn abroad.
weall-, weal-stân, *st. m.* **wall-stone,** stone for a wall, corner-stone.

weal-steall, *st. m.* a **wall** or wall-place (whereon a ruin stands).
weall-stêap, *adj.* **wall-steep,** steep-walled, steep like a wall. [wall.
weall-wâla, *w. m.* **wall,** parts of a
weal-sâda, *w. m.* cord for binding (**Welshmen** or) slaves? (Ps.139:5).
wêan? Ps. 68: 27.
weard, *adv.* **ward,** toward, to.
weard, *st. m. & f.* **ward,** watch, protection, waiting for, lurking ambuscade; possession.
weard, *st. m.* **warden,** watchman, guardian, protector, lord.
weardian, *w. v.* 1. to **ward,** guard, heed, protect, preserve. — 2. to hold, occupy, inhabit, sojourn in. 3. lâst (swađe) **weardian,** to hold or guard one's footsteps = (1.) to follow closely (B. 2164); — (2.) to leave behind, abandon, remain behind.
wearg, wearh, werg, *st. m.* 1. wolf. 2. outlaw, criminal.
wearg-træf, -treaf, *st. n.* house of the damned, hell.
wearm, *adj.* **warm.**
wearmian, *w. v.* to become **warm.**
wearmlic, *adj.* **warm.**
wearn (?), multitude, many.
wearn, *st. f.* denial; refusal, renunciation (B. 366). — 2. resistance. 3. reproaches, abuse.
wearnian, warnian, *w. v.* to guard one's self, be on one's guard against, deny one's self.
wearning, warning, *st. f.* 1. warning. — 2. foresight, caution.
wearod. See **warud** (shore).
wearp, *st. m.* **warp** (in weaving).
wêas, *adv.* accidentally, by chance.
wêa-spell, *st. n.* **woe-spell,** evil tidings.
wêa-tâcen, *st. n.* **woe-token,** evidence of misery.
wêa-þearf, *st. f.* woful misery, need.
weax, *st. n.* **wax.**

weâx = weâcs = wâces, *gen. n.* of **wâc,** weak, soft. Rid. 46: 1.
weaxan, *st. abl. v.* IV. to **wax,** increase, grow, strengthen, become more powerful.
â-**weaxan,** to grow up, become full grown, arise, originate.
be-, bi-**weaxan,** to overgrow.
ge-**weaxan,** to **wax,** grow up.
weaxan, to consume, devour? B.3115.
wêo, weo-bedd. See **wôh, wigbed.**
wêod, wiod, *st. n.* **weed.**
weodewe. See **widwe** (widow).
wêod-mônad, *st. m.* **weed-month,** August. Men. 138.
weogas, weog, weola. See **weg, wig, wela.**
weolme, *st. f.* choice, selection, pick of one's fellow-creatures. Cri. 445.
weoloras. See **weleras** (lips).
weor, *adv.* (cf. **worse**), meanly, cowardly.
weora, *gen. pl.* of **wer** (man).
weorc, worc, werc, *st. n.* 1. **work,** deed, labor. — 2. trouble, **work** (Lat. *labor*), difficulty, strait.
weorce, *adj.* difficult, heavy, painful.
weorce, *adv.* the same as above.
weorcean. See **wyrcan, -ean.**
weorc-sum, *adj.* oppressive, hard, hurtful, irksome.
weorc-þeow, 1. *st. m.* **workman,** servant, slave.— 2. *st. f.* female slave, maid (Gen. 2260).
weoren, *part.* of **wesan** (to be).
weorfan. See **hweorfan** (to move).
weorm, *st. m.* **worm.**
weorn (?). Az. 185; An. 677, 1492. [from **weor** or **worn?**]
weornan. See **wyrnan** (to refuse).
weornian, *w. v.* to wilt, wither, dwinfor-**weornian,** to rot, decay. [dle.
weorod, weorold. See **weorud, weoruld** (world).
weorpan, worpan, wyrpan, wurpan, (Ger. *werfen*), *st. abl. v.* I. to cast, throw.

â-weorpan, to throw from, off, out, or down; to expel, remove; to contest, refute.

be-, bi-weorpan, 1. to cover over, surround.— 2. to throw, cast down.

for-weorpan, 1. to cast out, cast down, drive off.— 2. to squander, throw away (B. 2872).

ge-weorpan, 1. to throw, cast down.— 2. (*reflex.*), to rise, to lift one's self up.— 3. to turn round, alter, change (Cri. 188).— 4. to pass by, pass away (Gn. Ex. 77).

ofer-weorpan, 1. to throw over, upon, or at.— 2. to throw down, overthrow.— 3. *intrans.* to stumble, fall over.

tô-weorpan, to break in pieces, dissipate, destroy, frustrate, avert; *intrans.* to pollute one's self. Gn. Ex. 191. [diate.

wid-weorpan, to reject, repu-
ymb-weorpan, to throw around, surround.

weorpere, *st. m.* thrower, caster.

weord, wurd, *st. n.* 1. worth, price, value, ransom, purchase-money.— 2. honor, worth, dignity (Bed. Sm. 545: 6).

weord, word, *st. m.* street, lane; corridor, hall, way, vestibule.

weordan, wiordan, wurdan, wyrdan, (Ger. *werden*), *st. abl. v.* I. to be or become, happen, occur;— *w. past. part.* of trans. verbs = passive voice;— *w. past. part.* of intrans. verbs = circumlocution for the ordinary preterite. Cf. **worth** in "woe **worth** the day!"= exclamation.

for-weordan, to perish, pass away, vanish.

ge-weordan, 1. to be or become, happen, occur.— 2. *impers. w. acc.* of *pers.* to become, take place, happen, occur to, seem, appear; please.

weord-ful, *adj.* **worthful**, highly esteemed, glorious.

weord-georn, *adj.* ambitious, desirous of glory.

weordian, wurdian, wyrdian, *w. v.* 1. to hold **worthy**, esteem, respect, honor, revere, adore.— 2. to magnify, praise.— 3. to honor, distinguish, deck, adorn, present.

ge-weordian, 1. to distinguish, honor, adorn, furnish, present.— 2. to magnify, praise.

weordig, wordig, *st. m.* street, lane, way; area, ground or soil upon which an estate lies; court.

weord-, wurd-lic, *adj.* worthy, reverend, venerable, distinguished.

weord-, wurd-lice, *adv.* the same.

weord-, wurd-, wordmynd, -mynd, -mynt, *st. f.* & *n.* honor, dignity, memorial.

weord-, wyrd-scipe, *st. m.* worthship, worship, honor, dignity.

weordung, *st. f.* honor, distinction, appreciation.

weorud, weorod, werud, werod, wered, *st. n.* troop, band, folk, multitude.

weorudân (?). Wy. 93.

weorud-lêast, werod-lêst, *st. f.* lack of men or warriors.

weoruf-, woruf-tord, *st. m.* dung, excrement of cattle.

weoruld, weorold, woruld, worold, world, *st. f.* 1. **world** (inclusive of all temporal things, all things betwixt heaven and hell; and, in a biblical sense, all that is earthly, sensible, sensuous.— 2. men, humanity.— 3. life, temporal or worldly life (Met. 10: 70; Sch. 22).— 4. lifetime, century.

weoruld-, worold-âr, (Ger. *ehre*), *st. f.* worldly honor or favor before the world.

weoruld-, world-bearn, *st. n.* world-bairn, man, person.

weoruld-, woruld-bliss, *st. f.* worldly bliss, joy of earth.
weoruld-, woruld-búend, *part. & subs.* world-inhabiter.
weoruld-bysgung, -bisgung, *st. f.* worldly misery, trouble.
weoruld-, woruld-candel, *st. f.* world-candle, sun.
weoruld-, woruld-cræft, *st. m.* world-craft, earthly wit and wisdom.
weoruld-, world-cund, *adj.* worldly, earthly.
weoruld-, worold-cyning, *st. m.* worldly king, earthly potentate.
weoruld-, woruld-déad, *adj.* dead.
weoruld-, woruld-dréam, *st. m.* earthly joy.
weoruld-driht. See weoruld-riht.
weoruld-dryhten, -drihten, *st. m.* lord of the world, God.
weoruld-, woruld-duguđ, *st. f.* earthly or worldly good.
weoruld-, woruld-ende, *st. m.* end of the world.
weoruld-, woruld-earfođ, *st. n.* earthly misery.
weoruld-, woruld-feoh, *st. n.* earthly goods, wealth.
weoruld-fréond, *part. & subs.* earthly or worldly friend.
weoruld-, woruld-ge-dâl, *st. n.* separation from the world, death.
weoruld-, woruld-ge-sǽlig, *adj.* rich in worldly goods.
weoruld-ge-sǽld, *st. f.* worldly happiness, earthly bliss.
weoruld-, woruld-ge-sceaft, *st. f.* 1. earthly creature. — 2. world. Gen. 110.
weoruld-, woruld-ge-stréon, *st. n.* earthly or worldly treasures.
weoruld-ge-swinc, *st. n.* earthly toil, misery.
weoruld-, woruld-gitsere, *st. m.* earth-seeker, coveter of worldly things.

weoruld-gitsung, *st. f.* earth-greed, desire for worldly things, covetousness.
weoruld-, woruld-hyht, *st. m.* worldly or earthly joy.
weoruld-, woruld-lic, *adj.* worldly, earthly.
weoruld-, woruld-, world-lif, *st. n.* world-life, life in the world.
weoruld-, woruld-mâgas, *st. m. pl.* worldly or earthly kin.
weoruld-, woruld-man, *st. m.* man, human being.
weoruld-, woruld-nytt, *st. f.* worldly use, profit, or advantage.
weoruld-, worold-rǽden, *st. f.* world's intent, destination, destined use, order.
weoruld-, world-rice, *adj.* rich in worldly power or goods.
weoruld-, woruld-, world-rice, *st. n.* 1. world-realm, world. — 2. earthly kingdom. Cf. Ger. *reich.*
weoruld-riht, woruld-ryht, *st. n.* secular or civil right, law. Gû. 28.
weoruld-, woruld-sǽld, *st. f.* earthly or worldly happiness, blessing.
weoruld-, woruld-sceaft, *st. f.* worldly or earthly creature, creation.
weoruld-, woruld-spêd, *st. f.* world-speed, success in the world.
weoruld-, woruld-strengu, *st. f.* worldly strength, power.
weoruld-, woruld-stund, *st. f.* time, season, or life in this world.
weoruld-, world-þearfa, *w. m.* poor in worldly goods.
weoruld-, woruld-þearfende, *part.* the same as above.
weoruld-wela, *w. m.* world-wealth, riches of earth.
weoruld-, woruld-widl, *st. m. & n.* (?) world-filth, foulness, dirt.
weoruld-, woruld-wite, *st. n.* torture, martyrdom.

weoruld-, woruld-wuniende, *part.* dwelling in the world.
weoruld-, woruld-yrmdu, *st. f.* worldly or earthly wretchedness.
wêos, weota, weotian, wibed. See **wig, wita, witian, wigbed.**
wic, *st. n.* -**wick,** dwelling-place, camp, stopping-place, house, bed, lair.
wican, *st. abl. v.* V. to yield, give way, fall down. (Ger. *weichen*.)
   ge-wican, to yield, slide down or aside, refuse, deny, renounce.
wic-cræft, *st. m.* **witchcraft,** magic.
wiccung-dôm, *st. m.* same as above.
wic-eard, *st. m.* residence, dwelling-place.
wic-freodu, *st. f.* protection or defense of the residence.
wicg, wycg, *st. n.* horse.
wician, *w. v.* to dwell, tarry, sojourn, rest in.
   ge-wician, *intrans.* to dwell, have a dwelling, live.
   ymb-wicigean, to surround, beleaguer, beset.
wicing, *st. m.* **wicking,** sea-robber, pirate.
wic-stede, *st. m.* residence, dwelling.
wic-steal, *st. m.* camp, camping-ground.
wic-stôw, *st. f.* residence, dwelling-place.
wic-tûn, *st. m.* vestibule; atrium, court.
wid, *adj.* **wide,** extensive, broad, long.
wid-brâd, *adj.* **wide and broad,** immense.
wid-cûd, *adj.* widely-known.
wide, *adv.* **widely,** far-spread.
wide-ferd, -ferhd, -fyrhd, *st. m. & n.* long life, long time.
wide-feorh, -ferh, -ferg, *st. m. & n.* the same as above.
widewe. See **widwe** (widow).

wid-fædme, *adj.* comprehensive, broad-bosomed, ample.
wid-fêrende, *part.* **wide-faring,** coming from afar.
wid-floga, *w. m.* **wide-fier,** dragon. B. 2346.
wid-folc, *st. n.* great nation, widespread folk.
wid-gal, -gel, -gil, -giell, *adj.* **1.** widespread, extensive.— **2.** wandering, vagabond, roaming. Rid. 21: 5.
wid-gangol, -gongel, *adj.* **wide-going,** wandering far.
widl, *st. m. & n.?* filth, dirt.
widlan, *w. v.* to soil, befoul, pollute.
wid-land, -lond, *st. n.* **wide land.**
wid-lâst, *st. m.* long wandering, long way or road.
wid-lâst, *adj.* extending far, far-stretching.
wid-mǣre, *adj.* known afar, well-known.
wido. See **widu** (wood).
wid-rynig, *adj.* far-running? wide-flowing? An. 1509.
wid-sceap, *adj.* extended, large, great, considerable.
wid-sid, *st. m.* **1.** wide or extensive journey.— **2.** the Far-traveled One (name of A.-S. poem, I).
widu, wido = wudu (?), **wood,** branch. (Met. 13: 55; Rid. 57: 2).
widwe, wydewe, weodewe, wudwe, wuduwe, *w. f.* **widow.**
wid-wegas, *st. m. pl.* **wideways,** long roads or journeys.
wif, *st. n.* (*f.*), **wife,** woman, lady, spouse.
wifel, *st. m.* chafer, scarab, dung-beetle (**weevil**).
wif-gift, *st. f.* **wife-gift,** dower, outfit.
wif-hâd, *st. m.* female sex.
wif-lufe, *w. f.* **wife-love,** love for one's wife.
wif-man, -mon, wimman, *st. m. & f.* **woman.**

wíf-wyne, *st. m.* love for a woman.
wífre, *w. f.* female **weaver** (webster).
wíg, wíh, weoh, weg, *st. m.* idol, image; fane, sanctuary, temple, altar.
wíg, wígg, *st. m. & n.* **1.** war, battle. **2.** warlike ability.
wíga, *w. m.* warrior, contestant, fighter.
wígan, *st. abl. v.* V. to contend, fight, make war.
    ge-wígan, to dwindle, vanish? Rim. 76.
    ofer-wígan, to outdo, conquer, vanquish.
wíg-, wí-, weo-, weoh-bed, *st. n.* altar, place of sacrifice.
wíg-bealu, *st. n.* war-bale, horrors of war.
wíg-bil, *st. n.* war-bill, battle-sword.
wíg-blác, *adj.* brilliant in battle equipments.
wíg-bord, *st. n.* war-board, war-shield.
wíg-cirm, -cyrm, *st. m.* war-cry, noise of battle.
wíg-cræft, *st. m.* war-craft, ability.
wíg-cræftig, *adj.* skilled in war, able to fight.
wígend, -wíggend, *part. & subs.* warrior, fighter, contestant.
wíg-freca, *w. m.* war-wolf, hero.
wíg-fruma, *w. m.* warrior, war-prince.
wíg-getawe, *st. n. pl.* war-equipments, gear, accouterments.
wígg, wíggend. See **wíg, wígend**.
wíg-gryre, *st. m.* war-horror, battle-dread, fearfulness.
wíg-, wíh-gyld, *st. n.* idol.
wíg-, wí-haga, *w. m.* war-hedge, wall of shields, phalanx, *testudo.*
wíg-hete, *st. m.* war-hate, hostility.
wíg-heafola, *w. m.* battle-headpiece, helmet.
wíg-heáp, *st. m.* war-troop, **heap** of warriors.

wíg-heard, *adj.* inured to war, brave in battle.
wíg-hryre, *st. m.* falling in fight, defeat.
wíg-hyrst, *st. f.* war-gear, accouterments, ornament.
wíg-leód, *st. n.* war-lay, battle-cry, battle-signal.
wíg-líc, *adj.* warlike.
wíg-neafola. See **wíg-heafola**.
wíg-nyt, *st. n.* success in or profit from battle or war.
wíg-plega, *w. m.* war-**play**, conflict, battle.
wíg-rád, -ród, *st. f.* war-road, path of war or road for armies.
wíg-ræden, *st. f.* state or condition of war; battle, war.
wíg-síd, *st. m.* war-expedition, campaign.
wíg-sigor, *st. m.* triumph, victory.
wíg-smið, *st. m.* idol-**smith**, maker of idols.
wíg-smið, *st. m.* war-smith, warrior, man of war.
wíg-spéd, *st. f.* success in war.
wíg-steal, *st. n.* rampart, bulwark.
wíg-trod, wítrod, *st. f.* expedition, raid.
wíg-þracu, *st. f.* onslaught in battle.
wíg-þrist, *adj.* bold in battle.
wíg-, weoh-weorðung, *st. f.* idol-worship, idolatry.
wíh, wíhaga. See **wíg (weoh), wíg-haga** (phalanx).
wiht, wuht, wyht, *st. f. & n.* **1.** wight, whit, creature, animal, thing.—**2.** thing (especially in neg. clauses); — **ne-wiht** = naught, (*acc.*), not, not at all;—so also in instr. and w. comparatives.
wíl-bec, *st. m.* brook or stream of tears, lamentations? Rim. 26.
wíl-boda, *w. m.* messenger of joy, angel.

wil-cuma, *w. m.* welcome one, cherished guest.
wild, *adj.* wild, savage.
wil-dæg, *st. m.* day of joy.
wild-dêor, wildêor, *st. n.* wild beast.
wilde, *adv.* wildly.
wil-der, *st. n.* wild beast. Cf. deer.
wil-fægen, *adj.* fain, glad.
wil-gæst, -gest, *st. m.* welcome guest.
wil-, will-ge-brôðor, *st. m. pl.* beloved brothers.
wil-, will-ge-dryht, *st. f.* willing troop, ready band, retinue.
wil-ge-hlêða, *w. m.* intimate and willing friend or companion.
wil-, will-ge-sið, *st. m.* the same.
wil-, will-ge-steald, *st. n.* riches, wealth.
wil-, will-ge-sweostor, *st. f. pl.* beloved sisters.
wil-, will-ge-þofta, *w. m.* willing or ready companion.
wil-, will-gifa, -geofa, -giefa, *w. m.* giver of joy. king. [ant.
wil-hrêdig, *adj.* glad-hearted, exultwill. See well.
willa, *w. m.* 1. will, wish, longing, joy, good pleasure.— 2. something wished for, object of desire.
willan, wyllan, to will or wish;— *irreg. v., pres. indic. sg.* 1, 3. wille, wile, wyle, wylle.— 2. wilt, wylt; *pl.* willað, wyllað; *subj. sg.* wille, wile, wylle; *pl.* willen, wyllen, wylle; *pret.* wolde.
wille-burne, will-flôd. See wylleburne, wyllflôd (wellspring, &c.)
willian, *w. v.* to will, wish, desire, long for.
wiln, wyln, *st. f.* maid, maid-servant.
wilnian, *w. v.* 1. to will, desire, demand, wish, supplicate, entreat.— 2. (local), long to go. An. 283; Met. 20: 159.
wilnung, *st. f.* longing, yearning.

wil-, will-sele, *st. m.* pleasant dwelling.
wil-, will-sið, *st. m.* wished-for journey, much-desired trip.
wil-, will-spel, *st. n.* glad message, good tidings.
wil-sum, *adj.* desirable, wished-for, delightful.
wil-þegu, *st. f.* agreeable fare or food.
wil-wang, will-wong, *st. m.* delightful field, plain, or expanse.
wil-weg, *st. m.* chosen way, pleasant path.
wim-man. See wifman (woman).
win, winn, *st. n.* 1. strife, contention, conflict, battle, uproar.— 2. toil, labor, trouble.
win, *st. n.* wine. [hall.
win-ærn, *st. n.* wine-hall, drinkingwin-burg, *st. f.* wine-burg, castle or town in which wine-feasts are held.
wincan, wincian, *w. v.* to wink, close the eyes, nod to.
wincel, *st. m.* corner. (Ger. *winkel.*)
wind, *st. m.* wind.
win-dagas, *st. m. pl.* days of toil or misery, life in this world.
windan, *st. abl. v.* I. 1. to wind, twist, turn one's self, move, stir, fly, roll.— 2. *intrans.* to move hesitatingly hither and thither (Gû. 265).— 3. to wind, turn, swing;— wunden gold, twisted gold, gold wrought into rings, &c.
â-windan, to wind out of, to escape, to withdraw, run away.
æt-windan, the same as above.
be-, bi-windan, 1. to bewind, wind about, surround, shut in.— 2. to fit in, imprint, impress (An. 58; Jul. 234).
ge-windan, 1. to wind, turn about, entangle.— 2. *intrans.* to turn or twist one's self, flee away, betake one's self off.

on-windan, 1. to unwind, loosen, open.— 2. to turn round, return. An. 531.
ymb-windan, to clasp round, hold, grasp.
wind-bland, -blond, *st. n.* wind-blending,(the) commingled winds, roaring of the wind.
windig, *adj.* windy, breezy.
win-drinc, *st. m.* wine-drink.
win-druncen, *part.* wine-drunken.
wind-sele, *st. m.* wind-hall; hall of misery, hell.
wine, *st. m.* friend, intimate, beloved lord and husband.
wine-dryhten, -drihten, *st. m.* dear lord, lord and friend.
wine-gêomor, *adj.* mourning for friends.
wine-lêas, *adj.* friendless.
wine-mæg,*st. m.*dear relation,blood-friend.
wine-scipe, *st. m.* friendship.
wine-trêow, *st. f.* true to one's friend; conjugal fidelity.
wine-þearfende, *part.* needing friends, friendless.
win-gâl,*adj.* wine-mad, intoxicated, exhilarated with wine.
win-ge-drinc, *st. n.* wine-drinking, feast of wine.
win-geard, *st. m.* vineyard.
win-hâte, *w. f.* invitation to wine, wine-feasting. Jud. 8.
winia, winiga, winigea, *gen. pl.* of wine (friend).
winn. See win (struggle).
winnan, wynnan, *st. abl. v.* I. 1. to strive, struggle, fight, resist, oppose.— 2. to toil, exert one's self, labor, compete with.— 3. *w. acc.* to endure, bear. [endure.
â-winnan, to win, gain, attain,
ge-winnan, 1. *intrans.* to fight, struggle (Gû. 421).— 2. *w. acc.* to vanquish, conquer.— 3. *w. acc.* or *gen.* to win, gain, attain.

win-ræced, -reced, *st. n.* wine-hall, hall for drinking.
win-sæd, *adj.* wine-sated, intoxicated.
win-sæl, *st. n.* wine-hall, drinking-hall.
win-sele, *st. m.* the same as above.
winster, wynster, *adj.* left, on the left hand.
winter, *st. m. & n.* winter;—in pl. = years.
winter-biter, *adj.* wintry-bitter, cold.
winter-ceald, *adj.* wintry-cold.
winter-cearig, *adj.* grieved or troubled on account of great age, laden with years.
winter-dæg, *st. m.* winter-day.
winter-fylled, October. Men. 184.
winter-ge-rim, *st. n.* number of winters or years (counted by winters).
winter-getæl, *st. n.* same as above.
winter-ge-wæde, *st. n.* winter-weeds, snow.
winter-ge-weorp, -geworp, *st. n.* snowstorm.
winter-rim,*st. n.* number of winters or years.
winter-scûr, *st. m.* winter-shower.
winter-stund, *st. f.* winter time, season, or hour.
win-þegu, *st. f.* wine-feast, convivial drinking.
wir, *st. m.* wire, ornaments of wire or filagree.
wir-boga, *w. m.* twisted or bent wire.
wircan, -ean. See wyrcan (to work).
wis, *adj.* withered? Crä. 13.
wis, *adj.* wise, sage, experienced, certain, fully conscious.
wis, *st. f.* wise, fashion.
wisa, *w. m.* director, guide, leader.
wisan, *w. v.* to guide, direct, point out, show? Dan. 35.
wis-bôc, *st. f.* law-book, book of wisdom.

wiscan. See **wýscan** (to wish).

wis-dôm, *st. m.* wisdom, knowledge.

wise, *w. f.* **1. wise,** fashion, guide, custom, habit, mode of acting.— **2.** condition.— **3.** state or circumstances of a case.— **4.** direction. **5.** species of song, melody. (Ger. *weise.*)

wis-fæst, *adj.* wise, discreet, sage.

wis-fæstlic, *adj.* the same as above.

wis-hycgende, *part.* wise-thinking, sagacious, circumspect.

wis-hydig, *adj.* the same as above.

wisian, *w. v.* to direct, refer, show, lead, guide.

    ge-wisian, to direct, prescribe, guide.

wislic, *adj.* certain, secure, trustworthy.

wis-lic, *adj.* wise, sagacious.

wis-wisslice, *adv.* certainly, surely, decidedly.

wislice, *adv.* wisely, sagaciously.

wisnian, *w. v.* in

    for-wisnian, to rot, decay, age, wither.

wis-sefa, *adj.* (Grein), wise-souled, sagacious. Sol. 138.

wist, *st. f.* **1.** being, existence.— **2.** well-being, wealth, happiness, abundance (B. 1735).— **3.** food, nourishment, feed.

wist-fyllo, *st. f.* abundant food, nourishment.

wit, wyt, *dual pron.* we two;— **wit Adam twâ, wit Scilling** = Adam (Scilling) and I;— *gen.* **uncer;**— *dat.* **unc;** *acc.* **uncit, unc.**

wit, *st. n.* **wit,** understanding, intellect, sense.

wita, weota, *w. m.* sage, wise man, philosopher, counselor, adviser, senator.

witan, wytan, to know, be acquainted with; **wit, wot;**— *pret. pres. indic. sig.* **1, 3, wât.**— **2. wâst,** **wæst;** *pl.* **witon;** *subj.* **wite;** *pret.* **wiste, wyste, wisse.**

    be-witan, to lead, guide, care for, attend to.

    ge-witan, to wit, wot, know.

witan, *st. abl. v.* V. **1.** to look, behold, see (Gen. 511).— **2.** to follow with the eyes or glance (accompanied by motions), start out for, begin a journey, go (Met. 24: 52). **3.** to rebuke, reproach, reprimand.

    æt-witan, to twit, reproach, taunt, censure.

    ge-witan, to behold, cast one's eye in a certain direction (Ps. 79: 14); to move, start, go; then as *general verb of motion,* with or without reflexive dative; followed by inf. of a verb of motion, or a verb expressing an action involving motion or the end or aim of motion; with local prepositions, or adverbs, or alone.

    ôd-witan, to blame, scold, reproach, censure.

wite, *st. n.* punishment, death-penalty or punishment, torture, distress, misery, hell.

wite-bend, *st. m. & f.* bonds of torture or punishment.

wite-brôga, *w. m.* tormenting dread, torturing terror.

wite-dôm, *st. m.* prophecy, prediction, presage.

wite-hrægl, *st. n.* penitential garb or dress of one who expiates a crime or an offense, or who pays a penalty.

wite-hûs, *st. n.* torture-house, hell.

wite-lâc, *st. n.* punishment, death-penalty, punishment by death.

wite-lêast, *st. f.* immunity or freedom from punishment, penalty, &c.

wite-scræf, *st. n.* hole or pit of torment, hell.

wite-swing, *st. m.* scourging, flogging, punishment.

wite-þéo, *st. m.* tortured slave.
witga. See **witiga** (prophet).
witian, weotian, *w. v.* to order, dispose, arrange, destine, conclude, establish, attend to.
    be-witian, to care for, attend to, prepare, execute, effect, perceive.
witian, *w. v., w. gen.,* to visit (?). Gû. 488.
witig, wittig, *adj.* witting, cognizant, wise.
witiga, witega, witga, *w. m.* prophet, seer, predicter.
witig-dôm, *st. m.* prophecy, prediction, prescience.
witigian, witgian, *w. v.* to prophecy, predict.
witnian, *w. v.* to punish, chastise, correct, scourge.
    ge-witnian, the same as above.
witodlice, *adv.* certainly, undoubtedly.
wit-rod, wittig. See **wig-trod, witig** (wise).
wid, I. *prep.* against (= **with** in withstand). — **1.** *w. gen.* (*a.*), toward, to; — (*b.*), against (cf. protection, defense). — **2.** *w. dat.* (*a.*) toward, to; — (*b.*) against, opposed to, contrary (of hostility, resistance, or sentiment); — (*c.*), against, from (protection, defense, security); (*d.*), from (separation); — (*e.*), for, in exchange for (exchange, purchase, sale, compensation; — (*f.*), at, to, beside, by, with. — **3.** *w. acc.* (*a.*), to, toward, up to (to lean upon or beside, to support one's self upon; — (*b.*), toward and against (hostility and friendliness); (*c.*), against, from (protection, defense, guarding; to be one's friend, defend one's self against); — (*d.*), beside, by, with; — (*e.*), at, upon (B. 3049); — (*f.*), through, through and through. — *dat. & acc.* often

interchange: no case found in *Fä.* 50 (= against, in opposition to.
wider, *prep.* against. (Ger. *wieder, wider.*
wider-breca, -breoca, *w. m.* antagonist, opponent.
wider-brôga, *w. m.* same as above.
wider-cwide, -cwyde, *st. m.* contradiction, objection.
wider-cyr, *st. m.* return. (Ger. *wiederkehr.*)
wider-feohtend, *part. & subs.* antagonist, foe.
wider-gyld, -gild, *st. n.* compensation, return, recompense.
wider-hycgende, *part.* refractory, stubborn, perverse, hostile-minded.
wider-hydig, *adj.* same as above.
wider-léan, *st. n.* compensation, recompense.
wider-méde, *adj.* hostile-minded, inimical.
wider-médo, *st. f.* hate, enmity, antagonism.
wider-ræhtes, *adv.* opposite, over against.
wider-sæc, *st. n.* contradiction, opposition, strife.
wider-steall, *st. m.* resistance, opposition.
wider-trod, *st. n.* return.
wider-weard, *adj.* opposing, antagonizing, hostile, refractory, stubborn, rebellious, bad.
wider-weardnes, *st. f.* opposition, enmity, hostility.
widre, *st. n.* resistance, opposition.
wid-steall, *st. m.* the same as above.
wiod, wiolena, (*gen. pl.* of **wela**), **wiordan.** See **wêod, wela, weordan.**
wlæclice, *adv.* tranquilly, gently (?) (Ps. 148: 5), for **wræclice.**
wlanc, wlonc, *adj.* rich, stately, glad, lively, proud, insolent.

wlátian, *w. v.* to look, glance, gaze.
  be-wlátian, to look at, contemplate, inspect.
wlenco, wlencu, wlence, *st.f.* wealth, glory, pomp; pride, arrogance, haughtiness.
wlencan, *w. v.* in
  ge-wlencan, to render proud, adorn, decorate.
wlitan, *st. abl. v.* V. to look, glance, gaze. see.
  and-wlitan, the same as above.
  be-wlitan, the same as above.
  geond-wlitan, 1. to look beyond, look over, to contemplate.— 2. *intrans.* to look about, look around. Cri. 60.
  þurh-wlitan, to look through.
wlite, *st. m.* form, figure, aspect, look; beautiful form, beauty, glory, ornament.
wlite-andet (?), fitting or appropriate acknowledgment, confession. Ps. 103: 2.
wlite-beorht, *adj.* brilliant or lovely of form or appearance.
wlite-léas, *adj.* without beauty, ugly.
wlite-séon, *st. f.* sight, aspect, object.
wlitig-torht, *adj.* brilliant, lovely.
wlitig, *adj.* beauteous, lovely.
wlitige, *adv.* the same as above.
wlitig-fæst, *adj.* of unfading beauty.
wlitigian, *w. v.* 1. to beautify, ennoble. — 2. to become beautiful. Seaf. 49.
  ge-wlitigian, to adorn, beautify, embellish.
wló, wlóh, *st. n.* fringe, tuft, tatter; to characterize a small matter (Gû. 1127) = bit (*adverb acc.*)
wlonc, wô. See wlanc, wôh.
wôcor, *st. f.* progeny, posterity, descendants, race.
wôd, *adj.* (wood), raging, mad, senseless.
woddor, *st. n.* throat, gorge, gullet.

Wôden, *st. m.* (cf. Wednesday), the god Wuotan, Odin. Gn. Ex. 133.
wôd-þrag, *st. f.* attack of insanity, time of an attack; madness, rage.
wôh, wô, *adj.* 1. bent, curved, twisted, distorted, wrong. — 2. twisted, perverse, eccentric, unequal, unjust, bad, mean, injurious.
wôh-bogen, *adj.* bent, crooked, curved.
wôh-fremmend, *part.* committing injustice, doing evil.
wôh-godu, *st. n. pl.* false gods, idols.
wôh-hæmed, *st. n.* unlawful cohabitation, adultery.
wolcen, *st. m. n.* (welkin), cloud.
wolcen-faru, *st. f.* flying (of) clouds, cloud-drift.
wolcen-ge-hnást, *st. n.* cloud-collision (in a storm).
wol-dæg, *st. m.* day of pestilence.
wollen-teâr, *adj.* with welling tears.
wom. See wam (blemish, &c.)
wôm, *st. m.* howling, shouting, lamentation.
wôma, *w. m.* noise, tumult, brawling, horror, terror;— swefnes wôma, dream-tumult, vision, dream.
womb, won (wonn), wong, wonge, wonian. See wamb, wan, wang, wange, wanian.
wôp, *st. m.* (whoop?), cry, lamentation, weeping, shrieking.
wôp-dropa, *w. m.* drop of pity, tear.
wôpig, *adj.* weeping, lamenting.
worc. See weorc (work).
word, *st. n.* word.
word, *st. n.* injury, loss (?). Gn. Ex. 65.
word-béot, *st. n.* promise in words, plighted word.
word-béotung, *st. f.* same as above.
word-cræft, *st. m.* word-craft, art of speech, poetic art.
word-cwide, -cwede, -cwyde, *st. m.* speech, language, rhetorical expression, utterance.

word-ge-bêot, *st. n.* promise in words, plighted word.
word-ge-mearc, *st. n.* word-definition or characterization, limitation by words.
word-ge-rŷne, *st. n.* **word-rune,** secret expressed in or by words.
word-gid, -gyd, *st. n.* song, melodious speech, language, saying.
word-glêaw, *adj.* **word-**clever, eloquent in words, fluent.
word-hlêodor, *st. m.* word-clangor, speech, language; sermon.
word-hord, *st. n.* **word-hoard,** treasury of words.
word-latu, *st. f.* laxity in fulfilling commands, hesitation in obeying orders.
word-ladu, *st. f.* converse, speech, language.
word-lêan, *st. n.* word-recompense, reward for song.
word-loca, *w. m.* **word-hoard;** speech.
word-riht, *st. n.* 1. **word-right,** the written law, law.—2. right or fitting word (B. 2631).
word-snottor, *adj.* wise in words.
worhte, *pret.* of **wyrcan** (to work).
wôrian, *w. v.* to roam, ramble, move, roll in ruins.
world. See **weoruld** (world).
worn, *st. m.* multitude, number.
worn-ge-hât, *st. n.* promise of multitude, of numerous descendants. Gen. 2364.
worpan. See **weorpan** (to cast).
worpian, *w. v.* to cast, throw, throw at or upon, pelt with missiles.
word, wordig. See **weord, weordig.**
woruf, woruld, -old. See **weoruf, weoruld.**
wôd, *st. f.* voice, tone, cry, song.
wôd-bora, *w. m.* orator, speaker, singer, minstrel, prophet.
wôd-cræft, *st. m.* oratory, art of speech or song.

wôd-gifu, *st. f.* gift of voice, speech, or song.
wôd-sang, *st. m.* song.
wrace, *st. f.* (**wreaking**) vengeance. Ps. 93:1.
wracu, *w. f.* (**wreaking**) persecution, vengeance, punishment, misery, torture, pain.
wræc, *st. n.* exile, banishment, persecution, oppression, misery, grief.
wræc, *st. m.* exile, fugitive (B. 2613), émigré, outcast.
wræcca, wrecca, wreccea, wreca, *w. m.* **wretch,** exile, fugitive, stranger.
wræc-fæc, *st. n.* time of exile, banishment, misery.
wræc-hwîl, *st. f.* the same as above.
wræc-, wrec-lâst, *st. m.* path of exile, banishment.
wræc-lic, *adj.* 1. foreign, strange, unfamiliar.— 2. unusual, uncommon, extraordinary.— 3. wretched, grievous (Gen. 37).
wræclice, *adv.* 1. in exile, abroad. 2. strangely, wondrously.
wræc-mæcg, *st. m.* exile, outcast, wretch.
wræc-mæcg, *w. m.* same as above.
wræc-man, *st. m.* exile, fugitive.
wræc-setl, *st. n.* place for exiles, penal colony.
wræc-sid, *st. m.* exile, banishment, misery, woful fate, wretchedness.
wræc-stôw, *st. f.* place of exile or punishment.
wræd, wræd, *st. f.* **wreath,** band, ribbon.
wræne, *adj.* extravagant, lax, voluptuous, libidinous.
wræn-nes, *st. f.* extravagance, dissoluteness, lust, revelry.
wræsnan, *w. v.* to alter, change, modulate.
wræst, *adj.* fixed, firm, lasting, able, strong.

wrǽstan, *w. v.* to wrest, twist, turn, set in motion.
wrǽste, *adv.* fixedly, firmly.
wrǽt, *st. f.* fret (?), fretwork, ornament, oddity, jewel, work of art.
wrǽtlic, *adj.* artistic, ornamental, strange, singular, rare.
wrǽtlíce, *adv.* the same as above.
wrǽd. See **wrǽd** (wreath).
wrǽd-, wred-studu, *st. f.* studding, column, pillar, support.
wráð, *adj.* 1. **wroth,** angry, cruel, hostile. — 2. crooked, mean, cowardly, bad.— 3. urgent, insistent, violent.
wráðe, *adv.* the same as above.
wráðlíc, *adj.* bitter, vehement, woful.
wráðlíce, *adv.* hostilely.
wráð-mód, *adj.* **wroth-minded,** angry.
wráð-scræf, *st. n.* mean and woful hole; pit of misery or wrath.
wraðu, *st. f.* strengthening material, support, help, maintenance.
wreca. See **wrǽcca** (exile).
wrecan, *st. abl. v.* III. 1. to drive, push, urge, force.— 2. to expel, drive out or away.— 3. to bring before, deliver, utter, pronounce, sing.—4. to punish, **wreak,** avenge. 5. to press forward, hurry, hasten to.
   á-wrecan, 1. to drive off, out, away.— 2. to strike, hit, pierce.— 3. to bring forth, deliver, utter, pronounce.
   be-, bi-wrecan, 1. to drive, bring, fetch.— 2. to overturn, push over or about, strike, flog.
   for-wrecan, to drive forth, expel, banish.
   ge-wrecan, *w. acc.* to **wreak** vengeance on, to punish.
   tó-wrecan, to drive asunder, scatter, dissipate.
   þeod-wrecan, to **wreak** or avenge on a whole people, take summary revenge. B. 1278.
wrecca. See **wrǽcca** (exile).
wreccan, *w. v.* to wake, rouse, set up; to urge, press, torment.
wreccea, wrec-lást. See **wrǽcca, wrǽc-lást** (exile).
wrêgan, *w. v.* to set in lively motion, excite, stir up.
   ge-wrêgan, the same as above.
wrenc, wrence, *st. m.* 1. **wrench,** crook, bending, curve.— 2. crookedness, deceit, cunning, intrigue. —3. modulation, song (Ph. 133; Rid. 9: 2).
wrencan. *w. v.* to spin intrigues, controversies; — to "wirework."
wrenna, *w. m.* spy's or scout's horse. Rim. 7.
wredian, *w. v.* to support, sustain, uphold, strengthen, render firm.
   á-wredian, the same as above.
   under-wredian, same as above.
wred-studu. See **wrǽd-studu.**
wrêon, wrion, *st. abl. v.* V. & VI. to cover, conceal, hide, cover over, protect, defend.
   be-wrêon, to cover over, hide.
   on-wrêon, to uncover, reveal.
wreoðen-hilt, *adj.* **wreathen-hilted,** with twisted hilt.
wriceð, *3d pers. sg. indic. pres.* of **wrecan** (to drive).
wridan, wriðan, *st. abl. v.* V. to increase, germinate, wax, grow up.
wridian, wriðian, *w.v.* same as above.
wrigels, *st. n.* cover, veil.
wrigian, *w. v.* to strive, struggle, press forward, endeavor, dare, venture.
wrihan, *st. abl. v.* V. to cover over, hide, conceal, keep secret.
   be-, bi-wrihan, same as above.
   in-wrihan, to uncover, reveal, disclose.
   ofer-wrihan, to **over-rig,** cover over, conceal.

on-wríhan, to unrig, uncover, disclose.
writ, *st. n.* writ, writing.
wrítan, *st. abl. v.* V. to scratch, incise, scribble, write.
   â-wrítan, 1. to write out, put down in writing.— 2. to describe (El. 91).— 3. to form, fashion, copy (An. 726).
   be-wrítan, to write about, describe, inscribe.
   for-wrítan, to cut to pieces.
wrida, *w. m.* ring. Cf. wreath.
wrídan, *st. abl. v.* V. to wreathe (writhe), turn, bind, fetter, tie.
   â-wrídan, to turn, get ready, prepare.
   be-wrídan, to wind about, bewreathe, surround, envelop.
   ge-wrídan, to bind or tie on, attach to.
   on-wrídan, to unwreathe, ununbind, loosen, disclose.
wrídan, wrídian. See wrídan, wrídian (to grow).
wrixl, *st. f.* exchange, change, barter.
wrixlan, wrixlian, *w. v.* to change, exchange, alternate, barter.
   ge-wrixlan, 1. to get by exchange, barter for.— 2. to compensate, recompense.
wrion. See wréon (to cover).
wrôht, *st. m. & f.* 1. accusation, censure, blame, reproach.— 2. crime, sin, mischief, injustice, misery, provocation, anger.— 3. strife, enmity, hostility, discord.— 4. harm, hurt, damage, injury, misfortune.
wrôht-bora, *w. m.* originator or stirrer up of strife or crime; monster, devil.
wrôht-dropa, *w. m.* drop, bloodshed that brings sin or crime with it.
wrôht-ge-tême, *st. n.* injustice, wrong, crime, guilt.
wrôht-scipe, *st. m.* crime, outrage, misdeed.

wrôht-smid, *st. m.* worker of crime or misdeeds, evil-doer, devil.
wrôht-stæf, *st. m.* mischief, misdeed, crime, outrage.
wrôtan, *st. red. v.* to root up, turn, rummage.
wuce, *w. f.* week.
wudig, *adj.* woody.
wudu, *st. m.* 1. wood.— 2. tree.— 3. forest, woods.
wudu-bât, *st. m.* woodboat, wooden boat.
wudu-bêam, *st. m.* forest tree.
wudu-bearu, *st. m.* (woodbarrow), grove, forest.
wudu-blêd, *st. f.* tree-blossom.
wudu-fæsten, *st. n.* wood-fastness, ship.
wudu-feld, *st. m.* woody field.
wudu-fugol, *st. m.* woodfowl, forest bird.
wudu-holt, *st. n.* woodholt, forest, grove.
wudu-rêc, *st. m.* wood-reek, smoke from the wood of the funeral pyre.
wudu-telga, *w. m.* wood-twig or branch.
wudu-trêow, *st. n.* wood-tree.
wuduwe, wudwe, wuht. See widwe, wiht.
wuldor, *st. n.* glory, praise, fame.
wuldor-blæd, *st. m.* fullness of glory, ecstatic glory.
wuldor-cyning, *st. m.* king of glory or praise, God.
wuldor-drêam, *st. m.* heavenly rapture, joy of heaven.
wuldor-fæder, *st. m.* father of glory, God.
wuldor-fæst, *adj.* glorious, splendid, illustrious, noble.
wuldor-fæste, *adv.* same as above.
wuldor-gâst, *st. m.* spirit of glory, angel. Holy Ghost.
wuldor-ge-steald, *st. n. p'.* glorious possession, dwelling-place, realms of glory.

wuldor-gifen, -geofun, *st. f.* glorious gift, gift of glory, noble intellectual power.
wuldor-gifu, *st. f.* same as above.
wuldor-gim, *st. m.* glory-gem, sun.
wuldor-hama, *w. m.* garb of glory, brilliant robe.
wuldor-lêan, *st. n.* glorious recompense, (loan).
wuldor-lic, *adj.* glorious, splendid.
wuldor-mâga, *w. m.* kinsman in or of glory.
wuldor-mago, *st. m.* son of glory, illustrious son.
wuldor-micel, *adj.* gloriously great.
wuldor-nyttig, *st. f.* remarkable service, profit, gain.
wuldor-spêd, *st. f.* fullness of glory, glorious wealth.
wuldor-spêdig, *adj.* glorious, famous.
wuldor-torht, *adj.* glory-bright, brilliant, shining, clear.
wuldor-þrym, *st. m.* heavenly glory, hight of glory, majesty.
wuldor-weorud, *st. n.* noble army, heavenly host or inhabitant.
wuldor-word, *st. n.* word of glory, glorious word.
wuldrian, *w. v.* **1.** to glorify, magnify.— **2.** to boast, brag.
ge-**wuldrian,** to render glorious, marvelous; to magnify.
wulf, *st. m.* wolf.
wulf-heafod-trêo, *st. n.* wolf-headed tree; cross, gallows. Rid. 56: 12.
wulf-heort, *adj.* wolf-hearted, hard-hearted, cruel.
wulf-hlið, *st. n.* (*pl.* hleoðu), wolf-slope, mountain-slope where wolves or monsters live.
wull, *st. f.* wool.
wund, *st. f.* wound.
wund, *adj.* sore, wounded.
wunden-feax, *adj.* curly-haired or maned. B. 1400.
wunden-heals, *adj.* with twisted or curved neck. B. 298.

wunden-heord, *adj.* curly-locked? B. 3151.
wunden-locc, *adj.* same as above.
wunden-mæl, *st. n.* sword damascened with twisted or complicated patterns.
wunden-stefna, *w. m.* ship with curved prow.
wundian, *w. v.* to wound.
for-**wundian,** same as above.
ge-**wundian,** same as above.
wundor, *st. n.* wonder, marvel, monster, strange deed or work, work of art;—*instr. pl.* **wundrum,** wondrously, strangely.
wundor-âgræfen, *part.* wondrously graven or chiseled.
wundor-bebod, *st. n.* wonderful command, puzzling order.
wundor-bêacen, *st. n.* wonder-beacon, strange sign.
wundor-blêo, *st. n.* wondrous hue or color.
wundor-clam, -clom, *st. n.* wonder-clamp, fetter, strange band or bond.
wundor-fæt, *st. n.* (vat), vessel of wondrous workmanship.
wundor-gifu, *st. f.* wonder-gift, wondrous endowment.
wundor-lic, *adj.* wonderlike, wonderful.
wundor-lice, *adv.* same as above.
wundor-maððum, *st. m.* wondrous jewel.
wundor-sêon, -sion, *st. f.* wonderful sight.
wundor-smið, *st. m.* smith that executes wonderful work.
wundor-tâcen, *st. n.* wonder-token.
wundor-weorc, *st. n.* wonder-work, marvelous deed.
wundor-woruld, *st. f.* wonderful world.
wundor-wyrd, *st. f.* wonderful event, happening.

wundrian, *w. v.* to **wonder,** marvel, admire, stare (at).
  â-wundrian, to turn in a wonderful wise. El. 581.
wundrung, *st. f.* **wondering,** wonder, admiration.
wunian, *w. v.* **1.** (Ger. *wohnen*), to dwell, abide, sojourn in.— **2.** to stand, consist, remain, last, persevere, hold out.
  ge-wunian, 1. to dwell, tarry, sojourn, be, in;—*past part.* living, dwelling, abiding.— **2.** to stand, consist, remain, last, hold out;— *w. acc.* to stand by, cling to, be dependent on.— **3.** to accustom one's self, be wont (Ger. *gewöhnen*).
þurh-wunian, to persevere, hold out, continue.
wunn, wurd. See **wyn, wyrd.**
wurma, *w. m.* (**worm**), *murex* that affords the Tyrian dye; purple.
wurpan. See **weorpan** (to cast).
wurd, wurdan, wurdian. See **weord, weordan, weordian.**
wutan, wuton, wutun, utan, uton, (properly, **1.** *pers. pl.* of **witan,** used as hortatory subj.), *w. inf.* come on! go to! cheer up! *allons!* let us go! well! well then! let's!
wycg, wydewe, wyht. See **wicg, widwe, wiht.**
wyldan, *w. v.* in
  ge-wyldan, to tame, control, bring into subjection.
wylf, *st. f.* she-**wolf.**
wylfen, *adj.* **wolf**ish.
wyll, *st. m.* **well,** spring.
wylla, *w. m.* the same as above.
wyllan. See **willan** (to wish).
wyllan, *w. v.* **1.** to **well** up, to gush or leap forth.— **2.** *reflex.* to wallow, roll round.
wylle, *w. f.* **well,** spring.
wylle-, wille-burne, *w. f.* the same as above.

wylle-, wille-ge-spring, *st. n.* **well**-spring, water-flood.
wyll-, will-flôd, *st. m.* same as above.
wylm, *st. m.* **welling,** surging, billowing; surf, flood.
wylm-hât, *adj.* surging-**hot,** fervent.
wyltan, *w. v.* (to **welter**), roll, turn.
wyn, wynn, wenn, wunn, *st. f.* joy, rapture, delight, delightfulness;—*w. gen.* the joy, delight of, favorite.
wyna, *w. m.* name of an animal or plant. Run. 37.
wyn-bêam, *st. m.* joy-beam, tree of delight (holy cross).
wyn-burg, *st. f.* happy or delightful burgh, town, castle.
wyn-candel, -condel, *st. f.* joy-candle, pleasant light (sun).
wyn-dæg, *st. m.* **day** of joy, **win**some day.
wyn-ele, *st. m.* joy-giving **oil, win**some oil.
wyn-fæste, -feste, *adv.* joyfully firm or fixed.
wyn-ge-sid, *st. m.* winsome, pleasant companion.
wyn-grâf, *st. m. & n.* delightful grove.
wyn-land, -lond, *st. n.* land of delight.
wyn-lêas, *adj.* joyless.
wyn-lic, *adj.* delightful, rapturous, pleasant, sweet.
wyn-lice, *adv.* the same as above.
wyn-mǽg, *st. f.* winsome maiden.
wynnan. See **winnan** (to strive).
wyn-psalterium, *st. n.* psalm of joy.
wyn-rôd, *st. f.* **rood** of bliss, blessed cross.
wynster. See **winster** (left).
wyn-, winsum, *adj.* **winsome,** delightful.
wyn-sumlic, *adj.* same as above.
wyrcan, wyrcean, weorcean, wercan, wircan, *w. v.* **1.** *w. acc., gen.,* or *instr.* to **work,** act, do, make,

get, prepare, institute, cause.—
2. *w. acc.* or *gen.* to work out,
merit, deserve.

be-, bi-wyrcan, to bring about,
accomplish, get, adorn.

for-wyrcan, to lose by misdeed,
forfeit; to condemn, curse.

ge-wyrcan, 1. *w. acc.* to **work,**
make, do, manufacture, construct,
fabricate.— **2.** *w. acc.* to do, make,
accomplish, perform, commit.— **3.**
to work out, win, effect, deserve.
4. *w. gen.* to carry out, execute.
Sol. 386.

in-wyrcan, to **work in,** produce
effect, exert influence; to direct,
fix, appoint.

wyrcend, *part. & subs.* **worker,**
doer.

wyrd, wird, wurd, *st. f.* **1. Weird,**
(one of the Norns or goddesses of
Fate), fate, providence, destiny.—
2. event, fact, transaction.

wyrdan, werdan, *w. v.* to spoil, injure, hurt, oppress, annihilate, kill.

â-wyrdan, the same as above.

ge-wyrdan, the same as above.

wyrdan, *w. v.* in

and-wyrdan, to answer.

wyrd-stæf, *st. m.* decree of **weird**
or fate.

wyrfan = **hwyrfan,** to go, wander?
Met. 24: 44.

wyrgan, *w. v.* in

â-wyrgan, to **worry,** throttle,
stifle, strangle, destroy. injure, disfigure.

wyrgan, wyrgean, wyrigan, *w. v.*
to scold, abuse, imprecate, execrate,
bewitch, curse, condemn.

wyrgnes. See **wyrignes.**

wyrgdu, *st. f.* curse, imprecation,
malediction.

wyrhta, *w. m.* **wright,** worker, originator, creator. artist, artisan.

wyrig, *adj.* evil, vicious, bad, malignant.

wyrignes, wyrgnes, *st. f.* abuse,
execration, reviling invective.

wyrm, *st. m.* **worm,** serpent, dragon.

wyrm-cynn, *st. n.* kith and **kin** of
worms, serpents, dragons.

wyrm-fâh, *adj.* particolored, inlaid
or adorned with serpentine lines
of ornamentation.

wyrm-geard, *st. m.* **wormyard,**
dwelling-place of worms or serpents.

wyrm-hât, *st. n.* **worm-heat,** heat
of the dragon. B. 897.

wyrm-hord, *st. n.* dragon-hoard.

wyrm-lic, *st. n.* serpent-body.

wyrm-sele, *st. m.* hall of serpents,
hell.

wyrman, *w. v.* to **warm.**

wyrnan, weornan, *w. v.* to reject,
refuse, repudiate, reserve, withhold.

for-wyrnan, 1. to reject, refuse,
decline, repudiate.— **2.** *w. acc.* of
thing: to repel, hold at a distance,
escape from. B. 1142.

wyrp, *st. m.* throw, cast, fling,
blow.

wyrpan. See **weorpan** (to throw).

wyrpan, *w. v.* **1.** to return, come
back, turn.— **2.** to refresh one's
self, rest, recover. Exod. 130.

wyrpe, *st. m.* revolution, change,
alteration, remedy, relief.

wyrpel, *st. m.* varvels, silver rings
put on a hawk's leg, foot-ring.
Wy. 87.

wyrrest, *adv.* **worst.**

wyrresta, *adj.* the same as above.

wyrs, *adv.* **worse.**

wyrsa, wirsa, *compar. adj.* **worse,**
meaner, &c.

wyrslic, *adj.* bad, mean, evil.

wyrst, *superl.* of **wyrs** (worse).

wyrt, *st. f.* **1. wort,** vegetable,
kitchen herb, sweet-smelling herb.
2. root.

wyrt-cynn, *st. n.* **wort-kind,** species of fragrant herb.
wyrtian, *w. v.* in
 ge-**wyrtian,** to spice, season, perfume.
wyrt-truma, wyrtruma, *w. m.* root, root-stock.
wyrt-wâla, -wêla, *w. m.* root.

wyrd, wyrde, *adj.* **worth, worthy,** honored, dear, precious.
wyrd, wyrd-, wyrdan, wyrdian. See **weord** (*n.*), **weordan, weordian.**
wŷscan, wiscan, *w. v.* to **wish,** desire, aspire to, struggle for.
wyt. See **wit** (we two).

Y

ŷcan, ican, icean, iecan, *w. v.* to **eke,** increase, enlarge.
 ge-**ŷcan,** the same as above.
ŷce, *w. f.* toad, frog.
ydwe, *pl.* intestines, entrails? Ps. 108: 18.
yfel, *st. n.* **evil,** ill.
yfel, *adj.* **evil,** bad.
yfel-dǽd, *st. f.* **evil deed.**
yfele, yfle, *adv.* ill, badly.
yfelian, yflian, *w. v.* to hurt, harm, bring evil upon.
 ge-**yfelian,** the same as above.
yfe-mest, yf-mest, *adj. & adv.* **overmost,** uppermost.
yfle, yflian, ŷht, ylca, yld. See **yfele, yfelian, ieht, ilca, yldu.**
yldan, eldan, *w. v.* **1.** *intrans.* to hesitate, be irresolute.— **2.** *trans.* to delay, defer, put off, procrastinate, detain, prolong.
 for-**yldan,** to delay, put off.
ylde, ilde, *st. m. pl.* men, humanity.
ylding, *st. f.* delay, procrastination.
yldra, yldest. See **eald** (old).
yldra, *w. m.* **1.** *sg.* father (El. 492). **2.** *pl.* one's elders, parents, ancestors, forefathers.
yldu, yldo, yld, *st. f.* **1.** lifetime, era, age.— **2.** *pl.* one's age or years (Ps. 89: 11).— **3.** old age, age.
ylf, *st. f.* **elf,** incubus.
ylfete, ylfetu, *st. f.* swan.
ymb, ymbe, *prep.* I. *w. acc.* **1.** local: about, around, along.— **2.** over, concerning, of, in respect of, in relation to (w. vbs. of speaking, striving, caring, thinking, &c.).— **3.** temporal: about, around (B. 219); after; before (Sat. 426, 571).— II. *w. dat.* about, around, concerning. —In I. and II. it is often placed after the word governed: occurs also without a case—adverbially.
ymbe-sittend, *part. & subs.* one sitting or settled around, a near neighbor.
ymb-hoga, *w. m.* care, anxiety, apprehension.
ymb-hwearft, -hwerft, *st. m.* rotation, revolution.
ymb-hwyrft, *st. m.* **1.** rotation, revolution (Met. 28: 20).— **2.** surrounding, environment, circle, circuit, extent.— **3.** circle, globe, earth.
ymb-lyt, *st. m.* circle, circuit, circumference, extent? Sat. 7.
ymb-sittend, *part. & subs.* one settled in or around, neighbor.
ymb-sprǽce, *adj.* **spoken** about, much spoken of.
ymb-standende, *part.* **standing** about or around.
ymb-ûtan, *adv. & prep.* about, around.
ymen, ymn, *st. m.* **hymn,** sacred song.
yppan, *w. v.* to open, disclose, reveal.
 ge-**yppan,** to unveil, reveal, betray.

yppe, *adj.* open, public, manifest, known.

yppe, *w. f.* tribune, daîs, high seat in the hall.

ypping, *st. f.* heaping up, accumulation, extent, expanse.

yr, *adj.* irate, angry.

yr, *st. m.* 1. bow.— 2. name of the Rune y.

yre-þweorh, *adj.* irate, ireful, cross, brusque. Jul. 90.

yrfe, *w. n.* inheritance, heritage. (Ger. *erbe.*)

yrfe-lâf, *st. f.* 1. property left, inheritance.— 2. heir, guardian of the inheritance. Exod. 403.

yrfe-land, *st. n.* hereditary land, heritage in land.

yrfe-stôl, *st. m.* hereditary seat (stool), estate.

yrfe-weard, *st. m.* heir, inheritor.

yrgdo, yrhdo, *st. f.* cowardice.

yrman, *w. v.* to render miserable or wretched. (Ger. *arm.*)

 ge-yrman, the same as above.

yrmen, yrmen-þeod. See eormen, eormenþeod.

yrming, *st. m.* wretch, beggar, needy one, pauper.

yrmdu, *st. f.* wretchedness, misery.

yrnan. See irnan (to run).

yrre, *st. n.* ire, wrath, fury.

yrre, ierre, *adj.* 1. wrong, erring, bewildered, lost, confused.— 2. irate, wroth. [ire.

yrre-môd, *adj.* angry of mind, full of

yrre-weorc, *st. n.* ire-work, work or deed of wrath, fury.

yrringa, *adv.* irefully, wrathfully, furiously.

yrsian, *w. v.* to get angry or irate, to pour forth indignation. Gû. 171.

yrsung, irsung, *st. f.* ire, wrath, passys. See is (to be). [sion.

ysle, *w. f.* powder, dust, ashes.

ŷst, *st. f.* storm, tempest, hurricane.

ŷstig, *adj.* stormy (cf. the "yeasty waves.") [treme.

yte-mest, yt-mest, *adj.* utmost, ex-

ŷð, *st. f.* wave, billow.

ŷð, *compar. adv.* of êaðe: more easily; —*superl.* ŷðast, -ost.

ŷðan, *w. v.* (cf. Ger. *ôde*), to waste, ravage, destroy, annihilate, clear away, strip.

ŷðan, ŷðian, *w. v.* to surge, rise in billows; to roar, rage.

ŷð-bord, *st. n.* wave-board? ship? shore? Crä. 57.

ŷðe, *adj.* easy.

ŷðelice, *adv.* the same as above.

ŷð-faru, *st. f.* wave-current, water-path, flowing waves. [find.

ŷð-fynde, *adj.* easily found, easy to

ŷð-ge-bland, -ge-blond, *st. n.* turmoil or tumult of waves.

ŷð-ge-sêne, *adj.* easily seen, visible.

ŷð-ge-win, *st. n.* battling waves, tumultuous seas.

ŷð-hof, *st. n.* water-dwelling, ship, vessel.

ŷð-lâd, *st. f.* water-course, path over the sea.

ŷð-lâf, *st. f.* wave-leavings, sand, shore, beach.

ŷð-lid, *st. n.* ship, vessel.

ŷð-lida, *w. m.* the same as above.

ŷð-mere, *st. n.* (mere), sea, ocean.

ŷð-mearh, *st. m.* sea-horse (mare?) ship.

ŷð-naca, *w. m.* boat, vessel.

ŷwan, *w. v.* to show, reveal, point out, announce.

 æt-ŷwan, 1. to show, exhibit, disclose, announce.— 2. to become visible, appear.

 ge-ŷwan, to show, exhibit, reveal, present, offer.

 ôd-ŷwan, 1. to show, exhibit, disclose.— 2. to show one's self, to appear.

zefferus, *st. m.* zephyr (wind).

AN OUTLINE OF ANGLO-SAXON GRAMMAR.*

§ 1.—**Alphabet.**—The Old English, after their conversion to Christianity, adopted the Roman alphabet with slight changes. d was crossed to represent **dh** and the Runic characters **thorn** and **wên** (= **th** and **w**) were retained. ð and þ afterwards became in sound indistinguishable; that is, either character was used to represent either sound, **dh** or **th**.

§ 2.—**Pronunciation.**—The pronunciation of these signs must be studied from (1) the standpoint of other Germanic languages; and (2) the traditional pronunciation of Latin as it was spoken in England during and after the seventh century. Modern English can give but little help.

§ 3.—**Accent.**—The stress or accent is generally on the root-syllable, or significant element. "A secondary accent may fall on the tone-syllable of the lighter part of a compound or on a suffix."

§ 4.—**Quantity.**—Vowels and diphthongs are both short and long. Length of vowel, however, can not be determined by the Mss. To designate a long vowel some editors, like Sweet and Sievers, use an acute accent á; others, like March and Zupitza, prefer the more customary circumflex â.

§ 5.—**Umlaut.**—This is the change in an accented vowel produced by a vowel or a semi-vowel (i, w) in the following syllable. Exs. sēcan (Goth. *sốkjan*); ciest (from cēosan); liofað (from libban); men (from mann); helpan (root hilp); bealu (O.H.Ger. *balo*); seofon (Goth. *sibun*), &c. Sievers finds a palatal-umlaut in rieht (riht, ryht), from reoht, cnieht, cniht, from cneoht. See Sievers' *Angelsächsische Grammatik*, § 101.

§ 6.—**Breaking.**—Breaking is a change of an accented vowel brought about by a consonant or consonants in the same syllable. Exs. eall, earm, eorl, leoht, &c. What is called Breaking by Grimm and others is considered u- and o-umlaut by Holtzmann and Sievers. Cf. bealu, eafor, &c.

§ 7.—**Sounds.**—(A). Vowels.—In Old English there are the following vowels and diphthongs: a, æ(ä), e, i, o, u, y, œ, ea(ia), eo(io), and ie(ei). Of these, ea(ia), eo(io), and ie(ei), are likewise used as diphthongs. a, o, u, are gutturals; æ, e, i, œ, y, are palatals. All diphthongs begin with a palatal sound.

a	=	a	in	far;	â	=	a	in father.
æ(ä)	=	a	"	hat;	ǣ	=	a(ai)	" fate (air).
e	=	e	"	men;	ê	=	ey	" they.
i	=	i	"	pin;	î	=	i	" pique.
o	=	o	"	not;	ô	=	o	" note.
u	=	u	"	full;	û	=	oo	" fool.
y†	=	u	"	sur (Fr.);	ŷ	=	ü	" grün (Ger).

* This Outline is specially indebted to the masterly works of March and Sievers.   † Later y and ŷ = i and î.

œ ǽ (Kentish and Northumbrian) = e ê (West Saxon).
ea = e + a,— earm (e-úrm); —êa = ǽ + a, —êast (ú-árst).
eo = e + o,— weorc (wŭ-ork); —êo = a + o, —dêop (dä-op).
(B.) Consonants.—1. *Liquids*—l, r.—2. *Semi-Vowels*—j, w.—3. *Nasals*—m, n.—4. *Mutes* (*a*), *Labials*—p, b, f, v; (*b*), *Dentals*—t, d, ð, þ, s; (*c*), *Gutturals* and *Palatals*—c (k, q, x), g, h (x).

l was pronounced as modern l.

r was a strong trill, as in modern French.

j. There was no special sign for j (yot). This sound was most frequently represented by i, g, ge, and ige = y in yea.

w was pronounced as modern w.* So likewise m, n, p, b, t, d.

f (v) have the sound of both f and v in modern English. Exs. of f: fæder, findan, woffian, hæft, ræfsan, wulf, fif, &c. Exs. of v: ofer, gifan, hláford, sealfian. v is sometimes found in foreign words.

ð, þ. Both characters at first represented th; but later they stood for dh too. In print þ is initial, and ð medial and final. This custom was introduced by Grimm.

c (k is seldom found in the Mss.) is generally the sharp guttural; as in cld, cyning, circe. In some cases, however, it had become palatal: mêceas, sêcean, êcium, drencium,—that is, when i or e follows.

g is either a flat guttural: galan, gold, guma, gylden, glæd, gnorn, grafan; or a broad palatal (before e, ea, eo, i): geldan, gieldan, geaf, gêafon, gêotan, gift.

For g = j, see under j. gg is always written cg. ng is thus pronounced engel (= eng-gel).

h. Initial h is a breathing: hê, hláf, hring, hwæt, &c. Medial and final h is guttural (palatal) = German *ach* and *ich*.

x = cs or hs.

s had originally the sharp hissing sound: sunu, sittan, stondan, smæl, &c. Later it sometimes got the sound of z: llesde, ræsde, &c.

sc seems to vary between a guttural and a palatal pronunciation: sceal, sceaft, sceat, sceáp, sceolde, as well as scær, scæron, scolde, sculan. There seems to be no rule to determine the use of sc and sce: sceacan, scêoc, sceacen, and scacan, scôc, scæcen, are both found.

INFLECTIONS.

§ 8. **Declension of Substantives.**—In Old English the declension of substantives shows more decay than in any other Germanic language. The declension of a Germanic word is brought about by suffixing different kinds of determinating elements to a Root or Stem. If this word-stem end in a vowel, we have—I. The Vowel-Declension; if it end in a consonant, we have II. The Consonant-Declension.

§ 9. **Gender.**—There are three Genders—Masculine, Neuter, and Feminine. Gender is partly natural (sex), partly grammatical. Sometimes grammatical gender is shown by the endings: the suffixes -a, -dôm, -hád, are Masculine: -e, -nes, -ing, -ung, are Feminine. But most often gender can be determined only by the article. Compounds follow the gender of the last element.

---

* It was always pronounced before l and r.

AN OUTLINE OF ANGLO-SAXON GRAMMAR.

§ 10. **Number.**—There are three Numbers—Singular, Dual, and Plural. Outside of Pronouns, the Dual is not found.

§ 11. **Case.**—There are five cases—Nominative, Genitive, Dative, Accusative, and Instrumental. In substantives the Dative and Instrumental are alike. It is incorrect to print the Instr. sg. with a long e (ê). Sometimes in substantives and frequently in pronouns we find a pure Instrumental form: **folcy, ceapi; hwȳ, þȳ.** In Syntax, however, Dative and Instrumental are distinct.

§ 12.—I. **The Vowel (Strong) Declension.**

Here only three vowels are concerned—**a, i, u**. Hence the vowel-declension is divided into three classes: (*a.*) The **a**-declension; (*b.*) The **i**-declension; (*c.*) The **u**-declension. Of these only the **a**-declension is found entire. The other two had gone over more or less into it.

§ 13. **The a-declension.**—1. **Monosyllabic Words.**

(*a.*) MASCULINES.

Sg. N. A.	stân (stone).	drêam (joy).	dæg (day).
G.	stanes,	drêames,	dæges,
D. I.	stâne,	drêame,	dæge,
Pl. N. A.	stânas,	drêamas,	dagas,
G.	stâna,	drêama,	daga,
D. I.	stânum,	drêamum,	dagum.

(*b.*) NEUTERS.

Sg. N. A.	geoc (yoke).	scip (ship).	fæt (vessel).	word (word).
G.	geoces,	scipes,	fætes,	wordes.
D. I.	geoce,	scipe,	fæte,	worde,
Pl. N. A.	geocu, -o,	scipu,	fatu,	word,
G.	geoca,	scipa,	fata,	worda,
D. I.	geocum,	scipum,	fatum,	wordum.

§ 14.—Like **stân** and **drêam** decline:—

âd, oath.	gâr (spear).	slǣp, sleep.
cnif, knife.	hæft, prisoner.	stôl, chair.
dêad, death.	helm, helmet.	strêam, stream.
dôm, judgment.	hring, ring.	þeof, thief.
earm, arm.	mûd, mouth.	wind, wind.
eorl, man.	rim, number.	wulf, wolf.

§ 15.—Like **dæg** decline **hwæl**, whale; **pæd**, path; **stæf**, staff; that is, words with æ before one consonant. Before two consonants æ is generally retained in the plural: **æsp**, asp; **cræft**, strength; **gæst**, guest, &c., have pl. **æspas, cræftas, gæstas** (seldom **gastas**).

§ 16. Like **geoc** and **scip** decline:—

col, coal.	lot, cunning.	lid, member.
dor, gateway.	sol, dung.	twig, twig.
geat, gate.	spor, trace.	gebed, prayer.
hof, courtyard.	brim, sea.	gebrec, noise.
hol, hole.	clif, cliff.	geset, seat.
hop, hiding-place.	hlid, cover.	gesprec, conversation.
geflit, strife.	genip, darkness.	gewrit, writing. &c.

These Neuters, with **e** or **i** before a single consonant (from **brim** to **gewrit**, inclusive), frequently have **eo** or **io**, instead of **e** or **i** in the plural: **gebeodu, cliofu, liodu**, &c., as well as **gebedu, clifu**, &c.

§ 17.—Like **fæt** decline—

bæc, back.	glæs, glass.	stæd, seashore.
bæd, bath.	græf, grave.	þæc, roof.
cræt, crate.	hæf, sea.	træf, tent.
dæl, dale.	sæl, hall.	swæd, track.

Occasionally **æ** is found in the plural instead of **a**: **stædu, scræfu** (**stadu, scrafu**), &c.

§ 18.—Like **word** decline all neuters that are long, either by position, (that is, before two consonants), or by nature:—

bân, bone.	hǽr, hair.	lēoht, light.
bearn, child.	hilt, hilt.	lîf, life.
dêor, animal.	hors, horse.	lîc, body.
fŷr, fire.	hûs, house.	scêap, sheep.
folc, people.	lâc, play.	weorc, work.
gôd, good.	lêaf, foliage.	wîf, wife.
	wîn, wine, &c.	

§ 19.—REMARK 1.—In Northumbrian and in older West Saxon, the Gen. sg. ended in -**æs**: **domæs, heofonæs**. In Northumbrian **a** is also found: **biscobas, roderas**. Sometimes for -**es** we find -**ys**: **wintrys** (B. 516). Later, in West Saxon, this form became quite common.

REM. 2.—The Dat. sg. ending -**e** is sometimes dropped: **hâm**, seldom **hâme**.

REM. 3.—Words ending in -**h** lose the **h** in inflection:—

Nom.	mearh.	Gen. meares.
"	feorh.	" feores.
"	seolh.	" seoles.

If a vowel precedes the **h**, contraction takes place:—

Nom.	eoh.	Gen. êos.	
"	þeoh.	" þêos.	
"	feoh.	" fêos.	
"	scôh.	pl. scôs.	
"	hôh.	" hôas.	Dat. hôum.

REM. 4.—Some words ending in a double consonant lose one consonant in the Nom. and Acc., but it remains in the oblique cases: **weal, wealles; ful, fulles**, &c.

REM. 5.—Three Neuters regularly strengthen the stem in the pl. by -**er**: **ǽg**, egg; **cealf**, calf; **lamb**, lamb. They are thus declined: Sg. N. A. **ǽg**, G. **ǽges**, D. I. **ǽge**, Pl. N. A. **ǽgru, ǽgeru**, G. **ǽgra**, D. I. **ǽgrum**, &c. Sometimes **cild** has a pl. **cildru**; but in West Saxon it is usually declined like **word**. In Northumbrian it is also masculine; hence **cildo** and **cildas**.

AN OUTLINE OF ANGLO-SAXON GRAMMAR.

§ 20.—(c.) FEMININES:—

Sg. N.	âr (honor).	gifu, -o (gift).	sacu (strife).
G.	âre,	gife,	sace, sæce.
D. I.	âre,	gife,	sace, sæce.
A.	âre,	gife,	sace, sæce, sacu.
Pl. N. A.	âra, -e,	gifa, -e,	saca, sace, sæce,
G.	âra, -ena,	gifa, -ena,	saca.
D. I.	ârum,	gifum,	sacum.

§ 21.—Like âr decline—

dûn, hill.
folm, hand.   lâr, love.   þrâg, time.
fôr, journey.   mearc, boundary.   glôf, glove.
feoht, fight.   sorg, sorrow.   wund, wound.
heall, hall.   rest, ræst, rest.   þeod, people.
hwîl, while.   stund, hour.   spræc, speech.

§ 22. Like gifu, decline—

cearu, care.   lufu, love.   scolu, school.
fremu, advantage.   nosu, nose.   sceamu, shame.
                      þegu, taking.

§ 23.—Like sacu decline—

cwalu, death.   ladu, invitation.   talu, tale.
faru, journey.   racu, narrative.   þracu, violence.
lagu, law.   swadu, trace.   wracu, revenge.
                      wradu, support, &c.

REM. 1.—Rarely a Gen. sg. in -ys is found: helpys (Ps. 101: 9). In the oldest monuments the oblique cases of the sg. and the Nom. Acc. pl. ended in -æ. In the Gen. pl. the regular ending is -a. -ena, however, is often found; and sometimes -na, -ona. These forms have come from the Consonant-Declension.

§ 24.—2. POLYSYLLABIC WORDS.—(a.) MASCULINES:—

Sg. N. A.	mâdum (treasure).	heorot, heort (hart).	nægel (nail).
G.	mâdmes,	heorotes, heortes,	nægles,
D. I.	mâdme,	heorte, heorte,	nægle,
Pl. N. A.	mâdmas,	heorotas, heortas,	næglas,
G.	mâdma,	heorota, heorta,	nægla,
D. I.	mâdmum,	heorotum, heortum,	næglum.

§ 25.—(b.) NEUTERS.

Sg. N. A.	hûsel, hûsl (sacrifice).	wæter (water).	weofod (altar).
G.	hûsles,	wæteres, wætres,	weofodes,
D. I.	hûsle,	wætere, wætre,	weofode,
Pl. N. A.	hûsl, hûslu,	wæteru, wætru,	weofodu,
G.	hûsla,	wætera, wætra,	weofoda,
D. I.	hûslum,	wæterum, wætrum,	weofodum,

Here we have chiefly to do with derivatives in -ad, -ed, -els, -al, -ol, -ul, -um, -on, -en, -er, -or. If the stem is long, the vowel of the suffix is lost in inflection. If the stem is short, the vowel of the suffix is sometimes kept, sometimes lost. Usage varies. Examples:—

§ 26.—(*a.*) Masculines: **æppel**, apple; **bétel**, beetle; **ceafor**, chafer; **dêoful**, devil; **hungor**, hunger; **hrôdor**, consolation; **finger**, finger; **hamor**, hammer; **heofon**, heaven; **hæled**, warrior; **hagal** (-ol), **hægel**, **hægl**, hail; **regen**, rain; **þunor**, thunder, &c.

§ 27.—(*b.*) Neuters: **bêacen**, beacon; **fôdur** (-er), fodder; **gaful** (-ol), tribute; **hêafod**, head; **heolstor**, shadow; **leger**, resting-place; **mordur** (-or), murder; **setel**, seat; **tungol**, star; **wolcen**, welkin; **wundor**, wonder, &c.

§ 28.—Rem. 1.—When **e** is protected by position (that is, before two consonants, though it is sometimes retained before a single consonant) it is retained. Exs.: **fæsten, mæden, mægen, nŷten, hengest, færeld, fætels,** &c.;—gen. sg. **fæstennes, mægenes, færeldes, fætelses,** &c.

Rem. 2.—Words ending in -ad, -ed, -els, frequently discard the pl. suffix -as. Exs.: six **monad**; **hæled, fætels**.

§ 29.—(*c.*) Feminines:—

Sg. N.	frôfor (consolation).	ides (woman).	mǣrdu, -o (glory).
G.	frôfre,	idese,	mǣrdu, -o,
D. I.	frôfre,	idese,	mǣrdu, -o,
A.	frôfre,	idese,	mǣrdu, -o,
Pl. N. A.	frôfra, -e,	idesa, -e,	mǣrda,
G.	frôfra,	idesa,	mǣrda,
D. I.	frôfrum,	idesum,	mǣrdum,
Sg. N.		strengu, -o (strength).	
G.		strenge, -u, -o,	
D.		strenge, -u, -o,	
A.		strenge, -u, -o,	
Pl. N. A.		strenge, -a, -u, -o,	
G.		strenga,	
D. I.		strengum.	

Here belong Abstracts ending in -ing, -ung, -nes, -u (o), -du (do), and Derivatives in -ul, -ol, -el, -or, -er, &c.

Words of two syllables, if the stem is long, lose the vowel of the suffix in inflection. If the stem is short, there is no syncope. This suffix must end in a simple consonant. Exs.: **sâwul** (-ol), **sâwle**; **firen, firene,** &c. The vowel of the suffix is protected by position in such words as—**candel, candelle; byrgen, byrgenne; ræden, rædenne,** &c.

§ 30.—Rem. 1.—When syncope has already taken place in the Nom., the words are declined like **âr**. Exs.: **âdl**, disease; **nædl**, needle; **stefn**, voice; **earfod**, labor; **fæhd**, feud; **geogud**, youth; **strengd**, strength, &c.

Rem. 2.—Abstracts in -ung have the Dat. sg. in -a. This ending is also found in the Gen., and sometimes even in the Acc. sg.: **leornung, leornunga,** &c.

Rem. 3.—Words ending in -du (-do) are declined like **mǣrdu**. Many, however, have lost the -u (o), and then they are declined like **âr**. (See Rem. 1, above.) Both forms are frequently found: **cŷd, cŷddu; fæhd, fæhdu; strengd, strengdu; mǣrd, mǣrdu,** &c. These were originally words of three syllables, ending in Gothic in -iþa.

AN OUTLINE OF ANGLO-SAXON GRAMMAR. 261

REM. 4.—Some of the Abstracts ending in -u (-o) belonged originally to the Consonant-declension; but in Old English they have for the most part been taken into the a-declension. Such words are: ǽdelu, nobility; brǽdu, breadth; byldu, boldness; feorhtu, fright; hǽlu, health; mengu, menigo, crowd, many; ieldu, age; strengu, strength; snyttru, wisdom, &c.

§ 31.—3. -ja-STEMS.—(a.) MASCULINES.

Sg. N. A.	here, army.	hirde, herdsman.	secg, warrior.
G.	heriges, herges, heres,	hirdes,	secges,
D. I.	herige, herge, here,	hirde,	secge,
Pl. N. A.	herigas, herigeas, hergas,	hirdas,	secgas, -eas,
G.	herga, heriga, herigea,	hirda,	secga, -ea,
D. I.	hergum, herigum,	hirdum,	secgum, -ium.

(b.) NEUTERS.

Sg. N. A.	rice, kingdom.	cyn (n), race.
G.	rices,	cynnes,
D. I.	rice,	cynne,
Pl. N. A.	ricu, riciu,	cyn (n),
G.	rica, ricea,	cynna,
D. I.	ricum, ricium,	cynnum.

§ 32. (a.)—Like hirde decline—
    ende, end.
    esne, servant.
    lǽce, leech.
    mêce, sword.

Like secg decline—
    dyn (n), noise.
    hyl (l), hill.
    hrycg, ridge.
    wæcg, wedge, &c.

And all derivatives in -ere and -scipe, as—
    bôcere, scribe.
    bæcere, baker.
    fiscere, fisher.
    frêondscipe, friendship, &c.

§ 33.—(b.) Like rice decline—
ǽrende, errand; inne, inn: stycce, piece; wǽge, cup; wite, punishment; yrfe, bequest: and formations with ge-, as in gemyrce, boundary; getimbre, building; gewǽde, dress; &c.

§ 34.—Like cyn (n) decline—
bed (d), bed; bil (l), war-ax; flet (t), ground; neb (b), nib; net (t), net; rib (b), rib; wed (d), pledge; spel (l), story; wicg, horse, &c.

Words whose stems ended originally in -ja (aja) form the Nom. Acc. sg. in -e. This is j vocalized. In all other cases the endings are added to the stem without showing any sign of original j, except in the umlaut of the root-vowel. Fore the oldest monuments have i, as in heri, endi, rici (Sievers). The neuter hig, hêg, hay, has retained j (= g) in all its forms.

§ 35.—(c.) FEMININES.

Sg. N.	ben (n), (wound).	gyrd, (yard).
G.	benne,	gyrde,
D. I.	benne,	gyrde,
A.	benne, benn,	gyrde,
Pl. N. A.	benna, -e,	gyrda, -e,
G.	benna,	gyrda,
D. I.	bennum,	gyrdum.

§ 36.—Like **ben** decline—

brycg, bridge.	hell, hell.	secg, sword.
cribb, crib.	nyt, use.	syll, sill.
ecg, edge.	sib, peace.	sæcc, strife.
fit, song.	syn, sin.	wyn, joy.

§ 37.—Like **gyrd** decline—

bend, band.	hild, war.	ȳd, wave.
cȳll, bottle.	hind, hind.	blids, bliss, bliss.
eax, ax.	hȳd, booty.	lids, liss, grace.
hǣd, heath.	wylf, wolf (f.)	milds, milts, kindness.

REM.—The short stems assimilate the **j** to the consonant immediately preceding. This gemination is generally simplified in the Nom. Sg. The long stems show signs of original j only in the umlaut of the root.

§ 38.—(a.)—4. wa-STEMS.—MASCULINES.

Sg. N.	bearu, -o, (grove).	þeow, þeo, (servant).	snâw, snâ, (snow).
G.	bearwes,	þeowes, þeos,	snâwes,
D. I.	bearwe,	þeowe, þeo,	snâwe,
A.	bearu, -o,	þeow, þeo,	snâw.
Pl. N. A.	bearwas,	þeowas,	
G.	bearwa,	þeowa,	
D. I.	bearwum,	þeowum.	

§ 39.—(b.) NEUTERS.

Sg. N.	searu, -o, (equipment).	trêow, trêo, (tree).
G.	searwes,	trêowes,
D. I.	searwe,	trêowe, trêo,
A.	searu, -o,	trêow, trêo,
Pl. N. A.	searu, -o,	trêow, -u, trêo,
G.	searwa,	trêowa,
D. I.	searwum,	trêowum.

§ 40.—(a.) Like **bearu** decline: **horu**, filth; **heoru**, sword; &c. **sǣ** has the Dat. **sǣwe**, Gen. **sǣs**.

Like **þeow** decline: **lâreow**, teacher; **lâttêow**, guide, &c.

Like **snâw** decline: **briw**, broth; **bêaw**, gadfly; **dêaw**, dew; **hlâw**, **hlǣw**, grave-mound; **þeaw**, custom, &c.

(b.) Like **searu** decline: **bealu**, evil; **ealu**, beer; **meolu**, meal; **smeoru**, lard; **teoru**, tar; **cwudu**, cud; **cnêow** is declined like **trêow**.

Sg. Nom. **hrâw, hrâ, hrǽw, hrǽ,** (corpse).
Gen. **hrâwes, hrǽwes, hrǽs,** &c.
Dat. **hrǽwe, hrǽ**.
Acc. **hrâw, hrâ, hrǽw, hrǽ**.
Pl. Nom. Acc. **hrâw, hrǽw, hrêaw, hrâ, hrǽ**.
Gen. **hrǽwa**.
Dat. **hrǽwum**.

REM. 1.—In the Oblique cases **o** or **e** is frequently found before **w**, as **bearowes, bealowes, melowe, bealewa, bealewum,** &c.

REM. 2.—Final **w** is sometimes retained, sometimes lost, as **trêow, trêo**. After consonants it is vocalized, and frequently written **u** or **o**, as **bealu, searo**.

§ 41.—(c.) FEMININES.

Sg. N.	**beadu, -o,** (war).	**stôw,** (place).
G.	**beadwe,**	**stôwe,**
D. I.	**beadwe,**	**stôwe,**
A.	**beadwe,**	**stôwe,**
Pl. N. A.	**beadwe, -a,**	**stôwe, -a,**
G.	**beadwa,**	**stôwa,**
D.	**beadwum,**	**stôwum.**

§ 42.—Like **beadu** decline: **nearu**, strait; **sceadu**, shadow; **seonu**, sinu, sinew; **fratu**, adornment; **gearu, geatu**, equipment. The three last occur almost always in the Pl. **fraetwe, gearwe, geatwe**.
Like **stôw** decline: **hrêow**, repentance; **trêow**, truth.
Many have rejected the **w**, and are then in the Sg. indeclinable, as **sǽ**, sea; **êa**, water; **bêo**, bee; **þrêa**, threat, throe, &c. These have **-m** in Dat. Pl., as **êam, sǽm**, &c.

REM.—Sometimes **o** or **e** appears before **w**, as **beadowe, nearowe, fraetewum, geatewa**.

§ 43.—(B.) The **i**-declension.

There are only a few remains of the **i**-declension, for it had passed over almost altogether into the **a**-declension. In all the words of this declension some forms of the **a**-declension are found in the Sg., and all the forms of the Pl. frequently belong to the **a**-declension. It shows **i**-umlaut wherever it can appear.

§ 44.—(a.)—1. PURE **i**-STEMS.—MASCULINES.

Sg. N. A.	**byre,** (son).	**wyrm,** (worm).
G.	**byres,**	**wyrmes,**
D. I.	**byre,**	**wyrme,**

Pl. N. A. byre, -as,   wyrmas,   Engle, Angles.
    G.   byra,   wyrma,   Engla,
    D.   byrum,   wyrmum,   Englum.

§ 45.—(b.) Neuters.

Sg. N. A. sife,   Pl. N. A. sifu,
    G.   sifes,   G.   sifa,
    D. I. sife,   D.   sifum.

§ 46.—(a.) Like **byre** decline many Masculines with short stems: **bere**, barley; **bite**, bite; **bryce**, breach; **bryne**, brand; **byre**, event; **cwide**, speech; **cyre**, choice; **drepe**, stroke; **dryne**, noise; **ege**, fear; **flyge**, flight; **gryre**, fright; **gripe**, gripe; **gyte**, outpouring; **hryre**, fall; **lyre**, loss; **ryne**, course; **scride**, step; **sige**, victory; **slide**, fall; **scyte**, shot, &c.; **ele**, oil; **mene**, neck-ornament; **mete**, meat; **sele**, hall; **stede**, place; **hæle**, man; **hype**, hip; **hyse**, youth; **ciele**, keel; **hyge, myne**, mind, thought; **þyle**, speaker; **wlite**, countenance, &c.

Like **wyrm** decline all long stems: **frist**, time; **gist**, guest; **lyft**, air; **steng**, pole; **streng**, string; **þyrs**, giant; **lig**, flame; **swêg**, noise; **feng**, grasp; **rêc**, smoke; **smêc**, smell; **steno**, odor; **sweng**, blow; **wrenc**, wrench; **drync, drinc**, drink; **swylt**, death; **wyrp**, throw; **hwyrft**, turn; **hyht**, hope, &c.

Like **Engle** decline folk-names: **Se(a)xe**, Saxons; **Myrce (Mierce)**, Mercians; **Norð-hymbre**, Northumbrians; **Egipte**, Egyptians, &c. And a few plurals: **ylde, lêode, ielfe, -ware, cantware, burh-ware**. -ware has likewise a weak form—**waran**.

§ 47.—Like **sife** are declined **gedyne**, din; **gedyre**, doorpost; **gemyne**, care; **gewile**, will; **ofdele, ofdæle**, declivity; **oferslege**, lintel; **wlæce**, tepidity.

A few long stems are to be found: **gehygd**, thought; **gemynd**, mind; **gewyrht**, deed; **wiht, wuht**, creature; **geþyld**, patience; **gecynd, gebyrd**, nature; **ǽrist**, resurrection; **fulluht**, baptism; **lyft**, air; **forwyrd**, destruction; **genyht**, abundance; **gesceaft**, creature; **geþeaht**, thought. They are declined like **word**, but have Nom. Pl. in -u. Originally they were feminines. See Cook's Sievers's Grammar of Old English, § 262, § 263, § 267.

The short stems have retained the i of the stem, but weakened to e. In the other cases the i has dropped off, though not till it had caused umlaut.

The Nom. Pl. ends regularly in -e, but the ending -as is also found, as **byras, hysas**. The long stems have i-umlaut to show their origin. Otherwise they follow the a-declension.

§ 48.—(c.) Feminines.

Sg. N. A. glêd, (gleed).   dǽd, (deed).
    G.   glêde,   dǽde,
    D. I. glêde,   dǽde,
Pl. N. A. glêde, -a,   dǽde, -a,
    G.   glêda,   dǽda,
    D.   glêdum,   dǽdum,

§ 49.—Like dǽd decline: ǽ, law; bysen, command; benc, bench; cwên, queen, woman; dryht, crowd; hȳd, hide; lyft, air; nȳd, need; tîd, time; þrȳd, strength; wên, hope; wiht, wuht, thing; wyrd, fate; wyrt, wort, root, and many abstracts—fyrd, army; spêd, speed; gehygd, gemynd, mind; gewyrht, deed; geþyld, patience; ǽht, possession; niht, night; gesceaft, creation; êst, favor; wist, food; ȳst, storm; ǽrist, resurrection, &c.

ǽrist and lyft are likewise masculine. Many nouns of this class are to be found, but they all end in consonants in the Nom. Sg. In the other cases the i has either been weakened to e or disappeared. In all cases, however, it has wrought Umlaut.

§ 50.—2. MIXED STEMS.—(a.) MASCULINES.

Sg. N. A. tôđ, (tooth).
G. tôđes,
D. & I. têđ,
Pl. N. A. têđ,
G. tôđa,
D. tôđum.

Like tôđ decline fôt (foot), and mann, monn (man).—mann has also a weak form—manna.

§ 51.—(b.) FEMININES.

Sg. N. bôc, (book).   burh, -g, (city).
G. bêc,   burge, byrig,
D. & I. bêc,   byrig, byrg, burge,
A. bôc,   burh, -g,
Pl. N. A. bêc,   byrig, burge, -a,
G. bôca,   burga,
D. bôcum,   burgum.

Like bôc decline âc, oak; brôc, breeches; gât, goat; gôs, goose; lûs, louse; mûs, mouse; sulh, plow; turf, turf; wlôh, fringe.

REM.—cû has Gen. Sg. cû, cȳ, cûs; Pl. Nom. cȳ, cȳe; Gen. cûna; Dat. cûm.—niht is indeclinable, though a Gen. Sg. used adverbially, nihtes, is found.

§ 52.—(c.) THE U-DECLENSION.

The u-declension shows only an occasional word and a few forms of other words.

(a.) MASCULINES.

Sg. N. sunu, -o (son).   feld (field).
G. suna,   felda, -es,
D. I. suna, -u, -o,   felda, -e,
A. sunu, -o,   feld,
Pl. N. A. suna, -u, -o,   feldas,
G. suna,   felda,
D. sunum,   feldum.

The few words belonging here are: **breogu**, prince; **heoru**, sword; **lagu**, lake; **magu**, boy; **meodu**, mead; **siodu**, custom; **wudu**, wood. The words **friodu**, peace; **liodu**, member; **headu**, battle, are u-stems only in the first member of a compound.

Like **feld** decline **ford**, ford; **weald**, forest; **sumor**, summer; **winter**, winter.

REM. 1.—In the Gen. Sg. we find later also **-es**, as **wudes**; and also in Nom. Pl. **-as**, as **wudas**, **sunas**.

REM. 2.—**winter**, though always masculine in the Sg., has the Pl. forms **wintru**, winter.

§ 53.—(*b.*) FEMININES.

Sg. N. A.	duru, (door).	hand, (hand).
G.	dura,	handa, -e,
D. I.	dura, -u,	handa, hande, hand,
Pl. N. A.	dura, -u,	handa,
G.	dura,	handa,
D.	durum,	handum.

Sometimes an Acc.—as **nosu** (nose)—is met with; but otherwise this word is declined like **gifu**.

§ 54.—(*c.*) NEUTERS.

No neuters are found: only a few forms are left, as **feolu**, **feolo**, **feola**, **fela**.

§ 55.—II. THE CONSONANT (WEAK) DECLENSION.

THE -n-DECLENSION.

	Masculine.	Neuter.	Feminine.
Sg. N.	hunta, (hunter).	êage, (eye).	tunge, (tongue).
G.	huntan,	êagan,	tungan,
D. I.	huntan,	êagan,	tungan,
A.	huntan,	êage,	tungan,
Pl. N. A.	huntan,	êagan,	tungan,
G.	huntena,	êagena,	tungena,
D.	huntum,	êagum,	tungum.

Like **hunta** decline: **bana**, murderer; **cempa**, fighter; **cuma**, comer, guest; **flêma**, fugitive; **guma**, man; **hana**, cock; **hara**, hare; **môna**, moon; **nefa**, nephew; **oxa**, ox; **sefa**, thought; **steorra**, star; **þeowa**, servant; **wiga**, warrior; **wrecca**, exile, &c.

Like **êage** decline **êare**, ear; **wonge**, cheek.

Like **tunge** decline **cêace**, cheek; **cycene**, chicken; **cyrice**, church; **eorðe**, earth; **heorte**, heart; **hlæfdige**, lady; **lufe**, love; **molde**, earth; **nunne**, nun; **sirce**, coat-of-mail; **sangestre**, songstress; **sunne**, sun; **þeowe**, female servant; **wicce**, witch; **wise**, wise, &c.

§ 56.—REM. 1.—Occasionally strong forms are found, as **stearres**, **brydgumes**.

REM. 2. **-ena** is the regular ending of the Gen. Pl., but sometimes we find **-ana**, **-ona**,—seldom **-una**. A contracted form, **-na**, also occurs.

Rem. 3.—When the final consonant is lost, contraction takes place, as—

1. Masculines.

frêa, lord; gefêa, joy; lêo, lion; twêo, doubt; Swêon, Pl. Swedes; Gen. Dat. Acc. Sg. frêan, twêon; Dat. Pl. frêaum, lêoum, &c.

2. Feminines.

bêo, bee; flâ, arrow; rêo, covering; sêo, pupil; râ, roe; tâ, toe; Sg. Gen. Dat. Acc. tân, tâan; Pl. Nom. Acc. tân, tâan; Gen. tâna; Dat. tâ(n)um; Gen. bêon, &c. The word flâ is weak, but we find a strong form belonging to the a-declension—flân, Gen. flânes.

§ 57.—III. Anomalies.—(*a*.) r-stems.

The declension of these stems is mixed with the vowel-declension. They are thus declined:—

Masculines.

Sg. N. fæder, (father).   brôðor(-ur, Ps.), (brother).
G. fæder, -res,   brôðor,
D. I. fæder,   brêðer,
A. fæder,   brôðor,
Pl. N. A. fæderas,   brôðor, -dru,
G. fædera,   brôðra,
D. fæderum.   brôðrum.

Feminines.

Sg. N. môdor, -ur, (mother). dohtor, (daughter). sweostor, (sister).
G. môdor, -er,   dohtor,   sweostor,
D. I. mêder,   dehter,   sweostor,
A. môdor,   dohtor,   sweostor,
Pl. N. A. môdra,   dohtor, -tru, -tra,   sweostor,
G. môdra,   dohtra,   sweostra,
D. môdrum,   dohtrum,   sweostrum.

Rem.—Instead of -or we find frequently -er.

§ 58.—(*b*.) nd-stems.

Sg. N. frêond, (friend).
G. frêondes,
D. I. frêonde,
A. frêond,
Pl. N. A. frêondas, frêond, frŷnd,
G. frêonda,
D. frêondum.

Participles used as nouns are thus declined: fêond is declined like frêond. As a rule they follow the a-declension; but in Nom. Acc. Pl. they show weak forms—frêond, fêond; and also forms of the i-declension—frŷnd, fŷnd.

Rem.—Words of two syllables have the Nom. Pl. sometimes in -e, as hettend or hettende; and the Gen. Pl. in -ra, as wigendra.

§ 59.—Declension of Proper Names.

1. Names of Persons.

Masculine Proper Names, if they end in a consonant or -e or in -sunu, follow the vowel-declension, as **Aelfric, Hrôdgâr, Ine, Leofsunu**, &c. Those in -e follow the i-declension; and compounds in -sunu, the u-declension.

Rem.—Masculines in -a are weak, as **Offa, Offan; Aetla, Aetlan**. Feminine Proper Names, if they end in a consonant or in u-, follow the a-declension, as **Begu, Hild, Hygd**.

Rem.—Those ending in -e are weak, as **Eve, Evan; Marie, Marian**, &c.

Foreign Proper Names sometimes follow the custom of Anglo-Saxon Names; sometimes they are declined as in the language from which they come; and sometimes they are not declined at all. The Gen. and Dat. have generally English inflection, as **Herodes, Agustine**.

§ 60.—2. Names of Peoples.

Folk-names seldom occur in the Sg., as **ân Bret**. They are generally plural, and end in -as, -e, and -an. Those in -as and -e are strong; those in -an are weak. The Sg. is generally represented by an adjective with a noun, as **egyptisc man, ides**. Often a collective noun with Gen. Pl. is used, as **Seaxna þeod; Filistea folc**.

§ 61.—3. Names of Countries.

Names of Countries are seldom found, as **Angel, Bryton**. Generally we find a preposition with the folk-name in an oblique case or the Gen. Pl. depending on **land, rice, êdel**, &c.; as **on Frisum, of Seaxum, Francena rice, Nordhymbra rice**.

§ 62.—4. Names of Cities.

Names of Cities are sometimes declined, but generally they are used with appellations like **burh, ceaster, wic, hâm, tûn**, &c.

CHAPTER II.
DECLENSION OF ADJECTIVES.

§ 63.—Adjectives have two Declensions,—a Vowel (Strong), and a Consonant (Weak) Declension. The endings of the Weak Declension agree exactly with those of weak substantives. Most adjectives can be inflected in either way. The weak inflection is used after the definite article and demonstratives generally. Adjectives have three genders, and five cases.

§ 64.—(A.) THE STRONG DECLENSION.

The strong inflection of Adjectives has been materially influenced by the pronominal declension. The a-declension has almost completely absorbed the i- and the u- declension.

§ 65.—1. a-DECLENSION.—(*a.*) SHORT STEMS.

	Masculine.	Feminine.	Neuter.
Sg. N.	til, (useful).	tilu, til,	til,
G.	tiles,	tilre,	tiles,
D.	tilum,	tilre,	tilum,
A.	tilne,	tile,	til,
I.	tile,	(tilre),	tile,
Pl. N. A.	tile,	tile,	tilu, -e,
G.	tilra,	tilra,	tilra,
D. I.	tilum,	tilum,	tilum.

(*b.*)	Masculine.	Feminine.	Neuter.
Sg. N.	glæd, (glad).	gladu, -o,	glæd,
G.	glades,	glædre,	glades,
D.	gladum,	glædre,	gladum,
A.	glædne,	glade,	glæd,
I.	glade,	(glædre),	glade,
Pl. N. A.	glade,	glada, -e,	gladu, -o,
G.	glædra,	glædra,	glædra,
D. I.	gladum,	gladum,	gladum.

§ 66.—(*b.*) LONG STEMS.

(*a.*)	Masculine.	Feminine.	Neuter.
Sg. N.	gôd, (good).	gôd,	gôd,
G.	gôdes,	gôdre,	gôdes,
D.	gôdum,	gôdre,	gôdum,
A.	gôdne,	gôde,	gôd,
I.	gôde,	(gôdre),	gôde,
Pl. N. A.	gôde,	gôda, -e,	gôd,
G.	gôdra,	gôdra,	gôdra,
D. I.	gôdum,	gôdum,	gôdum.

(b.) Masculine. Feminine. Neuter.
Sg. N. blind, (blind). blind, -u, blind,
G. blindes, blindre, blindes,
D. blindum, blindre, blindum,
A. blindne, blinde, blind,
I. blinde, (blindre), blinde,
Pl. N. A. blinde, blinda, -e, blind, -e,
G. blindra, blindra, blindra,
D. I. blindum, blindum, blindum.

§ 67.—(c.) Polysyllabic Stems.

Sg. N. hâlig, (holy). hâligu, -o; hâlgu, -o; hâlig,
G. hâlges, hâligre, hâlges,
D. hâlgum, hâligre, hâlgum,
A. hâligne, hâlge, hâlig,
I. hâlge, (hâligre), hâlge,
Pl. N. A. hâlge, hâlga, -e, hâligu, -o; hâlgu,-o;
G. hâligra, hâligra, hâligra, [hâlig.
D. I. hâlgum, hâlgum, hâlgum.

§ 68.—Like til decline dol, dull; hol, hollow; cwic, quick, alive; tam, tame; wan, wan, &c.; and all adjectives ending in -lic and -sum.

§ 69.—Like glæd decline bær, bare; blæc, black; hwæt, sharp; hræd, quick; læt, late; smæl, small; spær, spare; wær, ware, &c.

§ 70.—Like gôd and blind decline all long stems: blâc, pale; brâd, broad; dêaf, deaf; dêop, deep; rûm, roomy; sâr, sore; beald, bold; beorht, bright; ceald, cold; eald, old; forht, timid; grimm, fierce; wlanc, proud, &c.

§ 71.—Like hâlig decline all derivatives in -ol, -el, -or, -er, -en, and -ig. These sometimes retain the e of the suffix, as fæger; Gen. fægeres, fægres. Exs.: êadig, blessed; fâmig, foamy; hrêmig, noisy; manig, many; lytel, little; micel, much; yfel, evil; hnitol, butting; sticol, sharp; sweotol, clear; bitter, bitter; fæger, fair; snottor, wise; hǽden, heathen; gilpen, boastful; gylden, golden; iren, iron; stænen, stony;—as well as the preterit participles of many verbs, &c. Those in -ol rarely contract.

§ 72.—The principal differences between the declension of Strong Adjectives and that of Strong Substantives are these: The Adj. has the Dat. Sg. Masc. and Neut. in -um (subs. in -e); the Gen. and Dat. Sg. Fem. in -re (subs. in -e); in Acc. Sg. Masc. the ending is -ne (subs. uninflected); in the Pl. Nom. Acc. Masc. the ending is -e (subs. -as); in Nom. Acc. Neut. -u or -e (subs. -u, or uninflected); in the Gen. -ra (subs. -a). The Instrumental Sg. Masc. and Neut. ends in -e (subs. like the Dat.).

§ 73.—Rem. 1.—Adjectives in -en have Acc. Sg. Masc. in -ne, as hǽdenne, âgenne, âgene. Those in -er have Dat. Sg. in -erre, as fægerre; Gen. Pl. in -erra, as fægerra, or fægera.

REM. 2.—Words in -h, as fáh, hostile; hêah, high; hrêoh, rough; wôh, bent; rûh, rough (G. rûwes); þweorh, diagonal, &c., lose the h in forms of more than one syllable.

	Masculine.	Feminine.	Neuter.
Sg. N.	hêa (h), (high).	hêa (h),	hêa (h),
G.	hêa (ge) s,	hêarre,	hêa (ge) s,
D.	hêa (g) um,	hêarre,	hêa (g) um,
A.	hêanne,	hêa (ge),	hêa (h),
I.	hêa (ge),	(hêare),	hêa (ge),
Pl. N. A.	hêa (ge),	hêa (ge),	hêa (gu),
G.	hêarra,	hêarra,	hêarra,
D. I.	hêa (g) um,	hêa (g) um,	hêa (g) um.

§ 74.—2. ja-DECLENSION.—(a.) SHORT STEMS.

Original short stems are inflected like those of the a-stems with double consonantal ending, as mid, middle (middes); nyt, useful; gesib, akin; niwe, new (niwne, niwra, or nêowne,&c.); frio, free (G. friges; D. frigum; N. Pl. frige, G. D. Sg. Fem. friore; G. Pl. friora; N. & A. Pl. Masc. frio; A. Sg. Masc. frione, &c.

§ 75.—(b.) LONG STEMS.

	Masculine	Feminine.	Neuter.
Sg. N.	grêne, (green).	grênu, -o,	grêne,
G.	grênes,	grênre,	grênes,
D.	grênum,	grênre,	grênum,
A.	grênne,	grêne,	grêne,
I.	grêne,	(grênre),	grêne,
Pl. N. A.	grêne,	grêna, -e,	grênu, -o.
G.	grênra,	grênra,	grénra,
D. I.	grênum,	grênum,	grênum.

Words like gifre, sýfre, fǽcne, &c., insert a vowel when an unlike consonant follows, as sýferne, fǽcenra; but A. Sg. Masc. fǽcne; G. Pl. sýfra.

§ 76.—Like grêne decline—

blíðe, blithe; brême, celebrated; cêne, bold; dyrne, dark, secret; yrre, mad; fǽcne, sinful; sêfte, soft; swête, sweet; clǽne, clean; êce, eternal; mǽre, renowned; sýfre, sober. Also verbal adjectives like genge, current; genǽme, agreeable; and derivatives in -bǽre, -ede, -ihte, &c.

3. wa-DECLENSION.

	Masculine.	Feminine.	Neuter.
Sg. N.	gearu, (ready).	gearu, -o,	gearu, -o,
G.	gearwes,	gearore,	gearwes,
D.	gearwum,	gearore,	gearwum,
A.	gearone,	gearwe,	gearu, -o,
I.	gearwe,	(gearore),	gearwe,
Pl. N. A.	gearwe,	gearwa, -e,	gearu,
G.	gearora,	gearora,	gearora,
D. I.	gearwum,	gearwum,	gearwum.

§ 77.—(a.) Words with a simple consonant before the **w**, change this **w**, when final, to **-o, -u (-a)**; when before a consonant, to **-o**. So are declined **earu**, swift; **calu**, bald; **fealu**, fallow; **basu**, brown; **hasu**, hazel; **mearu**, tender; **nearu**, narrow; **salu**, sallow; &c.

§ 78.—(b.) Words with a long vowel or a diphthong before the **w**, retain this **w** in all the forms, but do not otherwise differ from the inflection of the a-declension. So are declined **glêaw**, prudent; **hnêaw**, stringy; **rêow**, wild; **rôw**, gentle; **slâw**, slow; &c.

The i-declension and the u-declension present so few remains that a paradigm can not be formed from them. See Sievers's *Angelsächsische Grammatik*, § 302, § 303.

§ 79.—(B.) THE WEAK DECLENSION.

This is just like the weak declension of substantives, with the exception of the G. Pl. Here we generally find **-ra**: **-ena** is occasionally found.

Sg. N.	se gôda,	sêo gôde,	þæt gôde,
G.	þæs gôdan,	þǽre gôdan,	þæs gôdan,
D.	þâm gôdan,	þǽre gôdan,	þâm gôdan,
A.	þone gôdan,	þâ gôdan,	þæt gôde.

	Masc., Fem., Neut.
Pl. N. A.	þâ gôdan,
G.	þâra gôdra, -ena, -ana,
D.	þâm gôdum.

§ 80.—Participles, both Present and Preterit, are declined like Adjectives.

§ 81.—COMPARISON OF ADJECTIVES.

The Comparative and Superlative are formed by **-or, -ost (-ir, -est, -ust)**. Sometimes a Superlative in **-ma, -dema**, is found. The Comparative of the Adjective is always weak, as **-ra, lêofra, lêofre**.

Exs.—**heard, heardra, heardost; lêof, lêofra, lêofost; glæd, glædra, gladost; fæger, fægerra, fægrost.**

§ 82.—EXAMPLES WITH UMLAUT.

Positive.	Comparative.	Superlative.
eald,	ieldra,	ieldest,
lang,	lengra,	lengest,
strang,	strengra,	strengest,
sceort,	scyrtra,	scyrtest,
hêah,	hierra, hêrra,	hiehst, hêhst,
geong,	gingra,	gingest.

§ 83.—IRREGULAR COMPARISON.—(a.) MIXED ROOTS.

gôd,	bet(e)ra,	bet(o)st,
yfel,	wyrsa,	wyrrest, wyrst,
micel,	mâra,	mǽst,
lytel,	lǽssa,	lǽsest, -ast, lǽst,
......	sélla, sélra,	sélost, sélesta.

§ 84.—(*b.*) From Adverbs and Prepositions:—

feor, far.	fierra, fyrra,	fierrest,
ǽr, ere.	ǽrra,	ǽrest,
fore, before.	......	fyrst,
(sid, late).	sidra,	sidemest, sidest,
(inne, within).	inn(e)ra,	innemest,
(ûte, without).	ût(er)ra,	ȳtemest, ûtemest,
(nord, northward).		nordmest,
(sûd, southward).		sûdmest,
(êast, eastward).		êastmest,
(west, westward).		westmest.

§ 85.—Numerals.

Cardinal.
ân, one;
twâ, two;
þrêo, three;
fêower, four;
fîf, five;
six, six;
seofon, seven;
eahta, eight;
nigon, nine;
tȳn, tên, ten;
endleofan, eleven;
twelf, twelve;
þrêo-têne, -tȳne, thirteen;
fêower-tȳne, fourteen;
fîf-tȳne, fifteen;
six-tȳne, sixteen;
seofon-têne, seventeen;
eahta-tȳne, eighteen;
nigon-tȳne, nineteen;
twentig, twenty;
ân-and-twentig, twenty-one;
þri-tig, þrittig, thirty;
fêower-tig, forty;
fîf-tig, fifty;
sixtig, sixty;
hund-seofon-tig, seventy;
hund-eahta-tig, eighty;
hund-nigon-tig, ninety;
hund,
hundred, } hundred;
hund-têon-tig,
hund-endleofan-tig, hundred and ten;
hund-twelf-tig, hundred and twenty;
þûsend, thousand.

Ordinal.
forma, first;
ôðer, second;
þridda,
fêowerða, fêorða,
fîfta,
sixta,
seofoða,
eahtoða,
nigoða,
têoða,
endlyfta,
twelfta,
þrêotêoða,
fêowertêoða,
fîf-têoða,
etc.

§ 86.—ân is declined like an adjective.

	Masculine.	Feminine.	Neuter.
N. A.	twegen,	twâ,	twâ, tû.
G.		twega, twegra,	
D.		twǽm, twâm.	

So decline begen, bâ, bû, both.

	Masculine	Feminine	Neuter
N. A.	þri, þrie, þrŷ,	þrêo,	þrêo,
G.		þrêora,	
D.		þrim.	

The Cardinals, from 4 to 19, are not generally inflected. All Cardinals are most often neuter substantives, with the genitive after them. Those in -tig are sometimes declined like adjectives: Gen. -ra; Dat. -um. Sometimes they are declined like substantives: þritiga sum.

§ 87.—PRONOUNS.
1. PERSONAL PRONOUNS.

Sg.	N.	ic, (I).	þû, (thou).
	G.	min,	þin,
	D.	mê, me,	þê, þe,
	A.	mec, mê, me,	þec, þê, þe,
Du.	N.	wit,	git,
	G.	uncer,	incer,
	D.	unc,	inc,
	A.	uncit, unc,	incit, inc,
Pl.	N.	wê, we,	gê, gie, ge,
	G.	ûser, ûre,	êower,
	D.	ûs,	êow,
	A.	ûsic, ûs,	êowic, êow.

§ 88.

		Masculine.	Feminine.	Neuter.
Sg.	N.	hê,	hêo, hie, hi,	hit,
	G.	his,	hiere, hire, hyre,	his,
	D.	him,	hiere, hire, hyre,	him,
	A.	hine,	hie, hêo, hi,	hit.
Pl.	N. A.	hie, hêo, hi, (hig).		
	G.	hiera, hira, hyra, heora, heara.		
	D.	him, heom.		

§ 89.—2. REFLEXIVES.

Reflexives are supplied by the Personal, either with or without self. self is declined like blind, and is often weak in the Nom.

§ 90.—3. POSSESSIVES.

The Possessives are min, þin, sin, ûser, ûre, uncer, êower, incer. They are declined like Strong Adjectives (ûre like grêne).

AN OUTLINE OF ANGLO-SAXON GRAMMAR.

§ 91.—4. DEMONSTRATIVES.

	Masc.	Fem.	Neut.
Sg. N.	sê, se,	sêo,	þæt,
G.	þæs,	þǽre,	þæs,
D.	þǽm, þâm,	þǽre,	þǽm, þâm,
A.	þone,	þâ,	þæt,
I.	þŷ, þon,		
Pl. N. A.		þâ,	
G.		þâra, þǽra,	
D.		þǽm, þâm.	

This word is generally used as the Definite Article.

§ 92.

	Masculine.	Feminine.	Neuter.
Sg. N.	þes, (this).	þeos,	þis,
G.	þis(s)es, þys(s)es,	þisse,(þeosse, þisre),	like Masc.
D.	þiosum, þis(s)um, þys(s)um,	þisse,(þeosse, þisre),	" "
A.	þiosne, þisne, þysne,	þâs,	þis,
I.	þŷs, þis,		
Pl. N. A.		þâs,	
G.		þissa, þeossa,	
D.		þiosum, þis(s)um, þyssum.	

§ 93.—5. RELATIVES.

þe is the usual Relative, and it is used either with or without the Personal Pronouns: þe ic, I who; þe his, whose; þe him, whom; or simply þe. sê is also frequently used as a Relative.

§ 94.—6. INTERROGATIVES.

	Masculine.	Neuter.
Sg. N.	hwâ,	hwæt,
G.	hwæs,	hwæs,
D.	hwǽm, hwâm,	hwǽm, hwâm,
A.	hwone,	hwæt,
I.		hwŷ, hwi.

Only the Masculine and Neuter forms are found. hwæder and hwilc (hwylc) are declined like Adjectives.

§ 95.—7. INDEFINITES.

"Some" is expressed by sum. See ADJECTIVES.

In interrogative and negative sentences hwâ, hwæder, and hwelc, can be used indefinitely. ælc, each; ǽnig, any; nǽnig, no, none;—are declined like Adjectives.

CHAPTER III.
VERBS.

§ 96.—In Old English, verbal inflection is very circumscribed. Auxiliary verbs play an important part.

§ 97.—VOICE.—There are two Voices—Active and Passive. To show present from past time the Active has independent forms: the Passive has to make use of **wesan** (**bêon**) and **weorðan**.

§ 98.—MOOD.—There are three Moods—Indicative, Subjunctive, and Imperative. The so-called Infinitive Mood ends in -**an**, but shows a regular Dative inflection in -**anne** (-**enne**).

§ 99.—TENSE.—There are two Tenses—Present and Preterit. Already in Old English, however, a periphrastic Future, with **sculan**, is occasionally to be met with. There are likewise the beginnings of the modern so-called Perfect and Pluperfect, with **habban**. Intransitives frequently have **wesan** instead of **habban**. But generally the Present is used both for present and future time, and the Preterit is the general tense of past time.

§ 100.—NUMBER.—There are two Numbers—Singular and Plural. When the Plural Pronoun follows the Verb (both Indicative and Imperative), the form of the Verb is most frequently changed: **wê bindað**, but **binde wê**; **gâð!** go! but **gâ gê!** go ye!

§ 101.—CONJUGATION.—There are two Conjugations—Strong and Weak. They are distinguished by the formation of the Preterit.

Strong Verbs form the Preterit, either—I. by Vowel-change Ablaut; or II., by Reduplication. Weak Verbs form the Preterit by means of the verb **dôn**, whose root is **da-, ta-**.

§ 102.—I.—STRONG VERBS.

	Indicative.			Subjunctive.		
Pres. Sg.—1.	binde,	helpe,	bidde,	binde,	helpe,	bidde,
2.	bindest, bintst,	hilp(e)st,	bidest, bitst,	binde,	helpe,	bidde,
3.	bindeð, bint,	hilp(e)ð,	bideð, bit,	binde,	helpe,	bidde,
Plur.—	bindað,	helpað,	biddað,	binden,	helpen,	bidden.
Pret. Sg.—1.	band,	healp,	bæd,	bunde,	hulpe,	bǣde,
2.	bunde,	hulpe,	bǣde,	bunde,	hulpe,	bǣde,
3.	band,	healp,	bæd,	bunde,	hulpe,	bǣde,
Plur.—	bundon,	hulpon,	bǣdon,	bunden,	hulpen,	bǣden.

Imperative.			Infinitive.		
Sg.—2. bind,	help,	bide,	bindan,	helpan,	biddan.
Plur.—2. bindað,	helpað,	biddað.			

PARTICIPLES.

Present.	Preterit.
bindende, helpende, biddende.	bunden, holpen, beden.

Traces of a Passive are found in **hâtte**, plural **hâtton**,—which signifies both *I am called* and *I was called*.

§ 103.—Contract Verbs are those whose stems ended originally in **h**. This has fallen out, thus bringing together two vowels, which are contracted. Such verbs are—**têon, þeon, wrêon, lêon, sêon, flêon, têon, gefêon, plêon, sêon, lêan, slêan, þwêan**, and **fôn, hôn**, &c. The Present Indicative goes thus:—

Sg. 1. **têo, têo, sêo, slêa, fô**.
2. **tihst, tiehst, siehst, sliehst, fêhst**.
3. **tihð, tiehð, siehð, sliehð, fêhð**.
Pl. **têoð, têoð, sêoð, slêað, fôð**.

In the Preterit the **h** is retained: Sg. 1, 3, **tâh**; 2, **tige**;—1, 3, **têah**; 2, **tuge**;—1, 3, **seoh**; 2, **sâwe**;—1, 3, **slôg(h)**; 2, **slôge**;—1, 3, **feng**; 2, **fenge**. Pl. **tigon, tugon, sâwon, slôgon, fengon**.

§ 104.—Rem. 1.—Verbs with Breaking, like **feallan, weorpan**, are sometimes modified by i-umlaut in the Second and Third Persons Sg. Ind.; as **feallest** and **felst**; **fealleð** and **feld**.

Rem. 2.—Umlaut regularly occurs in the Second and Third Persons Sg. of the Present Ind.; and by syncope of the connecting vowels certain euphonic changes are brought about:—

1.—In the Second Sg. when the stem ends in the dental sound **d** or **ð**, **s** or **t**, the dental is lost before the ending -**st**; as **hladan, hlest; cwedan, cwist; cêosan, ciest; berstan, birst**, &c. But if the stem ends in **t**, this **t** is retained, as **blôtan, blêtst**; if in -**nd**, the -**nd** is changed to -**nt**, as **standan, stentst**.

2. In the Third Sg. when the stem ends in -**t** or -**st**, the ending -**th** is dropped, as **blôtan, blêt; berstan, birst**. If the stem ends in -**d** or -**nd**, the ending is dropped, and the **d** changed to **t**, as **hladan, hlet; standan, stent**. If the stem ends in -**ð** one **ð** is dropped. as **cwedan, cwið (cwideð)**.

Rem. 3.—"Grammatical change" is frequently found in the Pres. Pl. This affects **h, s**, and **ð**, especially, and they are changed respectively to **g, r**, and **d**, as **cêosan, cêas, curon, coren; lidan, lâd, lidon, liden; têon, têah, tugon, togen**, &c.—**sêon** has Pret. Pl. **sǽgon** or **sâwon**; and Part. **sewen** or **segen**.

Rem. 4.—An old Preterit Pl. in -**un** is occasionally found. A Pret. Pl. in -**an** (= **on**) occurs frequently.

Rem. 5.—In later texts -**on** often takes the place of the older Subjunctive Pls. in -**en**. This -**on** also becomes -**an**.

§ 105.—I. Ablauting Verbs.

All the different classes show alike four stems: 1, The Present Stem; 2, The First Preterit; 3, The Second Preterit; and 4, The Stem of the Preterit Participle. The regular vowel-change in these four stems gives rise to six different classes. Koch divides these Verbs as follows:—

§ 106.—FIRST CLASS.
(Sievers's Third Class.)*

Present Stem.	1st Pret. Stem.	2d Pret. Stem.	Pret.-Part. Stem.
i, e, eo.	a, ea, ae.	u.	u, o.
bindan,	band,	bundon,	bunden,
helpan,	healp,	hulpon,	holpen,
steorfan,	stearf,	sturfon,	storfen,
bregdan,	brægd,	brugdon,	brogden.

§ 107.—SECOND CLASS.
(Sievers's Fourth Class.)

i, e.	a, æ.	ǣ, â.	o (u).
beran,	bær,	bǣron,	boren,
niman,	{ nôm,† { nam,	{ nâmon, { nômon,	numen,
stelan,	stæl,	stǣlon,	stolen,
cuman,	c(w)ôm,†	c(w)ômon,	{ cumen, { cymen.

§ 108.—THIRD CLASS.
(Sievers's Fifth Class.)‡

i, e.	æ, a.	ǣ.	e.
biddan,	bæd,	bǣdon,	beden,
gifan,	geaf,	gêafon,	gifen,
cwedan,	cwæd,	cwǣdon,	cweden,
sêon,	seah,	{ sâwon, { sǣgon,	{ sewen, { sawen.

§ 109.—FOURTH CLASS.
(Sievers's Sixth Class.)§

a, ea.	ô.	ô.	a, ea.
hebban,	hôf,	hôfon,	hafen,
wadan,	wôd,	wôdon,	waden,
hlihhan,	hlôh,	hlôgon,	hleahhen,
slêan,	slôg,	slôgon,	{ slegen, { slægen.

* Sievers divides his Third Class into four subdivisions. (1) Verbs with the stem ending in a nasal + a consonant, as **bindan**. (2) Verbs with l + a consonant, as **helpan**. (3) Verbs with r or h + a consonant, as **weorpan, wearp, wurpon, worpen**; or **feohtan, feaht, fuhton, fohten**. (4) Other variations are shown by the following verbs: **bregdan, stregdan, berstan þerscan, frignan, murnan, spurnan (spornan)**.

† These two Verbs have an exceptional long Vowel in Pret. Sg.

‡ Sievers divides his Fifth Class into three subdivisions. (1) Those verbs like **metan, mæt, mǣton, meten**. (2) The verbs **gefêon, plêon, sêon**. (3) The verbs **biddan, licg(e)an, sittan**, &c.

§ In like manner his Sixth Class he divides into four subdivisions. (1) Those verbs like **faran, fôr, fôron, faren**. (2) The verbs **lêan, slêan, þwêan**, &c. (3) **standan**, which loses n in the Pret. **stôd, stôdon**. (4) The verbs **swerig(e)an, hebban, hlihhan, scyppan, steppan, sceddan**, &c., which have in the Pres. a j.

§ 110.—FIFTH CLASS.
(Sievers's First Class.)

1.	â.	i.	i.
slítan,	slât,	slíton,	slíten,
wrêon,	wrâh,*	wrigon,	wrigen,
snídan,	snád,	snidon,	sniden.

§ 111.—SIXTH CLASS.
(Sievers's Second Class.)

eo, û.	êa.	u.	o.
bêodan,	bêad,	budon,	boden,
cêosan,	cêas,	curon,	coren,
lûcan,	lêac,	lucon,	locen.

For further examples of the different Classes, see *List of Irregular Verbs.*

§ 112.—II.—Reduplicating Verbs.

Of the forty verbs in Gothic which plainly showed reduplication, only a few have traces of it in Old English. Exs. **heht, leolc, reord, leort,(on)-dreord.** These Preterits have younger forms. Contraction has taken place until there are only two classes left: (*a*) êo-preterits; (*b*) ê-preterits.

The four stems can be recognized; but the first and fourth have the same vowel, and the second and third are alike.

(*a.*) êo-PRETERITS.

Infinitive.	Pret. Sg.	Pret. Pl.	Pret. Part.
ea :—			
feallan,	fêoll,	fêollon,	feallen,
healdan,	hêold,	hêoldon,	healden.
êa :—			
bêatan,	bêot,	bêoton,	bêaten,
hlêapan,	hlêop,	hlêopon,	hlêapen.
â :—			
blâwan,	blêow,	blêowon,	blâwen,
cnâwan,	cnêow,	cnêowon,	cnâwen.
ô :—			
flôwan,	flêow,	flêowon,	flôwen,
rôwan,	rêow,	rêowon,	rôwen,
wêpan(by umlaut).	wêop,	wêopon,	wôpen.

(*b.*)—ê-PRETERITS.

â :—			
hâtan,	hêt,	hêton,	hâten.
ǽ :—			
lǽtan,	lêt,	lêton,	lǽten.
a :—			
blandan,	blênd,	blêndon,	blanden,
fôn (by contraction)	feng,	fengon,	fangen,
hôn,	heng,	hengon,	hangen.

These are conjugated like other Strong Verbs.

---
* Sometimes confused with the Sixth Class—**wrêah, wrugon, wrogen.**

§ 108.—WEAK VERBS.

There are three classes of Weak Verbs, divided, according to Sievers, into (1), the **jo**-class; (2), the **ō**-class; (3), the **ai**-class. There are three stems distinguishable in Weak Verbs—the Present, the Preterit, and the Past Participle.

§ 109.—1. THE **jo**-CLASS.

	Indicative.		Subjunctive.	
Pres. Sg.—1.	nerie,	dême,	nerie,	dême,
2.	neres(t),	dêm(e)st,	nerie,	dême,
3.	nered,	dêm(e)đ,	nerie,	dême,
Plur.—	neriađ,	dêmađ,	nerien,	dêmen.
Pret. Sg.—1.	nerede,	dêmde,	nerede,	dêmde,
2.	neredes(t),	dêmdes(t),	nerede,	dêmde,
3.	nerede,	dêmde,	nerede,	dêmde,
Plur.—	neredon,	dêmdon,	nereden,	dêmden.

	Imperative.		Infinitive.	
Sg. 2.	nere,	dêm.	nerian,	dêman.
Plur. 2.	neriađ,	dêmađ.		

PARTICIPLES.

Present.		Past.	
neriende,	dêmende.	nered,	dêmed.

nerian represents short stems, and **dêman** long stems. Wherever it is admissible i-umlaut occurs in all forms of the Present. Long stems retain this i-umlaut in the Preterit.

§ 110.—By suffixing the **-de** certain euphonic changes are brought about, as—

-ndde	becomes	-nde,	as	in	sende,	from	sendan.
-llde	"	-lde,	"	"	fylde,	"	fyllan.
-tde	"	-tte,	"	"	mêtte,	"	mêtan.
-pde	"	-pte,	"	"	dypte,	"	dyppan.
-cde	"	-hte,	"	"	tæhte,	"	tæcan.
-ssde	"	-ste,	"	"	cyste,	"	cyssan.
-xde	"	-xte,	"	"	lixte,	"	lixan.
-rw(e)de	"	-rede,	"	"	gyrede,	"	gyrwan.

§ 111.—The Past Participle generally contracts; as **send, mêtt, tæht, wend; seted**, plur. **sette; treded, tredde; dêmed, dêmde; gegyrwed, gegyrede**. The ending **-ed** is, however, frequently retained; as **fylled, dypped, hŷred, cŷded**, &c.

AN OUTLINE OF ANGLO-SAXON GRAMMAR. 281

§ 112.—In like manner conjugate—

ferian, (carry).	ferede,	(ge)-fered,
werian, (defend).	werede,	(ge)-wered,
fremman, (do).	fremede,	(ge)-fremed,
þennan, (extend).	þenede,	(ge)-þened,
sceddan, (hurt).	scedede,	(ge)-sceded,
cnyssan, (strike).	cnysede,	(ge)-cnysed,
lecg(e)an, (lay).	legde, (lêde),	(ge)-legd, (lêd),
wecg(e)an, (awake).	wegede,	(ge)-weged,
treddan, (tread).	tredde,	treded,
settan, (set).	sette,	seted,
cŷdan, (make known).	cŷdde,	(ge)-cŷded,
sendan, (send).	sende,	send,
fyllan, (fill).	fylde,	fylled,
nemnan, (name).	nemnde,	nemned,
gyrwan, (prepare).	gyrede,	(ge)-gyrwed,
cigan, (call).	cigde,	(ge)-ciged.

§ 113.—The following verbs have not been affected by i-umlaut in the Preterit:—

cwellan, (kill).	cwealde,	(ge)-cweald,
sellan, (sell).	sealde,	(ge)-seald,
tellan, (tell).	tealde,	(ge)-teald,
bycg(e)an, (buy).	bohte,	boht,
þenc(e)an, (think).	þôhte,	þôht,
þync(e)an, (appear).	þûhte,	þûht,
wyrcan, (work).	worhte,	worht,
bringan, (bring).	brôhte,	brôht,
rêc(e)an, (care).	rôhte,	rôht,
sêcan, (seek).	sôhte,	sôht.

§ 114.—A few have i-umlaut also; as—

cwecc(e)an, (vibrate).	cweahte,	cwehte,	cweaht,
drecc(e)an, (vex).	dreahte,	drehte,	dreaht,
recc(e)an, (tell).	reahte,	rehte,	reaht,
wecc(e)an, (awake).	weahte,	wehte,	weaht,
þecc(e)an, (thatch).	þeahte,	þehte,	þeaht,
tæc(e)an, (show).	tâhte,	tæhte,	tâht, tæht, &c.

§ 115.—2. THE ô-CLASS.

	Indicative.	Subjunctive.
Pres. Sg.—	1. lufi(g)e,	lufi(g)e,
	2. lufast,	lufi(g)e,
	3. lufađ,	lufi(g)e,
Plur.—	lufiađ,	lufi(g)en.
Pret. Sg.—	1. lufode,	lufode,
	2. lufodest,	lufode,
	3. lufode,	lufode,
Plur.—	lufedon, -odon,	lufoden.

Imperative.   Infinitive.
Sg. 2. lufa,   lufian.
Plur. 2. lufiađ.

PARTICIPLES.
Present.   Past.
lufiende.   lufod.

Instead of **lufian**, we frequently find **lufigan, lufigean**.

A large number of Verbs belongs to this class. The Preterit ends in -ode (-ade, -ude, -ede); — the Past Participle in -od (-ad, -ud). In inflected forms -ed- is found.

So conjugate **âscian**, ask; **lôcian**, look; **macian**, make; **scêawian**, behold· **sealfian**, anoint; **tâcnian**, betoken; **weorđian**, honor, &c.

§ 116.—3. THE ai-CLASS.

	Indicative.		Subjunctive.	
Pres. Sg.—	1. hæbbe,	{ libbe, lifge,	hæbbe,	{ libbe, lifge,
	2. hafas(t),	liofas(t),	hæbbe,	lifge,
	3. hafađ,	liofađ,	hæbbe,	lifge,
Plur.—	habbađ, hæbbađ,	libbađ, lifg(e)ađ,	hæbben	{ libben, lifgen.

Pret. Sg.—1. hæfde, lifde, &c., like **dêmde**.

Imperative.   Infinitive.
Sg. 2. hafa,   liofa.   habban, { libban, lifgan.
Plur. 2. { habbađ, { libbađ,
         { hæbbađ, { lifg(e)ađ.

PARTICIPLES.
Present.   Past.
hæbbende, { libbende, lifgende.   gehæfd, gelifd.

This class contains only a few remains of the original **ai**-class. Besides the above two, there belong here **secg(e)an**, say; **hycg(e)an**, think; and perhaps **þrêag(e)an**, threat; **smêag(e)an**, think; **frêog(e)an**, free. They are all conjugated in full in "Cook's Sievers's Grammar of Old English," p. 212.

§ 117.— 4. Preterit-Presents.

These Verbs are old Strong Preterits, with Present signification. From these, new Weak Preterits have been formed, which are inflected like other Weak Preterits.

willan.

	Indicative.	Subjunctive.
Pres.—1.	wille, wile,	wile,
2.	wilt,	wile,
3.	wile, wille,	wile,
Plur.—	willađ,	willen.
Pret.—	wolde, walde,	wolde.

The Present **wille** was originally a Subj. Preterit, and hence **willan** is not strictly to be classed with the Preterit-Presents.

nyllan.

	Indicative.	Subjunctive.
Pres.—1.	nele, nyle,	nyle, nel(l)e,
2.	nelt, nylt,	nyle,
3.	nele, nyle,	nyle,
Plur.—	nellađ, nyllađ,	nylen.
Pret.—	nolde, nalde,	nolde.
Imper. Sg.—	nelle, nyl.	
Plur.—	nyllađ.	

1. witan.

	Indicative.	Subjunctive.
Pres. Sg.—1.	wât, (know),	wite,
2.	wâst, wǽst,	wite,
3.	wât,	wite,
Plur.—	witon,	witen.
Pret. Sg.—	wiste, wisse,	wiste.
Plur.—	wiston.	

Imp. **wite, witađ.** Inf. **witan.**
Participles.— Present, **witende.** Past, **witen.**
With **ne** (not) = **nât, nâst, nyton (-un), nysse, nyste,** &c.

AN OUTLINE OF ANGLO-SAXON GRAMMAR.

INDICATIVE.						PARTICIPLES.	
Pres.	Pret.	Subj.	Imp.	Inf.		Present.	Past.
2. 1, 3, âh (g), (possess). 2. âht, âhst, âgon,	âhte,	âge,	âge,	......		......	âgen, (only as ǽgen [adj. *own*
3. 1, 3, dêah (g). (avail). 2. ...... dugon,	dohte,	duge, dyge,	......	dugan,		dugende,	......
4. 1, 3, an, (grant). 2. ...... unnon,	ûðe,	unne,	unne,	unnan,		unnande,	(ge)unnen,
5. 1, 3, cann, (know). 2. canst, cunnon,	cûðe,	cunne,	......	cunnan,		......	cunnen. cuð, (only as [adj. *known*.)
6. 1, 3, þearft, (need). 2. þearft, þurfon,	þorfte,	þurfe, þyrfe, durre,	......	þurfan,		......	......
7. 1, 3, dear, (dare). 2. dearst, durron,	dorste,	dyrre,	......	......		......	......
8. 1, 3, sceal, (shall). 2. scealt, { sculon, sceolon,	sc(e)olde,	{ scyle, scule, sceole,	......	{ sculan, sceolan,		......	......
9. 1,3, (ge)man, (remember). 2. manst, munon,	munde,	{ munc, myne,	{ gemune, gemyne,	munan,		munende,	(ge)munen.
10. 1, 3, mæg, (can). 2. { meaht, miht, magon,	{ meahte, mihte,	mæge,	......	......		......	......
11. 1, 3, -neah, (it suffices). 2. ...... -nugon,	-nohte,	{ mage, muge, -nuge,	......	......		......	......
12. 1, 3, -môt, (may). 2. môst, môton,	môste,	môte.	......	......		......	......

The missing forms are not found.

§ 118.—5. ANOMALIES.

1. wesan, (to be).

	Indicative.		Subjunctive.	
Pres. Sg.—	1. eom,	bêo,	sie,	bêo,
	2. eart,	bist,	sie,	bêo,
	3. is,	bið,	sie,	bêo,
Plur.—	sind.	bêoð.	sien.	bêon.

	Pret. Sg.			
Pret. Sg.—	1. wæs,		wǽre,	
	2. wǽre,		wǽre,	
	3. wæs,		wǽre,	
Plur.—	wǽron.		wǽren.	

Imperative.	Infinitive.
wes, wesað,	wesan,
bêo, bêoð.	bêon.

PARTICIPLES.—Present, **wesende**. Past, **gewesen**.

For a variety of forms in the different dialects, see "Cook's Sievers's Grammar of Old English," § 427.

The contracted forms are **neom, neart, nis, næs, nǽron, nǽren**, &c.

§ 119.—2. dôn, (to do).

	Indicative.	Subjunctive.
Pres. Sg.—	1. dô,	dô,
	2. dêst,	dô,
	3. dêð,	dô,
Plur.—	dôð.	dôn.

Pret. Sg.—	1. dyde,		dyde,
	2. dydes(t),		dyde,
	3. dyde,		dyde,
Plur.—	dydon.		dyden.

Imper. **dô, dôð**. Inf. **dôn**.

PARTICIPLES.—Present, **dônde**. Past, **gedôn**.

For other dialect forms, see "Cook's Sievers's Grammar of Old English," § 429.

§ 120.—3. gân, (to go).

	Indicative.	Subjunctive.
Pres. Sg.—	1. gâ,	gâ,
	2. gǽst,	gâ,
	3. gǽð,	gâ,
Plur.—	gâð.	gân,
Pret.—	êode,	êode.

like **nereðe**.

Imper. **gâ, gâð**. Inf. **gân**.

PARTICIPLES.—Present, **gânde**. Past, **gegân**.

§ 121.—ADVERBS.

Adverbs, derived from Adjectives, generally have the ending -e; as hearde, hard; lange, long; sôde, truly; wide, widely. If the Adjective ends in -e, the Adverb has the same form. Many Adverbs are formed with the suffix -lice (-ly); as heardlice, hardly; sôdlice, truly; sweatullice, clearly. Still another class has the ending -a; as fela, very; singala, always; sôna, soon; tela, teala, properly. The endings -unga, -enga, -inga, are also used to form Adverbs; as ânunga, -inga, entirely; semninga, suddenly; eallunga, entirely; hôlinga, secretly; wêninga, perhaps.

Of Nouns the Gen., Dat., Acc., and Instr. cases are freely used as Adverbs. Comparison of Adverbs is like that of Adjectives. Adverbs of place answer to the three questions—Where? Whither? Whence?—as, þǽr, there; þider, thither; þonan, thence; hwǽr, where; hwider, whither; hwonan, whence; hêr, here; hider, hither; heonan, hence; &c.

LIST OF IRREGULAR AND ANOMALOUS VERBS.

Infinitive.	Present.	Preterit.	Participle.
	1. âh,	âhte,	âgen, (*adj.*)
	2. âhst, âht.		

âgan (own, ought). Pl. âgon.   Subj. Pres. âge, âgen (on).

bannan (command).	2. bannest,	bên (un),	bannen.
bonnan (*red.*)	2. banst, benst.	bêon (un).	
	3. banned, 3. band.	bêonnon.	
bêatan (beat, *red.*)	2. bêatest, bŷtst,	bêot,	bêaten.
	3. bêated, bŷt.	bêoton.	
belgan (be angry). I.	2. bilgst, bilhst,	1. bealg(h),	bolgen.
	3. bilgd, bilhd, bylgd.	2. bulge, bulgon.	
beran (bear). II.	2. birest, birst, byrst,	1. bær,	boren.
beoran,	3. bired, bird, byr(e)d.	2. bǣre, bǣron.	
berstan (burst). I.	2. birst,	1. bærst.	
	3. birsted, birst,	2. burste,	borsten.
	3. byrst, bierst.	burston.	
bêodan (bid). VI.	2. bêodest, bŷtst, bŷst,	1. bêad,	
biodan,	3. beoded, bŷtt, bitt.	2. bude, budon.	boden.
bêon (be).	1. bêom, bêon, bêo,	1. wæs,	(ge-) wesen.
bion,	2. bist, byst,	2. wǣre,	
	3. bid, byd, bêod.	wǣron.	

     Pl. bêod, biod, biad.   sint,   Pres. Subj. bêo, bio.   si, sŷ, sig,
     sind.   Pl. bêon.   sie, sêo, sêo.

     Imper. bêo (d).   sindon.   Pl. sien, sie, sŷn, sin, sêon.

288 *LIST OF IRREGULAR AND ANOMALOUS VERBS.*

Infinitive.	Present.	Preterit.	Participle.
beorcan (bark).	I. 3. byrcð.	bearc, burcon.	borcen.
beorgan (save,) (protect).	I. 2. byrgst, byrhst, 3. byrgeð, byrgð, 3. byrhð.	1. bearg(h), 2. burge, burgon.	borgen.
beornan (burn), byrnan,	I. 1. beorne, byrne, 2. beornest, beornst, 2. byrnest, byrnst, 3. beorneð, beornð, 3. byrneð, birnð(y). Pl. beornað.	barn(ea, o), burne, burnon.	bornen.
bidan (bide).	V. 2. bidest, bitst, bist, 3. bideð, bitt.	1. bâd, 2. bide, bidon.	biden.
biddan (ask).	III. 2. biddest, bidst, bitst, 3. bidded, bit, byt, bitt, Pl. biddað.	1. bæd, 2. bæde, bædon.	beden.
bindan (bind).	I. 2. bindest, bintst, binst, 3. binded, bint, Pl. bindað.	1. band (o), 2. bunde, bundon	bunden.
bitan (bite).	V. 2. bitest, bitst, 3. biteð, bitt, bit.	1. bât, 2. bite, biton.	biten.
blǽtan(bleat,*red.*). blandan(blend,*red*). blondan,	3. blǽt. 2. blandest, 3. blanded, blent.	...... blênd, blênde, blêndon.	...... blanden, blonden.
blâtan (to be blue- [pale, *red*).	2. blâtest, blǽtst, 3. blâted, blǽt.	1. blêot, blêt, 2. blête, blêton.	blâten.
blâwan(blow,*red.*).	2. blâwest, blawst, 2. blǽwest, blǽwst, 3. blâwed, blâwd, 3. blǽwed, blǽwd. Pl. blâwað.	blêow (ê). blêowon.	blâwen.

LIST OF IRREGULAR AND ANOMALOUS VERBS.

Infinitive.	Present.	Preterit.	Participle.
blican (glitter). V.	2. blicest, blicst, 3. bliceđ, blicđ.	1. blâc, 2. blice, blicon.	blicen.
blinnan (cease). I.	2. blinnest, blinst, 3. blinneđ, blinniđ, blinđ.	blan (o), blann, blunne, blunnon.	blunnen.
blôtan (sacrifice). (red.)	2. blôtest, blêtst, 3. blôteđ, blêt, &c.	1. blêot, 2. blêote, blêoton.	blôten.
blôwan (bloom). (red.)	2. blôwest, blêwst, 3. blôweđ, blêwđ, &c.	1. blêow, 2. blêowe, blêowon.	blôwen.
brecan (break). II.	2. bricest, bricst, 3. briceđ, bricđ, &c.	1. bræc, 2. bræce, bræcon.	brocen.
bredan (braid, swing). I.	2. britst, brist, 3. brit, bret, &c.	1. bræd, brudon.	broden, breden.
bregdan (move). I. bredan,	1. bregde, 2. -est, 3. -đ, &c.	1. brægd. brugdon,	brogden, bregden.
brengan* (bring).	2. brengest, brengst, 3. brengeđ, brengđ, brencđ, &c.	1. brôhte, 2. brôhtest, brôhton.	gebrôht.
brêatan (break). (red.)	2. brêatest, brŷtst, 3. brêateđ, brŷt, &c.	1. brêot, brêoton.	brêaten.
brêotan (break). VI.	2. brêotest, brêotst, brŷtest, brŷtst, 3. brêoteđ, brêot, brŷteđ, brŷtt, &c.	1. brêat, 2. brute, bruton.	broten.
brêođan (ruin). VI.	2. brêođest, brŷst, 3. brêođeđ, brŷđ, &c.	1. brêađ, brudon.	broden

Infinitive.	Present.	Preterit.	Participle.
bringan (bring).	I. 1. bringe, brincge, 2. bringst, 3. bringeð, brincgð, bringð, &c.	1. brang (o). 2. brunge, brungon.	brungen.
brinnan (burn).	I.	1. bran, brunnon.	brunnen.
brûcan (use).	VI. 2. brûcest, brŷcst, brîcst, 3. brûceð, brŷcð,	1. brêac, 2. bruce, brucon, bude.*	brocen.
bûan (dwell). bûwan	VI. 2. bûst, Pl. bûað.	Pl. buan(=buwon),	gebûn, gebud.*
bûgan (bow).	VI. 2. bûgest, bŷhst, 3. bûgeð, bŷhð, bŷgð, &c.	1. bêag(h), 2. buge, bugon.	bogen.
bycgan* (buy). bicgan,	1. bycge, bicge, 2. bygest, 3. bygeð, &c.	1. bôhte, bôhton.	gebôht.
ceorfan (carve).	I. 2. ceorfest, cyrfst, 3. ceorfeð, cyrfð, &c.	1. cearf, 2. curfe, curfon.	corfen.
cêosan (choose). ciosan	VI. 2. cêosest, cŷst, 3. ceoseð, cŷst, cist, &c.	1. cêas, cês, 2. cure, curon.	coren.
cêowan (chew).	VI. 2. cêowest, cywst, 3. cêoweð, cŷwð,	1. cêaw, cuwon.	cowen.
clêofan (cleave, split).	VI. 2. clŷfst, 3. clŷfð, &c.	1. clêaf, clufon.	clofen.
clifan (cleave, stick).	V. 2. clifest, clifst, 3. clifeð, clifð,	1. clâf, clifon.	clifen.
clingan (cling, shrink up).	I. 2. clingst, 3. clingð, &c.	1. clang, clungon.	(ge-) clungen.

LIST OF IRREGULAR AND ANOMALOUS VERBS. 291

Infinitive.	Present.	Preterit.	Participle.
(on)cnáwan (know).	2. -cnáwest, -cnǽwst,	-cnéow,	-cnáwen.
(red.)	3. -cnáwed, -cnǽwd, &c.		-cnéowon.

cnéodan (give). VI. 3. cnéoded, &c. cnéad. cnoden.

créodan (crowd). VI. 2. créodest, crýtst, crýst, 1. créad, croden.
    3. créoded, crýded, crýtt, 2. crude,
        &c. crudon.

créopan (creep). VI. 2. crýpest, crýpst, créap, cropen.
    créopest, créopst.
    3. crýped, crýpd, cripd, crupon.
    créoped, créopd, &c.

crincan (yield). I. 2. crincst, cranc, cruncen.
    3. crincd, &c. cruncon.

cringan (cringe, fall). I. 2. cringest, cringst, crang (o), crungen.
crincgan, 3. cringed, cringd, &c. crungon.

cuman (come). II. 2. cymst, cymest, 1. cóm, cwóm, cumen,
    3. cumed, cymd, 2. cóme, cymen.
    cymed, cimd, cómon, cwómon.
    Pl. cumad.

cunnan (can). 1. can, con, cann, conn, cúde, cúd,
    2. canst, const, cúdon. (on-cunnen).
    Pl. cunnon.

cwellan * (kill). cwealde. cweald.

cwelan (die). II. 2. cwilst, cwǽl, cwolen.
    3. cweld, cwild, cwyld. cwǽlon.

cwedan (quoth). III. 2. cwedest, cwedst, cwǽdst, 1. cwǽd, cweden.
    cwidst, cwydst, cwist, cwyst, 2. cwǽde.
    3. cweded, cwed, cwǽdon.
    cwid (d), cwyd, &c.

delan (sink). II. dæl, dolen.
    dǽlon.

delfan (delve). I. 2. delfest, dilfst, 1. dealf, dolfen.
    3. delfed, dilfd, &c. 2. dulfe,
    dulfon.

Infinitive.　　　Present.　　　　　　　　Preterit.　　　Participle.
dôn (do, *red.*).　1. dô,　　　　　　　　1. dyde,dide,dæde,(ge)dôn,
　　　　　　　　2. dêst,　　　　　　　　2. -est, -on, -en.　　dên.
　　　　　　　　3. dêd.
　　　　　　Pl.　　dôd.　Imper. dô (-d).　Pres. Subj. dô,
　　　　　　　　　　　　　　　　　　　　　　　　　　dôn.

(on)drǣdan(dread). 2. drǣdest, drǣtst, drǣst,　(drêord),drêd, drǣdon.
　　　(*red.*) 3. drǣded, drǣtt, &c.　　　drêdon.

dragan(drag,draw).IV. 2. drægest,drægst,dræhst,　drôg(h), dragen.
　　　　　　　　　3. dræged,drægd,dræhd,&c.　drôgon.

drepan (strike). III. 2. drepest,dripest,dripst,　1. drep,dræp,　drepen,
　　　　　　　　3. dreped,driped,dripd,&c. 2. dræpe,　dropen.
　　　　　　　　　　　　　　　　　　　dræpon.

drêogan(do,suffer). VI. 2. drêogest, drŷhst,　1. drêah(g),　drogen.
　　　　　　　　3. drêoged,drŷhd,drigd, 2. druge,
　　　　　　Pl.　drêogad.　[drihd.　drugon.

drêopan(drop). VI. 2. drŷpst,　　　　dreap,　　　dropen.
　　　　　　　3. drŷpd,　　　　　　drupon.
　　　　　Pl.　drêopad.

drêosan (fall). VI. 2. drŷst,　　　　dreas,　　　droren.
　　　　　　　3. drêosed, drŷst, &c.　druron.

drifan (drive). V. 2. drifest, drifst,　1. drâf,　　drifen.
　　　　　　3. drifed, drifd, drift, &c.　2. drife.
　　　　　　　　　　　　　　　　　　drifon (eo).

drincan(drink). I. 2. drincest,　　　dranc,　　　druncen.
　　　　　　3. drincd, dryncd, &c.　　druncon.

dûfan (dive). VI. 2. dŷfst,　　　　1. dêaf,　　dofen.
　　　　　　3. dŷfd, &c.　　　　　2. dufe,
　　　　　　　　　　　　　　　　dufon.

dugan (do, avail). 1. dêag(h),　　　dôhte,
　　　　　　　2. duge,　　　　　　-on.
　　　　　Pl.　dugon.

dwelan (err). II. 2. dwelest, dwilst,　1. dwæl,　　dwolen.
　　　　　　3. dweled, dwild, &c.　　2. dwǣle,
　　　　　　　　　　　　　　　　　dwǣlon.

LIST OF IRREGULAR AND ANOMALOUS VERBS. 293

Infinitive.	Present.		Preterit.	Participle.
etan (eat).	III.	2. etest, etst, itst, ytst, ætst, 3. yt, ytt, et, ett, eted, ieted, 3. yted, ited, itt.	1. æt, 2. æte, 	eten, (eton). æton.
	Pl.	etad.		
eam, &c. (am).		1. eom, eam. 2. eart, eard, eartþu, earttu.	See bêon and wesan.	
	Pl.	earon, earun.		
faran (fare).	VI.	2. farest, færest, færst, færst, 3. fared, færed, færd.	fôr, [færstd.] fôron.	faren.
	Pl.	farad.		
feccan* (fetch). feccean, fæccan.			1. feahte, fehte, 2. -est, -on.	feaht, feht.
fecgan (seize). III.			feah.	
felgan (fall into). I.		2. filgst, filhst, 3. filgd, filhd,	fealg(h), fulgon.	folgen.
	Pl.	felgad.		
fealdan (fold, red.)		2. fealdest, fylst, 3. fealded, fylt.	fêold, fêoldon.	fealden.
feallan (fall, red.)		2. feallest, fealst, felst, fȳlst, 3. fealled, feald, fild, fyld,	fêol (l), fêollon.	feallen.
	Pl.	feallad.		
fêogan* (hate). flogan, fêon, flon.		fêoged, fêod. Pl. fêogad, fêogead.	fêode, fêodon (-un, -an).	
feohan (rejoice). III. fêon,		 -fihd.	feah(-feh), fegen fǽgon (-fêgon).	
feohtan (fight). I.		2. feohtest, 3. feohted, fiht, &c.	1. feaht, 2. fuhte, fuhton.	fohten,
fêolan (hang). II. fiolan, felan,			fæl, fǽlon, fêlon.	folen, feolen.

LIST OF IRREGULAR AND ANOMALOUS VERBS.

Infinitive.	Present.	Preterit.	Participle.
findan (find). I.	2. findest, findst, fintst, finst,	fand(o), funde,*	funden.
	3. finded, fint, &c.	fundon.	
flêogan (fly). VI.	2. flêogest,	1. flêog(h),	flogen.
fliogan,	3. flêoged, fligd, &c.	2. fluge, flugon.	
flêon (flee). VI.	1. flêo,	1. flêah,	flogen.
flêohan,	2. flihst, flȳhst,	2. fluge,	
flêogan,	3. flihd, flȳhd.	flugon.	
flion. Pl.	flêod, fliod, flȳhd.		
flêotan (float). VI.	2. flȳtst,	flêat,	floten.
	3. flȳt.	fluton.	
flitan (strive). V.	2. flitest, flitst,	flât,	fliten.
	3. flited, flit, &c.	fliton.	
flôwan (flow, red.)	2. flôwest, flêwst,	flêow,	flôwen.
	3. flôwed, flêwd, &c.	flêowon.	

folgan * (follow). 1. folgige, folgode, fyl(i)gde, gefolgod.
                2. folgast, fylgst,
                3. folgad, fylgd.
          Pl. folgiad.   Imper. folga (-iad).

fôn (grasp, red.)	1. fô,	1. fêng,	fangen,
	2. fêhst,	2. fênge,	fongen.
	3. fêhd.	fêngon.	
	Pl. fôd.		
	Imper. fôh,	Subj. Pres. fô,	Pret. fênge,
	fôd.	fôn,	fêngen.

| fragan (learn). IV. | | | gefrægen, |
| (gefragan). | | | gefregen. |

fretan (eat up). III.	2. fritest, fritst,	1. fræt,	freten.
	3. freted, frited,	2. fræte,	
	fritt, fryt.	fræton.	

frêogan * (free).	frêo, &c.	frêode,	frêod.
frêon,	frêod,	-on.	
	Pl. frêogad.		
	Imper. frêo.	Subj. Pres. frêoge.	

… LIST OF IRREGULAR AND ANOMALOUS VERBS. 295

Infinitive.		Present.	Preterit.	Participle.
frícgan (ask).	III.	2. frígest, frígst, frihst,	1. fræg,	ge-frigen,
frícgean,		3. fríged, frígd, frihd, &c.	2. frǣge,	-fregen,
frícggan.			frǣgon.	-frǣgen,
	Imper.	frige, &c. Subj. Pres. frícge, &c.		

frignan (ask).	I.	2. frígnest,	1. frægn (-en,-in),	frugnen.
		3. frígned, &c.	fræng, fregen (-n),	
			2. frugne,	
			frugnon.	
	Imper.	frígn (-ad). Subj. Pres. frígne, &c.		

frínan (ask).	I.	2. frínest,	1. frân,	frunen.
		3. fríned, &c.	2. frune,	
			frunon.	
	Imper.	frín (ad). Subj. Pres. fríne (-en).		

| fringan (ask). | I. | | -(ge)-fringon (Beo. 1667.) | |

| galan (sing). | IV. | 2. gǣlest, gǣlst, | gôl, | galen. |
| | | 3. gǣled, gǣld, &c. | gôlon. | |

gân (go).		1. gâ,	*	
		2. gǣst,	1. eode,	gegân.
		3. gǣd.	2. eodest,	
	Pl.	gâd.	eodon.	
	Imper.	gâ (-d). Subj. Pres. gâ, gân.		

gangan (go).		1. gange, gonge,	gêong, giong,	gangen,
gongan (red).		2. gangest, gongest,	gieng, gêng,	gongen.
gancgan,		3. ganged, gonged.		
	Pl.	gangod, gongod.	gêongon, giongon,	
	(Usually contracted into gân).	giengon, gêngon.		

gellan (yell).		1. gelle, gille, gielle, gylle,	geal,	gollen.
giellan (red.)		2. gilst, gielst, gylst,	gullon.	
gyllan,		3. gilled, gild, gield,		
gillan,		gylled, gyld.		
	Pl.	gellad (i, ie, y).		

Infinitive.	Present.	Preterit.	Participle.
gerwan*(prepare).	gearw(i)e (gearuwe),	gearwode(-ade, -ede),	gegired,
gærwian,		girede, &c.	ge-gearwod,
girwan,		-odon.	(-ad, -ed).
gierwan,			
gyrwan,			
gearwian.	Pl. gearwað.		

gêopan (take up). VI.	2. gŷpst,	gêap,	gopen.
	3. gŷpð.	gupon.	
	Pl. gêopað.		

gêotan (pour). VI.	2. gŷtst,	gêat, gêt,	goten.
	3. gŷt.	guton.	
	Pl. gêotað.		

gifan (give). III.	1. gife, &c.	1. geaf, gæf, gef,	gifen,
giefan,	2. gifest, gifst,	2. gêafe, gêfe,	giefen,
gefan,	3. gifeð, gifð.	gêafon, gêfon.	gyfen.
geofan,			
giofan,	Pl. gifað.		
gyfan.			

gildan (pay). I.	2. giltst, gieltst,	geald,	golden.
gieldan,	gyltst, gilst,	guldon.	
gyldan,	3. gilded, gilt,		
geldan,	gielt, gylt, &c.		

gilpan (boast). I.	2. gilpst, gielpst, gylpst,	gealp,	golpen.
gielpan,	3. gilpð, gielpð.	gulpon.	
gylpan,	Pl. gilpað (ie, y).		

ginan (yawn). V.	1. gine,	gân,	ginen.
	2. ginest, ginst,	ginon.	
	3. gineð, ginð.		
	Pl. ginað.		

ginnan (begin). I.	2. -ginnest, ginst,	1. -gann (o),	-gunnen.
gynnan,	3. -ginneð, ginð, gined, &c.	2. -gunne,	
		-gunnon.	

LIST OF IRREGULAR AND ANOMALOUS VERBS. 297

Infinitive.	Present.	Preterit.	Participle.
gitan (get). gietan, gytan, geotan.	III. 1. -gite (y, ie), 2. -gitst, 3. -git, -gitt. Pl. -gitađ (y, ie).	-geat, ·gêaton.	giten.
glidan (glide).	V. 2. glidest, 3. glided, glit, &c.	glâd, glidon.	gliden.
grætan (bewail). grêtan. (*red.*)	1. grǽte, 2. grǽtest, &c.	grêt, grêton.	grǽten, grêten.
grafan (dig).	IV. 1. grafe, grǽfe, 2. grǽfest, grǽfst, 3. grǽfeđ, grǽfđ. Pl. grafađ.	grôf, grôfon.	grafen.
grêosan (frighten).	VI. 2. grŷst, 3. grŷst. Pl. grêosađ.	grêas, gruron.	groren.
grêotan (weep).	VI. 2. grŷtest, grŷtst, 3. grêoteđ, grŷt, &c.	grêat, gruton.	groten.
grimman (rage, hasten).	I. 2. grimst, 3. grimmeđ, grimđ, &c.	gramm (o), grummon.	grummen.
grindan (grind). gryndan.	I. 2. grintst, grinst, 3. grint, &c.	1. grand (o), 2. grunde, grundon.	grunden.
gripan (grasp).	V. 2. gripest, gripst, 3. gripeđ, gripđ, &c.	grâp, gripon.	gripen.
grôwan (grow, *red.*)	2. grôwest, grêwst, 3. grôweđ, grêwđ, &c.	grêow, grêowon.	grôwen.
habban (have).	1. hæbbe (hafa, -o, -u), 2. hæfst (hafast, hafest), 3. (hafađ, hæfeđ), hæfđ. Pl. habbađ (æ). Imper. hafa, habbađ (æ).	hæfde, -on.	(ge)hæf(e)d. Subj. Pres. hæbbe (a), -en, -on (æ).

Infinitive.	Present.	Preterit.	Participle.
hâtan (bid, *red*).	2. hâtest, hǣtsđ (?),	hêht, hêt,	hâten.
	3. hâteđ, hât, hǣtt, &c.	hêhton, hêton.	
hâtan*(be called).		hâtte (Pres. & Pret.)	
		hâtton.	
hebban (raise). IV.	1. hebbe (æ),	hôf,	hafen (æ).
hæbban.	3. hefeđ, hefđ.	hôfon.	
	Pl. hebbađ.		
	Imper. hebe, hebbađ.		
helan (conceal). II.	2. hilest (y),	1. hæl,	holen.
		2. hǣle,	
	3. hilđ.	hǣlon.	
	Pl. helađ.		
helpan (help). I.	2. helpst,	1. healp,	holpen.
	3. helpeđ, hilpđ (ie),&c.	2. hulpe,	
		hulpon.	
herian (praise).	1. herige, herge,	heređe (-ode), heređ.	
hergan, hæran,		heređon.	
hergian, herian.	3. heređ.		
	Pl. herađ, heriađ, herigađ.	herigeađ, hergađ.	
	Imper. hera (e).		
hêafan (mourn, *red*.)		hêof, hôf,	
		hêofon.	
healdan(hold, *red*.)	2. healdest,	1. hêold,	healden.
haldan.	3. hilt, healt, hylt,	2. hêolde,	
	Pl. healdađ.	hêoldon (io).	
hêawan (hew, *red*.)		hêow,	hêawen.
	3. hêaweđ,	hêowon.	
	hiwđ (ie).		
	Pl. hêawađ.		
hladan (load). IV.	1. hlade,	hlôd,	hladen.
	2. hlætst,		
	3. hladeđ, &c.	hlôdon (u, a).	

LIST OF IRREGULAR AND ANOMALOUS VERBS.   299

Infinitive.	Present.	Preterit.	Participle.
hlehhan (laugh). IV. 1.	hliche, &c.	1. hlôh,	-hlahen,
hlihhan,		2. hlôge,	-hleahen.
hlihan,			
hlyhhan.		hlôgon (a, u).	
	Pl. hlihgađ, hlihađ (ie).		

hlêapan (leap, run). 1.	hlêape, &c.	hlêop,	hlêapen.
(red.)	3. hlêapeđ, hlêapđ, hlipđ, &c.	hlêopon (u).	

hlêotan (cast lots). 1.	hlêote,	hlêat,	
(red.)	2. hlêotest, &c.	hluton.	

hlidan (cover). V.		-hlâd,	hliden.
		-hlidon.	

hligan (call).   V. 3. -hliđ. ....

hlimman (resound). I.		hlamm,	......
hlymman.	3. hlimmeđ, hlymmeđ, &c.	hlummon.	

hlôwan (low, red.) 3. hlêwđ.	hlêow,	......
	hlêowon.	

hnâtan (strike, red.)   hnêot.   ......

hnêappan (break, red.)	-hnêop,	-hnêapen.
	hnêopon.	

hnigan (bend). V.	hnige, &c.	hnâg (h),	hnigen.
		hnigon.	

hnitan (knock). V		hnât,	hniten.
		hniton.	

hôn (hang, red.)		hêng,	hangen.
	Pl. hôđ.	hêngon.	
	Pl. Imper. hôh (-đ).		

hrêosan (fall). VI. 1. hrêose,	hrêas,	hroren.
3. hrŷsđ, hrŷst, hrist (ê).	hruron.	

hrêođan (cover). VI.	......	hroden.
(hrêođan).		

300 LIST OF IRREGULAR AND ANOMALOUS VERBS.

Infinitive.	Present.	Preterit.	Participle.
hrêowan (rue).	VI. 3. hriwð,	hrêaw (êo).	......
(Impers. often).	3. hrêowed.		
	Pl. hrêowð.		
hrinan (touch).	V. 1. hrine (o),	hrân,	hrinen.
	3. hrined, hrind.	hrinon.	
hrindan (push).	I.	hrand,	......
		hrundon.	
hrôfan (cry, call, red.)		hrêop,	
		hrêopon (-u).	
hrûtan (make a noise).	VI. hrûte, &c.	hrêat,	......
		hruton.	
hûdan (rob).	VI.	-hêad,	-hoden.
		-hudon.	
hwelan (howl),	II.	hwæl.	
hwylan.	3. hwiled.		
hwettan* (whet).	1. hwette, &c.	hwette,	
	3. hwæt, hwæted, hweted.	hwetton.	
hweorfan (turn, move),	I. 1. hweorfe,	hwearf, hwærf,	hworfen.
hworfan,	2. hwearfest,	hwurfon (o, eo).	
hwurfan.	3. hwirfð, hweorfed, &c.		
hycgan* (think),	1. hycge (i), &c.,	hogade (-ode, -ede),	
hicgan (-ean).	3. hycged, hyged.	[hogde,	
	Pl. hycgað (ead).	hogedon (-odon, -dan),	
		hogdan.	
irnan (run, flow).	I. 3. irnð, irned, yrned.	1. arn,	urnen.
		2. urne,	
	Pl. yrnað.	urnon.	
lâcan (jump, move),		1. lêolc (-lêc),	-lâcen.
(red.)	3. lâced, &c.	2. lêolce,	
		-lêcon.	

LIST OF IRREGULAR AND ANOMALOUS VERBS.   301

Infinitive.	Present.	Preterit.	Participle.
lǽtan (let, red.),	1. lǽte,		
lêtan.	2. lǽtest, lǽtst,	lêt (lêot),	lǽten.
	3. lǽteđ, lǽtt, lêteđ.	lêton.	
	Imper. lǽt (-ađ).		

leccan* (moisten).		leohte.	leoht.

lecgan* (lay).	1. lecge,	legđe (-lêđe),	ge-leged,
	2. legest,	legdon (æ).	ge-lêd.
	leged.		
	Pl. lecgađ.		

| lesan (pick). | III. | lǽs, | -lesen. |
| | | -lǽson. | |

| lêan (scold). | IV. 3. lyhđ. | lôg (h), | -leahen. |
| | | lôgon. | |

| lêodan (grow), | VI. | lêad, | -loden. |
| líodan. | | ludon. | |

| lêofan (love?). | VI. (Dan. 56). | Pl. lufan (?). | |

lêogan (lie).	VI.	lêag (h),	-logen.
	3. lȳhđ, lêogeđ.	lugon.	
	Pl. lêogađ.		

| lêosan (lose). | VI. 3. -list. | lêas, | -loren. |
| | | -luron. | |

libban* (live),	1. libbe (Sweet, lxxv.),		
lybban.	2. leofast (i),	lifđe (y),	-lifd,
	3. leofađ (i).	leofode,	-lyfd.
	Pl. libbađ.	lifđon (a, y),	ge-leofod.
		leofodon.	
	Pres. Subj. libbe (-en, -on). Imper. leofa (i),		
	libbađ.		

licgan (ean), (lie down). III. 2. ligst,
  3. licgeđ, ligeđ, ligđ, ligđ (-et), lǽg,   -legen.
                                   [lid. lǽgon (â), (un, an).
          Pl. ligađ (-ead).

| lídan (grow). | V. 3. lídeđ. | ...... | ...... |

302 LIST OF IRREGULAR AND ANOMALOUS VERBS.

Infinitive.	Present.	Preterit.	Participle.
lifian* (live),	1. lifige, lifge,	(See libban).	
lyfian,	2. leofast,		
lifgan (-ean).	3. lifađ, lyfađ, leofađ.		
leofian.			
	Pl. lifiađ, lifigeađ, lifigađ, lifgađ.		
	Imper. leofa.		
lihan (lend),	V. 3. -lihđ (-lŷhđ).	lâh (g), lêah, -lihen.	
lŷhan.		-ligon.	
limpan (happen).	I. 3. limpeđ, limpđ, &c. (Impers.)	lamp (o), -lumpon.	gelumpen.
linnan (yield),	I. 2. linnest, linst,	1. -lan,-lon(un), -lunnen.	
lynnan.	3. -linđ,	2. -lunne,	
	-linneđ, linniđ, &c.	lunnon.	
liđan (go).	I.	-lâđ,	-liđen,
		-liđon (-lidon).	-liđen.
lûcan (lock).	VI.	-lêac,	locen.
	3. lŷcđ, &c.	lucon.	
lûtan (bow).		lêat,	(ge)loten.
	3. lûteđ, lŷtt, &c.	lutan (-un).	
magan (may).	1. mæg,	1. meahte, mehte, mihte,	
	2. meaht, miht.	2. meahtes,	
	Pl. mâgon, mǣgon, mâgan, mâgum, mâgun.	meahtum (-on, -an), mihton (-en).	
	Subj. Pres. mǣge.	Subj. Pret. meahte, mihte,	
	Pl. mǣgen, mǣge.	meahte, meahtes (-t), meahton, mihton, meahtan, meahten, mihten, meahte, mihte.	
mâwan (mow, *red.*)		-mêow.	-mâwen.
meltan (melt).	I. 3. melteđ,	mealt, multon (-an).	-molten.

LIST OF IRREGULAR AND ANOMALOUS VERBS.

Infinitive.	Present.	Preterit.	Participle.
metan (measure). III.		mæt, mǣton.	meten.
meornan (mourn, care). I. (u).		mearn, murnon.	mornen.
miđan (hide). V.		mâđ, -miđon.	miđen.
môtan (may, must).	1. môt, 2. môst. Pl. môton (-an, -en, -um, -un). Subj. Pres. môte. Pl. môten (-an, -e).	môste. -on.	
munan (think).	1. man, mon 2. manst. Pl. munon. Subj. Pres. mune, -an.	munde. -on.	
nabban (not to have). (ne + habban.	1. næbbe, 2. nafast, næft, 3. nafađ, næfđ. Pl. nabbađ.	næfde, næfdon.	
nâgan, (ne + âgan).	1. nâh, Pl. nâgon (-an).	nâhte, nâhton (-an).	
nâpan (red.) in genâpan (attack?).		-nêop, -nêopon.	neopen.
nesan (survive, endure). III.	3. -nist, -nesed, &c.	-næs, nǣson.	genesen.
neam, neom (am not). (= ne + eam).	3. nis, nys, Pl. nearon. Pres. Part. nǣrende.	næs.	
nêotan (enjoy, use). VI. niotan.		-nêat, -nuton.	-noten.

LIST OF IRREGULAR AND ANOMALOUS VERBS.

Infinitive.	Present.	Preterit.	Participle.
nillan,	1. nelle, nele,	1. nolde,	
nellan (=ne+willan),	nylle, nyle,	2. noldest (-s),	
nyllan.	2. nelt, nylt.		
	Pl. nellað (g).	noldon (-an).	
	Imper. nyle, nyllað. Pres. Subj. nyle, nelle,		
		nyllen, nellon.	

niman (take). II.	1. nime,	1. nam, nom, numen.
(y, eo, io).	2. nimest,	2. name,
	3. nimeð (y), nimð.	namon (-an),
		(noman).
	Pl. nimað (y).	

nipan (grow dark). V.   -nâp,   -nipen.
                             -nipon.

nitan (y, e), (not to know). 1. nât,	1. nyste, nysse,
(= ne + witan). 2. nâst.	2. nysses,
	nyston.
Pl. nyton, neton.	

-nugan (have at com-   -neah.   -nohte.
    [mand.)
             Pl. -nugon.

rǽcan* (reach, attain),		ræhte,	-ræht.
rǽcean.		ræhton.	

rǽdan (advise, red.). 1. rǽde,   rêord.
                      2. rǽdest,
                      3. rǽded, rǽt, &c.

rafan (rob). IV.   -rôf,   -rafen.
                                      rôfon.

rêcan* (reck),	2. rêcst,	rôhte,
rêccan.	3. rêcð, rêced, &c.	rôhton (-un).

reccan* (rule, say).	1. recce,	reahte, rehte,	-reaht,
	2. recest,	-on.	-reht.
	3. recð, receð, &c.		
	Imper. rece (-að).		

LIST OF IRREGULAR AND ANOMALOUS VERBS. 305

Infinitive.	Present.	Preterit.	Participle.
rêocan (reek, exhale). IV.	Pl. rêocađ.	......	......
rêodan (redden). VI.		...... Pl. rudon.	......
rêofan (break). VI.		-reaf, -rufon.	rofen.
rêotan (weep). VI.	3. rêoteđ. Pl. rêotađ.	reat, ruton.	-roten.
ridan (ride). V.	1. ride, &c., 3. rideđ, &c.	1. râd, 2. ride, ridon (-an).	riden.
ridan (get ready). V.		-râd, ridon.	-riden.
rinnan (run, flow). I.		ran, runnon.	-runnen.
risan (rise). V.	3. rist, &c.	1. râs, 2. rise, rison.	risen.
rôwan (row, red.)	1. rôwe, 3. rôweđ, rêwđ, &c.	rêow, rêowon, rêon.	
sacan (fight). IV.		sôc, sôcon.	sacen.
sâwan (sow, red.)	3. sâweđ, sǽwđ. Pl. sâwađ.	sêow (slow), sêowon (-an).	sâwen.
scâdan (separate), scêadan. (red.)	3. scêadeđ, scâdeđ, &c.	scêd (êo), scêdon.	scâden, scêaden.
scânan (shine? red.) See scinan.		Pl. scionan.	

LIST OF IRREGULAR AND ANOMALOUS VERBS.

Infinitive.	Present.	Preterit.	Participle.
sceppan (shape, do). IV. (i, y, eo).	2. scyppest, 3. scipd, &c.	1. scôp (êo), 2. scêope, scôpon(eo).	sceapen, scepen, scapen.
sceran(eo), (shear). II.		scær, scer (ea), scǽron.	scoren.
scerwan (squander). III.		......	scerwen.
sceacan (shake, move), IV. scacan.	sceaced, scæced, &c.	scôc (êo), scêocan (an).	sceacen, scacen, scæcen.
sceadan (scathe). IV.		scôd (eo), scôdon (-un, -an).	sceaden.
scêotan (shoot, move), VI. sciotan.	3. scȳt, scitt, Pl. scêotað.	scêat, scuton.	scoten, sceoten.
scinan (shine). V.	3. scined, scȳned, &c.	scân (êa), scinon, scionon (B. 303?).	scinen.
scrifan (shrive). V.	3. scrifed, scrifd, &c.	scrâf (ea), scrifon.	scrifen.
scridan (stride). V.	3. scrided, scrid, &c.	scrâd, scridon (-un).	scriden.
scûfan (shove). VI.	3. scȳft. Pl. scûfað.	scêaf, scufon (-un).	scofen.
sculan (shall).	1. sceal (ll), scal, scel (ll), 2. scealt, scealtû (=scealt þû). Pl. sculon (-un, -an), sceolon (-un, -an). Pres. Subj. scyle, scile. Pl. scylen, scylan, scyle, sceole.	sceolde, scolde, sciolde.	-on.
sêcan, sêcean* (seek), sêccan, seôccan, sǽcan.	3. sêcd, &c.	sôhte, sôhton (-un, -an).	gesôht.

LIST OF IRREGULAR AND ANOMALOUS VERBS.

Infinitive.	Present.	Preterit.	Participle.
secgan*(say), seccgan, secgean, sæcgean.	1. secge, sæcge, &c. 3. seged, sæged, secged. Pl. secgað, secgeað (æ). Imper. sege, sæcgeað, secgeað.	sægde, sæde, sægd, sægdon, sædon. sæd.	
sellan(i,y),*(give,sell).	1. selle, sille, 2. selest, sylest, 3. seld, sild, seled, syled. Pl. syllað. Imper. Sg. sæle, syle, sile.	1. sealde, 2. -est (-es), sealdon (-un).	geseald.
sendan*(send).	1. sende, 2. senst (æ), sendest (æ), 3. sended, sent, &c.	sende, sendon.	gesended, gesend.
serwan*(contrive), serian, syrwan (i).	2. syrwst. Pl. syrewað, serwað.	syrwde, syrede, serede, syrwedan, geserod, -ed. syredan (-on), seredon (i).	
sêon (see), sion.	III. 1. sêo, 2. sihst, 3. sið, syhð, sihð. Pl. sêoð, sioð. Imper. seoh, syh, sioh.	1. seah, 2. sâwe, sâwon, sægon, [sêgon (-un).	gesegen, -sewen.
sêon (strain).	V. ...... Pl. (ge-)sêoð.	......	(be)sêon.
sêoðan (seethe).	VI. 3. sêoðed. Pl. sêoðað.	1. sêað, 2. sude, sudon.	soden.
sigan (sink).	V. 3. sigð, siged. Pl. sigað.	sâg(h), sigon.	sigen.

308 LIST OF IRREGULAR AND ANOMALOUS VERBS.

Infinitive.	Present.		Preterit.	Participle.
sincan (sink).	I.		1. sanc (o), 2. sunce, suncon.	suncen.
singan (sing).	I.		1. sang, 2. sunge, sungon.	sungen.
sinnan (think).	I.		sann (-u), sunnon.	......
sittan (sit).	III.	1. sitte, 2. sitest, sitst, sittest, 3. sited, sitt. Pl. sittađ. Imper. site, sittađ.	1. sæt, 2. sǣte, sǣton(e).	seten.
slǣpan (sleep, red.) (â, ê).		2. slǣpst, 3. slǣped, slǣpđ. Pl. slǣpađ.	slêp(slǣpte),*(slâpen). slêpon.	
slêan (strike), slagan.	IV.	3. slihđ. Imper. sleah, sleh. Pl. slêađ.	slôg (h), slôgon(-un).	slagen, slægen, slegen.
slidan (slide).	V.	1. slide, 2. slidest, slitst, 3. slided, slit. Pl. slidađ.	slâd, slidon.	sliden.
slitan (slit).	V.	1. slite, &c., 3. slited, slit. Pl. slitađ.	slât, sliton.	sliten(y).
sliđan (injure).	V.	...... Pres. Part. sliđend.	......	......
slûpan (ê), (slip).	VI.		slêap, slupon.	slopen.

LIST OF IRREGULAR AND ANOMALOUS VERBS. 309

Infinitive.	Present.	Preterit.	Participle.
smêocan (smoke). VI.	1. smêoce, 3. smȳcð.	smêac, smûcon.	smocen.
smitan (smite, sail). V.		smât, smiton.	smiten.
smûgan (flow, penetrate). VI.	-smȳhð.	......	......
snadan (?). IV. (Cf. B. 1944).		snôd.	
sniðan (cut). V.		snâð, snidon.	sniden.
spanan (entice, *red.*)	3. spaneð, -spend, &c.	spôn (êo), spônon (êo).	spanen (o).
spannan (join, *red.*)		spêon.	spannen.
speornan (spurn), I. spornan.		spearn, spurnon.	spornen.
spiwan (spew). V.		spâw.	......
spôwan (succeed, *red.*)		spêow, spêowon.	......
sprecan (æ), (speak). II.	1. sprece (æ, i), 2. spricest, sprycst, 3. spricð, spriceð, spreceð. Pl. sprecað.	1. spræc, 2. spræce, spræcon, spæcon.	sprecen.
sprêatan (sprout, *red.*)		-sprêot.	......
sprêotan (sprout). VI. (Cf. sprȳtan).		sprêat, spruton.	sproten.
springan (spring). I.	3. springð, &c.	sprang (o), sprungon.	sprungen.
standan (o), (stand). IV.	3. stondeð, standeð, stent (y). Pl. standað.	stôd, stôdon (-an, -un).	standen.
stapan (step). IV.		stôp, stôpon.	stapen.

LIST OF IRREGULAR AND ANOMALOUS VERBS.

Infinitive.	Present.	Preterit.	Participle.
stelan (steal).	II. 3. steled, steld (y). Pl. stelad.	stæl, stǽlon.	stolen.
stellan*(place).		stealde, stalde.	gesteald.
stigan (move, go).	V. 3. stigd, stiged, stihd, &c.	stâg (h), stigon.	stigen.
stincan (stink).	I.	stanc (o), stuncon.	stuncen.
stingan (sting).	I.	stang, stungon.	stungen.
streccan*(stretch).	1. strecce, 2. strecest, 3. streced, strecd. Pl. streccad.	streahte, strehte.	streaht, streht.
stredan (scatter).	I. 3. streded. Pl. stredad.	2. -strude (?).	
stregdan (strew).	I. 3. stregded (i).	2. -strugde.	......
strican (move).	V. 3. striced.	......	......
strûdan (ravage).	VI.	strêad, strudon.	stroden.
styrian (i)*(stir), styrgan (i).	styrge, &c. Pl. styriad.	styrode (ede), styredon.	styred (i).
sûcan (suck).	VI.	sêac, sucon.	sôcen.
sûgan (suck).	VI.	sêag, sugon.	sogen.
sûpan (swallow).	VI.	sêap, supon.	sopen.
swapan (sweep, drive, *red.*)		swêop.	......
swâpan (sweep, *red.*)		swêop, swêopon.	swâpen.

LIST OF IRREGULAR AND ANOMALOUS VERBS. 311

Infinitive.	Present.	Preterit.	Participle.
swebban*(put to sleep).	3. swebed. Pl. swebbad.	swefede.	swefed.
swefan (sleep). III.	3. swefed, swifed, &c.	swæf, swæfon.	......
swelgan(eo), (swallow). I.		swealg(h), swulgon.	swolgen.
sweltan (die). I.	1. swelte, 2. sweltest, 3. swelted, swylted, &c.	swealt, swulton (-an).	......
swerian(swear). IV.	3. swered. 1. swerige, swerge, Pl. sweriad.	swôr, swêor, (swerede*), swôron.	sworen.
swercan (darken). I.		swearc, swurcon.	sworcen.
sweorfan (wipe). I.	3. swyrft.	......	sworfen.
swican (move, leave off). V.	1. swice, 2. -est, -st, 3. swicd, -ed, &c.	swâc, swicon.	swicen.
swifan (roam). V.	3. swifed.	swâf.	......
swimman(y), (swim). I.	3. swimd. Pl. swimmad.	swamm (o), swummon.	
swincan (toil). I.	1. swince, &c., 3. swincd. Pl. swincad.	swanc, swuncon.	......
swingan (beat, swing). I.	3. swinged, &c.	swang, swungon.	swungen.
swôgan (rustle, red.)	Pl. swôgad.	......	......

312   LIST OF IRREGULAR AND ANOMALOUS VERBS.

Infinitive.	Present.	Preterit.	Participle.
tǽcan*(-ean),(teach).	3. tǽcð, &c.	tǽhte.	tǽht.
teldan (cover).	I.	teald, tuldon	tolden.
tellan*(tell,count).	1. telle, 2. telest, 3. teleð. Pl. tellað.	tealde, tealdon.	teald, teled.
teran (tear).	II. tere, &c.	tær, tǽron.	toren.
têon (draw), tion.	VI. 1. têo, 2. týhst(i), 3. týhð, têhð. Pl. têoð.	têah(g),têh, tugon.	togen.
tihan (accuse), têon	V. 2. týhst, 3. týhð(i).	têah.	tigen.
tingan (press).	I.	tang.	......
tredan (tread).	III. 1. trede, &c. 3. tritt, treded (ie,i,y). Pl. tredað.	1. træd, 2. trǽde. trǽdon(-an).	treden.
þeccan*(cover).	3. þeceð. Pl. þeccað.	þeahte, þehte.	þeaht.
þencan*(-ean),(think).	1. þence, 2. -est, -st, 3. -ed, -d. Pl. þencað (-ead).	1. þôhte, 2. -est, -on (-an).	geþôht.
þerscan (thresh).	I. 3. þirsceð(-d).		
þêon(i),(thrive).	VI. 1. þêo. Pl. þêoð.	þêah, þugon.	þogen.
þêotan (howl).	VI. ...... Pl. þuton.	......	......

LIST OF IRREGULAR AND ANOMALOUS VERBS.

Infinitive.	Present.	Preterit.	Participle.
þicgan (-ean), (take). III.	......	þeah, þah,	þigen.
	3. þiged.	þǣgon.	
þicgan (take).		þigde,*	......
		þigdon*(edon).	
þíhan (thrive). V.	þíhđ.	þáh (-g),	þǣh.
þindan (swell). I. 3.	þint.	þand,	þunden.
		þundon.	
þingan (thrive). I.		þang,	geþungen.
		þungon.	
þrêotan (become weary). VI.		þrêat,	þroten.
	3. þrýt.	þruton.	
þrêowan (throw). VI.			þrowen.
þringan (press). I.		þrang,	þrungen.
		þrungon.	
þurfan (need, dare). 1. þearf,		þorfte.	
2. þearft,			
3. þearf.			
Pl. þurfon.			
Pres. Subj. þurfe.			
Pl. þurfe, þyrfen.			
þweran (beat, forge). II.		þwær,	þworen,
		þwǣron.	þuren.
þweahan (wash), IV. 1. þwêa (-h),		þwôg (h),	þwagen (æ).
þwêan. 2. -hst (y, e),			
3. þwehđ (y, i).		þwôgon.	
Pl. þwêađ.			
þwitan (cut out). V. 3. þwited.			
Pl. þwiton.		......	......
þyncan (-ean),*(seem),		þúhte,	
þincan. 3. þyncđ, þinced(y), þincđ.		þúhton.	geþúht.
Pl. þincađ (-ead).			
unnan (grant). 1. an, ann, onn,		úđe.	
2. unne.			
Pl. unnon.			

314 LIST OF IRREGULAR AND ANOMALOUS VERBS.

Infinitive.	Present.	Preterit.	Participle.
wâcan (originate). IV.		wôc, wôcon.	wacen.
wadan (go). IV.		wôd, wôdon.	waden.
wascan (wash). IV. 3. wæsced.		......	......
wâwan (blow, *red.*)		(wêow).	wâwen.
weccan (-ean)*(arouse).	3. wecd, weced. Pl. weccad.	weahte, wehte.	weaht.
wefan (weave). III.		wæf, wǽfon.	wefen.
wegan (bear). III.		wæg, wǽgon.	wegen.
wêpan (weep, *red.*)	3. wêped, wêpd. Pl. wêpad.	wêop, wêopon.	......
wesan (be). III. (See bêon and eam).	1. wæs, 2. wǽre, wǽron (-un, -an),	wesen, (weoren). (wêron).	
	Pres. Subj. wese, wesen (an).	Imper. wes, wesad.	
wealcan (roll, *red.*)		wêolc.	wealcen.
wealdan (a), (wield).	1. wealde, (*red.*) 2. -est (a), 3. wilt, 3. wealded (a), &c.	wêold (1o), wêoldon (an), (wioldon).	wealden.
weallan (well up).	(*red.*) 3. wealled. Pl. weallad.	wêoll (l), wêollon.	weallen.

LIST OF IRREGULAR AND ANOMALOUS VERBS. 315

Infinitive.　　　　Present.　　　　　　　Preterit.　　Participle.
weaxan (grow, wax). IV.　　　　　　　wêox, wôx, weaxen.
　　　　3. weaxed, wexed, wexd, wixt. wêaxon (-an).
　　　　Pl. weaxad.

weorpan (throw). I.　　　　　　1. wearp,　　worpen.
　(o, y, u).　　3. weorped, wyrpd (i).　2. wurpe,
　　　　　　　　　　　　　　　　　　　　　wurpon.
　　　　Pl. weorpad.

weordan (become), I. 2. wyrdest,　　1. weard,　　worden.
　(io, u, y).　　3. (weord), wird, weor-　2. wurde,
　　　　　　　　　[ded (u), (wyrd).　　wurdon (-an, -um).
　　　　Pl. weordad.
　　　　Imper. weord (-ad). Pres. Subj. weorde,
　　　　　　　　　　　　　　　　　　　　weorden (-an).

wican (yield). V.　　　　　　　　　wâc,　　wicen.
　　　　　　　　　　　　　　　　　　　wicon.

willan (y), (will). 1. & 3. wille, wile, wyle, wylle, wolde.
　　　　2. wilt, wylt.
　　　　Pl. willad (y).
　　　　Pres. Subj. wille, wile, wylle,
　　　　　　　　willen (-on), wyllen, wylle.

windan (wind). I. 3. wint, &c.　　　wand (o),　wunden.
　　　　　　　　　　　　　　　　　　　wundon.

winnan (y), (strength). I.　　　　1. wan (o), wann, wunnen.
　　　　3. winned, wind.　　　　　2. wunne,
　　　　　　　　　　　　　　　　　　　wunnon.
　　　　Pl. winnad (y).

witan (y), (know.) 1. wât,　　　　wiste (y), (wisse). witen.
　　　　2. wâst, wæst.
　　　　Pl. witon.
　　　　Pres. Subj. wite (-en, -on). Imper. wite (ad).

witan (see, move). V. 1. wite,　　1. wât,　　witen.
　　　　2. witest, witst,　　　　　2. wite,
　　　　3. wited, witt.　　　　　　witon.
　　　　Pl. witad
　　Subj. Imper. wutan, wuton, wutun, utan, uton (= let us).

Infinitive.	Present.	Preterit.	Participle.
wlitan (see).	V. 2. wlitest, 3. wlited. Pl. wlitað.	wlát, wliton.	wliten.
wrecan (push, wreak).	III. 3. wricð, &c.	wræc, wrǽcon.	wrecen.
wreon (io), (cover).	V. 1. wreo.	wreah, wrugon.	
wridan (ð), (increase).	V. Pl. wridað.		wriden.
wrihan (cover).	V. 2. wrihst, 3. wrihð.	wráh, wrigon.	wrigen.
writan (scratch, write).	V.	wrát, writon.	writen.
wriðan (wreathe).	V. 3. wrið. Pl. wráð.	wráð, wridon.	wriden.
wrótan (root, *red.*)	Pl. wrótað.	......	......
wyrcan*(-ean),(work), weorcean, wercan (i).	3. wyrcð.	1. worhte, 2. -est, -on.	geworht.
ŷcan*(increase), ican (-ean).	2. icest, 3. iced (ŷ). Pl. ŷcað (ie).	yhte, ihte, icte, iecte, icton, ihtan.	
ywan*(show).	1. ŷwe, 2. ŷwest, ŷwst, 3. ŷwed, ŷwð. Pl. ŷwað.	ŷwde, ŷwdon.	ŷwed.

LIST OF IRREGULAR AND ANOMALOUS VERBS.   317

NOTES.

1. Verbs marked *, though they are not Strong Verbs, are given here on account of certain vowel irregularities.

2. First Person Sg. Pres. Ind. is generally regular; and in the Preterit the First and Third Pers. Sg. are alike. The Subj. Pret. has the stem-vowel of Ind. Pret. Pl.

3. The Vowel of Second Pers. Sg. Pret. usually coincides with the Vowel of the Pret. Pl.

4. Many Verbs are defective, or occur only in certain Persons or Tenses.

5. The dialect forms in various spellings are very numerous: hence only the more *regular* forms in Pres., Pret., and Participle have been given.

6. The Roman Numeral after a Verb indicates the class to which the Verb belongs. (Koch's classification.)

7. The Verb-forms, from a to hwi, have been compiled from Bosworth-Toller's Lexicon, and from Groschopp; from hwi on, from Grein's Lexicon, supplemented by Bosworth-Toller, as far as the latter extends. The orthography has been corrected, as far as possible, by the lists of Verbs given in Sweet's *Anglo-Saxon Reader*.

ADDITIONAL LIST.

The following list of Weak Verbs is here added as presenting peculiarities.

	Present.	Preterit.	Participle.
cȳdan (know).	3. cȳd(d).	cȳdde, cȳdde.	gecȳded, gecȳdd.
fyllan (fill).	3. fyld.	fylde.	gefyld.
lǣdan (lead).	3. lǣtt.	lǣdde.	gelǣded, gelǣdd.
lǣran (teach).	3. lǣrd.	lǣrde.	gelǣred.
gelífan (believe).	3. gelífd.	gelífde.	gelífed.
nemnan (name).	3. nemned.	nemnde, nemde.	genemned.
rǣsan (rush).	3. rǣst.	rǣsde.	......
wēnan (hope).	3. wēnd.	wēnde.	
wendan (turn).	3. went.	wende.	gewended, gewend.
lettan (hinder).	3. lett.	lette.	gelett.
mētan (meet).	3. mētt.	mētte.	gemētt.
settan (set).	3. sett.	sette.	gesett.
dyppan (dip).	3. dypd.	dypte.	......
rīpan (reap).	3. rīpd.	rīpte.	......
lixan (shine).	3. lixt.	lixte.	......
(nea)lǣcan (approach).	3. lǣcd.	-lǣcte, -lǣhte.	-lǣht.

NOTE.—smēagan (smēan), þrēagan (þrēan), twēon, þēon, contract; as hē, hī, smēad, twēod; þrēade, twēode, geþrēad, &c.

---

*_** The typographical execution of this Dictionary is from the very competent hands of Mr. THOMAS P. PEABODY, 6 Reade Street, New York. Mr. P. has displayed taste and skill in the typesetting and carefulness in the proofreading, and the editors are indebted to him for many valuable suggestions.

www.ingramcontent.com/pod-product-compliance
Lightning Source LLC
Chambersburg PA
CBHW030016240426
43672CB00007B/976